THE PRENTICE HALL SERIES IN MARKETING

Philip Kotler, Series Editor

Fifth Edition

Research
for Marketing
Decisions

Paul E. Green
University of Pennsylvania

Donald S. Tull
University of Oregon

Gerald Albaum
University of Oregon

PRENTICE HALL, Englewood Cliffs, New Jersey 07632

Library of Congress Cataloging-in-Publication Data

Green, Paul E.
    Research for marketing decisions.

    Includes index.
    1. Marketing research.   I. Tull, Donald S.
II Albaum, Gerald   III. Title.
HF5415.2.G68 1988   658.8'3   88-5800
ISBN 0-13-774175-8

Editorial/production supervision and
    interior design: Rob DeGeorge
Cover design: Lundgren Graphics, Ltd.
Manufacturing buyer: Margaret Rizzi

© 1988 by Prentice-Hall, Inc
A Division of Simon & Schuster
Englewood Cliffs, New Jersey 07632

Printed in the United States of America

10   9   8   7   6   5   4   3   2   1

ISBN 0-13-774175-8

Prentice-Hall International (UK) Limited, *London*
Prentice-Hall of Australia Pty. Limited, *Sydney*
Prentice-Hall Canada Inc., *Toronto*
Prentice-Hall of Hispanoamericana, S.A., *Mexico*
Prentice-Hall of India Private Limited, *New Delhi*
Prentice-Hall of Japan, Inc., *Tokyo*
Simon & Schuster Asia Pte. Ltd., *Singapore*
Editora Prentice-Hall do Brasil, Ltda., *Rio de Janeiro*

Contents

Preface

In the original (1966) edition of this book, our Preface contained the following comments:

> Any field which is subject to systematic inquiry can be characterized by: (a) content—what the researcher attempts to study; (b) method—the conceptual basis or strategy of inquiry; and (c) techniques—the procedures or tactics by which the strategy is implemented.
>
> The motivation for this book has arisen from our feeling that marketing research has now reached a stage of development where traditional methods and techniques require synthesis and extension. We believe this book is novel in two major respects.
>
> With respect to method, the unifying concept of this book is that marketing research is a cost-incurring activity whose output is information of potential value for management decision.
>
> With respect to technique, this book again departs from tradition in terms of the relatively large coverage given to newer research procedures. . . . We hope that discussion of these techniques—which are either omitted entirely or given more limited description in most current marketing research texts—will help close the gap between textbook coverage and the content of contemporary professional journals devoted to the advancement of research technique in marketing.

The fifth edition of the book may appropriately be called the *broadening* edition. While we have updated the content of the preceding editions, the most significant changes entail a broadening of the book's methodological scope in the sense that the treatment of research design, data collection techniques, and measurement has been expanded. We have tried to respond to the wishes of readers of previous editions by providing a considerably simpler and more streamlined version.

The book still emphasizes, relatively, the place of modern analytical tools, such as multivariate analysis, in the design and conduct of marketing research. Moreover, packaged computer programs for analyzing data are described and their results interpreted in the context of illustrative marketing problems. The current edition continues to present this material from primarily a pragmatic and user-oriented (rather than research technician) perspective.

Cases have been placed at the end of each of the five major parts of the book. Although each case is designed for use with the material in the preceding part, a case may draw upon discussions from earlier parts. Some rather "technical" material, which may be elementary to some readers but new to others, has been presented in an appendix to the chapters.

Part I of the book is mainly concerned with problem formulation and marketing decision making. Here we discuss the basic concepts of decision models, including the role of Bayesian analysis in assessing the value versus cost of marketing research information. We look at marketing problems from the standpoint of the marketing executive and then from the perspective of the researcher. A new chapter in the book deals with an overview of the research process and what is involved in planning a research project. We show how the researcher's view of the problem is translated into a research design, and what potential errors the researcher should be aware of.

Part II is directed toward implementation of the research design through the collection of data. We discuss the preparation of questionnaires, procedures for gathering marketing information, the fundamentals of measurement and scaling techniques, and respondent sampling methods. A new chapter covers design and implementation of experiments.

Part III is devoted to the analysis of collected data via the better-known techniques of cross tabulation, chi square, regression, and the analysis of variance and covariance. Each procedure, as it is introduced, is described conceptually and applied numerically to a data set that is small enough to enable the reader to work through the calculations easily and quickly.

Part IV is concerned with the more advanced tools of data analysis—discriminant analysis, probit and logit, automatic interaction detection, factor analysis, clustering methods, multidimensional scaling techniques, and conjoint analysis. However, again we try to present this material as simply as possible, consistent with its higher technical level.

Part V discusses selected activities in marketing research—forecasting, market segmentation studies, and tools for designing new marketing strategies. A number of actual case studies, drawn from various consulting experiences, are used to show how the multivariate methods of Parts III and IV can be applied to marketing problems.

Appendix A provides the basic statistical tables used in the text.

In conclusion, the fifth edition maintains our interest in providing the student with a modern discussion of marketing research. Moreover, we feel that the present edition does this with relatively less concentration on the more esoteric aspects of research methodology.

Many people helped shape the content and style of the present edition. Thorough critiques of the fourth edition were provided by Professors Gary T. Ford, University of Maryland, and Robert J. Meyer, University of California, Los Angeles.

Extensive and insightful reviews of the present edition were provided by Professor Meyer and, in addition, by Professors Arno Rethans, Pennsylvania State University; Frank Carmone, Drexel University; S. W. Swanson, California State University, Sacramento; and Robert Krapfel, Jr., University of Maryland.

Manuscript typing was expertly carried out by Janet Clayton and Diane Collins. The marketing and production staff of Prentice Hall cooperated in ways too numerous to catalog.

To all of these benefactors we extend our sincere thanks and appreciation. We hope that the final product reflects well on the efforts of the many talented people who helped us produce it.

PAUL E. GREEN
DONALD S. TULL
GERALD ALBAUM

1

Marketing Research—Content and Strategy

INTRODUCTION

Marketing is a restless, changing, dynamic field. Since 1920 many important and dramatic changes have taken place in marketing. Thousands of new products, including those of entire new industries such as plastics and electronics, have appeared on the market. Two completely new national communication media have been introduced and supported entirely by marketing expenditures. The corporate chain form of organization, the widespread application of the self-service principle, automatic vending, and computerized checkout systems are but a few of the developments (at the retail level) that have led to sweeping changes in marketing methods. During this same period the proportion of the labor force engaged in performing marketing activities has increased substantially, and it is now estimated to be as high as 33%.[1]

Concomitant with these changes has been the gradual but pronounced shift in the orientation of firms from production to marketing. Moreover, the role of marketing itself has been changing. The various crises of the 1970s and 1980s—material and energy shortages, inflation, economic stagnation, high unemployment, dying industries—together with rapid technological changes in certain industries, have forced the marketing executive to assume a wider range of responsibilities that have grown in complexity. An ever-increasing premium has been placed on making sound marketing decisions, and companies are becoming more *market-driven* in their strategic decision making. In response to this requirement a formalized means of acquiring information to assist in the making of such

[1] Robert F. Lusch and Virginia N. Lusch, *Principles of Marketing* (Boston: Kent, 1987), p. 6.

decisions has emerged and, in many ways, has reached a stage of maturity. This means is *marketing research*, the subject of this book.

In this chapter we describe the nature of marketing research and its relation to decision making. Emphasis is placed throughout on the general problem of rational decision making under conditions of uncertainty and on the informational needs of the marketing executive. Special attention is given to the concept of the value of information in reducing the costs of uncertainty associated with managerial decision making.

In the first section we deal with the nature and content of marketing research. We then examine the characteristics of marketing management from the standpoints of the components of decisions and the generic types of decisions that have to be made. Problem-situation models are introduced and the meaning of the term "information" is examined.

In order to develop satisfactorily the concept of the value of information, we introduce the reader to some of the formal notions of decision theory. We cover such topics as personalistic probability, expected value, and introductory comments on the Bayesian approach to decision making under uncertainty. In addition, other common choice-criterion models are covered in the appendix to this chapter.

Final topics covered are the role of marketing research in what has come to be known as a marketing information system (MIS), and the nature of the manager-research dialogue.

THE CONTENT OF MARKETING RESEARCH

What Is Marketing Research?

Research connotes a systematic and objective investigation of a subject or problem in order to discover relevant information or principles. It can be considered to be primarily "fundamental" or primarily "applied" in nature. *Fundamental research*, frequently called *basic* or *pure research*, seeks to extend the boundaries of knowledge in a given area with no necessary immediate application to existing problems; an example is the development of a research method that would be able to predict what people would be like *X* years in the future. *Applied research*, also known as *decisional research*, attempts to use existing knowledge as an aid to the solution of some given problem or set of problems: for example, the use of the research method by an appliance manufacturer to predict what consumers' life-styles will be five years in the future, thus starting the planning and development cycle for new products.

In a problem-solving context the emphasis is on applied or decisional research. For the purposes of this book, therefore, the following definition is a useful one:

> *Marketing research* is the systematic and objective search for and analysis of information relevant to the identification and solution of any problem in the field of marketing.

Some comments are needed concerning this definition. Marketing research is a *systematic* search for and analysis of information. Careful planning through all stages of the research is a necessity. Starting with a clear and concise statement of the problem to be researched, good research practice requires that the information sought, the methods to be used in obtaining it, and the analytical techniques to be employed be systematically and carefully laid out in advance if at all possible.

Objectivity in research is all-important. Marketing research has sometimes been defined as "the application of scientific method of marketing." The heart of scientific method is the objective gathering and analysis of information. Research projects that are carried out for the purpose of "proving" that a prior opinion is correct are, at best, a waste of time and resources; if research is intentionally slanted to arrive at predetermined results, a serious breach of professional ethics is involved. Research done with such an underlying motive is a specific example of what has been called *pseudoresearch,* which is research done to satisfy needs other than aiding the making of marketing decisions. The motives behind pseudoresearch have been categorized as organizational politics, service promotion, and personal satisfaction.[2] Research practitioners must resist all efforts made to get them to perform research for such purposes.

It will be noted that the definition adopted contains no reference to a "thorough" search for and analysis of information. When the nature of the problem requires it, thoroughness is, of course, desirable. For many marketing problems, however, the time and money spent to obtain and analyze thoroughly the information relevant to their solutions would be completely out of proportion to the benefits gained. The thoroughness with which the research is conducted, therefore, depends on the nature of the problem.

The term "problem" is used in the broadest of contexts. That is, there does not have to be something wrong; it only means that a marketing decision has to be made. Such a decision, of course, may have arisen so that a problem can be prevented.

Although the definition given above is useful, it is by no means the only definition of marketing research, nor is it necessarily the most useful one for other purposes (see Exhibit 1-1). The management of a company, for example, would be well advised to choose a less general and more detailed statement to define the specific functions of its marketing research department. The following statement is as valid today as it was when it was put forth many years ago:

Exhibit 1-1   The American Marketing Association Redefines Marketing Research*

> The Board of Directors of the American Marketing Association has approved the following as the new definition of marketing research:
>
> Marketing research is the function which links the consumer, customer, and public to the marketer through information—information used to identify and define marketing opportunities and problems; generate, refine, and evaluate marketing actions; monitor marketing performance; and improve understanding of marketing as a process.
>
> Marketing research specifies the information required to address these issues; designs the method for collecting information; manage and implements the data collection process; analyzes the results; and communicates the findings and their implications.

*Reported in "New Marketing Research Definition Approved," *Marketing News,* 21 (January 2, 1987), 1.

[2] See Stewart A. Smith, "Research and Pseudo-Research in Marketing," *Harvard Business Review,* March–April 1974, pp. 73–76. For a different perspective, see Barry Orton, "Phony Polls: The Pollster's Nemesis," *Public Opinion,* 5 (June/July 1982), 56–60.

The task of research is: to provide and maintain for management the research system, to work with management in such a way as to be able to understand its needs, to help define informational requirements, to specify the filter and generate, through application of professional methodology, meaningful information in the most efficient manner. Its role is to broaden managerial decision alternatives and reduce the range of decision error through application of the scientific method to analysis of data and evaluation of information.[3]

In short, research must be viewed as an aid to, not as a substitute for, decision making.

Marketing Research in Practice

Very broadly, the functions of marketing research include *description* and *explanation* (which are necessary for *understanding*), *prediction,* and *evaluation.* More narrowly, the function of marketing research within a company is to provide the informational and analytical inputs necessary for effective (1) *planning* of future marketing activity, (2) *control* of marketing operations in the present, and (3) *evaluation* of marketing results.

Marketing research projects are conducted on a broad array of topics by a variety of types and sizes of organizations. They are performed by companies for internal use, by commercial marketing research firms, and by government and nonprofit institutions.[4]

We know a great deal about the nature of marketing research projects conducted and who conducts them as a result of research carried out in this area. As shown in Table 1-1, a sizable amount of research is done to *identify* marketing problems. More than 90% of the 599 respondent companies conduct studies of market potential, market share, market characteristics, and business trends and perform sales analyses to help determine if their sales performance is at the appropriate level. Slightly less than 90% of all companies also have short- and long-range forecasts prepared to help identify future problems as opportunities in the marketing of their products.

As indicated in Table 1-1, the marketing research department conducts more than 80% of the studies of market potential, market share, and market characteristics. The remaining percentage of these types of projects is carried out by other departments within the company and by outside firms. (The outside firms that conduct such studies are commerical marketing research firms, management consultants, and advertising agencies.)

The marketing research department is responsible for performing two-thirds of the sales analyses and studies of business trends, and about one-half of the forecasts. From one-fifth to one-third of such projects are carried out by other departments inside the company—primarily accounting and finance departments—and a small percentage is conducted by outside agencies.

Table 1-2 shows what types of research projects are carried out to help *solve*

[3]Murray Cayley, "The Role of Research in Marketing," *Business Quarterly,* 33, No. 3 (Autumn 1968), 36.

[4]Many nonprofit organizations avoid marketing research because of certain myths. For a discussion that disputes these myths, see Alan R. Andreasen, "Mythological Barriers to the Use of Marketing Research by Small and Non-Profit Organizations," University of Illinois, College of Commerce and Business Administration, Faculty Working Paper No. 70, 1981.

TABLE 1-1   Problem Identification Research Conducted by and for Respondent Companies*

	PERCENTAGE OF COMPANIES DOING	PERCENTAGE OF STUDIES DONE BY:		
		Marketing Research Department	*Other Departments*	*Outside Firms*
Market potential	97	88	4	5
Market share	97	85	6	6
Market characteristics	97	88	3	6
Sales analysis	92	67	23	2
Short-range forecasting	89	51	36	2
Long-range forecasting	87	49	34	4
Studies of business trends	91	68	20	3

*599 companies responded.

Source: Adapted from D. W. Twedt, *1983 Survey of Marketing Research* (Chicago: American Marketing Association, 1983), p. 41.

marketing problems and who does them. Over two-thirds of the responding companies do studies in one or more aspects of product, pricing, distribution, and advertising and sales research. For example, Johnson Wax did extensive marketing research in the late 1970s prior to the national launch of Agree Shampoo. Research helped identify the opportunity, define the target user, define the positioning and strategy, and define the attributes and features the product should have. In addition, the marketing plan was tested.[5]

Similarly, Saab–Scania AB, the Swedish-based automobile manufacturer, conducts a great deal of marketing research in the United States market using a commerical marketing research firm. Surveys are conducted among current and prospective owners to determine their wants and needs, likes and dislikes. Clinics are run in which buyers can compare Saab with other competitive makes. Specific customized studies are done to analyze the demographic characteristics of buyers of Saab and competitive automobiles. On occasion multidimensional scaling is used to forecast in the company's designated market segment. Results of such research are used in product design, advertising, market segmentation, and sales training.[6]

The extent to which the marketing research department is responsible for conducting problem-solving research projects varies considerably by problem area. As shown in Table 1-2, whereas almost three-fourths of all competitive-product studies are done by the company's marketing research department, the department is involved in only about one-seventh of sales-compensation studies. Some areas of problem-solving research in marketing seem to be destined for other departments or outside agencies—for example, certain types of advertising research (often done by the company's advertising department

[5]"Key Role of Research in Agree's Success Is Told," *Marketing News,* January 12, 1979, pp. 14–15.

[6]Bernie Whalen, " 'Tiny' Saab Drives Up Profits with Market-Niche Strategy, Repositioning," *Marketing News,* 18 (March 16, 1984), Sec. 1, pp. 14–16.

TABLE 1-2   Problem-Solving Research Conducted by and for Respondent Companies*

	PERCENTAGE OF COMPANIES DOING	PERCENTAGE OF STUDIES DONE BY:		
		Marketing Research Department	Other Departments	Outside Firms
Product research				
Competitive-product studies	87	71	10	6
New-product acceptance and potential	76	59	11	6
Testing existing products	80	55	19	6
Packaging research	65	44	12	9
Pricing research	83	34	47	2
Advertising and sales research				
Establishment of sales quotas, territories	78	23	54	1
Studies of advertising effectiveness	76	42	5	29
Sales-compensation studies	60	13	43	4
Promotional studies of premiums, deals, etc.	58	38	14	6
Copy research	61	30	6	25
Media research	68	22	14	32
Distribution research				
Distribution-channel studies	71	32	38	1
Plant and warehouse location studies	68	29	35	4

*599 companies responded.

Source: Adapted from D. W. Twedt, *1983 Survey of Marketing Research* (Chicago: American Marketing Association, 1983), p. 41.

or its advertising agency) and research involving costs and quotas (often done by the accounting department).

Our discussion so far of marketing research in practice has been directed primarily to the "traditional" product-based companies. There are in addition many companies in the service and "nontraditional" product industries that use a great deal of marketing research. These companies are from such diverse industries as transportation, health care, interior home design, real estate development, military recruiting, and financial institutions such as banks and brokerage houses. For example, a large national brokerage and financial services company uses marketing research techniques to ascertain client needs for services such as order-execution, market-monitoring, financial-advising, and information-providing services. The company uses a customer-profiling information system to enhance its market segmentation activities and better match clients and "products."

Another area where marketing research is increasingly being used is in providing legal evidence. When designed properly and relevant to the issues being litigated, *survey* research results can be used as evidence. However, such survey data must be based on designs that are precise in their attention to the legal logic to which the survey's results will be subjected. Major areas of use have been trademark protection and advertising claims. Courts tend to prefer surveys that measure behavior; the behavior must be apparent to the court and not imputed. Despite this preference, there is more receptivity to surveys describing psychological states than to those that describe objective reality. Since this is still a relatively new phenomenon, not much is known about the extent of use of surveys in legal proceedings.[7]

Government agencies, trade associations, trade periodicals, and colleges and universities are other organizations that do marketing research. Such agencies of the federal government as the Federal Trade Commission, the Antitrust Division of the Department of Justice, the Food and Drug Administration, and the Interstate Commerce Commission carry out studies in specific marketing problems from time to time. Trade associations and trade periodicals often collect and disseminate marketing research data on the industries with which they are concerned. Bureaus of business and economic research at universities also regularly conduct research projects of interest to marketers, as do chambers of commerce, brokerage houses, railroads, airlines, and such reporting services as Standard and Poor's, Moody's, and Dun and Bradstreet. For the most part, these agencies provide secondary data, a topic that is discussed in Chapter 4.

THE CHARACTERISTICS OF MARKETING MANAGEMENT

A primary characteristic of management is *decision making*. Decisions and decision making underlie and permeate the management process. Since the terms "decision making" and "managing" are so closely interwoven, we shall use them as though they were synonymous. In considering the characteristics of marketing management, it is appropriate that we examine the decision-making process. We shall first be concerned with the types of decisions to be made. We shall then consider the role of problem-situation models in decision making and the meaning of the term "information."

---

[7]See Irving Crespi, "Surveys as Legal Evidence," *Public Opinion Quarterly*, 51 (Spring 1987), 84–91; Robert J. Lavidge, "Survey Research in Trademark Cases Gets More Attention," *Marketing News*, 20 (September 12, 1986), 54, 57; and Solomon Dutka, "Bringing Polls to Justice," *Public Opinion*, 5 (October/November 1982), 47–49.

Types of Management Decisions

Six types of management decisions may be usefully distinguished:

1. *Deciding what the problems are:* recognizing and defining the problems currently faced by the organization.
2. *Selecting the immediate problem for solution:* determining priorities according to the importance of the problems and the timing of their solution.
3. *Solving the problem selected:* finding alternative solutions, evaluating the consequences of each, and selecting the most favorable one.
4. *Implementing the solution:* making the decisions necessary to carry out the solution decided upon.
5. *Modifying the original solution based on observation of results:* deciding whether, when, and how original solutions should be modified after experiencing results.
6. *Establishing policy:* deciding which problems occur often enough and are sufficiently similar to warrant a policy decision; making the policy decision.

The primary activity of marketing management is making such decisions with regard to marketing problems. Problems in the areas of product design, price, distribution, and promotion must be identified; the more important and pressing ones selected for solution; the best possible solution reached, based on the information available; the solution implemented; the solution modified when additional information obtained from experiencing results so dictates; and, where required, policy established to act as a ready-made solution for a recurrence of the problem.

Problem-Situation Models and Decision Making

Suppose that a marketing manager is considering increasing the advertising appropriation for one of the company's products. As long as one of the company's objectives is to increase profits, the decision to increase the appropriation will be at least partially dependent on the amount of net additional sales generated. Net additional sales will in turn depend on such factors as the nature of the campaign, the advertising-sales response relationship, and the actions of competitors.

A necessary part of the process of this decision—or of any one of the generalized types of decisions discussed in the preceding section—is the formulation of a problem-situation model. The model may take many forms, ranging from implicit models that the decision maker may not even be aware of using to elaborate mathematical models solved with the aid of a computer. Regardless of form, one or more models *must* be used each time a decision is made.

What, then, is a *model?* Although the word has many connotations, some of which are taken up in Chapter 3, we shall use it here to refer to a conceptual scheme that specifies a measure of the outcome(s) to be achieved, the relevant variable, and their functional relationship to the outcomes(s).

We may define a problem-situation model in symbolic form as follows:[8]

$$U = f(A_i, S_j)$$

where U = the measure of the outcomes, the payoff, of each alternative course of action
         A_i = the variables that are under the control of the decision maker—i.e., the variables that define the alternative courses of action
         S_j = the environmental factors, either variables or constants, over which the decision maker has no control (alternative descriptions of the environmental factors comprise the *states of nature* of the problem)
         f = the functional relationship between the dependent variable U and the independent variables (and constants) A_i and S_j

To return to our example of the decision concerning increasing the advertising appropriation, what kind of a problem-situation model might be appropriate? We have already indicated that the nature of the decision-making process requires that some model or models be used. In this case the executive may have a set of intuitive, nonformalized judgments, which might be expressed somewhat as follows: "Assuming that nothing else changes, as advertising for this product is increased, sales will increase in the form of a 'flat S' curve. I think we are on the lower end of the curve."

If pressed further, the executive might agree that his conception of the sales-advertising relationship could be represented by a graph. Some specification of the level of the other controllable variables and of the environmental variables would have to be made; let us assume that they are all held at their present levels. The graph would be of the general nature of Figure 1-1, with present sales and advertising designated as *s* and *a,* respectively.

Figure 1-1   Model of Sales-advertising Relationship

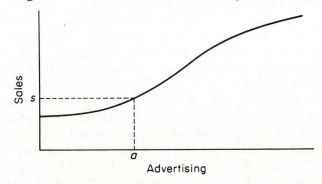

[8]This definition of a problem-situation model is based on that given in R. L. Ackoff, Shiv Gupta, and J. S. Minas, *Scientific Method: Optimizing Applied Research Decisions* (New York: John Wiley, 1962).

Or, an analysis of the sales-advertising relationship in the past might indicate that it takes the form of a Gompertz-type (S-shaped) curve such that the equation

$$\log Y = \log k + (\log G)B^p$$

where Y is sales response, p is amount of advertising, and k, G, and B are constants, provides a reasonably good predictive equation over the range of advertising of interest to the decision maker.

Several points concerning this example are worth noting. First, we have been dealing with *explicit* forms of a model. It should be clearly understood, however, that if the conceptualization of a specific problem by the decision maker remains *implicit*, it is no less a model. It may be, in fact, that an explicit model is not worth the cost of formulation.

The second point concerns the form in which explicit models may be expressed. In our example, the same basic explicit model was described by a verbal statement, a graph, and an equation. Models described verbally are known simply as *verbal models*. Those that are expressed as a graph or diagram are known as *diagrammatic models,* and those expressed as a logical sequence of questions are called *logical flow models*. Models represented in equational form are called *symbolic (mathematical) models*. All explicit models may be described in one or more of these forms (see Exhibit 1-2).

A third point relates to the degree of simplification of models. Models are necessarily simplifications and abstractions to some degree of the reality of the problem situation. It is not possible to examine either all the variables or all their possible interactions in the illustrative problem just considered—or, for that matter, in any marketing problem. Rather, the decision maker attempts to abstract the important elements of the problem situation and represent them so that they are simple enough to be understood and manipulated, yet realistic enough to portray the *essentials* of the situation.

This point leads in turn to an examination of the manner in which problem-situation models are used. The general form of the model, $U = f(A_i, S_j)$, in theory permits predictions of U for continuous values (within appropriate limits) for each of the variables in the A and S subsets. As a practical matter, however, neither the nature of the functional relationships nor the value of some of the environmental variables can usually be determined well enough to make such predictions worthwhile. Often, a more realistic and viable way of using a problem-situation model is to structure the problem into a relatively small number of discrete *courses of action* and *states of nature*. That is, we designate the courses of action we want to consider by specifying two or more levels of one or more of the controllable subset of variables (A) while holding the others constant. Similarly, we designate the states of nature under which outcomes are to be predicted by specifying two or more levels of one or more of the environmental (S) subset of variables. The problem-situation model is then applied to predict the outcome for each action-state pair.

A simplified application will help to illustrate this procedure. Suppose that a change in the marketing program for a product is being considered which would allocate a part of the current advertising trade media expenditures to hiring and supporting an additional salesperson to call upon retailers. To make such an action worthwhile, a net increase in

Exhibit 1-2   Three Types of Models

VERBAL MODEL:
   "If I change my price my competitor will match my price unless it would cause him to lose money."

LOGICAL FLOW MODEL:

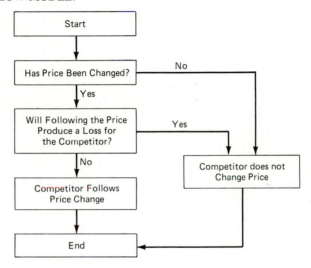

MATHEMATICAL MODEL:

$$\overline{P}_c = (1 - I)P_c + IP_m$$

$$I = \begin{cases} 0, \text{ if } P_mQ_c - C_c < 0 \\ 1, \text{ if } P_mQ_c - C_c \geqslant 0 \end{cases}$$

$\overline{P}_c$ = competitor's new price

P_c = competitor's old price

P_m = price of firm ("my" firm)

Q_c = quantity of sales competitor could sell at P_m

C_c = competitor's total cost of producing and selling Q_c

Source: David B. Montgomery and Glen L. Urban, *Management Science in Marketing* (Englewood Cliffs, N.J.: Prentice-Hall, 1969), p. 11.

TABLE 1-3   Marketing-Program Illustration

ACTION	S_1: NEW MARKETING PROGRAM SUPERIOR	S_2: OLD MARKETING PROGRAM SUPERIOR
A_1: adopt new	$U_{11} = 15$	$U_{12} = -7$
A_2: retain old	$U_{21} = -2$	$U_{22} = 4$

sales would have to result. Whether or not additional sales *will* result will depend on the effectiveness of the new salesperson in convincing existing retailer customers to purchase more and in getting new dealers to stock the product, the possible loss of sales from the reduction in advertising expenditures, competitor actions, and other factors.

Assume that the problem has been structured into the two courses of action and two states of nature shown in Table 1-3. Note that the two courses of action—adopting the new marketing program or retaining the present one—are concerned with two controllable variables: amount of advertising expenditure and adding a new salesperson. No change is contemplated in any of the other controllable variables.

The two states of nature shown in Table 1-3 reflect different environmental conditions. In state S_1 the environment is such that retailer purchases will increase more as a result of the salesperson than they decrease as a result of the reduction in advertising expenditures. The reverse is true in state S_2. Other environmental variables may be assumed to be the same between the two states.

Although Table 1-3 illustrates the application of the problem-situation model, it immediately raises another question, How does one go about selecting a course of action without knowing which state of nature is the true state? If the new promotional program in our example is adopted, there is a potential gain of 15 units *if* S_1 is the true state and a loss of 7 units if it is not. Similarly, if the old program is retained, a loss of 2 units will result *if* S_1 is the true state and a gain of 4 units if it is not.

The answer to the question of which alternative to choose, given the conditional payoffs of each, lies in the choice criterion adopted. *Choice-criterion models* have been developed by decision theorists to illustrate this problem. We consider several such models in the appendix to this chapter.

A further comment about models is in order. We have already noted that they may be either implicit or explicit. We have also observed that sometimes the cost of explicating an implicit model is greater than the benefit received. When the cost of formulation is justifiable, however, explicit models are preferable for several reasons. The most important of these are the following:

1. *Clarification*. Explication usually results in the clarification of relationships and interactions. The need for more rigorous definitions of key variables often becomes apparent.
2. *Objectivity*. As a correlative of clarification, the process of explicating the model often discloses rationalizations and unfounded opinions that had not been recognized as such before.

3. *Communication.* When alternative implicit models of the same problem situation are held by different people, discussion frequently results without common points of reference, and communication problems arise. Explication reduces these problems.

4. *Improvement of models.* Explicit models can be tested by different persons and in differing situations to see if the results are reproducible. The degree of adaptability and range of applicability can thus be extended.

5. *Guide to research needs.* Formulating models explicitly can better pinpoint information gaps and thus aid in determining the nature of research needs.

Having considered problem-situation models and introduced the concept of choice-criterion models, we will now specify more completely what is meant by the term "information."

Information and Decision Making

Information as used here refers to *recorded experience that is useful for decision making.* In other words, it consists of that recorded experience which will reduce the level of uncertainty in making a decision.

This definition clearly makes the existence of information dependent on the decision maker and the context of the decision. The model that is being used for a specific problem situation defines both the information required for solution and the way in which it will be interpreted (Exhibit 1-3).

At this point we can state that from a *practical* point of view, information must possess certain characteristics if it is to be useful for decision making.[9] That is, information must be

- *Accurate.* This refers to the degree to which information reflects reality. Accuracy should be judged as a relative criterion in terms of the specific decision at hand.
- *Current.* This is the degree to which information reflects events in the *relevant* time period, past and present.
- *Sufficient.* Information must be complete and/or detailed enough to allow a decision to be made.
- *Available.* Information must be available *when a decision is being made.*
- *Relevant.* This refers to the pertinency and applicability of information to the decision and is the single most important characteristic.

Realistically, tradeoffs must often be made among the characteristics of accuracy, currentness, sufficiency, and availability. For example, the requirement of sufficiency may be relaxed to increase accuracy. However, relevancy is the one characteristic that can never be compromised. To do so would make information useless.

[9]See Robert A. Peterson, *Marketing Research* (Plano, Tex.: Business Publications, 1982), pp. 10–12.

Exhibit 1-3   A Model and Related Research

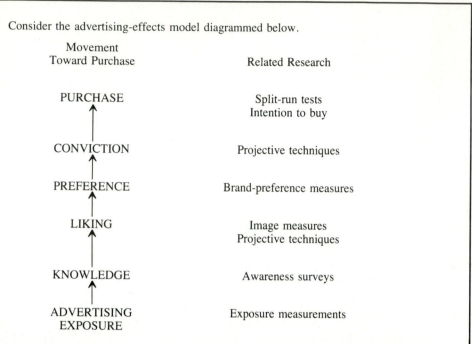

Consider the advertising-effects model diagrammed below.

This model represents a view that has been widely held in advertising circles for many years. It conceptualizes the psychological processes the typical consumer is believed to undergo after exposure to advertising. The research techniques related to each step in the progression indicate the kinds of information that can be obtained to provide a measure of advertising "effectiveness."

If this model is correct, at least two important implications result. First, measures at any one of the intermediate stages should show a high correlation with sales. This permits dispensing with the difficult and costly research that attempts to measure directly the sales effects of advertising. Second, a time lapse is implied, suggesting that there is a lagged effect of advertising on sales. Both of these implications are of obvious importance in decisions as to what kinds of data to obtain and how to interpret them.

Source: Adapted from K. S. Palda, "The Hypothesis of Hierarchy of Effects: A Partial Evaluation," *Journal of Marketing Research,* 2 (February 1966), 13–24; and R. C. Lavidge and G. A. Steiner, "A Model for Predictive Measurements of Advertising Effectiveness," *Journal of Marketing,* 25 (October 1961), 59–62.

Many companies develop more or less "formal" systems for obtaining, processing, and disseminating decision information. Such a system, known as a Marketing Information System or simply MIS, is designed to increase the likelihood that decision information will possess the desired characteristics. The nature of an MIS and the role played by marketing research is discussed later in this chapter.

It is apparent that information can never be available to the extent that the decision maker would desire if no costs were involved. Since obtaining information is a cost-incurring activity, rational decision making necessarily involves consideration of the *value* of information. The *amount* of information is important only as it affects the value. The notion of the value of information is introduced later in this chapter and discussed more fully in Chapter 3.

There are basically three levels of decision making that affect marketing research: marketing management (e.g., brand management activities), strategic marketing planning, and corporate strategy and allocation planning. Traditionally marketing research has dealt primarily with the marketing management level, although more recently it is being used for strategic marketing planning. By default or otherwise, marketing research will become more active in providing information relevant to overall company strategic decision making. In many companies no one else can do this, as units that have dealt with so-called business research are disappearing. This means that marketing research departments will have to broaden their scope and conduct research on issues that are nonmarketing in nature.[10]

PROBABILITY THEORY AND DECISIONS

Underlying all managerial decision making is the use of *probabilities*. Sometime probability is formally introduced into the decision-making process, while perhaps equally as often, if not more often, it is only informally or implicitly used. Much depends on the choice-criterion model that is being used.

Probability theory, the foundation of statistics, is perhaps as controversial a subject as one could find when it comes to the interpretive aspects of its own concepts. Of course, one can study probability theory strictly as an abstract system and hence avoid the problems of interpretation. When it comes to interpreting probabilities in the real world, however, we might ask the reader how he or she would react to the following statements:

1. I will assign a probability of 1/6 to the appearance of a six on the next throw of a well-balanced die.
2. I have observed, over a long period, a process that produces metal parts. The defective proportion of metal parts produced so far is 0.08. I am willing to assume that the probability of this process's producing a defective part in the immediate future is 0.08.
3. I personally feel that the chance of my going to Mexico this year is 0.05.

Our experience with tossing dice suggests that almost everyone would agree with the first probability statement. Our agreement stems from the large amount of empirical evidence that has been assembled on die tossing and, perhaps, an examination of the way in which the die is constructed (symmetrically). Most of us would feel reasonably com-

---

[10]"In Strategic Phase, Line Management Needs 'Business' Research, Not Market Research," *Marketing News*, 17 (January 21, 1983), Sec. 1, pp. 2, 22.

fortable in assigning the same probability (0.08) to the production of a defective part, particularly if additional knowledge suggests that the process can be treated as stable over time and we have no reason to believe that the appearance of a good or bad part changes the probability of the next part's being good or defective. But perhaps many of us would feel uneasy about statement 3; we are not at all sure about the relevancy of the experience underlying this probability assignment and how our personalistic probability would be modified in the light of new information.

Judgment pervades all measurements and interpretations of probability. Two of the major views of probability theory are the relative-frequency view and the personalistic view. The *relative-frequency* view defines probability as the limit of a sequence of relative frequencies as the sequence approaches infinity. Before going further, however, we must agree that in any practical situation we can observe only a finite number of trials; hence, we must *postulate* this limit. Experience with tossing symmetrical dice and coins neither substantiates nor refutes the notion of a limiting frequency. We should be clear on the central point that probability is *not an observed relative frequency;* moreover, the relative-frequency view, strictly speaking, does not tell us what to expect on a *single* toss (the probability of a six would be either 1 or 0 according to this point of view).

Our more limited experience with the metal-part production process may arouse more disagreement about using the observed proportion of defective parts as an estimate of the probability. We might be more inclined, for example, to change this probability assignment as more experience with the process accumulates than we would be to change our probability assignment of 1/6 to the toss of a six as more evidence against this assertion accumulates. Of course, if we had reason to suspect the "trueness" of the die, we might behave in the same manner as we would regarding the production process. But, compared with the production process, the past experience gained in tossing symmetrical dice is overwhelming.

The *personalistic view* of probability is more like the view held by the person on the street. Those who subscribe to the personalistic view find it quite natural to assign probabilities to unique events. Personalistic or subjective probability relates to the degree of belief or confidence one has in the occurrence of a particular state of the world, as expressed in decision-making terms. Several procedures have been described for eliciting this degree of belief. One of these, suggested by Schlaifer,[11] is that the decision maker conceptualize a "standard lottery" of, say, 100 numbered balls in an urn and a corresponding set of numbered lottery tickets. The decision maker has a (conceptual) right to receive some worthwhile prize if he or she draws a ticket whose number corresponds with the number of a ball drawn from the urn. The personalistic probability assigned, for example, to the occurrence of a trip to Mexico this year is derived by imagining the number of lottery tickets (in this case, five) which he or she would wish to have in the standard lottery in order to be indifferent to receiving the prize provided by winning the lottery or receiving the same prize if the event "trip to Mexico this year" occurred.

The personalistic approach admits the assignment of probabilities to unique as well

---

[11]Robert Schlaifer, *Probability and Statistics for Business Decisions* (New York: McGraw-Hill, 1959), pp. 11–13. Also see Robert Schlaifer, *Analysis of Decisions under Uncertainty* (New York: McGraw-Hill, 1969); and Howard Raiffa, *Decision Analysis* (Reading, Mass.: Addison-Wesley, 1968).

as repetitive events. In some cases the probability assignments will be based on more or less "public" experience in the sense that most people would assign the same or nearly the same probability to the event. In most marketing problems, however, the particular experience involved will be possessed by one or at most a few individuals. If such is the case—*and no additional information can be gathered*—the approach recommends action consistent with these beliefs. When additional data can be collected, these initial judgments may be modified according to procedures to be introduced in Chapter 3. As we shall see, the incorporation of new information, if economically justified, tends to bring into much closer correspondence opinions that may initially be at wide variance, a comforting thought to the reader who is uneasy about the subjective aspect of this view of probability.

The Bayesian Approach

The Bayesian approach[12] to decision making under uncertainty embodies several notions that may not be familiar to the student of traditional statistics. As mentioned earlier, in traditional statistics use was made of the relative-frequency view of probability (i.e., the limit of a sequence of relative frequencies over the long run).

In contrast, the Bayesian approach makes use of personal probabilities—for example, the confidence that the decision maker has in the truth of a specific proposition, where this confidence is expressed numerically and where the expressed judgments obey certain rules of consistency. The Bayesian approach, in effect, treats "uncertainty" problems as if they were "risk" problems by using personal probabilities in lieu of relative-frequency probabilities. For introductory purposes, let us apply this approach to the marketing-program illustration and assume that the decision maker's prior probabilities of S_1 and S_2 occurring are 0.6 and 0.4, respectively. The results are shown in Table 1-4.

By multiplying each payoff by the appropriate probability and summing the products—one obtains an expected value. For example, if the decision maker chooses act A_1, his or her expected value is 6.2 units; that of act A_2 is, of course, 0.4 unit. If the decision maker wished to adopt the choice criterion of maximizing expected value, the choice would be act A_1. The decision maker would make this choice despite believing that there is a 40% chance for S_2 to occur, which would result in a loss of 7 units.

TABLE 1-4 Application of Bayesian Approach

Action	$P(S_1)$	S_1: New marketing program superior to old	$P(S_2)$	S_2: Old marketing program superior to new	Expected value
A_1: adopt new	0.60	15	0.40	−7	6.2 (max.)
A_2: retain old	0.60	−2	0.40	4	0.4

[12]So named for its frequent use of Bayes' theorem, developed by an eighteenth-century clergyman, Thomas Bayes.

The marketing executive is usually dealing with events that are unique. No two marketing problems are ever precisely the same, and most have substantive differences from the closest analogous situation faced by the executive in the past. There is little opportunity, therefore, to determine relative-frequency, objective-type probabilities.

The Bayesian approach considers both objective probabilities, where applicable, and personalistic probabilities. In a situation where a decision maker possesses partial information about the relevant probabilities, he or she may elect a strategy of collecting more information before making a final choice among the courses of action. *The decision maker will do so only, however, if the value of the additional information is greater than the cost of obtaining it*. The value versus the cost of information is a central issue in marketing research. The Bayesian approach provides a framework for the formal treatment of this problem and operationalizes the measurement of information value. We describe this framework and the Bayesian approach to the determination of information value in Chapter 3.

MARKETING RESEARCH AND MARKETING INFORMATION SYSTEMS

Many years ago Malcolm McNiven, then with Coca-Cola USA, stated:

> Every marketing oriented company has a functioning marketing information system which is generally designed around the requirements of the senior marketing manager. These systems vary as the individuals vary. In many companies the systems may consist only of sales analysis data which tracks the product from the manufacturer through the distribution chain. In other companies it may include information about consumers and the effects of marketing variables on consumption of the product. In other companies, the system may include environmental analysis and predictions of changes in the distribution and marketing system. . . .[13]

To a large extent in many companies, such systems are not formally structured and/or are equated with the activity of marketing research.

There is more to marketing information than marketing research, as it is defined. The concept of a marketing information system (MIS) is illustrated in Figure 1-2. As shown, marketing research is but one subsystem—the others are concerned with the following:

- *Internal Reports*. The internal accounting system that reports such items as sales and orders
- *Marketing Intelligence*. Provides information about relevant developments in the marketing environment

---

[13]Malcolm A. McNiven, "Marketing Research and Marketing Information Systems," in *Marketing and the New Science of Planning,* ed. Robert L. King (Chicago: American Marketing Association, 1968), pp. 170–71.

• *Analytical Marketing*. Consists of advanced techniques for analyzing data and problems; includes a statistical bank and a model bank

The activities performed by an MIS and its subsystems include information *discovery, collection, interpretation* (which may involve validation and filtering), *analysis,* and *intracompany dissemination* (storage, transmission, and/or dumping).[14]

More specifically, the MIS can be tied directly to the decision process.[15] A good MIS will contribute in some way to every part of this process, although not necessarily equally. The MIS should have the capability to:

1. Store and retrieve data easily.
2. Generate reports and analyses, both standard and ad hoc as required.
3. Provide modeling and "what-if" (i.e. spreadsheet-type) analysis.
4. Create high quality visual aids (e.g. graphics).
5. Integrate all of the functions listed above.

Often the MIS is developed as a computer-based system, particularly with the increasing use of the personal computer with networking capability. The system must be able to be operated by any decision maker without that person having to become a technical computer expert (i.e., it must be "user-friendly"). There must be structure and flexibility built in to allow the orderly transfer of information and quick response to program changes. Finally, as marketing research becomes increasingly tied to overall corporate strategic planning, the MIS must have the capability to link with corporate information systems.

Figure 1-2   The Marketing Information System

Source: Philip Kotler, *Marketing Management: Analysis, Planning, and Control,* 5th ed. (Englewood Cliffs, N.J.: Prentice-Hall, 1984), p. 189.

---

[14]For one view of this, see Gerald Albaum, "Information Flow and Decentralized Decision Making in Marketing," *California Management Review,* Summer 1967, pp. 59–70.

[15]Raymond Kaupp, "Avoid Frustration, Use a Good Information System" *Marketing News,* 20 (March 19, 1986), 50.

The MIS is concerned with all information (internal and external) relevant to solving marketing problems and making marketing decisions. Based on the degree of collection effort used, which is determined by the extent of the user's knowledge of the need for information, marketing information may be either *planned* or *unsolicited*. Planned information exists when a need is recognized and, therefore, a request is made that it be provided. In contrast, unsolicited information is that which may in fact exist within and is obtainable from within the company, but which potential users do not know is available unless they happen to chance upon it. A manager is dependent on others in his or her organization as suppliers and transmitters of this type of information. Using this framework, it is obvious that marketing research is concerned with planned information.

Inasmuch as decision makers, as a rule, dislike being surprised, it is not totally unexpected that the "ideal" MIS is one in which a maximal proportion of information used in decision making is planned information. This, however, requires that decision makers make their needs known and that a clear dialogue be established between the information users (e.g., marketing managers) and the information providers (e.g., marketing researchers). We discuss this dialogue in the next section.

Closely related to the MIS is what is called the marketing decision support system (MDSS). A marketing decision support system is a "coordinated collection of data, systems, tools, and techniques with supporting software and hardware by which an organization gathers and interprets relevant information from business and environment and turns it into a basis for marketing action."[16] Components are a *data bank, models, statistics,* and techniques for *optimization*. The desired end result is the application of computers and marketing science to work on increasing the productivity of marketing activities.[17]

MANAGER-RESEARCHER DIALOGUE

Problem formulation is probably the single most critical aspect of the research process. If the problem has not been formulated properly any research that is done, although sound in method, is worthless to the decision maker. As we shall show in Chapter 2, problem formulation involves interaction between researcher and decision maker.

As shown in Table 1-5, conflict between researchers and management may arise in a number of important areas. To minimize conflict it is essential that managers and researchers communicate with each other. If research is to make a contribution to managerial decision making, neither side can be effective without the other. That is, there must be a reconciliation of opposing positions on key issues. Further evidence of potential managerial-researcher conflict is provided by a study of managers' attitudes toward mar-

[16]John D. C. Little, "Decision Support Systems for Marketing Managers," *Journal of Marketing,* 43 (Summer 1979), 11.

[17]For further discussion, see ibid., pp. 9–26. The Summer, 1987 issue of *Decision Sciences* is devoted entirely to expert systems and DSS.

[18]Danny N. Bellenger, "The Marketing Manager's View of Marketing Research," *Business Horizons,* June 1979, pp. 59–65.

TABLE 1-5   Areas of Top Management–Marketing Research Conflict

Top Management Position	Area	Marketing Research Position
• MR lacks sense of accountability. • Sole MR function is as an information provider.	Research Responsibility	• Responsibility should be explicitly defined and consistently followed. • Desire decision-making involvement with TM.
• Generally poor communicators. • Lack enthusiasm, salesmanship, and imagination.	Research Personnel	• TM is anti-intellectual. • Researchers should be hired, judged and compensated on research capabilities.
• Research costs too much. • Since MR contribution is difficult to measure, budget cuts are relatively defensible.	Budget	• "You get what you pay for" defense. • Needs to be continuing, long-range TM commitment.
• Tend to be over-engineered. • Not executed with proper sense of urgency. • Exhibit ritualized, staid approach.	Assignments	• Too many nonresearchable requests. • Too many "fire-fighting" requests. • Insufficient time and money allocated.
• MR best equipped to do this. • General direction sufficient . . . MR must appreciate and respond. • Can't help changing circumstances.	Problem Definition	• TM generally unsympathetic to this widespread problem. • Not given all the relevant facts. • Changed after research is under way.
• Characterized as dull with too much researchese and qualifiers. • Not decision-oriented. • Too often reported after the fact.	Research Reporting	• TM treats superficially. • Good research demands thorough reporting and documentation. • Insufficient lead-time given.
• Free to use as it pleases . . . MR shouldn't question. • Changes in need and timing of research are sometimes unavoidable. • MR deceived by not knowing all the facts.	Use of Research	• TM use to support a predetermined position represents misuse. • Isn't used after requested and conducted . . . wasteful. • Uses to confirm or excuse past actions.

Source: John G. Keane, "Some Observations on Marketing Research in Top Management Decision Making," *Journal of Marketing,* 33 (October 1969), 13.

keting research (see Table 1-6)[18]. Although managers exhibited relatively positive attitudes toward marketing research in general, there do appear to be areas where managers perceive that changes need to be made. Overall, only 22 percent of the managers agreed that they are getting what they need from marketing research (38 percent disagreed with this contention). Major concerns were the manner in which results are presented, problem definition, cost, and lack of communication. Recent studies by Deshpande and Zaltman confirm the importance of research-manager interaction (i.e., communication), attributes

TABLE 1-6   Managers' Attitudes Toward Marketing Research

STATEMENTS	PERCENT AGREE OR DISAGREE
	AGREE
Marketing researchers are more concerned with techniques than with problem solving.	31.1
Marketing research is frequently too complex to be useful.	23.5
Marketing research often takes too long to be of use to managers.	35.8
Many marketing research techniques are too technical to be of use to me.	33.9
Marketing research reports are too technical	20.2
	DISAGREE
Managers are getting what they need from marketing research.	38.1
The cost of marketing research is generally reasonable.	20.0
They typical marketing researcher would never distort results to fit preconceptions.	23.0
Marketing researchers can usually relate their findings to the managers' problem.	14.8
Marketing research approaches are consistent with the needs of managers.	19.8
I generally would not make a major decision without doing marketing research.	30.1

Source: Adapted from Danny N. Bellenger, "The Marketing Manager's View of Marketing Research," *Business Horizons,* June, 1979, p. 62.

of the final report, and technical quality.[19] One further issue is the matter of surprise. Researchers are not as concerned as managers about the level of surprise in research results. Moreover, researchers tend to perceive projects as having a much more exploratory purpose than do managers.

The message should be clear. There must be interaction between the manager and the researcher. Each can contribute a specific type of knowledge and experience to the formulation and solution of the problem. Although this may sound commonplace, the truth of the matter is that the marketing researcher is seldom asked—or even permitted—to assist in the structuring of a managerial problem. Instead the researcher may be given the following type of directive: "Find out all you can about the market for tranquilizers." If the researcher can implement this type of request, he or she must serve principally as a "fact finder," unaware of the use to which the findings are to be put, the scale of effort to be devoted to the inquiry, and the accuracy required in his or her findings.

Further complications arise when the researcher is not a member of the manager's company but instead belongs to private external research firms and agencies.[20] For such researchers effective communication with managers is critical to their being able to market their research project. A dialogue will establish for the researchers what the researchable issues are, how they should be addressed, when the client wants results delivered, and so on.

[19]Rohit Deshpande and Gerald Zaltman, "Factors Affecting the Use of Market Research Information: A Path Analysis," *Journal of Marketing Research,* 19 (February 1982), 14–31; and Rohit Deshpande and Gerald Zaltman, "A Comparison of Factors Affecting Researcher and Manager Perceptions of Market Research Use," *Journal of Marketing Research,* 21 (February 1984), 32–38.

[20]See Deshpande and Zaltman, "Comparison of Factors."

SUMMARY

In this chapter we examined the nature of marketing research and its relationship to the making of marketing decisions under uncertainty. The strategy of using marketing research to provide information whenever the expected value exceeds the estimated cost was introduced, as were basic concepts to be developed in depth in subsequent chapters.

We next considered the characteristics of marketing problems. We discussed the basic components of a problem situation—objectives, environment alternatives, and state of doubt—and the generic types of decisions managers must make. We examined problem-situation models and the necessity for using some problem-solving model, whether implicit or explicit, for decision making. The basic requirement of a model became more evident as we considered the meaning of the term "information" and role of the model in specifying the information needed for decision making. The concept of value of information was stressed in this discussion.

We discussed the basic concepts of probability theory and its meaning for decisions, and we then showed, by means of a simplified example, how a problem could be structured for application of the Bayesian approach.

We next viewed the role of marketing research within the context of a total marketing information system. It was pointed out that marketing research is one of four subsystems, and these subsystems are both independent of each other and interdependent.

The chapter concluded with a discussion of the type of dialogue that can fruitfully be undertaken between manager and researcher. This dialogue can encompass objectives, courses of action, and environmental variables affecting decision outcomes.

Appendix 1-1

DECISIONS UNDER UNCERTAINTY—CHOICE-CRITERION MODELS

We have already considered problem-situation models. It is now appropriate to consider *choice-criterion* models—the models concerned with choosing a course of action, given the outcomes for each alternative action under the various states of nature.

In recent years several theories have been proposed for dealing with the problem of making rational decisions under uncertainty. By *rational* is meant choice behavior consistent with the assumptions underlying the model—nothing more. The fact that several different theories exist for making decisions under uncertainty is an indication of the many possible models according to which one can choose courses of action. In this context we use the term "model" to represent an ideal of how people should behave if they agree that the assumptions underlying the model are intuitively appealing. No claim is made in any of these theories that people *do* behave as the model implies or that the model represents how people *should* choose for all time; rather, these *prescriptive models* represent the frameworks currently proposed by people who have taken the notion of decision making under uncertainty as a serious problem for research.

TABLE A   Application of Maximin Criterion

ACTION	S_1: NEW MARKETING PROGRAM SUPERIOR TO OLD	S_2: OLD MARKETING PROGRAM SUPERIOR TO NEW	MINIMUM PAYOFF
A_1: adopt new	15	-7	-7
A_2: retain old	-2	4	-2 (max.)

The choice-criterion models with which we shall be concerned are the maximin, the minimax regret, and the Laplace.

The Maximin Criterion

The *maximin criterion* is so named because it requires the decision maker to choose the action that *maxi*mizes the *min*imum payoff. That is, the decision maker determines what the worst outcome could be for each action–state of nature pair and chooses the course of action whose worst outcome could be, for each action, better than that of any other action. When using this criterion, it is assumed that the decision maker has no meaningful information on which to base probability assignments to the various states of nature. Application of the maximin model to the previously described marketing-program problem (see Table 1-3) is illustrated in Table A.

The new marketing program in this illustration involved the use of a salesperson in lieu of a portion of media advertising. Since the worst payoff if the new program is adopted is -7, while if the old program is retained it is only -2, the decision maker who uses the maximin model will choose act A_2: retain the old program.

This model is clearly a conservative one, as it assumes, in effect, that the worst that can happen will happen. It is difficult to imagine any new commercial venture that does not have a negative payoff for some state of nature. Consequently, persistent use of the maximin criterion would prevent such ventures from being initiated. When one considers that this is the case even when the potential loss is small and the gain large, one must question the consistent use of this model for choice among alternative actions.

The Minimax Regret Criterion

The *minimax regret model* is a closely related, if somewhat more sophisticated, version of the maximin model. The name for this model is coined from the decision rule it employs: it requires that the decision maker *minimize* the *maximum regret* that could be incurred.

This decision criterion, formulated by L. J. Savage,[21] uses the maximin criterion

---

[21]L. J. Savage, "The Theory of Statistical Decision," *Journal of the American Statistical Association,* 46 (March 1951), 56–67.

TABLE B   Application of Minimax Regret Criterion

Action	S_1: New marketing Program Superior to Old	S_2: Old Marketing Program Superior to New	Maximum Regret
A_1: adopt new	0	11	11 (min.)
A_2: retain old	17	0	17

but applies it to a choice among outcomes expressed as levels of "regret." The same assumption is made that the worst possible outcome will occur, given each state of nature.

To apply this criterion, therefore, we must first transform the payoff matrix to a regret matrix. We do so by assuming in turn that each state of nature will be the true state, and then determining the resulting conditional regret associated with each action. In our illustration, if state S_1 is the true state we would have incurred *no* regret by choosing action A_1, since 15 units is the maximum outcome we could have realized under that state of nature. However, we would incur 17 units (15 + 2) of regret by having chosen action A_2. Applying the same reasoning to state S_2, we arrive at the regret matrix shown in Table B for our marketing-program problem.

The decision based on this criterion, then, is to choose act A_1: adopt the new program, since this choice minimizes the maximum regret that can be incurred.

The minimax regret criterion is subject to the same criticism as the maximin rule: it assumes a persistently malevolent nature.

The Laplace Criterion

The *Laplace* criterion, unlike the maximin or minimax regret criteria, employs assignments of probabilities to the occurrence of each state of nature. These probabilities are based on the principle of insufficient reason, however, and are restricted to a single type of probability set as a result. The *principle of insufficient reason* states that, if there is no evidence to suggest that any one event from a mutually exclusive and exhaustive set of events is more likely to occur than any other, each event should be considered to have the *same* probability of occurrence. Application of this criterion is shown in Table C.

TABLE C   Application of the Laplace Criterion

Action	$P(S_1)$	S_1: New marketing Program Superior to Old	$P(S_2)$	S_2: Old Marketing Program Superior to New	Expected Value
A_1: adopt new	0.5	15	0.5	−7	4.0 (max.)
A_2: retain old	0.5	−2	0.5	4	1.0

As the table shows, assignment of equal probabilities over the states of nature, S_1 and S_2, results in assigning $P = 0.5$ to each state. If one then takes a weighted average of the payoffs assigned to each state of nature for a given act, an expected value is obtained. For act A_1, the expected value or payoff is 4.0 units [$4.0 = 0.5(15) + 0.5(-7)$]; the expected value for act A_2 is found similarly. The Laplace criterion requires that the course of action with the highest expected value be chosen. Thus, in our example the decision would be made to adopt the new marketing program.

The major criticism of this decision rule is that it is not necessarily independent of the number of states of nature specified in the model. Since equal probabilities are assigned to each state of nature, the probability for each state will be $P = 1/n$, where n is the number of states of nature. As n changes, the probabilities attached to each state change, and except in special cases, the expected values change.

For most real problems there are many possible listings of states of nature. For example, we could easily and reasonably increase the number of states in our illustration by adding a third one, S_3, defined as "new and old marketing programs equally effective." With the addition of the third state the probability of each becomes $P = 0.33$. Similarly, we could expand to four states of nature by dichotomizing the present S_1 and S_2 definitions into "greatly superior" and "moderately superior," respectively. With this structuring of the model, the probability of each state becomes $P = 0.25$.

Each of the three preceding criteria assumed "total ignorance" about the true state of nature. If a research project were being conducted to obtain information for a decision to be made using any one of these choice-criterion models, it would be limited to developing alternative actions, defining states of nature, and estimating the payoffs of the action–state pairs. No consideration would be given to obtaining information to help decide which state of nature is likely to be the true state.

In practice, however, it is a rare situation in which the decision maker does not possess *some* information about the likelihood of the occurrence of each state. The fact that the decision maker has included certain states of nature in structuring the problem argues that he or she has assigned some probability greater than zero to the occurrence of each. It seems even more unusual that a decision maker would not want information that would help him or her assess more precisely the probability of occurrence of each state.

ASSIGNMENT MATERIAL

1. Assume that you are faced with the alternative of changing a package design for a firm marketing frozen peas. Describe the major environmental conditions that could affect sales and cost considerations associated with changing over to the new design.

2. It has been suggested that the distinction between basic research and decisional research is that the purpose of the former is to answer a question and the purpose of the latter is to solve a problem. Comment.

3. Give several examples of research projects dealing with human behavior that might be either basic or decisional, depending on who the "client" of the project is.

4. Six types of management decisions were identified. For each, give examples of marketing research that might be done for a company manufacturing bicycles.

5. What practical characteristics must information have to be useful for making decisions? Can we really say one is more important than the others?

6. Of what value is it to the marketing researcher to explore with a client the actions that would be taken, given alternative research outcomes, *before* the contemplated research is undertaken?

7. Using the operation of a household thermostat as a model, construct a theory for modeling call frequency of salespeople on key accounts.
   a. What is your measure of effectiveness?
   b. What are the control variables?
   c. What functional relationship appears plausible?
   d. Criticize the thermostat model as an appropriate "analogy" in this context.

8. Suppose that you have the following conditional payoff table for establishing a franchising operation in the restaurant field.

	S_1		S_2		S_3	
ALTERNATIVE	*Probability*	*Payoff*	*Probability*	*Payoff*	*Probability*	*Payoff*
A_1: establish franchises in 20 states	0.2	+$250	0.5	+$100	0.3	−$400
A_2: establish franchises in 10 states	0.2	+$100	0.5	+$ 40	0.3	−$100
A_3: do not establish franchises	0.2	0	0.5	0	0.3	0

What decision would you make if you used a
   a. Maximin decision rule?
   b. Minimax regret decision rule?
   c. Laplace decision rule?
   d. Bayesian decision rule?

2

The Tactics of Marketing Research—Planning the Research Project

INTRODUCTION

In this chapter we provide an overview of the research process and what is involved in planning a research project. In Chapter 1 we made a distinction between basic and decisional (i.e., applied) research. This distinction is important in that the difference in usage of information (i.e., to provide information for a pending decision vs. increasing level of knowledge in a given area) affects the way research is conducted.

There are essentially four broad determinants of how a research project should be conducted: the nature of the *problem,* the *researcher,* the *respondent,* and the *client.* It is not difficult to think of basic- and decisional-research projects dealing with the same problem, being conducted by the same researcher, and using the same respondents to provide information. A consumer-motivation study or a voting behavior study are potential examples. These projects would have different clients, however, and it is there that we must look for the source of method and design difference requirements.

It is clear that all clients, regardless of who they may be, would *like* information whose errors are small but *need* information whose errors or potential errors can be measured with reasonable accuracy. Information of unknown accuracy may be worse than none at all. Similarly, it is apparent that all clients would like to have objective measures of the potential error.

It is the differences in the level of allowable error of basic- and decisional-research clients and the ways in which they go about assessing the level of actual error that give rise to process and method differences in the two types of research. The "client" of a basic survey research project is the scientific community to which it is reported. It is typically a large group of people who might more properly be referred to as a "clientele" than as a "client." It normally will not have commissioned the research, nor, as a group if not as individuals, will it be affected personally by the outcome. The researcher may or may not be known to the majority of those to whom the results of the project are reported.

Scientists historically have insisted upon eliminating as much error as possible and obtaining objectively verifiable measures of the remaining potential error. Ideally, the research must have been conducted with full disclosure of procedures that provide for investigator independence. The capability of replication of the project by other investigators from the report is a means of ensuring that these requirements are met.

The client of the decisional-research project would always choose as little error as possible and objective measurement of the residual potential error if these options were available at no additional cost. However, as the financial sponsor of the research as well as the user of it, such a client may find that beyond some point added accuracy is not worth the cost of obtaining it. The same conclusion may also be reached about objective measurement of residual error.

The decisional-research client also has an added means of assessment of research information not generally available to his or her basic-research counterparts. The client will typically have been closely associated with the project from the inception, in many cases even to the point of having chosen the principal researcher or researchers involved. He or she will, therefore, have had many opportunities to assess both the general competence of the researchers and the manner in which the project has been conducted. The need for objective measurement of error and for investigator independence in procedures may have become less as a result.

Finally, there is rarely a need for replication in decisional-research projects. Most research projects conducted for decision-making purposes are concerned with problems that are essentially unique and nonrecurring. A new product to be evaluated before deciding whether to introduce it, or the determination of the proportion of the electorate who favor a political candidate, may require decisions at a later date, but the circumstances will inevitably have changed. Including features in the research plan that incur added costs solely to permit replication are, therefore, seldom reasonable objectives in decisional projects.

Thus, differences in client requirements often give rise to different requirements in basic- and decisional-research projects. The value versus cost orientation of decisional research, which will be examined in Chapter 3, is an outgrowth of these differences.

We now turn to a discussion of the broad research process and what a research project entails. In planning a project it must be remembered that the overriding concern facing the researcher is error. Consequently, the practice of marketing research may be viewed as involving the management of *total error*. The concept of total error is discussed in Chapter 4.

For purposes of planning, the research process can be viewed as consisting of a number of interrelated steps, as shown in Figure 2-1. Although presented in a hierarchical format, some of the steps may be performed simultaneously. There are times, in addition, when alternatives for "later" decisions influence decisions that are made early in the

Figure 2-1   The Research Process

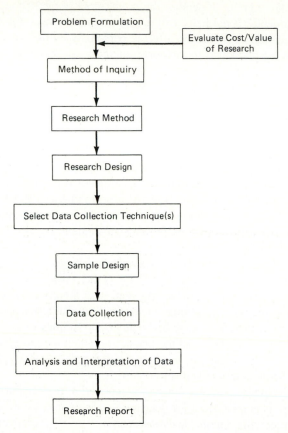

process. For example, desired analysis techniques often influence the selection of data collection techniques (e.g., measurement) and sample design.

PROBLEM FORMULATION

In a very real sense, problem formulation is the "heart" of the research process. As such it represents the single most important step to be performed. Problem formulation from the researcher's point of view represents translating the *management problem* into a *research problem* (see Table 2-1). In order for this to occur the researcher must understand the origin and nature of management's problem and then be able to rephrase it into meaningful terms from an analytical point of view. The end result is not only a management problem that is analytically meaningful but one that often points the way to alternative solutions—i.e., specifying the types of information needed to help solve the management problem.

TABLE 2-1   Examples of Management and Research Problems

MANAGEMENT PROBLEMS	RESEARCH PROBLEMS
Allocate advertising budget among media	Estimate awareness generated by each media type
Decide whether to keep office open on Saturday	Evaluate use of services on Saturday and determine if customers can do these on weekdays
Introduce a new health service	Design a concept "test" through which likely acceptance and use can be assessed
Change the marketing program	Design a test-marketing situation such that the effect of the new program can be estimated
Increase the sales of a product	Measure current image of the product

In order for the research problem to be formulated there must be a dialogue between the researcher and the manager, as we discussed in Chapter 1. Without such a dialogue there is a great risk that the problem will not be defined properly. If this happens, even the best planned and implemented project will produce information that has no value, in a Bayesian sense. A few years ago Seagram was marketing a new wine and the vice-president of marketing requested a survey of the U.S. wine market.[1] Discussion between "management" and the research department led to the decision that the survey should produce advertising copy strategy, target groups, an image of the brand compared with that of other wines, and a media mix. According to Robert W. Beller, vice-president of marketing services:

> It's fundamental, but I think we would have not done anybody involved any favor if we had just done a survey when we were asked to do a survey. It is up to the marketing and research people involved to, up front, build action intentions or objectives into the research.

After the research results were combined with other data to develop an advertising campaign, sales of the brand increased 74% in two years while category sales increased only 13%.

Closely related to problem formulation is the development of hypotheses or, more properly, "working hypotheses." While hypotheses are crucial for basic research because they tell the researcher, in effect, what to do, the concept of a hypothesis is useful in decisional research. In most cases the marketing researcher will not explicitly state hypotheses for testing. However, implicit hypotheses will often serve as guidelines for the research.[2]

At all times it must be remembered that management and the researcher are interacting on potential research involving decisions that must be made under conditions of

---

[1]"Action-Oriented Research Spells Success for New Seagram Wine," *Marketing News,* 15 (January 1981), 7.

[2]The nature of problems, problem statements, and hypotheses is presented in Fred N. Kerlinger, *Foundations of Behavioral Research* 2nd ed. (New York: Holt, Rinehart & Winston, 1973), Chap. 2.

uncertainty. We now discuss problem formulation under such conditions from both the manager's and the researcher's viewpoints.

The Manager's Viewpoint

Informational needs as viewed by the marketing executive will arise in connection with a variety of marketing problems:

1. What media should be employed in next year's advertising campaign?
2. Should the new product, now undergoing test marketing, be commercialized?
3. If I reduce the price of the larger package size, will my total profits be increased?
4. Should my distributors be given exclusive territories in the Southwest?

Questions such as these presuppose opportunities for choice. But the consequences attached to the choices are not known with certainty. As a matter of fact, the marketing executive frequently faces problems in areas where little or no directly related information is available. This executive often deals with more or less unique events, and the experience gained in dealing with earlier problems must somehow be searched and analyzed for relevance to his or her current problem situation.

Components of a Problem

As implied earlier, a problem consists of a set of specific components: (1) the decision maker(s) and his or her (their) objectives; (2) the environment or context of the problem; (3) alternative courses of action; (4) a set of consequences that relate to courses of action and the occurrence of events not under the control of the decision maker; and (5) a state of doubt as to which course of action is best.

The Decision Maker and Objectives.   The decision maker may not always be represented by a single individual; marketing decisions may be made by a marketing group of two or more people. Moreover, some members of the group may not agree with the choice made because of differences either in objectives (i.e., valued outcomes) or in their appraisal of the effectiveness of means chosen to achieve the objectives. In other situations an individual may be performing the role of agent for some superior or group of superiors.

In later chapters we shall be describing decision theory and its applications as though only a *single* individual represented the decision maker, knowing full well that a gross simplification is being made. Not that the theory cannot be extended to deal with group decision making; but such an extension would require knowledge of the group's objectives and a means of combining conflicting objectives or conflicting viewpoints as the preferable course of action. These extensions would carry us far beyond the scope of this book.

The objectives of the decision maker provide motivation for the decision. These objectives, or goals, may range from a desire to maintain or increase company profits and market share to personal goals concerned with maintaining prestige and a desire to advance in the corporation. However, most of the objectives with which we shall deal involve only monetary considerations (e.g., net profits, cash flow, return on investment) and, hence, represent another simplification of the real world.

The decision maker's objectives may also be characterized by their hierarchical nature at any given moment and their evolution over time. For example, an increase in the firm's profits may come about through an increase in the firm's sales, which, in turn, may be accomplished by the firm's sales personnel contacting a greater number of new accounts per month. The goal for the salesperson may be to increase sales contacts 10% over those made in some base period, but this represents a subgoal, consistent, it is hoped, with a higher-level objective. The decision theorist also faces the problem of estimating changes in objectives over time. Current value theory generally assumes that objectives remain stable over the relevant decision period, again a simplifying assumption.

Finally, we shall be assuming that the decision maker really knows what his or her objectives are and that these can be communicated to the market researcher. In practice, such is often not the case. One of the major jobs of the research practitioner is to attempt to draw out these objectives and to ascertain the relevance of the proposed research to the decision maker's goals and state of information.

Environment of the Problem. Every problem exists within a context of the characteristics of the company and of the market—consumer tastes and preferences, level of income and rate of growth in the market areas, the degree of competition and competitor action and reaction, and the type and extent of governmental regulation. These environmental factors may individually and collectively affect the outcome of the decision made. The researcher must assist the manager in identifying these relevant environmental factors.

Consider the problem of deciding whether to introduce a new consumer product. Some of the environmental factors that could affect the decision are as follows:

- The types of consumers that comprise the potential market
- The size and location of the market
- The prospects for growth or contraction of the market over the planning period
- The buying habits of consumers
- The current competition for the product
- The likelihood and timing of entry of new competitive products
- The current and prospective competitive position with respect to price, quality, and reputation
- The marketing and manufacturing capabilities of the company
- The situation with respect to patents, trademarks, and royalties
- The situation with respect to codes, trade agreements, taxes, and tariffs

Although this listing is by no means exhaustive, it illustrates some of the more important environmental factors that could influence the outcome of the decision and so must be considered in the problem statement. Each problem has a comparable set of environmental factors to be considered.

Alternative Courses of Action.   A *course of action* is a specification of some behavioral sequence, such as the construction of a new warehouse, the adoption of a new package design, or the introduction of a new product. All courses of action involve, either implicitly or explicitly, the element of time. For example, "Construct a warehouse, starting next week" is a different course of action from "Construct a warehouse, starting next year." A course of action that indicates "Do nothing new" is just as much a course of action as one denoting a change from the status quo.

Actions, of course, can be taken only in the present. A decision to *stipulate* a program of action becomes a commitment, made in the present, to follow some behavioral pattern in the future. The implementation of this course of action may well extend over time as, for example, a program involving the construction of a new plant. Courses of action may thus range in complexity from a single act to be implemented immediately to a large set of related acts proceeding either in parallel or sequentially over time. The time interval, which becomes a part of the course of action, may be highly important, since both the costs of implementation and the probabilities of alternative outcomes will typically vary as a function of time. Forecast error usually increases as a function of time. Frequently, however, implementation of some action may be delayed pending the receipt of better information with relatively little cost associated with this delay.

Two additional points about courses of action will be mentioned briefly here and then developed more fully in later chapters. First, courses of action can be spelled out in greater or lesser degree, depending on the problem under consideration. For some purposes it may be sufficient merely to state the course of action: "Add two new salespeople in the Chicago district starting next month." In other instances a more detailed specification (regarding the type of salespeople to be hired in terms of previous experience, education, product familiarity, etc.) may be required. Second, courses of action may include *decision rules,* that is, various conditional statements in the program of action. For example, a course of action may be: "Start designing a new plant; if sales from the existing plant exceed 100,000 units by the end of next year, start new plant construction; if not, reconsider the decision to build a new plant." We shall call this type of course of action a *contingency plan,* since its implementation is dependent on some unknown even at the time of stipulation. Although we have a *recipe* for reacting to each possible event, we do not know *which* act will be implemented until one of the possible events occurs.

The Consequences of Alternative Courses of Action.   The world of uncertainty is a common world for the marketer. When choosing a course of action, a marketer can rarely be certain of the consequences, since the choice is usually based on incomplete information about the various factors that influence the decision's outcome. A primary job is thus to list the possible outcomes of various courses of action. But these outcomes will depend on various environmental factors. For example, suppose that a manufacturer of industrial belting is interested in increasing the tensile strength of this product. Presumably, higher production costs will be incurred in effecting this increase in strength. The decision to modify the product will be dependent on additional sales anticipated through marketing a stronger product. The additional sales will obviously depend on how customers react to the modification, the actions that competitors take, and so on.

As discussed earlier, the phrase "state of nature" is frequently used to refer to alternative descriptions of the decision maker's environment. Moreover, as was shown in Chapter 1 (Table 1-4), each action–state pair leads to a set of consequences that can ultimately be expressed as a payoff.

As before, the term "consequence" is relative. In the marketing-program example, the immediate consequence or outcome may represent sales of so many physical units. The final payoff of the decision maker, however, may represent the cash flow generated by these additional sales. As such, it would include assumptions about price, production costs, and the time span and pattern of cash inflows and outflows. If the decision maker were also to treat these assumptions as states of nature, it is clear that an expansion of Table 1-4 would be required.

It should now be apparent that the choice of courses of action, states of nature, and the details of the consequences of combining each course of action with each state of nature depend on the decision maker's model of the problem. Expansion of each class of variables can take place either *intensively* (specifying each variable in greater detail) or *extensively* (increasing the number of courses of action, states of nature, etc.). The primary notion to keep in mind is that all these entities are *conceptual* and no rules exist about how detailed the problem's structure should be. That is, no one model of the problem can be considered to be the "correct" one.

State of Doubt.   To solve a problem is to select the best course of action for attaining the decision maker's objectives. A state of doubt as to which course of action is best can arise under three main classes of conditions:

1. *Certainty* with respect to each course of action leading to a specific outcome. The problem here, however, is that the number of courses of action may be so large (even infinite) that some mathematical means is necessary to identify the best alternative.

2. *Risk* with respect to each action leading to a set of possible outcomes, each outcome occurring with a "known" probability. For example, if a fair coin is tossed, we may assume that over the long run the proportion of heads will approach one-half; however, on any single toss we cannot predict whether a head or a tail will appear.

3. *Uncertainty* with respect to outcomes, given a particular course of action. In this view of decision making we assume that the relative frequencies of the probabilities are *not* known. One version of this class of models, exemplified in the Bayesian approach to decision making (to be described later), assumes that the decision maker can express various "degrees of belief" as to the occurrence of alternative outcomes. Moreover, the decision maker may be able, in many cases, to collect more information regarding the "true" state of nature.

    Other versions of the uncertainty class (called total ignorance models) assume that the probabilities to be attached to alternative outcomes are either not applicable to begin with, or if they are, must be equal for each outcome that can occur.

Most marketing problems are characterized by a situation of *uncertainty*. The decision maker is usually dealing with a set of more or less unique conditions. Experience in dealing with broadly similar—if not identical—problems may permit the decision maker to assign various "degrees of belief" to the occurrence of various possible outcomes, given specific courses of action.

The Researcher's Viewpoint

A carefully formulated problem is a necessary point of departure for competently conducted research. There should be as clear and thorough an understanding as possible on the part of both the researcher and the decision maker as to the precise purposes of the research. In effect, this statement of purpose involves a *translation of the decision maker's problem into a research problem and study design*. The decision maker is faced with a problem for which he or she must recognize alternative courses of action, choosing among them to accomplish one or more objectives. The research problem is to provide relevant information concerning recognized (or newly generated) alternative solutions to aid in this choice. To determine what information is required, the researcher will try to identify and understand the major elements of the problem faced by the decision maker.

Determining Objectives

Objectives range from the very general, such as profit maximization, to the highly specific, such as obtaining a particular account. They also vary from jointly agreed-upon corporate objectives to the particularized objectives of each employee. In this section we shall be concerned with the objectives of the decision maker, whether general or particular, as they affect the formulation of the problem to be researched.

Suppose that the marketing manager says, "I need to know how effective our last advertising campaign was." Superficially, it may seem that this is an adequate statement of the objective of the research project to be initiated—to determine the effectiveness of the last advertising campaign. However, on reflection it is apparent that this statement does not state an objective at all. Why does the marketing manager want this information? If his or her purpose is to evaluate the agency's handling of the campaign, an entirely different kind of research may be appropriate than if the purpose is, say, to use the information to aid in deciding on the level and allocation of the advertising budget for the coming period. Knowledge of the specific objectives may well influence the kind of information desired and the degree of accuracy that is required. The research problem cannot be adequately formulated, therefore, without knowing the objectives of the client.

It is the exceptional project in which the objectives are explained fully to the researcher. The decision maker will seldom have formulated any objectives completely, and, even if he or she has, may not be willing to disclose all of them. *The researcher will normally need to take the initiative*, therefore, in developing a clear statement of objectives. This can frequently turn out to be a difficult task, but it is nonetheless a necessary and valuable one.

Direct questioning of the executive concerned about objectives can only be successful in those cases where he or she is able and willing to disclose them. Since we have already indicated that these conditions are seldom fully met, it is usually necessary to resort to direct methods of determining objectives. Two techniques are useful in this indirect approach.

The first of these is the "explosion" of the problem through exploring with the decision maker what is meant exactly by the terms in the statement of the problem. For example, in the statement, "I need to know how effective our last advertising campaign was," the researcher must know what the marketing manager means by the word "effective" in order to ensure that the problem statement formulated specifies the kinds of information that the manager needs. Does the manager mean the extent to which the campaign *informed* the audience of the content of the advertising? If so, the research project will need to be designed to measure such variables as audience level, recall, and level of knowledge. If the manager means the degree to which the campaign *persuaded* the audience of the merits of the product, then a different kind of research project is needed. In this case, a measurement of changes in attitudes and/or preferences will need to be made and linked with exposure to the advertising. Or, if the manager means the volume of *sales* resulting from the campaign, still another kind of research project will be required. By raising such questions, noting the answers, and probing where required, the researcher can be much further along toward a clear formulation of the problem in terms of the appropriate measurements required. By this process the researcher may also provide a valuable service by helping the manager to understand more fully the possible objectives and to sort out the important ones.

A second approach to clarification of the objectives is to raise questions with the manager as to what actions would be taken, given specified outcomes of the study. If the research shows that the last campaign was ineffective, will the advertising budget be increased? Different appeals used? Allocation of the budget among media changed? A new agency given the account? It is often helpful to raise such questions with subordinates or other appropriate members of the organization as well, in terms of what actions they think *would* be taken, as a result of the possible outcomes of the research.

It should be apparent at this stage that problem formulation is not and cannot be delayed in its entirety until after the research problem has been selected. In fact, these two activities, and design of the research as well, must be done at least somewhat simultaneously, rather than sequentially. Careful problem formulation may well eliminate some problems as candidates for research.

Alternative Courses of Action and Statement of Hypotheses

As discussed earlier, alternative courses of action are the various possible solutions to the problem. It is usually desirable that as many alternatives as possible be recognized during the problem-formulation stage and stated in the form of research hypotheses to be examined.

A *hypothesis* is an assertion about the "state of nature" and, from a practical standpoint, often implies a possible course of action with a prediction of the outcome if the course of action is followed. The prediction thus becomes an assertion about a state (or states) of nature, frequently stated in terms of the objective (or objectives) to be accomplished. For example, if a decision is to be made concerning whether or not to adopt a new package, and the immediate objective is to obtain a 15% share of the market, a hypothesis may be stated that adoption of the proposed new package *will* result in a market share of at least 15%. It will then become the task of the researcher to obtain information to test this assertion (by developing hypotheses concerning acceptance on a trial-market basis) and thus to assist in the process of deciding whether or not to change to the new package.

How does the researcher recognize relevant alternative courses of action and thus develop hypotheses? It is clear that this process is at least as much an art as it is a science, as it is dependent to a significant extent on the experience, judgment, and creative capabilities of the individuals concerned. It is also apparent that relevant alternative courses of action should be closely related to the objectives to be achieved.

There is perhaps no better illustration of this relationship than the general problem of diversification of products. While there is almost always the general objective of increasing profit through the addition of new products, other objectives are invariably present as well. Utilization of excess capacity in one or more of the functional areas of the business (manufacturing, marketing, etc.), reducing seasonal or cyclical fluctuations in sales, and rounding out the product line are a few of the possible objectives for diversification. If one of the major objectives is to utilize excess manufacturing capacity, this may greatly limit the number of possible products that should be considered. The relevant possible courses of action are therefore closely tied to the objectives of diversifying.

The identification of possible courses of action is closely related to the problem-situation model. Once the objectives have been agreed upon, the formulation of the model consists of

1. Determining which variables *affect* the solution to the problem.
2. Determining which of these variables are *controllable* and to what extent control can be exercised.
3. Determining the *functional relationship* of the variables. The nature of this relationship will indicate which variables are critical to the solution of the problem.

Examples of failures to follow through on these three aspects of the problem-situation model are not difficult to find.

CPC International met some resistance when it tried to sell its dry Knorr soups in the United States. The company had test marketed the product by serving passersby a small portion of its already-prepared warm soup. After the taste test, the individuals were questioned about possible sales. The research revealed U.S. interest, but sales were very low once the packages were placed on grocery-store shelves. Further investigation indicated that the market tests had overlooked the American tendency to avoid most dry soups. During the testing, those interviewed were unaware they were tasting a dried soup. Finding the taste quite acceptable, the interviewees indicated they would be willing to buy it. Had they known the soup was sold in a dry form and that during preparation it required 15–20 minutes of occasional stirring, they would have shown less interest in the product. In this particular case, the preparation was extremely important, and the failure to test for this unique difference resulted in a sluggish market.[3]

Taste was certainly not the critical variable in this problem.

The Environment of the Research Problem

The effects of the environment of the problem—those factors which both *affect* the outcome and are *uncontrollable*—cannot be predicted with certainty. However, for a given problem it may be sufficient to consider only a few of the many possible outcomes for each of the alternatives. For example, in a decision concerning whether or not to introduce a new product, the executive may be interested only in whether the sales volume is likely to exceed or not exceed some desired level.

We shall find that many ways exist to formulate a problem in terms of the set of mutually exclusive and exhaustive states of the problem environment that are to be considered. In fact, one of the jobs of the market researcher is to assemble information concerning the firm's environmental variables to assist in identifying the states of nature that should be considered. The possible states may range from fairly detailed descriptions to broad, summarizing descriptions in which data are condensed into a relatively small number of potential sales levels over a specific time period.

In summary, the marketing researcher, to be effective as an information supplier, must work closely with his or her client in effecting a transformation of the client's problem into a research problem. Since the researcher's and client's interests are both concerned with the potential value versus cost of the research findings, the researcher must become aware of, and *assist in,* the identification of objectives, courses of action, and environmental variables, insofar as they affect the design of the research investigation. For that matter, the researcher's efforts should be oriented toward helping the manager decide whether *any* investigation is justified.

Evaluate Cost/Value

At some point during the problem formulation process (perhaps only at the end of it), there is need to decide whether a formal investigation is justified. This decision is also one that involves communication between the manager and the researcher. Of interest to the decision maker is whether a decision should be made using only experience, judgment, and existing knowledge or whether the decision should be delayed until the proposed project is completed. We have suggested that this situation involves comparing

[3]David A. Ricks, *Big Business Blunders: Mistakes in Multinational Marketing* (Homewood, Ill.: Dow Jones-Irwin, 1983), p. 129.

Exhibit 2-1   Problems and Hypotheses

The criteria of good research problems and problem statements, and hypotheses, are:

Problem and Problem Statements

1. The problem should express a relation between two or more variables.
2. The problem should be stated clearly and unambiguously in question form.
3. The problem and problem statement should be such as to imply possibilities of empirical testing.

Hypotheses

1. The hypothesis should be a statement about the relation between two or more variables, and should always be in declarative statement form.
2. The hypothesis should carry clear implications for testing the stated relation —i.e., variables must be measurable or potentially measurable.

Source: Adapted from Fred N. Kerlinger, *Foundations of Behavioral Research,* 2nd ed. New York: Holt, Rinehart & Winston, 1973), pp. 17–18.

the additional value to the decision that the research will provide with the cost of conducting the research. We discuss this process, particularly the Bayesian approach introduced in Chapter 1, in greater detail in Chapter 3.

METHOD OF INQUIRY

In establishing investigative methods in the behavioral sciences, researchers turned to the natural sciences for guidance and method of inquiry. The name *scientific method* was borrowed along with the procedures. While this method was never the only one used, it quickly became accepted and entrenched as the standard against which other investigative methods were to be measured. The hallmark of a scientific methodologist, whom we shall refer to as an *objectivist* in the behavioral sciences, is to run a hypothesis test using publicly stated procedures that are investigator independent. Other investigators differ in kind or degree of requirement with respect to these criteria. The *subjectivist* requires a hypothesis test but is not as strict in the requirement for publicity of procedures or investigator independence. The *Bayesian* also tests hypotheses, using either objectivist or subjectivist methods in addition to his or her prior judgments. Therefore, the Bayesian will insist that procedures cannot be either fully publicly available or investigator independent. The *phenomenologist* has been insisting for the past seventy-five years that hypotheses not be tested, that the procedures for inquiry need not be public, and that the process of inquiry cannot be investigator independent.

The objectivist, subjectivist, and Bayesian follow the same steps: formulating a problem, developing a hypothesis, making predictions based on the hypothesis, devising a test of the hypothesis, conducting the test, and analyzing test results. While the terminology used is that associated with basic research, the reader will recognize that the process described is analogous to that of decision making. Substitution of the word *alternative* for *hypothesis* accomplishes most of the rephrasing required to transpose it to a decisional context. Although the steps are the same, there are differences in the way in which the steps are performed and in the underlying assumptions of behavior (Exhibit 2-2). For example, the essential difference between the objectivist and the subjectivist is the latter's allowance for use of subjective judgments when both collecting data and analyzing them.[4] The distinction has very practical meaning, particularly when considering the use of outside research suppliers. There are commercial research firms that tend to specialize in one or the other method of inquiry.

Implicit in the objectivist and subjectivist designs are the assumptions that (1) the likelihood obtained from the test is the only probability statement that is to be included in the test, and (2) the costs of errors are adequately reflected in the significance levels chosen. Bayesians disagree with both assumptions. As will be shown in Chapter 3, the Bayesian believes that prior judgments should be included as a part of the test and that a client who has ordered a study and an investigator who has reached the point of developing hypotheses for the study each have reasonably well developed judgments about the alternatives to be investigated.

The method of inquiry resulting in the greatest degree of investigator independence is that of phenomenology. A difference of kind in belief between the objectivist-subjectivist-Bayesian on the one side and the phenomenalist on the other is with respect to the role of the explanatory hypothesis. The discussion to this point has emphasized the centrality of the hypothesis and the testing of it to each of the three methods of inquiry. The phenomenalist is opposed to the use of explanatory hypotheses. Hypotheses represent preconceived ideas of the phenomenon and, as such, are viewed as leading to selective perception and distortion of measurement.

Therefore, a legitimate question is, What *is* the method of phenomenology? An answer is that, although there is no one universally accepted "method" as such, four steps are recognized by enough phenomenalists to qualify as representative of the approach generally followed:[5]

1. Suspension of prior conceptions
2. Description of the phenomenon
3. Determination of universal elements
4. Apprehending of relationships

In a real sense, this method of inquiry is analogous to what many researchers call a "fishing expedition" without knowing anything about the body of water. Some marketing

---

[4]For an excellent review article of the positions of objectivists and subjectivists, see Paul Diesing, "Objectivism vs. Subjectivism in the Social Sciences," *Philosophy of Science,* 33 (March–June 1966), 124–33.

[5]See Herbert Spiegelbug, *The Phenomenological Movement* (The Hague: Martinus Nijhoff, 1969), Vols. 1 and 2.

Exhibit 2-2   The Objectivist, Subjectivist, and Bayesian Methods of Inquiry in the Behavioral Sciences

STAGE	OBJECTIVIST	SUBJECTIVIST	BAYESIAN
1. Develop hypothesis	The hypothesis is based on a model held by the investigator concerning the subject to be investigated. The model may be private or public. The existence of such a model implies a prior probability attached to the truth of the hypothesis by the investigator. This prior probability is ignored.	Same as objectivist.	Same as objectivist/subjectivist except that prior probabilities are recognized and expressed formally when the hypothesis is formulated.
2. Make prediction(s)	Predictions must involve only behavior that can be observed. The behavior to be recorded must be specified.	Prediction need not be limited to observable behavior. The behavior to be recorded need not necessarily be specified in advance.	May be objectivist, or subjectivist, or a combination of both.
3. Devise test	The test must be made by observing and recording overt behavior (real or simulated) by specified method. Criteria for acceptance or rejection of hypothesis are specified. Testing methods commonly in use include controlled experiments, survey research using random samples, structured interviews, and simulations.	The test must be made by observing overt behavior, but the investigator has at least some freedom of selection of behavior to be recorded. Test may be partially ad hoc in nature conditional on results in early stages. Criteria for acceptance or rejection of hypotheses are somtimes exstablished on ex post basis. Testing methods advocated and used include a priori deductions, participant observation, uncontrolled experiments, and survey research using population samples and unstructured interviews.	May be objectivist or subjectivist or a combination of both.

Stage	Objectivist	Subjectivist	Bayesian
4. Conduct test	Procedures must be public. The findings must be investigator free in that they are capable of being replicated by other investigators.	Procedures often cannot be made fully public and findings may or may not be capable of being replicated, since they may be investigator dependent.	May be objectivist or subjectivist or a combination of both.
5. Analyze test results	Analysis is conducted using methods of descriptive and inferential statistics. Hypothesis is rejected or not on the basis of the criteria specified earlier.	Analysis is conducted using methods of descriptive and where applicable, inferential statistics. Hypothesis is rejected or not based on specified or ex post criteria.	Analysis may proceed initially along either objectivist or subjectivist lines. If the initial analysis is objectivist in nature, the prior probability that the hypothesis should be rejected is revised formally by the use of specified mathematical procedures. If the initial analysis is subjectivist in nature, the prior probability that the hypothesis should be rejected is revised informally.

research involves characteristics of this method, since the "problem" may represent desiring to know something that no one knows anything about.

RESEARCH METHOD

What is an appropriate method of inquiry for a research problem depends in large part on the nature of the problem itself and the extent or level of existing knowledge. In addition to selecting a method of inquiry, the research planner must also select a research methodology. Two broad methodologies can be used to answer any research question—*experimental* research and *nonexperimental* research. The major difference between the two methodologies lies in the control of extraneous variables and manipulation of at least one variable by the intervention of the investigator in experimental research. In nonexperimental research, there is no intervention beyond that needed for purposes of measurement.

RESEARCH DESIGN

Once the methodology has been selected, the next step is to develop a research design. A research design is defined as *the specification of methods and procedures for acquiring the information needed*. It is a plan or organizing framework for doing the study and collecting the data. Whereas an objectivist, subjectivist, or Bayesian approach to a study may use either methodology, research designs are unique to a methodology. We discuss research design in Chapters 4 and 6.

DATA COLLECTION TECHNIQUES

The research design begins to take on detailed focus as the researcher selects the particular techniques to be used in solving the problem formulated and in carrying out the strategy or method selected. There are a number of techniques available for collecting data, and these can be used with either methodology. Some techniques are unique to a method of inquiry, whereas others can be used across such methods. For example, many of the so-called qualitative research techniques (e.g., projective techniques) are used only in subjectivist-type research.

In general, data collection uses the process of either *communication* or *observation*. Communication involves asking questions and receiving (it is hoped) a response. This process can be done in person, by mail, or by telephone, and in most instances constitutes the broad research technique known as the *survey*. In contrast to this process, data may be obtained by observing present or past behavior. Regarding past behavior, techniques will include looking at secondary data (e.g., company records, published studies by external sources, etc.) and physical traces (e.g., erosion and accretion).

In order to communicate or observe there must be a means of recording responses or behavior. Thus, the process of measurement and the development of a measurement instrument are closely connected to the decision of which data collection technique(s) should be used. The relationship is two-way. That is, while the structure and content of the measurement instrument can depend on the data collection technique, measurement considerations often influence technique selection.

SAMPLE DESIGN

Rarely will a marketing research project involve examining the entire population that is relevant to the problem. For the most part, practical considerations (e.g., absolute resources available, cost vs. value, etc.) dictate that a sample, or subset of the relevant population, be used. In other instances the use of a sample is derived from the tradeoff between systematic and variable errors.

In designing the sample, the researcher must specify three things: (1) where the sample is to be selected from, (2) the process of selection, and (3) the size of the sample.

The sample design must be consistent with the relevant population, which is usually specified in the problem formulation stage of the research process. This allows the data obtained from the sample to be used in making inferences about the larger population.

DATA COLLECTION

Once the previous six steps have been performed, data collection can begin. Data collection, whether by communication or observation, requires the use of people, which then raises questions regarding managing these people. Because data collection can be costly, firms often utilize outside limited service research suppliers. This is particularly

TABLE 2-2   The Supplier/Client–Field Service Communication Process

(A)
Perceived Determinants of Breakdown

REASONS	PERCENT OF RESPONDENTS ($N = 107$)
Insufficient Information supplied by Client	64
Supplier Serving as an Intermediary Between the Client and Field Firm	43
Client's Insufficient Interest in Data Collection	34
Isolation of Field Service Firm	25
Client's Desire to Maintain Control Over Project	21
Lack of Field Experience by Client	17
Constant Change While Project in Progress	2
Rigidity of Supplier to Make Adjustment	2
Other Reasons	17

(B)
Suggestions for Improvement

SPECIFIC SUGGESTIONS	PERCENT OF RESPONDENTS ($N = 107$)
Clients Providing More Information to Suppliers and Field Firms	76
Field Service Consulted on Pertinent Issues	68
Establishing/Renewing Two-Way Communication With Suppliers	51
Direct Contact Between Involved Personnel (Field and Project Director)	42
More Active Role by Project Director	22
Other Ways	11

Source: Madhav N. Segal and Cedric Newberry, "On the Field Service Agency—Supplier/Client Relationship: Problems and Perspectives," *Journal of Data Collection*, 23 (Winter 1983), 58, 59.

prudent when the extent of in-house research activity does not warrant the cost of having permanent data collection personnel. Also, there are times when the design of the project requires specialized data collection, and this can best be obtained from an outside supplier.

It is obvious that the working relationship between the data collection agency (e.g., a so-called field service) and the research supplier/client is a major factor affecting the quality of field work and data collection. A study of marketing research firms found that the major barriers in the communication process as information flows from clients to research suppliers to field service firms were insufficient information supplied by the client, the research supplier as an intermediary between client and field firm, and lack of client interest in data collection (see Table 2-2A). Not surprising, then, is that the major suggestion for improving communication is for clients to provide more information to suppliers and field firms, as shown in Table 2-2B. Another widely suggested way to overcome communication barriers is for the field service to be consulted on such major issues as scheduling, costs, and purpose of the study.

ANALYSIS AND INTERPRETATION

The data that have been obtained, presented in the same form as originally collected, are seldom useful to anyone. Data must be analyzed. Once obtained, the data must be edited, coded, and tabulated before formal analyses (e.g., statistical tests) can be performed. The types of analyses that can be performed (i.e., that can be "properly" performed) are a function of the sampling procedures, measurement instrument, and data collection techniques used. Consequently, it is imperative that the techniques of analysis be selected *prior* to data collection.

RESEARCH REPORT

The culmination of the research process is the research report. Everything that has been done and the results, conclusions, and—whenever possible—recommendations for courses of action should be included and presented clearly, accurately, and honestly. Two critical attributes of the report are that it provides all the information readers need using language they understand (*completeness*) and that at the same time the researcher must be selective in what is included (*conciseness*). These attributes are often in conflict with each other. According to one observer, "the vast majority of reports falls short of meaningfully interpreting the data to management in a way that useful action can be taken."[6]

Two approaches can be taken in order that the "conflict" not be a problem. One approach involves preparing two reports: (1) a *technical* report that emphasizes the methods used and underlying assumptions, and presents the findings in a detailed manner, and (2) a *popular* report that minimizes technical details and emphasizes simplicity. The

---

[6]James H. Nelems, "Report Results, Implications, and Not Just Pounds of Data," *Marketing News,* 12 (January 12, 1979), 7.

second approach is concerned with how the report is communicated. This is clearly summarized in the following statement:

> Because people vary a great deal in how they are affected by different forms of communication, the ideal reporting process should try to encompass all major forms. Thus, a written report, by itself, I feel to be totally inadequate and only an invitation to inaction. There are simply a lot of people who, for various reasons, don't respond to the printed word. And there are still more that, although they may respond, will often misunderstand the meaning of what is written. For these reasons, it is vitally necessary to try and get management to sit down with you, the research manager, or with you and the outside research firm, in a face-to-face audio-visual type of reporting situation.[7]

ADDITIONAL CONSIDERATIONS

Some researchers may become more concerned with finding an application for their techniques and technologies than with supplying information for decision making. The researcher must protect against testing for its own sake using the most sophisticated techniques. Useful information may not allow the researcher to use all the advanced technologies and new statistical techniques, but it is what decision makers want. In short, research basics must not be overlooked (Exhibit 2-3).

The internationalization of business is one of the dominant trends today. In many ways, information is even more important for effective decisions in developing international marketing strategy than it is for domestic marketing. At the very least managers cannot draw upon an intimate knowledge of the environment within which they operate (and which in the domestic situation they have "grown up" in) because they lack such knowledge. In approach, the international marketing research process does not differ from that already described. However, there are certain unique considerations, as shown in Figure 2-2.

A number of conceptual, methodological, and organizational issues that impede data collection and the conduct of research for international marketing decisions have been identified.[8] These are as follows:

- The complexity of research design, due to operation in a multicountry, multicultural, and multilinguistic environment,
- The lack of secondary data available for many countries and product markets,
- The high costs of collecting primary data, particularly in developing countries,

[7]E. Dean Howard, "Producing Information That Management Can't Ignore," paper presented at the 1973 Spring Conference of the American Marketing Association, pp. 10–11.

[8]See Susan P. Douglas and Samuel Craig, *International Marketing Research* (Englewood Cliffs, N.J.: Prentice-Hall, 1983), pp. 15–30.

- The problems associated with coordinating research and data collection in different countries,
- The difficulties of establishing the comparability and equivalence of data and research conducted in different contexts,
- The intrafunctional character of many international marketing decisions,
- The economics of many international investment and marketing decisions.

As marketers increase and broaden their participation in overseas markets, the issue of comparability takes on special importance. To an extent, each overseas market may be characterized by a unique pattern of sociocultural behavior patterns and values. Conse-

Exhibit 2-3   Research Basics

As technology advances, marketing researchers are continually looking for ways to adapt such advances. Both hardware and software are involved in adaptations. However, researchers must never forget that research basics cannot be overlooked. Rather, what must be done is adapt the new techniques and technologies to these basics. All studies must address the following basic issues:*

- *Ask the right questions.* This is the essence of project design, and is the heart of proper planning. The research planner must remember that every project is in some way(s) unique, and as such must be in tune with the user's needs.
- *Ask the right people.* Sample design should be such that only those people who are of interest to the research user are contacted, and that those who are contacted are reasonably representative of the group of interest.
- *Ask questions the right way.* It is not enough to be able to ask the right questions; they must be asked in the right way. This is the essence of questionnaire design. The researcher can use all the aid(s) available with the new technologies. One basic that is overlooked all too often is pretesting the questionnaire; this is crucial for ensuring that responses are the ones that are needed to address the problem.
- *Obtain answers to questions.* The process of data collection is central to all marketing research. Techniques used should be selected for how each bears on nonresponse and response alike.
- *Relate answers to the needs of the research user/client.* Data seldom speak for themselves. Proper data analysis is needed if a study is to have any value to the user. It is in this aspect where there is a risk in letting advanced techniques become the master of the researcher rather than the opposite. Common sense is a valuable tool for the researcher when considering alternative analysis approaches for any project.
- *Communicate effectively.* Many good projects are ruined in this stage. The information that is reported to the user should be in a form that is understandable to the user so that he or she can tell that it is relevant to the issues at hand.

*John F. Anderson, Douglas R. Berdie, and Rebecca M. Liestman, "Hi-Tech Techniques OK, but Don't Forget Research Basics," *Marketing News*, 18 (January 16, 1984), Sec. 2, p. 12.

Figure 2-2 International Dimension of the Marketing Research Process

Problem Definition	Development of Research Plan	Data Collection	Data Interpretation	Summary of Findings and Report

Tasks to be carried out

Problem Definition:
Problems must be defined (and re-defined) and reasons for research clearly determined
Avoid
1. Vague terms of reference
2. Stating wrong problem
3. Trivial research projects
4. Research where underlying purpose is withheld or unknown

Development of Research Plan:
1. List objectives
2. Specify tasks to be undertaken
3. Evaluate alternative methodologies
4. Select most appropriate methodology
5. Formulate detailed plans and review
6. Specify possible "pay offs"

Data Collection:
1. Identify sources
   a. Internal
   b. External
2. Conduct interviews/ questionnaires (as relevant)
3. Deal with response error
4. Collate data

Data Interpretation:
1. Distil the essentials
2. Tabulate, classify, and cross classify
3. Integrate and organize relevant data
4. Examine for significant relationships

Summary of Findings and Report:
1. Summarize findings in easily understandable form
2. Communicate to one's "audience"

Additional points relating to international dimension

Problem Definition:
1. Ensure concurrence about terms of reference among all concerned
2. Prepare "research authorization" document
3. Identify priorities for funds allocation

Development of Research Plan:
1. Undertake preliminary "desk research" to identify best opportunity area for "in depth" studies
2. Define comparability differences
3. Select methodology with minimum comparability problems
4. Screen research agencies with international experience

Data Collection:
1. Attach weights to data to eliminate national/ cultural differences
2. Identify local biases including interviewer's biases

Data Interpretation:
1. Watch for results comparability
2. Ensure that unexpected findings are not due to special local biases

Summary of Findings and Report:
1. Think of international reader and communicate accordingly
2. Watch language and terms
3. Avoid offensive conclusions to local sensitivities

Source: Simon Majaro, *International Marketing: A Strategic Approach to World Markets*, rev. ed. (London: George Allen & Unwin, 1982), p. 64.

49

TABLE 2-3   Characteristics of Emic Versus Etic Approaches

| | APPROACH | |
CHARACTERISTIC	Emic	Etic
Perspective taken by researcher	Studies behavior from within the system	Studies behavior from a position outside the system
Number of cultures studied	Examines only one culture	Examines many cultures, comparing them
Structure guiding research	Structure discovered by the analyst	Structure created by the analyst
Criteria used to compare behavior in the culture(s)	Criteria are relative to internal characteristics	Criteria are considered absolute or universal

Source: Adapted from John W. Berry, "Introduction to Methodology," in *Handbook of Cross-Cultural Psychology,* Vol. 2, *Methodology,* ed. Harry C. Triandis and John W. Berry (Boston: Allyn & Bacon, 1980), pp. 11–12.

quently, attitudes and behavior may be expressed uniquely. Relevant constructs and their measures will be unique to a particular country. At the other extreme, there may be similarities. This situation is the *emic* (culture-specific) versus *etic* (culture-free) issue in cross-national research, which has implications for the appropriate research process (see Table 2-3).[9] The international marketer is most likely to prefer the "etic" approach in international marketing research, with the prime emphasis on constructs and methods that are comparable across countries and cultures.[10] However, one can never assume equivalence. To illustrate, an American company, assuming that a similar language must indicate similar tastes, tried to sell after-shave lotion in England. The product never got off the ground, and it was discovered (unfortunately after the fact) that the average British male saw no functional value in the use of after-shave lotion.[11]

COMPONENTS OF THE RESEARCH PLAN

It should be obvious from our discussion of the research process that each step must be carefully planned and that the relationship between the steps must be formally recognized. What this means is that a formal plan for the project must be developed and put in *writing*. As such, the research plan becomes the "master" guide for implementing and controlling the research project.

The components of a research plan are outlined in Table 2-4. Most of the components have been discussed in previous sections of this chapter and/or are self-explanatory. A useful device for showing the time schedule is a graphic work plan (Figure 2-3), which

[9]*Ibid., pp.* 133–37.
[10]*Ibid.,* p. 134.
[11]Ricks, *Big Business Blunders,* p. 133.

TABLE 2-4   Outline of Research Plan

Objectives
The primary and secondary objectives of the study are stated precisely. Included are operational objectives and more general aims.
Problem Analysis
This aspect involves a statment of the research problem(s) and question(s) and the hypothesis or hypotheses relevant to the stated problem (i.e., testable hypotheses). The researcher must be able to show the relation of the objectives to the problem at hand.
Research Plan and Design
A. *Research methodology.* How the investigation is to be made is described in general terms. In addition, there should be justification shown for selection of the methodology that will be used.
B. *Research techniques.* The methods and procedures to be used in collecting the data are described in some depth. Who is to be solicited, how contact is to be made, special techniques to be used, and so on are to be covered. Forms to be used to collect data should be discussed and, if already developed, included with the plan.
C. *Sample design and selection.* The size of the total sample and any proposed subsamples must be stated. Describe in detail the procedure to be used to ensure a representative (or other appropriate) sample of survey respondents or experimental subjects. Any technical notes, e.g., how the sample size was determined, can be shown in an appendix to the plan.
D. *Proposed analysis.* General tabulation procedures, and cross-analysis tabulations, should be described. If not obvious, the reasons for such tabulations must be shown. Also included should be discussion of proposed methods of statistical analysis together with reasons why such analyses will be used. If possible, show dummy tables with the "stubs" that will be used.
Personnel Requirements
This section of the plan gives a complete list of all personnel who will be involved with the project. The exact assignment of each person, the time to be spent, and pay should be shown.
Time and Cost Requirements
A budget and time schedule for the major activities involved in conducting the study are presented.

---

indicates the relevant tasks and the time to be allotted to each. Not only is this work plan a useful planning device but it can also serve as a control mechanism.

The research plan may also be viewed as a research *proposal*. This is so particularly when the research supplier is an external firm, but it may also be so for "in-house" suppliers when management must be convinced to allocate money for the project at hand. To a large extent, the contents of a proposal will be the same as those of a research plan, although the proposal format will contain less technical material and will not be as detailed. Although style and format will differ among research suppliers, the following topics should be included (not necessarily in the order shown):[12]

- Background
- The Problem
- Statement of Research Objectives

[12]See A. B. Blankenship and Raymond F. Barker, "The Buyer's Side of Marketing Research: Guidelines for Obtaining and Evaluating Proposals," *Business Horizons*, August 1973, pp. 73–80.

Figure 2-3 Graphic Presentation of Work Plan

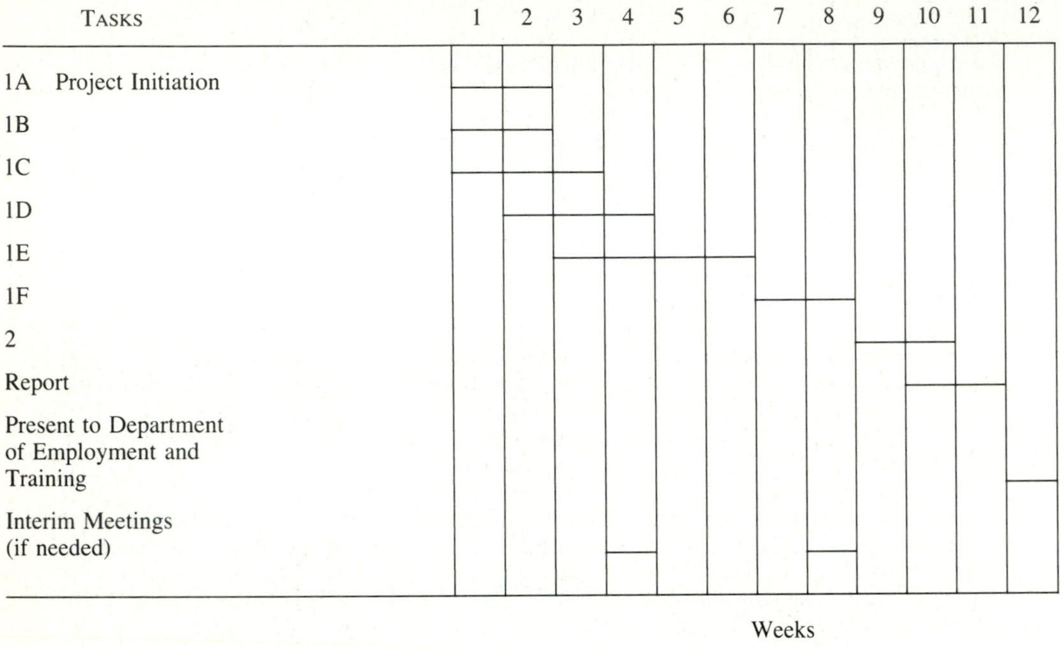

Tasks	1	2	3	4	5	6	7	8	9	10	11	12
1A Project Initiation												
1B												
1C												
1D												
1E												
1F												
2												
Report												
Present to Department of Employment and Training												
Interim Meetings (if needed)												

Weeks

- Research Methods
- Nature of the Report
- Timing and Costs
- Special Areas (e.g., biographies of professional staff)

There is no uniform guideline for how a proposal should be presented. It may range from a short letter covering the minimum necessities to an extensive document. The nature of the project and client will largely determine how elaborate a proposal should be. An illustration of a proposal (in condensed form) is shown in the appendix to this chapter.

SCHEDULING RESEARCH ACTIVITIES

To formally schedule a research project, the marketing researcher must be able to isolate the major activities to be performed and determine a sequencing of tasks. Some tasks must be performed before others can be started, whereas some activities can be carried on concurrently.

One approach to scheduling research activities is to use an activity flow chart. The work plan presented in Figure 2-3 is an illustration of such a flow chart. Another approach uses the *critical path method* (CPM). This is a network approach in which the component activities are diagrammed in sequence of performance and a time estimate for each activity is presented. A modification of the critical path method is the program evaluation and review technique (PERT). PERT is a probabilistic scheduling approach using three time estimates: optimistic, most likely, and pessimistic. Whether CPM or PERT is used, the critical path is the sequence of activities resulting in the longest project completion time.[13]

SUMMARY

In this chapter we discussed the research process and its individual components. Very simply, the process begins with formulating the problem and ends with the research report and the presentation of results to management. This chapter dealt in some detail with problem formulation. The other individual components form the basis for the remainder of the book.

Appendix 2-1

ILLUSTRATION OF A RESEARCH PROPOSAL

Nature of the Problem

Wine produced in South Africa is beginning to appear in stores in various parts of the United States. Although South Africa has produced wine for more than three centuries and its total annual production is equal to that of West Germany, relatively few sales have been made to North America. South African producers appear to be planning a campaign that they hope will give them a significant share of the United States market.

Yankee Traders[14] is becoming involved in importing South African wines, including table wines, champagne, and liquors (e.g., rum and brandy). Initial targeted markets are New York, Chicago, and Washington, D.C. Of immediate concern is market acceptance of these products, on the part of both distributors and consumers.

The process of gaining market acceptance, and thus a profitable share of market, is often time-consuming and requires that many hurdles be overcome. In the South African wine situation there is the general problem of awareness, which results because consumers, and perhaps distributors, do not think of South Africa as being a wine-producing area. Thus, an issue of "trust" may be involved. Related to this is that unlike major wineries in the United States, France, West Germany, and Italy, specific wineries in South Africa are totally unknown to the general wine-consuming public. This may also exist to a significant extent among wine distributors.

Regarding South Africa, there is another major potential hurdle that does not confront products imported into the United States from most countries. This problem stems

---

[13]For more complete discussion, see James H. Myers and A. Coskun Samli, "Management Control of Marketing Research," *Journal of Marketing Research*, 6 (August 1969), 267–77.

[14]The company name is disguised.

from South Africa's political and socioeconomic policies toward certain segments of its population. The issues have been exposed widely throughout the United States as being concerned with "human rights." Thus, public feelings in the United States toward the South African government may carry over into prejudices against products from that country. The nature of such prejudices, and the extent to which they exist, will affect market acceptance of South African wines.

Objective of the Study

The proposed study is designed to provide information helpful to Yankee Traders in planning and implementing a marketing approach for South African wines. More specifically, the study will attempt to provide answers to the following research questions:

1. What is the state of awareness among distributors about South African wines, what are their attitudes and beliefs about such wines, and to what extent are they likely to purchase such wines?
2. What general images are held by consumers regarding products made in South Africa, and what are their attitudes about purchasing such products? One concern here is the extent to which general prejudices carry over to products, specifically wine.
3. What is the likelihood that wine drinkers will purchase South African wines, and what factors affect the likelihood?

These three research questions are broadly stated and will serve as a guide to the specific kinds of information to be sought.

Method

The study will be conducted in two parts: (1) the distributor study and (2) a survey of the general public. The geographic areas to be considered are the New York, Chicago, and Washington, D.C., metropolitan areas, including the core city and selected suburbs.

Distributor Study. The study of distributors will be conducted as a telephone survey of a random sample of wine distributors in the three market areas. The specific questionnaire to be used will be constructed once the project is approved. Information will be obtained to answer research question 1. This phase of the study will serve the additional role of being a situation analysis and informal investigation for the consumer survey. As such, then, the questions to be asked will include more open-end types. It is felt that a sample size of ten in each market area will be sufficient.

Consumer Survey. This phase of the study will be conducted as a mail questionnaire survey. At first thought, it would appear that since prejudice is somewhat fluid and can change rapidly, the use of the telephone to collect data would be most appropriate. However, in this case it is felt that the nature of the prejudice involved is not something that can easily be changed. Also, product and brand images do not change very rapidly unless one has had a bad experience with the product and/or brand. A third reason for choosing the mail survey approach is that some of the information to be requested can be viewed as "sensitive," and anonymity is necessary for good response rates and quality. The mail survey provides the highest degree of anonymity. Finally, cost considerations enter.

The approach to be used can be summarized as follows:

1. Introductory post card to mention the study and inform the potential respondent that he or she will soon receive a questionnaire.
2. The initial mailing of the questionnaire with a cover letter and return envelope. Also included will be a post card to be returned independently. This card will inform us that a particular person has responded, so that he or she will not be sent a follow-up questionnaire.
3. A reminder post card will be sent to the sample members.
4. A second questionnaire (i.e., a follow-up) will be sent to those sample members who have not responded.
5. A sample of those potential respondents who have not responded after the follow-up will be contacted by telephone for purposes of nonresponse validation.

Recent studies using this design have realized a response rate of 40 percent or better.

The sample will be developed on an area basis. Within each of the central cities and selected suburbs, sample members will be chosen by random sampling techniques from appropriate sample frames (e.g., telephone directories). The primary sampling element will be the household. Since the population to be sampled is the general public, both drinkers and nondrinkers of wine will be included. This is deliberate, since non-drinkers may be potential drinkers, and they also have an effect on overall attitudes within a community.

Based on normal response rates for surveys of this type, and considering costs, an original sample size of 500 in each market area should provide sufficient returns to have reliable results. For example, with an original sample of 500, a response rate of 200 should be obtained. If we assume a wine consumption incidence of 50%, this should provide at least 100 drinking and 100 nondrinking respondents in each market. The obtained sample of 200 with a .50 proportion will generate no more than a $\pm 5\%$ error with 95% confidence. Naturally, if greater accuracy is desired the original sample size can be increased.

The specific questionnaire will be constructed once the project is approved. The questionnaire will be developed in accordance with generally accepted survey research principles and will employ the "funnel sequence," which results in ordering questions from the most general to the most specific. Image data will be collected by using a set of semantic differential or Stapel scales; these involve survey respondents describing a particular object. Such scales have widely been used in determining images of, and attitudes toward, products made in foreign countries. Also to be used are Likert scales, which involve respondents indicating the extent of agreement with statements. This format will be best for measuring prejudice. Of course there may be a standard scale for measuring prejudice that is appropriate for the study. Although a preliminary search of the literature has not yet revealed such a scale, we will search further. More direct questions will be used to obtain the usual demographic and socioeconomic information as well as wine consumption and purchase data.

Cost and Time

Following the procedures outlined above, the study should be completed within eight to ten weeks from the date of acceptance of the proposal. The total cost will be $18,500.

ASSIGNMENT MATERIAL

1. Four methods of inquiry were discussed in this chapter. Which methods are more appropriate for basic research and which are more suited for decisional research? Explain.
2. For each of the following stated management problems, suggest some likely research questions and research problems:
   a. Decide whether to allow a bank to install an automated teller machine (ATM) outside the premises.
   b. Develop a package for a new product.
   c. Allocate the advertising budget among sales territories.
   d. Expand product distribution to a new area.
   e. Set up a plant in an overseas market area.
3. Why is it difficult to do research on marketing problems?
4. When doing research on international marketing problems there is often need to do cross-national research—i.e., research in a number of countries dealing with essentially the same problem. A problem of comparability may arise which has implications for the equivalence of various aspects of the research process. Discuss the process of establishing data equivalence within the context of constructs, measures, and sampling.
5. How does a research proposal differ from a research plan?

3

Marketing Research—The Value and Cost of Decision-Making Information

INTRODUCTION

In Chapter 1 we introduced Bayesian decision theory, and in the appendix to that chapter we described the maximin, minimax regret, and Laplace models for making decisions under uncertainty. Of these, only the Bayesian model is designed to evaluate the addition of *new information* to the decision process. Indeed, the Bayesian approach provides a formal way for evaluating marketing research as an information-supplying and cost-incurring activity. But it is not the only approach (see Exhibit 3-1).

This chapter discusses the fundamentals of Bayesian decision theory in terms of the problems it is designed to solve and the kinds of marketing research applications for which it is useful. To set the stage, we first present a very simple example of Bayesian decision theory—an example that nevertheless demonstrates all the basic principles. We then proceed to a more realistic illustration that deals with the potential use of marketing research in determining whether a new product should be introduced.

The next section discusses the nature of the payoff entries that figure so prominently in Bayesian calculations. We discuss such topics as net present value and attitudes toward risk, as formally incorporated into utility functions.

Also included is a discussion of the cost of conducting research. Of concern are the various cost categories that may be involved in a research project.

The chapter concludes with a discussion of the practical aspects of Bayesian decision theory and its application to actual business problems.

Exhibit 3-1   Non-Bayesian Approaches to Value of Information

There are several methods of establishing the value of marketing research information. Each is applicable primarily to the individual project rather than the total research effort. Some methods are applied before doing any research, some after. Ideally, value should be established before the research is conducted, but this is not always feasible.*

Simple Savings Method

This method assumes that management can make a *single* reasonably accurate estimate of the cost of making a wrong decision as well as estimate the chance of making such an incorrect decision. The value of information is determined as follows:

$$Value = E(Cost)_n - E(Cost)_I$$

where
$E(Cost)_n$ = estimated cost of mistake using no additional information
$E(Cost)_I$ = estimated cost of mistake using additional information

Return on Investment

Another approach views research as an investment and calculates a return on this investment after the research has been completed and acted upon.

Present Value Method

This method also treats research expenditures as an investment. Incremental cash benefits (receipts due to the research minus costs of the research) expected over the life of "the investment" are discounted by the marginal cost of capital. It seems clear that this approach can be applied to individual projects and a total marketing research effort by an organization.

Cost Benefit Approach

This approach places determining value into a cost-benefit framework and suggests that evaluation be done by (1) setting a cost figure and maximizing benefits from that cost, (2) establishing a desired level of benefits and minimizing cost, or (3) maximizing benefits. Generically, this method is non-Bayesian in structure. However, it can be used very effectively with a Bayesian approach; the expected value of perfect information places an upper limit on benefits to be obtained.

*These methods are discussed in great detail in James H. Myers and A. Coskun Samli, "Management Control of Marketing Research," *Journal of Marketing Research,* 6 (August 1969), pp. 267–277.

THE ESSENTIALS OF BAYESIAN DECISION THEORY

As already indicated in Chapter 1, today's marketing manager is being faced with both a growing number of specialized procedures for performing marketing research and a greater need for obtaining relevant information about the consequences of alternative marketing courses of action. What would appear to be needed is some framework for measuring the effectiveness of alternative marketing research studies. Fortunately, such a framework is available from the field of applied statistics.

Statistical methodology is no stranger to the marketing researcher. The computation of averages and measures of dispersion as well as the use of probability sampling has been commonplace in marketing research, almost since its inception. What is newer to marketing research, however, is the increasing emphasis being placed on *analytical*—as opposed to descriptive—statistics. In particular, the Bayesian decision model, briefly described in Chapter 1, has provided a way to deal analytically with many types of marketing problems. For the practical businessperson, the books by Schlaifer[1] and Chernoff and Moses[2] stand out as key references on Bayesian theory.

Ironically, one of the foundations of Bayesian decision theory was built more than 200 years ago. At that time an English clergyman, Thomas Bayes, proposed a procedure for combining new information about the likelihood of alternative *states of nature* being the true state with judgments existing *before* receipt of the new information. Although modern Bayesian theory bears little relationship to Thomas Bayes' pioneering work, the name has stuck.

Virtually all decision making—marketing or otherwise—takes place under conditions of uncertainty about the variables that will influence the consequences of the decision. Will the new product, now undergoing test marketing, fail or succeed if introduced nationally? Will ad A or ad B pull more reader attention? If we raise the price of our product's economy package by five cents, what will happen to unit sales volume and profits? The illustrations are endless.

Like it or not, the marketing manager is usually forced to *take chances* and consequently runs the risk of making wrong decisions. Of course, the more certain one is of the outcomes, the lower the risk. Moreover, the better some course of action is over competing options, under a wide variety of possible environmental conditions, the lower the risk of incurring sizable costs if the manager *is* wrong.

Frequently the marketing manager can obtain additional information related to the consequences of the alternatives being considered. Usually the information is not perfectly accurate and costs something to collect and analyze. Moreover, the manager frequently has available several information-gathering options of varying cost and accuracy. The questions that Bayesian decision theory is designed to answer are basically two:

1. How should the manager choose among alternative information-gathering options, including the option of gathering no additional information at all?
2. Having made this choice, what action should the manager finally take?

[1]Robert Schlaifer, *Probability and Statistics for Business Decisions* (New York: McGraw-Hill, 1959).
[2]H. Chernoff and L. E. Moses, *Elementary Decision Theory* (New York: John Wiley, 1959).

Behind these common-sense questions there exists a large body of detailed and technical theory. Our purpose here is to discuss only the barest outlines of the Bayesian approach, by means of a simple gambling example. We shall then step from this artificial world to the real environment of managerial decision making and marketing research.

A Simplified Example

One nice thing about gambling illustrations is that they have almost universal appeal even if the context seems artificial. The following "game" contains all the essential concepts of Bayesian decision theory; that is, its *structure* is similar to many real-world marketing problems, although its content is rather trivial.[3]

Assume that we have three small boxes that we shall call *A, B,* and *C.* Outwardly the boxes look alike. We are told that box *A* contains two gold coins, box *B* contains a gold and a silver coin, and box *C* contains two silver coins. The boxes are put in random order on a table and we are allowed to perform a simple experiment, to choose a box at random and, without observing the contents of the box, draw a single coin. Suppose that the coin happens to be gold. Based on this experimental evidence we are asked to state the probability that the remaining coin is also gold or, in other words, that box *A* was chosen.

We can reason as follows. Before we were given the datum that the first coin drawn was gold, our prior probability of drawing box *A* was 1/3. This assumes that our state of knowledge with respect to the characteristics of each box led to the assignment of an equally likely measure over all states of nature: *A, B,* and *C.* (A person who thinks that he or she possesses extrasensory perception might not wish to make an equiprobable assignment at all; Bayes' theorem handles either case.)

We can next ask ourselves the question, Given the choice of each box, *A, B,* and *C,* respectively, how likely is it that we would have observed a gold coin? Had we chosen box *A,* it is clear that we must observe a gold coin on a single draw from the box, since *both* coins in *A* are gold; thus, a probability of one is correct. Given that box *B* was chosen, the probability is 1/2 that our first draw would have produced a gold coin, since box *B* contained one gold and one silver coin. Given that we chose box *C,* it is clear that the chances of drawing a gold coin are zero, since both coins in *C* are silver. These probabilities are *conditional* probabilities. For example, the probability of drawing a gold coin, conditional upon having picked up box *B,* is 1/2.

From here it is but a short step to Bayes' theorem. Figure 3-1 shows a diagrammatic representation of the problem. The area of the rectangle is first divided into three vertical strips of equal area, which represent the prior probabilities of drawing box *A, B,* and *C.* Next, the relevant probabilities are pictured by shading the area of each strip in proportion to the probability of observing a gold coin. Thus, all of strip *A* is shaded, half of strip *B* is shaded, and none of strip *C* is shaded.

---

[3]See P. E. Green, "Bayesian Decision Theory in Advertising," *Journal of Advertising Research,* 2 (December 1962), 33–41. For a slightly different example, see Barbara Bund Jackson, *The Value of Information* (Boston: Division of Research, Graduate School of Business Administration, Harvard University, 1979), pp. 3–12.

Figure 3-1   Pictorial Presentation of Probabilities—Box Problem

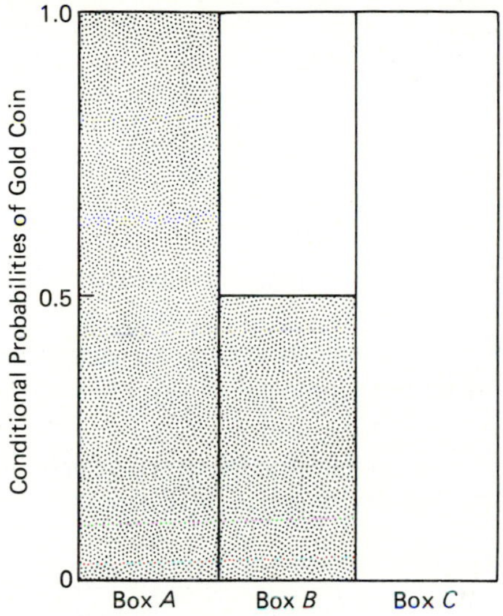

Source: Reprinted, with permission, from P. E. Green, "Bayesian Decision Theory in Advertising," *Journal of Advertising Research,* 2 (December 1962), 33–41. Copyright © 1962 by the Advertising Research Foundation.

Since, in performing our experiment, we have *observed* a gold coin, we must revise our prior probabilities to reflect this new information; that is, only the shaded area is now relevant. Moreover, the shaded area under each vertical strip represents the combined occurrence of (1) choosing a particular box and (2) getting a gold coin. These are joint events. Now, if we divide the shaded area between the relevant boxes *A* and *B,* it is clear that two-thirds of this total area is contained in the vertical strip *A;* hence the revised probability of having drawn box *A* is now 2/3 versus a 1/3 probability of having drawn box *B*. Obviously, given our information that the coin is gold, we have *not* drawn box *C*.

Bayes' Theorem[4]

Bayes' theorem merely formalizes this approach. Suppose that we wanted to find, for example, the probability that box *A* was drawn, given the observance of a gold coin. We can use the following formula (Bayes' theorem), where $P(g|A)$ stands for the conditional probability of observing a gold coin, given that we have drawn box *A*; $P(A)$ stands for the probability of drawing box *A* in the first place; and $P(A|g)$ stands for the conditional probability of having drawn box *A*, given the information that the coin was gold. Other symbols are defined analogously.

---

[4]The reader may find it helpful to review the basic notions of probability shown in the appendix to this chapter.

$$P(A|g) = \frac{P(g|A) \cdot P(A)}{P(g|A) \cdot P(A) + P(g|B) \cdot P(B) + P(g|C) \cdot P(C)}$$

$$= \frac{1 \cdot 1/3}{(1 \cdot 1/3) + (1/2 \cdot 1/3) + (0 \cdot 1/3)}$$

$$= 2/3$$

From our previous discussion we already know that this solution, 2/3, agrees with our intuitive analysis of the problem. Notice that the revised or "posterior" probability is conditional upon a *particular* observed event; the appearance of a silver coin would have changed the posterior probability assigned to box *A* from 2/3, in the gold coin case, to zero.

More generally, given some observed sample event *E*, Bayes' theorem states that the conditional probability of a particular state of nature S_j being true (i.e., the posterior probability) is

$$P(S_j|E) = \frac{P(E|S_j) \cdot P(S_j)}{\sum\limits_{i=1}^{n} P(E|S_j) \cdot P(S_j)}$$

$P(S_j)$ is the *prior* probability of state of nature S_j and $P(E|S_j)$ is the *conditional* probability of observing the event *E*, given that S_j is true. (In the preceding example, *E* denotes the gold coin, while the S_j's are boxes *A, B,* and *C.*) Finally, the product $P(E|S_j) \cdot P(S_j)$ is the *joint* probability of observing *E* under state of nature S_j. If *E* denotes the gold coin and S_j denotes box *A*, then $P(E|S_j) \cdot P(S_j)$ is the joint probability of drawing a gold coin from box *A;* as we know, it is $1 \cdot 1/3$, or 1/3.

So much for probability revision. We must now determine how the approach is used in evaluating courses of action.

The criterion for choosing among courses of action under the Bayesian approach is: choose the act that leads to the highest expected or weighted average payoff. We can modify our example to illustrate this criterion.

Assume that we have the option to bet or not bet that we will choose box *A* from the three boxes on the table. Suppose that we would win $1.00 if *A* were drawn but would lose $0.60 if box *B* were drawn and would lose $0.50 were we to draw box *C*. Suppose further that we are not allowed to run an experiment before betting; that is, not allowed to observe one of the two coins in each box.

A pictorial representation of these initial ground rules appears in the upper branch of the *tree diagram* shown in Figure 3-2. Looking at the extreme right of the upper branch, we note the conditional payoffs, $1.00, −$0.60, and −$0.50, associated with drawing box *A, B,* or *C*, respectively. To find the *expected* payoff associated with "bet," we merely multiply these payoffs by our prior probabilities, 1/3, 1/3, and 1/3, and sum the products, leading to a negative expected payoff of −$0.03: That is, we would lose

Figure 3-2 Decision Tree—Box-betting Problem

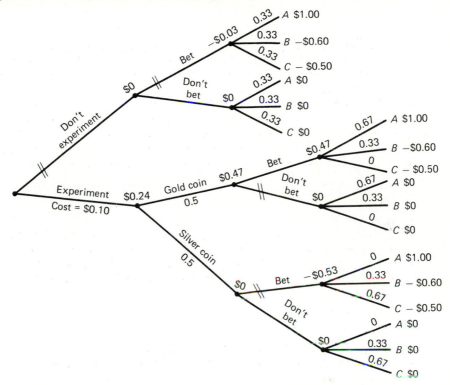

Source: Reprinted, with permission, from P. E. Green, "Bayesian Decision Theory in Advertising," *Journal of Advertising Research,* 2 (December 1962), 33–41. Copyright by the Advertising Research Foundation.

3 cents per bet on the average. Obviously, if maximizing expected monetary value is our criterion, we would select the "no bet" action with an expected payoff of zero. Therefore, we put a double slash through the "bet" branch to indicate that this act is not taken.

Consider another modification of the problem. Assume that *before* we decide whether to bet or not we are allowed to observe one coin from the box chosen. To conduct this experiment we are charged $0.10. Conditional payoffs are the same as before. The major difference is that we can delay our choice of whether to bet or not until *after* we have observed the results of our experiment and it will cost us $0.10 to run the experiment.

The lower branch of the tree diagram of Figure 3-2 summarizes the features of this strategy. If we look at the extreme right portion of the lower branch, following the subbranch labeled "gold coin," we note the probabilities: 0.67, 0.33, and 0. These represent the *posterior probabilities* derived from applying Bayes' theorem on the assumption that a gold coin is observed. Notice that the expected payoff associated with "bet" is $0.47, clearly higher than that associated with "don't bet." Therefore, the double slash through the "no bet" subbranch indicates that, if we observed a gold coin, we would choose the "bet" rather than "no bet" act.

TABLE 3-1   Calculation of Joint and Marginal Probabilities for Box Problem

	Box *A*	Box *B*	Box *C*	Marginal
Gold coin	1/3	1/6	0	1/2
Silver coin	0	1/6	1/3	1/2
Marginal	1/3	1/3	1/3	1

Before the fact, however, it is possible that we may observe a silver rather than a gold coin. If we follow this branch and look at the posterior probabilities—0, 0.33, and 0.67 for *A, B,* and *C,* respectively—the expected payoff associated with "betting" is very poor, − $0.53. It is clearly to our advantage *not* to bet if we observe a silver coin— hence, the double slash through the "bet" subbranch. But we must still compute the probabilities of getting a gold versus silver coin. These are known as *marginal probabilities,* and they represent the sum of a set of joint probabilities involving mutually exclusive events. Their calculation, along with the calculation of the joint probabilities, is shown in Table 3-1.

Now we may obtain the expected payoff of $0.24 by again averaging over the payoffs associated with the *best* act taken after the observance of each possible result of the experiment, that is, $0.24 = (0.5 × $0.47) + (0.5 × $0). The expected payoff must then be reduced by $0.10, the cost incurred in using this strategy, leading to a *net* expected payoff of $0.14. This figure is still higher than the $0 associated with the best act under "don't experiment"; hence, we double-slash the upper main branch of the tree.

To summarize, our best strategy is (1) to conduct our experiment and (2) to take the best act after observing the experimental results; this means that we bet if a gold coin appears and do not bet if a silver coin appears. If we do this, our average payoff per play, after deducting the cost of the experiment, is $0.14.

Before leaving this example, let us introduce one additional complication. Suppose that we could enlist the services of a shill who, for a payment of $0.25, could secretly give us a signal that would indicate *without error* the nature of the box we picked up before we had to decide whether or not to bet. What is the net value of this *perfect* information?

Inasmuch as the shill cannot influence our choice process (but only tell us *after* we have picked up a box which box it is), about one-third of the time we pick up box *A* and, being given its identification, will decide to bet. We will make $1.00. Two-thirds of the time we will pick up box *B* or box *C* and, upon being told this, will not bet. On these occasions we will make $0. Thus, our average *gross* payoff per play will be

$$1/3 × \$1.00 + 2/3 × \$0 = \$0.33$$

Since our shill charges $0.25 per play for his service, our expected net payoff is only $0.33 − $0.25, or $0.08. We note that this is less than the $0.14 payoff of the second option. Here is a case in which the net value of even *perfect* information is *less* than the net value of less reliable (but cheaper) information.

The *expected value of perfect information* (EVPI) is an important concept in Bayesian analysis. In general, to compute EVPI we can reason as follows: if we had perfect information about which state of nature prevails, we would always take the best action available to us. In the preceding example we would bet under box *A* conditions and would not bet under box *B* or box *C* conditions. However, *before* the fact we do not know which event will occur. Hence, we must multiply each of the best payoffs under *A, B,* or *C* conditions by the prior probability that further inquiry (e.g., use of the shill's services) will reveal the true state. This reasoning leads to the $0.33 gross payoff noted above.

The *difference* between $0.33 and the best expected payoff under the *prior* probabilities case (in the sample problem it is *not* to bet, carrying an expected payoff of zero) is defined as EVPI and represents an upper bound on what we should pay for even perfect information.

From Gambling Game to the Real World

As simple as the preceding example appears, it nonetheless demonstrates some significant points about the economics of decision making. Consider the situation of a marketing manager faced with the problem of whether to increase the level of product advertising in a particular marketing area. Like the gambler, the manager has alternative courses of action. We also assume that the manager wants to achieve certain objectives, such as earning a maximum return on his or her advertising investment.

In reflecting on this problem, however, our manager realizes that, under some levels of response to increased advertising effort, the additional advertising would more than pay for itself in terms of the profits from increased sales volume. Under other levels of response—certainly under no increase in sales at all—payoffs would be higher if the manager did not increase the advertising expenditures. Presumably the manager's deliberations include the possible effects of competitors' options for changing *their* levels of advertising and the resultant impact on total industry sales and his or her firm's market share. The trouble is that our decision maker does not know for certain what *will* happen and must deal with payoffs that are conditional upon one of *several* possible events.

In most situations, however, the decision maker has had experience in facing at least broadly analogous situations and has been exposed to the events preceding a particular problem situation. For example, the decision maker may well feel that some of the possible events are more likely to occur than others. Bayesian decision theory formalizes this notion by assuming that it is possible to assign numerical weights, in the nature of betting odds, such that they obey certain requirements for consistency. These numerical weights, called *prior probabilities,* may be based on long-run, "objective" experience with very similar problems; in other instances they may be more "subjective."

But, like our mythical gambler, the manager can often attempt to improve his or her view regarding the likelihood that each state of nature is the "true" underlying event *before* having to take final action. That is, he or she may elect to "experiment" before making a final choice among alternatives. The marketing manager might conduct a test campaign before deciding whether to increase the total level of promotion.

Gathering additional data usually involves a cost, however, and rarely are data so accurate as to foretell perfectly the true state of nature. Decision makers must usually cope with both experimental (sampling) and systematic error. Thus, the manager is forced to weigh the cost of the test campaign against its potential value in supplying information.

THE COST AND VALUE OF RESEARCH INFORMATION

Let us now take a more realistic example in which Bayesian decision theory can be used to assess the value versus cost of marketing information. Moreover, our approach will be more formal and detailed than the simple gambling illustration. We shall describe three types of analyses:

1. *Prior analysis,* which concerns which act should be chosen under conditions involving the decision maker's prior (before receipt of any new information) probabilities only.
2. *Posterior analysis,* which deals with which act should be chosen after the receipt of new information bearing on the states of nature. Bayes' theorem provides the means to obtain posterior probabilities which are conditional probabilities of states of nature, given information about states of nature likely to exist.
3. *Preposterior analysis,* which deals with the strategic question of whether new information should be purchased (and, if so, how much) before making a final, or terminal, decision. It should be obvious that the primary concern for marketing research is preposterior analysis, although often prior and posterior analysis must first be conducted.[5]

Suppose that the research and development phase of a new-product candidate is nearing completion and a decision must be made concerning whether the product should be commercialized. The alternative strategies are the following:

- *Strategy 1:* Make the decision concerning whether to introduce the new product on the basis of prior probabilities only.
- *Strategy 2:* Conduct the test marketing operation and make the decision of whether to introduce the new product on the basis of both prior and additional information.

The decision process involved is summarized in Figure 3-3.

Expected Payoff before Research—Evaluation of Strategy 1

In evaluating strategy 1, suppose that the prior analysis is that shown in Table 3-2. As shown there, three payoff levels have been judged to be relevant if the product is introduced; that is, a 15% market share, for which the payoff is estimated at $20 million; a 5% market share with an estimated payoff of $5 million; and a 1% market share, with

---

[5]Technically, there is a fourth type of analysis, *sequential decision making,* which applies preposterior analysis to multistage decision processes to be taken over time. For example, there could be an option to conduct two studies, and whether the second one would actually be done will depend on the results from the first study.

Figure 3-3   A Bayesian View of the Decision Process

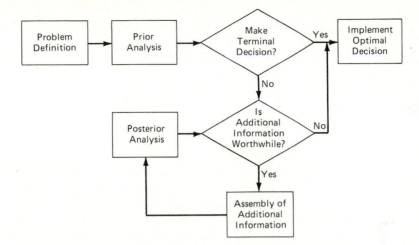

Source: Adapted from Keith Cox and Ben Enis, *The Marketing Research Process* (Pacific Palisades, Calif.: Goodyear Publishing Co., 1972), p. 60.

a payoff estimated at $-\$10$ million. The prior probabilities attached to each of these possible states of nature are 0.3, 0.5, and 0.2 respectively. The expected payoff (EV) of introducing the product (in the light of current information only) is

$$0.3(\$20 \text{ million}) + 0.5(\$5 \text{ million}) + 0.2(-\$10 \text{ million}) = \$6.5 \text{ million}$$

The payoff of not introducing the product is, of course, 0. Thus, the *prior* analysis suggests that the new product be introduced.

TABLE 3-2   Prior Analysis—New-Product Introduction

				State of Nature				
		S_1			S_2		S_3	
Alternative	$P(S_1)$	15% Market Share (millions of dollars)	$P(S_2)$	5% Market Share (millions of dollars)		$P(S_3)$	1% Market Share (millions of dollars)	Expected Payoff (millions of dollars)
A_1: introduce the product	0.3	20	0.5	5		0.2	-10	6.5
A_2: do not introduce the product	0.3	0	0.5	0		0.2	0	0.0

Expected Payoff after Research—Evaluation of Strategy 2

In evaluating strategy 2, our task would be simplified if we could assume that the additional information we obtain from the market test is perfect—that is, that we could identify with certainty the optimal act under strategy 2. If, after collection of the market test data, we could conclude with certainty which act, A_1 or A_2, is the better act, then the expected payoff would be equal to

$$0.3(\$20 \text{ million}) + 0.5(\$5 \text{ million}) + 0.2(0) = \$8.5 \text{ million}$$

Since we have already calculated the best expected payoff without additional information and found it to be \$6.5 million, the *expected value of perfect information* (EVPI) would be

$$\boxed{\text{EVPI} = \text{EV (with perfect information)} - \text{EV (without any information)}}$$

or

$$\$8.5 \text{ million} - \$6.5 \text{ million} = \$2.0 \text{ million}$$

Even if we were assured of getting perfect information, we would be well advised not to spend more than \$2 million to obtain it.

Realistically, however, we know that the information obtained will not be perfect; there will almost always be some uncertainty present as to which is the preferable act after collecting additional information. How, then, can we determine the expected payoff after collecting the information when we recognize that the information we obtain will be imperfect?

To do this, it is necessary that a *preposterior analysis* be made. Before we proceed with an example, it may be helpful to set down the procedural steps that we will have

TABLE 3-3   Assignment of Conditional Probabilities to Possible Outcomes of Market Test Operations—New-Product Introduction

	POSSIBLE OUTCOME		
STATE OF NATURE	Z_1: *Market Share in Test* $10\% \leqslant M.S.$	Z_2: *Market Share in Test* $3\% < M.S. <10\%$	Z_3: *Market Share in Test* $M.S. \leqslant 3\%$
S_1: 15% market share	0.6	0.3	0.1
S_2: 5% market share	0.3	0.5	0.2
S_3: 1% market share	0.1	0.2	0.7
Total	1.0	1.0	1.0

TABLE 3-4   Calculation of Joint and Marginal Probabilities of States of Nature and Market Test Outcomes—New-Product Introduction

STATE OF NATURE	MARKET-TEST OUTCOME			TOTAL $P(S_i)$
	Z_1	Z_2	Z_3	
S_1	$0.3(0.6) = 0.18$	$0.3(0.3) = 0.09$	$0.3(0.1) = 0.03$	0.30
S_2	$0.3(0.3) = 0.15$	$0.5(0.5) = 0.25$	$0.5(0.2) = 0.10$	0.50
S_3	$0.2(0.1) = \underline{0.02}$	$0.2(0.2) = \underline{0.04}$	$0.2(0.7) = \underline{0.14}$	$\underline{0.20}$
Total—$P(Z_j)$	0.35	0.38	0.27	1.00

to take to determine the expected payoff *after* receiving the research information from the test market. These steps are as follows:

1. For each of the possible relevant outcomes that the market test could yield, determine the marginal probability of getting each specific outcome. (In our example, the marginal probabilities are calculated in Table 3-4.)

2. For each specific outcome of the market test, calculate the posterior probabilities. (The posterior probabilities in our example are calculated in Table 3-5.)

3. Calculate the expected payoff of each possible act under the strategy involving additional data collection (via the market test) and select the act that leads to the highest expected payoff on the basis of the information when available. Multiply the expected payoff, conditional upon which outcome occurs, by its marginal probability of occurrence. Sum the products to obtain an expected payoff after the market test. (These calculations are made in Figure 3-4.)

As noted in the prior analysis, it was decided that three possible states of nature were relevant: S_1, a market share of 15%; S_2, a market share of 5%; and S_3, a market share of 1%. Let us assume that the following possible outcomes of the market test are the relevant ones with respect to drawing inferences concerning the true state of nature: Z_1, a test market share of 10% or more is indicated; Z_2, a test market share between 3% and 10%; and Z_3, a test market share of 3% or less. Let us suppose that we assign the

TABLE 3-5   Calculation of Posterior Probabilities of States of Nature and Market Test Outcomes— New-Product Introduction

STATE OF NATURE	MARKET-TEST RESULTS		
	$P(S_i|Z_1)$	$P(S_i|Z_2)$	$P(S_i|Z_3)$
S_1	$0.18/0.35 = 0.5143$	$0.09/0.38 = 0.2368$	$0.03/0.27 = 0.1111$
S_2	$0.15/0.35 = 0.4286$	$0.25/0.38 = 0.6579$	$0.10/0.27 = 0.3704$
S_3	$0.02/0.35 = \underline{0.0571}$	$0.04/0.38 = \underline{0.1053}$	$0.14/0.27 = \underline{0.5185}$
	1.0000	1.0000	1.0000

Figure 3-4   Determination of Expected Payoff after Market Test—New-product Introduction (Payoffs in Millions of Dollars)

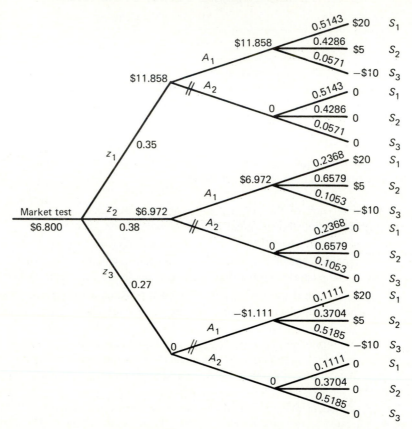

probabilities shown in Table 3-3 to each of these outcomes, conditional upon the given state of nature being the true state. For example, the conditional probability assigned to getting outcome Z_1, given state of nature S_1, is $P(Z_1|S_1) = 0.6$. Conditional probabilities associated with S_2 and S_3, respectively, are $P(Z_1|S_2) = 0.3$ and $P(Z_1|S_3) = 0.1$.

Having made this assignment of conditional probabilities, we are now in a position to calculate the *joint probability* of a given state of nature's being the true state *and* its being identified as such by a given test market outcome. The joint probability for each of the states of nature and each of the test-market outcomes is calculated and shown in Table 3-4. For example, the joint probability of S_2's being the true state of nature *and* being identified correctly by outcome Z_2 is

$$P(S_2 \text{ and } Z_2) = P(S_2) \cdot P(Z_2|S_2) = 0.5 \times 0.5 = 0.25$$

Note that the sum of each row is the marginal probability of that state of nature's being the true state and is equal to the prior probability assigned initially (Table 3-2). Note also that the sum of each column is the *marginal probability* of getting each specific outcome from the market test. The probability of getting outcome Z_1, indicating a test market share of 10% or more, for example, is 0.35. The marginal probabilities $P(Z_j)$ are required to implement the first step in the procedure outlined above.

We may now calculate the posterior probabilities of each state of nature's being the true state, given a specific outcome of the market test. These calculations are made in Table 3-5. For example, it may be seen that the (conditional) probability of state S_1, given outcome Z_1, is 0.5143; $P(S_1|Z_1) = 0.5143$. These probabilities are central to our analysis, as they are the revised probabilities incorporating the additional information that would be obtained from the market test. As illustrated in the coin example, they are computed from Bayes' theorem.

Now that the *posterior probabilities* $P(S_i|Z_j)$ have been determined, we may apply them to determine the expected payoff of each act, conditional upon the outcome of the market test. As shown in Figure 3-4, the optimal act for outcomes Z_1 and Z_2 is A_1 (introduce the product), as the payoffs are $11.858 and $6.972 million, respectively. The optimal act for outcome Z_3 is A_2 (not to introduce the product), as the payoff of introduction is negative in this case.

A final step (see Figure 3-4) is needed to find the expected payoff *after* research. We may calculate this value by multiplying each of the conditional payoffs by its marginal probability of occurrence. Thus, the *unconditional payoff* is

$$0.35(\$11.858) + 0.38(\$6.972) + 0.27(0) = \$6.800 \text{ million}$$

By conducting the market test, therefore, we obtain a gross expected payoff of $6.800 million. It should be kept in mind that this payoff does *not* take into account the cost of the research—in this case, the market test.

Net Expected Payoff of Research

The *net expected payoff of research* is defined as the expected value of additional information minus the expected cost of acquiring it.

The *expected value of additional information* is the difference between the expected payoff of the best act *before* research and that of the best strategy *after* research. We found that the best act before research was to introduce the product and that the expected payoff *before* research was $6.500 million. The best strategy, given the research, is to introduce the product under survey outcomes Z_1 and Z_2, but not under outcome Z_3. The expected payoff *after* research was $6.800 million. The expected value of additional information (EVI) is therefore $300,000. This can be interpreted as the maximum amount that can be spent on the research, given the assumed uncertainty, and still have added value.

Let us suppose that the expected cost of conducting the market test is $150,000. The net expected payoff of research is then $300,000 – $150,000 = $150,000. Since the net expected payoff of research is positive, it is clear that the market test should be carried out before deciding whether to introduce the new product.[6]

A Special Case[7]

The new-product-introduction example illustrates a special decisional situation known as a *venture* problem—i.e., it is one in which the choice of alternatives finally rests between the two actions of "GO" or "NO GO." The uniqueness of this type of problem rests with the following:

1. There will always be a most "unfavorable" state (S_j) with a negative outcome.
2. The outcomes for the NO GO alternative will always be zero (0).

As discussed so far, the Bayesian approach is not limited to this type of situation. We have presented it in such a context only to simplify the discussion and needed calculations.

When one is facing a venture situation and there is an option to acquire additional information, preposterior analysis can be performed directly without having to go through posterior analysis first, as we have done above. The venture analysis problem can be summarized in a conditional payoff table, as shown in Table 3-6. The conditional probabilities $P(Z_1|S_1)$ and $P(Z_2|S_2)$ would then be the probabilities associated with correct prediction, and the conditional probabilities $P(Z_1|S_2)$ and $P(Z_2|S_1)$ would be the probabilities of the predictive errors. These probabilities are simply an assessment of the predictive accuracy or validity of the information whose acquisition is being considered.

It can be shown that, for venture analysis problems, the expected value of perfect information is

$$\text{EVPI} = |P(S_2)V_{12}|$$

Moreover, it can also be shown that the expected value of imperfect information (EVI) is given by the expression

$$\text{EVI} = \left(\frac{L - L^*}{1 - L^*}\right)\text{EVPI}$$

where

$$L = P(Z_2|S_2),$$

[6]If *other* research options were available, we would of course choose the option that carried the *highest* net expected payoff.

[7]This section is based on material from Gerald Albaum and Donald S. Tull, "Management Style and Information Valuation in a Venture Situation: Some Propositions," paper presented at the annual meetings of the Western Division, Academy of Management, Santa Barbara, Calif., April 1976. See also Gerald J. LaCava and Donald S. Tull, "Determining the Expected Value of Information for New Product Introduction," *Omega*, 10 (1982), 383–89.

TABLE 3-6 Conditional Payoff Table for Contemplated Venture

| | STATE OF NATURE | | | |
| | "Favorable" (S_1) | | "Unfavorable" (S_2) | |
COURSE OF ACTION	Prob.	Payoff	Prob.	Payoff
A_1 ("Go")	$P(S_1)$	$V_{11} > 0$	$P(S_2)$	$V_{12} < 0$
A_2 ("No Go")	$P(S_1)$	0	$P(S_2)$	0

which is the *probability of correctly accepting the "null" hypothesis that state* S_2 *is the true state* (i.e., the "no go" action should be taken);

$$L^* = \frac{W \cdot P(S_1)V_{11}}{W \cdot P(S_1)V_{11} + |P(S_2)V_{12}|}$$

which is the minimum value of L for the information to be of any value at all;

$$W = \frac{P(Z_2|S_1)}{P(Z_1|S_2)} = \frac{\text{Type II Error Probability}}{\text{Type I Error Probability}} = \frac{\beta}{\alpha};$$

and EVPI is as derived above.

Looking at the venture analysis situation as one of hypothesis testing greatly simplifies the problem. Since $P(Z_2|S_2) + P(Z_1|S_2) = 1$, it is obvious that $L = 1 - \alpha$. By making appropriate substitutions, the expression for EVI can be rewritten as

$$\text{EVI} = \text{EVPI} - \alpha |P(S_2)V_{12}| - \beta \cdot P(S_1)V_{11}$$
$$= (1 - \alpha)\text{EVPI} - \beta \cdot P(S_1)V_{11}$$

That is, *the expected value of information is equal to the expected value of perfect information minus the expected cost of the errors*. For such a two-state problem, EVI can be estimated from the tabular values contained in Table 3-7.

This approach is also applicable to a three-state problem. To calculate EVI in such a situation, it must be recognized that there are two Type II errors to be considered:

$$\text{EVI} = (1 - \alpha)\text{EVPI} - \beta_1 P(S_1)V_{11} - \beta_2 P(S_2)V_{12}$$

where EVPI is now defined as $|P(S_3)V_{13}|$, β_1 is $P(Z_3|S_1)$, and β_2 is $P(Z_3|S_2)$.

TABLE 3-7 Expected Value of Information for Two-State Venture Problem

Chance of GO Alternative Being a Success Is*

Ratio of Estimated Gain if Successful to Loss if Unsuccessful

The Maximum Percentage of the Potential Loss That Can Safely be Spent on Marketing Research Is

Chance that the research project being considered will indicate correctly whether or not the product should be introduced is*	50 Percent					60 Percent					70 Percent					75 Percent					80 Percent				
	1.0	2.0	3.0	4.0	5.0	1.0	2.0	3.0	4.0	5.0	1.0	2.0	3.0	4.0	5.0	1.0	2.0	3.0	4.0	5.0	1.0	2.0	3.0	4.0	5.0
55 percent	5.0																								
60 percent	10.0	zero																							
65 percent	15.0					5.0																			
70 percent	20.0	5.0				10.0	zero																		
75 percent	25.0	12.5				15.0					5.0	zero													
80 percent	30.0	20.0	10.0			20.0	8.0				10.0					5.0	zero								
85 percent	35.0	27.5	20.0	12.5	5.0	25.0	16.0	7.0			15.0	4.5				10.0					5.0	zero			
90 percent	40.0	35.0	30.0	25.0	20.0	30.0	24.0	18.0	12.0	6.0	20.0	13.0	6.0			15.0	7.5				10.0	2.0			
95 percent	45.0	42.5	40.0	37.5	35.0	35.0	32.0	29.0	26.0	23.0	25.0	21.5	18.0	14.5	11.0	20.0	16.2	12.5	8.7	5.0	15.0	11.0	7.0	3.0	

*For intermediate values, the percentage of total loss can be interpolated from the tabled values.

To illustrate this approach, we return to the new-product introduction example (see Tables 3-2 and 3-3). First, we calculate EVPI as follows:

$$\text{EVPI} = |P(S_3)V_{13}| = |0.2 \times -\$10| = \$2 \text{ million}$$

The other values needed for the EVI calculation are

$$\alpha = 1 - P(Z_3|S_3) = 1 - 0.7 = 0.3; \beta_1 = P(Z_3|S_1) = 0.1; \beta_2 = P(Z_3|S_2) = 0.2$$

The value of additional information for the venture problem is calculated as

$$\text{EVI} = (1 - 0.3) \times \$20 - 0.1 \times 0.3 \times \$20 - 0.2 \times 0.5 \times \$5 = \$0.3 \text{ million}$$

As we would expect, the added value of $300,000 derived from direct preposterior analysis is the same as that derived from the general Bayesian approach.

MEASURING CONDITIONAL PAYOFFS

So far, the examples in this chapter and the appendix to Chapter 1 have assumed that the conditional payoffs associated with each act and state of nature were given. In practice, however, these payoffs might be quite difficult to obtain. Our concern now is with the following types of questions:

1. What classes of revenues and costs are relevant for decision making?
2. What is the influence of the time period over which the payoffs are anticipated?
3. What are the various ways in which payoffs can be expressed?
4. How can the problem of risk be handled within the payoff framework?

Future Outlays and Opportunity Costs

In the usual business situation, the payoffs will be expressed in monetary terms. In determining what revenues and costs are relevant for deriving conditional payoffs, a guiding principle is to *include only those revenues and costs that are affected by the alternatives being evaluated*. For many problems a useful way to view the payoff figures is in terms of cash flow. For this purpose the firm can be viewed as a giant cash register in which cash outflows and cash inflows are anticipated. Concern with future revenues and outlays implies that we are not interested in "sunk" costs but only in those costs that would be changed by changes in the course of action presently pursued.

In some cases relevant costs will be of an *opportunity loss* nature, that is, the cash inflow that could be generated in the most productive alternative use of the firm's resources. For example, if the outlay required to increase promotional expenditures precluded the opportunity to use this cash in a research program aimed at product improvement, the opportunity forgone under this course of action might represent the relevant alternative payoff for the firm to consider.

The Time Horizon and Net Present Value

So far we have been rather vague with respect to how far in the future we wished to compute the conditional payoffs associated with various courses of action. In some problems, the *time horizon* may correspond to the time period of promotional expenditure budgeting—for example, one year. In capital budgeting problems, however, where sizable outlays for new plant and equipment or executive work force are involved, the planning horizon may be much longer, and consideration should be given to discounting cash flows to present value.

As a simple illustration of *present-value analysis,* assume that a firm is faced with the problem of determining whether it should set up production facilities for printing a promotional catalog or have the catalog printed by an outside firm. Assume that the necessary printing machinery costs $30,000 and has an anticipated life of five years. In addition, working capital (recoverable at the end of five years) of $50,000 would be required. Salvage value of the machinery at the end of five years is assumed to be zero.

We assume that the firm projects the cash savings (from using its own machinery rather than outside printing) anticipated at the end of each year as shown in Table 3-8. We assume that all cash savings (over the cost to have the catalogs printed by an outside firm) occur at year-end and that the recovery of working capital is included at the end of five years as a "cash savings." Discounting each cash inflow or outflow to present value (annual interest rate equal to 10%) yields a figure of $11,767. This figure is interpreted as the cash generated beyond that required to pay back all outlays and yield an average annual return of 10% on the present value of those outlays. Since the net

TABLE 3-8   Catalog Printing Investment Proposal, 10% Interest Rate

YEAR	YEAR-END CASH SAVINGS ($)	OUTLAYS ($)	DISCOUNT FUNCTION	NET PRESENT VALUE ($)
0		(−)35,000	1.000	−35,000
1	10,000	—	0.909	9,090
2	12,000	—	0.826	9,912
3	12,000	—	0.751	9,012
4	12,000	—	0.683	8,196
5	17,000	—	0.621	10,557
				11,767

present value is positive, the investment would be undertaken. This calculation represents a numerical illustration of the formula

$$\text{NPV} = \sum_{i=0}^{n} \frac{R_i - O_i}{(1 + r)^i}$$

where NPV = net present value

R_i = cash inflow at the end of time period i

O_i = cash outflow at the end of time period i

r = firm's cost of capital, expressed in decimal form

In computing present values the marginal cost of capital[8] is often used, since it is relatively easy to determine and incorporates an allowance for risk. However, in dealing with decision problems via the Bayesian approach *several* conditional net present values may have to be calculated, depending on the alternative states of nature that are postulated. Once calculated, the resultant conditional payoffs could then be handled in a manner similar to any other problem in Bayesian analysis.

Expected Monetary Value versus Utility Considerations

So far we have been assuming that the decision maker desires only to maximize expected monetary value (or expected payoff). This criterion assumes a rather *special set of risk attitudes* on the part of the decision maker.

To illustrate the nature of this assumption, suppose that a decision maker were faced with the alternatives shown in Table 3-9. If we calculate the expected values of the alternatives A_1 and A_2, we find that

$$EV(A_1) = 0.5(\$50,000) + 0.5(-10,000)$$

$$= \$20,000$$

$$EV(A_2) = 0.5(\$10,000) + 0.5(-2,000)$$

$$= \$4,000$$

TABLE 3-9 Two Investment Alternatives with Different Expected (Monetary) Values and Dispersions

A_1: receive $O_1 =$ $50,000 with $P(O_1) = 0.5$
receive $O_2 = -\$10,000$ with $P(O_2) = 0.5$
A_2: receive $O_3 =$ $10,000 with $P(O_3) = 0.5$
receive $O_4 = - \$2,000$ with $P(O_4) = 0.5$

[8]This is the rate that would have to be paid to obtain financing of a project with its anticipated level of risk.

If the decision maker were to follow the criterion of maximizing expected monetary value, he or she would choose act A_1. It is quite possible, however, that in some situations the decision maker could not afford to risk a possible loss of $10,000, even though this alternative carries a higher expected value. If this situation does prevail, some other set of values would have to be substituted for monetary payoffs in order to reflect the decision maker's attitudes toward risk.

Decision theorists have been concerned with this problem, and several procedures have been proposed for dealing with it. We shall discuss briefly only one such procedure: the *standard gamble,* or von Neumann–Morgenstern utility.[9]

Von Neumann–Morgenstern utility is a scale used in a rather special way to make predictions concerning a decision maker's preference for gambles involving specific payoffs whose attainment is subject to risk. To return to the data of Table 3-9, suppose that we were to ask our decision maker to rank in order of preference the following set of conditional outcomes:

$$O_1 = \$50,000$$

$$O_2 = -\$10,000$$

$$O_3 = \$10,000$$

$$O_4 = -\$2,000$$

The decision maker replies that he or she would prefer the receipt of O_1 to O_3 to O_4 to O_2. Suppose that we arbitrarily assign "utilities" (index numbers) to outcomes O_1 and O_2, the *highest* and *lowest* outcomes in the decision maker's array of preferences, as follows:

$$U(O_1) = 1$$

$$U(O_2) = 0$$

We would then ask the decision maker to visualize a choice between receiving outcome O_3 versus a one-time gamble involving the receipt of O_1 with probability P and the receipt of O_2 with probability $1 - P$. What probability would have to be associated with the outcome O_1 such that the decision maker would be just indifferent toward receiving O_3 for certain and participating in the gamble with O_1 and O_2 as the only possible outcomes?

Suppose that the decision maker replies that this "indifference" probability is 0.8. Then we define the decision maker's utility for outcome O_3 by the equation

$$
\begin{aligned}
U(O_3) &= P(O_1) \cdot U(O_1) + [1 - P(O_1)] \cdot U(O_2) \\
&= 0.8(1) + 0.2(0) \\
&= 0.8
\end{aligned}
$$

[9]A lucid discussion of utility theory can be found in W. J. Baumol, *Economic Theory and Operations Analysis,* 4th ed. (Englewood Cliffs, N.J.: Prentice-Hall, 1977).

Figure 3-5   Hypothetical Utility Functions

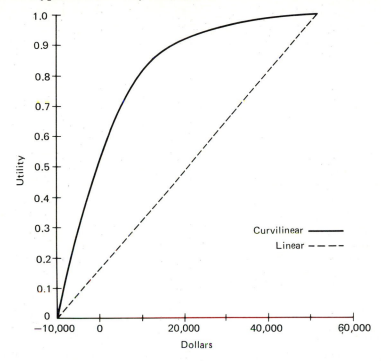

Similarly, we could determine the "indifference" probabilities for other outcomes O_4, and so on, so as to arrive at the decision maker's utility as a function of monetary payoff. Suppose that the utility function (indicated by the solid line) shown in Figure 3-5 results from this set of hypothetical gambles. A linear function (dashed line) is also drawn, for comparison, on the same chart. In practice, we would determine both lines from a limited set of gambles and interpolate between points. To summarize the procedure, all outcomes are evaluated numerically relative to the best and worst. Utility measures obtained are *relative,* not absolute, measures and the numbers themselves are a function of the limits arbitrarily selected for the best and worst outcomes.

We are now ready to discuss an important assumption that underlies the use of the following criterion: "Choose that course of action that maximizes expected (monetary) value."

Use of expected (monetary) value assumes that the decision maker's utility function is linear with respect to money.

To illustrate, we now return to the two investment alternatives of Table 3-9 and translate the conditional monetary outcomes into utilities by reading off the utility value (ordinate scale) for each monetary value (abscissa scale) and then determining the expected utility for each gamble under the curvilinear utility function and the linear utility function, respectively. The expected utility under the *curvilinear utility function* is

$$EU(A_1) = 0.5(1) + 0.5(0)$$

$$= 0.50$$

$$EU(A_2) = 0.5(0.8) + 0.5(0.44)$$

$$= 0.62$$

and under the *linear utility function*

$$EU(A_1) = 0.5(1) + 0.5(0)$$

$$= 0.5$$

$$EU(A_2) = 0.5(0.33) + 0.5(0.13)$$

$$= 0.23$$

Notice first that the curvilinear utility function is concave downward; that is, marginal utility declines with increasing quantities of money. We can say that this individual is *risk averse*. Using this function, the second alternative [with expected utility $EU(A_2) = 0.62$] would be chosen. As can be noted, this choice is the opposite of that which would be made if the decision maker were attempting to maximize expected (monetary) value.[10] In the case of the linear utility function, however, the choice is *not* reversed. It can be shown mathematically that the adoption of the criterion "Maximize expected (monetary) value" implies that the decision maker's utility function is *linear* with respect to money (at least over the monetary range in question).

The Practical Use of Utility Functions

The theoretical aspects and mathematical assumptions that underlie utility functions go well beyond the scope of this book. By this brief exposition we have intended merely to acquaint the reader with the notion and show the mechanics of eliciting utility functions by means of interrogating the decision maker regarding a set of hypothetical gambles.[11]

We shall continue to use the criterion of maximizing expected (monetary) value while realizing that in some situations this criterion may not be applicable. But work in the *empirical* derivation of utility functions has been quite meager to date. To the authors' knowledge, no industrial firm is employing utility calculations routinely as a basis for decision making. A study of marketing research directors in 200 *Fortune* 500 companies

---

[10]It should also be pointed out that utility functions for "risk-seeking" persons—where marginal utility increases with increasing quantities of money—could occur in some cases. This curvilinear function would be concave *upward*.

[11]Another approach, one that is simple and convenient for approximating an individual's utility for money, is Bernoullian utility. This approach is based on the premise that the utility of money is a function of the amount the individual already has. A good approximation of this is to use the logarithm of the amount of money. See, for example, Alfred Oxenfeldt, David Miller, Abraham Shuchman, and Charles Winick, *Insights into Pricing* (Belmont, Calif.: Wadsworth, 1961), pp. 15–20.

and chief marketing executives from the other 300 *Fortune* 500 firms indicated that less than 20% of the research directors and less than 7% of the marketing executives reported that a utility function had been determined for at least one of the executives within the company during a preceding 12-month period.[12] The theoretical and practical problems in employing these procedures still present major difficulties. Our purpose in presenting even this brief discussion is to show not only that expected (monetary) value is of importance to the decision maker but that the *dispersion* and, perhaps, the *whole shape of the distribution of conditional payoffs* may be important as well. For the present, if the marketing research analyst believes the maximization of expected (monetary) value to be inappropriate, he or she should attempt to present the whole distribution of conditional payoffs to the decision maker in cases where the dispersion and/or shape of these distributions differ markedly among the alternatives under consideration.

COSTS OF CONDUCTING A RESEARCH PROJECT

In a previous section of this chapter the net expected payoff of research was defined as the difference between the expected value of additional information and the expected cost of acquiring it. Compared with determining the value of information, determining the cost of acquisition is relatively simple. In fact, if the research is to be done by an outside supplier (e.g., an independent research firm, advertising agency, etc.) there is no problem—the cost is the price asked by the supplier.

If a project is to be done in-house, however, what is needed is accurate internal accounting data and good information about the costs of purchasing from outside the required materials, including any subcontracting for performing necessary activities (e.g., use of a field service to collect data for a survey). The research manager must know all the activities that will be performed in the project, starting with problem formulation and ending with preparation and presentation of the research report. In short, there must be a definite research plan formulated, or at least an outline of such a plan, in order that the relevant cost categories can be determined. Whether or not the research manager must present the plan as a formal proposal depends on the organizational structure of the firm. For example, some companies, such as DuPont and General Electric, have centralized research departments from which users in the company "buy" research. This arrangement is similar to purchasing research from an outside supplier and would require that a formal proposal be submitted with a price for doing the project.

The types of costs that may arise in any project can be categorized as *operational* and *creative*.[13] Operational costs are those involved in implementing the project itself and would include such items as, for example in a survey, costs of mailing questionnaires, interviewing, and printing of research materials. Creative costs, on the other hand, are

---

[12]Gerald Albaum, Donald S. Tull, and James W. Hanson, "The Expected Value of Information: How Widely Is It Used in Marketing Research?" *1979 Educators' Conference Proceedings*, ed. Neil Beckwith et al. (Chicago: American Marketing Association, 1979).

[13]H. Robert Dodge, Sam D. Fullerton, and David R. Rink, *Marketing Research* (Columbus, Ohio: Charles E. Merrill, 1982), pp. 46–48.

those related to planning the project and would include such tasks as problem formulation, research and sample design, drawing a sample, and analyzing obtained data. Operational costs may be most easily determined, since they are *direct* costs—i.e., costs that are incurred only because the project will be undertaken. In contrast, creative costs tend to involve cost categories that are more or less joint in nature, and to attach them to a specific project requires an allocation procedure. For example, the tasks involved are those done basically by research personnel who are paid a fixed salary. Joint costs are not limited to creative tasks, however. The cost involved in using a piece of apparatus in an experiment, such as a psychogalvanometer, is a joint cost if the company uses the equipment for other projects. It would, however, be a direct cost if it had to be purchased for the contemplated project and would have no other use in the research activities of the company.

An important question is, Which costs are relevant? Certainly, all direct costs must be included in estimating the total cost of a proposed research project. Whether allocation of joint costs should be included essentially involves a question of managerial philosophy—i.e., total versus contribution costing. For purposes of determining the net expected payoff of research ideally the following criterion should be applied:

The total cost of a project should include all direct and allocated joint costs.

Since it is often difficult to attach certain creative costs to a specific project, it may not be possible to follow this criterion to the fullest extent.

EVALUATION OF THE BAYESIAN APPROACH

We can now observe that the Bayesian approach emphasizes the key role of *managerial judgment* in the whole decision process that involves the relationship of marketing research to managerial action (Exhibit 3-2). Indeed, the manager is placed in the position of "make or buy" with regard to information. The manager can elect to *make*—use his or her prior experience and other less formal means of information—or to *buy* additional information through the utilization of marketing research (which can be supplied by either internal groups or outside consulting firms).

Second, this kind of orientation also suggests that the marketing researcher must work closely with the user of the information to be able to bring his or her own particular type of expertise to bear on the problem. The marketing researcher's skills can be utilized in a variety of ways within the theoretical decision format. These functions include (1) problem identification, (2) the search for and identification of relevant courses of action, (3) the estimation of alternative consequences of a given course of action and the probabilities associated therewith, and (4) the estimation of the accuracy and cost of alternative investigations. Consequently, the Bayesian approach provides a means to check for logical consistency in the decision-making process. In addition, explicit consideration and formalization of the elements of a decision problem lessens the likelihood that relevant facts or relationships will be overlooked.

Exhibit 3-2   Management Style and the Valuation of Information

For the most part, the literature dealing with the value of information has tended to focus on the problem situation as the major determinant of the value of information. This is certainly an appropriate emphasis, as the size and nature of the problem set the limits of the value of information in solving it. We suggest here, however, that variations in *managerial attitudes* and *attributes* (i.e., variations in what we call "management style") may also produce substantial differences in the valuation of information. We have already shown this for one attribute, risk aversion.

In more formal terms, *management style* can be defined as a "recurring set of characteristics that are associated with decisional processes." While it may be useful to think of this in the context of the individual, it is equally useful to focus on the firm. That is, acts of decision often are characteristic of organization behavior as contrasted with individual behavior.

There are at least seven style dimensions that affect valuation and utilization of information. They arise from the degrees of

(1) *Behavioral (market) versus technological (production) orientation*—influences the setting of priorities on types of decisions to be made;
(2) *Planning versus improvisation*—a determinant of the time period covered by the decision;
(3) *Innovation versus imitation*—affects the development of alternative courses of action;
(4) *Complexity (many variables) versus simplicity (few variables)*—influences the determination of outcomes or payoffs;
(5) *Risk acceptance versus risk aversion*—affects the choice of decision rules used for choosing among alternatives;
(6) *Intuition and informal empiricism (experience and judgment) versus rationalism and statistical empiricism*—influences the manner in which the decision rule is applied in choosing among alternatives; and
(7) *Individual versus group decision making*—defines with whom responsibility rests and how it is shared.

Each of these elements of management style affects the valuation of information for a particular decisional situation. Propositions about the relationship between the elements of management style and the value of information can be summarized as follows:

- For a given level of predictive validity, information is valued most highly by the management concerned with *behavioral* and/or *planning* problems, evaluating *innovative* alternatives, and/or engaging in complex decision making.
- Information is valued more highly by the management that is risk averse, rationalist in its approach to decision making, and/or engaging in individual decision making.

Source: Adapted from Albaum and Tull, "Management Style and Information Valuation in a Venture Situation."

Like many models, the value of the Bayesian framework would seem to lie more in the types of *questions* that its utilization generates than the kinds of answers it provides. Although applying the model to actual business problems may often require fairly sophisticated procedures—for example, computer simulation or mathematical statistics—the basic logic agrees with common sense. Its major impact is to force the manager and the researcher to look at marketing research in terms of its value in reducing the costs of wrong decisions. Dogmatic statements such as "Take a 10% sample of all households" and "Get the most accurate data available" thus become suspect within a framework that attempts to compare the value of the information with the cost of acquiring it.

The implications of the Bayesian approach suggest that marketing research studies should be geared to the costs incurred in making decisions in the absence of additional information; that is, the breadth and cost of marketing research studies should relate to *other* components of the decision situation. For example, if prior uncertainty and the costs of wrong decisions are both low, a small-scale investigation (or no investigation at all) may be indicated. If the potential information is so inaccurate as to produce little reduction in prior uncertainty, again the study may not justify its cost. In other instances, of course, the stakes, the initial uncertainty, and the anticipated accuracy of the market study may justify large expenditures for additional information.

Extent of Use

Now that we have discussed the conceptual basis of the Bayesian model, illustrated its application, and described its implications from the standpoint of marketing manager and researcher interaction, some comments should be made on the present stage of its application in industry.

Many techniques that can be used in marketing research are not widely used, and Bayesian analysis is no exception. One study reported that only 12% of 269 responding companies indicated using this approach in marketing research.[14] In a similar study done at about the same time, 27% of European firms reported using the technique.[15] These two studies did not inquire explicitly into the use of the Bayesian approach for determining the value of information. In a study designed to determine the extent to which the expected value of information (EVI) was formally calculated for a proposed project at least once during a 12-month period, 11% of the responding research director subsample and 20% of the marketing executive subsample reported that this was done.[16] The calculation was made for a variety of marketing problems—e.g., distribution, advertising/sales promotion, product development, and pricing—although not to the same extent for all.

Many reasons why the Bayesian approach has not been accepted more readily can

---

[14]B. A. Greenberg, J. L. Goldstucker, and D. N. Bellenger, "What Techniques Are Used by Marketing Researchers in Business?" *Journal of Marketing,* 41 (April 1977), 62–68.

[15]S. Permut, "The European View of Marketing Research," *Columbia Journal of World Business,* Fall 1977, pp. 94–102.

[16]Albaum, Tull, and Hanson, "Expected Value of Information."

be offered. For instance, the decision maker may be uncomfortable in acknowledging and quantifying uncertainty; there may be a shortage of executives who are sufficiently familiar with the technique; there may be problems in implementation concerning the quantification of prior probabilities, conditional probabilities, and utility functions; and there may be associated problems that arise when the assumptions inherent in the Bayesian model do not appropriately reflect the decision situation.[17] In short, the lack of use may reflect a lack of understanding, a lack of capability, or a lack of need for more sophisticated techniques. The comment made by one marketing executive may very well represent the feeling of many businesspeople:[18]

> I have no quarrels with the discipline of estimating the value of information in some general broad way to see whether a project should be considered. But I object to a formalized rigid approval system based on EVI because:
>
> (a) Most of the numbers are imaginary, subject to bias and easy manipulation. Once established, this practice may shift the real basis of decision making to something absolutely nonsensical.
> (b) Once established, the practice may change the nature of decision making process in a company from the orientation of an artistic undertaking with a leaning toward scientific discipline to one of pseudo scientific exercise. It is my opinion when this change in orientation occurs, a business imagination becomes a bureaucratic, rather than an entrepreneurial entity.

As suggested earlier in this chapter, in some decision situations the expected monetary value may not be applicable as the criterion of choice. This may arise when possible consequences are extreme—i.e., "too good" or "too bad." Consequently, decision makers may be risk averse, rather than risk neutral. Risk aversion, of course, is a matter of degree. If a utility function can be determined, then an alternative to not using Bayesian analysis is to use a more appropriate choice criterion, namely, the *certainty monetary equivalent of information* (CMEI), which is the risk-adjusted expected value of information. As Tull demonstrates,[19] the value of information (in monetary terms) is higher for the risk averse person than it is for the risk neutral person. Using an assumed utility function for a person who is average with respect to risk aversion, it was shown that when the problem parameters were such that EVI was calculated to be $1.75, CMEI was $13.51.

---

[17]Gert Assmus, "Bayesian Analysis for the Evaluation of Marketing Research Expenditures: A Reassessment," *Journal of Marketing Research,* 14 (1977), 562–68.

[18]Albaum, Tull, and Hanson, "Expected Value of Information."

[19]Donald S. Tull, "Should a Marketing Manager Who Is Risk Averse Be Willing to Pay More, About the Same, or Unwilling to Pay as Much for a Research Project Than One Who Is Risk Neutral?" unpublished paper, n.d. For simplified discussion of the procedure for calculating CMEI, see Donald S. Tull and Del I. Hawkins, *Marketing Research: Measurement and Method,* 3rd ed. (New York: Macmillan, 1984), pp. 728–31.

Industrial Applications

As with any new approach, the time lag between methodological innovation and regular use is frequently long. Reported applications of the Bayesian approach are still sparse, with one of the reasons undoubtedly being corporate security. We comment briefly on the nature of some of these applications.

Introduction of New Products

One of the earliest applications of Bayesian analysis involved a new-product study. The management of a large chemical firm was faced with the question of whether to introduce a new product (a packaging material designed for further processing by industrial fabricators) on the basis of the data then available regarding its chances of commercial success.[20] There were two questions:

1. Should the decision as to whether the product should be introduced be made "now" or one year later?
2. Given the answer regarding proper timing of the decision, what size of plant and what pricing policy should be followed?

The product in question was designed to compete in some 20 end-use markets. Estimates of sales were prepared for three sets of environmental conditions—most probable, optimistic, and pessimistic. Three pricing strategies and two plant sizes were considered, in all combinations, as tactical alternatives.

The venture was run as a simulation under a variety of environmental conditions. It turned out that the choice of plant size and pricing policy was insensitive to variations in the environment; that is, given commercialization (now or one year hence), a particular pricing strategy-plant size combination was best. Under the pessimistic set of conditions, however, even this "best" alternative would not yield a satisfactory return.

The second part of the analysis was concerned with the wisdom of delaying commercialization of the new product until one year hence when, presumably, more reliable data could be obtained regarding the chances of the new product's commercial success. Delaying the decision would defer the start of revenues—if the product were successful— and hence the opportunity to earn a return on these cash flows. Moreover, an additional out-of-pocket expense (of $2.6 million) would be involved in keeping the development going and obtaining further commercial data on acceptance of the product by fabricators who were cooperating in end-use tests.

What was not known was the *accuracy* that had to be associated with the new data to justify delay of the venture, but the analyst did have enough information to solve for this accuracy level. The answer turned out to be 90%; that is, management would need *almost perfect information* regarding the occurrence of the appropriate state of nature to justify delay.

Figure 3-6 shows the structure of the analysis. As can be seen from the tree diagram,

---

[20]This example is drawn from Wroe Alderson and P. E. Green, *Planning and Problem Solving in Marketing* (Homewood, Ill.: Richard D. Irwin, 1964), p. 229.

Figure 3-6   Influence of Delay on Decision to Build Plant

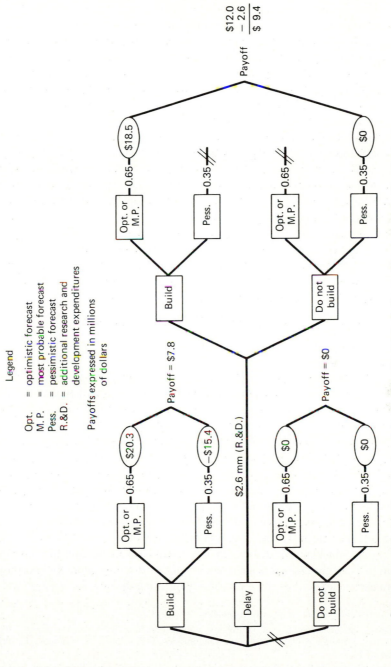

Legend

Opt. = optimistic forecast
M.P. = most probable forecast
Pess. = pessimistic forecast
R.&D. = additional research and
        development expenditures

Payoffs expressed in millions
of dollars

Source: Reprinted, with permission, from W. Alderson and P. E. Green, *Planning and Problem Solving in Marketing* (Homewood, Ill.: Richard D. Irwin, 1964), Chap. 8, p. 229.

given "no delay," the best present decision was to build the (already determined best-sized) plant. If so, an expected cash flow of $7.8 million was indicated. Given a one-year delay, *with perfect information,* the payoff could only be increased to $9.4 million. It was hardly surprising that management did not feel that information of anywhere near the high accuracy required to justify the delay could be obtained over the next year. Thus, the expected costs of delay exceeded the expected value of delay.

Test Marketing

A question arising when test marketing new products is when to stop the testing and make a final decision whether to market the product or drop it. This can be viewed as a sequential sampling problem and can be analyzed in a Bayesian framework.[21] A complicating factor, however, is that competitors often monitor results and may very well develop a product and decide to enter the national market before the testing firm does. Then the final decision is based not only on expected sales but also on the magnitude and timing of competitive reaction.

Johansson and Roberts show how test marketing under these conditions can be handled as a dynamic programming problem incorporating Bayesian sampling and probabilistic competitive actions.[22] Figure 3-7 shows the structure of this problem in the form of a decision tree. In addition to the three alternatives facing the firm (GO, DROP, TEST), competitors will either start production and distribution (COGO) at a particular point or wait for additional information (CONOGO). Assuming that competitors will find out about the potential market only by the testing firm's test or entry, Johansson and Roberts point out that competitors cannot enter prior to the second period. In addition, once a competitor has entered, the test option disappears for the first firm.

To see how the model framework could be used in an applied setting, simulated cases were run. Although not an actual application, this framework can easily be applied and solutions can easily be obtained where reasonable parameter values can be assessed by managers.

Decision Trees

Decision tree analysis—with or without probability revisions—has many users in marketing research. As an illustration, Villani and Morrison show how a decision tree can be constructed to estimate demand for a new product formulation, such as a different type of chocolate in a candy bar or a different type of coffee blend.[23]

As Villani and Morrison point out, potential customers for the new brand are drawn from two categories—users and nonusers of the current formulation. A consumer selected from each category has some probability of trying the new formulation and, having tried

---

[21]We cover the Bayesian approach to sampling in Chapter 9.

[22]Johny K. Johansson and Donald M. Roberts, "Competitive Reaction in Test Marketing: A Bayesian Solution," University of Illinois, College of Commerce and Business and Business Administration, Faculty Working Papers #188, 1974.

[23]K.E.A. Villani and D.G. Morrison, "A Method of Analyzing New Formulation Decisions," *Journal of Marketing Research,* 13 (August 1976), 284–88.

Figure 3-7 Test Market Problem Tree Diagram

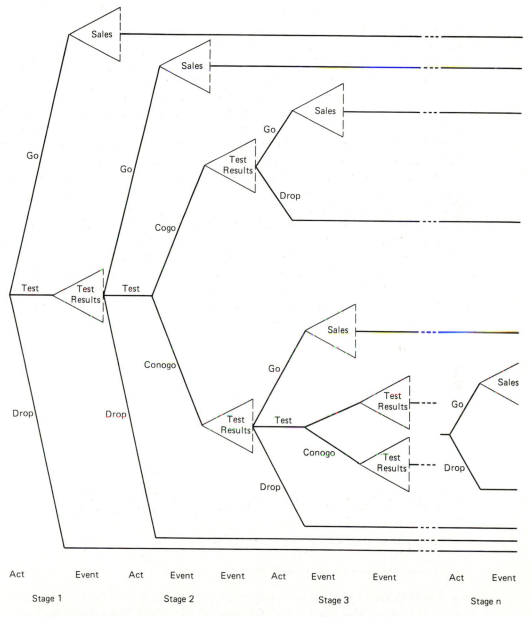

Source: Johansson and Roberts, "Competitive Reaction in Test Marketing."

Figure 3-8   Decision Tree for Demand Estimation

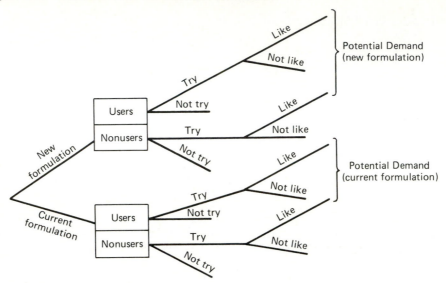

Source: Adapted, with permission, from K.E.A. Villani and D.G. Morrison, "A Method for Analyzing New Formulation Decisions," *Journal of Marketing Research,* 13 (August 1976), 284–88, published by the American Marketing Association.

it, some probability of liking it. Since the two pools of potential customers (users versus nonusers) are likely to vary in initial size and in their trying and liking probabilities as well, the authors propose that the category sizes and probabilities be estimated separately for each group.

Figure 3-8, adapted from Villani and Morrison's article, shows how the decision tree provides a useful tool for portraying the needed inputs to their model. For example, the expected number of customers for the new formulation, as obtained from the users category, is found by multiplying the number of people in that category by the probability of trying the new formulation, which, in turn, is multiplied by the conditional probability of liking, given that one has tried the new formulation.

Note that the decision tree of Figure 3-8 provides a simple way of showing the steps needed to develop the demand estimates. One can easily see, for example, how demand for the new formulation depends on consumers drawn initially from users and nonusers of the current formulation.

Design of Advertising Experiments

Blattberg shows how Bayesian analysis can be applied to the design and evaluation of advertising experiments.[24] The problem involves a company trying to decide between

[24]Robert C. Blattberg, "The Design of Advertising Experiments Using Statistical Decision Theory," *Journal of Marketing Research,* 16 (1979), 191–202. Also see James L. Ginter, Martha C. Cooper, Carl Obermiller, and Thomas E. Page, Jr., "The Design of Advertising Experiments Using Statistical Decision Theory: An Extension," *Journal of Marketing Research,* 18 (1981), 120–23.

two advertising spending levels for the next year—the present level and an increased amount. The experimental design is a randomized design with two sets of markets. Blattberg shows the procedure for calculating the expected value of sample information (EVSI), which is the same as EVI in our terminology. An actual example is given for an experiment run with seven control (i.e., present level of expenditures) and seven experimental (increased amount) markets.

SUMMARY

This chapter presented the fundamentals of the Bayesian approach to decision making under uncertainty. Our motivation was to use this model as a means of assessing the value versus cost of information that can be provided by marketing research. Two numerical examples—one highly simplified and the other more detailed—were used to illustrate the following basic ideas:

1. Prior analysis
2. Posterior analysis
3. Preposterior analysis, including the computation of the expected value of perfect information

We showed how various information-gathering options could be evaluated in terms of their net expected payoffs.[25]

We then discussed the related topics of determining the payoff entries and the role that utility functions could play in quantifying attitudes toward risk. A brief explanation of relevant cost concepts followed in which a distinction was made between operational and creative cost categories.

This led to a discussion of the potential value of Bayesian analysis in the context of an overall evaluation including extent of current use. The chapter concluded with brief descriptions of industry applications of Bayesian decision analysis and related methods.

Appendix 3-1

BASIC NOTIONS OF PROBABILITY

As a set of axioms, probability can be described or explained as follows:

1. A real number between 0 and 1 (including the end points) that is assigned to an event, j. In symbols, $0 \leqslant P_j \leqslant 1$.

---

[25]More extensive discussion of Bayesian methods can be found in Howard Raiffa's introductory text, *Decision Analysis, Introductory Lectures on Choices under Uncertainty* (Reading, Mass.: Addison-Wesley, 1968); and in the more technical book by John Pratt, Howard Raiffa, and Robert Schlaifer, *Introduction to Statistical Decision Theory* (New York: McGraw-Hill, 1965).

2. The sum of probabilities that are assigned to a set of n mutually exclusive (nonoverlapping) and collectively exhaustive events equals 1. In symbols

$$\sum_{j=1}^{n} P_j = 1$$

3. The probability of an event that can be decomposed into a set of mutually exclusive subevents is the sum of the probabilities assigned to the subevents. Bayesian analysis utilizes conditional, joint, and marginal probabilities. Also, two basic theorems—the addition and multiplication theorems—provide the foundation.

In the case of mutually exclusive events, the *addition theorem* states: If E_1 and E_2 are any two mutually exclusive events, the probability that either E_1 or E_2 occurs is $P(E_1 \cup E_2) = P(E_1) + P(E_2)$, where $(E_1 \cup E_2)$ stands for set union—i.e., the set of elements that are either E_1 or E_2, or both. Since in this case E_1 and E_2 have no elements in common, we are dealing with the exclusive "or."

More generally, if E_1 and E_2 are two (not necessarily mutually exclusive) events, the probability that either E_1 and/or E_2 occurs is

$$P(E_1 \cup E_2) = P(E_1) + P(E_2) - P(E_1 \cap E_2)$$

where $(E_1 \cap E_2)$ stands for set intersection, the set of elements that are both E_1 and E_2. Notice that in the mutually exclusive version of the formula the set $(E_1 \cap E_2) = \emptyset$, where the symbol $\emptyset$ stands for the null set (containing no elements). The distinction between the mutually exclusive and not mutually exclusive situations can be visualized as follows:

Mutually Exclusive   *Not Mutually Exclusive*

The general form of the addition theorem can be extended to deal with more than two events. In the case of three events, for example, the formula is

$$P(E_1 \cup E_2 \cup E_3) = P(E_1) + P(E_2) + P(E_3) - P(E_1 \cap E_2) - P(E_1 \cap E_3)$$
$$- P(E_2 \cap E_3) + P(E_1 \cap E_2 \cap E_3)$$

The *multiplication theorem,* in the special case of two independent events, states: If E_1 and E_2 are two independent events, then the probability of their joint occurrence is

$$P(E_1 \cap E_2) = P(E_1) \cdot P(E_2)$$

To generalize this formula for the case of dependent events, we require the use of conditional probability, written as $P(E_1|E_2)$ or the probability of event E_1 occurring, given the occurrence of event E_2. In the case of independent events (as first assumed above) $P(E_1|E_2) = P(E_1)$ and $P(E_2|E_1) = P(E_2)$, provided that $P(E_1), P(E_2) > 0$. We can then state the general version of the multiplication theorem as follows: If E_1 and E_2 are two events (not necessarily independent), then the probability of their joint occurrence is

$$P(E_1 \cap E_2) = P(E_1|E_2) \cdot P(E_2), P(E_2) > 0$$

We call $P(E_1 \cap E_2)$ a *joint* probability, $P(E_1|E_2)$ a *conditional* probability, and $P(E_2)$ a *marginal* (or unconditional) probability.

The multiplication theorem can be generalized beyond two events as follows: If k is an integer ($k \geq 2$) and $E_1, E_2, \ldots, E_k$ are any k events for which $P(E_1, E_2, \ldots, E_{k-1}) > 0$, then

$$P(E_1 \cap E_2 \cdots \cap E_k)$$
$$= P(E_1) \cdot P(E_2|E_1), \ldots, P(E_k|E_1 \cap E_2 \cap \cdots \cap E_{k-1})$$

ASSIGNMENT MATERIAL

1. Bernard B. Bayes, a sophisticated marketing research analyst, is charged with the assignment of recommending whether his firm should produce a new Christmas toy, the Mechanical Frump. His boss feels that a 60–40 chance exists that the toy will be successful. The payoff table (entries in thousands of dollars) is as follows:

Action	$P(S_2)$	S_1	$P(S_2)$	S_2
A_1: produce	0.6	150	0.4	−100
A_2: do not produce	0.6	0	0.4	0

Two market survey firms have submitted bids for doing the field work of interviewing toy store owners. The Alpha Company is known to conduct highly accurate surveys (at rather high cost), whereas the Beta Company's accuracy is somewhat lower but so is its cost. Pertinent conditional probabilities of survey results Z_1 (indicating S_1) and Z_2 (indicating S_2) are as follows:

Firm	Conditional Probabilities	Cost ($)
Alpha Company	$P(Z_1\|S_1) = P(Z_2\|S_2) = 0.9$	50,000
	$P(Z_1\|S_2) = P(Z_2\|S_1) = 0.1$	
Beta Company	$P(Z_1\|S_1) = P(Z_2\|S_2) = 0.7$	30,000
	$P(Z_1\|S_2) = P(Z_2\|S_1) = 0.3$	

Mr. Bayes has the following options: conduct no survey; buy Alpha's survey; buy Beta's survey.

a. Evaluate the expected payoff of each option. Prepare appropriate decision trees.

b. What is the expected value of perfect information?

c. Would your answer to part (a) change if the prior probability assignment over S_1 and S_2 were 0.9 and 0.1, respectively? If so, how?

2. The Bronstein Abacus Corporation is considering a proposal to develop a new calculator. The initial cash outlay would be $1 million. Development time is one year. If successful, the firm anticipates revenues (over the life cycle of the product) as follows:

- end of year 2: $200,000
- end of year 3: 300,000
- end of year 4: 400,000
- end of year 5: 500,000

If the new calculator is unsuccessful, the firm anticipates cash inflows of zero. The firm feels that a 90–10 chance exists for success of the product. Given a 10% annual cost of capital, should the venture be undertaken?

3. The Kiefer Oil Corporation is faced with the decision of whether to delay a decision regarding a new venture, pending the receipt of additional information on its success, given commercialization. The payoff matrix (entries in millions of dollars) is as follows:

Action	S_1	S_2
A_1: commercialize	20	−10
A_2: do not commercialize	0	0

The firm would incur a $3 million cost if the decision regarding the project were delayed. The conditional probabilities of Z_1 (indicating S_1) and Z_2 (indicating S_2), given the information anticipated to be developed in the delay period, are

$$P(Z_1|S_1) = P(Z_2|S_2) = 0.8$$

$$P(Z_1|S_2) = P(Z_2|S_1) = 0.2$$

Management elected to delay the venture. What can we infer from this action about the prior probabilities $P(S_1)$ and $P(S_2)$, assuming that in the *absence* of the survey management would have chosen act A_1?

4. Respond to the following statement: "The concept (and measure) Expected Value of Perfect Information has no practical value to marketing researchers and decision makers but is good for theory."

5. What cost categories could be relevant for any study where data are collected by telephone or personal interview?

6. How might the Bayesian model be used to examine actual decision makers' reactions to the receipt of new information in a decision problem under uncertainty?

7. For a venture analysis situation explain the relationship between research accuracy, prior beliefs, and the value of information.

4

The Tactics of Marketing Research—Research Design

In Chapter 1 we described marketing research as an activity concerned with acquiring and analyzing information related to the identification and solution of marketing problems. The tactics of research were introduced in Chapter 2 by describing the research process and planning a research project and the strategy of research—utilizing the Bayesian framework of cost versus value of information—was discussed in Chapter 3.

In this chapter we turn to the problem of research tactics as concerned with the sources and means available for acquiring marketing information and the types of research designs appropriate for organizing and analyzing this information. We first consider the characteristics of research design and the role it plays in information collection. Exploratory, descriptive, and causal studies are defined and discussed. We then present an introductory treatment of the general sources of information, in which we consider in turn (1) secondary information, (2) respondents, (3) natural experiments, (4) controlled experiments, and (5) simulation. This chapter's treatment of these five sources of marketing information is descriptive in nature and is for the purpose of giving a broad overview of alternative sources. We examine surveys of respondents and controlled experiments—two of the major sources of information—in subsequent chapters.

Next covered are the potential errors that can affect research design. We conclude the chapter by returning to the problem of the economics of research design and examining it within the context of the cost and value of information.

RESEARCH DESIGN

A *research design* is the specification of methods and procedures for acquiring the information needed to structure or to solve problems. It is the overall operational pattern or framework of the project that stipulates what information is to be collected, from which sources, and by what procedures. If it is a good design, it will ensure that the information obtained is relevant to the research problem and that it was collected by objective and economical procedures. A research design might be described as a series of advance decisions that, taken together, form a specific master plan or model for the conduct of the investigation.

Although research designs may be classified by many criteria, the most useful one concerns the major purpose of the investigation. On this basis we may identify the broad classes of designs as exploratory, descriptive, and causal.

Exploratory Studies

The major purposes of *exploratory studies* are the identification of problems, the more precise formulation of problems (including the identification of relevant variables), and the formulation of new alternative courses of action. An exploratory study is often the first in a series of projects that culminate in one concerned with the drawing of inferences that are used as the basis of management action. That is, an exploratory study is often used as an introductory phase of a larger study and results are used in developing specific techniques for the larger study.

The design of exploratory studies is characterized by a great amount of flexibility and ad hoc versatility. By definition, the researcher is involved in investigating an area or subject in which he or she is not sufficiently knowledgeable to have formulated detailed research questions. No clear hypotheses have been developed about the problem. The researcher is seeking information that will enable him or her to formulate specific research questions and/or to state hypotheses about the problem. In short, the researcher seeks to gain familiarity and/or achieve new insights into the problem situation.

For a given problem situation the results of an exploratory study may indicate that further research can be reduced and/or certain aspects of the larger study can be eliminated. This will result from the narrowing of the problem area. Although rare, it may be that the problem, if clear-cut, can be solved based on an exploratory study. For example, the researcher may discover that another study exists which provides the needed information.

An example of an exploratory study is one conducted by a major manufacturer of kitchen ranges. The purpose of the research was to "investigate the design of our ranges to see if it can be improved functionally." One part of the project design involved setting up a booth in department stores handling the brand and inviting women to simulate the cooking of a meal calling for one menu item to be boiled, another fried, another simmered, and so on. It was discovered that the women almost invariably used the same burners for the same type of cooking: for example, the left front burner for frying, the left back burner for boiling, and the right back burner for simmering. These exploratory research findings led to a prototype redesign of burners and additional research on them, along with research on preferences and usage patterns of ranges with respect to baking and the storage of cooking utensils.

Despite the necessity for flexibility in exploratory study design, we can distinguish three separate stages that are usually included in exploratory studies and typically conducted in the sequence listed: (1) a search of secondary information sources, (2) interviews with persons who are knowledgeable about the subject area being explored, and (3) the examination of analogous situations.

Search of Secondary Sources

Secondary sources of information, as used in this section, are the rough equivalent of the "literature" on the subject. (We shall use this term in an expanded sense later in this chapter.)

It is the rare research problem for which there is no relevant information to be found by a relatively quick and inexpensive search of the literature. If the question to be answered by the research project referred to above is, "How might we improve the functional design of our ranges?" it is likely that information bearing on this question will have been published. Studies performed on this subject by home economists at universities, by governmental agencies, or by women's magazines will probably have been made and published.

Secondary sources for exploratory studies are not limited to external sources. Search should also be made of company records. For larger firms this may be difficult, since operations may be spread out geographically. Despite such complications a search should be attempted, as various company operational units often face similar problems and it may be that one unit has recently done research pertaining to the problem at hand. One large company, for example, often used outside consultants for projects relevant to new-product decisions. This practice was stopped when it was realized that these consultants obtained much of their information directly from company records.

A later section of this chapter deals with secondary sources of information in greater depth.

Obtaining Information from Knowledgeable Persons

The stage of the exploratory investigation that relates to obtaining information from knowledgeable persons is a natural complement to the use of secondary information. After having searched secondary sources, it will usually be desirable to talk with persons who are well informed in the area being investigated. Such persons can be company executives as well as persons outside the organization.

This survey is sometimes called an *experience survey* or a *pilot survey*.[1] Rarely is it structured in the sense of a formal questionnaire being prepared, a probability sample selected, or the sample size specified in advance. Rather, the usual procedure is to look for competent, articulate individuals and talk with them about the problem. They will often suggest others who should be reached; a "referral" sample frequently results. The investigator continues these interviews until it is felt that the marginal return in information becomes less than the costs involved.

With respect to the redesign of ranges, knowledgeable persons—housewives—were asked to provide information. A convenience sample was taken of housewives who were shopping in the department stores where booths were installed. Observations were made until it was established that there was a consistent behavior pattern with respect to the use of each burner. Once this finding was established, this phase of the exploratory study was terminated.

[1]For a more complete discussion of the experience survey, see Claire Selltiz, Lawrence S. Wrightsman, and Stuart W. Cook, *Research Methods in Social Relations*, 3rd ed. (New York: Holt, Rinehart & Winston, 1976), pp. 94–97.

A widely used technique in exploratory research is the *focus group*. A focus group interview is one in which a group of people jointly participate in an interview that does not use a structured question-and-answer methodology. The group, which usually consists of 8 to 12 persons (but may have as few as 5 or as many as 20), is generally selected purposively to include persons who have a common background or similar buying or use experience that relates to the problem to be researched. The interviewer, or *moderator* as he or she is more often called, attempts to focus the discussion on the problem areas in a relaxed, nondirected manner. The objective is to foster involvement and interaction among the group members during the interview that will lead to spontaneous discussion and the disclosure of attitudes, opinions, and information on present or prospective buying and use behavior.

Focus groups are used primarily to define problems, to provide background information, and to generate hypotheses rather than to provide solutions for problems. Areas of application include the examination of new product concepts, the generation of ideas for improving established products, the development of creative concepts for advertising, and the determination of effective means of merchandising products.[2] Focus-group interviews are often held to help determine the subject areas on which questions should be asked in a later, large-scale, structured-direct interview (Exhibit 4-1).

During the development of Agree Creme Rinse and Agree Shampoo, Johnson Wax conducted many focus groups among all types of women, but experience with them led to concentration on the young woman. According to Neil DeClark, associate marketing research manager of Johnson Wax:

> Using focus groups to further our understanding of users' problems and perceptions—and also to get early reactions to some product concepts—we found that we were on the right path. The oiliness problems were major, and our ideas were regarded as important by the potential users.[3]

Furthermore, focus groups were used by Johnson Wax in copy development and provided the first exposure to their ultimate theme. These groups provided insight into the virtues of alternative reasons why a shampoo would keep hair cleaner longer.

The focus-group methodology is discussed further in Chapter 5.

Examination of Analogous Situations

It is also logical that one will want to examine analogous situations to determine what can be learned about the nature of the problem and its variables. Analogous situations consist of case histories and simulations. Examination of case histories is one of the older methods of marketing research, whereas the use of simulations is one of the newer methods.

---

[2]If the sole purpose is to generate ideas, then *individual interviews* may be a better alternative than focus groups. Limited research on this issue suggests that the number and quality of ideas may be greater from such interviews. (See Edward F. Fern, "The Use of Focus Groups for Idea Generation: The Effects of Group Size, Acquaintanceship, and Moderator on Response Quantity and Quality," *Journal of Marketing Research*, 19 [February 1982], pp. 1–13.)

[3]"Key Role of Research in Agree's Success Is Told," *Marketing News*, January 12, 1979, p. 14.

Exhibit 4-1 An Application of Focus Groups in Exploratory Research

A most important function of focus group interviewing is as a device to guide the design and conduct of a subsequent large-scale quantitative survey. In this context, group interviews are used:

1. To identify and understand consumer language as it relates to the product category in question. What terms do they use? What do they mean?
2. To identify the range of consumer concerns. How much variability *is* there among consumers in how they view the product and in the considerations which lead them to accept or reject the product?
3. To identify the *complexity* of consumer concerns. Are there a few simple attitudes which govern consumer reaction toward the product, or is the structure complex, involving many contingencies?
4. To identify specific methodological or logistical problems which are likely to affect either the cost of the subsequent research, or one's ability to generate meaningful, actionable findings at all.

Volvo of America Corporation in 1976 commissioned a study to explore the differences between Volvo *buyers* and Volvo *considerers* (people who thought about buying a Volvo, but in the end bought some other car). We wanted to learn the *reasons* for buying a Volvo, and the *resistances* to buying a Volvo. The research design called for two phases of research:

1. An exploratory stage, involving four group interviews—two with Volvo buyers and two with Volvo considerers (prior research has shown that buyers and considerers don't mix well; buyers dominate the sessions by proselytizing about Volvo).
2. A quantification phase involving telephone interviews with 400 first-time Volvo buyers and 200 Volvo considerers.

A great deal of research had been done by Volvo in the past which had generated a number of hypotheses about what makes a considerer become a Volvo buyer. In spite of this, important things were learned in the focus groups which led to conducting a quantification study which was both *more insightful* and *less expensive* than would otherwise have been conducted.

One of the most important things learned was that there are a number of different ways in which considerers considered Volvo. Thus, it was felt the quantification study should include questions designed to segment considerers according to the *degree* to which they seriously considered Volvo and the methods they used to arrive at their purchase choice. To that end, a question was designed to determine which specific actions were taken in considering Volvo, such as talking with the Volvo owners, reading evaluative articles in magazines, paying more attention to Volvo advertising, visiting a Volvo showroom, negotiating over price, and others.

The group interviews strongly suggested that the primary variable differentiating the Volvo buyer from the Volvo considerer was the set of *concerns* that individual brought with him to the car-buying process. Further, it was readily apparent from the groups that these concerns varied widely, implying that it would be necessary in the quantification to measure the importance to the consumer of a number of characteristics of a car, such as safety, exterior styling, anticipated cost of service, and so forth. In consequence, a list of 26 automobile attributes was prepared—some drawing from prior research and some new ones based upon the group session findings—to present to consumers in the quantification study. However, the desirability of this approach led to a methodological dilemma. It was important that not only the importance of these 26 factors to Volvo buyers and considerers be determined, but also how considerers compared Volvo, on the factors they considered important, to the car actually bought. The logical alternative, after having the respondent rate all 26 factors for importance was to have him rank the five factors which played the largest role in the automobile selection decision, and then rate Volvo versus the competitive car on those top five factors. Clearly, it would be expecting too much to have the respondent perform this task in a telephone interview. It was critical that the respondent have the 26 factors in front of him while he was going through the rating process.

This situation together with problems that arose in recruiting respondents for the focus group sessions led to the decision to conduct the quantification study as a mail survey—a decision which permitted collecting the rating information which could not be collected over the telephone, while at the same time saving Volvo a considerable sum of money (estimated at about $10,000). The mail survey went smoothly, the quantification verified some of the hypotheses generated in the group sessions (and refuted others), and the results of the study played an important role in the development of Volvo advertising and marketing strategies for 1976.

This example illustrates the value of conducting exploratory focus-group interviews prior to a larger, quantified study. Such an exploration will not always pay for itself in a more efficient final research design, as this one more than did, but it will nearly always lead to a subsequent survey richer in content, more adroit in interpretation, and more actionable to marketing management.

Source: Adapted from Thomas D. Dupont, "Exploratory Group Interview in Consumer Research: A Case Example," in "Advances in Consumer Research, Vol. III, ed. Beverlee B. Anderson (Association for Consumer Research, 1976), 431–33.

Case histories that are similar in content are generally available and provide a fruitful area of investigation for the exploratory study. They are well suited for use in exploratory studies in that the examination of another actual case problem will often help clarify the nature of the problem at hand, suggest which variables are relevant, and give indications of the nature of the relationship of the variables. This method of investigation is widely used in the behavioral sciences, where it is called the "case study."

However, the results of the investigation of case histories are always to be considered as suggestive rather than conclusive. Since the examination is being conducted on an after-the-fact basis, it is not possible to manipulate the independent variables or to randomize treatments and the selection of groups concerned. For these reasons the interpretations reached concerning the relevancy and relationships of variables are judgmental and always subject to error.

In the case of the problems concerning redesign of kitchen ranges, ready-made case histories may well be available in the form of previous design changes made by competitors. We might be able to observe what happened to the sales of one or more competitors' ranges following design changes. As always in case studies, we would have to examine the situation(s) carefully to try to identify and assess the effect of any other independent variable changes (price, advertising, changes in income, etc.) on sales. Tentative conclusions can be reached, however, and a hypothesis stated. This hypothesis can be tested in a subsequent causal study designed for that purpose if it is desired to do so.

Simulation of the general problem situation (discussed briefly later in the chapter) may also be useful for providing a better understanding of the problem and its components. Simulation involves the construction of a model representing the situation and, in effect, experimenting with it rather than the actual situation.

Descriptive Studies

Much research is concerned with *describing* market characteristics or functions. A market-potential study is made that describes the number, distribution, and socioeconomic characteristics of potential customers of a product; a market-share study is conducted to determine the share of the market received by both the company and its competitors; or a sales analysis is made that states sales by territory, type of account, size or model of product, and the like. Descriptive studies are also made in product research (a listing and comparison of the functional features and specifications of competitive products, for example), promotion research (the demographic characteristics of the audience being reached by the current advertising program), distribution research (the number and location of retailers handing the company's products that are supplied by wholesalers versus those supplied by the company's distribution centers), and pricing research (competitors' prices by geographic area). It is obvious that the examples of descriptive research given thus far cover only a few of the possibilities.

These studies often involve the description of the extent of the association between two or more variables. A frequency distribution of sales by the income levels of consumers is an example. This type of information may be used to draw inferences concerning the relationship between the variables involved. It may also be used for purposes of prediction.

Although associations can be used only to infer, and not to establish, a causal relationship, they are often useful for predictive purposes. It is not always necessary to understand causal relations in order to make accurate predictive statements. Descriptive information often provides a sound basis for the solution of marketing problems, even though it does not "explain" the nature of the relationship involved. The basic principle involved is to find correlates of the behavior it is desired to predict that are measurable at the time the predictive statement is made.

Descriptive research, in contrast to exploratory research, is marked by the *prior formulation of specific research questions*. The investigator already knows a substantial amount about the research problem, perhaps as a result of an exploratory study, before the project is initiated. Thus the investigator should be able to define clearly what it is that he or she wants to measure and to set up appropriate and specific means for measuring it.

An example of a descriptive study is one performed by a company that was considering entering the greeting card industry. A previous exploratory study had revealed that only 2% of the sales of greeting cards was made through supermarkets. Since the potential of this type of outlet is large, and other outlets were heavily franchised or otherwise dominated by well-entrenched companies in the field, a descriptive study was performed to answer the specific question, "What are the major problems of selling greeting cards in volume through supermarkets?" The answers obtained resulted in the company's developing a greeting card vending machine that is being used successfully in supermarkets.

Another example of a descriptive study is one conducted by a school-employees credit union in order to gain information useful in providing better service to its members. Management knew very little about the members other than they were school employees, family members of employees, or former employees. In addition, the credit union knew very little about members' awareness and use of—and attitudes toward—individual services available to them. Consequently, a study was undertaken to answer the following research questions:

1. What are the demographic and socioeconomic characteristics of primary members?
2. How extensively are existing services being used and what are the attitudes toward such services?
3. What is the interest for specific new services?

The answers proved helpful to management in evaluating the financial and nonfinancial services offered and in deciding which new services to add.

Descriptive research is also characterized by a preplanned and structured design. As contrasted with the flexibility of the exploratory study, the descriptive study should be planned carefully with respect to the sources of information to be consulted and the procedures to be used in collecting information. Since the intent of the study is to provide answers to specific questions, more care is normally exercised against the possibility of systematic (nonrandom) errors than is the case with the exploratory study. The designs used in descriptive research can employ one or more of the five general sources of information. Furthermore, they may be cross-sectional (at a point in time) or longitudinal (over time) in nature.

For descriptive studies (and causal studies as well) proposed data analysis and project output are critical aspects of research planning. One approach to the inclusion of such output planning into research design is illustrated in Table 4-1, which is from the research design for a survey conducted for a meat packer to test the market potential of a new sport-related hot dog. What was unique about the product concept was that it featured a winter sport—ice hockey—rather than the more usual link with baseball. As illustrated, this aspect of the design should include analysis procedures for each question, an assessment of their information value, and an explanation of how the information may be used.[4]

---

[4]Benjamin D. Sackmary, "Data Analysis and Output Planning Improve Value of Marketing Research," *Marketing News*, January 23, 1983, Sec. 1, pp. 6–7.

TABLE 4-1 Illustration of Proposed Analysis for New Hot Dog Study

Question Number(s) and Variable Name(s):

Questions #5.0 and 5.1 asking number of packages of hot dogs consumed per month by household and usual number of hot dogs per package plus number of loose links per month. Variable name is USAGE.

Information Content of Questions:

Computer coding will multiply number of packages per month by dogs per package plus links to obtain the total household usage of hot dogs per month.

Reasons for Including Question(s):

These questions provide information needed in order to segment the population of hot dog users into submarkets based on usage level. Usage volume can serve as an excellent predictor of future purchase patterns, may be related to interest in proposed new hot dog product and may support media selection that will reach high-usage households at least cost.

Primary Analysis and Information Value:

I. FREQUENCY DISTRIBUTION: Indicates number of dogs used per month for all respondents. These will be coded into three categories: LIGHT, MODERATE, AND HEAVY USERS.
II. RELATION TO DEMOGRAPHICS: Usage types will be cross-tabulated with size of household, age of household shopper, total income, sex and education of shopper in order to identify the characteristics of the three user segments. Statistic = Chi square.
III. RELATION TO PRICE: Usage will be systematically related to responses on purchase probability under different pricing conditions. This will tell us the importance of price for the user segments and help in estimating volume of sales at different price points.

Additional Analysis and Information Value:

RELATION TO IMPORTANCE OF PRODUCT FEATURES: User segments will be compared in terms of their mean responses to the 10-point importance-attribute scales including package, brand name, quality, contents, taste, texture, smell, shape, and color of the hot dogs. This will provide information on the relative importance of attributes and assist in formulating advertising approaches for the target segments.

Source: Adapted from Sackmary, "Data Analysis and Output Planning Improve Value of Marketing Research," Sec. 1, p. 6.

Causal Studies

Causal Relationships

Although descriptive information is often helpful for predictive purposes, where possible we would like to know the *causes* of what we are predicting—the "reasons why." Further, we would like to know how these causal factors relate the effects that we are predicting. In part, this is undoubtedly because we each have an innate desire to understand. Of a more direct and practical consequence, however, is the fact that if the causes of the effects we want to predict are understood, our ability both to predict and to control these effects is almost invariably improved.[5]

Suppose that a particular manufacturer of color television sets reduces the wholesale price of its sets by 10% and that this reduction is passed on to the consumer. Further, assume that sales to the consumer rose by 15% during the succeeding three months as compared with a like period prior to the price reduction. Did the price cut *cause* the increase in sales?

Deterministic Causation

Real-world events occur in and are affected by a real-world environment. The nature of this environment determines the "rules" that describe the relationship between events. The nature of the relationship between price and quantity of television sets sold by the state-owned monopoly in the Soviet Union is quite different from that for an individual producer in the United States.

Suppose that we establish a functional relationship between two events, X and Y, such that "Y is some function of X." This statement may be written

$$Y = F(X)$$

Further, suppose that we know the environment of these two events well enough to determine the "rule" that relates them, and thus specify F. Once we specify X, we have completely determined Y. In this case we may say that X is both a *necessary* and a *sufficient* condition for Y. We must specify X, but only X, to determine Y. We may, therefore, say that X is a *deterministic cause* of Y. We may define a deterministic cause as any event that is necessary and sufficient for the subsequent occurrence of another event.[6]

Returning to our example, would it be realistic to conclude that the price cut was a deterministic cause of the sales increase? Clearly, it would not. Many factors other

---

[5]Many of the notions of causality are described in Thomas D. Cook and Donald T. Campbell, *Quasi-Experimentation: Design & Analysis Issues for Field Settings* (Chicago: Rand McNally College Publishing, 1979), pp. 9–36; and Richard P. Bagozzi, *Causal Models in Marketing* (New York: John Wiley, 1980), Chap. 1.

[6]This definition, and the definition of probabilistic cause in the next section, follow that in R. L. Ackoff, Shiv Gupta, and J. S. Minas, *Scientific Method: Optimizing Applied Research Decisions* (New York: John Wiley, 1962), Chap. 1.

than price affect the level of sales; a change in price is, therefore, not a sufficient condition for determining the level of sales. More generally, the multivariate nature of the complex world of marketing would seem to indicate that deterministic causes are quite rare. Yet, there are occasions when companies do research on phenomena that border on deterministic causation. For example, Wrangler Jeans is a company that sponsors sports, such as rodeo and dirt bike racing. In measuring the impact of its sports marketing dollars, it proceeds as follows:

> Consumer interviews are conducted before the company gets involved to figure out how many pairs of Wrangler jeans are being purchased by spectators of that sport. After sponsorship is undertaken, follow-up interviews are conducted to measure incremental purchase in Wrangler purchases.
>
> The rate of increased purchasing is multiplied by the company's profit margin per pair of jeans to compute the sponsorship's sales contribution to the company. That figure is compared to the cost of sponsorship. If a loss results, continued sponsorship may not occur.[7]

Probabilistic Causation

Our discussion of problem-situation models in Chapter 1 permits us to generalize beyond the last example: relationships in marketing usually involve several variables. As further complications, these relationships are almost invariably complex, subject to change, and difficult to measure.

Consider now a multivariable relationship of the form

$$Y = F(X_1, X_2)$$

where X_1 and X_2 are independent. Assuming that we are able to specify F, the variables X_1 and X_2 become *jointly* necessary and sufficient to determine Y.

Suppose that we know the value of X_1 but do not know the value of X_2. Since X_1 and X_2 are assumed to be independent, no inferences can be drawn about the value of X_2 from the known value of X_1. Note that, in this situation, the only statements we can make about the value of Y must be conditional upon the unknown value of X_2. The effect on Y of a known change in X_1 may be reinforced, counteracted, or left the same, depending on what happens to X_2. X_1 is not sufficient to determine Y.

Where multivariable relationships exist, we may say that any one of the independent variables X_j is a *probabilistic cause* of the effect of Y. The term *producer* is sometimes used, and will be used here, as being synonymous with probabilistic cause. When the term "producer" is used, the resulting effect is referred to as a *product*.

In the more general case, we may define a probabilistic cause, or producer, as any event (e.g., X_1 or X_2) that is necessary but not sufficient for the subsequent occurrence of another event, Y.

[7]Kevin Higgins, "Olympics and Other Sports May Be a Bonanza—but for Whom?" *Marketing News*, 18 (June 22, 1984), 6.

Are we to conclude that the price reduction was a producer of the sales increase (product) in our example? Given that we believe that the price level and amount of sales of television sets are inversely and functionally related, we are, in fact, drawing that conclusion.

The reader should be careful not to read more into the last statement than is actually there. Note that it does *not* say that the price reduction determined the amount of the sales increase, or that it was even a major factor in bringing about any increase in sales. It may have been that a newly redesigned model series prompted a concomitant change in advertising and in price, and the other changes were more important producers of the sales increase than the price change.

Bases for Inferring Causal Relationships

What kinds of evidence can be used for drawing inferences about causal relationships? There are three types of such evidence: (1) associative variation, (2) sequence of events, and (3) absence of other possible causal factors. In addition, the cause and effect have to be related. That is, there is a logical implication (or theoretical justification) to imply the specific causal relation.

Associative Variation. *Associative variation*, or "concomitant variation," as it is often termed, is a measure of the extent to which occurrences of two variables are associated. Two types of associative variation may be distinguished:

1. *Association between two variables*—a measure of the extent to which the presence of one variable is associated with the presence of the other.
2. *Association between the changes of two variables*—a measure of the extent to which a change in the level of one variable is associated with a change in the level of the other.[8]

As an example, suppose that the brand manager of a particular brand of detergent notices that sales have shown an unusually large increase in the third quarter, and suppose that he or she is also aware that a number of detergent sales personnel took a retraining course during the second quarter. How may the brand manager determine if the retraining was a producer of the sales increase?

Two basic approaches, with variations on each, can be followed to obtain evidence concerning this relationship. The first is to start with the hypothesized producer (salesperson retraining) and see if there is an associated variation with the product ("large" territorial sales increase). This could be done by determining which salespeople had been retrained during the second quarter and comparing the net changes in sales between the second and third quarters in their territories with the corresponding net changes in sales of those salespeople who were not retrained during the second quarter.

---

[8]It has been argued that two other conditions exist, particularly for continuous variables: (1) the presence of one variable is associated with a change in the level of the other, and (2) a change in the level of one variable is associated with the presence of the other. See Jack Feldman, "Considerations in the Use of Causal-Correlational Techniques in Applied Psychology," *Journal of Applied Psychology*, 60 (1975), 663–70.

The second approach is to start with the product ("large" territorial sales increase) and work back to the producer (salesperson retraining). If this approach were used, all territories with "large" sales increases would be examined to determine whether they were predominantly those of salespeople who had been retrained during the second quarter.

Suppose that one of these approaches was used to collect information that showed a high degree of association between "large" territorial sales increases and salesperson retraining. Would this information constitute experimental "proof" of a causal relationship?

The answer to this question is, unfortunately, "No, it would not." The reasons why this is the case are discussed in detail in later chapters. It is sufficient to state here that this associated variation might be the result of random variation or the result of both variables being associated with some extraneous variable (a change in the point-of-sale displays provided to the salespeople who took the retraining course, for example). If we have no basis for believing that either of these situations exists, then we may use the associated variation as a basis for inferring—but not scientifically testing—that there is a causal relationship.

Sequence of Events.   A second characteristic of a causal relationship is the requirement that the causal factor occur first; the producer must precede the product. In order for the salesperson retraining to have resulted in an increase in sales, the retraining must have taken place prior to the sales increase.

The fact that a possible producer precedes a product does not establish that a causal relationship exists between the two, however. It might be that it was simply a coincidence that the retraining took place prior to the sales increase. It might also be that sales training and sales increases are associated but not causally related. (A salesman may shave every day before going to work, but shaving is not a cause of his going to work.)

It is not always easy to determine the sequence of events. In such cases where an actual causal relationship does exist, it is difficult to determine which is the producer and which is the product. The relationship between shelf space and sales is an example. Other factors being equal, those brands having the larger relative amounts of shelf space tend to have higher sales. Other factors being equal, those brands having the higher sales tend to be allotted the larger relative amounts of shelf space.

Absence of Other Possible Causal Factors.   A final basis for inferring causation is the absence of any possible causal factors (producers) other than the one or ones being investigated. If it could be demonstrated, for example, that no other factors present could have caused the sales increase in the third quarter, we could then logically conclude that the salesperson training must have been responsible.

Obviously, in an after-the-fact examination of a situation such as the detergent sales increase, it is impossible ever to clearly rule out all other factors. One could never be completely sure that there were no competitor, customer, or company-initiated causal factors that would account for the sales increase.

In experimental designs in which control groups are used, it is possible that some of the variables that might otherwise obscure or lead to a misinterpretation of the relationship(s) under study can be controlled. In addition, a soundly designed experiment will include an attempt to balance the effects of the uncontrolled variables on the experimental results in such a way that only random variations resulting from the uncontrolled variables will be measured.

For example, an experiment might be designed in which salespeople who have not yet undergone retraining are matched in pairs with respect to age, past sales history, type of territory, and other variables believed to be possible determinants of sales performance. A control group could then be chosen by selecting one salesperson from each pair at random who would not be retrained during the period of the experiment. The experimental group would then consist of the other salesperson from each of the pairs, who would be retrained. An analysis of the differences in sales results for the two groups during the period of the experiment could then be made to test the hypothesis that salesperson retraining does result in a significant increase in sales.

Conclusions Concerning Types of Evidence

No one of the three types of evidence, nor, indeed, all three types combined, can ever demonstrate conclusively that a causal relationship exists. However, we *can* obtain evidence that makes it highly reasonable to conclude that a particular relationship exists.

The accumulation of evidence from various investigations will, if all findings point to the same conclusion, increase our confidence that a causal relationship exists. A diversity of types of evidence is also convincing in this respect. If evidence of all three of the types discussed above can be obtained, the resulting inference is more convincing than if the evidence is of only one type.

Causal Inference Studies

Over the last few pages we have considered the nature and meaning of causation and the types of evidence that can be useful for drawing inferences about causal relationships. We now turn to a consideration of the design of causal studies.

There are two broad classes of designs for causal inference research: (1) natural experiments and (2) controlled experiments.[9] The distinguishing feature between the two is the extent of intervention by the investigator in the situation under study. As the name implies, a *natural experiment* may not require investigator intervention in the situation at all and, at most, will involve intervention only to the extent required for measurement. A *controlled experiment* will require investigator intervention to control and to manipulate variables of interest as well as to measure the response.

The salesperson-retraining example (as originally described) is an illustration of a natural experiment. In this case no intervention was involved in the situation; the measurements made were conducted as a normal part of doing business. Had the investigator

[9]Causation also can be inferred from nonexperimental methods, such as path analysis (causal modeling, structural equations) and cross-lagged panel correlation. See Hubert M. Blalock, Jr., *Causal Inferences in Non experimental Research* (Chapel Hill: University of North Carolina Press, 1964); Cook and Campbell, *Quasi-Experimentation*, Chap. 7; and Kent B. Monroe and Susan M. Petroshius, "Developing Causal Priorities in Marketing," unpublished working paper, n.d.

wanted to measure results other than those normally measured—the amount of shelf space in retail stores the company's detergents had in the affected territories before and after the retraining of salespeople, for example—there would necessarily have been investigator intervention to the extent required to perform such measurements.

One possible controlled experiment for assessing the effect of sales retraining on the level of sales has already been described. Investigator intervention was involved in matching the salespeople in pairs and randomly selecting one from each pair for inclusion in the test group. The experimental procedures were, therefore, the determinant of which salespeople were to be retrained. Clearly, intervention of this kind is not always practical or even possible.

It is apparent from the discussion thus far that causal studies presuppose a considerable amount of knowledge by the investigator about the variables being studied. The design of causal inference studies is also highly formalized. The experiment just described uses a form of "before–after with control group" design. We shall describe some specific designs of both natural and controlled experiments in Chapter 6.

Since we have already considered the three general classes of marketing research designs (exploratory, descriptive, and causal), it is appropriate that we now consider the major sources of information used in marketing research studies.

THE SOURCES OF MARKETING INFORMATION

There are five major sources of marketing information: (1) secondary sources, (2) respondents, (3) natural experiments, (4) controlled experiments, and (5) simulation. In this section we shall introduce and briefly describe each so that the reader will have an overview and an introduction to subsequent chapters that describe some of these sources in more detail.

Secondary Sources of Information

Secondary information is information that has been collected by persons or agencies for purposes other than the solution of the problem at hand. If a furniture manufacturer, for example, needs information on the potential market for furniture in the Middle Atlantic states, many secondary sources of information are available. The federal government collects and publishes information on the numbers of families, family formation, income, and the number of sales volume of retail stores, all by geographic area. It also publishes special reports on the furniture industry. Many state and local governments collect similar information for their respective areas. The trade associations in the furniture field collect and publish an extensive amount of information about the industry. Trade journals are a valuable source of secondary information, as are special studies done by other advertising media. These and other sources will yield much information of value to the researcher concerned with this problem.

Reasons for Obtaining Secondary Information

As a general rule, no research project should be conducted without a search of secondary-information sources. This search should be conducted early in the problem investigation and prior to any organized collection of information from primary sources. There are several reasons for this.

1. *Secondary information may solve the problem.* If adequate data are available from secondary sources, primary data collection will not be required. For example, Campbell Soup Company has based an advertising campaign on the theme "soup is good food." This theme emerged from working with federal government data pertaining to eating habits, nutritional health, and related topics that were collected over a period of 15 years.[10]

2. *Search costs are substantially lower than primary collection costs.* A comprehensive search of secondary sources can almost always be made in a fraction of the time and cost required for the collection of primary information. Although many marketing problems do not warrant the expenditures involved for primary information collection, it is a rare situation in which obtaining secondary data is not worth the time and cost invested.

3. *Secondary information has important supplementary uses.* Even when the secondary information obtained is not adequate for solving the problem involved, it often has valuable supplemental uses. These include
   a. Helping to define the problem and formulate hypotheses about its solution. The assembling and analyzing of available secondary data will almost always provide a better understanding of the problem and its context and will frequently suggest solutions not considered previously.
   b. Helping to plan the collection of primary data. An examination of the methods and techniques employed by other investigators in similar studies may be useful in planning the present one. It may also be of value in establishing classifications that are compatible with past studies so that trends may be more readily analyzed.
   c. Helping to define the population and select the sample in primary information collection.

The researcher must be careful when using secondary data, particularly as the only source of data. To be useful, secondary data must be available, relevant to the information needs (which includes being timely), accurate, and sufficient to meet data requirements for the problem at hand.[11] Potential sources of bias that have been identified include *selective recording, deliberate original distortion,* and *selective survival.*[12] While such

[10]"Soup Researcher Defends Ad Claims by Citing Federal Data," *Marketing News,* 18 (February 3, 1984), 13.

[11]See Donald S. Tull and Del I. Hawkins, *Marketing Research: Measurement and Method,* 4th ed. (New York: Macmillan, 1987), pp. 66–68.

[12]Lee Sechrest and Melinda Phillips, "Unobtrusive Measures: An Overview," in *Unobtrusive Measurement Today,* ed. Lee Sechrest (San Francisco: Jossey-Bass, 1979), pp. 5–6.

types of errors may not exist for a given piece of secondary data, the researcher never-theless should always be aware that any one or more may exist. Consequently, it is important that the researcher know something about how secondary data were collected. Despite this warning, if the right techniques are used, creative secondary research can provide at least a partial answer to almost any information question.

Secondary information falls into two categories, the distinguishing feature being whether it is available within the company (internal) or must be obtained from outside sources (external).

Internal Secondary Information

All companies collect information in the everyday course of conducting business. Orders are received and filled, costs are recorded, warranty cards are returned, sales-people's reports are submitted, engineering reports are made—these are but a few of the many sources of information, collected by companies for other purposes, that are often useful to the researcher.

A basic source of information, one that is all too often overlooked, is the sales invoice. By simple analyses of the information available on the company's sales invoice, one can determine the level and trend of sales quite easily by such characteristics as

1. Model and size of product by territory, type of account, and industry
2. Average size of sale by territory, type of account, industry, and sales volume
3. Proportion of sales volume by model, size of product, territory, type of account, size of account, and industry

For example, a retailer selling waterbeds could get some idea of the type of people purchasing waterbeds by using its sales invoices to determine where in the community its customers live. Once this information is known, certain general demographic and socioeconomic characteristics can be estimated by examining government census data (external information) broken down into census tracts, blocks, and so on.

Not all internal secondary information is of this accounting type. Company files are often "loaded" with special reports, previous marketing research studies, special audits, and other reports purchased from outside suppliers for past problems. Any one may be relevant to current problems. The key, of course, is knowing where they are and how to access them. In order that this can be done efficiently, the firm must have an effective marketing information system.

External Secondary Information

External secondary information is available in a staggering array and amount. It also is applicable to all the major types of marketing research projects and is mainly concerned with the noncontrollable aspects of the problem: the total market size, market characteristics, and competitor products, prices, promotional efforts, and distribution methods.

The major sources of external secondary information are (1) governmental (federal, state, and local), (2) trade associations and trade press, (3) periodicals, (4) institutions, and (5) commercial services. The federal government is by far the largest single source. Both governmental and trade sources are so important that the experienced and competent researcher will be thoroughly familiar with them in his or her field of specialization. Periodicals and the publications of research projects conducted by universities and research institutes frequently provide valuable information. Commercial services of many types are available that are highly useful for specific research problems.

Market performance studies on consumer products, for example, will normally require such demographic information as the number of consumers (or consuming units) by age group, income class, sex, and geographic area. Such data are usually available on a reasonably recent basis from censuses conducted by federal, state, and local governments. The *Census of Population* and the *Census of Housing* taken by the U.S. Department of Commerce every ten years are the most comprehensive of such censuses. Up-to-date estimates are made periodically within the ten-year period, often by nonfederal government agencies.

Direct market performance (e.g., size) studies are often conducted by trade associates, media, firms in the industry, and private research organizations. These studies are published and made available to interested parties. Industry-type studies may be concerned with such types of information as total market size, market characteristics, market segments and their size and characteristics, and similar types of information. As with other secondary sources, these studies may contain bias, and the researcher must know as much as possible about the research process used, although not necessarily in great detail. To illustrate, it was claimed in 1984 that the sporting goods market was considerably larger than the $19 billion annual retail volume projected by some industry analysts. In fact, reported size could have been a 35%–50% understatement of actual industry volume. This understatement is attributed to four factors:

1. Researchers focus on sports participants when a particular product category may be dominated by nonparticipants (e.g., running shoes).
2. Large, syndicated media studies involve lengthy questionnaires, resulting in high percentages of incomplete responses.
3. Consumer mail panels inadequately represent young singles who are active sports participants and consumers, and it is difficult to recruit these for such panels.
4. People younger than 18 often are excluded from samples even though they are a significant part of most sporting goods markets. [13]

Information on new products and processes are available from such sources as patent disclosures, trade journals, competitors' catalogs, testing agencies, and the reports of such governmental agencies as the Food and Drug Administration, the Department of Agriculture, and the National Bureau of Standards.

[13]"Studies Are Greatly Underestimating Size of Sporting Goods Market, Company Finds," *Marketing News,* 18 (June 22, 1984), 9.

An extensive amount of information is available concerning advertising. Through the *Publishers Information Bureau,* for example, one can obtain a compilation of expenditures by medium for each competitor. The *Audit Bureau of Circulation* provides data on the numbers of magazine copies sold under specified conditions. The reports of the *Standard Rate and Data Service* provide complete information on the rates and specifications for buying advertising space and time. A number of commercial services, such as the *Arbitron Radio and Television Market Reports,* the *Nielsen Radio-Television Index,* the *Hooperating, Trendex,* the *Starch Advertising Readership Service,* and *AdTel* supply measures of audience exposure to specific advertisements or programs (Exhibit 4-2).

There are also a substantial number of sources and amounts of data available for distribution research. The *Census of Business* provides information on retail and wholesale sales by type of outlet and geographic area. The *Census of Manufacturers* lists geographical and industry data on manufacturers including costs of materials and quantities of products produced. *County Business Patterns* gives the locations of businesses by a large number of classification. Commercial organizations and trade associations also provide such data.

An unfailing earmark of the experienced researcher is his or her knowledge of specific sources and efficient search procedures for other published sources of relevant information. This personal knowledge is indispensable in finding, evaluating, and using information from secondary sources. With the mass of secondary information currently being published, however, even experienced researchers will often need to refer to general reference works, bibliographies, indexes, and other guides to ensure that they have obtained all the secondary information relevant to the particular problem on which they are working.

With the increased usage of the personal computer has come the development of *commercial electronic data bases.* Thousands of such data bases are available from numerous systems, such as DIALOG, NEXIS, or Dow Jones News/Retrieval, and access is by subscription. In general, there are five categories of commercial data bases:

1. *Bibliographic:* indexing of publications.
2. *Financial:* detailed information about companies.
3. *Statistical:* demographic, econometric, and other numeric data for forecasting and doing projections.
4. *Directory/encyclopedia:* factual information about people, companies, and organizations.
5. *Full Text:* an entire document can be printed out.

The advantages of such current data bases are obvious. All that is needed is a personal computer, a modem, and appropriate software.[14]

---

[14]See Carol Tanzer Johnson, "Information Brokers: New Breed with Access to Secondary Research," *Marketing News,* 21 (February 27, 1987), 14.

Exhibit 4-2   Starch Readership Reports

The Starch Readership service reports on the reading of advertisements in more than 90 consumer, business, trade and professional magazines and newspapers. More than 100,000 people are personally interviewed each year on their reading of over 75,000 advertisements. Approximately 1000 individual issues are studied annually.

SAMPLE

Each Starch Report utilizes a minimum sample size of 100 men and/or women readers. Adults, 18 years and older, are personally interviewed face-to-face for all publications except those which are directed exclusively to special groups, i.e., for young girls, etc. For these publications, only the appropriate age group is interviewed. Interviews are assigned to parallel the geographic circulation of each study publication. Between 20 and 30 urban localities are used for each study issue. Starch Readership data is based on interviews with issue readers.

SELECTION OF ADVERTISEMENTS TO BE STUDIED

The length of an interview is held to 90 items or less in order to prevent respondent boredom. When an issue contains more than 90 items, only selected advertisements are studied. Advertisements are selected for study on the basis of advertiser and agency interest in Starch data. When required to study more than 90 items, an additional sample of respondents is interviewed. Each respondent is questioned on only a portion of the total items in the issue. In this way, it is possible to report on more than 90 advertisements but not interview any one person on more than 90 items.

INTERVIEWING METHODOLOGY

Starch Readership studies employ the "recognition" method. With the publication open, the respondent tells to what extent he or she had read each ad prior to the interview. For each advertisement, respondents are first asked, "Did you see or read any part of this advertisement?" If "Yes," a prescribed questioning procedure is followed to determine the observation and reading of each component part of the advertisement (illustration, headline, signature and copy blocks). After these questions are asked, each respondent is classified as follows:

"Noted" Reader: A person who remembered having previously seen the advertisement in the issue being studied.

"Associated"
    Reader: A person who not only "Noted" the advertisement but also saw or read some part of it which clearly indicated the brand or advertiser.

"Read Most"
    Reader: A person who read half or more of the written material in the ad.

After all ads are asked about, interviewers record basic classification data on sex, age, occupation, marital status, race, income, family size and composition so that sampling can be checked and cross-tabulations of readership can be made.

BASIC FORM OF STARCH REPORTS

Reports are compiled issue by issue and contain:

1. A copy of the issue with the studied ads clearly labeled to show the readership levels for the ads-as-whole, and also the noting or reading of the major components—illustrations, headlines, signatures and copy blocks.
2. A Summary Report listing all the studied ads in the issue. The advertisements are arranged by product category and show the Starch percentages for the ads-as-whole (as well as cost efficiency data for most publications). By arranging the ads by product category, it is more convenient to compare the readership levels of competing advertisements.
3. Starch Adnorms tables show the average readership levels derived from a previous series of studies on the publication. These tables list average ad-as-a-whole percentages by product category, size and color of space. This data provides a benchmark for comparing current advertisements. Starch Adnorms are not available on newly studied publications.

Source: Used with the permission of Starch INRA Hooper, Inc.

Syndicated Services

Some of the commercial services mentioned above are examples of what are called *syndicated services*. Research organizations providing such services collect and tabulate specialized types of marketing information on a continuing basis for purposes of sale to a large number of firms. In general, syndicated data are made available to all who wish to subscribe. Reports are made available on a regular basis (e.g., weekly, monthly, quarterly). Since these data are not collected for a particular firm for use in a specific research problem situation, they can properly be viewed as secondary data. Syndicated services are widely used in such areas as movement of consumer products through retail outlets, direct measures of consumer purchases, social trends and life-styles, and media readership, viewing, and listening.

Syndicated data may be obtained by personal interviews, direct observation, self-reporting and observation, or use of certain types of mechanical or electronic reporting or measuring devices. One of the most widely used approaches is the *continuous panel,* which refers to a sample of individuals, households, or firms from whom information is obtained at successive time periods. Continuous panels are commonly used for the following purposes:

1. As *consumer purchase panels,* which record purchases in a consumer "diary" and submit them periodically

2. As *advertising audience panels,* which record programs viewed, listened to, and/or publications read

3. As *dealer panels,* which are used to provide information on levels of inventory, sales, and prices

Of these types of panels, the consumer purchase panel is the most often used and has the widest range of applications. Such panels have been established by many different organizations, including the federal government, various universities, newspapers, manufacturers, and marketing research firms. The largest of the consumer panels is maintained by NPD Research, Inc. This panel is comprised of 13,000 families and is national in coverage. NPD also maintains self-contained panels in 29 local markets. Other large and well-known national consumer panels are maintained by such companies as Market Research Corporation of American (MRCA), Market Facts, and National Family Opinion (NFO).

The typical consumer purchase panel furnishes information at regular intervals on continuing purchases of the products covered. The type of product, brand, weight or quantity of unit, number of units, kind of package or container, price per unit, whether special promotion was in effect, store name, and date and day of week are reported for each product bought. In the NPD and MRCA panels these data are recorded in "diaries," which are mailed in each month.

Advertising audience panels are undoubtedly more widely publicized than other panels. It is from these panels that television and radio program ratings are derived. These panels are operated by independent research agencies rather than the media—both for reasons of economy and to avoid any question of partisanship. Traditionally, audience panels have used the diary method for collecting data. In 1987 A. C. Nielsen switched to the use of a "people meter," which is a microwave computerized rating system that transmits demographic information overnight to measure national television audiences. The people meter provides information on what TV shows are being watched, how many households are watching, and which family members are watching. The type of activity is recorded automatically; household members merely have to indicate their presence by pressing a button. The sample will be 2,000 households. A major Nielsen competitor, AGB Television Research, announced that it would start using such a meter in 1988.

Dealer panels are sponsored by both individual firms and independent research agencies. The Nielsen Retail Index is prepared from audits conducted regularly on a fixed national sample of food and drug stores. Each store in the sample is audited to obtain information on purchases, inventories, sales, special promotions, and prices of each brand of each product class of interest. The resulting data are compiled, analyses are made, and reports are distributed to clients.

The 1980s saw the widespread emergence of scanner technology and its use in retail stores, particularly grocery stores, for packaged consumer goods. With this development came the ability to collect data on products purchased. As the product is scanned at checkout, the Universal Product Code (UPC) information, and unit and price information, are recorded electronically. Companies such as National Brand Scanning obtain this information from supermarket chains where it is edited, tabulated, and projected for on-line delivery (through a service called NABSCAN-ON-LINE) for hard-copy reports.

Various types of data are provided by such sales tracking: product category sales, geographical area sales, new-product sales, new-product activity, competitor action, and so on. In addition to regular weekly sales data, other types of studies possible are trade promotion evaluation, price elasticity research, in-store experimentation, and so on. In addition to general syndicated services, there also are companies that provide scanner-based data using a type of statistically designed continuous panel.

The information obtained from the types of syndicated services described above has many applications. The changes in *level of sales to consumers* may be analyzed directly without the problem of determining changes in inventory levels in the distribution channel. Trends and *shifts in market composition* may be analyzed, both by type of consumer and by geographic areas. A continuing *analysis of brand position* may be made for all brands of the product class. Analyses of trends of sales by *package* or *container* types may be made. The relative importance of types of *retail outlets* may be determined. Trends in *competitor pricing* and *special promotions* and their effects can be analyzed along with the effects of the manufacturer's own price and promotional changes. *Heavy purchasers* may be identified and their associated characteristics determined. Similarly, *innovative buyers* may be identified for new products and an analysis of their characteristics made to aid in the prediction of the growth of sales. *Brand-switching* and brand-loyalty studies may be made on a continuing basis.

It is apparent that panels established for advertising audience measurement and dealer panels have similar advantages that accrue from the collection of data at regular intervals. Audience-measurement panels provide a continuous record of the size and composition of the audience for the medium measured. If television viewing is being measured, for example, a week-by-week measurement of the audience for each program is provided, permitting trends to be spotted quickly. Similarly, in the case of dealer panels, inventory buildups or depletions may be determined and corrective measures taken long before this requirement would have been recognized from factory sales data.

There are many organizations that provide syndicated services using methods other than the continuous panel. Many of these studies are done annually. The Gallup Organization, for example, conducts multiclient or syndicated surveys ranging from descriptive studies of the "market for . . . " to major analytical investigations. An annual study of changing social values (as many as 35 social trends) and how they can affect consumer marketing (almost 300 marketing aspects) is available from the *Yankelovich Monitor,* a service of Yankelovich, Skelly and White, Inc. Similarly, SRI International provides a syndicated segmentation scheme known as *Values and Lifestyles Segmentation* (VALS). VALS combines demographic and attitudinal data for segmentation, according to VALS-defined segments. One reported use of this syndicated service has been to design products for specific segments.[15]

As we have already stated, many organizations offer a wide range of syndicated services. Our discussion of specific sources and types of data has been illustrative rather

---

[15]Interestingly, syndicated segmentation schemes used in selecting consumer targets have been criticized as being too simple, too remote, too rigid, and too unreliable. See Sonia Yuspek, "Syndicated Values/Lifestyles Segmentation Schemes: Use Them As Descriptive Tools, Not to Select Targets, *Marketing News,* 18 (May 25, 1984), Sec. 2, p. 1; and "SRI's Response to Yuspek: Demographics Aren't Enough," *Marketing News,* 18 (May 25, 1984), Sec. 2, p. 1.

than comprehensive.[16] These are viable alternatives to primary data collection, and a firm should make sure that the information it requires is not already being gathered by one or more syndicated services. Since there is cost-sharing, syndicated data are usually less costly than the same data gathered by the firm itself. Moreover, there may be certain kinds of information where the syndicated method is the only feasible method for data collection.

Information from Respondents

A second major source of information is that obtained from respondents. Asking questions and observing behavior are primary means of obtaining information whenever people's actions are being investigated or predicted. The term *respondent* literally means "one who responds; answers." For our purposes it will be useful to include both verbal and behavioral response in the usage of the term. That is, we shall consider both the information obtained from asking people questions and that provided by observing behavior or the results of past behavior as comprising information from respondents.

Information from Communication with Respondents

The *survey,* in its many forms, is a widely used and well-known method of acquiring marketing information through communicating with a group of respondents. Information is obtained from consumers, industrial users, dealers, and others who are knowledgeable about the problem at hand. People are asked questions through personal interviews, telephone interviews, and mail questionnaires. They are asked for information as either part of a self-contained, "one-time" survey or repetitively as part of a continuing panel.

Questioning of respondents is virtually a necessity if one wants to obtain information about level of knowledge, attitudes, opinions, and motivations, or intended behavior. If, for example, a bank were considering providing for its depositors a service of direct payment of utility and credit card bills, the only practical way of determining how much the depositors knew about this type of service, their attitudes and opinions about it, and whether they intended to use it would be to ask them.

Although questioning of respondents is often the most efficient and economical way to obtain information, it requires considerable skill and care in application if the information is to be of maximum value. At best, people will respond with information that they are *able* to provide. At worst, misleading and highly biased information may result.

The kinds of information that may be obtained from respondents, the different means of communicating with respondents, and the errors associated with each are discussed in Chapters 5 and 7.

Information from Observation of Respondents

Relevant information for many marketing problems may be obtained by observing either present behavior or the results of past behavior. The researcher who requires

---

[16]For a detailed listing of the leading syndicated sources of marketing data, see Thomas C. Kinnear and James R. Taylor, *Marketing Research: An Applied Approach,* 3rd ed. (New York: McGraw-Hill, 1987) pp. 152–163.

information on the color and style preferences for men's shoes may well find the observation method ideally suited for this purpose.

Observational methods make it possible to record behavior as it occurs and thus to eliminate errors arising from the reporting of the behavior. For example, the researcher who observes the number of units and brands of a product class actually bought in supermarkets by a sample of housewives rather than questioning the housewives later will have avoided the errors inherent in relying on respondents' memories.

For reasons that are apparent, observing people's behavior cannot be used effectively to obtain information about the level of knowledge, opinions, and motivations, or the intended behavior of respondents. In some instances where the behavior is private or impossible to observe, it cannot be used at all.

Observation of respondents is discussed in detail in Chapter 5.

Information from Natural and Controlled Experiments

The subject of natural and controlled experimental designs was briefly treated earlier in this chapter. Three types of evidence were described as providing the bases for drawing inferences about causal relationships: associative variation, sequence of events, and absence of other possible causal factors (producers). Either natural or controlled experimental designs are capable of providing the first two, but only controlled experiments can provide reasonably conclusive evidence concerning the third, the absence of other possible producers.

A *natural experiment* is one in which the investigator intervenes only to the extent required for measurement. That is, there is no manipulation of an assumed causal variable. The investigator merely looks at what has happened. As such, the natural experiment is a form of *ex post facto* research. In this type of study, the researcher approaches data collection as if a controlled experimental design were used. The variable of interest has occurred in a natural setting and the researcher looks for respondents who have been exposed to it and, if a control group is desired, respondents who have not been exposed. Measurements can then be made on a "dependent" variable of interest. For example, if the impact of a television commercial on attitudes were desired, the investigator would contact a sample of people after the commercial was shown. Those who saw the commercial would constitute the experimental group, and those who did not see it would be a type of control group. Differences in attitudes could be compared as a crude measure of impact. Unfortunately, one can never be sure whether the obtained relationship is causal or noncausal, since what is observed may be due to the presence of other variables.[17]

In *controlled experiments,* investigator intervention is required beyond that for measurement purposes. Specifically, two kinds of intervention are required:

1. Manipulation of at least one assumed causal variable
2. Random assignment of subjects to experimental and control groups

[17]For a brief discussion of natural experiments, see Daniel Katz, "Field Studies," in *Research Methods in the Behavioral Sciences,* ed. Leon Festinger and Daniel Katz (New York: Holt, Rinehart & Winston, 1953), pp. 78–80; and Barry F. Anderson, *The Psychology Experiment: An Introduction to the Scientific Method,* 2nd ed. (Belmont, Calif.: Brooks/Cole, 1971), pp. 39–42.

Manipulation of at least one variable is required in order to administer the treatment(s) whose effects it is desired to measure. Randomized assignment of subjects to groups is for the purpose of controlling differences arising from extraneous variables.

The nature of experimentation, potential errors affecting experimental designs, and natural experimental, pre-experimental, quasi-experimental, and true experimental designs are treated in Chapter 6.

Simulation

The expense, time involved, or other problems associated with field experimentation may preclude it as a source of information for a particular operational situation. In such cases it may be desirable to construct a model of the operational situation and to "experiment" with it instead of the real-world situation. The manipulation of such models is called *simulation*.

This approach to obtaining information has a long history in, and is borrowed from, the physical sciences. An example of using physical analogs for simulative purposes is the use of scaled replicas of aircraft in a wind tunnel. The model can be tested under widely varying simulated conditions of wind velocity, altitude, and speeds, and its performance can be observed. It is far less expensive and time-consuming to use such simulation procedures than to construct and test actual prototype aircraft on test flights.

Physical analogs are seldom used in marketing, but conceptual models are constructed and manipulated to obtain information on the effect of varying combinations of the variables involved in specified ways. The information obtained consists of numerical outputs from the simulation models. As such, it differs from that provided by secondary sources, respondents, and field experimentation. The latter sources provide information directly from the situation being investigated. Simulation provides information from an *imitation* of this situation.

Simulation can be defined as a *set of techniques for manipulating a model of some real-world process for the purpose of finding numerical solutions that are useful in the real process that is being modeled*. Models that are environmentally "rich" (that is, that may contain complex interactions and nonlinear relationships among the variables, probabilistic components, time dependencies, etc.) are usually too difficult to solve by standard analytical methods such as the calculus or various mathematical programming techniques. Rather, the analyst views a simulation model as an *imitation* of the process or system under study and attempts to run the system on paper (or by means of a computer) to see "what would happen if" a particular policy were put into effect.

Simulations may be used for research, instruction, decision making, or some combination of these applications. Their use as an aid in decision making is our primary concern here. As a historical illustration of a market simulation developed for that purpose, the Simulmatics Corporation[18] reported on the development of a "marketing microcosm" consisting of almost 3,000 (hypothetical) persons who purportedly were representative of the U.S. population. The analyst could then study the impact of various media schedules on the reading characteristics of this "toy" population and could attempt to extrapolate

[18]*Simulmatics Media-Mix: Technical Description* (New York: Simulmatics Corporation, 1962).

these findings to the total universe. The microcosm was stratified by such characteristics as age, sex, educational level, race, and political affiliation. By means of the computer model, alternative media schedules could be "tested" on the microcosm and summary figures prepared on the type of audience and projected size and frequency with which the population is exposed to each media schedule.

Kotler and Schultz[19] describe 15 selected simulations developed during the 1960s for marketing decision-making applications. Seven of these were simulations of marketing systems (including the one by Simulmatics just described), seven were simulations to help make decisions concerning marketing-mix elements (new-product, price, advertising, and sales-force decisions), and one was a simulation of interviewing costs in marketing surveys. During the 1970s the reports of marketing simulations included three dealing with marketing systems[20] and three concerned with one or more of the mix elements.[21]

For the marketing researcher, the import of the various research studies being conducted in computer simulation should not be ignored. It is becoming increasingly apparent that the marketing researcher's role will be expanded to deal not only with the traditional tasks of data gathering but also with the manipulation and extensive analysis of the data.

TYPES OF ERRORS AFFECTING RESEARCH DESIGNS

A useful way of looking at the marketing research process (and research design) is that it involves the management of error. At all stages from problem formulation through report preparation potential errors can arise. It is rare that a research project will be error free. Consequently, the research designer must adopt a strategy for managing this error. As we shall see in the next section of this chapter, alternative strategies can be followed.

The objective underlying any research project is to provide information that is as accurate as possible. Maximizing accuracy requires that *total study errors* be minimized. Total Study error has two components—*sampling error* and *nonsampling error*—which can be expressed as follows:

$$\text{Total Error} = \text{Sampling Error} + \text{Nonsampling Error}$$

[19] Philip Kotler and R. L. Schultz, "Marketing Simulations: Review and Prospects," *Journal of Business,* 43 (July 1970), 237–95.

[20] M. R. Lavington, "A Practical Microsimulation Model for Consumer Marketing," *Operational Research Quarterly,* 21 (March 1970), 25–45; A. Kitchener and D. Rowland, "Models of a Consumer Product Market," *Operational Research Quarterly,* 22 (March 1971), 67–84; and J. W. Bryant, "A Simulation Model of Retailer Behavior," *Operational Research Quarterly,* 26 (April 1975), 133–49.

[21] D. H. Gensch, "Different Approaches to Advertising Media Selection," *Operational Research Quarterly,* 21 (June 1970), 193–217; J. J. Lambin, "A Computer On-Line Marketing Mix Model," *Journal of Marketing Research,* 9 (May 1972), 119–26; and R. L. Schultz and J. A. Dodson, Jr., "A Normative Model for Marketing Planning," *Simulation & Games,* 5 (December 1974), 363–81.

Total error is usually measured as total error variance, also known as the mean-squared error:[22]

$$(\text{Total Error})^2 = (\text{Sampling Error})^2 + (\text{Nonsampling Error})^2$$

Sampling error refers to the variable error resulting from the chance specification of population from elements according to the sampling plan. Since this introduces random variability into the precision with which a sample statistic is calculated, it is often called *random sampling error*.

Nonsampling error consists of all other errors associated with a research project. Such errors are diverse in nature. They are often thought of as resulting in some sort of bias, which implies *systematic* error. However, there can be a random component of nonsampling error. For example, misrecording a response during data collection would represent a random error, whereas using a "loaded" question would be a systematic error. Nonsampling errors arise from nonresponse and response.

To a large extent these major error components are related in an inverse manner. Increasing the sample size to reduce sampling error can lead to increasing nonsampling error in that, for example, there are more instances where such things as recording errors can occur, and the impact of loaded (i.e., nonobjective) questions and other systematic errors will be greater. This inverse relationship lies at the heart of our concern for total error.

Ideally, efforts should be made to minimize each component. Considering time and cost limitations, this can rarely be done. The researcher must make a decision that involves a tradeoff between sampling and nonsampling errors. Unfortunately, very little is known empirically about the relative size of the two error components, although there is some evidence that nonsampling error tends to be the larger of the two. In a study comparing several research designs and data collection methods, Assael and Keon concluded that nonsampling error far outweighs random sampling error in contributing to total survey error.[23] Similarly, Lipstein has stated:

> Over the years I have used a simple rule of thumb that the true mean square error of field studies is at least twice the size of reported theoretical sampling error, though there is evidence to suggest that it is larger in many commercial surveys.[24]

We now consider briefly eight major types of errors that can influence research results. These are defined in Table 4-2. Each is discussed in more detail in other sections of the book.

---

[22]For the statistical issues involved, see Henry Assael and John Keon, "Nonsampling vs. Sampling Errors in Survey Research," *Journal of Marketing*, 46 (Spring 1982), 114–23.

[23]Ibid.

[24]Benjamin Lipstein, "In Defense of Small Samples," *Journal of Advertising Research*, February 1975, p. 39.

TABLE 4-2   Types of Errors in the Research Process

Population Specification. Noncorrespondence of the required population to the population selected by the researcher.

Sampling. Noncorrespondence of the sample selected by probability means and the representative sample sought by the researcher.

Selection. Noncorrespondence of the sample selected by nonprobability means and the sought representative sample.

Frame. Noncorrespondence of the sought sample to the required sample.

Nonresponse. Noncorrespondence of the achieved (or obtained) sample to the selected sample.

Surrogate Information. Noncorrespondence of the information being sought by the researcher and that required to solve the problem.

Measurement. Noncorrespondence of the information obtained by the measurement process and the information sought by the researcher.

Experimental. Noncorrespondence of the true (or actual) impact of, and the impact attributed to, the independent variable(s).

Population Specification

Population specification error occurs when the researcher selects an inappropriate population or universe from which to obtain data. For example, a corporate aircraft manufacturer desiring to learn what features should be added to a proposed new aircraft might conduct a survey of purchasing agents from major corporations that now own such aircraft. This would be an inappropriate universe, since pilots undoubtedly play the key role in the purchase decision. Similarly, packaged goods manufacturers often conduct surveys of housewives because they are easy to contact and because it is assumed they make the decisions about what is to be purchased and do the actual purchasing. In this situation there often is population specification error, since for many packaged goods the husband makes a significant share of the purchases and may have a significant direct and indirect influence on what is bought.[25] Population specification is discussed in Chapter 9.

Sampling

Sampling error occurs when a *probability* sampling method is used to select a sample and this sample is not representative of the population concerned. For example, a random sample of 500 people composed only of people aged 35 to 55 would not be representative of the adult general population.

Sampling error is affected by the homogeneity of the population being studied and sampled from and by the size of the sample. In general, the more homogeneous the

[25]Haley, Overholser & Associates, *Purchase Influence Measures of Husband/Wife Influence on Buying Decisions*, 1975.

population, the smaller the sampling error; as sample size increases, sampling error decreases. If a census were conducted (i.e., all elements of the population were included), there would be no sampling error. Sampling error is discussed in Chapter 9.

Selection

Selection error is the sampling error for a sample selected by a *nonprobability* method. There is a natural tendency for investigators to select those respondents who are the most accessible and agreeable whenever there is latitude to do so. Such samples are often composed of friends and associates whose characteristics more or less resemble those of the desired population, or people who are most easily reached, are better dressed, have better-kept homes, and have more pleasant personalities. Samples of these types are seldom representative of the desired population. Selection error is discussed further in Chapter 9.

Frame

A *sampling frame* is a means of accounting for all the elements in the population. It is usually a listing of the elements but need not be a printed list. The sample frame for a study using the shopping mall technique, for instance, would be all those shoppers in the mall during the period of data collection. A perfect frame identifies each population element once, but only once, and does not include elements not in the population. A commonly used frame for consumer research that introduces error is the telephone directory. Many elements are not included (unlisteds, new arrivals), some people are listed more than once, and nonpopulation elements are included (businesses, people who have left the area). Sample frame is discussed further in Chapter 9.

Nonresponse

Nonresponse error can exist when the obtained sample differs from the original selected sample. There are two ways in which nonresponse can occur: (1) *noncontact* (i.e., the inability to contact all members of the sample) and (2) *refusal* (i.e., nonresponse to some or all of the items on the measurement instrument).

Errors arise in virtually every survey from the inability to reach the respondent. The inaccessibility of some respondents occurs because they are not at home (NAH) on the initial call and call-backs. Others have moved or are away from home for the period of the survey. Not-at-home respondents are typically younger with no small children. There is a much higher proportion of working wives than among those households with someone at home. People who have moved or are away from the survey period have a higher geographic mobility than the average of the population. Thus, errors from noncontact of respondents can be anticipated in most surveys.

Refusals may be by item or for the entire questionnaire. Income, religion, sex, and politics are topics that may elicit item refusals. Some respondents refuse to participate because of time requirements, a past experience in which an "interviewer" attempted to sell them a set of encyclopedias, their own ill health, or other reasons. A kind of refusal that is specific to the method is the nonresponse to a mail questionnaire. Nonresponse to mail questionnaires sometimes runs as high as 90% of the initial mailing even after several successive mailings. Methods for dealing with nonresponse error are discussed in Chapter 5.

Surrogate Information

In many problem situations in marketing research it is necessary to obtain information that is a surrogate for that which we really require. The necessity to accept substitute information arises from either the *inability* or the *unwillingness* of respondents to provide the information we need.

Decisionally oriented behavioral research is always concerned with prediction of behavior, usually nonverbal behavior. This limits most marketing research projects to using proxy information. We cannot observe future behavior, so a surrogate must be used. Typically, one or more of several different kinds of information are obtained which are believed to be useful in predicting behavior. We may obtain information on past behavior because it is believed that there is sufficient stability in the underlying behavior pattern to give it reasonably high predictive validity. We may ask about intended behavior as a means of prediction. Or we may obtain information about attitudes, level of knowledge, or socioeconomic characteristics of the respondent in the belief that they individually or collectively have a high degree of association with future behavior.

Since the type of information required is identified during the problem-formulation stage of the research process, minimizing this error requires as accurate a problem definition as possible. This has been discussed in previous chapters.

Measurement

Measurement error is error generated by the measurement process itself and represents the difference between the information generated and the information wanted by the researcher. Such error can potentially arise in any stage of the measurement process from the development of an instrument through the analysis of the findings. To illustrate, Figure 4-1 depicts the stages at which errors in eliciting information may arise in interviewing respondents in a survey.

In the transmittal stage there may be errors due to faulty wording of questions or preparations of nonverbal materials, to interviewer effects of the way the question is asked of the respondent, or the way in which the respondent interprets the question. In the response phase, errors may occur because the respondent gives incorrect information, the interviewer interprets it incorrectly, or there are errors in recording it. In the analysis stage, errors of incorrect editing and coding and descriptive summarization and inference can contribute substantially to measurement error.

Measurement error is particularly troublesome for the researcher, since it can arise

Figure 4-1 Potential Sources of Measurement Error in a Survey

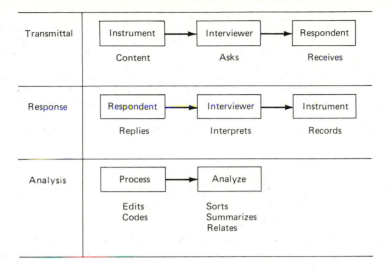

from many different sources and take on many different forms. These are discussed in more depth in Chapters 7 and 8.

Experimental

When an experiment is conducted the researcher attempts to measure the impact of one or more manipulated independent variables on some dependent variable of interest while controlling for the influence of all other (i.e., extraneous) variables. Unfortunately, control over all possible extraneous variables is rarely possible. Consequently, what may be measured is not the effect of the independent variable(s) but the effect of the experimental situation itself. This is the meaning of experimental error, which can arise from many varied sources. Experimental errors and the alternative ways of attempting to deal with them are discussed in Chapter 6.

Another Viewpoint

A useful way of summarizing the types of errors that can influence research results is that they arise from five sources: the researcher, the sample, the interviewer, the instrument, and the respondent (Table 4-3).

METHODS FOR DEALING WITH POTENTIAL ERRORS

For any research project, recognizing that potential errors exist is one thing, but doing something about them is another matter. There are two basic approaches for handling

TABLE 4-3   A Classification of Errors

	Source		Error Type
I	RESEARCHER		Myopia (wrong question)
			Inappropriate analysis
			Misinterpretation
			Experimenter Expectation
			Communication
II	SAMPLE		Frame (wrong target)
			Process (wrong method)
			Response (wrong people)
III	INTERVIEWER		Interviewer bias
			Interpretation
			Carelessness
IV	INSTRUMENT		
		Scale	Rounding
			Truncating
		Questionnaire	Positional
			Confusion
			Evoked Set
			Construct–Question Congruence
V	RESPONDENT		Consistency/Inconsistency
			Ego/Humility
			Fatigue
			Lack of Commitment
			Random

Source: James Hulbert and Donald R. Lehmann, "Reducing Error in Question and Scale Design: A Conceptual Framework," *Decision Sciences,* 6 (1975), 168.

potential errors: (1) minimizing errors through research design and (2) estimating or measuring the error or its impact.

Minimize Error

Two different approaches can be taken in attempting to minimize total error. The first involves using research design to minimize the errors that may result from each of the individual error components. Much of the material in Chapters 5 through 10 of this book discusses effective research methods and as such involves techniques designed to minimize individual errors. This is consistent with our view of research design as involving error management. This approach is often limited by the amount of the budget allotted to a project.

The second approach is based on the recognition that individual error components are not necessarily independent of each other. Thus, attempts to minimize one component may lead to an increase in another. Reducing sampling error by increasing sample size, for example, leads to potentially greater nonsampling error. This means that the research designer must tradeoff errors in developing a research design that minimizes total error. For a fixed project budget, therefore, it may be prudent for the research designer to choose a smaller sample size (which will increase sampling error) if the cost savings by doing this can be used to develop techniques that will reduce nonresponse and/or improve the measurement process. If the reduction in these nonsampling errors exceeds the increase in sampling error, there will be a reduction in total error.

Estimate or Measure Error

Even though the researcher has designed a project to minimize error, seldom, if at all, will it be eliminated. Consequently, for every project the error that does exist must be estimated or measured. This is recognized for sampling error when probability samples are used, but nonsampling errors typically are ignored. Although estimating and/or measuring errors is better than ignoring them, there may be times when ignoring nonsampling error may not be that bad. For example, it has been shown that, if nonsampling error is viewed as a multiple of sampling error, ignoring nonsampling errors up to an amount equal to one-half of sampling error reduces a .95 confidence level only to .92.[26]

Estimating and/or measuring individual component and total error is not easy, primarily due to the nature of nonsampling errors. There is a body of accepted sampling theory that allows the researcher to estimate sampling error for a probability sample, but there is nothing comparable for nonsampling errors. Consequently, subjective or judgmental estimates must be made. One approach that is useful for choosing among alternative research designs is presented in the appendix to this chapter. This approach is a method of combining nonsampling and sampling errors to arrive at total error.

For individual error components, many diverse procedures can be used to estimate and measure their impact, as illustrated in Table 4-4. Since these are discussed where appropriate in subsequent chapters, we shall not discuss them here.

CHOOSING A RESEARCH DESIGN

The overview of research designs and sources of marketing information just presented should make it apparent that, given a specified problem, many competing designs can provide relevant information. Each design will have an associated expected value of information and incurred cost.

Suppose, for example, that a researcher is assigned the task of determining the market share of the ten leading brands of cigarettes. There are many possible ways of measuring market share of cigarette brands, including questioning a sample of respondents, observing purchases at a sample of retail outlets, obtaining sales figures from a sample of wholesalers, obtaining sales figures from a sample of retailers and vending

---

[26]Donald S. Tull and Gerald S. Albaum, *Survey Research: A Decisional Approach* (New York: Intext Educational Publishers, 1973), pp. 66–67.

TABLE 4-4 Selected Methods for Handling Nonsampling Errors

		METHOD		
TYPE OF ERROR	Design to Avoid	Measure	Estimate	
Surrogate information	Strive for realism	No method of direct measurement, as event has not yet occurred	Use track record of studies Use surrogate variables	
Measurement				
1. Instrument-induced	Pretest, alternative wording, alternative positions, etc.	Experiment by using alternative wording, alternative positioning, etc., in a subsample	Estimate will likely be for no bias but some variable error	
2. Interviewing-associated, e.g., bias, recording, cheating	Select and train interviewer correctly	Reinterview subsample using expert interviewer	Estimate will be for both bias and variable error	
	Use same editor for all of interviews by one interviewer Use cheater questions	Analysis of variance Use cheater questions Use computer program to analyze for patterns Use interpenetrating sample		
	Use computer program to analyze for patterns of responses by interviewer			
3. Response	Randomized response technique	Compare with known data	Have interviewer evaluate respondent	

	Prevention methods	Checking method	Residual error
	Ask for verification checks Cross-check questions Use mail-back technique		Estimate will be for both bias and variable error
4. Editing	Prepare editing manual Train editors Require daily return of data	Use master editor to edit subsample	Estimate will be for limited bias, some variable error
5. Coding	Pre-code Use coding manual Use computer program to clean data	Use master coder to check subsample	Some bias and variable error
6. Tabulation	Use verifier with different "keypuncher"	Recheck sample of forms	Variable error
7. Analysis	No remedy except competence	Use more competent analyst	
Frame	Use multiple frames	Take subsample of excluded segments	Use compensating weights Use past data
Selection	Make sample element and sample unit the same Use probability sample	Compare with known population	Use compensating weights
Nonresponse	Use call-backs Call at appropriate time Use trained interviewers	Take subsample of nonrespondents	Use Politz-Simmons method Use "wave" analysis

machine operators, obtaining tax data, subscribing to a national consumer panel, sub-scribing to a national panel of retail stores, and, possibly, obtaining data directly from trade association reports or a recent study by some other investigative agency.

That this listing is not exhaustive is illustrated by the approach to this problem taken by one imaginative, if somewhat naive, researcher, who hired a group of small boys to pick up empty cigarette packages beneath the stands at John F. Kennedy Stadium in Philadelphia during an Army–Navy football game. He had a sample of 100,000 persons and concluded that, with this large a sample, a counting of empty packs of each brand should provide a very good estimate of market share. He neglected to consider that he had a self-selected sample from a universe of sports enthusiasts, a highly disproportionate representation of military personnel, and that only a few brands of cigarettes were sold at the concession booths.

The selection of the "best" design from among the alternative designs is no different in principle from choosing among the alternatives in making any decision. The associated expected value and cost of information must be determined for each contending design. If the design is such that the project will yield information for solving more than one problem, the expected value should be determined for all applicable problems and summed. The design with the highest, positive, net expected payoff of research should be selected.

SUMMARY

In this chapter we dealt with a subject of central importance to the research project—the research design. We described what a research design is, discussed the classes of designs, and examined the major sources of marketing information that the various designs employ. Finally, we considered the errors that affect research designs.

Treating these topics has provided the opportunity to present an introduction and an overview of the next several chapters. These chapters deal with major sources of marketing information—respondents, experimentation—and the means of obtaining and analyzing information from them.

Appendix 4-1

ESTIMATION OF NONSAMPLING ERRORS

Form of the Estimates[27]

Suppose we let r represent the recorded sample value and t the true value. The *accuracy* of the estimate may then be expressed as the ratio

$$\frac{r}{t}$$

[27]This section draws heavily from Rex V. Brown, *Research and the Credibility of Estimates* (Boston: Harvard University, 1969); and Charles Mayer, "Assessing the Accuracy of Marketing Research," *Journal of Marketing Research,* 3 (August 1970), 285–91.

For a particular sample this ratio will reflect the combined effects of the sample and all other variable and systematic errors present.

Estimation of the errors in the process generating r will allow us to draw inferences about the value of r/t. The sampling distribution in classical statistics is a conditional probability distribution of $p\,(r/t)$ which includes only sampling error. An analogous distribution for our purposes is the conditional probability distribution

$$p\left(\frac{r}{t}\middle|\,t\right)$$

and one that includes both sampling and nonsampling errors.

For many research projects the value of r/t will be independent of t. When such independence exists it is not necessary to condition by t, and the distribution used can be $p(r/t)$.

We may then make estimates for each of the nonsampling error components using this distribution when r/t is independent of t. It will be a *prior* distribution in the Bayesian sense, as it will be subjectively determined. The amount of estimated systematic error will be shown as the difference of the expectation of this distribution and t. Both the variable errors in the generation process and the uncertainty of the estimate are reflected in the variance of the estimate.

We can describe the prior distribution of each nonsampling error component precisely if we are willing to assume that it is normal and specify the mean and the variance of it. In most instances the assumption of normality does no great violence to reality. A log-normal distribution may be used when the prior is skewed to the right.[28]

It is convenient to express variance in *rel-variance* units. Rel-variance is the variance divided by the mean squared or

$$rv = \frac{\sigma^2}{\mu^2}$$

It may be more familiar as the square of the coefficient of variation.

The rel-variance is most easily estimated by use of the credible interval of the investigator. A *credible interval* is defined as the subjective confidence interval for some designated level of confidence. A 95% confidence level ($\pm$ two standard errors approximately) is one with which it is seemingly easy for most investigators to work, although any confidence level may be used.

The rel-variance is estimated for a 95% confidence level by taking one-fourth of the credible interval, dividing it by the expectation of the error component distribution, and squaring. For an error component e, the formula is

$$rv = \left(\frac{CI}{4E(e)}\right)^2$$

[28]See Brown, *Research and the Credibility of Estimates*, Appendix IIB.

where $E(e)$ is the expected value of the error component. One-fourth of a 95% credible interval is equal to the subjective standard deviation of the distribution.

Model for Combining Estimates

We may obtain the distribution of r/t by estimating the expected value and rel-variance of each of the error components and then combining them. The model for combining the expectations is

$$\left(\frac{r}{t}\right) = \left(\frac{m}{t}\right) \times \left(\frac{f}{m}\right) \times \left(\frac{s}{f}\right) \times \left(\frac{a}{s}\right) \times \left(\frac{r}{a}\right)$$

where

r is the value recorded from the sample

t is the population value

m is the value that would result if a census were taken using this measurement technique

f is the value that would result if every element in the sampling frame were measured using this measurement technique

s is the expectation of the sampling distribution of the *selected* sample values and

a is the expectation of the sampling distribution of *achieved* sample values

It follows that

- $1.0 - m/t$ is the noncorrespondence of achieved to sought information—the measurement error
- $1.0 - f/m$ is the noncorrespondence of sought to required sample—the frame error
- $1.0 - s/f$ is the noncorrespondence of selected to sought sample—the selection error
- $1.0 - a/s$ is the noncorrespondence of achieved to selected sample—the nonresponse error and
- $1.0 - r/a$ is the random sampling error

The above model could be expanded to allow for surrogate information error. However, surrogate information error results from the process of *application* of the estimate of t rather than the *estimation* of t. It is best to deal with it separately.

The formula for combing rel-variances is[29]

$$rv = \prod_{i=1}^{n} (1 + rv_i) - 1$$

[29]Ibid., p. 132.

However, a satisfactory approximation is obtained from a simple addition of the rel-variances of the error components. In most instances the correction term is so small as to be negligible.

An Example of Error Estimation

Suppose that personal interviews are to be taken of 250 bank depositors to obtain information pertinent to a decision regarding a new revolving loan plan. The information desired is the amount of money borrowed by depositors in small loans during the past year. A 10% noncontact and refusal rate is anticipated, resulting in a usable sample of 225 depositors. The sampling frame is to be a list of present depositors of the bank.

The estimation of nonsampling errors can be made either before or after the survey is run. Estimation before conducting the survey permits using the estimates in the choice of the research design as well as for adjustment of the actual survey results when completed. Estimation after the survey allows the experience gained during the survey to be incorporated into the estimates. Estimates made after the survey are solely for the adjustment of the results.

In the example used it will be assumed that the estimation occurs before the survey is run.

1. *Determination of error components to be included.* Reflection suggests that *measurement, nonresponse,* and *random sampling* errors are present. There is no *selection error,* since a random sampling process is being used. If one assumes that the present depositors either are the population of interest or are fully representative of the depositor population after the extra reserve plan is initiated, no *frame error* is present. This assumption seems valid.

2. *Estimation of the mean of the ratio of actual to error-free measurement, credible intervals, and calculation of rel-variances.* Drawing upon published validation studies regarding loan behavior, the researchers find that measurement errors ranged from 3.5% to 59.0%. The principal error source was the nonreporting of debts by respondents. However, the investigators in one of the studies experimented with the technique of handing the respondent one envelope with the part of the questionnaire concerning outstanding loans and amounts enclosed. The respondent was asked to complete the questionnaire and mail it. For the respondents for whom this technique was used, measurement error was reduced to only about one-fifth of that for those respondents for whom it was not used. For those respondents who reported loans, the response error ranged from underreporting of 8% to overreporting of 10% with a mean of almost zero.

Assuming that these experiences provide a reasonable guide for measurement error estimation in the extra-reserve study and that the envelope technique will be used, the mean of the measurement error distribution is assessed as .75. The 95% credible interval is judged as .75 $\pm$ .40. The resulting rel-variance is $[.40/(4 \times .75)]^2 = .0177$.

Concerning the *nonresponse* error, validation studies indicate that noncontacted and refusing respondents each had somewhat larger debts than those who responded. The amount of underestimation of the mean debt that resulted was approximately 2% for each. The investigator assesses the mean of the noncontact and the refusal distributions as .98

and the credible interval of each as .98 ± .02. The rel-variance for each is calculated as .0001.

   3. *Calculation of the standard error and the rel-variance of the sampling distribution.* Since an unbiased estimate of the population mean is provided by a simple random sample, the expectation of the sampling distribution is 1.0.

   Using amount of money borrowed, the mean and standard deviations of the population are estimated as $\hat{\mu}$ = $125 and $\hat{\sigma}_x$ = $175. The estimated standard error of the mean is then

$$\hat{\sigma}_{\bar{x}} = \frac{\hat{\sigma}_x}{\sqrt{n}} = \frac{\$175}{\sqrt{225}} = \$11.67$$

and the coefficient of variation of the sampling distribution is

$$CV = \frac{\hat{\sigma}_{\bar{x}}}{\hat{\mu}} = \frac{\$11.67}{\$125} = \$.094$$

   An additional source of random error other than that introduced by the process of sampling elements is possible and appears to be present in this situation. This is the variability in responses that would occur if the interviews were replicated to a large number of times with the same respondents. The factor to allow for this source of variability is assessed at 1.2. Multiplying the coefficient of variation by 1.2 and squaring gives a rel-variance of sampling of .0127.

   4. *Combination of the estimates of the error component distribution.* The estimates are assembled in Table A. The mean of the combined distribution, .72, is obtained as the product of the means of the individual distributions.

   5. *Estimation of the rel-variance of the combined distribution.* The rel-variance of the combined distribution, .0307, is also shown in Table A. It was obtained by summing the individual component distribution rel-variances.

TABLE A   Assessment of Errors of Projected Personal Interview Survey

ERROR SOURCE	MEAN	CREDIBLE INTERVAL LIMITS	REL-VARIANCE
Measurement	.75	.55–.95	.0177
Frame	1.00	1.00–1.00	—
Selection	1.00	1.00–1.00	—
Noncontact	.98	.96–1.00	.0001
Refusal	.98	.96–1.00	.0001
Random sampling	1.00	not applicable	.0127
Correction term			.0001
Combined assessments	.72	.47–.97*	.0307

*The limits are derived from the values of the combined mean and combined rel-variance.

The correction term is shown for information only; it was obtained from the formula, subtracting the value obtained from summing the rel-variances from it. One logically either uses the sum of the rel-variances and ignores the correction term or uses the above formula.

The result of the error estimation is to emerge with a probability distribution, $P(\overline{X}/\mu)$, which permits us to allow for all the systematic and variable errors of the survey. Our best estimate of the population mean will be $\mu = 1.00/.72\ \overline{X}$ (since $\overline{X}/\mu = .72/1.00$). Further, we can assert with a 95% level of confidence that the true population mean will lie between $\overline{\mu} - [1.96(.1752)]$ and $\overline{\mu} + [1.96(.1752)]$, since the coefficient of variation is

$$\sqrt{.0307} = .1752$$

ASSIGNMENT MATERIAL

1. A consumer durable goods manufacturer makes a public announcement that it will raise the price of its most popular model in 30 days. During this period sales of the product at the retail level increase 40% above prior forecasted levels.

   a. What kind of evidence is necessary to *prove* that the announced price change caused the increase in sales?

   b. Is such evidence available?

2. You are a senior analyst in the marketing research department of a major steel producer. You have been requested to make a forecast of domestic automobile production for the forthcoming calendar year and, from this forecast, to make a forecast of the total tonnage of steel that will be used by the automobile manufacturers.

   a. Is this an exploratory, descriptive, or causal study?

   b. What data would be useful for making the forecast of steel tonnage to be used by domestic automobile manufacturers next year?

   c. How would you design the study to obtain these data?

   d. How would you go about locating sources of secondary data useful for the forecast?

   e. What external secondary data are, in fact, available that would be useful for this purpose? From what sources can they be obtained?

3. You are product manager for brand M margarine, a nationally distributed brand. Brand M has been declining in absolute level of sales for the past four consecutive months. You ask the marketing research department to do a study to determine why sales have declined.

   a. Is this an exploratory, descriptive, or causal study?

   b. What data would be useful for determining why sales have declined?

   c. How would you design the study to obtain these data?

    d. How would you go about locating sources of secondary data useful for determining why sales have declined?

    e. What external secondary data are, in fact, available that would be useful for this purpose? From what sources can they be obtained?

4. You are the manager of product planning and marketing research for the personal appliances department of a large and widely diversified corporation. You have under consideration a proposal to produce and market a hearing aid, an appliance line in which your company currently does not have a product. You have assigned one of the analysts to work on this project.

    a. Is this an exploratory, descriptive, or causal study?

    b. What data would be useful for making the decision concerning whether or not to develop and introduce a hearing aid?

    c. How would you design a study to obtain these data?

    d. How would you go about locating sources of secondary data useful for this purpose?

    e. What external secondary data are, in fact, available that would be useful to you? From what sources can they be obtained?

5. Discuss the extent of the surrogate information error present in each of the following research situations:

Information Required	*Information Sought*
a. Consumer purchases of medium-priced table wines during the next 12 months	Consumer purchase intentions over the next 12 months
b. Purchases of ten-speed bicycles during the next 12 months	Actual purchases during the past 12 months

6. Explain what is meant by the following statement: "The planning and conducting of a marketing research project is essentially an exercise in error management."

CASES FOR PART I

I-1

PATTERNS, INC.

Patterns, Inc., is a small company whose product line consists of patterns for home sewing. The company has been in operation for two years, and sales are starting to increase as the company's products become better known. Although there have been no profits as yet, it is anticipated that the turning point will soon be reached and that the third year will show a profit.

For two years Patterns, Inc., has been marketing sewing patterns for women's clothing items. All the patterns have been designed by Sue Johnson, who together with her husband, Colin, operates the company. There are no other regular employees. All "production" is handled by a local printer. At certain times the Johnsons hire a part-time employee to help package the patterns into the final product. Distribution is through retail outlets that sell fabrics and materials and by mail order. Prices are competitive with those of other patterns.

Sue Johnson has designed a new set of patterns which she calls "For Kids Only." These patterns have been in development for some time, having started as something for her own family, friends, and neighbors. The availability of patterns for young children's items has been very limited.

Initially, the "For Kids Only" patterns are to include unique, "lovable" creations that are full-size patterns and represent quality for a reasonable price. At the present time, patterns for the following items are being considered: (1) weatherproof backpack, (2) carpenter belt with stuffed tools, (3) soft ball toy that is squeezable, (4) happy counting clock with movable hands, and (5) quilts. There are a few other sewing patterns for children that Sue is in the process of designing.

All the patterns come with complete instructions and a materials list. The detailed instructions for each item are contained in a three-page insert included with the pattern.

1. Does a small company such as Patterns, Inc., have need for marketing research?
2. If it does have need, explain how the company can make use of marketing research. If not, explain why marketing research may be of no value to Patterns, Inc.

I-2

THE BAYSTAT CHEMICAL COMPANY

Recently the Baystat Chemical Company developed a new dye compound for noncel-lulosic–natural fiber blended fabrics. The dyestuff, trade-marked Hue-Lock, was then produced in only pilot plant quantities. Baystat personnel felt that the product had superior properties but did not consider them sufficiently superior to establish a price premium over competitive dyes. Also, Baystat personnel believed that established channels would have to be used in marketing the product, and that little flexibility existed in regard to the magnitude of promotional efforts.

Baystat faced two principal decisions: Should the product be made on a commercial scale? And if so, how large should the initial facilities be? Both decisions hinged on unknown events or states of nature—that is, future sales of Hue-Lock.

The marketing management of the company believed that because of the nature of the product and the time required for full market penetration, a planning period of five years should be used as a basis of evaluating the attractiveness of the proposed venture.

Consultation with process engineers indicated that two plant sizes—10 and 5 million pounds per year—represented the range of feasible capacities. Although economies of scale were associated with the higher-capacity plant, investment costs and break-even costs were likewise higher. If sales were high, payoffs obviously would favor the larger plant, but if sales were low, the smaller plant would be more profitable. If, however, the smaller capacity were chosen, and sales turned out to be high, lead time and high costs of plant conversion would be too high to make capacity additions within the five-year period feasible. After five years capacity could be enlarged, but such possibilities were assumed too tenuous for consideration in the present evaluation.

Baystat's process group assembled production cost estimates as a function of unit sales volume. If introduced, the product was to be priced at the current market level of $1 per pound over the five-year planning period. Management agreed to consider net present value (net cash flow discounted at a rate of 6% annually) as the relevant payoff measure. The major unknown was, of course, yearly sales.

Marketing was asked to prepare a forecast of sales over the five-year period. From experience in launching similar products, the conclusion was reached that Hue-Lock's ultimate market share would be realized by the end of the third year. Further, they felt that modest sales gains during the following two years would reflect increases in total market demand only, and that sales during the first two years would represent 60% and 85% respectively, of the third-year sales.

Third-year sales volume thus became the key variable to be forecast. While Baystat personnel knew that sales during the third year could fall at any point within a wide range, they believed that some sales levels were more likely to occur than others and that subjective probabilities could be attached to different values of third-year sales.

As shown in Table 1, marketing personnel believed that third-year sales would fall between 1 and 11 million pounds, with the greatest probability (0.40) falling between 3.0 and 4.9 million pounds. Yet sales could amount to only 1.0 to 2.9 million pounds (0.20 probability) or as much as 9.0 to 11.0 million pounds (0.10 probability).

With these and the earlier estimates it was possible to prepare a conditional-payoff table. A conditional payoff was estimated for each act being considered for each level of demand for Hue-Lock in the third year. The estimates are shown in Table 2.

After reviewing the conditional-payoff table, Baystat management decided to have a customer survey conducted. For a total cost of $20,000, a random sample of 100

TABLE 1   Third-Year Sales Probabilities

SALES VOLUMES (MILLIONS OF POUNDS)	PRIOR PROBABILITY
1.0–2.9	0.20
3.0–4.9	0.40
5.0–6.9	0.20
7.0–8.9	0.10
9.0–11.0	0.10

TABLE 2 Conditional Payoff Table for Hue-Lock Commercialization—Demand in Third Year (millions of pounds)

| | 9.0–11.0 (S_1) | | 7.0–8.9 (S_2) | | 5.0–6.9 (S_3) | | 3.0–4.9 (S_4) | | 1.0–2.9 (S_5) | |
ACT	$P(S_1)$	Payoff (millions of dollars)	$P(S_2)$	Payoff (millions of dollars)	$P(S_3)$	Payoff (millions of dollars)	$P(S_4)$	Payoff (millions of dollars)	$P(S_5)$	Payoff (millions of dollars)
A_1: build 10 million-pound plant	0.10	4.55	0.10	2.23	0.20	(0.59)	0.40	(3.40)	0.20	(6.23)
A_2: build 5 million-pound plant	0.10	2.50	0.10	2.35	0.20	1.96	0.40	0.36	0.20	(3.05)
A_3: do not commercialize	0.10	0	0.10	0	0.20	0	0.40	0	0.20	0

potential customers out of a total customer population of 1,200 was presented with test fabrics that had been dyed with the new material. Survey response indicated that the average third-year sales would be 2,100 pounds with a standard deviation of 7,000 pounds. Thus, based on the total customer population (1,200), total third-year sales would amount to 2.52 million pounds (1,200 × 2,100).

1. If no additional information had been obtained, what decision should have been made about the commercialization of Hue-Lock?
2. Should the management of Baystat have authorized the survey?
3. Given that the survey was to be taken, was this the proper size sample to take?
4. Given the results of the actual survey, what decision should have been made about the commercialization of Hue-Lock?

I-3

SYD COMPANY (A)

The market for women's hair shampoos has become highly specialized and segmented. In recent years a large number of special-purpose shampoos have appeared on the market, each promising to provide various hair-care benefits to the potential user. The Syd Company[30] is a diversified manufacturer of consumer packaged goods. At this time the firm has no women's shampoo in its product line.

The company's marketing research personnel met recently with a small research firm, FC Associates, and discussed the possibility of a study of young female adults living in a large city in the eastern part of the United States.

The Syd Company had established—through a series of recently completed interviews with small groups of women consumers—that "body" (apparently connoting hair thickness or fullness) in a hair shampoo was frequently mentioned as a desired characteristic. Armed with this still rather sketchy information concerning the desirability of "body" in a shampoo, the firm's laboratory personnel had set to work on developing some prototypical compounds that appeared potentially capable of delivering this characteristic to a greater extent than brands currently on the market.

During the initial conversations between Syd and FC Associates, the following managerial problems came to light:

1. Assuming that laboratory personnel could produce a women's shampoo with superior "body," is the market for this product large enough to justify its commercialization?
2. What benefits in addition to "body" should be incorporated into the new shampoo?

[30]Disguised name.

3. What are the characteristics—product usage, hair type, demographics—of people who are particularly attracted to a shampoo with "body"? (Knowledge of these characteristics would be desirable in defining the target segment for the new product.)

4. How should the concept of "body" in shampoo be communicated; what does the *consumer* mean by "body" in shampoo? (Knowledge of the connotations of "body" would be valuable in the design of promotional messages and point-of-purchase materials.)

Since Syd had no entry in the shampoo market, the company had relatively little to go on in the way of secondary sources of information. While various market statistics could be obtained for existing brands, the firm was primarily interested in characteristics appropriate for a relatively new concept in the marketplace—a shampoo that emphasized "body."

Problem Structuring

Although formal statistical decision analysis was not applied in this case, it became apparent that the firm faced three primary courses of action:

1. Continue technical development of a new shampoo that delivers the consumer benefit: "body."

2. Terminate technical development related to this characteristic and switch effort to some other shampoo benefit.

3. Discontinue all effort in women's shampoo products.

Continuation of technical development on "body," in turn, is based on two considerations: (1) that the new product can be developed successfully from a technical standpoint, and (2) that the new product can be sold in sufficient quantities to justify future development outlays, start-up expense, ongoing production and marketing costs, plus earning an appropriate return on invested funds.

Informal analysis indicated a high probability of technical success during the ensuing 12 months with relatively modest additional outlays in technical resources. The major problem appeared to be one of market potential—more specifically, whether a target segment of sufficient size was available to warrant continued technical development and eventual commercialization.

Cost and Value of Marketing Research

Current uncertainties about potential demand for the new product suggested the desirability of conducting marketing research beyond the preliminary consumer group interviews that had recently been conducted by the firm. Crude estimates of the cost versus value of additional information (including such aspects as the costs of continuing technical development and start-up, the probability of technical and marketing "success," and the likelihood that survey results would correctly identify the appropriate state of nature) clearly indicated the advisability of further marketing research.

The problem was not whether more marketing research could be justified—the quickest and crudest estimates demonstrated its potential value—but rather, what *kind of research* should be done that seemed most likely to answer management's questions. Indeed, the main purpose of the marketing personnel's visit to FC Associates was to discuss an exploratory study that could be helpful in designing the main study that would eventually be conducted on a national, probability-based sample. What should the main study cover? How could management's questions be translated into a research design? What additional research questions should be raised?

Agreement was reached that FC would do the exploratory study.

Research Design

Given the exploratory character of the research, questions of adequate sample size and representativeness were not of primary importance. What was germane to the pilot research was the need for FC to translate management's questions into operational terms and, in the process, to develop additional questions of relevance to the design of the main piece of research that would be undertaken after the pilot results were analyzed.

The principal focus of the exploratory research was to be on shampoo benefits. In the course of conducting preliminary consumer group interviews the client's marketing research personnel had assembled a list of approximately 30 benefits that either had been advertised or were thought by at least some consumers to be relevant in the choice of a hair shampoo. Not surprisingly, many of the benefit descriptions were redundant; hence, the first step was to trim down the list to a smaller set. Table 1 shows the 16 benefits that emerged from the culling process. The preliminary research seemed to indicate that the first 10 benefits were probably the most important of the 16. Indeed, the preliminary

TABLE 1   List of 16 Hair Shampoo Benefits Used in Questionnaire

1. Hair Stays Clean a Long Time
2. Hair Stays Free of Dandruff or Flaking
3. Hair That Looks and Feels Natural
4. Hair That Has Body
5 Manageable Hair That Goes Where You Want It
6. Hair with Sheen or Luster
7. Hair with No Split Ends
8. Hair with Enough Protein
9. Hair That Doesn't Get Oily Fast
10. Hair That's Not Too Dry
11. Hair with Fullness
12. Hair That's Not Frizzy
13. Hair That Holds a Set
14. Hair with Texture
15. Hair That's Easy to Comb When It Dries
16. Hair That Looks Free and Casual

research suggested that the first 6 benefits probably constituted the "core set"—i.e., those benefits of really primary importance to consumer choice.

A second matter of importance concerned the nature of respondents to be interviewed. The study's sponsor suggested a purposive sample of young female adults—aged 18 through 30—with an approximate 60–40 split between married and single. Only consumers who shampooed their hair at least twice a month, on the average, were to be interviewed. In brief, the sample was to be aimed at a specific age group of relatively active users of shampoo.

Key Research Questions

Given the emphasis placed on product benefit preferences, particularly the benefit of "body," a number of ancillary research questions were developed from the primary ones indicated by the client:

1. How do consumers of hair shampoos perceive various benefits as commonly (or rarely) available in shampoos *currently* on the market?
2. Given freedom to make up her own "ideal" shampoo, what "bundles" of benefits do consumers want? Specifically, how often is "body" included in their ideal benefit bundles?
3. Assuming that a consumer desired and could get a shampoo that delivered "body," what *other* benefits are also desired in the same brand?
4. What is conjured up by the phrase "shampoo body" and its various connotations—that is, what words are elicited on a free-association basis?
5. How do preferences for "body" in shampoos relate to
   a. Frequency of hair shampooing (i.e., heavy versus light users of shampoos)?
   b. Perceptions of its availability in current shampoos?
   c. Preference for other benefits in addition to "body"?
   d. Hair physiology and wearing style?
   e. Demographics (e.g., age, marital status, education, etc.)?

These questions set the stage for FC Associates to develop the questionnaire.

Administration

The questionnaire was first pretested. Following this, the questionnaire was administered on a personal, in-the-home basis by interviewers. Respondents were drawn from the city on a purposive basis. Interview time averaged about half an hour; all data were collected over the span of one week.

Assume that you are the research and development manager for the Syd Company.

a. How would you criticize the study in terms of its usefulness to you?
b. If you had the opportunity to design the pilot project from *your* viewpoint, what questions would you want to include in the questionnaire?

I-4

SAN A/S

SAN A/S, an incorporated company in Denmark, manufactures electric heating products for the industrial market. The company was founded in 1950 and was involved in a limited way in the production of heating elements. Its primary activity originally consisted of acting as a trading company handling products for other manufacturers. This relationship has gradually been reversed and the company now generates the greatest part of its sales volume from its own production, handling only a few products of other manufacturers which complement its own production. Production, sales, and profitability have grown steadily, and by the early 1970s the company had a dominating share of the Danish market for its products.

Growth since this time has been achieved mainly by a growth in export sales, which at present account for one-third of the company's sales. It is anticipated that exports will increase to about one-half of corporate sales by 1990. The company's recent export expansion is the result of increasing involvement in larger-scale projects. Production of small products will remain unchanged in the coming years (although share of company sales will decrease from two-thirds to one-half), and the company has not actively sought to export these small products due to intense competition in local overseas markets.

Company Objectives

The company has stated its primary function as being the coverage of industrial needs for electric heating products in Denmark and abroad. The company seeks to compete primarily on the basis of its know-how, product development, and service. Expansion is sought through export, as the Danish market no longer offers expansion possibilities. The company aims to increase its sales by at least 15% per year, and this expansion is not to occur through competition with mass-producers.

The Company's Products, Resources, and Organization

SAN A/S develops and produces custom-made load resistors and electric heating systems, and standard heating elements and cables. The company describes this as a narrow, deep, and consistent product mix. Heating systems are designed to customer specifications and include heaters for water, fluid, chemical, plastic, and oil heating; industrial ovens, air duct heaters, unit and battery heaters, defrosting elements, space heating, and tunnel ovens. The know-how acquired through the development of heating systems to customer specifications enables the company to develop new standard heating elements and cables that have a technological lead over similar products. The products are consistent in that they have similar production requirements, distribution channels, and, with the exception of load resistors, the same market.

The company is economically sound, and its steady expansion has not caused profit or financing problems. Sales were approximately 30 million Danish Kroner in 1987 and are expected to increase to 40 million Kroner in 1990 due in large part to growth in exports.[31] The company now operates at its full production capacity and is in the process of expanding its production facilities. In spite of this capacity expansion, the company anticipates that its continuing sales growth will result in a continued full utilization of capacity. This high-capacity utilization has led to delivery delays in the past, and the company has now decided that delivery time for its standard products must not exceed six weeks.

The company is a 100% privately owned Danish company, with its own production facilities located near Copenhagen. At present there are 50 employees, of whom five are civil engineers and six are technicians. Product development is typically organized in project groups. The company sells directly to customers in Denmark, and both directly and through import agents overseas.

Market

The company's customers are mainly in the process industry, where heat processes have almost countless applications. The petrochemical industry and industries with a drying process are of particular importance in SAN's market. The company concentrates solely on electric heating processes. These can be divided into those in which heating requirements can be covered by standard and mass-produced products, and those in which requirements demand the development of tailor-made products or systems.

The market for standard and mass-produced heating elements and cables is well developed; there are established producers in all industrialized countries and competition is intense. The buyer is seeking a product that can fulfill specifications that can be met by many suppliers. The market demands high quality, quick delivery, good parts availability, and a competitive price. The buying decision is typically made by an engineer seeking to reduce operating costs. Competition in the market for special products and systems is less intense, as there are fewer suppliers. Here the buyer is seeking a supplier whose know-how will help to develop a product/system that can fulfill new specifications—e.g., higher heating temperatures, better heat-to-energy ratios, resistance to corrosion, which are not available with existing products. The buyer still demands high quality and good back-up (parts availability and service) but is not seeking quick "off-the-shelf" delivery. Price is also of less importance, as the product/system is required to pay for itself through either reduced operating costs or increased productivity. Again the buying decision is typically made by an engineer. Direct contact between the buyer and the supplier is important in the buying process, as the product development becomes a new task for both parties.

Export Markets

SAN is a niche marketing company and has had a typical export history. As the home market became saturated, the company started exploiting the possibilities in the

---

[31]For comparison purposes, assume an exchange rate of $1 = 7 Danish Kroner.

geographically and culturally close markets through import agents. Exports started with the Scandinavian countries and has since expanded by agents to most of western Europe (except West Germany and the United Kingdom), Poland, Greece, and North America. At the present time the company has no international investments in the form of sales or production companies or joint ventures. As export now accounts for a rapidly increasing share of sales, management is becoming increasingly interested in being able to control its international marketing efforts. The company's expansion strategy, therefore, is to establish sales companies wherever economically possible, and agents are seen as a second-best solution.

The growing share of sales accounted for by project-export has also led to a changing emphasis in marketing strategy. While import agents have fulfilled a useful role in establishing SAN's export of small products, their use in project-export is much more limited, as direct information exchanges between the supplier and the buyer are very important. For the company this means that increased expansion will lead to increased direct involvement in foreign markets. In some foreign markets there is a dual-distribution system where SAN is responsible for projects and special products and agents are responsible for small and standard products.

Expansion to Australia

As part of its long-term expansion strategy, SAN is considering entering markets in other parts of the world. One such market is Australia, where it has had no export experience. Due to the company's present expansion in Scandinavia and Western Europe, it has limited resources to devote to the Australian market. The company is somewhat cautious and is not anxious to expand too quickly. In the short term, therefore, if the company were to enter the Australian market its goals would be (1) to establish the company's reputation in Australia, with a view to more intensive market development at a later stage when resources permit, and (2) to obtain a quick return on its investment in order to avoid delays in its expansion in other markets as a result of a financial overextension in Australia.

Management has authorized a comprehensive market study with the following objectives: (a) Analyze the Australian market and determine the sales potential for the company's products; (b) Evaluate the different marketing strategies and policies that might be used; and (c) Choose the strategy and policies that harmonize best with the company's expansion strategy and current resource availability.

1. *Explain how secondary information can be used to meet the objectives of the market study.*
2. *What kind(s) of data and sources of such data would be useful?*

5

Information from Respondents

INTRODUCTION

Respondents are a major source of marketing information. It will be recalled from Chapter 4 that we defined the term *respondent* to include a person who provides information passively through observation of his or her behavior as well as actively through verbal response. We shall therefore be concerned with both information obtained by asking questions of people and that provided by observing behavior or the results of past behavior.

In this chapter we shall first examine the types of information that can be obtained from respondents. Our concern will be with those types of information that can be used for predicting what actions marketing participants would take, given that a particular course of action is chosen in solving a specific marketing problem. The types of information relevant to predicting behavior are categorized as *behavioral correlates* and *non-behavioral correlates*.

We then turn to the *means* of obtaining information from respondents. How may we obtain this information? The general answer to this question is that the same methods are used that we use in our everyday, informal association with people. If we want to find out something from someone, we either ask them, observe their behavior (or results of their behavior) in the area in which we are interested, or do both. Formal research has simply formalized these methods. To be sure, many techniques, some of them highly ingenious, have been developed and are in use. All of these techniques, however, ultimately reduce to some form of communication and/or observation.

Interpersonal communication and observation are activities in which each of us is highly experienced. Much of our time each day is spent in communicating and observing. We ask and respond to questions, usually verbally and in formal face-to-face situations. We observe the actions of others each time we are in visual contact with them.

Casual reflection on our experiences in asking and replying to these everyday-type questions and in making informal observations would suggest to most of us that we are relatively skilled in the roles of both questioner–observer and respondent. To be sure, we are aware that we often receive less information than we need, and that the information we get is not always entirely accurate or clear. We are also aware than on occasion we give out misinformation and misinterpret what we have observed. Evaluating our experiences as a whole, however, most of us feel reasonably competent to obtain and to provide information via communication, and to obtain information by observation.

When viewed against this background of informal experience, it seems almost paradoxical that the asking of seemingly straightforward questions and receiving straightforward answers, or the observing of people's behavior in a formalized information-seeking context, could be attended by serious problems. Yet the subtleties and complexities of obtaining information from respondents are such that they have been the subject of extensive investigation and experimentation for the past forty years.

In this chapter we shall consider in turn the processes of communication and observation as means of obtaining information.

TYPES OF INFORMATION THAT CAN BE OBTAINED FROM RESPONDENTS

All marketing decisions involve recognizing alternatives and making predictions that always involve to some extent the prediction of the behavior of *market participants*. Choose any marketing problem, and the decisions made to solve it will ultimately turn, in whole or in part, on a prediction of the behavior of consumers, industrial users, marketing intermediaries, or competitors.

Consider such marketing problems as deciding whether to introduce a particular new product, to raise the price of an existing product, to change distribution channels, or the determination of the advertising budget. The solution to each of these problems involves forecasting the behavior of one or more groups of market participants.

We now consider the types of information that can be obtained from these market participants for use in forecasting behavior.

Behavioral Correlates

Past Behavior

Past behavior is a type of information that has wide usage as a predictor of future behavior. Each of us relies heavily upon this method of prediction in our everyday relationships with our family, friends, and associates. When we state that we "know" someone well, we are implicitly saying that we believe we are able to predict his or her behavior over a wide range of social situations. This ability to predict stems to a considerable extent from observations of past behavior. In more formal applications, the use of trend, seasonal, and cyclical data for forecasting (*persistence model methods*) is an example of the use of recorded information of past behavior to predict future behavior.

Regardless of the nature of the variable or variables to be forecasted, a basic premise involved in the use of information on past behavior in the prediction of future behavior is that there is a relationship between the two that to some extent is stable. This relationship may or may not be understood, in the sense that the underlying causal factors relating the two are identified and measured. Recognizing that the degree of stability is sometimes difficult to determine and that the extent of our understanding of the relationship is always imperfect, we nonetheless must believe that there is some continuity and stability in the behavior patterns of people. To believe otherwise would require us to abandon predictions concerning behavior and to preclude our making decisions in which such predictions play an essential part.

The record of past behavior may have been obtained from a natural situation or a controlled experiment. The assumption that there is a continuing and relatively stable relationship between past and future behavior is basic to and explicitly recognized in the use of controlled experiments in marketing. Test marketing operations are carried out involving such variables as product variations, differing prices, and varying levels of advertising for one basic purpose—to obtain information on customer and/or competitor response to the differing levels of the variables involved. This recorded response is used to predict future responses, even though in many cases allowances must be made for expected changes in conditions.

Information on the past behavior of respondents, whether obtained via experimental or nonexperimental methods, is frequently sought. The typical consumer study, for example, concerns itself in part with determining such "facts" as what brands have been used, the last brand bought, where and with what frequency purchases are made, what the exposure to company advertising has been, and similar aspects of past behavior. A formal classification of types of information with respect to past behavior toward products is concerned with three categories—*acquisition, use,* and *possession.* Within each of these behavioral areas information on what, how much, how, where, when, in what situation, and who becomes useful for understanding consumption patterns for the product. The requirements of the particular study will dictate which of these types of information will be required. Table 5-1 shows the requirements for a study on tomato juice to determine, among other things, whether a new type of container should be developed.

Intended Behavior

Intentions may be defined as presently planned actions to be taken in a specified future period. What more logical method of predicting the future behavior of respondents could be used, it might be asked, than to determine what their intentions are? After all, intentions are self-predictions of behavior, and thus, if obtained from the people whose behavior we want to predict, they would seemingly be the most direct and reliable method of prediction.

Intentions are a relevant and commonly sought type of information. However, consideration of our own experiences in terms of what we have planned to do vis-à-vis

TABLE 5-1. Information on Past Behavior Exploratory Study of Tomato Juice Usage Patterns

	ACQUISITION	USE	POSSESSION
What	What brand of tomato juice did you buy last time? What is your regular brand?	What dishes do you cook, or prepare with tomato juice?	What brands of tomato juice do you now have on hand?
How much	What size can of tomato juice do you usually buy? About how often do you buy tomato juice? About how many cans do you buy at a time?	About how much juice does your family drink in a week? For which purpose, drinking or cooking, does your family use more juice?	Do you now have any unopened cans of tomato juice on hand? (If "Yes") About how many cans do you now have?
How		How does your family use tomato juice? Beverage _____ Cooking _____ Both _____	How do you store tomato juice after it is opened? Can _____ Bottle _____ Plastic container _____ Other _____
Where	Do you usually do your food shopping at a particular store or supermarket? (If "Yes") What is the name of the store?		
When	About how long has it been since you last bought tomato juice?		
In what situation		Do you ever serve tomato juice as a beverage to friends?	
Who	Who in your family usually does the shopping?	Who in your family drinks tomato juice?	

TABLE 5-2. Expected and Actual Purchase Rates During a 60-Day Period

PRODUCT/SERVICE	INTENTIONS-BASED EXPECTED PURCHASE RATE (%)	PURCHASE (%)	DIFFERENCE
Ride local public transportation	22.5	21.7	−0.8
Purchase tax-sheltered investment	11.4	7.2	−4.2
Purchase stereo system	17.6	15.6	−2.0
Trip on cruise ship	4.2	3.7	−0.5
Purchase new automobile	14.3	14.1	−0.2

what we have actually done later should serve to raise some questions concerning the reliability of intentions as a predictive tool. The question "What will you do?" must always be answered conditionally. The degree of assurance that can be given that planned actions will be translated into actual actions varies widely, depending on circumstances and future happenings, many of which are outside the respondent's control.

The results of a hypothetical study of expected and purchase rates of a few products and services are shown in Table 5-2. Intentions data were collected from a sample drawn from a consumer panel using a 0-to-10 scale to measure purchase probabilities. Verbal definitions were assigned to each point on the scale. A 10 was defined as "absolutely certain of buying" and a 0 as "absolutely no chance of buying." The definition of a 5 was given as "five chances out of ten of buying" and the other points between 1 and 9 inclusively were similarly defined.

Expected purchase rates were calculated as the average purchase probability for each item. The actual rate was determined by reinterviewing the panel members 60 days later to find out what purchases had actually been made.

Many judgments and expectations are bound up in a concurrently valid statement of intentions to buy. Such variables as expected change in financial status, price expectations, general business forecasts, and predictions of need all contribute to the final intention decision. Since each of these is (to some extent, at least) a random variable, it seems plausible to suppose that the intender views them as such and that his or her stated intention is based on a subjective probability of purchase. This supposition is supported by the fact that intentions data with assigned probabilities have generally proven to be more accurate than those expressed in "either/or" form. Verbal attitude scales and variously calibrated probability scales (such as the one used in collecting the data for Table 5-2) have been used. A commonly used verbal attitude scale consists of five categories: (1) definitely will buy, (2) probably will buy, (3) might buy, (4) will not buy, and (5) don't know. Numerical scales of up to 101 (including 0) points have also been used.

A major use of intentions data has been in forecasting sales. In general, forecasts of sales of industrial products using intentions data have been better than those for consumer products. The difference between expected and actual purchase rates of the items in Table 5-2 in terms of forecast error (using actual as the base) range from a low of 1.4% for automobiles to a high of 58.3% for the tax-sheltered investment.

A study sponsored by *Newsweek* magazine involved a telephone survey of households with stereos to determine the early outlook for the compact disc player, a new type of audio product, and to forecast market growth.[1] The results of this study suggested certain guidelines to follow when consumer purchase intent is to be studied in such a high technology product class. Included were the following:

1. Understand the technology and its role.
2. Understand the consumer motivations and the context in which the product will be bought and used.
3. Make sure the survey is of consumer behavioral groups with the greatest purchase potential.
4. Go beyond the simplistic and traditional "intent to purchase" questions.

Regarding this last guideline, a better estimate of intent to buy was obtained by using a series of *filters* (e.g., varying time frames and cost; replicating the purchase process) to separate "yea-sayers" from true potential buyers. Although 25% of the sample indicated intent to buy at a specific low price, this dropped to 9% when considering a firm commitment to a decision. Further, when purchase actions already taken were considered, the proportion dropped to 2%.

Nonbehavioral Correlates

So far we have discussed what people have done and what they intend to do as correlates of what they will do. We now need to examine the nonbehavioral correlates that are useful for predicting what they will do.

Socioeconomic Characteristics

Why is information on the social and economic characteristics of respondents often useful for forecasting what they will do? The answer to this question, if not already obvious, can be readily suggested by an illustration. The Radio Corporation of America, in introducing color television in the fifties, was very much interested in the age, income, educational, and occupational composition of the market. They judged that the initial market for color television sets would be comprised of families that were proportionally higher in income and educational levels and that were older on the average than either the black-and-white set owners or the population as a whole. These judgments were subsequently confirmed by a study of the early purchasers of color sets. This information was useful for both pricing and promotional decisions, since certain characteristics were found to be correlates of purchase behavior. That is, an association was found to exist between families with these characteristics and purchase of color television sets.

In studies of consumers where there is a basis for believing that such an association

---

[1]A. Shapiro and J. Schwartz, "Research Must Be as Sophisticated as the Products It Studies," *Marketing News,* 20 (January 3, 1986), 2.

might exist, information is obtained on one or more socioeconomic characteristics. The ones on which information is most frequently obtained are income, occupation, level of education, age, sex, marital status, and size of family. While socioeconomic characteristics are by far the most widely used bases for classification of consumers, other bases exist and their use is increasing. Among these are preferences, personality traits, perceived risk, and such measures of actual buying behavior as amount purchased and brand loyalty.

In general, the identification of consumer classifications is useful in marketing so long as (1) there is differential purchase behavior among the segments of the market identified, (2) there are practicable means of differentiating the marketing effort among segments, and (3) it is worthwhile to do so. It may be interesting to know, for example, that owners of vans show different personality traits than owners of standard models; such knowledge will be useful in marketing automobiles, however, only if it can be used in developing and evaluating appeals for each type of buyer.

Two commonly used and widely accepted classifications of consumers are by stage of the life cycle and by life-style. The *life-cycle stages* experienced by most households in the United States consist of the following:

1. Young unmarrieds
2. Young marrieds, no children
3. Young marrieds, children, youngest child under six
4. Older marrieds, children, youngest child six or over
5. Older marrieds, children maintaining separate households
6. Solitary survivor, older single people[2]

Some writers have expanded the number of stages by distinguishing whether in the last two stages a person is in the labor force or retired.

The life-cycle stage has obvious implications with respect to purchases associated with family formation (furniture, appliances, household effects, and housing) and addition of children (food, clothing, toys, expanded housing). Other, less obvious relationships exist as well. New-car buying reaches its peak among the older married couples whose children have passed the age of six. A second stage of furniture buying takes place when children begin to date and have parties at home. Dental work, travel, and purchases of insurance are examples of service purchases associated with the life cycle.

Life-style has a close association with membership in a social class. It is a basis for segmenting customers by values, attitudes, opinions, and interests, as well as by income. These differences tend to be expressed through the products bought and the stores patronized as well as the section in which one lives, club membership, religious affiliation, and other means. These media are used, either consciously or subconsciously,

---

[2]Of the many good articles dealing with the life-cycle concept, one of the most comprehensive is W.D. Wells and George Gubar, "Life Cycle Concept in Marketing Research," *Journal of Marketing Research*, 3 (November 1966), 355–63. Also see Patrick E. Murphy and William A. Staples, "A Modernized Family Life Cycle," *Journal of Consumer Research*, 6 (June 1979), 12–22; and Janet Wagner and Sherman Hanna, "The Effectiveness of Family Life Cycle Variables in Consumer Expenditure Research," *Journal of Consumer Research*, 10 (December 1983), 281–91.

as symbolic representations of the class to which the person perceives he or she belongs (or would like to belong).

A common designation of social classes is the one originally used by Warner, or some close variant thereof.[3] These are the by now familiar *upper, middle,* and *lower* class designations, each divided into upper and lower segments. Thus, the Warnerian classification results in six classes ranging from the UU (upper upper) down through the LL (lower lower). More recently the value and life-styles (VALS) schema has been developed, which classifies the American public into the following life-style groups: survivors, sustainers, belongers, emulators, achievers, I-am-me's, experientials, societally conscious, integrateds.[4]

Although less direct and more subtle than life-cycle stage in its effect on overt buying behavior, there can be little question but that an upper-middle-class household will show more similarity in purchasing and consumption patterns of food, clothing, furniture, and housing to another upper-middle-class household than it will to a blue-collar, upper-lower-class household. The media to which the managerial–professional, upper-middle-class family is exposed and the appeals to which it responds are also likely to be closer to those of other managerial–professional families than to those of the blue-collar family. Similarly, on the basis of VALS, a processor and packager of tofu may find that because "experientials" have a great appreciation for natural things, they are heavier users of tofu. The marketer can then direct the product at this life-style group.

Classification of consumers is vital if we are to learn more of consumer behavior and to utilize this information in developing more efficient marketing techniques. Empirical classification procedures, while by no means commonly employed, are beginning to be more widely used in marketing studies. Such techniques as regression analysis, factor analysis, discriminant analysis, cluster analysis, and canonical analysis are described in later chapters. Examples of the use of the techniques for consumer classification purposes are given in these chapters also.

Although the discussion thus far has focused on consumers, similar classification requirements exist and are used in studies of industrial users and marketing intermediaries. Comparable characteristics of these firms include sales volume, number of employees, and the type of products manufactured or handled.

Information on Extent of Knowledge

The assertion that the *extent of knowledge* about a situation is one of the determinants of the behavioral response to it borders on being a tautology. So long as the action taken is at all rational, the amount that is known (or believed to be known) about the situation will influence the action. Translated into terms of the color television example, the extent of the prospective purchasers' knowledge about the quality of picture, reliability, and price undoubtedly influenced their decision to purchase or not purchase. The extent of the purchasers' knowledge concerning the relative levels of these variables among brands also undoubtedly played a major role in their choice of brand.

[3]See W.L. Warner et al., *Social Class in America* (New York: Harper & Row, 1960), esp. pp. 6–32: and S.J. Levy, "Social Class and Consumer Behavior," in *On Knowing the Consumer,* ed. J.W. Newman (New York: John Wiley, 1966), pp. 146–60.

[4]A. Mitchell, *The Nine American Lifestyles* (New York: Macmillan, 1983).

Prediction of what actions respondents will take, therefore, is often aided by knowing "how much they know." This is especially so in making advertising budget and media allocation decisions, for example, where the decisions are strongly affected by the levels of awareness and the extent of knowledge of potential audiences concerning the product and its attributes.

Information on Attitudes and Opinions

Extensive studies of attitudes and opinions have been made by investigators in the fields of psychology, sociology, and political science over a wide range of subject areas. The most widely known opinion studies are the public opinion polls that have been conducted regularly since the 1930s.

The study of people's behavior in business and economic contexts is also a behavioral science. As such, it has been a natural consequence that many of the techniques employed in these related fields have been adopted, adapted, and applied to business problems. Marketing research has made wide use of opinion–attitude studies to obtain information applicable for the solution of marketing problems.

The terms "attitude" and "opinion" have frequently been differentiated in psychological and sociological investigations. A commonly drawn distinction has been to view an *attitude* as a predisposition to act in a certain way and an *opinion* as a verbalization of the attitude. Thus, a statement by a respondent that he or she prefers viewing color to black-and-white television programs would be an opinion expressing (one aspect of) the respondent's attitude toward color television.

When used to predict actions that the respondent will take, this distinction between "attitude" and "opinion" rapidly becomes blurred. Since the major purpose of attitude–opinion research in marketing is to predict behavior, this differentiation is, at best, of limited usefulness. We shall therefore use the terms interchangeably.

Attitude research in marketing has been conducted with the use of both qualitative and quantitative techniques. In either form, problems are encountered that are more severe than those involved in obtaining any of the other types of descriptive information discussed. Despite these problems, which we shall discuss in later chapters in some detail, attitude–opinion research has been widely used to provide information for choosing among alternatives. Its greatest use has been in the areas of product design and advertising. Other uses have been in the selection of store locations, developing service policies, and in choosing company and trade names.

The attitudes and opinions of prospective buyers clearly affect purchase decisions. Consequently, the marketing manager should be as well informed as possible about both the nature of the relevant attitudes and opinions and the intensity with which they are held.

COMMUNICATION

Interviews in marketing research are usually classified by two major characteristics. An interview is either *structured* or *unstructured,* depending on whether a formal questionnaire has been formulated and the questions asked in a prearranged order. An interview is also either *direct* or *indirect* as a result of whether the purposes of the questions asked are intentionally disguised. Cross-classifying these two characteristics provides four different types of interviews. That is, an interview may be (1) structured and direct, (2) unstructured and direct, (3) structured and indirect, or (4) unstructured and indirect. Types 1 and 2 are basically objectivist, types 3 and 4, subjectivist.

We discuss each type of interview in turn (although the discussion of the two indirect types of interviews is combined). We then discuss the media through which interviews may be conducted.

Structured–Direct Interviews

The usual type of interview conducted during a consumer survey to obtain descriptive information is one using a formal questionnaire consisting of nondisguised questions, a questionnaire designed to "get the facts." If the marketing research manager of a television set manufacturer wants to find out how many and what kinds of people prefer various styles of television cabinets, for example, the manager may have a set of questions drawn up that asks for these facts directly. Assuming that personal interviewing is being used, each interviewer will be instructed to ask the questions in the order given on the questionnaire and to ask only those questions. The resulting interviews will be *structured– direct* in nature.

A portion of a questionnaire designed to obtain information on furniture styles owned, television cabinet design preferences, and socioeconomic characteristics follows:

Which of the styles of furniture shown in these pictures is most nearly similar to your furniture?
> *(show folder with furniture pictures)*
> *Style A   Style C   Style E*
> *Style B   Style D   Style F*

Which of the styles of television cabinets shown in these pictures do you like best?
> *(show folder with cabinet pictures)*
> *Style H   Style J   Style L*
> *Style I   Style K   Style M*

What is (your)(your husband's)(your wife's) occupation?
About how much was the total income of you and (your husband)(your wife) last year from salary and other sources?
> *Less than $10,000 _____ $20,000 to $29,999 _____*
> *$10,000 to $14,999 _____ $30,000 to $39,999 _____*
> *$15,000 to $19,999 _____ $40,000 and over   _____*

For a problem of this type, the structured–direct interview has many desirable features. Since the questions are formulated in advance, all the required information can be asked for in an orderly and systematic fashion. The exact wording of the questions can be worked out carefully to reduce the possibility of misunderstandings and influencing the answer by the phrasing used. Pretests can (and should) be made on the questionnaire to discover any problems in the wording and/or ordering of questions before the questionnaire is in its final form.

The same questions are asked each of the respondents in the same order. This serves to provide maximum control of the interviewing process and to reduce the variability in results caused by differences in interviewer characteristics. This type of interview is less demanding so far as the abilities of the interviewer are concerned, permitting less-skilled interviewers to be used and a resulting lower cost per interview. Editing, tabulating, and analyzing the information obtained are also facilitated, since standardized, direct questions are asked and the answers are recorded in a uniform manner.

The major problems associated with this type of interview are those involved with wording questions properly and the difficulties encountered in getting unbiased and complete answers to questions concerning personal and motivational factors. Despite these problems, the structured–direct interview is by far the most commonly used type of interview in marketing research.

Unstructured–Direct Interviews

In the *unstructured–direct* method of interviewing, the interviewer is given only general instructions on the type of information desired. He or she is left free to ask the necessary direct questions to obtain this information, using the wording and the order that seems most appropriate in the context of each interview.

Unstructured–direct interviews are often used in exploratory studies. Many research projects that use a formal questionnaire for the final interviews go through an exploratory phase in which respondents are contacted and unstructured interviews are held. These interviews are useful in obtaining a clearer understanding of the problem and determining what areas should be investigated. To use again the color television example, the company that is considering entering the field will want to know what consumers' experiences with color television have been, what their attitudes are toward it, suggestions they have for improvement, and so on. Pilot interviews that are unstructured and direct at the beginning of such a project are often helpful in determining which topics should be included on the final questionnaire.

This type of interview is also often useful for obtaining information on motives. If the owner of a color set is asked the free-answer question, "Why did you buy your color television set?" the answer is almost certain to be incomplete and may be worthless. Consider, for example, answers such as "Because we needed a television set," "Our old set wasn't working well," or "Because it was on sale." These answers are expressions of proximate causes rather than motivational causes. When motivations are given, such as "We enjoy color television more than black-and-white television," they are rarely complete. The added enjoyment may be because the picture is more lifelike, because of the aesthetic effect of color, because of the prestige the owner attaches to having a color set, or some combination of these and other factors. In addition, it is probable that motives other than "enjoyment" influenced the purchase.

When used to establish motives the unstructured–direct interview is known as a *depth interview,* the terminology being borrowed from the field of psychology. The interviewer will continue to ask probing questions of the type "What did you mean by that statement?" "Why do you feel this way?" and "What other reasons do you have?" until he or she is satisfied that all the information that can be obtained has been obtained, considering time limitations, problem requirements, and the willingness and ability of the respondents to verbalize motives.

It should again be noted that there is always the danger that people will consciously or unconsciously offer wrong answers to prestige questions or to questions about why they took a particular action. Although the depth interview using direct questions may assist the respondent to recognize and to verbalize motives that otherwise would not have been disclosed, it still does not satisfactorily solve this problem in all cases.

The unstructured interview is free of the restrictions imposed by a formal list of questions. The interview may be conducted in a seemingly casual, informal manner in which the flow of the conversation determines which questions are asked and the order in which they are raised. The level of vocabulary used can be adapted to that of the respondent to ensure that the questions are fully understood and that rapport is developed and maintained. The flexibility inherent in this type of interview, when coupled with the greater informality that results when it is skillfully used, often results in information being disclosed that is not obtained in a structured–direct interview.

In the structured–direct interview, the questionnaire is, in effect, the dominant factor in the interview. The interviewer's role is simply that of a question asker. In the unstructured interview, the interviewer must both formulate and ask questions. The unstructured interview can therefore be only as effective in obtaining complete, objective, and unbiased information as the interviewer is skilled in formulating and asking questions. The major problem in unstructured–direct interviews is accordingly that of ensuring that competent interviewers are used. Higher per-interview costs result, both as a result of this requirement and the fact that unstructured interviews generally are longer than those in which a questionnaire is used. In addition, editing and tabulating problems are more complicated as a result of the varied order of asking questions and recording answers.

Structured– and Unstructured–Indirect Interviews

Psychologists have long recognized that direct questioning of patients is frequently of little value for diagnostic purposes. The patient is usually unable and often unwilling to give accurate answers to direct questions. To solve this problem, a number of techniques have been devised to obtain information by *indirect* means. Most of these techniques employ the principle of *projection*. That, is, the subject is given a nonpersonal, ambiguous situation and asked to describe it. The person giving the description will tend to interpret the situation in terms of his or her own needs, motives, and values. The description, therefore, involves a projection of characteristics of personality to the situation described. These techniques include *word association, sentence completion tests, interpretation of pictorial representations,* and other devices that have been developed as a means of inducing people to project their feelings (see Table 5-3). They have been most widely used for studies on those consumer products that are similar in quality, performance, and price—notably for such products as automobiles, soaps and detergents, gasoline, cigarettes, food products, beverages, and drug sundries.

TABLE 5-3. Classification of Projective Techniques

TECHNIQUE	RESPONSE REQUESTED
Construction	
Thematic Apperception Test (TAT)	The respondent is asked to respond for or to
Item Substitution Test	describe a character in a simulated situation.
Association	
Word-association test	The respondent is asked to reply to a
Rorschach Test	stimulus with the first word, image, or
Cloud pictures	percept that occurs to him or her.
Auditory projective techniques	
Completion	
Sentence-completion test	The respondent is given an incomplete
Picture completion study	expression, image, or situation and asked to
Psychodrama	complete it however he or she chooses.

Most indirect interviews are at least *partially structured* in that they are conducted by using a predevised set of words, statements, one or more cartoons, pictures, or other representations to which the subject is asked to respond. However, the interviewer is usually allowed considerable freedom in questioning the respondent in order to ensure a full response. Indirect interviews, therefore, are commonly neither fully structured nor unstructured; ordinarily they utilize both types of questions. Within the marketing research community these techniques constitute *qualitative* research techniques.

Focus-Group Interviews

Perhaps the best-known and most widely used type of indirect interview is that conducted with a *focus group*. As we mentioned in Chapter 4, a focus-group interview is one in which a group of people jointly participate in an interview that does not use a structured question-and-answer method to obtain information from these people. The interview is conducted by a trained moderator with a group of, ideally, 8–12 willingly recruited participants. The composition of the group varies according to the needs of the client, especially the "problem" under study.

Although the technique is widely used in exploratory research, it also is useful in nonexploratory research. Such applications include, broadly, direct exposure to consumers for firsthand knowledge, idea generation for management consideration (e.g., problems, unmet needs, ideas for new products), concept development and screening, tests for comprehension of promotion and communication material, and establishment of "opinion leader" panels. One example is provided by the development of an advertising and merchandising program to dealers of fiberglass radial tires.[5] Just prior to the introduction of the new glass radial tires, Owens-Corning Fiberglas conducted a series of 15 focus-group interviews with mass merchandise, oil company, and private-label dealers to see what the dealers perceived as being the key benefits and merchandising aids that would best help them sell the new type of tires. Previous research had indicated that consumers

[5]"Owens-Corning Listens to Dealers," *Sales Management,* 114 (March 3, 1975), 23.

would buy the glass radials provided they were less expensive than steel radials. Since glass radials were to be 15% to 20% lower in price than steel radials, Owens-Corning expected no problems with dealer acceptance of the new tires. Instead, in the focus interviews, they found that the dealers were afraid that the problems they had had with glass bias belted tires when they were introduced some eight years earlier would be repeated with the glass radial tires. As a result, sales themes and promotional copy were reworked to assure dealers that consumer acceptance of the new tires would be good, performance would be high, and they should have a minimum of problems with the new product.

Another example is the use of the focus group by Republic Health Corporation, which owns or manages 90 health institutions.[6] During the period 1983–1985 earnings increased 420%, and this was due to promotional packages (often pushing low prices) for the surgical procedures and services offered by its hospitals. Focus-group research played a major role in the development of the promotion.

It seems to be a well-accepted fact that focus groups do work, especially (but not limited to) when used with other techniques. For instance, focus groups involving children as young as five years of age are becoming the rule in the toy industry. These are followed by concept-fulfillment studies before a company commits itself to marketing a new toy.[7] A natural question, of course, is, Why do they work?[8] One practitioner's view is that clients are provided with a gut-level grasp of their customers. This means that there is gained a sense of what is unique about customers—their self-perceptions, desires, and needs that affect everything they do.[9]

When conducting a focus group the session is often video-taped for further in-depth analysis. At the very least the session is audiotaped. In some instances, clients observe the group session firsthand in a type of observation room. When this is done (or the client sees a videotape), the impact is as follows:

> . . . [there is] a powerful emotional force. Seeing and hearing consumers, only a few feet away, has an impact that no set of statistics, no written report alone can have. It makes the abstract real because it is human, individual. Qualitative research offers not just an intellectual comprehension of consumers but a vivid, visceral recognition that affects, on a very deep level, how clients see, feel about, and deal with their customers from then on.[10]

In addition to in-person group interaction, a focus group can be conducted over the telephone by use of a conference call.[11] Groups have included doctors, car dealers,

[6]"A High-Powered Pitch to Cure Hospitals' Ills," *Business Week,* No. 2910 (September 2, 1985), 60–61.

[7]K. Higgins, "Research, Marketing Not Playthings for Toymakers," *Marketing News,* 19 (July 5, 1985), 1ff.

[8]See, for example, E. Fern, "Why Do Focus Groups Work: A Review and Integration of Small Group Process Theories," *Proceedings of the Association for Consumer Research Annual Conference,* 1981, pp. 444–51. A complete treatise on the technique will be found in A. Goldman and S. S. McDonald, *The Group Depth Interview: Principles and Practice* (Englewood Cliffs, N.J.: Prentice-Hall, 1987).

[9]J. Langer, "Personal Encounters of the First-Hand Kind: Getting to Know the Consumer Through Qualitative Research," paper presented at the Annual Conference on Marketing Research, American Marketing Association, October 1985.

[10]Ibid., p. 11.

[11]"Focus Groups Are a Phone Call Away," *Marketing News,* 20 (January 3, 1986), 22ff.

accountants, travel agents, and others for projects relating to product development, promotion feedback, reasons why a product was not selling, and similar issues.

When conducting focus groups with professionals, however, the practical aspects of focus-group use are somewhat unique. Special attention must be given to recruitment, type of compensation or gratuity, convenience of the facility to be used, and the moderator. Unlike other types of focus groups, when professionals are involved the moderator's interaction must be such that he or she is presented as an authority on research in the field of the professional. At least a working knowledge of current technical terminology is necessary.

The Third-Person Technique

The simplest way of obtaining information through indirect questioning of a respondent is to ask for the view of a neighbor, an (unnamed) associate, or some other person whose views on the subject at hand might reasonably be known. This permits the respondent to project his or her own views with no feeling of social pressure to give an "acceptable" answer.

A study of flying that was performed for a commercial airline is a good example of the use of this technique. When respondents were asked, "Are you afraid to fly?" very few people gave any indication of fear. The major reasons given for not flying were cost and the inconvenience of getting to and from the airport plus the uncertainty of airline schedules during the winter due to bad weather. When, in a follow-up study, respondents were asked, "Do you think your neighbor is afraid to fly?" most of the neighbors who traveled by some other method of transportation were said to do so because they were afraid to fly.

An early study using a variation of this technique that has come to be regarded as a classic is the study by Haire on instant coffee. This study was conducted when instant coffee was being introduced (1949). The purpose of the study was to determine the motivations of consumers toward instant coffee in general and Nescafé, a brand of instant coffee, in particular.[12]

Interviews of consumers had been conducted using a questionnaire employing direct questions. Among the questions asked were "Do you use instant coffee?" and (if "No") "What do you dislike about it?" The majority of the unfavorable responses were of the general content "I don't like the flavor." This answer was suspected to be a stereotype rather than revealing the true reasons. An indirect approach was therefore decided upon.

Two shopping lists were prepared that were identical in every respect except that one contained "Nescafé instant coffee" and the other "Maxwell House coffee (drip grind)." These shopping lists were shown alternately to a sample of 100 respondents, each being unaware of the other list. Each subject was given the following instructions:

> Read the shopping list below. Try to project yourself into the situation as far
> as possible until you can more or less characterize the woman who bought
> the groceries. Then write a brief description of her personality and character.
> Wherever possible indicate what factors influenced your judgment.

[12]Mason Haire, "Projective Techniques in Marketing Research," *Journal of Marketing,* 14 (April 1950), 649–56.

The results were quite revealing. The descriptions given was summarized as follows:[13]

1. 48% of the people described the woman who bought Nescafé as lazy; 4% described the woman who bought Maxwell House as lazy.

2. 48% of the people described the woman who bought Nescafé as failing to plan household purchases and schedules well; 12% described the woman who bought Maxwell House this way.

3. 4% described the Nescafé woman as thrifty; 16% described the Maxwell House woman as thrifty; 12% described the Nescafé woman as spendthrift; 0% described the Maxwell House woman this way.

4. 16% described the Nescafé woman as not a good wife; 0% described the Maxwell House woman this way; 4% described the Nescafé woman as a good wife; 16% described the Maxwell House woman as a good wife.

The implications of these findings seem clear. The woman using the instant coffee was characterized as being lazier, less well organized, more of a spendthrift, and not as good a wife as the one using the conventional coffee. These imputed characteristics must have been the result of the respondents' projecting their own feelings toward instant coffee in their descriptions of the woman using it.

This study has been replicated a number of times. The general acceptance of instant coffee and the change in dietary habits since it was done originally have resulted in different findings in the more recent studies.[14]

Word Association Tests

Word association tests have been used since 1879 by psychologists and are considered to be the forerunner of more recent projective techniques.

The test consists of presenting a series of stimulus words to a respondent who is asked to answer quickly with the first word that comes to mind after hearing each. The respondent, by answering quickly, presumably gives the word that he or she associates most closely with the stimulus word.

A word association test was used by the American Telephone and Telegraph Company to choose the name that best communicated the service provided by long distance dialing. Seven names were tested, including "Nationwide Dialing," Customer Toll Dialing," and "Direct Distance Dialing." Responses to "Nationwide Dialing" were (somewhat surprisingly) weighted in the direction of "worldwide," an apparent interpretation that this new system would permit dialing telephone numbers all over the world. "Customer Toll Dialing" received a high response rate of "money" and "charges," indicating an unfavorably high association with the cost of making long distance calls. "Direct Distance Dialing" was chosen by AT&T since it seemed to convey the idea of long

[13]Ibid., p. 652.
[14]See, for example, G. S. Lane and G. L. Watson, "A Canadian Replication of Mason Haire's 'Shopping List' Study," *Journal of the Academy of Marketing Science,* 3 (Winter 1975), 48–59.

distance dialing without the use of an operator and did not have any unfavorable associations.

Sentence Completion Tests

Sentence completion tests are similar to word association tests, both in concept and in use. A sentence stem (the beginning phrase of a sentence) is read to the respondent, who is asked to complete the sentence quickly and with the first thought that occurs to him or her.

Sentence completion was one of the techniques used in a study of automobile buying. The purpose of the study was to probe the motivations of automobile buyers to provide a sounder basis for advertising. Such sentence stems were used as

People who drive a convertible. . .
Factory workers usually drive. . .
Most of the new cars. . .
When I drive very fast. . .

Some selected responses of men and women to two of the sentence stems illustrate how inferences of motivational influences can be drawn through the use of this technique.[15]

Sentence stem: When you first get a car. . .
  Women's responses:
     . . . you can't wait till you drive.
     . . . you would go for a ride.
     . . . you would take rides in it, naturally,
     . . . you would put gas in it and go places.
  Men's responses:
     . . . you take good care of it.
     . . . I want to make darn sure it has a good coat of wax.
     . . . check the engine.
     . . . how soon can I start polishing it.

Sentence stem: A car of your own. . .
  Women's responses:
     . . . is a pleasant convenience.
     . . . is fine to have.
     . . . is nice to have.
  Men's responses:
     . . . I would take care of it.
     . . . is a good thing.
     . . . absolutely a necessity.

---

[15]As reported in J. W. Newman, *Motivation Research and Marketing Management* (Cambridge, Mass.: Harvard University Graduate School of Business Administration, 1957), pp. 227–28.

The interpretation of these results was as follows:

> The women's responses indicated that for them a car is something to use and that pride of ownership stresses being seen in the car. For men a car was something for which they should be protective and responsible. Their emphasis was on examining the car and doing things to it. Men appeared to feel closer to their car and regarded it as more of a necessity than did women.[16]

Thematic Apperception Tests

The *Thematic* (for themes that are elicited) *Apperception* (for the perceptual–interpretative use of pictures) *Test* (TAT) consists of one or more pictures or cartoons that depict a situation relating to the product or topic being studied. Generally, one or more persons are shown in an ambiguous situation and the respondent is asked to describe or to assume the role of one of these people.

The most common form of the TAT as used in marketing research is the cartoon. The cartoons shown in Figures 5-1 and 5-2 were used to study the price–quality association of a sample of women with respect to a beauty cream. Each woman in the sample was

Figure 5-1

Figure 5-2

shown one of the cartoons (in random order) and asked to describe first the person in the cartoon and then to indicate what she thought the beauty cream shown would be like.

The general nature of the responses for the cartoon showing the 49-cent beauty cream are well summarized by the answers of one of the women:

> "Any female over 18 interested in her appearance who falls for the advertising claims and doesn't have too much money to spend on cosmetics." "It's a poor quality product that is probably greasy and oily."

For the cartoon showing the $5.00 cream, the responses given below are generally representative of those of the sample:

> "Someone who cares what she looks like—possibly a business girl interested in her appearance."
>
> "It's a cream that leaves your skin clear and refreshed. It probably would keep your skin young-looking by softening and cleansing the skin."

The reader may draw his or her own conclusions as to the association of price and quality for this product. (Before a sound conclusion can be reached, however, additional information is needed with respect to the size and nature of the sample used.)

The Depth Interview

There is substantial use of the unstructured, informal interview in marketing research to explore the underlying predispositions, needs, desires, feelings, and emotions of the consumer toward products and services. This method of interviewing was discussed earlier in this chapter and referred to as a "depth interview."

Insofar as obtaining information on motivations is concerned, the concept of "depth" refers to the level at which underlying motivations are uncovered. Both the method of interviewing and the term "depth interview" were borrowed from clinical psychology, where the method has been used to probe and assess the sources and nature of the problems of patients. In marketing research, the "depth" of the interviews has been varied but with a general level that is substantially less "deep" than the level used in the field of psychology.

The *depth interview* in marketing research may consist of either direct or indirect questions, or some combination of the two. The skilled interviewer will generally employ both types of questions. A direct, free-answer question such as "What are the major reasons why you bought your CB ratio?" might well be followed up, for example, with an indirect question such as "Why do you think people who own CB radios bought them?" By following leads and cues provided by respondents, phrasing questions to continue the flow and pattern of the conversation and to maintain the rapport established, the competent interviewer can explore and probe the underlying motivations of the respondent.

Many examples of the use of depth interviewing in marketing research could be cited. One, which again relates to coffee, is reported by Newman.[17] Depth interviews were the basic research technique used in a study done for the Pan-American Coffee Bureau by the Institute for Motivation Research. Exploratory depth interviews were conducted with 36 respondents, and an additional sample of 96 respondents were depth-interviewed later.

In each depth interview, "a trained interviewer encouraged the respondent to talk freely about his associations and feelings related to coffee. Direct questions seldom were asked. Instead the interviewer attempted by skillful probing to learn what was important to the respondent and to investigate the emotional facets that often determined apparently rational behavior."[18]

Interviewer instructions for the initial set of 36 interviews are given in Figure 5-3. These instructions are worthy of careful reading, since they illustrate both the major strength—adaptability—and the primary weakness—opportunity for subjective biases in interviewing and interpretation—of the depth interview.

Several recommendations were made as a result of the study. One of these was to change coffee, in psychological terms, from a "sinful and escapist" beverage to a positive, life-accepting product. Although many of the respondents showed a liking for coffee, they were afraid of drinking too much of it and reluctant about letting young people drink it. A second recommendation was to provide a greater variety of coffee flavors. Coffee should not just be "coffee"; restaurants should treat it as more of a specialty by listing

[17]Newman, *Motivation Research*, pp. 156–227.
[18]Ibid., p. 161.

Figure 5-3   Pan-American Coffee Bureau Study—Interviewer Instructions

Sample Note:

Of your two respondents, please make sure that you have represented one male, one female; one "dark strong" coffee drinker, one "light weak" coffee drinker; one "heavy drinker" (6–8 cups per day), one "light drinker" (2–3 cups per day).

Just for Your Information

There are 5 major practical questions that we want to answer in this study:

1. What is the real role of coffee drinking in people's lives today?
2. What people drink coffee more frequently, or less?
3. Why people prefer stronger, or weaker coffee brewing?
4. At what age levels and why is coffee drinking morally possible?
5. Any special feelings about coffee on the part of older people.

To answer these questions, we need to probe for the whole range of people's feelings about coffee and its real role in their lives. Encourage maximum spontaneity and feel free to probe any area that seems likely to be significant.

It would be most helpful for these initial interviews if you could just get people talking freely on all their feelings about coffee for an hour or so.

The areas below are to be probed only after fullest possible rambling free association is exhausted.

Some Suggested Research Areas

Among others, try to probe the following areas that we have found helpful in our preliminary field testing:

1. *Spontaneous Associations*—First try to encourage maximum free association with coffee, *everything that comes into people's minds as they think of coffee.* . . . Probe in detail for *all sensory* impressions, smell, taste, appearance, etc.
2. *Kinds of Coffee*—All impressions about different types of coffee—strong, weak, black, etc., difficulties in making coffee, how one brews coffee, etc. . . .
3. *Coffee Drinking Occasions*—When respondent drinks coffee and attitudes to coffee at all these specific occasions—when it is most wanted, best liked . . .
4. *Best Cup*—The *best* cup of coffee—how it tasted, etc. . . .
5. *Childhood*—Impressions of coffee in childhood—when first asked for some— parents' attitude—when he and friends first started drinking coffee—all impressions of that first cup, taste, smell, etc.
6. *His Children*—Any comments about or requests for coffee by his children—what he said—at what age allowed, or will be allowed, to drink coffee?
7. *Frequency*—Average number of cups per day— . . . .
8. *Health*—All feelings about coffee and health— . . . .

four or five varieties of coffee. A third recommendation was that coffee advertising should be more permissive about suggesting how people should make and drink their coffee, since people were proud of having individual tastes and, in some cases, resented authoritarian advertisements that told them the "right" way of making coffee.

To a large extent, in the past the individual depth interview has been used less extensively as the focus-group interview has become more prominent. However, dissatisfaction with the group influence and the high cost of focus groups ($3,000 or more), together with certain evolving factors in the marketing environment, have led to recent increased use of the individual depth interview.[19] The depth interview is ideal for obtaining from consumers anecdotes of times they used a product or service, and such "stories" provide the marketer with a good view of what products mean to consumers.[20] When used this way, the result of the interview is usually presented as a verbatim. Telephone interviewing has proved to be effective in obtaining such consumer stories.

The depth interview offers insights with depth, whereas focus groups offer information with breadth. Thus, each has its place in the total set of methodologies from which marketing researchers can draw.

Other Techniques

Other variations of projective techniques have been used that are similar in nature but different in form from those already described. The *repertory grid,* for example, is a partially structured technique that requires the respondent to compare objects along dimensions that he or she selects. The usual procedure is to present the interviewee with a pack of cards on which brand names are printed. The respondent is asked to cull unfamiliar brands from the pack, and three cards with familiar brand names are selected at random. Following this, the respondent is asked to describe a way in which any two of the familiar brands are like each other and different from the third. The respondent is then asked to rate all the brands with respect to this dimension. The response may be in the form of a paired comparison, a ranking, or a numerical rating on a scale. This process is repeated using three different brands until the dimensions of the respondent are exhausted. Additional respondents are interviewed until no new dimensions are given. On the average, 40 interviews are required to identify most of the relevant dimensions.[21] An example of the repertory grid technique appears in Chapter 18.

Story completion, a logical extension of the sentence completion technique, consists of presenting the beginning of a situational narrative to a respondent, who is asked to complete it. The general underlying principle is that the person will project his or her own psychological interpretation of the situation into the response.

Projection through *sketching* by the respondent has been used in a study of super-

---

[19]H. Sokolow, "In-Depth Interviews Increasing in Importance," *Marketing News,* 19 (September 13, 1985), 26ff.

[20]J. Langer, "'Story Time' Is Alternative Research Technique," *Marketing News,* 19 (September 13, 1985), 19ff.

[21]Reported in G. D. Hughes, "The Measurement of Beliefs and Attitudes," in *Handbook of Marketing Research,* ed. Robert Ferber (New York: McGraw-Hill, 1974), pp. 3–19.

Exhibit 5-1   Add Protocols to the Qualitative Research Tool Kit

A *protocol* is a record of a respondent's verbalized thought processes while performing a decision task or while problem solving. This record is obtained by asking the respondent to "think out loud" or talk about anything going through his or her head while performing the task at hand. Protocols can be collected either in a laboratory situation while the respondent is making a simulated purchase or in the field while an actual purchase decision is being made. This approach is the *concurrent protocol*. Another version is the *retrospective protocol* in which the verbalizing out loud is done just after the task has been finished.

In contrast to traditional survey methods, protocol methodology allows a person to respond freely in his or her own terms in relation to the actual choice task or decision situation. The form and particular stimuli to which the research subject should respond is not defined or specified by the researcher.

Consumer protocols have been collected on actual shopping trips or in simulated shopping environments. Protocols can be useful in studying brand choice, product categorization, product usage patterns and attitudes, and the impact of shopping environment and situational variables on behavior.

Since data are collected in an unstructured way there is the problem of interpretation. By its very nature protocol-based data are subjective. Thus, some form of content analysis will be needed. This could lead to incomplete information being provided. Although protocols can provide great detail and breadth of coverage, they are best suited for use with other techniques.

Source: Adapted from Susan P. Douglas and C. Samuel Craig, *International Marketing Research* (Englewood Cliffs, N.J.: Prentice-Hall, 1983), pp. 162–68. A more complete exposition is in K. Anders Ericsson and Herbert A. Simon, *Protocol Analysis: Verbal Reports As Data* (Cambridge, Mass.: MIT Press, 1984).

market layout and design.[22] A sample of 50 housewives was asked to "draw a supermarket" in conjunction with an interview. Some of the findings, of which the reader may make his or her own interpretations, were: (1) the meat department was omitted in about 1 out of 10 drawings, produce in 1 out of 5, and dry groceries in 1 out of 4; (2) the produce department was drawn first in about 2 out of 5 drawings, meats in 1 out of 5, dairy in 1 out of 6, and dry groceries in 1 out of 6; (3) the meat department was, on the average, drawn about 50% *larger* than the dry groceries department. Actually it is only about one-third as large as the dry groceries department in a store of the dimensions involved. Produce was drawn 80% as large as dry groceries, though it too occupies only about one-third of the space actually allotted to dry groceries.

INTERVIEWING MEDIA

Several alternative media are available for obtaining information from respondents through communication. Respondents may be interviewed in person or interviewed by telephone, or they may be mailed a questionnaire to which they are asked to respond.

[22]H. E. Krugman, "The 'Draw a Supermarket' Technique," *Public Opinion Quarterly,* 24 (Spring 1960), 148–49.

Response and Nonresponse Bias

A major concern of the research planner in choosing which medium to use is the potential systematic error (i.e., bias) that might arise. In Chapter 4 we discussed total error and looked at its major components. At this point it is useful to explore error further but in a slightly different context. Controlling errors related to the sampling process is discussed in Chapter 9. Our concern here is with nonsampling-based potential error. In communication, error may be due to the nature of response given and/or to the fact that the sample member has not responded.

Response Bias

Response as a source of error, or response bias, may arise because of carelessness in reporting and recording, measurement error, or lying.[23] For instance, questions that ask respondents to reconstruct past experiences also run a high risk of response bias. More specific is the possibility of a respondent *telescoping*, remembering when an event occurred during a short recent time period. One suggestion for reducing telescoping is to use *bounded recall* procedures, which involves asking questions about the events of concern in previous time periods, as well as the time period of research interest.[24]

A complex source of inaccuracy in response stems from the respondents' appraisal of the investigator and the opinions and expectations that are imputed to him or her. Although much remains to be learned about the nature of the cues from which respondents draw inference about investigators' opinions, there is sufficient evidence to conclude both that such inferences are drawn and that they influence responses.

The investigator's appearance and manner will often influence responses. A "classic" example is a cosmetics study that showed an unexpectedly high reported usage of luxury cosmetics among women from low-income families. In this case, one woman interviewer had conducted all the interviews in the low-income area. She was an exceptionally well dressed and carefully groomed person who was known to be a very competent interviewer. The director of the study hypothesized that the responding women had reported using more expensive cosmetics than they actually used because they thought that these were the kinds of cosmetics the interviewer used. To test this hypothesis, a matronly woman, dressed similarly to the women to be interviewed, was asked to call on the same respondents and use the same questionnaire on the following day. The reported brands of cosmetics used were much less expensive, on the average, in this series of interviews.[25]

The level of rapport established between the investigator and the respondent is an important factor in reducing response bias. There have been instances in which the

---

[23]See I. A. Lewis and W. Schneider, "Is the Public Lying to The Pollsters?" *Public Opinion*, 5 (April/May 1982), 42–47.

[24]S. Sudman, A. Finn, and L. Lannam, "The Use of Bounded Recall Procedures in Single Interviews," *Public Opinion Quarterly*, 48 (Summer 1984), 520–24. For a related discussion of how to deal with telescoping, see William A. Cook, "Telescoping and Memory's Other Tricks: Short-Term and Long-Term Strategies for Survey Methods Development," paper presented at the Fourth Annual Advertising Research Foundation Research Quality Workshop, September 15–16, 1986.

[25]E. G. Morgan, "The Right Interviewer for the Job," *Journal of Marketing*, 16 (October 1951), 201–2.

respondents reported later that they thought they were being interviewed for such purposes as establishing a credit rating, investigating past income tax returns, or determining whether their house met the requirements of the local building code. It is understandable that, under these conditions, the respondent might not be willing to give candid and informative answers to all the questions asked.

So far we have considered only the unwillingness of the respondent to provide accurate information. The investigator's side of the coin should also be considered. The investigator may be unwilling to obtain accurate information, even if the respondent is willing to provide it.

The most common form of this problem is interviewer cheating. The ways in which the interviewer may obtain inaccurate information deliberately and his or her motives for doing so are limited only by ingenuity and personality. It may be, for example, that an interviewer finds that a particular question is embarrassing to ask. As a result, the interviewer may decide to supply his or her own answer or to make an estimate or inference of what the respondent's answer would be if the question were asked. (It is probable that this happens relatively frequently with respect to the age and income of respondents.) At the other extreme, reports of "interviews" are occasionally submitted without the "interviewer" having taken the trouble to contact any respondents. A compromise between these extremes is the interviewing of friends but listing the names of the people that were supposed to be interviewed.

Like embezzling, interviewer cheating can be kept to a low level of incidence but not eliminated completely. Careful selection, training, and supervision of interviewers will eliminate much of the problem. In addition, control procedures can and should be established that will reduce it even more.

The simplest control procedure is the "call-back." If the interviewers are aware that a subsample of respondents will be queried after the interviewing reports have been turned in, the fear of being caught will discourage cheating. If the information on an initial interview is found to disagree significantly with that on the call-back interview, additional call-backs may be made on respondents originally interviewed by the same person.

Other control procedures include the analysis of responses obtained by each investigator and the use of "cheater" questions. In studies where the volume of information obtained makes it worthwhile to use machines for tabulation and analysis, analyses of the patterns of responses obtained by each interviewer can be made at very little additional cost. Significant variations from expected norms can then be investigated. In many telephone surveys, for example, this type of analysis is possible. Similarly, mall-intercept and other personal interview approaches involving respondents interacting with a personal computer can use these control procedures. Software packages such as CAPPA[26] and the Ci2 System are used to conduct interviews as well as to generate questionnaires.

The use of "cheater" questions in the questionnaire is a less widely used and publicized control device. Questions can be devised that will disclose fabricated answers with a reasonably high probability of success. Understandably, the research directors using this technique have not been interested in publicizing either the fact that they use

[26]P. E. Green, P. Kedia, and R. Nikhil, *Electronic Questionnaire Design and Analysis with CAPPA* (Palo Alto, Calif.: Scientific Press, 1985).

it or the type of questions they use. Response bias (in the context of inaccuracy related to the asking of questions) is also discussed in Chapter 7.

Nonresponse Error

A *nonresponse error* occurs when an individual is included in the sample to be taken but, for any of many possible reasons, is not reached. In most consumer surveys this is a source of a potentially sizable error.

Families who, after several attempts, cannot be reached generally have different characteristics than those who can be reached to provide information. For example, families in which all members are usually away from home during the day differ from those families in which at least one member can usually be found at home with respect to age, number of small children, and the proportion of time in which the wife is employed.

The seriousness of nonresponse error is magnified by the fact that the direction of the error is often unknown, and while the maximum error due to the nonresponse can be determined (by assuming that the nonrespondents would each have responded in a given way), it is difficult to estimate the actual magnitude of the error.

A method of estimating both the direction and the magnitude of the nonresponse error is that devised by Politz and Simmons.[27] In addition to the regular questions on the questionnaire, each respondent is asked on how many of k similar periods (evenings if the respondent is being interviewed in the evening) he or she would have been home.

For example, one typically sets up seven respondent groups, where the estimated proportion of the time persons in each group are at home is 1/7, 2/7, . . . ,7/7 of the time. Having done this, one estimates a total-sample mean by weighting the separate results of each group by the *reciprocal* of the estimated proportion of the time that the members of that group are at home. In this way respondents who are not often at home receive more weight (than those who are usually at home) in the calculation of the weighted mean.

So called not-at-homes are, of course, only one source of nonresponse bias. The other major source is refusals, which were discussed in Chapter 4.

The Personal Interview

As the name implies, the *personal interview* consists of an interviewer asking questions of one or more respondents in a face-to-face situation. The interviewer's role is to get in touch with the respondent(s), ask the desired questions, and record the answers obtained. The recording of the information obtained may be done either during or after the interview. In either case, it is a part of the interviewer's responsibility to ensure that the content of the answers is clear and unambiguous and that it has been recorded correctly.

While it is substantially more expensive on a per-completed-interview basis, the personal interview as a collection medium has several advantages relative to telephone interviews and mail questionnaires. It provides the opportunity to *obtain a better sample*,

---

[27]Alfred Politz and Willard Simmons, "An Attempt to Get the 'Not at Homes' into the Sample without Callbacks," *Journal of the American Statistical Association*, 44 (March 1949), 9–31.

since virtually all the sample units can be reached and, with proper controls and well-trained interviewers, nonresponse can be held to a minimum. It also gives the *opportunity to obtain more information*, as a personal interviewer can be of substantially greater length than either a telephone interview or a mail questionnaire. Finally, it permits *greater flexibility*. More freedom is provided for adapting and interpreting questions as the situation requires, especially in the case of unstructured personal interviews.

The limitations of the personal interview are the cost and the response bias that may be induced by poorly trained or improperly selected interviewers. The reader will recall the discussion of interviewer-induced response bias in the previous section. In a sense, the problems of the personal interview arise from its very nature in that it is bound up with social interaction and the communication of meaning in language.[28] A personal interview, after all, is an interaction between *strangers* often (but not always) on the respondent's territory, initiated by the interviewer.

For consumer research, major places of interviews for many studies are shopping malls, where the so-called mall-intercept method is used. This method involves having interviewers stationed at selected places in a mall and having them request interviews from people who pass by. Presumably the people are chosen on the basis of a predetermined sampling plan. At times, monetary incentives may have positive effects.[29]

To illustrate, Soft Care Apparel, a manufacturer of infant apparel, uses mall intercepts to test-market its new goods.[30] The company's new designs are compared with current designs and competitive designs in a type of simulated marketplace situation. The company feels that mall intercepts are effective because responses are obtained from all different types of people for assessing differences in regions.

The mall intercept method is perhaps the fastest-growing method of data collection in marketing research, whereas telephone interviewing is still the most widely used method. The two have many things in common but are also substitutable for each other. Bush and Hair compared the two methods in a study limited to one geographic area.[31] They found that the overall quality of data (completeness, depth) was about equal for each method. Yet the mall intercept yielded less distortion in data than the telephone approach. The telephone method seems to elicit more socially acceptable responses. A significantly lower participation refusal rate was obtained from the mall intercept. The following interesting conclusions were reached based on the methodological comparisons made:

- Mall intercept interviewing would be useful in obtaining personal information such as income, name, and telephone number in a face-to-face manner.

[28]The research interview as a form of complex social interaction is discussed in M. Brenner, "Interviewing: The Social Phenomenology of a Research Instrument," in *The Social Contexts of Method*, ed. M. Brenner, P. Marsh, and M. Brenner (New York: St. Martin's Press, 1978), pp. 122–39.

[29]F. Wiseman, M. Schafer, and R. Schafer, "An Experimental Test of the Effects of a Monetary Incentive on Cooperation Rates and Data Collection Costs in Central-Location Interviewing," *Journal of Marketing Research*, 20 (November 1983), 439–42.

[30]"Research Basic to Baby-Wear Business," *Marketing News*, 21 (February 13, 1987), 26, 28.

[31]A. J. Bush and J. F. Hair, Jr., "An Assessment of the Mall Intercept as a Data Collection Method," *Journal of Marketing Research*, 22 (May 1985), 158–67.

- More accurate and less distorted responses appear to be obtained in the mall intercept approach.
- The mall intercept would be a useful method for studies seeking information on forms of desirable and/or undesirable behaviors.
- Since mall intercept respondents are more frequent users of shopping centers, they may be better able to provide more brand and store-oriented information than the telephone respondent.

Although the mall intercept does not appear to be as well suited to probability sampling as other face-to-face interviewing methods, with control for frequency of shopping visit and use of quota sampling the mall intercept method can be a powerful approach for data collection.[32]

Closely related to the mall intercept for consumer research is data collection at the place of purchase. Such *in-store interviewing* asks questions about a just-made specific purchase decision and is conducted at the point of purchase. Obvious advantages of this method are (1) the respondent is usually in a proper state of mind, (2) the recall task is easier, (3) it is easier to contact actual purchasers of a target product category, (4) there are high response rates, and (5) the technique seems to be robust in its application. Applications include the study of competition, urgent marketing issues, and observation of consumer behavior.[33]

The Telephone Interview

Telephone interviews are often used in lieu of personal interviews, especially when the information must be collected quickly and inexpensively and the amount of information required is relatively limited.

The telephone interview is well suited to such research problems as determining "coincidental" viewing of television or listening to radio programs. In this type of study, calls are placed to a sample of telephone subscribers during the time the program is on the air. The person receiving the call is simply asked "Are you now watching television?" and, if so, "What program are you watching?" Other questions such as "How often do you watch this program?" "Who sponsors this program?" and the like may also be asked. The result is a rapid and inexpensive measurement of audience level. D'Lites of America, a restaurant chain, uses telephone tracking studies to gauge advertising awareness, product trial and retrial, and rejection of individual products or restaurants and to determine how D'Lites compares with its competitors with regard to service and quality.[34] Telephone interviews are also useful for early projections of the success of a new product. This type

---

[32]The issue of sampling is covered by S. Sudman, "Improving the Quality of Shopping Center Sampling," *Journal of Marketing Research*, 17 (November 1980), 923–31.

[33]See G. Meyers, "Consumers Offer 'Fresh' Purchase Data When Questioned in the Store," *Marketing News*, 21 (January 2, 1987), 28–29; and "PIT Stop Discovers Reason Behind Purchasing Habits," *Marketing News*, 20 (September 12, 1986), 1ff.

[34]"Restaurant Chain Credits Marketing for Growth," *Marketing News*, 19 (February 1, 1985), 21.

Exhibit 5-2   Almost All Types of Surveys Can be Conducted in Malls

Most marketing researchers realize that shopping-mall research facilities are useful for advertising and product tests. However, many such researchers do not seem to use malls for other kinds of marketing research, especially surveys. Person-to-person, mail, and telephone surveys are still the "favorites" of quite a number of researchers.

Shopping malls have become the new "main streets" of North America, visited by a broad cross-section of mobile consumers. If, indeed, a cross-section of consumers go to malls, it makes sense to use them for almost every type of marketing and social science survey. At the very least, it makes sense to include them among the viable alternatives being considered.

A research firm located in Winnipeg, Canada has done just this.* This firm opened its "permanent" facility in a mall in Winnipeg in 1970. At the time they interviewed 3,000 shoppers and asked a variety of demographic questions. Upon determining that the shoppers came from all over the area, the wisdom of doing personal interviews in the home, as opposed to the mall, was questioned. The company still uses other forms of data collection, when deemed appropriate.

The company's experience has been that with a *quota sample* by age, sex, and geographic location within a city or other area, and control questions to avoid interviewing the same people twice, the results have been excellent. Doing mall-situated research is faster and less costly than the telephone. Quality, too, is usually better. Often, many people seem to be more candid in malls than they are in other research environments. It may be that the mall is more anonymous and less threatening to them.

The Winnipeg research firm conducted a telephone survey of about 1,000 people throughout the province and found that 95% of the adults had visited one or more shopping centers during the year preceding data collection. At the time there were 30 malls in the province. In Winnipeg, where one-half of the province's population lives, 50% of the people had visited more than five malls during the year, and 70% had been to the one where the company had its facility. Since the company knows where nonusers of "its mall" are located, it can go to their malls when geographic reliability is needed.

*See P.M. Reid, "'Purists' May Disagree, But Almost All Types of Surveys Can Be Conducted in Malls," *Marketing News,* 18 (January 6, 1984), Section 1-p.5.

of interview was used for this purpose and to forecast market growth for the audio compact disc player.[35]

Either a *structured* or an *unstructured* interview may be held. Since the amount of information sought is usually well defined, nonconfidential in nature, and limited in amount, virtually all telephone interviews are structured in nature. This medium does not lend itself well to *indirect* interviews and has not been used much for this purpose.

The telephone interview has advantages in addition to speed and economy. It is frequently easier to get the cooperation of people over the telephone than in a personal interview. This is particularly true in industrial surveys, where an executive may be busy with appointments and unable to see an interviewer when he or she makes a personal call (if a prior appointment has not been made) but can be reached readily by telephone. Interviews by telephone may also successfully be conducted during evening hours, a time

[35]Shaprio and Schwartz, "Research."

TABLE 5-4. Telephone vs. Personal Interviewing

| | METHOD ATTRACTIVENESS | | | |
| | Telephone | | On-Site | |
CRITERIA	Quality	Cost	Quality	Cost
* Tuning-in to issues (getting a "feel" for the market)	2.5	3.0	3.0	1.5
* Open-ended questioning; probing (after the tuning-in process)	3.0	3.0	3.0	2.0
* Mode of analysis				
• Qualitative	3.0	3.0	3.0	2.0
• Statistical	3.0	3.0	2.5	1.5
* Sample size				
• Large	3.0	3.0	2.0	1.0
• Small	3.0	3.0	3.0	2.0
* Observation and/or demonstration	-0-	N/A	"10"	N/A
* Constituency-building (client relationship with key parties is reinforced)	2.5	3.0	3.0	2.0
* Quality control/administrative complexity	3.0	3.0	2.5	1.0
* Time pressure	3.0	3.0	2.5	1.5
* Cost/budget constraint	N/A	3.0	N/A	1.0
* Privacy/"anonymity"	3.0	N/A	2.5	N/A
* Minimal interruptions	3.0	N/A	2.5	N/A
* Response rate	3.0	N/A	2.5	N/A

Note: 3 = most attractive; 2 = acceptable; 1 = least attractive; "10" = absolute requirement; -0- = not appropriate; N/A = not applicable.

Source: J. J. Brock, "Phone Interviews Equal In-Person Methodology," *Marketing News*, 20 (January 3, 1986), 72.

when many people are reluctant to be interviewed personally. A recent study of national marketing research companies showed that for industrial marketing research (as well as general marketing research), telephone interviewing is usually as effective as personal interviewing for scope and depth of information that can be obtained (see Table 5-4).

The basic limitations of telephone interviews are the relatively limited amounts of information that can be obtained (at least compared with some alternative methods) and the bias that exists in any sample of subscribers. Subscribers have different characteristics than nonsubscribers, particularly with respect to income and location. The inability to include nonsubscribers in the sample may seriously affect the findings. Perhaps even more sample bias is introduced in the typical telephone survey by the high proportion of subscribers who are not listed in the directory, either because of having an unlisted number or as a result of moving. A technique for including unlisted telephone numbers in the sample frame is called random-digit dialing. This together with other telephone sampling approaches is discussed in Chapter 9.

Figure 5-4   Telephone Survey Response Decision Process

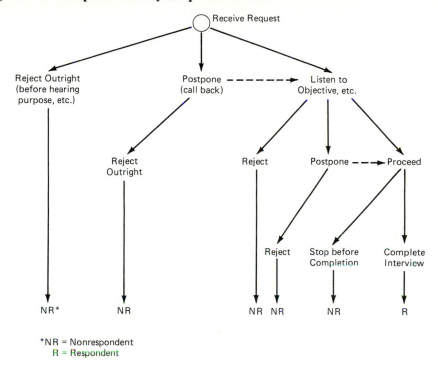

*NR = Nonrespondent
 R = Respondent

Additional problems associated with telephone interviewing are those of sample control and interviewer performance. Often this is manifested by inadequate efforts to complete interviews with some of the "harder-to-reach" respondents. Adding another sample is no substitute for dealing properly with the original sample. Usual control efforts require large clerical staffs to monitor results. Computerized control techniques that can more easily handle the factors involved are now available.[36] As computer-assisted telephone interviewing (CATI) becomes more prevalent, computerized control techniques become more essential.

An emerging aspect of telephone interviewing is the use of CATI.[37] By having the questionnaire on the computer the interviewer can proceed through it easily, which results in less interviewer-induced error. Software that allows this to be handled on personal computers is now available.

Telephone interviewing is an important methodology for marketing research. It is widely used but is sometimes "abused" by use of questionable techniques, particularly for consumer research. As shown in Figure 5-4, which is a schematic diagram of the

[36]M. A. Michetti and G. Kennedy, "On-Line Sample Control: Cost-Efficient Way to Raise Response Rates in Phone Surveys," *Marketing News*, 19 (January 4, 1985), 34; and E. Burg, "Computers Measure Interviewers' Job Performance," *Marketing News*, 20 (March 14, 1986), 36.

[37]The entire issue of *Sociological Methods & Research*, 12 (November 1983), is devoted to this topic.

telephone survey research response decision, only *one* of six possible outcomes results in a response. The researcher should strive to maximize the proportion of the original sample that does complete the interview.

The Mail Interview

Mail interviews have been widely used for a variety of purposes. Some indication of the extent of use, both by product or service and by geographic area, is provided by the fact that for several years the Soviet film industry has sponsored mail surveys to evaluate films.

Mail questions provide great versatility at relatively low cost. A questionnaire may be prepared and mailed to people in any location at the same cost per person: the cost of preparing the questionnaire, addressing the letter or card sent, and the postage involved. Unless the name is requested, the respondent remains anonymous and therefore may give confidential information that otherwise would be withheld. The respondent may also answer the questionnaire at his or her leisure, rather than being forced to reply at the time a personal or telephone call is made.

Serious problems are involved in the use of mail questionnaires, however. Perhaps the most serious is the problem of nonresponse. Typically, those people who are indifferent to the topic being researched will not respond. It is usually found necessary to send additional mailings to increase response. Even with added mailings, response to mail questionnaires is generally a small percentage of those sent; the modal response rate is often only 20 to 40%. Experiments involving preliminary contact by letter or telephone call, cover letters, and monetary inducements have increased response rates dramatically in some cases.

Other aspects of mail surveys that are of concern to research designers include follow-up, questionnaire format and length, survey sponsorship, type of postage, personalization, anonymity and confidentiality, deadline date premiums and rewards, and perceived time for task. Reported results of experiments involving these techniques vary, and there appears to be no strong empirical evidence that any one is universally better than the others except for the follow-up and use of monetary incentives.[38] There is no disagreement that use of a monetary incentive increases response rates significantly. Indeed, nonmonetary incentives also appear to have such a positive impact. A major concern, however, is how much the incentive should be. Typically, amounts range from twenty-five cents to one or two dollars. The key issue is whether a larger incentive is cost-effective. That is, Does it generate a sufficiently greater response to justify the added cost? For some studies, the use of a follow-up mailing may be an alternative to monetary

---

[38]Rather than try to summarize the findings of all the experiments we refer the reader to the following review papers, which are illustrative of those that have been prepared: T. A. Heberlein and R. Baumgartner, "Factors Affecting Response Rates to Mailed Questionnaires: A Quantitative Analysis of the Published Literature," *American Sociological Review*, 43 (August 1978), 447–62; R. A. Peterson and R. Kerin, "The Quality of Self-Report Data: Review and Synthesis," in *Annual Review of Marketing*, ed. B. Enis and K. Roering (Chicago: American Marketing Association, 1981), pp. 5–20; J. Yu and H. Cooper, "A Quantitative Review of Research Design Effects on Response Rates to Questionnaires," *Journal of Marketing Research*, 20 (February 1983), 36–44; and D. Jobber, "Improving Response Rates in Industrial Mail Surveys," *Industrial Marketing Management*, 15 (August 1986), 183–95.

Exhibit 5-3   Theories of Mail Survey Response

Why do people participate as respondents in a survey? The question is often asked by marketing researchers, perhaps all too often implicitly, and seldom is an answer provided other than in terms of specific techniques (including inducements) that have been used to increase participation. The following theories are among those proposed (and studied to varying degrees) as answers to the question raised at the start.

Exchange

The process of using mail survey techniques to obtain information from potential respondents can be viewed as a special case of "social exchange."* Very simply, social exchange theory asserts that the actions of individuals are motivated by the return (or rewards) these actions are expected to, or usually do, bring from others. Whether a given behavior occurs is a function of the perceived costs of engaging in that activity and the rewards (not necessarily monetary) one expects the other participant to provide at a later date. In order that survey response be maximized, then, three conditions must be present: (1) the costs for responding must be minimized, (2) the rewards must be maximized, and (3) there must be a belief by potential respondents that such rewards will, in fact, be provided.

Cognitive Dissonance

Cognitive dissonance theory appears to provide a mechanism for integrating, within a single model, much of the empirical research that has been done on inducement techniques for survey response.† As used for explaining survey response, the theory postulates that reducing dissonance is an important component of the "respond/not respond" decision of potential survey respondents.

The process is triggered by receipt of a questionnaire and cover letter asking for participation. Assuming that failure to respond might be inconsistent with a person's self-perception of being a helpful person, or perhaps at least one who honors reasonable requests, failure to respond will produce a state of dissonance which the potential respondent seeks to reduce by becoming a survey respondent. Since the decision process involves a series of decisions for some people, delaying the ultimate decision may be a way to avoid completing the questionnaire without having to reject the request outright and, thus, experience dissonance. Delaying a decision, therefore, may in itself be a dissonance-reducing response.

Self-Perception

Self-perception theory asserts that persons infer attitudes and knowledge of themselves through interpretations made about the causes of their behavior. Interpretations are made on the basis of self-observation. To the extent that a person's behavior is attributed to internal causes and is not perceived as due to circumstantial pressures, a positive attitude toward the behavior develops. These attitudes (i.e., self-perception) then affect subsequent behavior.

The self-perception paradigm has been extended to the broad issue of mail survey response.‡ To increase the precision of the paradigm the concepts of *salience* (behaviors one has attended to), *favorability* (the affect or feeling generated by a given behavioral experience), and *availability* (information in memory) are utilized. In addition, to enhance the effects of these on response, labels should be created. Labeling involves classifying people on the basis of their behavior such that they will later act in a manner consistent with the characterization. Self-perception would predict that labeling one's behavior would cause that person to view himself or herself as the kind of person who engages in such behavior; therefore, the likelihood of later label-consistent behavior is increased.

Commitment and Involvement

Of concern here are the ranges of allegiance an individual may be said to have for any system of which he or she is a member. Consistent behavior is a central theme, with the following characteristics: (1) persists over some period of time, (2) leads to pursuit of at least one common goal, and (3) rejects other acts of behavior.§ Consequently, the major elements of commitment are viewed as including the following:

1. The individual is in a position in which his or her decision regarding a particular behavior has consequences for other interests and activities not necessarily related to it.
2. The person is in that position by his or her own prior behavior.
3. The committed person must recognize the interest created by one's prior action, and realize it as being necessary.

A person who is highly committed to some activity is less likely to terminate the activity than one who is uncommitted.

The theory of commitment (or involvement) can be extended to explain survey response behavior. To do this requires recognition that commitment can be attached to many different aspects of a survey, such as the source or the sponsor, the researcher, the topic and issues being studied, and/or the research process itself. To a large extent, commitment is manifested by interest in what is being asked of the potential respondent. The following hypotheses (untested) can be proposed:

1. The less favorable the attitude toward a survey's sponsor, topic, etc., the less involvement with, and thus the commitment to, anything related to that study.
2. The less the extent of involvement, the more behavior productive of disorder (e.g., nonresponse, deliberate reporting of false information, etc.) is perceived as legitimate.

> 3. The more behavior productive of disorder is perceived as legitimate, the less favorable the attitude toward the survey.

*D. A. Dillman, *Mail and Telephone Surveys: The Total Design Method* (New York: Wiley-Interscience, 1978).

†D. Furse and D. Stewart, "Manipulating Dissonance to Improve Mail Survey Response," *Psychology and Marketing*, 1 (Summer 1984), 79–94.

‡C. Allen, "Perspectives on Mail Survey Response Rates: The Self-Perception Paradigm and Beyond," paper presented at the American Marketing Association Conference on Marketing Theory, 1982.

§H. S. Becker, "Notes on the Concept of Commitment," *American Journal of Sociology*, 66 (July 1960), 32–40.

Source: Adapted from G. Albaum and M. Venkatesan, "Explaining Survey Response Behavior," *Contemporary Research in Marketing*, Vol. 1, ed. K. Möller and M. Paltschik, Proceedings of the Annual Conference of the European Marketing Academy, June 1986.

incentives. That is, an initial mailing and follow-ups without an incentive may be more cost-effective and generate a greater response than one mailing with an incentive. One potential problem with using any incentive, monetary or nonmonetary, is that it may result in responses from people who otherwise might not respond, and the quality of such responses may be suspect.

When designing a mail survey, concern should be for the *total package* of survey procedures rather than any single technique.[39] Unfortunately, the literature rarely reports in this way. Instead, concern in the factorial experiments is for the significance of main and interaction effects. To illustrate how this can be misleading, consider a 2^4 factorial experiment. Traditional ANOVA analysis indicated no main or interaction effects. Yet the response rates for each of the "packages" ranged from 24% to 66%, giving rise to survey strategy differences.

Since the people responding to a mail questionnaire tend to do so because they have stronger feelings about the subject than the nonrespondents, biased results are to be expected. To measure this bias, it is necessary to contact a sample of the nonrespondents by other means, usually by telephone interviews. The low level of response, when combined with the additional mailings and telephone (or personal) interviews of nonrespondents, results in substantial increases in the per-interview cost. The initial low cost per mailing may therefore be illusory. On the other hand, *nonresponse validation* may indicate that population subgroups have not been omitted and that results may not be biased.

Additional limitations are the length of time required to complete the study and the inability to ensure that questions are fully understood and answers are properly recorded. Proper administration can hold this to a minimum.

[39]See D. A. Dillman, *Mail and Telephone Surveys: The Total Design Method* (New York: Wiley-Interscience, 1978).

By way of conclusion, we propose the following sequence of activities for an "optimal" mail survey:

1. Preliminary notification (letter, post card, telephone call)
2. First mailing
3. Reminder notice (post card, letter, telephone)
4. Follow-up mailing (one or more)
5. Nonresponse validation (based on a subsample of nonrespondents contacted by telephone)

Unpublished research has shown that the number of contacts positively affects response rates. Response varied from 10% using only stage 2 above to 24% using stages 1, 2, 3, and two follow-ups (stage 4). Thus, each additional contact seemed to generate an additional 3–4 percentage point increase in response rate.

Variations

A variation of the mail interview that is frequently used is the *warranty card*. Most consumer durables have a warranty card included in the package or crate. The buyer is instructed to fill out the card and send it to the manufacturer if he or she wishes to take advantage of the warranty. Information is usually requested on where the item was purchased, what kind of store or outlet sold it, and when it was purchased. If the item is of the type that may be used as a gift (an electric shaver, for example), information on the purpose of the purchase is also sought. Although warranty cards do not provide an extensive amount of information, response rates are substantially higher than for the usual mail questionnaire.

Another variation of the mail questionnaire is the use of *telegrams*. Although this method of requesting information is used infrequently, it has the advantage of rapidity and a relatively high rate of response. Apparently, people who receive telegrams requesting information are impressed and somewhat flattered by the trouble taken to solicit information from them. Offsetting these advantages, however, is the limitation on the amount of information that can be obtained and the obvious higher cost of the medium.

A third variation of the mail questionnaire is the questionnaire that is delivered personally and is either returned via a representative of the research organization or by mail. Dealer surveys are often conducted in this manner, the salespeople calling upon them being used to deliver the questionnaire.

A fourth variation is the questionnaire that is either printed or inserted in a newspaper or magazine. Potential respondents are requested to mail this back to a designated address. Among the many problems with this approach is the lack of any formalized control over the sample. Yet, despite this major limitation, the approach does have a possibility of better hitting the target population, depending on the match between the readership and the population of interest.

A similar method has been used for surveying audiences to classical entertainment.

Surveys are inserted into the program and the respondent is asked to complete the survey and leave it in a designated place. This approach can lower administration and return costs but can lead to greater costs in terms of technical quality. This can be minimized by sound control over the research procedure.[40]

Yet another variation that combines the monetary incentive and the questionnaire is the *answer check*. That is, the questions to be answered are printed on the back of a commercial bank check. The major benefit of this approach is reduced cost. This lower cost is obtained, however, at the expense of the amount of information obtainable and the low response to open-ended questions.

Potential survey respondents are being exposed directly to high technology and the electronic age in surveys. Automated polling machines, which are portable, are being used to conduct surveys in retail stores, hotels, casinos, shopping malls, and other places.[41] These are interactive machines whose reliability has proved to be very good.

Pretesting

A distinction should be made between a *pretest* and a *pilot survey*. Pretesting is an activity related to the development of the questionnaire or measurement instrument to be used in a survey or experiment. In contrast, a pilot survey is a small-scale test of what the survey is to be, including all activities that will go into the final survey.

Pretesting a questionnaire answers two broad questions: (1) whether or not we are asking "good" questions and (2) whether or not the questionnaire flows smoothly and the question sequence is logical. Pretesting does not, however, ensure that the questionnaire (or even the survey) will be valid, particularly content valid. It has been suggested that for most surveys, a pretest of 30–100 interviews is adequate, provided all subgroups in the main survey population are covered.[42] Ideally, the sample for the pretest should mirror in composition that of the main survey. We discuss questionnaire design per se in Chapter 7.

The pilot study is designed to ascertain whether all the elements in the survey fit together. Thus, questionnaire pretesting may be part of the pilot study but normally should not be. One aspect of the pilot survey is that it can help in deciding upon the size of the original sample for the main survey. Response to the pilot can be used together with the desired obtained sample size to arrive at what size the original sample should be.

Both pretesting and pilot surveys can provide information helpful in managing some of the sources of potential research error. Moreover, in the long run they can both cause a survey to be more efficient and effective.

---

[40]P. Acito and M. Clouthier, "Research in Performing Arts: 8 Tips," *Marketing News*, 19 (January 4, 1985), 4.

[41]See "Stores, Campuses Use Poles for Polls," *Marketing News*, 19 (May 24, 1985), 25ff; and P. Suneson and E. Cadotte, "Research Suggests Automated Polling Machines Yield Reliable and Valid Data," *Marketing News*, 18 (January 6, 1984), Sec. 1 pp. 8, 9.

[42]M. Dale, "Survey Pretesting Can Save Time, Money in the Long Run," *Marketing News*, 19 (March 19, 1985), 6.

THE USE OF PANELS

Panels are widely used in marketing research. In the preceding chapter we discussed the *continuous panel* as used by syndicated services such as Market Research Corporation of America. In this chapter we present some general characteristics of panels.

Although the panel concept has been used in industrial marketing research, by far its major application has been in studying consumer purchase and consumption patterns, as well as other aspects of consumer behavior. For example, effective use has been made of panels in developing early forecasts of long-run sales for new products. There are major commercial consumer panel organizations, and a number of consumer product companies maintain their own panels or create short-term "ad hoc" panels as the need arises to test new products. In addition, several universities now maintain consumer panels to obtain research data and to generate revenues by providing data to others. Moreover, the application of electronic and communications technology has encouraged new types of panels using advertising delivery via split-cable television and in-store scanner-recording of purchases.

The distinguishing feature of a panel is repeated data collection from a sample of respondents on the same topic.[43] The repeated collection of data from panels creates both opportunities and problems. Panel studies appear to offer at least three advantages over one-time surveys: (1) deeper analysis of the data is possible so that the researcher can, for example, determine whether an overall change is attributable primarily to a undirectional shift for the whole sample or reflects overlapping changes for subgroups; (2) additional measurement precision is gained from matching responses from one interview/data collection point to another; and (3) panel studies offer flexibility that allows later inquiries to explain earlier findings. Because responses are obtained at two or more times, the researcher assumes that "something" happens or can happen (i.e., changes may occur) during the time interval that is of interest. In fact, it is just such changes, analyzed in the form of a *turnover table,* that provide the heart of panel analyses.[44] Assume that we have changed the package in one market for a brand of tissue called Wipe and that we rank a survey of 200 people purchasing the product two weeks before the change (T_1) and a similar measure for the week after change (T_2). The results are shown in Table 5-5. Both (A) and (B) tell us that the gross increase in sales of Wipe over X (this represents all other brands) is 20 units (or 10%). However, only the turnover table from the panel in (B) can tell us that 20 former buyers of Wipe switched to X and that 40 former buyers of X switched to Wipe. In those instances where there is experimental manipulation (e.g., introduction of a new product or the use of split-cable advertising), the manipulation is presumed to cause changes between Time X and Time X + 1. We discuss panels and experimental design in Chapter 6.

Panel studies are a special case of longitudinal research, where respondents are typically conscious of their ongoing part in responding to the same or similar questions

---

[43]See S. Sudman and R. Ferber, *Consumer Panels* (Chicago: American Marketing Association, 1979).

[44]See B. Levenson, "Panel Studies," in *International Encyclopedia of the Social Sciences,* Vol. II, ed. D. Sills (New York: Macmillan and Free Press, 1968), pp. 371–79; and F. Nicosia, "Panel Designs and Analyses in Marketing," in *Market and Economic Development,* ed. P. Bennett (Chicago: American Marketing Association, 1965), pp. 222–43.

TABLE 5-5. Change in Sales of Wipe Between T_1 and T_2 (hypothetical data)

(A) Cross-Sectional

	T_1	T_2
Bought Wipe	100	120
Bought X	100	80
Number of Purchasers	200	200

(B) Panel

		T_1		
		BOUGHT WIPE	BOUGHT X	
at T_2	Bought Wipe	80	40	120
	Bought X	20	60	80
		100	100	$N = 200$

over a period of time. This consciousness of continuing participation can lead to *panel conditioning*, which may bias responses relative to what would be obtained through a cross-sectional study. As in any effort at scientific measurement, the researcher should be concerned with threats to internal validity, since internal validity is a precondition for establishing with some degree of confidence the causal relationship between variables. Another issue of concern is *panel attrition*, the extent of nonresponse that occurs in later waves of study interviewing. Some persons who were interviewed at the first time may be unwilling or unable to be interviewed later on.

Distinguishing characteristics of panel types are many. We have already mentioned different types of sponsoring organizations (e.g., commercial), permanence (continuous or ad hoc), and research design (nonexperiment). Panels can also be characterized by geographic coverage (ranging from national to local), whether a diary is used, data collection method (all types are used), sampling method employed for a given study (probability or not), and type of respondent.

A unique type of panel is the *scanning diary panel*. This panel involves recruiting shoppers in the target market area to participate in the panel, and each person typically is compensated for participation. An identification card (similar to a credit card) is given to each member of the panel household. At the end of a normal shopping trip in a cooperating store, the card is presented at the start of the checkout process. This identifies the respondent for input of purchases into the computer data bank. The types of information available from this type of panel are similar to those discussed in the preceding chapter for scanner-based syndicated services. An added advantage here, of course, is that there is a carefully designed sample providing purchase data.

One last comment about panels is that they are often used for a cross-sectional study. When used this way and only one measurement is made, the panel is merely the source of a sample (i.e., the sample frame).

OBSERVATION

The remaining major method of collecting information is through observation. *Observation* is used to obtain information on both current and past behavior of people. Rather than asking respondents about their current behavior, it is often less costly and/or more accurate if the behavior is observed. We clearly cannot observe past behavior, but the *results* of such behavior are often observable. For example, instead of asking such questions as "What brand of television set do you own?" and "Is it equipped to receive programs on UHF channels?" the best and simplest procedure may be simply to look at the set.

Observation may be used as the sole means of collecting data or, as is frequently the case, it may be used in conjunction with other means. It is a method that should always be considered in designing marketing research investigations that call for information on past or current behavior. In some circumstances, observation is the *only* means of collecting the data desired. Department managers in Lord and Taylor's department store in New York City will need information on the prices of similar products at Bloomingdale's if they want to ensure that their prices remain competitive. The observation of Bloomingdale's prices through "shopping" is the only means of collecting this information. As a matter of practice, both department stores continuously "shop" each other to determine prices.

In other circumstances, alternative methods of collecting information are available, but observation may be the preferable method from either considerations of *cost*, improved *accuracy*, or both. Respondents often cannot and sometimes will not report information accurately. In the example cited above the respondent may not remember the brand of the television set and may very well not understand what "UHF" means. Brands usage reports of well-established brands generally show a "halo effect," an upward bias reflecting the prestige the respondent associates with the use of the brand. The Johnson Wax Company, for example, has found that respondent reports of brand purchases of floor wax vary widely from the actual brand floor wax that the consumer has on hand.

TABLE 5-6.   Dimensions of Observational Techniques

Natural/Contrived:
    Natural observation involves observing behavior as it occurs normally in the environment, whereas
    Contrived observation involves observing behavior in an artifical environment.
Disguised/Undisguised:
    Disguise concerns whether or not the people to be observed are aware they are being observed.
Structured/Unstructured:
    The distinction is whether the approach to be followed is specified in detail including what behaviors
      are to be observed in the first place.
Direct/Indirect:
    Behavior can be observed as it occurs (direct) or in the form of a record of past behavior (indirect).
Human/Mechanical:
    The main distinction here is whether or not a human observer is used.

Source: Adapted from T. C. Kinnear and J. R. Taylor, *Marketing Research*, 3rd ed. (New York: McGraw-Hill, 1987), pp. 398–400.

The major applications of observation as an information-collection method may be classified into the categories of the *audit,* coincidental *recording devices,* and a general classification, *direct observation.* Within this classification schema, observation techniques can be distinguished on the basis of extent of naturalness, disguise, structure, directness, and human involvement (see Table 5-6).

The Audit

Audits are performed in practice on both distributors and consumers. The *distributor audit* is the more widely known of the two.

The commercially available Nielsen Retail Index, an audit of retail stores performed regularly, was described in Chapter 4. As indicated there, data from this and audits available through other research agencies provide estimates of *market size, market share, geographic pattern of the market, seasonal purchasing patterns,* and *results of promotional and pricing changes.*

Manufacturers often perform their own audits of distributors through their salespeople. Although the data collected are not as comprehensive as those described above, information on inventories and prices can usually be obtained and reported. These salesperson audits have the additional advantage of ensuring that the salespeople check inventories and prices as a routine part of their sales calls. Improved sales performance is an important co-product of such an auditing program.

Pantry audits of consumer homes is the second type of audit that is sometimes performed. In this type of audit, the field worker takes an inventory of the brands, quantities, and package sizes that the consumer has on hand. When this type of audit is performed on a recurring basis, inconspicuous labels may be attached to the package showing the date the item was first included in the inventory. When the audit is combined with questioning of the consumer, an estimate of usage may be made. The pantry audit is relatively expensive in terms of data obtained, compared with a self-reporting consumer panel, however. Its use has declined as the use of consumer panels has increased.

Recording Devices

A number of electromechanical devices for "observing" the behavior of respondents are in use in marketing research. Some of these devices are used primarily in laboratory-type investigations and others for recording behavior in its natural setting. Illustrative of the types of *recording instruments* used in laboratory studies are the eye camera, the pupilometric camera, and the psychogalvanometer. Three of the devices used in non-contrived situations are the motion-picture camera, the video camera, and the Audimeter.

The "observing" of respondent behavior in a laboratory situation with the aid of recording devices has been largely confined to the pretesting of advertising. *Eye cameras,* for example, are specially designed cameras that record eye movements in relation to the specific location of material on a page. Subjects may be given an advertisement and, through the use of the photographic record provided by the eye camera, analyses can be made of the pattern in which the advertisement is "read." A determination may be made of which parts of it tend to attract attention initially, the relative amounts of time spent in looking at the illustration versus that used for reading the copy, which portions of the copy are actually read, and so on.

The *pupilometric camera* photographs eye movements of an entirely different sort and for a different purpose. The dilation and restriction of the pupil of the eye has been found to correlate with the degree of interest aroused by the visual stimulus. Interest-arousing stimuli result in the dilation of the pupil. An advertisement or a product that has a pleasurably toned interest to the subject will be evidenced by dilation of the pupil. Further, there are indications that the *extent* of pupil dilation will indicate *degree* of interest. While this technique has not yet been fully validated, it shows some promise as a means of measuring consumer interest.

The *psychogalvanometer* is used for measuring the extent of the subject's "response" to the advertisement. The principle involved is that the perspiration rate of the body is increased by excitement. The amount of stimulation provided by an advertisement, there-fore, can be measured by recording changes in perspiration rate. This is done by measuring the change in electrical resistance in the palms of the subject's hands.

Other devices are also used for "observing" behavior under laboratory conditions. In general, all such devices have the advantage of permitting careful and detailed ob-servations of behavior that could not be made otherwise. They have the added advantage of providing permanent records of the behavior observed. In using these devices, however, one should always keep in mind two important questions: (1) Is the behavior we are observing a valid predictor of the behavior we want to predict? and (2) Are the subjects behaving as they would in a natural situation?

The answer to the second question can clearly be in the affirmative if the observation is made outside the laboratory and in the natural situation. Hidden *motion-picture cameras,* for example, are used in many situations to record respondent behavior. One such ap-plication was a study performed for a manufacturer of frozen juice concentrates who was considering changing the design and amount of information given on the label. Before this change was made, information was needed on the extent to which consumers actually read information on labels. Hidden cameras were stationed in a sample of supermarkets in front of the frozen food cases, and pictures were taken of consumers selecting frozen juice concentrates. An analysis of these pictures indicated that far more time was spent in the selection and more careful attention given to the label than had previously been believed to be the case.

The *Audimeter* is another device for recording respondent behavior under normal conditions. It is, in effect, an electromechanical equivalent of the consumer "diary" so far as obtaining a record of television viewing is concerned. It is used by the A. C. Nielsen Company to record automatically the times the television set is turned on and off and the stations which it is tuned. It is installed in the television sets of a selected panel of families. The tapes on which the recording is made are collected and the National Nielsen TV Ratings is issued every two weeks. Measurements of *total, average,* and *share* of audience are available to clients.

This method of recording the viewing behavior of set owners has some obvious advantages. It permits a complete and accurate record to be obtained of the programs to which each set included in the panel was tuned. Careful analyses can be made of switching during a program to determine the effect of competing programs and of commercial messages. It has the limitation shared by all fixed-sample collection procedures with respect to the inability of obtaining a completely random sample. It also fails to provide information concerning the number of viewers of the program that are tuned in or, indeed, whether the program is actually being watched at any particular time.

Direct Observation

Direct observation of people and how they behave in situations of interest is a commonly used method of collecting information. Many studies have been made of shopping behavior to determine the relative effects of such variables as displays, availability, and reliance on salesperson advice on the brand selected and the quantity purchased. Supermarkets and department store managers continually rely on observation of traffic flows and length of waiting lines to determine the proper location of the various lines of products and the number and location of salespeople and cash registers. An important consideration in the location of banks, retail stores, and entire shopping centers is the amount and pattern of traffic at alternative sites.

Information obtained from direct observation of purchasers can be highly useful in helping to answer such questions as

- Who actually buys the products?
- Do they appear to be influenced by an accompanying person?
- To what extent do brand choices appear to have been made earlier versus at the point of purchase?
- What proportion of shoppers appear to check prices?
- What proportion of shoppers study the package before purchase?

Direct observation of purchasers has some obvious limitations. Though perhaps more serious to the subjectivist that the objectivist, some of the limitations are important to both. It is apparent that the observers will selectively perceive and record those actions that seem meaningful to them. Thus, the selection of acts to record will depend on the behavioral model of the observer. Direct observation discloses *what* rather than *why*. Motivation must be inferred. Inferences are often difficult to substantiate as a result of lack of control over important variables

Participant observation, as the name implies, is a form of observation in which the observer actually participates in the activities of the group he or she wishes to study. Examples are anthropologists who live with native tribes, labor economists who join a union, and a sociologists studying poverty who move to a low-income neighborhood. This form of observation has been rarely used in marketing research, as by their nature marketing activities do not usually lend themselves well to such a technique. Participant observation studies of both industrial and retail salespeople have been made, however.

Unobtrusive Measures

Observation is the method of data collection underlying a set of methods known as *unobtrusive measures*. By their very nature these are nonreactive measures. Included are all the types mentioned in this section. In addition, other types of unobtrusive measures are *traces* and *archives*. Regarding traces, studies of garbage can tell much about consumers. There is the "classic" study of alcoholic beverage purchases in a "dry" community in which types and brands purchased and consumed were determined by examining residents' garbage.

Archives, which include published data and internal records, also are a form of observation. In fact, such data are the only way we can observe past behavior. Sales invoices disclose much about how buyers have behaved in the past.

For a more detailed discussion of these fascinating methods we refer the reader to other sources.[45] In many cases it is desirable to use these methods in conjunction with other more traditional ones. This is the process known as *triangulation*.

DIRECT VERSUS INDIRECT RESEARCH TECHNIQUES—AN ASSESSMENT

Opinion has been divided among practitioners about the role and relative merits of indirect research techniques in marketing research. This division reflects in marketing research the objectivist–subjectivist debate in the behavioral sciences in general. The controversy has largely centered on three areas: the applicability of the techniques, samples selection and sizes employed, and the accuracy of utilizing disguised modes of obtaining such information.

Applicability of Indirect Research Techniques

The basic premises leading to the *use* of indirect research techniques are as follows:

1. The criteria employed and the evaluations made in most buying and use decisions have emotional and subconscious content.
2. This emotional and subconscious content is an important determinant of buying and use decisions.
3. Such content is not adequately and/or accurately verbalized by the respondent through direct communicative techniques.
4. Such content is adequately and accurately verbalized by the respondent through indirect communicative techniques.

---

[45]See E. Webb, D. Campbell, R. Schwartz, and L. Sechrest, *Unobtrusive Measures: Nonreactive Research in the Social Sciences* (Chicago: Rand McNally, 1966); L. Sechrest, ed., *Unobtrusive Measurement Today* (San Francisco: Jossey-Bass, 1979); and T. J. Bouchard, Jr., "Unobtrusive Measures: An Inventory of Uses," *Sociological Methods & Research*, 4 (February 1976), 267–300.

How valid are these premises? From the earlier discussion of specific cases, we have already seen that they are valid for some problems. Conversely, it is not difficult to cite cases in which one or more of the premises are not valid. The general answer to the question of whether the premises are valid or not must then be that it "depends on the problem."

As it stands, this is a correct but not a very satisfactory answer. To extend it somewhat and to give it more meaning, it is useful to review the categories of situations in which information might reasonably be sought from respondents and to decide in which of these categories indirect research techniques are the proper ones to apply. Four situational categories can be distinguished in which information might be sought from respondents.

First is the category in which *the information desired is known to the respondent and he or she will give it if asked*. Direct questioning will therefore provide all of the needed information in this situation. If the reason a consumer does not buy brand X tires is because he believes they do not wear as well as they should, he will willingly say so given the opportunity.

Second, *the information desired is known to the respondent, but he or she does not want to divulge it*. Matters that are considered to be private in nature, that are believed to be prestige- or-status bearing, or that are perceived as presenting a potential respondent–investigator opinion conflict may not be answered accurately. That many people do not fly because they are afraid to do so; that stout people often do not diet because they are afraid that they will not gain the social acceptance they desire anyway; that otherwise quiet and retiring people sometimes buy powerful cars because it gives them a feeling of superiority on the highway are not reasons that will likely be expressed openly and candidly in response to direct questions. When underlying motivations of this general nature are believed to exist, indirect techniques are well suited to elicit such information.

Third, *the information desired is obtainable from the respondent, but he or she is unable to verbalize it directly*. When respondents have reasons they are unaware of, such as the association of the use of instant coffee with lack of planning and spendthrift purchasing, or the refusal to accept a palatable aspirin because of the association of effectiveness of headache remedies with the requirement that they be taken with water, properly designed and administered indirect techniques can be highly useful for uncovering such motivations.

Fourth, *the information desired is obtainable from the respondent only through inference from observation*. In some cases motivations of respondents are so deepseated that neither direct nor indirect methods of questioning will bring them to the surface. An experiment in which the same detergent package in three different-colored boxes resulted in the opinion of housewives using them that the detergent in the blue box left clothes dingy, that the one in the yellow box was too harsh, and that the one in the blue-and-yellow box was both gentle and effective in cleaning is an illustration of color association and its effect on assessment of product quality that very likely would not have been discovered through either direct or indirect questioning. In another experiment, orange-scented nylon hose placed on a counter in a department store next to identical, but unscented, hose were bought by approximately 90% of the women making purchases.

Questioning of the women who bought the scented hose as to why they preferred the hose they bought resulted in answers such as "of better quality," "sheerer," and the like.

Of these four informational categories, two of them lend themselves to the use of indirect research techniques. It remains, of course, for the analyst to decide in which one or more of these categories the information he or she requires will fall.

While not the universally applicable methodology nor the panacea that some proponents have claimed, indirect research techniques can provide information on some types of marketing problems that is not now obtainable by other means.

Sample Selection and Sizes

The subject of sampling is considered in detail in subsequent chapters. However, it is desirable to examine here the typical sampling procedures and practices that have been used in "motivation" or *qualitative* research studies, as this has been an area of considerable controversy.

Sample selection in motivation research studies has tended to be done on nonprobabilistic (purposive) bases rather than by probabilistic methods. Typically, selection has been on a judgement or quota basis. As an illustration, the instructions to interviewers in the Pan American Coffee Bureau study asked each interviewer to select two respondents: "one male and one female; one 'dark strong' coffee drinker, one 'light weak' coffee drinker; one 'heavy drinker' (6–8 cups); one 'light drinker' (2–3 cups per day)." Although this sample was selected for exploratory purposes, unfortunately it is not an isolated example.

Serious sampling errors can result from purposive sampling, and, in any case, the extent of the sampling error is unknown. One of the reasons often given for using purposive rather than probability sampling is the high nonresponse rate. To refer again to the coffee study cited above, the statement was made in the instructions to the interviewers, ". . . it would be most helpful . . . if you could just get people talking freely on all their feelings about coffee for an hour or so." One can well imagine that some sample members would be reluctant to spend this much time in an interview.

A second area of controversy over the samples typically taken in motivation research studies relates to their *size*. Generally, samples have been small, often ranging from 20 to 50 in size. The use of a small sample in a motivation research study suggests that the population of psychological attributes and motivations being sampled is sufficiently homogeneous that only a limited sample is required to provide an adequate representation of the population. However, the bulk of the evidence amassed by psychologists suggests that motivations are myriad and varied in their effect on behavior. To assume that the motivations of a very small group of people adequately represent those of the population at large is to ignore the high degree of variability that empirical studies have substantiated.

The Validity of the Findings

What about the validity of indirect research findings? How has their performance in these respects compared with that of the more conventional research methods?

The question of validity of findings is, of course, the heart of the issue here, as it is in the general objectivist–subjectivist controversy. Unfortunately, to raise the question is to beg it; no definitive answer can be given. As has already been indicated, the answer is necessarily conditional on the nature of the problem being investigated.

An observation does need to be made, however, about the differences in judging validity by the "clients" of basic research versus those of decisional research projects. The client of the basic research project is the professional in the field. Judgement of the validity of findings of a study is a highly impersonal process and one that is seldom urgent. The purpose of the project is either to make the best estimate of a population parameter or to conduct the best test of a hypothesis within the constraints of available resources. In the absence of data that can be used for direct validation, the basic research project is judged tentatively on the basis of method. The rules of evidence for a basic research study require that the *procedures be public,* the *results investigator-independent,* and the project *replicable.*

Since indirect research methods violate each of these requirements to some extent, there has been a reluctance on the part of some basic researchers to give even tentative acceptance to unvalidated findings of studies that employ indirect methods. They tend to look upon indirect research methods as a means of generating hypotheses for testing by objectivist methods rather than as a source of valid findings.

The client for a decisional research project has a different set of requirements. Rather than wanting to be assured that the best estimate of a parameter or the most definitive test of a hypothesis has been made, the client needs information that will assist him or her in making the *best decision* possible in the circumstances. The procedures of the investigation need not be public, and there is seldom a need for replication. The client works directly with the researcher and is able to raise any questions he or she has about the project. The client usually will have had the opportunity to judge the validity of the findings of past research projects conducted by either the researcher or the organization for which he or she works. An assessment of validity of the findings must be made *now;* to await the outcome to determine if the findings are valid would obviate the very purpose for which the research was conducted. Judgment of degree of validity therefore turns out to be a much more subjective process in decisional than in basic research.

Indirect techniques serve several useful purposes in marketing research. They can be used to obtain information from respondents unwilling or unable to provide it by direct methods, to check the validity of responses to direct techniques, and to provide supplemental information. Included in the supplemental information that is of value is that which suggests hypotheses that can be tested by direct methods.

SUMMARY

In this chapter we first examined the various types of information that can be obtained from respondents.

We then considered communication as a means of obtaining information from respondents. The types of respondent interviews—structured–direct, unstructured–direct, and structured– and unstructured–indirect— were discussed. In the indirect types of interviews we described the more commonly used projective techniques, including the third-person technique ("What does your neighbor think of . . . ?"), word association, sentence completion, Thematic Apperception Tests, and depth interviews.

The media through which interviews may be conducted were then considered. The personal interview, the telephone interview, and the mail interview were discussed, including the merits and limitations of each. Also, the use of panels was presented in a general context.

We then considered the means of obtaining information through observation of respondents. The various forms of audits, recording devices, and direct *observation* were described and their applications discussed.

Finally, an assessment was made of direct versus indirect research techniques from the standpoints of applicability to marketing problems, sample selection and sizes, and validity of findings.

ASSIGNMENT MATERIAL

1. Indicate whether or you agree or disagree with the following statement and defend your position: *One of the important reasons for the use of surveys is that they can obtain sound information on what people's actions in the future will be.*

2. State the conditions under which you believe information on (a) past behavior and (b) intentions can each be a reliable predictor of future behavior.

3. You are a senior analyst in the marketing research department of a major steel producer. You have been requested to make a forecast of domestic automobile production for the forthcoming calendar year and, from this forecast, make a forecast of the total tonnage of steel that will be used by the automobile manufacturers.

   a. What information, if any, that could be obtained from respondents would be useful for making the forecast of steel tonnage that will be used by the automobile manufacturers? If it is concluded that no useful information could be obtained from respondents, so indicate and do not answer questions (b) through (d).

   b. What techniques are applicable for obtaining each item of information?

   c. Design a survey to obtain the information desired. Prepare all instructions, collection forms, and other materials required to obtain such information.

   d. Estimate the cost of conducting the survey you have designed.

4. You are product manager for brand M margarine, a nationally distributed brand. Brand M has been declining in absolute level of sales for the last four consecutive months. What information, if any, that could be obtained from respondents would be useful for determining the cause or causes of this decline?

5. You are the manager of product planning and marketing research for the personal appliances department of a large and widely diversified corporation. You have

under consideration a proposal to produce and market a hearing aid, an appliance line in which your company currently does not have a product.

a. What information, if any, that could be obtained from respondents would be useful for deciding whether to develop and introduce a hearing aid? If it is concluded that no useful information could be obtained from respondents, so indicate and do not answer questions (b) through (d).

b. What techniques are applicable for obtaining each type of information?

c. Design a survey to obtain the information desired. Prepare all instructions, collection forms, and other materials required to obtain such information.

d. Estimate the cost of conducting the survey you have designed.

6. Many people believe that projective techniques belong only in clinical psychology. What is your position on this issue?

7. Comment on the following statement: *The proper role of qualitative research is to suggest rather than to test hypotheses.*

8. Is it true that observation is a technique that is more effective in objective survey research than in subjective survey research? Why?

6

Experimentation

INTRODUCTION

Experimentation is receiving increased attention in marketing research. Marketing experiments have been conducted in such diverse activities as evaluating new products, selecting advertising copy themes, and determining the frequency of salespeople's calls. The purpose of this chapter is to acquaint the reader with the objectives of experimentation and to illustrate techniques for designing and analyzing marketing experiments.

We first describe the general nature of experimentation within the framework of a decision model, including such aspects as determining the value of the criterion variable in the model (the estimation and measurement problem), the functional form of the model, and the relevancy of the predictor variables to the decision problem. Also described are the steps involved in conducting a marketing experiment.

We then examine the potential sources of invalidity that may arise in an experiment. Together with the variable whose effect is of interest, these sources cause variation in an experiment and affect the dependent measure (i.e., criterion variable) being used.

Some of the major designs used in experimentation are then discussed. Both single variable designs (e.g., after-only with control and before-after with control) and multi-variable designs (e.g., factorial, randomized blocks, latin squares, and switch-over) are described. An experimental design can be viewed as concerned with identifying the sources of variation in an experiment.

In the next section of the chapter we discuss some of the difficulties encountered in designing field experiments in marketing. These difficulties involve the lack of stability of the environment over time, the impact of uncontrolled variables on the response data at any given time, and the uncertainty of extrapolating experimental findings to the marketing population of interest.

The last sections of the chapter are concerned with the use of continuous panels as experimental designs, a discussion of the limitations of the experimental method, and consideration of certain ethical issues that arise.

THE NATURE OF EXPERIMENTATION

In Chapter 4 we discussed experimentation as a source of marketing information. Two general types of experimental designs were identified—natural and controlled. A *natural experiment* is one in which the investigator intervenes only to the extent required for measurement, and there is no deliberate manipulation of an assumed causal variable. "Nature" produces the changes. In contrast, in a *controlled experiment* two kinds of intervention are needed: (1) manipulation of at least one assumed causal variable and (2) random assignment of subjects to experimental and control groups. An experiment having both types of intervention is known as a *true experiment*. When there is manipulation of variables but there is not random assignment of subjects, the design is known as a *quasi-experiment*.

All true experiments have certain things in common—treatments (i.e., assumed causal variables), an outcome measure, units of assignment, and some comparison from which change can be inferred and, it is hoped, attributed to the treatment. Quasi-experiments, on the other hand, have treatment, outcome measures, and experimental units but do not use random assignment to create the comparisons from which treatment-caused change is inferred. Rather, such comparisons depend on groups that differ from each other in ways other than the presence of a treatment whose effects are being tested.[1]

Objectives

The term *experimentation* is used in a variety of ways and for a variety of objectives which, for our purposes, should be distinguished. Some marketing researchers use the term synonymously with market *measurement* and *estimation*. In this use of the term it is assumed that the analyst has already formulated a model of how the phenomenon under study behaves and is interested only in obtaining numerical values for some of the parameters of the model. Considered literally, "experimentation" in this context does *not* involve a possible rejection of the model itself.

In other cases, experiments may be conducted for the primary objective of determining the *functional form* that links some criterion variable to a set of input variables. For example, a marketing analyst may postulate that sales response to increasing amounts

[1]Thomas D. Cook and Donald T. Campbell, *Quasi-Experimentation: Design and Analysis Issues for Field Settings* (Chicago: Rand McNally College Publishing, 1979), pp. 5–6.

of advertising is either linear or quadratic over some range of interest. The analyst may conduct an experiment to establish which functional form better fits the data.

In still other cases the experimenter may not even know what variables are relevant. An experiment may be conducted for the purpose of *identifying relevant variables* as well as the functional form of the model that links these variables with the criterion variable under study. In the discussion of this chapter we shall use the term "experimentation" in this third context, realizing that the term has been and will probably continue to be used in other ways as well. Perhaps the characteristic that best distinguishes experimentation from observational studies (which are also employed in measurement and estimation) is that the former term denotes some intervention and control over the factors affecting the response variable of interest to the researcher.

We have already discussed the nature of the term "cause" in Chapter 4. Experimentation permits the establishment of *causal relationships*. In contrast, correlation analysis (a useful technique in observational studies) permits the analyst to measure the degree to which changes in two or more variables are *associated* with each other.

Although we cannot infer causality from simple associations alone, correlation techniques are still useful. If association is found, we can use the results of this preliminary analysis to provide possible candidate variables for later experimentation.

As an illustration of tying in correlation analysis with experimentation, a major chemical firm was interested in the relationship of its antifreeze sales to changes in total expenditures for advertising. By using multiple regression analysis, the firm was able to establish an association between its sales and (regional) variations in advertising expenditures. Unfortunately, historical variations in past advertising expenditures by region had been too small to enable the firm to construct a sales-response function over a range of advertising sufficiently broad to be useful for policy purposes. Accordingly, a field experiment was designed that revealed the nature of the response function over a wide enough range to determine the "best" advertising expenditure level. Thus, the regression analysis first served to give insight into the variables that were affecting the sales-response function and later paved the way for direct manipulation of advertising expenditures.

Some Industry Examples

The use of experimental design principles is on the increase in marketing. To illustrate, a large western petroleum refiner was recently interested in what type of merchandise catalog to send out to its credit card customers to induce them to purchase various kinds of gift merchandise.

An experiment was designed in which three test catalogs were prepared covering the same merchandise at the same prices. However, the catalogs differed in terms of layout and copy. A set of marketing regions were chosen as experimental "blocks," and an equal number of each of the three test catalogs were sent to a random sample of credit card holders in each region. In addition to recording sales response to each test catalog, each merchandise order was analyzed to determine the credit card holder's extent of past purchases of the firm's catalog merchandise over the previous year.

A randomized block design (to be described later in the chapter) with past purchases serving as a covariate was used to analyze the data. After statistically adjusting for the effect of past purchases on current sales response, it turned out that one of the test catalogs resulted in 50% more purchases than the second catalog and almost 80% more purchases than the third. Needless to say, the company adopted the winning catalog for national distribution.

As a second example, a national producer of packaged candies was interested in children's preferences for various formulations of one of its well-known candy bars. Type of chocolate, quantity of peanuts, and amount of caramel were independently varied in a factorial design of 2 types of chocolate by 3 quantities of peanuts by 3 amounts of caramel.

Paired comparisons involving the 18 combinations were made up and evaluated by various schoolchildren between 8 and 12 years of age. Interestingly enough, the company found that preferences for type of chocolate varied with the amount of caramel. In addition, while children preferred more peanuts to fewer peanuts, the intermediate level of caramel was the most preferred. The company modified its formulation to match the most preferred test combination.

Another example is provided by Johnson Wax's use of different types of experiments prior to the introduction nationally of Agree Shampoo.[2] For the product itself, the test design used a blind-paired comparison among members of a mail panel. Products were given to 400 women and each was to be used for two weeks. At the end of the use period a telephone interview determined overall preferences and ratings for key performance attributes.

Next, Johnson Wax used a *lab test market*. This technique simulates the awareness, trial, and repurchase sequences by using a finished advertisement and final label product and by providing a shopping situation in a simulated store, actual use, and simulated repurchase. The lab test market was conducted in Fresno, California, and in South Bend, Indiana. The model predicted a market share that met the objectives of the marketing plan.

Finally, the product was test marketed in Fresno and South Bend by using controlled store tests. The test market was used not only for measuring sales and market share but also for testing elements of the marketing plan. On the basis of test market results, the product was then launched nationally.

The final examples of experimentation in industry involve the use of scanners in supermarkets and cable television.[3] Using two cities as test markets, Information Resources, Inc., of Chicago developed a service based on monitoring purchases by 2,000 households in each market at selected supermarkets and a type of split-cable capability that cable television stations can selectively send commercials to participants on a house-by-house basis. In one test, the objective was to determine the cost-effectiveness of a product sample as either an alternative or an accompaniment to television commercials to sell a children's food product. The household panelists were split into four groups of

---

[2]"Key Role of Research in Agree's Success Is Told," *Marketing News*, January 12, 1979, pp. 14–15.
[3]"Market Research by Scanner," *Business Week*, May 5, 1980, pp. 113–16.

1,000 and various combinations of samples and advertising were used. Sales doubled in all the groups receiving samples, but the group also exposed to advertising was more brand loyal over time. Another test looked at whether a switch to television advertising would benefit household products marketed chiefly through price promotions.

Many other experiments have been carried out involving taste testing, package design, advertising type and quality, price sensitivity, and other marketing variables.

INGREDIENTS OF A MARKETING EXPERIMENT

In Chapter 2 the research process in general was discussed in the context of a series of interrelated steps. In a similar manner, an experiment involves interrelated steps, as shown in Figure 6-1 (note the similarity to Figure 2-1). Our concern in this chapter is primarily with defining variables, designing the experimental procedure, and conducting the experiment. The other steps are discussed elsewhere in this book, and for experimentation they do not differ from general concepts.

All experiments involve three types of variables. First, there is the variable whose effect upon some other variable the experiment is designed to measure. In a causal study this variable is the presumed cause. Since this is the variable that is manipulated, it is known as the *treatment,* although it is often referred to as the *independent* variable. Marketing experiments often involve more than one treatment variable. When this is the case, the researcher may be interested in observing the effects of combinations of treatment variables, in addition to the effect of each one individually. In short, there may be *interaction* effects. Interaction refers to the situation where *the response to changes in*

Figure 6-1   Components of an Experiment

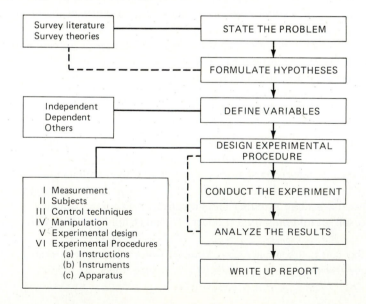

the levels of one treatment variable is dependent on the level of some other treatment variable(s) in the experiment. For example, suppose we design an experiment to measure the effects of price and advertising on the sales of a product. Not only will each of these two marketing variables, independent of the other, have an effect on sales, but the combination of the two may also have a separate effect.

The second broad type of variable in an experiment is the effect of interest. This is the outcome or *dependent* variable. In the preceding price and advertising example, the dependent variable was product sales.

The last category of variables consists of those other than the manipulated independent variable(s) that could influence the observed effects (i.e., dependent variable). These are known as *extraneous* variables, and unless controlled adequately they are the source of error(s) in an experiment. These will be discussed in a later section of this chapter.

The remainder of this chapter deals with designing the experimental procedure and conducting the experiment.

Measurement, Manipulation, and Experimental Procedures

A critical aspect of all experiments, indeed of all marketing research, is measurement. Our concern at this point is with the operational problems of measurement. The concepts, levels, and techniques of measurement, and scaling are covered in the next two chapters.

In a marketing experiment, it is the outcome or dependent variable that is measured. Generally, the operational measures used can be classified into verbal, electromechanical, and direct measures. *Verbal* measures include spoken and written responses. *Electromechanical* measures include those obtained from devices that measure such things as eye movements of advertising readership, pupil dilation, and responses to sensory stimuli obtained from using a psychogalvanometer or tachistoscope. Such devices are used in laboratory experiments. *Direct* measures are illustrated by dollar amount of sales, or profit, units of a product that are sold or consumed, and actual behavior of people under the conditions of the experiment.

Turning now to manipulation, an experimental treatment must be capable of variation. There are at least three ways in which variation in the independent variable can be achieved. First, there is the *presence versus absence* technique. This approach requires that the treatment be given to one group of subjects while another group does not receive the treatment. For instance, one group of people could be shown a new advertisement and their responses to an attitude measurement could be compared with the same type of response from a group that did not see the advertisement. Second, the *amount of a variable* can be manipulated, and different amounts are administered to different groups. This technique is used in such experiments as those where different prices for a product are "tested" and the outcome "units sold" is measured. Finally, the *type of variable* can be manipulated. For example, a company interested in the effect of image on some outcome measure could conduct an experiment by running a series of advertisements, each of which was designed to convey a different image of its product. Regardless of whether the dependent variable was attitude or sales, variation was generated in the type of image conveyed.

As with any approach to marketing research, all phases of an experiment should be carefully planned in advance. After decisions have been made concerning measurement, research subjects, experimental design, control techniques, and manipulation, there is the need to plan everything that will take place in the actual experiment itself through to the end of data collection. This includes the setting of the experiment, physical arrangements, any apparatus that will be used and its operation, data collection forms, instructions, recording of the dependent variable, and so forth.

Classical versus Statistically Designed Experiments

We are all familiar with the stereotype of the laboratory scientist who carefully fixes all factors (or treatment variables) assumed to affect the outcome of the experiment except the one whose effect he or she is trying to measure. If several factors are under study, the scientist then proceeds to fix all factors except the second one under study, and so on, until the effect of each factor is measured.

There are two things wrong with the "varying one factor at a time" approach. First, this procedure is inefficient in the sense that other experimental designs (to be described) yield more information per observation. Second, the procedure does not enable the researcher to measure any interactions that may exist among the experimental factors. For example, suppose that a laboratory scientist (working in the field of electrolytic chemistry) is attempting to study the effect of temperature and reagent concentration on the amount of copper deposited (per unit of time) on a steel bar. If the scientist holds the temperature constant, we assume that so many additional milligrams of copper are deposited per each increase of five percentage points in the electrolytic concentration. Similarly, holding the concentration of the electrolytic solution constant while varying the temperature results in so many milligrams of copper deposited per unit of time. If, however, the milligrams deposited per unit change in temperature *differ* among levels of electrolytic concentration, the "varying one factor at a time" approach will *not* reveal this tendency.

Both classical and statistically controlled experimental designs are discussed later in this chapter.

Difficulty of Control

In any experiment, extraneous factors could potentially affect the response. Those factors that probably would not influence the dependent variable can be ignored. On the other hand, those extraneous variables that might reasonably influence the dependent variable must be controlled in some way in order that error, and thus threats to valid inference, be minimized.

The concept of *control* has different meanings.[4] First, it may refer to the ability to control the situation in which an experiment is being conducted so as to keep out extraneous

---

[4]Cook and Campbell, *Quasi-Experimentation*, pp. 7–9.

forces. Used in this way, control is much easier to achieve in a laboratory environment than in a field setting. A second meaning of control refers to the ability to determine which subjects or test units receive a particular treatment at a particular time. Control over the treatment variable helps separate out the effects attributable to irrelevancies that are correlated with a treatment. The third meaning of control relates to a particular identified extraneous factor that the researcher has attempted to eliminate by the way the experimental procedures were designed and implemented or by measuring the factor and then in some manner using the measure in data analysis to remove its influence. The researcher working in the marketplace can more readily use control in our last two meanings than in the first one.

In general, then, control can be achieved by (1) designing the experiment appropriately, (2) making statistical adjustments through the use of such techniques as covariance analysis, and (3) incorporating one or more of the available control techniques into the design of the experiment. A problem in deciding how best to achieve control is that in a given experimental situation some extraneous factors will be known while others will be unknown.

In any experiment, control over all possible variables affecting the response is rarely possible. Even in the laboratory it is not possible to control *all* variables that could conceivably affect the outcome. But compared with the laboratory situation, the researcher who is working in the marketplace has a really difficult control job to do. In real-world market experimentation, it is not possible to come even close to holding other factors constant. Rather, the marketing researcher must try to design the experiment so that the effects of uncontrolled variables do not obscure and bias the nature of the response to the treatment variables that *are* being controlled.

An illustration should make this point clearer. Suppose that a marketing researcher is interested in conducting a series of taste-testing experiments for a new soft drink. Subjective interpretations of, say, "sweetness" may well vary from subject to subject. If half the subjects were asked to taste only an established soft-drink brand and the other half were asked to taste only the new brand, the average sweetness rating could mainly reflect the inherent perceptual differences between each group of subjects. A preferable procedure might be to have each subject taste each of two drinks on the assumption that intrasubject expressions of sweetness will affect each response approximately equally; that is, ratings will be expressed in terms of differences in sweetness over each subject. To avoid "ordering" effects on responses, the new and the control drink would be presented in randomized order or one-half of the group would follow the sequence "established-new" while the other one-half would use the sequence "new-established." To reduce carryover tendencies, the subject would be asked to take a sip of water between testing trials. This is the control technique known as *counterbalancing*.

Such attempts to control *confounding,* or the tangling effects of two or more levels of a treatment variable (or two or more treatment variables), are commonly used in experimentation. Ideally, the researcher would like to be able to show that the manipulated variables are related to direct measure of the underlying variables they have been designed to change and that such manipulations did not produce changes in measures of related but different constructs. The first situation is a widely used form of *manipulation check,* whereas the second condition refers to a *confounding check*. These two types of checks appear to have their greatest value during the pretest and/or pilot testing phases of an experiment. After all, they are of little use if the manipulation cannot be changed when a problem is identified.[5]

The fact remains, however, that confounding can *never* be entirely eliminated. Replicating (repeating) an experiment on a new test object or applying a second treatment to the same test object (after a "suitable" length of time) always leads to some confounding, since (1) obviously no two test objects will ever be exactly alike, and (2) the conditions of the environment will usually be different over the time lapse required to apply the second treatment, even if one assumed that a "treated" object could return to its original state after the first treatment.

A major contribution that statisticians have made to experimental design is the development of statistical models that feature *randomization* over uncontrolled variables so as to reduce the effect of these variables on *comparative* measures of response to the variables under the experimenter's control. In general, the use of "matched groups" (where subjects possess similar characteristics) and "before and after" experiments (where measurements are made before and after the treatments are applied) is to reduce variation in response through variables that are not of direct interest to the experimenter. Randomization is a useful device for ensuring, at least *on the average,* that uncontrolled variables do not favor one treatment versus others. Randomization is also useful for experiments using more classical designs. The purpose of randomization is to provide assurance that known and unknown extraneous factors will not cause systematic bias. Consequently, it is assumed that the effects of the extraneous variables will affect all groups in an experiment to the same extent.

The third major control technique is that of *matching,* which is sometimes called *balancing*. Matching is perhaps the best technique for increasing the sensitivity of the experiment—i.e., being able to detect the influence of the independent variable regardless of how small its influence may be. To increase sensitivity, the error variance must be reduced, and the best way for this to occur is to engage in some form of matching. For the marketing researcher, perhaps the most valuable types of matching are equating subjects and holding variables constant. In the former, subjects are equated on the variable or variables to be controlled. Thus, the composition of each group is essentially the same. In the taste-testing illustration, if it were felt that sex and age of subject would influence results, each group should have the same proportions of sex-and-age combinations. Matching by holding variables constant involves constancy of conditions for all groups. Again referring to the taste-testing experiment, the sex variable could be controlled by using only all males or females as subjects. If time of day is an important extraneous variable that could affect one's "taste buds," then subjects should be introduced into the experiment at approximately the same time on successive days. Similarly, if it were deemed desirable to control for experimenter effects, the same person might be used in all administrations of the taste experiment.

Test Objects

In the preceding discussion we have used the terms *test units, test objects,* and *subjects* frequently, and interchangeably all are used to refer to the units whose responses

---

[5]See B. C. Perdue and J. O. Summers, "Checking the Success of Manipulations in Marketing Experiments," *Journal of Marketing Research,* 23 (November 1986), 317–26.

to the experimental treatment are being studied. In marketing research the experimenter has a choice of three possible universes of test units—*people, stores,* and *market areas.* Which is most appropriate depends on the problem forming the basis of the experiment.[6]

The experimenter must contend with differences among the inherent properties of the test objects. For example, if a researcher is interested in the effect of shelf height on the sales of a packaged consumer product, it is to be expected that stores will vary in their amount of shopping traffic, placement of gondolas, and the like. If the experimenter is interested in the effect of various shelf heights on product sales over a variety of store sizes, several stores will have to be used in the analysis. If so, he or she may wish to use the technique of *covariance analysis,* in which responses to the controlled variables (shelf height) are adjusted for inherent differences in the test objects (stores) through measurement of these characteristics before (or during) the experiment.

In summary, the experimenter can use randomization, control groups, covariance analysis, and similar devices to reduce the impact of uncontrolled variations resulting from

1. Other environmental variables affecting response
2. Inherent differences among the test objects receiving treatments

so long as the interest is in *comparative* effects among the responses to variables under his or her control. In practice, however, the experimenter can never be sure that all uncontrolled sources of distortion have been guarded against or that even the very process of measurement does not distort the response of the test object being measured. The latter point is particularly true when the test object is a human being. It is not at all unusual to find distorted behavioral patterns when people know that they are participating in an experiment.

Our comments regarding the control of extraneous variables and the techniques used to achieve control are not exhaustive. We have, however, discussed some of the critical issues faced with such variables and we have covered the more widely used techniques for achieving control.[7] We now discuss the major extraneous variables that need to be controlled, as each poses a threat to the internal and/or external validity of an experiment.

SOURCES OF INVALIDITY

In Chapter 4 we briefly described experimental error as one of the major types of errors that can arise in the research process. At this point we discuss in more detail the various types of experimental errors. The way in which these errors arise is unique to the experimental method, although as an error source some may be part of other major types of error such as measurement, surrogate information, and sampling error.

---

[6]Some of the issues involved in the selection of type of test units are discussed briefly in Seymour Banks, *Experimentation in Marketing* (New York: McGraw-Hill, 1965), pp. 13–15.

[7]For a more in-depth treatment, see Larry B. Christensen, *Experimental Methodology,* 2nd ed. (Boston: Allyn & Bacon, 1980), Chap. 6.

Experimental errors relate to extraneous forces that can affect the outcome of an experiment. Each potentially has a bearing on the validity of an experiment and, consequently, they have often been called *threats* to validity. In the context of experimentation, validity essentially means the extent to which we really observe from an experiment what we say we observe. Four distinct types of validity have been identified—statistical conclusion, internal, construct, and external.[8]

A necessary condition for inferring causation is that there be covariation between the independent and dependent variables. *Statistical conclusion validity* involves the specific question as to whether the presumed independent variable, *X,* and the presumed dependent variable, *Y,* are indeed related.[9] This aspect of validity appears to be more closely related to tests of statistical significance used than magnitude estimates. After it has been determined that the variables covary, the question arises about whether they are causally related. This is the essence of *internal validity.* A given experiment is internally valid when the observed effect is due solely to the experimental treatments and not due to some extraneous variable(s). In short, internal validity is concerned with *how good the experiment is, as an experiment.* The third type of validity, *construct validity,* is essentially a measurement issue. The issue revolves around the extent to which generalizations can be made about higher-order constructs from research operations and is applicable to causes and effects.[10] Because construct validity is concerned with generalization, it is a special aspect of external validity. *External validity,* however, refers more broadly to the generalizability of a relationship beyond the circumstances under which it is observed. That is, external validity is concerned with how good an experiment is in terms of the extent to which conclusions can be made to and across populations of persons, settings, times, and so on.

To a large extent, the four kinds of validity are not independent of each other. That is, ways of increasing one kind may decrease another kind. Consequently, in planning an experiment it is essential that validity types be prioritized, and this varies with the kind of research being done. For applied research, our primary concern in marketing research, it has been observed that the priority ordering is internal, external, construct of the effect, statistical conclusion, and construct of the cause.[11] Accordingly, we now examine those extraneous factors that affect internal and external validity. Construct validity is discussed in Chapter 7, and factors affecting statistical conclusion validity are covered throughout the later sections of this book. The major potential sources of error that can affect internal and external validity are presented in Table 6-1.

Internal Validity

The kind of evidence that is required to support the inference that independent variables other than the one(s) used in an experiment could have caused the observed

---

[8]For a more detailed discussion, see Cook and Campbell, *Quasi-Experimentation,* Chap. 2.

[9]Robert Rosenthal and Ralph L. Rosnow, *Essentials of Behavioral Research: Methods and Data Analysis* (New York: McGraw-Hill, 1984), pp. 76–77.

[10]Cook and Campbell, *Quasi-Experimentation,* p. 38.

[11]Ibid., p. 83.

TABLE 6-1   Sources of Experimental Error

INTERNAL VALIDITY

1. History: The impact of an extraneous event that takes place between the pre-measurement and postmeasurement of the dependent variable.

2. Maturation: The results of an experiment are contaminated by changes within the participants with the passage of time.

3. Testing: The effect of a prior measurement on a later measurement.

4. Instrumentation: The effect of changes in the measuring instrument or process, including interviewers' instructions, over time.

5. Selection: Different kinds of research subjects have been selected for at least one experimental group than have been selected for other groups.

6. Mortality: The dropping out of different types of persons from experimental groups during the course of an experiment.

7. Statistical Regression: This may arise when experimental groups have been selected on the basis of extreme pretest scores or correlates of pretest scores.

8. Interactions with Selection: Independent effects of the interaction of selection with history and maturation.

EXTERNAL VALIDITY

1. Reactive Effect of Testing (Interaction): The impact premeasurement on the experimental subject's sensitivity or responsiveness to the treatment variable.

2. Reactive Effects of Experimental Situation: The effect(s) due to experimental subjects reacting to the experimental situation (such as setting, arrangements, and experimenter).

3. Interaction of History and Treatment: Measuring the dependent variable at a point in time that does not reflect the actual effect of the independent variable(s).

4. Interaction of Selection and Treatment: The extent to which the measured effect can be generalized to the population of interest.

effect(s) varies, depending on the independent variable(s) being investigated. However, there are some general classes of variables affecting designs that deserve mention (see Table 6-1). To illustrate each, suppose that the salesperson-retraining situation described in Chapter 4 had been set up as a controlled experiment. That is, one group of salespeople had taken a retraining course during a three-month time period while another group had not been retrained. The brand manager of a particular brand of detergent wanted to determine if the retraining was a producer (i.e., a cause) of sales performance. During the three-month period after retraining, sales of the detergent had shown an unusually large increase.

History deals with events outside the design that affect the dependent variable. History is therefore comprised of the producers that are extraneous to the design. In the salesperson-retraining example, the level of competitive promotion and advertising, the overall level of demand, or any one of many other producers may have changed substantially in some territories. Clearly, the longer the time period involved, the greater the probability that history will significantly affect the results.

Maturation is concerned with the changes that occur with the passage of time in the people involved in the design. For example, as time passes, salespeople gain more experience in selling and hence know their customers better, and the customers become better acquainted with the product. Again, the effect of maturation on the results is a direct function of the time period involved. Similarly, some biological and psychological changes within salespeople and customers over time can affect the performance of either.

Testing effect has to do with the effect of a first measurement on the scores of a second measurement. In particular, familiarity with a measurement (i.e., a test) can sometimes enhance performance because items and error responses are more likely to be remembered at later measurement sessions. Suppose that in both groups the attitudes of the salespeople toward their job, performance, the company, and so on, had been measured prior to and after the retraining program. There is the possibility that some responses obtained after the program was completed were due to remembering responses given on the first measurement rather than being independent responses at the time of measurement.

Instrument effect refers to the changes in the measuring instrument or process that may affect the measurements obtained. If total dollar sales volume per territory on a "before" and "after" basis were being used to determine the effect of retraining, a price change in the interim could clearly make a substantial difference. This is an obvious change in the measuring instrument, but many other and more subtle changes can occur. The learning process on the part of the investigators, a change in investigators, or simply boredom or fatigue may affect the measurements and thus the interpretation of results. A related issue arises when self-report instruments are used. When such instruments are used, it is the research subjects themselves who serve as recorders. Since subjects in the treatment group have had different experiences than control subjects (i.e., they have received the experimental treatment), there exists the possibility of a confounding of the instrument with the experimental treatment. This potential is strengthened when the purpose of the treatment is to change the subjects' understanding or awareness of the variable being measured. The salesperson-retraining program is of this type, as is an experiment designed to measure advertising's impact on attitude. An alternative to the pretest-posttest design is the *retrospective pretest-posttest* design. In this design, the pretest is given retrospectively after the treatment has been given. Not much is known about this technique, so we cannot generalize about its value in improving internal validity.[12]

Selection is concerned with the effect of the selection procedure for the test and control groups on the results of the study. If the selection procedure is randomized, the effect will be a measurable random variation. However, if the selection is by the investigator, self-selection, or some other nonrandom (purposive) procedure, the results will be affected in a nonmeasurable manner. Sizable systematic errors may well result. The concern, of course, is that the resulting groups may differ on important characteristics, and these differences may be influencing the dependent variable.

[12]See George S. Howard et al., "Internal Validity in Pretest-Posttest Self-Report Evaluations and a Re-evaluation of Retrospective Pretests," *Applied Psychological Measurement*, 3 (Winter 1979), 1–23.

Statistical regression may have an impact when experimental subjects are chosen on the basis of pretest scores. In this situation and when measures are unreliable, high pretest scorers will score relatively lower at the posttest and low pretest scorers will score higher. There is a tendency with repeated measures for scores to regress to the population mean of the group.[13] This could be operating in the retraining example if the group receiving retraining consisted of salespeople who had high and low attitude scores on the pretest. Similarly, it could be a factor if this group consisted of salespeople with the highest and lowest sales of the detergent.

Some of the foregoing error sources affecting internal validity can interact with selection to produce forces that might appear to be treatment effects. *Selection-maturation* results when experimental groups mature at different speeds. *Selection-history* can occur when the experimental groups come from different settings. For example, the salespeople receiving the retraining all come from one region of the country, whereas those not retrained come from some other region. In this situation, each group may have a unique local history that might affect outcome variables.

As previously mentioned, randomization takes care of many potential errors that can affect interval validity. There are, however, other so-called threats to internal validity that cannot be handled by randomization. These other threats may cause spurious differences or tend to obscure true differences. For a more detailed discussion of threats to internal validity the reader is referred to the excellent book by Cook and Campbell.[14] Although randomization is useful for true experiments, for quasi-experiments each potential error must be made explicit and then ruled out one by one.

External Validity

Reactive effect of testing refers to the learning or conditioning of the persons involved in the design as a result of knowing that their behavior is being observed and/or that the results are being measured. If salespersons know that they are being retrained as a part of a study to determine how effective retraining is, they may act differently than they would have otherwise. A frequent problem in research design is that a "before" measurement is desired, but it is recognized that making such a measurement may alert the subjects that they are participating in a study. If they surmise that an "after" measurement will be taken, they may become sensitized to the variables involved and behave differently as a result (see Exhibit 6-1). Similarly, if an experiment is being conducted on the impact of advertising, a premeasurement may sensitize an experimental subject to pay particular attention to a company's advertising, product(s), or both. Although this potential source of error may seem the same as that from testing, it is distinctly different in that it is an interaction of testing and treatment.

Reactive effects of experimental situation concern those effects that may arise from experimental subjects' reacting to the situation surrounding the conduct of an experiment rather than the treatment variable(s). By situation surrounding an experiment we mean

---

[13]Cook and Campbell, *Quasi-Experimentation,* pp. 52–53.
[14]Ibid., pp. 50–59.

Exhibit 6-1   Bias in Posttest Scores

In many marketing experiments, particularly the nonfield ones, the subjects take one or more attitude measures both before and after the experimental treatment. Because of a sensitization effect of the pretest, this pretest-treatment-posttest design may confound the treatment effect. Previous research suggests several sources of such bias in the posttest scores:

1. The pretest may raise the curiousity of subjects and thus have a motivational effect.

2. Pretesting may orient the subject's attention selectively toward certain aspects of the treatment. For example, subjects in an educational experiment may learn what to concentrate on during their study of the instructional materials.

3. Taking a pretest engages the subject in a form of public commitment and may therefore have an inhibitory influence on subsequent attitude change.

4. The pretest items may alert the subject to the intent of the investigator and may subsequently facilitate or inhibit opinion change depending on the subject's willingness to comply with the experimental demands.

5. The information contained in the pretest may induce the subject to consider the position implied by this information. This advertising or priming effect may facilitate attitude change.

Despite the plausibility of these explanations, the *empirical* evidence of a pretest treatment interaction bearing on attitude change research is, in general, meager.

Source: Adapted from Joh. Hoogstraten, "Pretesting as Determinant of Attitude Change in Evaluation Research," *Applied Psychological Measurement,* 3 (Winter 1979), 25.

such things as the setting within which the experiment is conducted, the arrangements made for the experiment (e.g., apparatus used), and the presence and behavior of an experimenter. These reactive effects involve both experimenter and subject effects.[15] An important consideration is the presence of demand characteristics (artifacts), which are defined as including "all aspects of the experiment which cause the subject to perceive, interpret, and act upon what he believes is expected or desired of him by the experimenter."[16] Included among experimenter effects, particularly in laboratory experiments, are such things as

1. Experimenter expectancies: biasing effects attributed to the expectancies of the experimenter regarding the outcome of the experiment; these are linked to the hypothesis as a self-fulfilling prophecy.

2. Early data returns: the effect of early data obtained on subsequent data obtained.

3. Experimenter modeling: the extent to which an experimenter's own performance of an experimental task determines his or her subjects' performance of that task.

[15]For a more complete discussion of subject-experimenter effects, see Rosenthal and Rosnow, *Essentials of Behavioral Research,* Chap. 9; and Christensen, *Experimental Methodology,* pp. 100–14.

[16]Alan G. Sawyer, "Demand Artifacts in Laboratory Experiments in Consumer Research," *Journal of Consumer Research,* 1 (March 1975), 20.

4. Experimenter attributes: these include effects that are *biosocial* (e.g., sex, age, and race of the experimenter); *psychosocial* (e.g., personality of the experimenter); and *situational* (e.g., experience in performing a given type of experiment).[17]

To a large extent, the effects of demand characteristics depend on the roles adopted by subjects, particularly when subjects become aware of, or believe they know, the experimental hypothesis (see Table 6-2). Ideally, the investigator would desire subjects who are faithful or naive (i.e., do not know the hypothesis).

Unfortunately, one can never be absolutely certain that demand characteristics will be present in the chosen experimental procedures. Research design, measurement of dependent variables, and use of procedures (e.g., deception and natural environments) will reduce such demand characteristics.[18]

History-treatment interaction can affect external validity when the dependent variable is measured at a point in time that is not representative of the timing as it relates to the effect of the treatment variable. Of concern is the issue of time periods to which a particular causal relationship can be generalized. If the retraining program had been run during the winter or early spring and detergent sales measured during the quarter following, results may have been misleading because sales would normally be expected to increase greatly during late spring or summer as outdoor activities increase. Similarly, if an experiment were conducted on the effectiveness of advertising and this experiment was run at a time close to any holiday, then a question could be raised whether the same cause-effect relationship would exist at some other point in time. Moreover, with some independent variables their effects may be long-run in nature, but typically dependent variable measurement occurs at one point in time.

Selection-treatment interaction refers to the categories of people to which a cause-effect relationship can be generalized. That is, can the observed effect(s) be generalized beyond the groups used to establish the relationship(s)? Even when research subjects belong to the target group of interest, the recruitment approach used may limit any

TABLE 6-2 Alternative Subject Roles

Good:	tries to confirm what is believed to be the experimental hypothesis.
Faithful:	has no intention to bias and is concerned only with following instructions.
Negative:	tries to disconfirm a suspected hypothesis by behaving in a contrary or intentionally random or neutral manner.
Apprehensive:	effects are ambiguous and unpredictable, since these types of subjects often worry about how their performance will be judged by others.

Source: Adapted from Sawyer, "Demand Artifacts."

[17]See M. L. Barnes and R. Rosenthal, "Interpersonal Effects of Experimenter Attractiveness, Attire, and Gender," *Journal of Personality and Social Psychology*, 48 (1985), 435–46.

[18]Sawyer, "Demand Artifacts," pp. 25–28.

Exhibit 6-2   Reducing Experimenter Expectancy Effects

Different strategies are available for the reduction of experimenter expectancy effects. These techniques are based on the premise that the mediation of such effects depends to some extent on various nonverbal communication processes that can be controlled or bypassed. These strategies are:

1. Increasing the number of experimenters
   decreases learning of influence techniques
   helps to maintain "blindness"
   minimizes effects of early data returns
   increases generality of results
   randomizes expectancies
   permits the method of collaborative disagreement
   permits statistical correction of expectancy effects
2. Observing the behavior of experimenters
   sometimes reduces expectancy effects
   permits correction for unprogrammed behavior
   facilitates greater standardization of experimenter behavior
3. Analyzing experiments for order effects
   permits inference about changes in experimenter behavior
4. Developing training procedures
   permits prediction of expectancy effects
5. Maintaining "blind contact"
   minimizes expectancy effects
6. Minimizing experimenter-subject contact
   minimizes expectancy effects
7. Employing expectancy control groups
   permits assessment of expectancy effects

Source: Adapted from Rosenthal and Rosnow, *Essentials of Behavioral Research*, pp. 113–14.

generalizations to only those who participated in a given experiment. Experiments, particularly laboratory experiments, rely heavily upon volunteers, paid or otherwise. There is some evidence that volunteer experimental subjects differ from nonvolunteer subjects in more or less systematic ways (see Table 6-3). In the salesperson-retraining example, this potential threat to external validity would arise if the company attempted to generalize the results to other types of salespeople, such as those who sell food items or small appliances.

MODELS OF EXPERIMENTAL DESIGN

A number of experimental designs have been developed to overcome and reduce the various sources of invalidity. Experimental designs can be categorized into two broad groups—classical and statistical. Classical designs consider the impact of only one in-

TABLE 6-3   Characteristics of the Volunteer Subject*

CONCLUSIONS WARRANTING MAXIMUM CONFIDENCE

1. Volunteers tend to be better educated than nonvolunteers, especially when personal contact between investigator and respondent is not required.

2. Volunteers tend to have higher social-class status than nonvolunteers, especially when social class is defined by respondents' own status rather than by parental status.

3. Volunteers tend to be more intelligent than nonvolunteers when volunteering is for research in general, but not when volunteering is for somewhat less typical types of research such as hypnosis, sensory isolation, sex research, and small-group and personality research.

4. Volunteers tend to be higher in need for social approval than nonvolunteers.

5. Volunteers tend to be more sociable than nonvolunteers.

CONCLUSIONS WARRANTING CONSIDERABLE CONFIDENCE

6. Volunteers tend to be more arousal-seeking than nonvolunteers, especially when volunteering is for studies of stress, sensory isolation, and hypnosis.

7. Volunteers tend to be more unconventional than nonvolunteers, especially when volunteering is for studies of sex behavior.

8. Females are more likely than males to volunteer for research in general, but less likely than males to volunteer for physically and emotionally stressful research (e.g., electric shock, high temperature, sensory deprivation, interviews about sex behavior).

9. Volunteers tend to be less authoritarian than nonvolunteers.

10. Jews are more likely to volunteer than Protestants, and Protestants are more likely to volunteer than Catholics.

11. Volunteers tend to be less conforming than nonvolunteers when volunteering is for research in general, but not when subjects are female and the task is relatively "clinical" (e.g., hypnosis, sleep or counseling research).

CONCLUSIONS WARRANTING SOME CONFIDENCE

12. Volunteers tend to be from smaller towns than nonvolunteers, especially when volunteering is for questionnaire studies.

13. Volunteers tend to be more interested in religion than nonvolunteers, especially when volunteering is for questionnaire studies.

14. Volunteers tend to be more altruistic than nonvolunteers.

15. Volunteers tend to be more self-disclosing than nonvolunteers.

(Continued)

---

*Derived from content analysis of published research. The extent of confidence about a conclusion refers to confidence in the relationship stated.

TABLE 6-3   Characteristics of the Volunteer Subject (*Continued*)

CONCLUSIONS WARRANTING SOME CONFIDENCE

16.   Volunteers tend to be more maladjusted than nonvolunteers especially when volunteering is for potentially unusual situations (e.g., drugs, hypnosis, high temperature, or vaguely described experiments) or for medical research employing clinical, rather than psychometric, definitions of psychopathology.

17.   Volunteers tend to be younger than nonvolunteers, especially when volunteering is for laboratory research and especially if they are female.

CONCLUSIONS WARRANTING MINIMUM CONFIDENCE

18.   Volunteers tend to be higher in need for achievement than nonvolunteers, especially among American samples.

19.   Volunteers are more likely to be married than nonvolunteers, especially when volunteering is for studies requiring no personal contact between investigator and respondent.

20.   Firstborns are more likely than laterborns to volunteer, especially when recruitment is personal and when the research requires group interaction and a low level of stress.

21.   Volunteers tend to be more anxious than nonvolunteers, especially when volunteering is for standard, nonstressful tasks and especially if they are college students.

22.   Volunteers tend to be more extroverted than nonvolunteers when interaction with others is required by the nature of the research.

Source: Robert Rosenthal and Ralph L. Rosnow, *The Volunteer Subject* (New York: John Wiley, 1975), pp. 88–90.

dependent variable at a time, whereas statistical designs allow for examining the impact of two or more independent variables.

Classical Designs

The major types of classical designs can be classified as pre-experiment, quasi-experiment and true experiment. Pre-experimental designs are so called because there is such a total absence of control that they are of minimal value in establishing causality. Quasi-experimental designs involve control but there has not been random assignment of subjects, as there is for true experiments. Where any given design fits will depend on whether the treatment variable has been deliberately manipulated, the nature of control, and whether there has been random assignment of subjects to experimental groups. The following notational system will be used in the discussion of classical experimental designs:

• *X* represents the exposure of test groups to an experimental treatment of a producer or event whose effect is to be observed and/or measured.

- *O* refers to the measurement or observation taken.
- *R* indicates that individuals have been selected at random for groups to receive differing treatments or that the groups have been assigned at random to differing treatments.
- Movement from left to right indicates a sequence of events. When *O*'s and *X*'s are found in a given row, they are to be interpreted as having occurred in sequence and to the same specific individual or group. Vertical arrangement of symbols is to be interpreted as the simultaneous occurrence of the events that they denote.

Three classes of designs seem to fit for pre- and quasi-experiments: (1) time-series and trend designs, (2) cross-sectional designs, and (3) combinations of the two.

Time-Series and Trend Designs

Time-series and trend designs are similar in concept, yet their differences in implementation and analytic procedures warrant a brief discussion. A *time-series design* involves obtaining data from the same sample (or population) for successive points in time. The common method of gathering primary data of this kind is to collect current data at successive intervals through the use of a continuous panel. One may, however, collect current and retrospective data from respondents during a single interview. If the latter technique is used, respondent recall must be depended on to reconstruct quasi-historical data. An alternative method of obtaining data for past periods, when available, is to use secondary sources.

Trend data differ from time-series data in that they are obtained from statistically matched samples drawn from the same population over time. Current data are gathered from each successive sample.

Both time-series and trend data are used to investigate the existence and nature of causal relationships based on associative-variation and sequence-of-events types of evidence. While individuals or households are the most commonly used sample units, data are also obtained from retail stores, wholesalers, manufacturers, and other units.

Since trend designs provide no continuity in the sample units from which data are obtained, there is no opportunity to observe changes over time in individual sample units. Trend data, therefore, can only be analyzed in the aggregated form in which they are collected. Time-series data generated from continuous panels and, to a lesser extent, from retrospective interviews permit analysis of effects by individual sample units. Microanalyses of this type can provide valuable information on buyer behavior including purchase rates, brand switching, and brand loyalty. The analysis of microeffects is called *longitudinal analysis*.

Time-series and trend designs involve, at a minimum, one treatment and a subsequent measurement. At the other extreme they may involve a large number of measurements with several interspersed treatments. We now describe and discuss four types of time-series and trend designs.

After-Only without Control Group   This design is often termed a "tryout" or "one-shot case study." It is the simplest of all designs, as it involves only one nonrandomly selected group, one treatment, and one measurement. Symbolically, it may be diagrammed as follows:

$$X \quad O \tag{1}$$

If not already apparent, the many weaknesses of this design may be illustrated by applying it to the salesperson-retraining problem. Assume that no prior measurement of sales volume of the salespeople to be retrained had been made. A group of salespeople are selected by a nonrandom method and retrained (X); a measurement (O) is made after the retraining.

Since no prior measurement of sales volume of each of the retrained salespeople was made, there is no method, short of making assumptions as to what would have happened in the absence of retraining, of estimating what the effect of retraining was. The effects of history, maturation, and selection are all potentially substantial and non-measurable.

It is hardly necessary to add that the use of this design is to be avoided if at all possible.

Before-After without Control Group   This design, as the name implies, is the same as (1) with the addition of a "before" measurement. In its simplest form it is shown as

$$O_1 \quad X \quad O_2 \tag{2}$$

and in an extended form as

$$O_1 \quad O_2 \quad O_3 \quad O_4 \quad X \quad O_5 \quad O_6 \quad O_7 \quad O_8 \tag{3}$$

Although design (2) is relatively weak, it is frequently used. It is a decided improvement over (1) in that the apparent effect of the treatment, $O_2 - O_1$, is measured. In terms of the salesperson-retraining illustration, a measurement (O_2) of sales volume of the retrained salesperson is made for the quarter after the sales retraining (X) and compared with a similar measurement (O_1) for the same quarter of the preceding year.

Design (3) is an improvement over design (2) in that data for a larger number of periods are available. The apparent results of the treatment (X) can be analyzed as either the difference of averages

$$\left(\frac{O_5 + O_6 + O_7 + O_8}{4} - \frac{O_1 + O_2 + O_3 + O_4}{4} \right)$$

or the difference in trends of "before" and "after" measurements. It is this type of design that is implicit in many of the aggregate analyses made of consumer-panel data.

The weaknesses of both designs (2) and (3) include neglect of the effects of history, maturation, testing effect, instrument effect, and selection. History can play a large role in determining the level of difference in the before-and-after measurements, as can maturation. Since measurements are made both before and after the treatment, both testing effect and instrument effect can be present. The testing effect can be particularly important in design (3). The effect of nonrandom selection is also potentially present in both designs. Careful investigation and close scrutiny are necessary to estimate the effect of each of these uncontrolled and unmeasured sources of variation.

Multiple Time Series   In using a time-series design the possibility of establishing a control group should always be investigated. It may be possible to find a comparable, if not equivalent, group to serve as a control against which to compare the results of the group that underwent the treatment involved. This design may be diagrammed as

$$O_1 \ O_2 \ O_3 \ O_4 \quad X \quad O_5 \ O_6 \ O_7 \ O_8$$
$$O_1' \ O_2' \ O_3' \ O_4' \qquad\quad O_5' \ O_6' \ O_7' \ O_8' \tag{4}$$

where the primed O's represent measurement of the control group. Note that the individuals constituting the groups were not selected at random. It may be possible, however, to select at random the group that will receive the treatment.

This design can easily be adapted to the sales-retraining evaluation problem. If it is assumed that the sales volume of each of the salespeople is measured during each period as a matter of course anyway, a group could be selected for retraining after period 4. Either a comparable group or all the rest of the salespeople could be selected as the control group. After the sales of both groups in the periods after the training had been measured, the apparent effect of the retraining would be shown by comparing the differences in average sales volume for the two groups before and after treatment.

This design is a substantial improvement over design (3) in that the control group, even though purposively selected, provides a basis for allowing for history, maturation, and testing effect. To the extent that the groups are similar, the effects of each of these factors will *tend* to affect both groups in the same manner. The nonrandom selection of the test and control groups, although less than ideal, may provide a practical and workable substitute for situations where random selection is not possible.[19]

Cross-Sectional Designs

Cross-sectional designs involve measuring the product of interest for several groups at the same time, the groups having been exposed to differing levels of treatments of the producer whose effect is being studied. Cross-sectional designs may be viewed diagramatically as follows:

$$
\begin{array}{cc}
X_1 & O_1 \\
X_2 & O_2 \\
X_3 & O_3 \\
\cdot & \cdot \\
\cdot & \cdot \\
\cdot & \cdot \\
X_n & O_n
\end{array}
\tag{5a}
$$

[19]In Chapter 12 we discuss an alternative form of dealing with test-object differences, called *covariance analysis*.

Examples of frequent applications of this design are studies of the effect of such variables as price or level of advertising in different geographic areas. This design can be used when direct manipulation of the producer involved is not possible or practical. When this is the case, the design is being used in a natural experiment. The effect of the different levels of treatment is measured by determining the degree of association between producer and product. The techniques that can be employed are discussed in later chapters.

A variation of this design is the *static-group comparison*. This is a design in which a group exposed to a treatment is compared with one that was not:

$$X \quad O_1$$
$$O_2 \tag{5b}$$

History may play a critically important role in cross-sectional designs. There may be a sizable differential effect of extraneous producers between the groups being measured. The effects of maturation and testing tend to be reduced to a minimal level, and the instrumentation effect is certainly no greater than in any other design.

Combination Cross-Sectional, Time-Series Designs

A number of designs employing a combination of time-series and cross-sectional treatment and measurement may be used in observational studies. The multiple-time-series design [design (4)] could be considered a combination of the two, as it involves measurements of a product for different groups at the same time as well as for the same group over time.

Combination designs are well adapted for use with consumer-panel data. One commonly used design is the *ex post facto* test-control group. In this design the test and control groups are not known until *after* the treatment has been administered. This design is illustrated as follows:

$$O_1 \quad X \quad O_3$$
$$O_2 \quad\quad O_4 \tag{6}$$

This design is widely used in connection with testing the sales effectiveness of price changes, "deals," and advertising. Data on the sales of the brand of interest are reported regularly by the members of the continuous consumer panel. After a given advertisement is run (X), panel members may be questioned to determine whether or not they saw it. Those who saw it are a part of the test group, since they have had exposure to the treatment involved. Those who did not see the advertisement become a part of the control group. The apparent effect is determined by comparing the difference in test and control-group purchases before with that after the advertising was run.

The *ex post facto* determination of test and control-group members is another selection method used as a substitute for random selection. Self-selection is involved; the individuals determine by their actions whether or not they will be included in the test or the control group. The self-selection feature of this design can be an important source of systematic error. It has been demonstrated in many studies of advertising, for example, that the individual who has seen the advertising for a particular brand is more likely to have purchased the brand *before* he or she saw the advertising than is the individual who did not see it.

A variation of the same general design is the *nonequivalent control group*. There is purposive selection in advance of the treatment, and measurements are made on the test and control groups. The selection of the two groups must of necessity be determined entirely by the problem environment.

An example of the use of this type of design occurred in the early stages of the development of network television. Advertising of a hand soap on network television was initiated at a time when only about one-half of the present number of cities were covered by stations. An analysis was made of sales to network versus nonnetwork cities and compared with sales to the same cities for a comparable period before television advertising was initiated. In this case it was evident that the test and control cities were not equivalent, since a larger amount was spent on advertising in other media in non-network cities than in network cities.

In addition to the error induced by the method of selection, testing effect may be a substantial contributor of error in this design. Despite these error sources, the design is a useful one. It can be adapted to a variety of situations to provide information relatively quickly and inexpensively, particularly when panel data are already available.

True Experimental Designs

As previously mentioned, for true experiments two kinds of investigator intervention are required:

1. Manipulation of at least one assumed causal variable
2. Random assignment of subjects to experimental and control groups

Through use of a random selection procedure, systematic errors due to selection are eliminated, and the effects of the many extraneous variables tend to be equalized between the experimental and the control groups as the size of these groups increases. Random selection permits the use of inferential statistical techniques for analyzing the experimental results. The most fundamental technique for this purpose is analysis of variance. The rationale and some applications of analysis of variance are treated in Chapter 12.

Three single-variable experimental designs are described below.

After-Only with Control Group   The simplest of all experimental designs is the *after-only with control group*. It requires only one treatment and an "after" measurement of both the experimental and the control group. Yet it has the essential requirements of the true experiment: manipulation of at least one variable and randomly selected test and control groups. It may be illustrated as follows:

$$R \quad X \quad O_1$$
$$R \qquad\quad O_2$$

(7a)

The absence of a "before" measurement is a feature that concerns many researchers about this design. Banks has described this concern and some possible explanations for it:

> The pre-test is a concept deeply imbedded in the thinking of research workers in the social sciences but it is not actually essential to true experimental designs. Almost all the agricultural experiments are run without pre-tests. In the social sciences, however, it seems difficult to give up the notion that the experimental and the control groups might have been unequal before differential experimental treatment and rely upon randomization to reassure us that there will be a lack of initial biases between groups. Perhaps this belief comes from the fact that we have not run many experiments in the social sciences and marketing.[20]

This design, by avoiding the "before" measurement, provides control over the testing and instrument effects. It is of major interest, therefore, when "before" measurements are impractical or impossible to obtain and/or when the testing and instrument effects are likely to be serious.

A common application of this design is in the testing of direct-mail advertising. Random-sampling procedures are used to select an experimental and a control group. Direct-mail pieces are sent to the experimental group and withheld from the control group. "After" measurements of sales to each group are made, and the differential is determined $(O_1 - O_2)$.

A variation of this design is the so-called *simulated before-and-after design*. Separate samples are used for the before-and-after measurements:

$$R \quad O \quad (X) \tag{7b}$$
$$R \quad \quad X \quad O$$

Although there is random assignment, this design is perhaps more properly classified as a quasi-experimental design. Weaknesses of this design are that history and maturation are not controlled. However, this design lends itself to modification by adding features to control specific factors. For example, if this design were repeated in different settings at different times, history would be controlled.[21]

Before-After with One Control Group   If "before" measurements are added to design (7a), we arrive at the following configuration:

$$R \quad O_1 \quad X \quad O_2$$
$$R \quad O_3 \quad \quad O_4 \tag{8}$$

---

[20]Seymour Banks, *Experimentation in Marketing* (New York: McGraw-Hill, 1965), p. 35.

[21]See Donald T. Campbell and Julian C. Stanley, *Experimental and Quasi-Experimental Designs for Research* (Chicago: Rand McNally, 1966), pp. 53–54.

This design is very similar to that of (6) but with an important difference: the experimental and control groups are randomly selected, rather than self-selected. Most of the sources of systematic error are controlled in this design. Maturation is controlled in the sense that it is present in both the experimental and control groups. The same observation applies to the testing effect, although it should be noted that no measurement of the testing effect is possible in this design. (Such a measurement is possible in the next design to be discussed.) History is controlled so long as the two "before" measurements (O_1 and O_3) and the two "after" measurements (O_2 and O_4) are made at the same time. A potential instrumentation effect is established, as is always the case when sequential measurements are made on the same subjects and the same measuring instruments are used.

This design offers three ways to evaluate the effect of the treatments: $O_2 - O_1$, $O_2 - O_4$, and $(O_2 - O_1) - (O_4 - O_3)$. If the results of each of these evaluations are consistent, the strength of our inferences about the effect of the experimental treatment is substantially increased.

An example of the use of this design is in advertising tests that use a dual cable television system with two consumer purchase panels (one from the subscribers to each cable). "Before" measurements can be made on the test and control panels, an experimental advertising treatment introduced on the test cable, and "after" measurements made for both panels.

Four-Group, Six-Study Design Suppose that we combine (7a) and (8) and arrive at the following design:

$$
\begin{array}{ccccc}
R & O_1 & X & O_2 & \\
R & O_3 & & O_4 & \\
R & & X & O_5 & \quad (9) \\
R & & & O_6 &
\end{array}
$$

This design provides the opportunity of not only testing the effect of the experimental variable but also testing the effect of testing and the combined effects of maturation and history.

The effect of the treatment can be evaluated in a number of ways, the usual ones being to determine the differentials $O_2 - O_1$, $O_2 - O_4$, $O_5 - O_6$, $O_4 - O_3$, and $(O_2 - O_1) - (O_4 - O_3)$.

The "after" measurements provide a useful basis for drawing inferences about the testing effect as well as that of the treatment. They can be placed into a 2×2 table as follows:

	No X	X
"Before" measurements taken	O_4	O_2
No "before" measurements taken	O_6	O_5

The effect of the treatment can be estimated from the difference in the column means. The difference in row means provides the basis for estimating testing effect. The

TABLE 6-4 Sources of Invalidity and Selected Experimental Designs

	Internal								External		
	History	Maturation	Testing	Instrumentation	Regression	Selection	Mortality	Interaction of Selection and Maturation, etc.	Interaction of Testing and X	Interaction of Selection and X	Reactive Arrangements
One-Shot Case Study X O	−	−				−	−			−	
One-Group Pretest-Posttest Design O X O	−	−	−	−	?	+	+	−	−	−	?
Time Series O O O OXO O O	−	+	+	?	+	+	+	+	−	?	?
Multiple Time-Series O O OXO O O O O O O O O	+	+	+	+	+	+	+	+	−	−	?
Static-Group Comparison X O O	+	?	+	+	+	−	−	−	−		
Nonequivalent Control Group Design O X O O O	+	+	+	+	?	+	+	−	−	?	?
Posttest-Only Control Group Design R X O R O	+	+	+	+	+	+	+	+	+	?	?
Separate-Sample Pretest-Posttest Design R O (X) R X O	−	−	+	?	+	+	−	−	+	+	+

224

TABLE 6-4 *(Continued)*

| | SOURCES OF INVALIDITY | | | | | | | | | | | |
| | Internal | | | | | | | | External | | | |
	History	Maturation	Testing	Instrumentation	Regression	Selection	Mortality	Interaction of Selection and Maturation, etc.	Interaction of Testing and X	Interaction of Selection and X	Reactive Arrangements
Pretest-Posttest Control Group Design R O X O R O O	+	+	+	+	+	+	+	+	−	?	?
Solomon Four-Group Design R O X O R O O R X O R O	+	+	+	+	+	+	+	+	+	?	?

Note: In the tables, a minus indicates a definite weakness, a plus indicates that the factor is controlled, a question mark indicates a possible source of concern, and a blank indicates that the factor is not relevant.
Source: Adapted from Campbell and Stanley, *Experimental and Quasi-Experimental Designs,* pp. 8, 40, 56.

differences in the individual cell means can be used for testing the *interaction* of testing and treatment. Analysis-of-variance procedures are useful for analyzing these results.

Summary of Classical Designs

There are many classical designs. In this section of the chapter we have discussed the more common designs.[22] A useful way to summarize what we have discussed is to look at each in terms of sources of potential error and whether such sources are controlled for, as shown in Table 6-4.

A quasi-experimental design used to determine the direction of causality between two variables measured at two or more points in time is the *cross-lagged panel correlation*

---

[22]For a more detailed discussion, see Cook and Campbell, *Quasi-Experimentation;* and Campbell and Stanley, *Experimental and Quasi-Experimental Designs.*

Figure 6-2   Cross-Lagged Panel Correlation Design

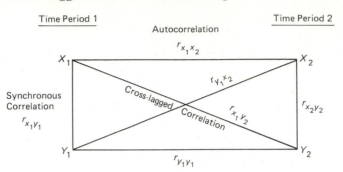

technique. A typical cross-lagged panel correlation design for two variables measured at two points in time is shown in Figure 6-2. The correlations of major interest are $r_{x_1y_2}$ and $r_{y_1x_2}$. Although the two cross-lagged correlations are the critical ones, how they are to be interpreted is directly affected by the autocorrelations and the synchronous correlations.[23] For the most part, this design is one of data analysis rather than a unique data collection design.[24]

Another design that has been used in the analysis of experimental data, perhaps even more widely than the cross-lagged panel design, is *path analysis* or *structural equation modeling*. At such, then, it is an alternative to analysis of variance. For the most part, data are collected by one of the more usual designs for data collection, although there are certain measurement implications if this analytical design is to be used.[25]

Statistical Designs

For the most part, statistical designs are "after-only" designs (design 7a) in which there are at least two treatment levels. In addition, such designs can examine the effects of more than one independent variable. Two principal aspects of statistical designs are (1) the experimental layouts by which treatment levels are assigned to test objects, and (2) the techniques that are used to analyze the results of the experiment. We briefly discuss now the major types of layouts used to obtain data. The analysis techniques, known generically as *analysis of variance and covariance,* are discussed in Chapter 12.

---

[23]Christensen, *Experimental Methodology*, p. 228.

[24]See Cook and Campbell, *Quasi-Experimentation*, pp. 308–21; and Richard P. Bagozzi, *Causal Models in Marketing* (New York: John Wiley, 1980), pp. 229–33.

[25]A detailed discussion of the structural equation model in experimental research is provided by Cook and Campbell, *Quasi-Experimentation*, Chap. 7; and Bagozzi, *Causal Models*, Chap. 7.

Completely Randomized Design

The *completely randomized design* is the simplest type of statistical design. In this design the experimental treatments are assigned to test units on a random basis. Any number of treatments can be assigned by a random process to any number of test units.

As an illustration, suppose that a marketer is interested in the effect of shelf height on supermarket sales of canned dog food. The marketer has been able to obtain the cooperation of a store manager to run an experiment involving three levels of shelf height ("knee" level, "waist" level, and "eye" level) on sales of a single brand of dog food, which we shall call Arf. Assume further that our experiment must be conducted in a single supermarket and that our response variable will be sales, in cans, of Arf dog food per some appropriate unit of time. But what shall we use for our unit of time? Sales of dog food in a single store may exhibit week-to-week variation, day-to-day variation, and even hour-to-hour variation. In addition, sales of this particular brand may be affected by the price or special promotions of competitive brands, the store management's knowledge that an experiment is going on, and other variables that we cannot control at all or would find too costly to control.

We shall address ourselves to some of these questions (and others) shortly, but for the time being, assume that we have agreed to change the shelf-height position of Arf three times per day and run the experiment over eight days. We shall fill the remaining sections of the particular gondola that houses our brand with a "filler" brand, which is not familiar to customers in the geographical area in which the test is being conducted. We shall assign the shelf heights at random over the three time periods per day and not deal explicitly with within-day and among-day differences. If so, our experimental design might look like that shown in Table 6-5. Here we let X_{ij} denote unit sales of Arf during the ith day under the jth treatment level.

The preceding example dealt with the simplest of statistical designs—classification by a single factor. This design is most applicable when it is believed that extraneous variables will have about the same effect on all test units, and when the marketer is interested in only one independent variable. Suppose, however, that our marketing re-

TABLE 6-5 Completely Randomized Design—Arf Dog Food Experiment

	SHELF HEIGHT	
Knee Level	*Waist Level*	*Eye Level*
X_{11}	X_{12}	X_{13}
X_{21}	X_{22}	X_{23}
X_{31}	X_{32}	X_{33}
X_{41}	X_{42}	X_{43}
X_{51}	X_{52}	X_{53}
X_{61}	X_{62}	X_{63}
X_{71}	X_{72}	X_{73}
X_{81}	X_{82}	X_{83}

TABLE 6-6   Factorial Design—Arf Dog Food Experiment

| | SHELF HEIGHT | | |
FACINGS	Knee Level	Waist Level	Eye Level
Level 1 (half width)	F_1H_1	F_1H_2	F_1H_3
Level 2	F_2H_1	F_2H_2	F_2H_3

searcher were interested in the effect of *other* point-of-purchase variables such as shelf "facings" (width of display) and shelf fullness on sales. Or, suppose that the researcher would like to generalize the results of the experiment to other sizes of stores in other marketing regions. It may be preferable to "ask many rather than few questions of nature" if the researcher would like to establish the most general conditions under which his or her findings are expected to hold. That is, not only may single-factor manipulation be difficult to do in practice, but it may be inefficient as well. We now discuss somewhat more specialized experimental designs, all of which are characterized by *two or more variables of classification.*

Factorial Designs

A *factorial experiment* is one in which an equal number of observations is made of all combinations involving at least two levels of at least two variables. This type of experiment enables the researcher to study possible *interactions* among the variables of interest. Suppose we return to our canned dog food illustration but now assume that the researcher is interested in studying the effects of *two* variables of interest: shelf height (still at three levels) and shelf facings (at two levels—that is, at half the width of the gondola and at full width of the gondola). The design is shown in Table 6-6. Note that each combination of F_iH_j occurs only once in the design. While the plan still is to use a single store for the experiment, the researcher intends to replicate each combination three times, leading to $3 \times 2 \times 3 = 18$ observations.

In the factorial experiment we can test for all main effects (i.e., facing, height), and in this case, where we have replicated each combination, for the interaction of the variables as well. If the interaction term is significant, ordinarily the calculation of main

TABLE 6-7   Latin-Square Design—Arf Dog Food Experiment

| VARIABLE A—SHELF HEIGHT | VARIABLE B—SHELF FACINGS | | | |
	B_1	B_2	B_3	B_4
A_1	C_1	C_2	C_3	C_4
A_2	C_4	C_1	C_2	C_3
A_3	C_3	C_4	C_1	C_2
A_4	C_2	C_3	C_4	C_1

effects is superfluous, since the experimenter will customarily be interested in the best *combination* of variables. That is, in market experimentation the researcher is typically interested in the combination of controlled variables that leads to the best payoff in terms of sales, market share, cash flow, or some other measure of effectiveness.

Latin Square

Latin-square designs are multivariable designs that are used to reduce the number of observations that would be required in a full factorial design. In using latin-square

Exhibit 6-3   Randomization of Latin-Square Design

To illustrate the procedures for randomization of a latin-square design, assume that we have four treatments. Also assume that we have the following four 4 × 4 latin-square designs:

(a)	(b)	(c)	(d)
A B C D	A B C D	A B C D	A B C D
B A D C	B C D A	B D A C	B A D C
C D B A	C D A B	C A D B	C D A B
D C A B	D A B C	D C B A	D C B A

In general, the procedure involves selecting at random one of the 4 × 4 squares, randomizing the rows and columns of the square, and assigning the treatments at random to the letters A–D.

Assume we have randomly selected square (a). Using a table of random numbers we can write down three random permutations of the numbers 1–4:

        (1) 1,3,4,2
        (2) 4,1,2,3
        (3) 2,4,3,1

Using permutation (1), we rearrange the rows of square (a) which gives us

    1 A B C D
    3 C D B A
    4 D C A B
    2 B A D C

We now rearrange the columns of this square in accordance with (2) above:

    4 1 2 3
    D A B C
    A C D B
    B D C A
    C B A D

Finally, if the treatments have been numbered 1–4, we rearrange them in accordance with (3). This results in:

    Permutation 2 4 3 1
    Treatment   A B C D

Thus treatment 2 is assigned A, etc., in the latin square.

Source: Adapted from Allen L. Edwards, *Experimental Design in Psychological Research,* 3rd ed. (New York: Holt, Rinehart & Winston, 1968), pp. 175–77.

designs the researcher is usually assuming that *interaction effects are negligible;* in so doing, all main effects can be estimated by this procedure.

As an illustration of a latin-square design, suppose that the researcher were interested in *three* variables (each at four levels) on store sales. For example, in the dog food illustration the researcher may be interested in the following:

A: shelf height—four levels—knee level, waist level, eye level, reach level

B: shelf facings—four levels—25%, 50%, 75%, and 100% of total width of gondola

C: shelf fullness—four levels—25%, 50%, 75%, and 100% of total height of gondola section

If the researcher were to run a full factorial experiment, with one replication only, there would be $(4)^3 = 64$ observations required. By using a latin-square design only 16 observations are required (with estimation of main effects only).

Table 6-7 (see page 228) shows one possible latin-square design for this experiment (see Exhibit 6-3). Notice in Table 6-7 that each level of treatment C (shelf fullness) appears once in each row and each column. Also the number of levels (four) is the same for each treatment.

Cross-Over Design

Cross-over design is the name given to a type of design in which different treatments are applied to the *same* test unit in different time periods. Although use of this type of design can reduce the effect of variation among test units, the experimenter must consider another problem—the possibility that successive observations may not be independent. That is, the experimenter may have to contend with a *carry-over* effect. If the researcher can assume that no carry-over effect exists, then a latin-square design could be used, as follows:

	TIME PERIOD		
TEST UNIT	*1*	*2*	*3*
1	A	C	B
2	C	B	A
3	B	A	C

In this design each test unit receives each treatment in "randomized" order over the three time periods, each treatment appearing once in each row and column.

In the case where carry-over effects *are* assumed to exist, the experimenter must make some assumptions about the nature of this carry-over effect. A particularly simple set of assumptions is that the effect obtained on a single test object in a specific time period is made up of

1. A quantity reflecting only the test object–time period combination, plus
2. A quantity reflecting only the treatment applied in that time period, plus
3. A quantity reflecting only the treatment applied in the preceding period.

TABLE 6-8   Latin-Square Design—Carry-Over Effect

	TIME PERIOD		
TEST UNIT	*1*	*2*	*3*
1	A	B	C
2	B	C	A
3	C	A	B
4	C	B	A
5	A	C	B
6	B	A	C

In the case described above, the experimenter would design the experiment so that (1) each treatment follows each other treatment the same number of times, and (2) each treatment occurs in each period and on each test unit. A design that meets these conditions is shown in Table 6-8. Notice that in Table 6-8 each treatment is followed by each treatment (except itself) the same number of times. This design, also known as *double change-over* design, consists of reversing the sequence of treatments in two orthogonal latin squares.

Randomized-Block Design

Randomized-block designs represent a frequently used experimental framework for dealing with multivariable classifications. These designs are typically used when the experimenter desires to eliminate a possible source of uncontrolled variation from the error term in order that the effects due to treatments will not be masked by a larger-than-necessary error term. For example, suppose that our researcher were interested only in the effect of shelf height on sales of dog food but had designed the experiment so that more than a single store was used in the study. The effect of store type could influence sales, and the experimenter might wish to remove this effect from the error term by "blocking" on store types. That is, each store would be considered a test unit and each level of shelf height would be tested in each store. To illustrate, if the researchers were interested in examining three levels of shelf height in each of four stores, results could be summarized in the form shown in Table 6-9. Table 6-9 indicates that we are dealing with a *two-variable* classification and can, accordingly, separate the block effect from

TABLE 6-9   Randomized-Block Design—Arf Dog Food Experiment

	TREATMENTS—SHELF HEIGHT		
BLOCKS—STORES	*Level 1*	*Level 2*	*Level 3*
1	X_{11}	X_{12}	X_{13}
2	X_{21}	X_{22}	X_{23}
3	X_{31}	X_{32}	X_{33}
4	X_{41}	X_{42}	X_{43}

the error term. Thus, if genuine treatment effects are present, this type of design will be more likely to detect them than a single-variable classification in which the block effect would become part of the error term.

Covariance Design

Covariance designs are appropriate in situations where some variable affects response but is *not subject to control* during the experiment. For example, if test units consist of human subjects and the response variable is the number of correct identification of trademarks that are shown on a projection screen (where such factors as length of exposure and clarity of focus are varied), it may be that response is affected by the general intelligence level of the viewing subject. Suppose that it is too costly to screen subjects, and only those with approximately the same intelligence quotient are selected. However, we shall assume that the researcher *is* able to measure each subject's IQ.

In this type of situation the researcher may use covariance analysis. Roughly speaking, the computational procedure is similar to a regression problem. The researcher, in effect, determines the effect on response resulting from differences (in IQ) among test units and removes this influence so that the effect of the controlled variables can be determined independently of the effect of test differences on response.

Recapitulation

As noted earlier, the study of experimental design is basically the study of two things: (1) various experimental layouts, such as single factor, factorial, latin-square, and randomized block designs; and (2) analysis-of-variance and covariance techniques for testing whether the various treatment effects are significant. Many other kinds of design layouts, including fractional factorial designs, balanced incomplete blocks, and partially balanced incomplete blocks, are available.[26] Excellent general discussions of these can be found in Davies and in Cox.[27] In addition, we have only described briefly the characteristics of some of the many specialized statistical designs. The reader interested in exploring the subject further should see more specialized books such as those by Davies and by Cox, as cited above.

Before we leave the subject of specialized experimental designs, some mention should be made of *experimental optimization techniques*. Briefly stated, experimental optimization techniques use an experimental framework for finding the combination of control variables that leads to an optimal response. This is usually done by a sequential design in which the response to a set of initial combinations is used to select the next set of combinations until an optimum is reached. *Evolutionary operations techniques* employ experimentation right along with production operations so that control settings

---

[26]In the context of marketing research, see P. E. Green, "On the Design of Choice Experiments Involving Multifactor Alternatives, *Journal of Consumer Research,* 1 (September 1974), 61–68.

[27]As illustrations, see O. L. Davies, *The Design and Analysis of Industrial Experiments,* 2nd ed. (New York: Hafner, 1956); and D. R. Cox, *Planning of Experiments* (New York: John Wiley, 1958).

can be optimally adjusted as environmental variables change. For details of these procedures the reader is referred to Myers' book.[28]

PANELS AND EXPERIMENTAL DESIGN

In Chapter 4 we discussed the use of the continuous panel by syndicated services.
Continuous panels also may be used for data collection in either a natural or a controlled
experimental design.

The Panel as a Natural Experimental Design

The normal course of operation of a consumer panel generates a continuing set of
natural experimental data. Buyer responses to changes in any of the controllable or
environmental variables affecting purchase decisions are recorded in the normal process
of conducting the panel. Audience and dealer panels provide similar response measurements.

Time-series, cross-sectional, and combination cross-sectional, time-series designs
are all inherent in panel data. To illustrate their application, suppose that we have increased
the price of our product in selected territories. We can analyze the price-increase effect,
at either the aggregated or individual household level, using the data from those territories
in which price was increased with either the after-only without control group or the before-
after without control group designs [classical designs (1) through (3)]. A cross-sectional
analysis may be made by comparing, for a given period after the increase, the purchase
data for the territories in which the price was raised with those in which no change was
made [classical design (5)]. A preferable approach here would be to use a combination
cross-sectional, time-series design and compare the change in purchases before and after
the price increase in the territories in which price was increased (test group) with the
change for those territories in which price was not changed (control group). Such a study
could employ either classical design (4) or (6).

The limitations of each of these designs discussed earlier apply when they are used
with panel data as well. A major difficulty, of course, is in sorting out the effect of the
price increase from the extraneous producers affecting purchases over time and among
territories. In this illustration selective price increases by territory would only have been
made in response to differing conditions among the sales territories (a price increase by
competitors, higher levels of demand, etc.). *History* variables must therefore be analyzed
carefully in using panel data.

Controlled Experimental Designs Using Panels

The controlled experimental design in conjunction with a panel is most often applied
to market tests of prospective new products, different levels of promotion, new campaign

---

[28]R. H. Myers, *Response Surface Methodology* (Boston: Allyn & Bacon, 1971).

themes, price changes, and combinations of two or more of these variables. Consider, for example, a market test of a general price increase. The requirement of random selection of test and control groups can be met by selecting territories at random in which to raise prices. The remaining territories automatically constitute the control group. Depending on the kinds of information desired, an after-only with control group [classical design (7a)], a before-after with one control group [classical design (8)], or a four-group, six-study [classical design (9)] may be used.

The general advantages and limitations of these designs were discussed earlier. We must, however, consider the limitations that arise from the use of the panel for measurement, applicable to both natural and controlled experimental designs.

The Limitations of Continuous Panels

Although panels can provide highly useful marketing information that is difficult to obtain by alternative research methods, there are some important limitations. The first of these limitations involves *selection* and stems from the difficulty of obtaining cooperation of the families or firms selected in the sample and the resulting effect on the degree of representativeness of the panel. To be most useful for drawing inferences about the population being studied, the sample should be drawn by a random process. The sample of families to comprise a consumer purchase panel may be chosen randomly, but the typical panel has experienced a high refusal rate during the period of establishment and a high attrition rate, once in operation. It has recently been reported (privately) for two of the major consumer panels that approximately 85% of sample families are retained through one year of operation.

Evidence indicates that the characteristics of both those families who refuse to participate and those who later drop from the panel are different from those who agree to participate and remain. In the MRCA panel, it was found that a significantly higher percentage of nonurban households agreed to participate than did urban households. In another consumer panel, it was found that a larger proportion of nonusers than users of the products about which purchase data were being reported dropped out after the first interview. To reduce the bias introduced by such nonrandom attrition, replacements are typically chosen from families with the same demographic and usage characteristics as those lost from refusals and dropouts.

An additional source of bias is the *testing effect* arising from continued participation in the panel. Since the individual is undoubtedly conditioned to some extent by the fact that data on purchases are reported, panel members may become atypical in their purchase behavior as a result of being a part of a panel.

Panel data may also be systematically biased through *instrument effects*. The majority of panels use *diaries* for reporting. These are self-administered, structured questionnaires. An attempt is made to have panelists record each purchase in the diary at the time it is made to avoid having to rely on the purchaser's memory. To the extent that this is not done, the accuracy of the data suffers. If properly filled out and submitted on schedule, the information is relatively inexpensive to obtain. However, in those cases where there are omissions or the diary is not mailed on time, either a follow-up personal or telephone interview must be made or the data must be omitted from the tabulation. If the follow-up interview is made, the cost of obtaining the data is increased considerably. If it is not made, possible biases are introduced and the total amount of data is decreased.

Despite these limitations, the use of data from panels has become widespread. If the panel is administered carefully, the resulting data are important additions to the information required for making sound marketing decisions.

FIELD EXPERIMENTATION IN MARKETING

Now that some of the techniques for designing experiments have been described, the reader may wonder if experimental methods are the wave of the future in the study of marketing phenomena. Unfortunately, the user of experimental procedures is beset by his or her own set of problems. When it comes to marketing, field experimentation may be

1. Quite expensive
2. Subject to large amounts of uncontrolled variation
3. Productive of results that are difficult to generalize to other products, market areas, or time periods

There is little question that field experimentation in marketing is a costly undertaking. Consider the case of a sales manager who wishes to determine the effects of varying amounts of sales effort on product sales of a nationally distributed brand. Sales in a given time period could be affected by point-of-purchase advertising, personal sales effort, broadcast promotion, competitors' selling efforts, relative prices, seasonal effects, past promotional expenditures, and so on. Suppose that the manager wished to consider only three levels each of the firm's point-of-purchase promotion, personal sales effort, and broadcast promotion. A full factorial experiment would require 27 market areas that, in turn, should be measured to account for differences in initial sales potential, competitive activity, and so on. Aside from the fact that regional managers may not like to see some of their market areas receive "low doses" of each of the variables, the administrative job of controlling the levels of the treatment variables, measuring response, adjusting response for different levels of various uncontrolled variables, and so on, is both time-consuming and expensive.

Suppose, however, that the initial cost of such an experiment could be justified and that the experiment yields a set of values for the three control variables which is deemed "optimal." Can the manager blithely assume that if this combination is introduced in *all* territories optimal profits will result? Not at all. First, some of the uncontrolled variables may be changing in some way different from that which existed at the time the experiment was conducted; that is, the environment may not be stable in terms of consumer tastes, consumer incomes, seasonal factors, and the like. Second, other producers may willfully change the competitive environment by changing the price or characteristics of their products. Third, the manager may find it is impossible to implement the "best strategy," since promotional expenditures cannot be altered quickly enough to ensure that essentially the same environmental conditions prevailing during the experiment are still in effect.

Earlier in the chapter we pointed out that the test units of marketing experiments can be broadly classified as involving (1) people, (2) stores, and (3) market areas. Each class of units presents its own set of problems for the experimenter.

In cases where people are the test units (e.g., product usage, advertising copy themes, package tests), the researcher must contend with such things as interview bias, subject conditioning, and subject dropouts. In experiments in which the test units are stores (e.g., pricing, couponing, point-of-purchase displays), the researcher must contend with the possible reluctance of store managers to implement the design, competitors' activities, contamination of the data of control stores by test store influences, and so on. In experiments emphasizing market areas, the problems of measurement and control became the most difficult of all. Seldom can market territories be partitioned without sales-response overlap and stimulus (sales promotion, pricing) overlap as well. Furthermore, there is a danger that any experiment may be conducted for too short a period of time so that the carry-over effect of such treatments as advertising and sales promotion is not appropriately measured.

Although the preceding paragraphs suggest a rather bleak picture for the future of field experimentation in marketing, the fact remains that experimentation and measurement provide the *only sound basis for model validation in marketing and the establishment of causal relationships*. It is to be hoped that as our knowledge of techniques improves and superior means are developed for measuring sales (e.g., via consumer panels, store audits, home audits, etc.), market experimentation will provide a significant tool for the development of information for decision-making purposes.

Sometimes a laboratory-type experiment may serve the needs of the marketer. For example, Entenmann's Inc., a baker of cakes, pastries, and cookies, entered the California market in 1984, launching first in San Diego. Prior to the San Diego launch, studies were conducted in a lab environment. About 20 consumers at a time were brought into the labs. Demographic and background information was recorded before respondents were exposed to the range of bakery goods available in their local supermarkets. Subjects were given seed money that could be used to buy any product. Consumers were asked why they chose as they did. This line of research indicated that the company's product would be successful in California. In a sense, San Diego was being viewed as a test market to test the marketing mix, as Los Angeles was to be the second market area.[29]

The Cost versus Value of Market Experimentation

Market experimentation represents a cost-incurring activity, just as any other form of information gathering. The manager (and researcher) must weigh the potential value of the information against this cost. One point of interest, however, is that, given a reasonably *stable* marketing environment, a field experiment can yield information that is useful for a *series of future decisions*. If so, the value of the research should be appropriately estimated over a time horizon involving a series of future decision choices.

---

[29]K. Higgins, "Baker Taking a Cautious Approach to Its Entry into West Coast Market," *Marketing News*, October 26, 1984, p. 20.

This value will, of course, depend on how cleverly the researcher can design the experiment along lines that are expected to remain reasonably stable over time.

The desire for determining causal relationships of some generality suggests that researchers may wish to include a fairly large number of variables in their field experiments so that they can gain pertinent information for making suitable transformations to other products, other markets, and other time periods. The problems involved in achieving this objective are hardly inconsequential, but the goal of developing *general* information that can be adjusted for specific situations appears more worthwhile than does a goal based on solving a "one-shot" problem.

Experimentation represents another way of information gathering and should be approached in terms of its cost versus value (compared with other techniques) for decision-making purposes, with regard to both present and anticipated problems. Unfortunately, it is much easier to state this objective than to design suitable techniques for implementing it.

SUMMARY

In this chapter our primary objectives were twofold: (1) to introduce the reader to the conceptual bases underlying marketing experimentation and (2) to discuss the various models of experimental design. The statistical machinery used to analyze experimental data will be discussed in Chapter 12.

The first section of the chapter covered the nature of experimentation. The critical aspects of this discussion were the various ingredients of an experiment. We next turned to the potential sources of invalidity, internal and external, associated with an experiment. These are the experimental errors that relate to extraneous factors that can affect an experimental outcome.

We next described some of the major classical and statistical experimental designs. Some of these designs—single-factor, factorial, randomized blocks, latin squares—were illustrated.[30]

We concluded the chapter with a discussion of some of the problems involved in marketing experimentation and the relationship of this means of data collection to the cost and value of information.

ASSIGNMENT MATERIAL

1. Which of the following questions can be tested experimentally and which cannot? Where a test is possible, briefly suggest an approach. Where a test is not possible, explain why.

   a. Do children from the urban inner core drink less milk than those from the suburbs?

[30]For more-advanced discussions of experimental design, see B. J. Winer, *Statistical Principles in Experimental Design*, 2nd ed. (New York: McGraw-Hill, 1962); and J. L. Myers, *Fundamentals of Experimental Design*, 2nd ed. (Boston: Allyn & Bacon, 1972).

b. Would frequent shoppers' reactions to a retailer changing its store layout differ from those of infrequent shoppers?

c. How will purchase behavior change if a manufacturer of greeting cards changes the package?

d. Why do clothing fashions change?

e. Should a gasoline company add a covering over the gasoline pumps at its retail outlets?

2. A mail-order marketer wanted to determine the effect that special promotional material pertaining to its products had on purchases of selected families. The procedure was to analyze changes in purchases for groups of families. Each group received a different number and kind of promotional material. What control problems are likely to emerge in such an experiment and how should they be handled?

3. Suppose that you are the manager of a supermarket and want to determine the sales effectiveness of the announcement of items over the public-address system in the store.

a. Describe how you would design an experiment to test the sales effectiveness of an announcement of frozen orange juice, using the before-after with one control group design.

b. Describe how you would design the same type of experiment using a statistically controlled design.

c. What sources of invalidity would be of major concern in each of the experiments in items a and b?

4. Users of credit cards not only benefit from the convenience of their use but can delay payment from the time of purchase through the billing and payment dates. If the customer is not charged for the use of the credit card, the seller must finance the purchase until payment is made. Such costs inevitably get reflected in prices, and so the customer who pays cash actually pays a part of the cost of financing credit card purchases as well. Recognizing that this was the case, Congress passed an amendment to the Robinson–Patman Act in 1976 which gave retailers permission to set cash discounts of up to 5%.

Exxon decided to test the effects of a 5% discount on cash and credit gasoline sales by conducting a market test. The test was to be conducted at Exxon stations in Abilene, Texas, and Charleston, South Carolina. It was planned to run the test for six months, after which a survey of dealers and customers would be conducted and the sales results analyzed. If the results were favorable, the cash discounts were to be introduced nationwide.

a. Was this an appropriate research design to test the use of the cash discount? Explain.

b. In your judgment, what would constitute sufficiently favorable results from the test using this design to warrant use of the cash discount at all Exxon stations?

5. What major difficulties are encountered in attempting to use field experimentation in marketing contexts?

7

Measurement in Marketing Research—General Concepts and Instrument Design

INTRODUCTION

As indicated in Chapter 5, survey procedures for obtaining respondent data represent one of the most prevalent sources of marketing research information. In many cases of practical interest—new-product-concept testing, corporate image measurement, ad copy evaluation, and the like—the researcher will be seeking information of a psychological nature—for example, how the new-product concept is evaluated by consumers or what the firm's image is. If useful data are to be obtained, the researcher must exercise care in defining what is to be measured, informed judgment in deciding how to make the measurements, and expertise in conducting the measuring operations and analysis of the resulting data.

Definitions play a significant role in scientific inquiry and especially so in the behavioral sciences. In the first section of this chapter we focus on operational defining and its use in research. Increasingly, behavioral scientists are paying greater attention to the working definitions of their particular disciplines. Operational definitions—that is, specification of the performances that are required to establish a concept—are thought by many to provide the means for making the behavioral sciences more rigorous and objective.

Closely allied to the process of defining is the process of measurement. In the next section we shall discuss various types of measurements and the relationship of measurement scales to the interpretation of statistical techniques. This section serves as useful background for the discussion of psychological scaling methods in the next chapter and for multivariate statistical techniques, to be covered in later chapters.

One of the major types of errors affecting research design discussed in Chapter 4 is measurement error. The overall quality of a research project depends not only on the appropriateness and adequacy of the research design and sampling techniques used but also on the measurement procedures used. The third section of this chapter looks at measurement error in the context of sources of variation in measurement. Next the concepts, and operational measures, of reliability and validity in measurement are covered.

Finally, we discuss some general principles and considerations in asking questions and designing a measurement instrument (known also as a *questionnaire*).

Throughout the chapter we emphasize procedures that typically (but not necessarily) lead to unidimensional scales, in which stimulus objects or people are scaled along a single continuum. Later chapters extend these procedures to analyses in which stimulus objects or people may be represented as points (or vectors) in a multidimensional space.

DEFINITIONS IN RESEARCH

An important part of the practice of research entails the construction, use, and modification of definitions. We cannot measure an "attitude," a "shelf facing," a "market share," or even "sales," without first having defined what is meant by each of these terms. More generally, measurement can proceed only after defining the variable(s) to be studied. An investigator must first know *what* must be measured before tackling the problem of *how* to measure it.

Two classes of defining can be distinguished. *Constitutive defining* is roughly similar to dictionary defining. Here we convey the meaning of a concept in terms of still other concepts whose meaning is assumed to be more familiar to the inquirer. One constitutive definition of *attitude*, for example, is "a learned tendency to respond in a consistent manner with respect to a given object of orientation."[1]

Operational defining establishes the meaning of a concept through specifying what is to be observed and how the observations are to be made. Generally this involves specifying (1) the class of persons, objects, events, or states to be observed; (2) the environmental conditions under which the observation takes place; (3) the operations to be performed in making the observations; (4) the instruments to be used to perform the operations; and (5) the observations to be made.[2] An attitude of consumers toward a given brand, for example, can be operationally defined as the results obtained from (1) consumers of the brand, (2) at a given time and in a given geographic area, who are (3) personally interviewed using a (4) specified attitudinal scale to obtain (5) the response information provided by the attitude scale.

Measurements and operational definitions often go together. Attitudes toward products may be defined operationally as numerical ratings on a like-dislike scale. Various

[1]L. A. Samovar, R. E. Porter, and N. C. Jain, *Understanding Intercultural Communication* (Belmont, Calif.: Wadsworth, 1981), p. 45.

[2]R. L. Ackoff, Shiv Gupta, and J. S. Minas, *Scientific Method: Optimizing Applied Research Decisions* (New York: John Wiley, 1962).

aspects of advertisement recall are often defined by having magazine readers go through an unmarked copy of the magazine and note those ads that they remember seeing and those they remember reading, at least in part. In other recall procedures the respondents are presented with cards showing the names of all products advertised in a particular issue of some magazine. Respondents are then asked to pick out those products for which they remember seeing an advertisement. This is followed by their (unaided) description of the ads, the copy points remembered, what information they got out of the ad, and so on.

In still other situations (e.g., theater tests) the effectiveness of a television commercial is defined in terms of the difference in the proportion of audience members who state a particular brand that they would like to receive (if they should turn out to be winners in a studio lottery) before and after watching a series of commercials about one or more of the brands of interest. The effective of direct-mail ads is often defined operationally in terms of the percentage of recipients who respond to the ad's offer. These have been only a few of the many examples that could be mentioned.

MEASUREMENT CONCEPTS

Measurement Defined

Consider the following set of incomplete statements: (1) *"The mean amount of shelf facing that our brand is currently receiving is . . ."*; (2) *"The Consumer Price Index for the first quarter of this year was . . ."*; (3) *"The preferred brand of this product class, as determined from a survey of consumers, is . . ."*; (4) *"The number of supermarkets carrying one or more of our brands in April was . . ."* What process is required to supply the missing information in each?

Most of us will agree that the answer to this question is "measurement." Yet if we reflect on why we gave that answer, it may not be immediately apparent. The first statement requires a determination of lengths to complete it, the second an observation of prices, the third a questioning of consumers, and the fourth an enumeration. Nor is there a common underlying metric for the measurement process. Statement (1) involves a universal standard, statement (2) an arbitrary standard, statement (3) a ranking, and statement (4) a categorization. (As we shall see shortly, these are examples of the use of different *scales* of measurement.)

It is only at a more abstract level that we find the common elements that led us to identify the process involved in completing each of the above statements as "measurement." Conceptually, *measurement* can be defined as a way of obtaining symbols to represent the properties of persons, objects, events, or states, which symbols have the same relevant relationship to each other as do the things represented. In each of the above instances it is necessary that symbols be obtained (numbers for the mean length of shelf facings and the price index, numbers or other symbols for the ranking of preferences and categorization of supermarkets). If they are to be useful as information, the symbols must be interpretable as having the same relevant relationship to each other as do the things represented.

Another way of looking at this is that measurement is "the assignment of numbers to objects to represent amounts or degrees of a property possessed by all of the objects."[3] If a characteristic or property or behavioral act is to be represented by numbers, there must exist a one-to-one correspondence between the number system used and the relations between various quantities (degrees) of that which is being measured. Three important characteristics or features of the real number series itself are

1. *Order*. Numbers are ordered.
2. *Distance*. Differences between numbers are ordered.
3. *Origin*. The series has a unique origin which is indicated by the number zero.

In measurement, then, numbers are assigned to objects (people) in such a way that the relations between the numbers reflect the relations between the objects (people) with respect to the characteristic involved. The end result is establishment of a scale of measurement, which allows the investigator to make comparisons of amounts and changes in the property being measured.

Measurement can be distinguished on the basis of level, according to the characteristics of order, distance, and origin. Measurement occurs at different levels according to the number of these characteristics possessed by the numbers.

Primary Types of Scales

To many people the term "scale" suggests such devices as yardsticks, pan balances, gasoline gauges, measuring cups, and similar instruments for finding length, weight, volume, and the like. That is, we ordinarily tend to think about measurement in the sense of well-defined scales possessing a natural zero and constant unit of measurement. In the behavioral sciences, however, the researcher must frequently settle for less-informative scales. For example, if a consumer is asked to rank a set of toothpaste brands according to overall desirability, the resulting "scale" does not possess the properties associated with most physical measures; for example, it is not meaningful to add two ranks together in order to get a third rank member.

Scales can be classified into the following major categories: (1) nominal, (2) ordinal, (3) interval, and (4) ratio. Each scale possesses its own set of underlying assumptions regarding the correspondence of numbers with real-world entities. These correspondences can progress from scale to scale as our knowledge about the phenomenon increases. Examples are the measurement of color and temperature.

Nominal scales are the least restrictive of scales. The nominal scale does not possess order, distance, or origin. In this type of scale the numbers serve only as labels or tags for identifying objects, properties, or events. For example, we can assign numbers to baseball players or telephone subscribers. In the first case each player receives a different number (any convenient numbers will do) and we have a simple legend for moving from number label to player's name. That is, we have a one-to-one correspondence between

[3]W. S. Torgerson, *Theory and Methods of Scaling* (New York: John Wiley, 1958), p. 19.

number and player and are careful in making sure that no two or more players receive the same number (or that a single player is assigned two or more numbers). Telephone numbers are another illustration of nominal scales, as are classifications into categories. The classification of supermarkets by "carry our brand" versus "do not carry our brand" categories is an illustration of the use of a nominal scale.

It should be clear that nominal scales permit only the most rudimentary of mathematical operations. We can count the number of stores that carry each brand in a product class and find the modal (highest number of mentions) brand carried. Also, we may make various contingency tests having to do with the likelihood that a member of one category is also a member of another category, but the usual statistical operations (calculations of means, standard deviations, etc.) are not empirically meaningful.

Ordinal scales are ranking scales and possess only the characteristic of order. These scales require the ability to distinguish between elements according to a single attribute and direction. For example, a person may be able to rank a group of floor polish brands according to "cleaning ability." If we assign the number 1 to the highest ranking polish, number 2 to the second highest ranking polish, and so on, an ordinal scale results. Note, however, that the mere ranking of brands does not permit us to say anything about the *differences* separating brands with regard to cleaning ability. We do not know if the difference in cleaning ability between the brand ranked 1 and the brand ranked 2 is larger, less than, or equal to the difference between the brand ranked 2 and the brand ranked 3. Thus, any series of numbers that preserves the ordering relationship (say 2, 4, 9, etc.) is as good as our original number assignment involving successive integers. Ordinal scales are thus unique up to a strictly increasing transformation (which is a function that preserves order).

An ordinal scale possesses all the information of a nominal scale in the sense that equivalent entities receive the same rank. Notice, however, that in dealing with ordinal scales, statistical description can employ positional measures such as the median, quartile, and percentile, or other summary statistics that deal with order among entities. The usual arithmetic averaging operations cannot be meaningfully interpreted with ranked data and the practice of calculating an overall index ranking (a weighted ranking of a set of brands according to several properties) is often suspect from an interpretative point of view. As an illustration, note the data summarized in Table 7-1.

TABLE 7-1   Illustration of the Misuse of Ranked Data

BRAND	RANK ON CLEANING ABILITY, X	RANK ON EASE OF APPLICATION Y	IMPORTANCE WEIGHTS		WEIGHTED-INDEX RANK
			w(X)	w(Y)	
A	1	2	0.2	0.8	1.8
B	2	3	0.2	0.8	2.8
C	3	1	0.2	0.8	1.4
A	2	11	0.2	0.8	9.2
B	20	100	0.2	0.8	84.0
C	50	10	0.2	0.8	18.0

From Table 7-1 we see that the brands A, B, and C are first ranked with respect to attribute X (cleaning ability) and then with respect to attribute Y (ease of application), where the number 3 denotes the highest ranked item. Numerical weights of 0.2 and 0.8 are then assigned to the attributes X and Y, respectively, to reflect the assumed relative importance of each attribute in contributing to overall evaluation. An overall index "rank" of each brand is then found. Notice, however, that by making two arbitrary order-preserving transformations in the lower half of the table, a different set of weighted indexes results, but, more importantly, this set does not have even the same *ordering* as the first set.

Interval scales approach the person-on-the-street's conception of measurement in that an interval scale does possess a constant unit of measurement. Interval scales permit one to make meaningful statements about *differences* separating two objects. This type of scale possesses the properties of order and distance, but the zero point of the scale is arbitrary. Among the most common examples of interval scaling are the Fahrenheit and centigrade scales used to measure temperature.[4] While an arbitrary zero is assigned to each temperature scale, equal temperature differences are found by scaling equal volumes of expansion in the liquid used in the thermometer. Interval scales permit inferences to be made about the differences between the entities to be measured (say "warmness"), but we cannot meaningfully state that any value on a specific interval scale is a multiple of another.

An example should make this point clearer. It is not empirically correct to say that an object with a temperature of 50°F is "twice as hot" as one with a temperature of 25°F. Remembering the conversion formula from Fahrenheit to centigrade,

$$T_c = \frac{5}{9}(T_f - 32)$$

we can find that the corresponding temperatures on the centigrade scale are 10°C and -3.9°C, which are not in the ratio 2 : 1. We *can* say, however, that *differences between values* on different temperature scales are multiples of each other. That is, the difference 50°F $-$ 0°F is twice the difference 25°F $-$ 0°F. Corresponding differences on the centigrade scale are 10°C $-$ (-17.7°C) = 27.7°C and -3.9°C $-$ (-17.7°C) = 13.8°C, which, aside from rounding error, are in the same ratio of 2 : 1.

Interval scales are unique up to a transformation of the form $y = a + bx; b > 0$. This means that interval scales can be transformed from one to another by means of a positive linear transformation. It turns out that *differences* between interval-scale values can be expressed in terms of multiples of one another because, by taking differences, the constant in the above linear equation drops out in the computations.

Most ordinary statistical measures to be discussed in later chapters (such as the arithmetic mean, standard deviation, and correlation coefficient) require only interval scales for their computation. For example, if we determine the average temperature in a certain city over a month and express it in either Fahrenheit or centigrade, those days of

---

[4]Various types of indexes, such as the Consumer Price Index, are typically interval scales. Also, the von Neumann–Morgenstern utility scale, described in Chapter 3, is an interval scale.

the month (if any) that are equal to the average will be the same days under each scale of measurement. (But some statistical measures, such as the geometric mean, would be empirically misleading if applied to interval-scaled data.)

Ratio scales represent the "elite" of scales, in that all arithmetic operations are permissible on ratio-scale measurements. These scales possess a unique zero point, and are the scales usually found in the physical sciences (e.g., scales for measuring length and weight). As the name suggests, equal ratios among the scale values correspond to equal ratios among the entities being measured. Ratio scales are unique up to a positive proportionality transformation (of the form $y = cx; c > 0$).

As an illustration of ratio-scale properties, we can see that it is meaningful to talk about 3 yards being three times 1 yard. If transformed to feet, then we can say that 9 feet and 3 feet are in the same ratio, that is, $3 : 1$. We can move from one scale to another merely by applying an appropriate positive multiplicative constant; this is the practice that we follow when we go from grams to pounds or from feet to inches. As would be surmised, a ratio scale contains all the information (class, order, equality of differences) of lower-order scales and more besides. All types of statistical operations can be performed on ratio scales.

Relationships among Scales

To give the reader some idea of the relationships among nominal, ordinal, interval, and ratio scales, Table 7-2 has been reproduced from Stevens' excellent articles on the subject of scaling.[5] From the standpoint of the marketing researcher interested in analyzing data from sample surveys and the like, it is appropriate to note from the table that most commonly used descriptive statistics (arithmetic mean, standard deviation) and tests of significance (*t* test, *F* test) assume that the data are (at least) interval-scaled.

Some further interpretation of this statement is needed. From a purely mathematical point of view one can obviously do arithmetic with *any* appropriate set of numbers—integer ranks, numbers used to label classes, and so on. Certainly the *computation* of a *t* statistic is no different in principle, if the numbers are ranks as opposed to interval-scaled measurements. What is at issue here is the *interpretation* of the results—that is, our ability to make meaningful empirical statements. For example, a *t* statistic will vary if some arbitrary rank preserving transformation is made of the data, but this type of transformation is quite permissible with the ordinal data.

SOURCES OF VARIATION IN MEASUREMENT

Variations in a set of measurements compiled from any measurement instrument arise from a variety of specific sources or factors. These sources may affect both the charac-

---

[5]S. S. Stevens, "Mathematics, Measurement and Psychophysics," in *Handbook of Experimental Psychology,* ed. S. S. Stevens (New York: John Wiley, 1962); and S. S. Stevens, "Measurement, Psychophysics and Utility," in *Measurement: Definitions and Theories,* ed. C. W. Churchman and P. Ratoosh (New York: John Wiley, 1959).

TABLE 7-2 Scales of Measurement

Scale	Mathematical Group Structure	Permissible Statistics	Typical Examples
Nominal	Permutation group $y = f(x)$ [$f(x)$ means any one-to-one correspondence]	Mode Contingency coefficient	Numbering of football players Assignment of type or model numbers to classes
Ordinal	Isotonic group $y = f(x)$ [$f(x)$ means any strictly increasing function]	Median Percentile Order correlation Sign test; run test	Hardness of minerals Quality of leather, lumber, wool, etc. Pleasantness of odors
Interval	General linear group $y = a + bx$ $b > 0$	Mean Average deviation Standard deviation Product-moment correlation t test F test	Temperature (Fahrenheit and centigrade) Energy Calendar dates
Ratio	Similarity group $y = cx$ $c > 0$	Geometric mean Harmonic mean Coefficient of variation	Length, weight, density, resistance Pitch scale Loudness scale

Source: Reproduced with permission from S.S. Stevens, "Mathematics and Psychophysics" in *Handbook of Experimental Psychology*, ed. S. S. Stevens (New York: John Wiley, 1962), p. 25; and S. S. Stevens, "Measurement, Psychophysics and Utility," in *Measurement: Definitions and Theories*, ed. C. W. Churchman and P. Ratoosh (New York: John Wiley, 1959), p. 27.

teristic or property of concern and the measurement process itself. In evaluating the results of any measurement, a major problem arises in attempting to distinguish the portion of the variation among individual scores that can be considered as representing true differences in that which is being measured from the portion of variation that represents error in measurement. Although there are many possible sources that can cause variations in scores, for information being collected from respondents (e.g., in a survey) they can be categorized as shown in Table 7-3. For any given research project, not all will necessarily be operative.

In the first place, variation within a set of measurements can represent only true differences in the characteristic being measured. This, of course, is the ideal situation. For instance, a company wanting to measure attitudes toward a possible new brand name and trademark would like to feel confident that differences in measurements concerning the proposed names represent the individuals' differences in this attitude, and that none of the differences are a reflection of chance variations or other attitudes, such as the individuals' attitudes toward the company itself.

TABLE 7-3 Sources of Variation in Measurement Scores

   I. *True differences in the characteristic or property.*
  II. *Other relatively stable characteristics of individuals which affect scores:* e.g., intelligence, extent of education, information processed.
 III. *Transient personal factors:* e.g., health, fatigue, motivation, emotional strain.
 IV. *Situational factors:* e.g., rapport established, distractions that arise.
  V. *Variations in administration of measuring instrument:* e.g., interviewers.
 VI. *Sampling of items included in instrument.*
VII. *Lack of clarity of measuring instrument:* e.g., ambiguity, complexity, interpretation.
VIII. *Mechanical factors:* e.g., lack of space to record response, appearance of instrument.
 IX. *Factors in the analysis:* e.g., scoring, tabulation, statistical compilation.
  X. *Variation not otherwise accounted for (chance):* e.g., guessing an answer.

Obviously, the ideal situation seldom, if ever, arises. Measurements often are affected by characteristics of individual respondents such as intelligence, education level achieved, and personality attributes. Therefore, the results of a study will reflect not only differences among individuals in the characteristic of interest but also differences in other characteristics of the individuals. Unfortunately, this type of situation cannot be controlled easily unless the investigator knows all the relevant characteristics of the members of the population such that control can be introduced through the sampling process.

Differences in measurement scores may also arise when personal factors such as health, mood, and state of fatigue vary among the respondents. These transient personal characteristics of people do not necessarily affect different measurement instruments in the same way. Closely related to these personal factors is the setting in which measurement occurs. For instance, if measurement is desired from married women, individual responses may vary depending on whether the husband or any other person is present at the time and place of measurement. Not only is this source of variation potentially present in cross-sectional marketing studies, it is often an even greater danger in longitudinal studies. The real danger lies in the investigator's being unaware that this source of variation is operative.

Other sources of variation in measurement scores come from the instrument itself. Any measuring instrument includes only a sample of items relevant to the characteristic or property of concern. Thus, if we attempt to analyze variations in a characteristic, for example, an attitude, that was measured by different instruments, we must recognize that the measures are not entirely comparable even though the same construct was supposedly being measured. The effect of this source should decrease as the number of relevant items included in the instrument increases.

Another source of variation in responses is the clarity of the measuring instrument itself. Ambiguity and complexity resulting from choice of words or context may mean that respondents have to interpret meaning. People tend to interpret statements differently and will respond accordingly.

The more mechanical aspects of measurement can also have an effect on measurement. These arise from both the construction of the instrument and the recording and analysis of responses. One must be extremely careful in performing tasks such as scoring, tabulation, and statistical manipulation if errors are to be prevented.

Finally, there may be some variation that is not otherwise accounted for. This may arise because respondents simply guess at answers. Consequently, responses are a result of chance.

The discussion in this section shows that there are many influences on a measurement other than the true characteristic of concern—that is, there are many sources of potential error in measurement. Measurement error has a constant (systematic) dimension and a random (variable) dimension. These two subtypes of measurement error affect the validity and reliability of measurement, to which we now turn.

VALIDITY AND RELIABILITY OF MEASUREMENT

As the reader has probably gathered by now, the measurement of perceptions, preferences, motivations, and the like is fraught with difficulty. Such questions as

1. Do the scales really measure what we are trying to measure?
2. Do subjects' responses remain stable over time?
3. If we have a variety of scaling procedures, are respondents consistent in their scoring over those scales that purport to be measuring the same thing?

are representative of the problems involved in establishing the validity and reliability of scaling techniques. Similar questions are applicable to other types of measurement, such as that designed to assess some type of behavior.

Our concern will be in looking at general concepts and measures of validity and reliability, which are frequently used in cross-sectional studies. There appears to have been little concern for issues of measure reliability and validity in developments in time-series analysis. Presumably, this is so because typical marketing time-series research involves nonpersonal variables like sales, advertising expenditures, and market share, and such variables are assumed to be not subject to the kinds of human-based things that can affect measurement. Yet, for all types of research unless there is prior evidence that a measure does what it is supposed to and does it well, steps should be taken to develop and assess the best measure possible.[6]

Validity

By *validity* the behavioral scientist means that the data must be unbiased and relevant to the characteristic being measured. We can thus view the validity of a scaling procedure (or measuring instrument, generally) in terms of its freedom from systematic error—that is, its ability to reflect "true" differences, either among individuals at a point in time or

---

[6]A procedure for developing and assessing measures of constructs in time-series research is presented in N. M. Didow, Jr. and G. R. Franke, "Measurement Issues in Time-Series Research: Reliability and Validity Assessment in Modeling the Macroeconomic Effects of Advertising," *Journal of Marketing Research, 21* (February 1984), 12–19.

within a single individual over time. Systematic error may arise from the instrument itself, the user of the instrument, the subject, or the environment in which the scaling procedure is being administered. Since in practice we rarely know "true" scores, we usually have to judge a scaling procedure's validity by its relationship to *other* standards that are thought to be relevant. To a large extent this process is circular.

As can be surmised, validity of a measuring instrument hinges on the availability of some external *criterion* that is thought to be correct. Unfortunately the availability of such "outside" criteria is often low. What makes the problem even more difficult is that the researcher often is not interested in the scales themselves but in the underlying *theoretical* construct that the scale purports to measure. It is one thing to *define* IQ as a score on a set of tests; it is quite another to infer from test results that a certain construct, "intelligence," is being measured.

In "testing" the validity of a scale, the researcher might use any or all of the following: (1) content validity, (2) criterion validity, and (3) construct validity.

Content Validation

The content of a measurement instrument concerns the substance, matter, and topics included as they relate to the characteristic that is being measured. Since a measuring instrument includes only a sample of the possible items that could have been included, content validation is concerned with how representative the scale or instrument is of the universe of the content of the property or characteristic being measured. For example, a bank that is contemplating initiating a new automatic overdraft plan might be interested in estimating need for such a plan by attempting to measure need of individuals for borrowing money. If the measurement instrument includes items concerned with annual income, age, size of family, education level achieved, occupation, number of times money borrowed during some previous time period, home ownership, and so on, the level of content validity of the instrument depends on how representative these surrogates are of need for borrowing money.

By its very nature, content validation is essentially judgmental. The behavioral scientist ordinarily attempts to measure content *validity* by the personal judgments of experts in the field. That is, several content experts may be asked to judge whether the items being used in the instrument are "representative" of the field being investigated. The results of this procedure reflect the "informed" judgments of experts in the content field. Closely related to this approach for assessing content validation is a method involving *known groups*. With this approach, validation comes from the known attitudes and other characteristics of antithetical groups, and not from specific expertise. For instance, if a scale were being constructed to measure attitudes toward a brand of a product, the questions could be tested by administering it to a group known to be regular buyers of the product, which presupposes a favorable attitude. The results would be compared with those from a group of former buyers or other nonbuyers who presumably have a negative attitude. If the scale does not discriminate between the two groups, then its validity with respect to measuring attitude is highly questionable. There is danger in using this method that there might exist other differences between relevant groups besides their known behavior, which might account for the differences in measurement. Therefore, this approach should be used cautiously.

A final approach to content validation is known as *logical validation*. This refers simply to a type of theoretical, intuitive, or common-sense analysis. This type of validation is derived from the careful definition of the continuum of a scale and the selection of items to be scaled. Thus, in an extreme case, the investigator reasons that everything that is included is done so because it is "obvious" that it should be that way. Because things often do not turn out to be as obvious as believed, it is wise not to rely on logical validation alone.

As an example of research lacking content validity we can turn to the Coca-Cola Company and its introduction a few years ago of "new Coke." Since the product represented a major change in taste, thousands of consumers were asked to taste "new" Coke. Overwhelmingly, people said they liked the new flavor. With such a favorable reaction, why did the decision to introduce the product turn out to be a mistake? Executives of the company acknowledge that the consumer survey conducted omitted a crucial question. The people who were asked if they liked the new flavor—remember, most said yes—were not asked if they were willing to give up the old Coke. In short, they were not asked if they would buy the new product in place of the old one.[7]

Criterion Validation

In pursuing the objective of *criterion validity,* the researcher attempts to develop or obtain an external criterion against which the scaling results can be matched. The outside criterion may, of course, be another scale. Criterion validity can be assessed by correlating the set of scaling results under study with some other set, developed from another instrument, that is administered at the same time. Alternatively, the correlation may be carried out with the results of another scaling procedure that is applied to a future testing occasion.

From a decision-making perspective criterion validity is known as *pragmatic* validity, and its two basic dimensions are known as *predictive* and *concurrent* validity. Decision makers are interested simply in whether the instrument works so that better decisions can be made with it than without it.

The "new" Coke example also illustrates criterion (i.e., predictive) validity. The measures of liking, and so on, were not very good predictors of purchase, which was the real measure of managerial interest.

Construct Validation[8]

In *construct validation* the researcher is interested not only in the question "Does it work?" (i.e., predict) but also in the development of criteria that permit answering theoretical questions of why it works and what deductions can be made concerning the theory underlying the instrument.

Construct validity involves three subcases: convergent, discriminant, and nomo-

---

[7]Reported in Arnold Rosenfeld, "Disaster at Coke: A Lesson for Us All," *Austin American Statesman,* July 21, 1985.

[8]An excellent review paper relevant to marketing studies is found in J. Paul Peter, "Construct Validity: A Review of Basic Issues and Marketing Practices," *Journal of Marketing Research,* 18 (May 1981), 133–145.

logical validity. In *convergent validity* we are interested in the correspondence in results between attempts to measure the same construct by two or more independent methods. (These methods need not all be scaling techniques.) *Discriminant validation* refers to properties of scaling procedures that *do* differ when they are supposed to—that is, in cases where they are measuring different characteristics of stimuli and/or subjects. As Campbell and Fiske[9] indicate, since characteristics of the subject and the measuring instrument can each contribute variation to the scaling results, more than one instrument and more than one subject characteristic should be used in convergent-discriminant validation work (see Exhibit 7-1). Discriminant validity concerns the extent to which a measure is unique and not simply a reflection of other variables, and as such it provides the primary "test" for the presence of method variance.

Nomological validity comes closest to what is generally meant by "understanding" a concept (or construct). In nomological validity the researcher attempts to relate measurements to a *theoretical model that leads to further deductions, interpretations, and tests*, gradually building toward a nomological *net*, in which several constructs are systematically interrelated. Since nomological validity is concerned with whether a measure behaves as expected, it is sometimes called "lawlike validity." Overall, it involves studying "both the theoretical relationship between different constructs and the empirical relationship between different measures of those different constructs."[10]

Ideally, the behavioral scientist would like to attain *construct* validity, thus achieving

Exhibit 7-1   Multitrait Multimethod Matrix (Correlations)

	M_A T_1 T_2 T_3	M_B T_1 T_2 T_3	M_C T_1 T_2 T_3
Method A Trait 1	R M M	C H H	C H H
Trait 2	R M	H C H	H C H
Trait 3	R	H H C	H H C
Method B Trait 1		R M M	C H H
Trait 2		R M	H C H
Trait 3		R	H H C
Method B Trait 1			R M M
Trait 2			R M
Trait 3			R

Convergence validity = C
Discriminant validity = difference between C and M correlations; size of H relative to C (ideally H should be approximately zero if traits and methods each are independent)
Reliability = R

[9]D. T. Campbell and D. W. Fiske, "Convergent and Discriminant Validation by the Multitrait–Multimethod Matrix," *Psychological Bulletin*, 56 (1959), 81–105.

[10]J. Paul Peter and G. A. Churchill, Jr., "Relationships among Research Design Choices and Psychometric Properties of Rating Scales: A Meta-Analysis," *Journal of Marketing Research*, 23 (February 1986), 5.

not only the ability to make predictive statements but understanding as well. Frequently the scientist must settle for only *content* validity or at best *criterion* validity. It should be evident, however, that the quest for construct validity may be well justified, particularly if the instrument is to be used in new situations with new groups of individuals. That is, *generalization* of a scale's validity over groups, situations, and times is most readily accomplished by establishing construct validity. Peter and Churchill conducted a meta-analysis of the relationships among research design variables and the psychometric measures of reliability and the three subclasses of construct validity as these relate to rating scales.[11] These researchers concluded that there are important differences between the conceptual and empirical relationships among variables involved. They feel that marketing researchers seem to be overly concerned with the magnitude of the empirical estimates of these psychometric properties which can hide the importance of judgments about nonempirical issues. Specifically, more emphasis should be placed on the theories, the processes used to develop the measures, and the judgments of content validity.

Reliability

By *reliability* the behavioral scientist means the extent to which scaling results are free from experimental error. In this case we are concerned with the consistency of test results over groups of individuals or over the same individual at different times. It need hardly be added that a scaling procedure may be reliable but not valid. Reliability, however, establishes an upper bound on validity. An unreliable scale cannot be a valid one.

In general, measurement of the reliability of a scale (or measurement instrument) may be obtained by one of three methods: (1) test-retest, (2) alternative forms, and (3) internal consistency.[12]

Test-Retest

In measuring the reliability of a scale, our interest may sometimes center on the extent to which *repeated applications* of the instrument achieve consistent results, assuming that the relevant characteristics of the subject(s) are stable over trials. The test-retest method examines the *stability* of response. One potential problem, of course, is that the first measurement may have an effect on the second one (i.e., there may be a testing effect and/or a reactive effect of testing as defined in Chapter 6). Such effects can be reduced when there is a sufficient time interval between measurements. If at all possible the researcher should allow a minimum of two weeks to elapse between measurements. Reliability may be estimated by any appropriate statistical technique for examining differences between measures.

---

[11]Ibid., pp. 1–10.

[12]The basics of reliability in a marketing context are reviewed in J. Paul Peter, "Reliability: A Review of Psychometric Basics and Recent Marketing Practices," *Journal of Marketing Research,* 16 (February 1979), 6–17.

Alternative Forms

The alternative forms method attempts to overcome the shortcomings of the test-retest method by administering successively to the same sample alternate equivalent forms of the measure. Equivalent forms can be thought of as instruments built in the same way to accomplish the same thing but consisting of different samples of items in the defined area of interest. The same types and structures of questions should be included on each form, but the specific questions should differ. In applying the forms of the measurement device they may be given one after the other or after a specified time interval depending upon the investigator's interest in stability over time. Reliability is estimated by correlating the results of the two "equivalent" forms.

Internal Consistency

The internal consistency method estimates reliability *within* single testing occasions. In a sense it is a modification of the alternative form approach, although it differs in that only scoring involves "alternatives." One application of the measurement instrument is sufficient to obtain the measure.

The basic form of this method is *split-half* reliability, in which items are divided into equivalent groups (say, odd- versus even-numbered questions or even a random split) and the item responses are correlated. In practice, any split can be made. To correct for the situation that a full-length scale will be more reliable than a split (i.e., any ratio of altered test length to the original length), the generalized Spearman–Brown formula is applied:

$$r_n = \frac{nr}{1 + (n - 1)r}$$

where

r_n is estimated reliability of the entire instrument,

r is the correlation between the half-length measurements,

n is the ratio of the number of items in the changed instrument to the number in the original.

When the length is doubled, as in the split-half method, the formula becomes

$$r_n = \frac{2r}{1 + r}$$

One obvious condition is that each split scale must contain enough items to be reliable itself. For a split-half scale this is often considered to be eight to ten items, which means that the entire scale should consist of at least sixteen to twenty items.

A potential problem arises for split-half in that results may vary depending on how the items are split in half. A way of overcoming this is to use *coefficient alpha,* which is a type of mean reliability coefficient for all possible ways of splitting an item in half.[13] Whenever possible, alpha should be used as a measure of the internal consistency of multi-item scales.

Another approach to measuring internal consistency utilizes estimation of variances. In this case reliability is defined as the proportion of the "true" variance to the total variance of the data obtained from a measurement instrument, or

$$r_{tt} = \frac{V_t - V_e}{V_t}$$

where r_{tt} is the coefficient of reliability, V_e is the error variance, and V_t is the total variance. If the measuring instrument is split into subsamples, such as a split-half, this formula gives results approximately the same as the Spearman–Brown correction.

A Concluding Comment

The achievement of scale reliability is, of course, dependent on how consistent the characteristic being measured is from individual to individual (homogeneity over individuals) and how stable the characteristic remains over time. Just how reliable a scaling procedure turns out to be will depend on the dispersion of the characteristic in the population, the length of the testing procedure, and its internal consistency. Also having an effect is research design. For example, Churchill and Peter concluded from their meta-analysis study that for reliability of rating scales, measure characteristics (e.g., number of items in a scale, type of scale, number of scale points, etc.) had a major influence on obtained reliability estimates, but sampling characteristics and measurement development processes had little impact.[14]

Although it is not our objective to pursue in detail the methods by which reliability or validity can be "tested," we hope that at least an appreciation of the difficulties encountered in designing and analyzing psychological measure has been conveyed to the reader.[15]

One question that has not been answered is, What is a satisfactory level of reliability or what minimum level is acceptable? There is no simple definitive answer to this question. Much depends on the investigator's or decision maker's purpose in measurement and on

[13]L. J. Cronbach, "Coefficient Alpha and the Internal Structure of Tests," *Psychometrika,* 16 (September 1951), 297–334.

[14]G. A. Churchill, Jr., and J. Paul Peter, "Research Design Effects on the Reliability of Rating Scales: A Meta-Analysis," *Journal of Marketing Research,* 21 (November 1984), 360–75.

[15]See, for example, Peter, "Reliability"; and R. Parameswaran, B. A. Greenberg, D. N. Bellenger, and D. H. Robertson, "Measuring Reliability: A Comparison of Alternative Techniques," *Journal of Marketing Research,* 16 (February 1979), 18–25. For comparisons in cross-national research, see A. Yaprak and R. Parameswaran, "Reliability Measurement in Cross-National Survey Research: An Empirical Investigation," *International Marketing Management,* ed. E. Kaynak (New York: Prager, 1984), pp. 172–93.

the approach used to estimate reliability. In trying to arrive at what constitutes satisfactory reliability, the investigator must at all times remember that reliability can affect (1) validity, (2) the ability to show relationships between variables, and (3) the making of precise distinctions among individuals and among groups.

ASKING QUESTIONS

Throughout this book we have discussed methodological issues in the context of error and ways to manage such error. At this point in our exposition we turn to asking questions of respondents and the sources of error that can arise due to the nature of the individual questions themselves (e.g., a structure, wording, etc.) and the way in which all questions are put together (i.e., the instrument itself).

The major source of error due to the instrument and individual question is *response error*.[16] This type of error occurs in the collection of information from an individual if the reported value differs from the actual value of the variable concerned. Strictly speaking, response error can also be due to the interviewer or investigator. This aspect of response error was discussed in Chapter 5.

It will be recalled that a respondent was defined as a person who either provides information actively through communication or passively through his or her behavior being observed. When we speak of response error, therefore, it should be understood that it is inclusive of errors arising through either communication, observation, or both.

What are the sources of response error? In answering this question it will be helpful to consider the stages involved in providing information. The information must first be *formulated;* that is, it must be assimilated and made accessible for transmission. Once this has been accomplished, it must be *transmitted*. Errors can arise in either stage or in both. We shall use the term *inaccuracy* to denote the errors arising in the formulation stage. The term *ambiguity* will be understood to mean the errors arising in the transmission stage.

Since the purpose of making this distinction in types of response errors is to help understand and thus to control this important source of error, it is appropriate that we examine each type of error in some detail.

Inaccuracy

We have agreed that "inaccuracy" refers to errors that are made in the formulation of information. Suppose that a male respondent is asked the question. "Do you intend to buy a new automobile within the next six months?" and that his answer is limited to "Yes," "No," or "Uncertain." A brief examination of possible answers and subsequent actions indicates that there are two different kinds of inaccuracies. If the respondent answers "Yes," but really has no intention of buying a car within this period or, conversely,

---

[16]Nonresponse error may also be relevant in this context if the instrument or individual questions are the cause of the potential respondent's *refusal* to participate. Nonresponse error was discussed in Chapters 4 and 5.

answers "No," but does intend to buy a car, then we may say that there is *concurrent inaccuracy* in his statement.

Suppose, however, that his present intention is to buy a new car; he so indicates in his answer, and then he does not, in fact, buy one within six months. Or, alternatively, he does not now intend to buy, he answers "No" to the question, and then buys a car within the six-month period. There is no concurrent inaccuracy in either case; the response has reflected the actual intention of the person. The intention, however, was not followed. In this situation we have what may be termed *predictive inaccuracy*.

Predictive inaccuracy as a source of response error is a special case related to intentions data. In each of the other types of information obtained from respondents (information on past behavior, socioeconomic characteristics, level of knowledge, and opinion–attitude), only concurrent inaccuracies occur as a source of error in formulating the desired information.

With the exception of the information on intentions, therefore, our major concern in understanding and reducing response errors resulting from inaccuracy will be with respect to concurrent inaccuracy.

What are the sources of inaccuracy? Both our everyday experiences and empirical evidence suggest that there are two basic sources. Inaccurate information may result from either the *inability* or the *unwillingness* of the respondent to provide the desired information. In those instances where observation is used, this statement may also be applied to the observer; the observer may be unable or unwilling to provide the desired information.

We can readily understand the inability of people to provide information because of its being inaccessible. Even such a simple and straightforward question as "What is the model year of your family car?" may result in an information-formulation problem, particularly if the car is several years old. If the additional question were asked, "What brand or brands of tires do you now have on your car?" most respondents would have even more difficulty in providing an accurate answer without looking at the tires. Finally, if the question were asked, "What reasons did you have for buying brand A tires instead of some other brand?" most respondents would have still more difficulty in providing an accurate answer.

When we move to the problem of *unwillingness* of respondents to provide accurate information, we are faced with a more complex topic. Here we are dealing with the motivations of people: why they are not willing to formulate accurately the information desired. No fully accepted "general theory" of motivation has yet emerged from the behavioral sciences to which we can turn to assist in explaining this type of behavior. The best we seem to have are the general theoretical concepts that attempt to explain survey response behavior. As we discussed in Chapter 5 any or none of these might be applicable in any given situation. There is no conclusive evidence favoring one theory to the exclusion of the others. However, by again applying everyday experiences to this problem, and adding some research findings and the accumulated experiences of practitioners, several reasons are suggested why people may not be willing to make accurate information accessible.

Except in those instances where the respondent provides information through being observed in a natural situation, there are always costs (negative utilities) attached to his or her formulating information. The *time* required is one such cost that is always present.

Others that are often present include *preceived losses of prestige* and some degree of *invasion of privacy*.

We may postulate that, when it is possible to do so, the respondent will tend to act in a manner that will reduce these costs. Such behavior will sometimes result in inaccurate information being provided.

Time Costs

Perhaps the most common reason for respondent unwillingness to provide accurate information is the result of the time required to make the information available. A person may simply be busy and wish to complete the interview as quickly as possible. In this circumstance it is not unusual for the respondent to decide that abrupt answers are the easiest and quickest way of terminating the interview. Rather than reflecting on or verifying the information provided, the respondent gives hasty, ill-considered answers and resists probing if attempted. Inaccurate information results.

Perceived Losses of Prestige

When information involving the prestige of the respondent is sought, there is always a tendency toward inaccurate formulation in the direction of the higher-prestige responses. Although this tendency is recognized by all experienced practitioners, two problems remain: (1) recognizing the items of information that the respondent will interpret as having prestige content, and (2) measuring the amount of the inaccuracy resulting therefore.

Some information items have prestige content associated with them by virtually all respondents. Among these are such socioeconomic characteristics as age, income, and educational level. Other informational items are more difficult to identify as having prestige content, however. Information on the place of birth or residence is an example. People who live in rural areas or in suburbs are prone to give the nearest city in answer to questions concerning where they live. In part, this no doubt reflects a belief that the investigator would not otherwise recognize the location given; in part, it may also reflect a higher level of prestige associated with being born or living in a large and well-known city.

An example of a still more subtle prestige association that resulted in a sizable error in information obtained is illustrated by the experience of a marketing research firm that conducted a study on nationally known brands of beer. One of the questions asked was, "Do you prefer light or regular beer?" The response was overwhelmingly in favor of "light" beer. Since sales data indicated a strong preference for "regular" beer, it was evident that the information was inaccurate. Subsequent investigation revealed that the respondents viewed people who drank light beer as being more discriminating in taste. They had, therefore, given answers that, in their view, were associated with a higher level of prestige.

The problem of measuring the amount of inaccuracy resulting from this source is usually difficult to solve satisfactorily. In the ideal case it requires that information be available on the item from sources that are external to the sample and, further, that these external data be more accurate than those obtained from the respondents. Clearly, in most cases such data are not available; if they were, the information would not have been collected from the respondents.

One approach to the solution to this problem is to ask for the information in two different ways. When one is obtaining information on respondents' ages, for example, it is a common practice to ask early in the interview, "What is your present age?" and later "In what year were you born?" or "In what year did you enter high school?" Another approach is to use indirect questions. In one study, when respondents were asked, "Are you afraid to fly?" very few people indicated any fear of flying. In a follow-up study when they were asked, "Do you think your neighbor is afraid to fly?" most of the neighbors turned out to have severe anxieties about flying.

A promising method for obtaining information about sensitive matters is the *randomized-responses* technique.[17] When using this technique the investigator presents two questions, either of which can be answered by a "Yes" or a "No," one innocuous (e.g., "Were you born in May?") and the other sensitive (e.g., "Did you shoplift any items from the Downtown Mall during the month of December?"). The respondent is asked to flip a coin or use some other randomizing device to select which question to answer, and then to answer the indicated question. The respondent is instructed *not* to tell or in any way communicate to the interviewer which question was answered.

The proportion of respondents who answered "Yes" to the sensitive question can be estimated from the formula

$$P(\text{yes}|\text{sens. quest.}) = \frac{P(\text{yes}) - P(\text{innoc. quest.})P(\text{yes}|\text{innoc. quest.})}{P(\text{sens. quest.})}$$

In the example, if the proportion of respondents who answered "Yes" is 0.06, the proportion born in May (determined from the Census of Population) is 0.08, and the probability of answering each question is 0.5, the estimated proportion who answered "Yes" to the shoplifting question would be

$$P(\text{yes}|\text{shoplifting question}) = \frac{0.06 - (0.5)(0.08)}{0.5} = 0.04$$

This is a point estimate of the (hypothetical) proportion of the population from which the sample was drawn who shoplifted at the place during the period specified.

This example of the randomized response technique is a simplified one. There are approaches that can use a single question, but the mathematical and statistical properties tend to be more complex. For most marketing applications the two-question structure will work nicely. All that is needed is a suitable randomizing device (for which the investigator knows the relevant distributions) and knowledge of the distribution of responses to the innocuous question. Although this technique is perhaps most easily ad-

---

[17]C. Campbell and B. L. Joiner, "How to Get the Answer without Being Sure You've Asked the Question," *American Statistician*, 27 (December 1973), 229–31.

ministered in person, there have been approaches developed that are suitable for telephone and mail administration.[18]

Invasion of Privacy

Clearly, some topics on which information is sought are considered to be private matters. When such is the case, both nonresponse and inaccuracy in the responses that are obtained can be anticipated. Matters about which respondents resent questions include money matters or finance, family life, personal hygiene, political beliefs, religious beliefs, and even job or occupation. Either indirect questions or the randomized-response technique can sometimes be used to avoid intrusion. If direct questions are used concerning such matters, they should be placed as near the end of the questionnaire as other considerations permit.

It should be recognized, however, that invasion of privacy is an individual matter. Thus, what one person considers to be sensitive information may not be viewed that way by others. In fact, it has been suggested that researchers often view topics as sensitive which a majority of respondents would not view as sensitive.[19] Because the response to the way in which questions are asked and the order in which they are asked will be affected by the "sensitivity" of the requested information, the investigator should attempt to determine sensitivity if it is suspected to be a problem. One way of handling this is in the pretest stage where questions can be added asking about extent of sensitivity of topics and specific questions.

Ambiguity

Ambiguity may be defined as the errors made in interpreting spoken or written words or behavior. Ambiguity, therefore, occurs in the transmission of information, through either communication or observation.

Now suppose we conduct an experiment. Before reading further, and without reading the preceding paragraph again, write what you understand the word "ambiguity" to mean. After you have finished, compare your definition with the first sentence in the preceding paragraph.

The experiment has two possible outcomes:

1. Your definition and the one given above have the same meaning. If this is the case, the definition is not ambiguous to you.
2. Your definition and the one given above do not have the same meaning. If this is the case, and you read the definition carefully the first time, the experiment has provided a personal example of ambiguity.

---

[18]See Donald E. Stem, Jr., and R. Kirk Steinhorst, "Telephone and Mail Questionnaire Applications of the Randomized Response Model," *Journal of the American Statistical Association*, 79 (1984), 555–64.

[19]Perhaps the most comprehensive treatment of sensitive information and how to ask questions about it is N. Bradburn and S. Sudman, *Improving Interview Method and Questionnaire Design* (San Francisco: Jossey-Bass, 1979).

Although the definition given above was not intended to be ambiguous, the careful reader might logically raise some questions about the interpretation intended, particularly if he or she were inclined to press a point here and there. Consider the following questions and answers:

Question: Did you intend the word "or" in the definition to mean "and/or," the inclusive disjunction, or just "or," the exclusive disjunction?

Answer: We intended it to mean "and/or." The meaning intended was "Ambiguity refers to errors made in interpreting spoken *and/or* written words *and/or* behavior."

Question: Why didn't you write it that way?

Answer: Because we thought it would be clearer to the average reader if we just used "or."

Questions: Were you aware that there are other words in your definition that have different usages?

Answer: Yes. Most words have different usages.

Question: Were you aware that "ambiguity" normally is used to refer to the condition that permits errors in interpretation rather than to the errors as such?

Answer: Yes. We used it to mean the errors as such because that was the meaning we wanted the word we used to have. "Ambiguity" was the best word we could think of to help convey that meaning.

Ambiguity is present in all languages and especially so in ours. The short discourse just completed contains examples of but a few of the difficulties encountered in attempting to express an idea clearly.

It is apparent that a single section of one chapter of a book on marketing research will not solve the general problem of ambiguity, or even the problem as it is encountered in research. This section will, however, point out the general areas in which it is encountered in marketing research, and describe methods that have been used successfully to identify and to reduce it.

Ambiguity in Communication

Unambiguous communication in research requires that the question asked and the answers given each mean the same thing to the questioner and the respondent. A two-step process is therefore involved:

1. Question as understood   *is same as*   Question as understood
   by questioner   by respondent
2. Answer as understood   *is same as*   Answer as understood
   by respondent   by questioner

The first step in this process is the controlling one. If the question is not clearly understood by the respondent, frequently the answer will not be clearly understood by the questioner. To illustrate this point, in an actual research project on tomato juice, the question

Do you like tomato juice?
        Yes □   *No* □   *Neither like nor dislike* □

was changed, after pretesting, to

Do you like the taste of tomato juice?
        Yes □   *No* □   *Neither like nor dislike* □

Even a careful reading of these two questions may not disclose any real difference in their meaning. If this is the case, it is clear that you are making the same assumption about the referent of "like" as did the analyst who drew up the question, that "like" refers to "taste." In pretesting, however, it was discovered that some housewives answered "Yes" with other referents in mind. They "liked" the amount of vitamin C their children get when they drink tomato juice, they "liked" the tenderizing effect that tomato juice has when used in the cooking of meat dishes, and so on. Note that if the wording of the question had not been changed, there would have been a complete misunderstanding in some cases of the simple, one-word answer "Yes."

Question understanding is an issue that goes beyond ambiguity. All too often a respondent may not understand a question but may have no opportunity to request clarification. In mail surveys, the extreme response is to not respond at all. In telephone or personal interview settings, the more captive individual might participate even though specific questions or topics were not fully understood. The quality of such data, of course, would be highly questionable.

How serious a problem this represents is subjective. The National Opinion Research Center reported a mean question understanding percentage of 78.9% for their social surveys conducted during the 1972–1980 period using personal interviews.[20] A study using telephone interviews reported a 74.9% incidence of question understanding, and such understanding varied systematically with the socioeconomic characteristics of respondents.[21] The danger, of course, lies in having a "significant" incidence of question understanding but not knowing it. Thus, examining question understanding should be a part of every survey whenever possible. Used in this manner it can help interpret and gain further insights into the data (Exhibit 7-2). Examining this issue in a pretest is not sufficient for improving overall data quality since in a pretest it addresses ambiguity only.

[20]National Opinion Research Center, *General Social Surveys Cumulative Codebook 1972–1980,* 1980. A study of ethical issues in biomedical research using household interviews reported respondent understanding for two questionnaire formats of 73% and 79% (G. Mellinger, C. Huffine, and M. Balter, "Assessing Comprehension in a Survey of Public Reactions to Complex Issues," *Public Opinion Quarterly,* 46 [1982], 97–109).

[21]R. A. Peterson, R. A. Kerin, and M. Sabertehrani, "Question Understanding in Self-Report Data," *An Assessment of Marketing Thought and Practice,* ed. B. J. Walker et al. (Chicago: American Marketing Association, 1982), pp. 426–29.

Exhibit 7-2   Using "Question Understanding" for Explanation

Consider the data below, which are raw responses to the question
  "Government regulation is necessary to protect and improve the quality of life."

QUESTION UNDERSTANDING	RESPONSE			
	Agree	*Uncertain*	*Disagree*	*Total*
MALE RESPONDENTS:				
Good	447	10	332	839
Fair/poor	128	11	33	172
FEMALE RESPONDENTS:				
Good	453	17	215	685
Fair/poor	248	20	72	340
TOTAL	1326	58	652	2036

From these data several percentages can be calculated. For example, while 65.1% of the total sample agreed with the statement, 61.8% of the males and 68.4% of the females agreed. However,

- of the males whose question understanding was "good," *59.2% agreed* with the statement.
- of the males whose question understanding was "fair/poor," *74.4% agreed.*
- of the females whose question understanding was "good," *66.1% agreed.*
- of the females whose question understanding was "fair/poor," *72.9% agreed.*

Generally, of the survey participants whose question understanding was "good," *62.3%* agreed with the statement. Hence, in certain instances question understanding can be used to enhance the interpretation of, and even, to a limited extent, "explain" item responses.

Source: Adapted from Peterson, Kerin, and Sabertehrani, "Question Understanding in Self-Report Data."

The question both initiates and gives direction to the communication process in research. In addition, the form and wording of the question, unlike that of the answer, can be completely controlled by the researcher. It is not surprising, therefore, that a large number of investigations have been carried out on both the form and wording of questions. It is appropriate that we consider both question form and question wording and their relationships to ambiguity.[22]

[22]A comprehensive treatment is found in the excellent book by H. Schuman and S. Presser, *Questions and Answers in Attitude Surveys: Experiments on Question Form, Wording, and Context* (New York: Academic Press, 1981).

Forms of Questions   Three basic forms of questions may be distinguished: the free-answer question, the dichotomous question, and the multiple-choice question. These forms are roughly analogous, respectively, to essay, true–false, and multiple-choice questions on examinations.

The *free-answer,* or *open, question* is, as the name implies, a question that has no fixed alternatives to which the answer must conform. The respondent answers in his or her own words and at the length he or she chooses. Interviewers are usually instructed to make a verbatim record of the answer.

An example of a free-answer question in the tomato-juice study already referred to is

What suggestions could you make for improving tomato juice?

The suggestions made included packaging it in glass containers, finding some way to keep it from separating, and improving the flavor through the use of such additives as lemon juice, salt, and vodka.

Free-answer questions are almost invariably shorter than multiple-choice questions and are usually shorter than dichotomous questions. A corollary characteristic is that free-answer questions are also invariably less complex in sentence structure than multiple-choice questions on the same issue, and are usually less complex than dichotomous questions.

Common sense suggests, and reading tests have confirmed, that short and simply structured sentences are more easily understood than long and complex ones. The tendency toward ambiguity of the long and complex sentence is accentuated, if anything, by *listening* to it rather than *reading* it. Further, there would seem to be no reason to believe that the findings would be any different for questions than for declarative statements. Based on these premises, we should be on reasonably sound grounds for drawing inferences about the relative probability of ambiguity in questions and answers based on length and complexity of structure.

Free-answer questions place greater demands on the ability of the respondent to express himself or herself. As such, this form of question provides the opportunity for greater ambiguity in interpreting answers. To illustrate, consider the following verbatim transcript of one female respondent's reply to the question:

What suggestions could you make for improving tomato juice?
I really don't know. I never thought much about it. I suppose that it would be nice if you could buy it in bottles because the can turns black where you pour the juice out after it has been opened a day or two. Bottles break, though.

Should the conclusion be drawn that she had "no suggestion," "suggested packaging in a glass container," or "suggested that some way be found to prevent the can from turning black around the opening"? Note that she seems to have made the implicit assumption that the bottle would *not* turn black around the opening.

From the criteria previously stated, we may tentatively conclude that the free-answer question provides *the lowest probability of the question's being ambiguous, but the highest probability of the answer's being ambiguous,* compared with the other two question forms.

The *dichotomous question* has two fixed alternatives of the type "Yes—No," "In favor—Not in favor," "Use—Do not use," and so on. It is the most frequently used form of question in marketing research. The question quoted earlier,

> *Do you like the taste of tomato juice?*
>   *Yes* ☐   *No* ☐   *Neither like nor dislike* ☐

is an example of a dichotomous question.

It will be observed that a third alternative has been added in the question in the example to allow for those people who do not have a definite liking or disliking for tomato juice. It is usually desirable to provide a category of this type to avoid forcing

Exhibit 7-3 Open-Ended Questions and Answers

The advantages of the open-ended format are considerable, but so are its disadvantages. In the hands of a good interviewer, the open format allows and encourages respondents to give their opinions fully and with as much nuance as they are capable of. It also allows respondents to make distinctions that are not usually possible with the fixed alternative formats and to express themselves in language that is comfortable for them and congenial to their views. In many instances it produces vignettes of considerable richness and quotable material that will enliven research reports.

The richness of the material can also be a disadvantage if there is need to summarize the data in concise form. For example, to reduce the complexity of the data to fewer or simpler categories and in order to treat the data statistically, responses must be coded into categories that can be counted. Coding of free-response material is not only time consuming and costly but also introduces some amount of coding error. This is known as content analysis.

Open-ended questions also take somewhat more time to answer than closed questions do and require greater interviewer skill in recognizing ambiguities of response and in probing and drawing respondents out—particularly those who are reticent and not highly verbal—to make sure that they give codable answers. Open-ended response formats may work better with telephone interviews, where close supervision of interview quality can be maintained, although there is a tendency for shorter answers to be given on the telephone. No matter how well controlled the interviewers may be, however, factors such as carelessness and verbal facility will generate greater individual variance among respondents than would be the case with fixed alternative response formats.

In general, the free-response format requires more psychological work on the part of respondents; that is, respondents must think harder about the question and pay more attention to what is being asked and marshal their thoughts in order to respond to the interviewers' questions. If the question comes more or less out of the blue, the respondents' thoughts will not be organized and may emerge somewhat haphazardly and in a confused fashion. What is reported first, however, may be important to the investigator as an indicator of the saliency of issues or the importance of things to the respondents.

Source: Adapted from S. Sudman and N.M. Bradburn, *Asking Questions* (San Francisco: Jossey-Bass, 1982), pp. 150–51.

the respondent to make a definite stand when he or she may really be neutral. Similarly, it may be desirable to add other types of categories such as "don't know," "no opinion," or "not applicable," as the nature of the question and question format dictates. Unfortunately there is a tendency to treat neutral, no opinion, and don't know responses as indicating the same thing, something that obviously they are not.

In the example above the implied alternatives are clear and do not have to be stated. For many issues, however, the alternatives must be stated in the body of the question, as they would not otherwise be clear. The following is an example of such a question:

> *Do you think that next year the price of cars will be higher, lower, or about the same as now?*

In terms of length and complexity of structure, the dichotomous question falls between the free-answered questions (shortest and least complex) and the multiple-choice questions (longest and most complex). The dichotomous question places the least demands on the respondent in terms of formulating and expressing an answer. With respect to ambiguity in dichotomous questions, therefore, we may tentatively conclude that this form of question provides roughly *an average probability of the question's being ambiguous, but the lowest probability of the answer's being ambiguous,* compared with the other two forms.

The *multiple-choice question* provides several set alternatives for the answer to it. In this respect it is in the middle ground between the free-answer and the dichotomous question.

An example of the multiple-choice type of question from the tomato juice study is as follows:

> *Would you say you use the brand you do because it is the most reasonably priced, or because it is a brand you are used to and can rely on, or because you like the taste, or because of some other reason?*
>
> *Reasonably priced* ☐   *Like taste* ☐
> *Used to and rely on* ☐   *Other*   ☐

It should be noted that this question could have been asked as a free-answer question. The choice between the free-answer and the multiple-choice forms of asking question must always be made if the same question is not asked in both forms.

The multiple-choice question must be longer and more complex than either the free-answer or dichotomous questions in order to state the several alternatives. The statement of the alternatives is provided to assist the respondent in recalling and in formulating his or her answer. In giving this assistance, however, added opportunities to misunderstand the question are also provided.

A common source of ambiguity in the multiple-choice question is the difficulty of making the alternatives mutually exclusive. In the above example this requirement was met reasonably well. (It might be argued, however, that one would have to be "used to" and be able to "rely on" the taste's being consistently the same in order to give the "taste" alternative as the answer.)

Another common source of ambiguity in multiple-choice questions is the implied restriction on alternatives. The example strongly implies that the respondent *should have a single, most important reason for using the brand.* This may very well not be the case.

There is a tendency for the alternatives appearing first and last in a multiple-choice question to be used as answers more frequently than those in other positions. This systematic error, often called *position bias* or *order bias,* may be indicative of ambiguity in the question. One experiment in which several alternatives were presented in different positions to matched samples of respondents resulted in the top position, on the average, outdrawing the middle position by 6 percentage points. The bottom position outdrew the middle position by 2 percentage points. In no instance did the middle position outdraw the top or bottom position.[23]

This problem can be solved satisfactorily in most cases by rotating the order of the alternatives. This may be done by printing cards for each of the desired different orders of alternatives and instructing the interviewers to use the cards in a prescribed sequence. For self-report instruments rotation means that different forms have to be prepared. Practical and economic considerations will limit the extent to which this can be done. The value of rotation in handling position bias has been questioned on the grounds that it is based on a "false" conception of bias and has been approached without reference to a statistical model of the data-generating process.[24] The criticism is based on a theoretical model, and alternative actions have not been proposed.

With respect to ambiguity in multiple-choice questions, we may tentatively conclude that this form of question provides the *highest probability of the question's being ambiguous, and an average probability of the answer's being ambiguous,* compared with the other two forms.

Table 7-4 summarizes our tentative conclusions concerning the form of question and the probability of ambiguity. These conclusions should not be used as the final arbiter on the choice of question form. Some question forms are suited better to eliciting certain kinds of information than others. In "reason why" questions, for example, one would normally use free-answer or multiple-choice questions rather than dichotomous ones.

Each question form has its proponents. Each has been used extensively. There is no one "best" form of question for obtaining all types of information from respondents.

TABLE 7-4 Form of Question and Relative Probability of Ambiguity

	RELATIVE PROBABILITY OF AMBIGUITY	
FORM OF QUESTION	*Question*	*Answer*
Free-answer	Lowest	Highest
Dichotomous	Average	Lowest
Multiple-choice	Highest	Average

[23]Reported in S.L. Payne, *The Art of Asking Questions* (Princeton, N.J.: Princeton University Press, 1951), pp. 84–85.

[24]Neils J. Blunch, "Position Bias in Multiple-Choice Questions," *Journal of Marketing Research,* 21 (May 1984), 216–20.

Question Wording The wording of questions is a critical consideration in obtaining information from respondents. Consider the following three questions and the percentage of affirmative responses to each from three matched samples of respondents:[25]

> *Do you think anything should be done to make it easier for people to pay doctor or hospital bills?*
>> (82% replied "Yes.")
>
> *Do you think anything could be done to make it easier for people to pay doctor or hospital bills?*
>> (77% replied "Yes.")
>
> *Do you think anything might be done to make it easier for people to pay doctor or hospital bills?*
>> (63% replied "Yes.")

These questions differ only in the use of the words *should, could,* and *might.* Although these three words have different connotations, they are sometimes used as synonyms. Yet the responses, at the extreme, are 19 percentage points apart. This difference is the same as the amount by which the *Literary Digest* was in error in predicting the percentage of the popular vote for Landon in 1936, a prediction that is used as a classic illustration of the dire results of improper sampling procedures.

The ability to construct clear, unambiguous questions is an art rather than a science. It has remained so despite the extensive investigations and accumulated experience of practitioners over the past four decades. Although principles of question wording have evolved, they are more indicative than imperative.

In general, we may summarize these principles by asserting that ambiguity in question wording arises from one or more of the following sources: (1) question length, (2) respondent unfamiliarity with one or more words, (3) ambiguity of one or more words in context, (4) two questions combined in one, and (5) lack of specificity. A brief discussion on each of these sources of ambiguity in question wording is in order.

1. *Questions that are too long.* There is a class of questions known as "flabbergasters" that are long, complex, and verge on being incomprehensible. A classic example is a reported 13-line question asking farm managers whether they used mostly inductive or deductive logic.

Each word in a question is a potential source of ambiguity. The greater the number of words, the more complex the structure of the question must become. For both these reasons, brevity in question construction is a virtue. As a general rule of thumb, questions should be held to no more than 20 words if at all possible.

The following question has been paraphrased from one actually used on a survey in a different field:

> *Do you think of new-car dealers as being independent businesspeople like appliance dealers and furniture merchants who own their own stores, or as being employees of the automobile companies?*

[25]Payne, *Art of Asking Questions,* pp. 8, 9.

Suppose, if you will, that this question is being read to you rather than your reading it. It refers to three different types of businesses, as well as to owning one's business versus being employed by a manufacturer. The researcher who constructed this question went to the trouble of using at least ten extra words which add opportunities of having the question misunderstood. Do you think that you would be more likely to understand the question above or this revised and shortened version?

> *Do you think of new-car dealers as owning their business, or as being employees of the automobile companies?*

2. *Questions that use one or more words that are unfamiliar to the respondent.* The vocabulary used in questions should match that normally used by the respondents as closely as possible. For example, the wording of the question

> *Do you think that the processing of dehydrated soups reduces the caloric content?*

might well be appropriate if it is to be asked of a group of food chemists. It would require a heroically optimistic researcher, however, to consider seriously asking this question of a sample of consumers. There are at least four words that individually, and in some cases collectively, would be unfamiliar to some consumers.

The principle of matching question vocabulary and respondent vocabulary is not always easy to follow. In the case of a group of food chemists, there is a similarity of training and a common usage of terms. It is probable that their individual vocabulary levels are uniformly high. For this group, question vocabulary and respondent vocabulary can be matched reasonably well. In the case of consumers, however, vocabulary levels vary widely.

When the sample of respondents is at all large and nonhomogeneous in background, it is desirable to word the question at the lowest vocabulary level represented in the sample. For consumers, this means that questions must be worded as simply as possible. The researcher must guard against the use of more difficult synonyms for their simpler equivalents such as "observe" instead of "see," "obtain" instead of "get," and "purchase" instead of "buy."

The question should be worded to be understood by the respondent—not to impress him or her with the researcher's vocabulary. Impressing other people through the use of an extensive vocabulary should be left to pedants.

3. *Questions that use one or more words that are ambiguous in context.* A common source of ambiguity of words in context is the way in which the question is constructed. Some illustrations of ambiguities arising from poor sentence structure are given below.

> *After receiving the Fisher stereo set you ordered, did a representative of the Sight and Sound Company telephone you promptly?* (Did the representative call after *the company* received the set or after *you* received it?)
>
> *Did you plan to buy a service policy after the set was one year old?* (Were your plans made to buy a policy before the set was one year old, or to buy

it after the set was one year old? Or were your plans made after the set was already one year old?)

A more serious and less easily corrected source of ambiguity of words in context is words that have two or more meanings. Most words have several meanings out of context, and we rely on the topic being discussed to indicate the intended meaning. For example, the word "set" used in the above question has more than 250 meanings. In these questions the meaning intended should be clear. In many cases, however, the intended meaning of a word is not clear form the context in which it is used. Consider the following question:

> *Have you been satisfied with the service provided by the Sight and Sound Company?*

In this question, both the words "you" and "service" are subject to misinterpretation. Does "you" mean the person being addressed only, or does it include this person's family? Does "service" refer to the assistance and consideration given the customer in making purchases or does it refer to the repair of equipment done by the company?

4. *Combined questions.* Careless question wording sometimes results in two questions being asked as one. A question asked of commuters is illustrative of such questions:

> *Which would you say is the more convenient and economical way to commute, by car or by train?*

It is obvious that the respondent who believed that one method was more convenient and the other more economical could not logically answer the question as it was asked.

Combined questions should be avoided. The above question should have been broken into two separate questions, one dealing with "convenience" and the other with "economy."

5. *Questions that lack specificity.* Ambiguity often arises because of the vagueness of questions. A question such as

> *Do you listen to FM stations regularly?*

will involve ambiguity because it is by no means clear whether "regularly" means three times a day, twice a week, once a month, or some other frequency of listening.

If the question is to be understood correctly, the desired information must be clearly specified.

Procedures for Recognizing and Reducing Ambiguity in Communication   Every research design that uses communication to obtain information should have as many safeguards against ambiguity as possible. Procedures should be employed to recognize where ambiguity may be present and to reduce it to the lowest practicable level.

Three procedural steps are useful for these purposes and should be considered in every project: (1) alternative question wording, (2) pretesting, and (3) verification by observation.

1. *Alternative question wording.* We have already seen that the present state of the art of question formulation cannot guarantee unambiguity. In questions where there is reason to suspect that ambiguity may exist, it is advisable to consider alternative wordings and forms of questions to be asked of subsamples of respondents.

The simplest application of this procedure applies to dichotomous questions. If it is believed that the order in which the alternatives are stated may influence the responses, the question can be asked of half the sample of respondents with the alternatives in one order, and of the other half with the order reversed. For example, the question

Which make of car would you say is more powerful, Ford or Chevrolet?

can be asked of half the respondents, and the question

Which make of car would you say is more powerful, Chevrolet or Ford?

of the other half. If the order of the alternatives does, in fact, affect the responses, this will become apparent and can be allowed for in interpreting the results.

The use of this simple experimental technique costs little more than having an extra set of questionnaires printed. It may reveal no significant differences in response. If so, it will usually be worth the cost involved simply to know that this is the case. Where significant differences in response are discovered, it will be even more worthwhile as a warning in interpreting the information.

2. *Pretesting.* Pretesting of questionnaires is a virtual necessity. The only way to gain real assurance that questions are unambiguous is to try them.

Pretesting is almost always done initially by asking proposed questions of associates. To be truly effective, however, pretesting of questions should be conducted by asking them of a group of respondents who are similar to those to be interviewed in the final sample.

It is the rule, rather than the exception, that questions will be revised as a result of pretesting. Several versions of a question may need to be considered as a result of pretesting before the final version is decided upon.

3. *Verification by observation.* Whenever cost, time, and the type of information desired permits, information obtained through communication should be verified by observation. The housewife may state that the only brand of floor wax she uses is Johnson's. Where possible, it is desirable to verify this statement partially by observing whether this is the only brand of floor wax she now has on hand.

Clearly, verification by observation is not always possible or practical. In the above example, the housewife may object to a pantry audit. Even greater difficulties would be involved in attempting to verify via observation her statement that she waxes the floors once each week.

Ambiguity in Observation

Although it has been suggested that, where practical to do so, information obtained by communication should be verified by observation, the implication should not be drawn that observation is free of ambiguity. If we conduct a pantry audit and find that Johnson's Wax is the only brand on hand, this in itself does not disclose whether it was purchased or received as a gift, whether it is used or not, or, if used, for what purpose.

In making observations we each select, organize, and interpret visual stimuli into a picture that is as meaningful and as coherent to us as we can make it. Which stimuli are selected and how they are organized and interpreted are highly dependent on both the backgrounds and frames of reference of the observer. If a customer, a floorwalker, and the department manager are each standing side by side on the mezzanine overlooking the jewelry department, what each "sees" will very likely differ markedly from what the others "see."

The trained observer will invariably "see" more that relates to his or her specialty in an ambiguous situation than the untrained observer. As an illustration, a few years ago a cereal manufacturer ran a promotional campaign involving a drawing contest for children. Each child who entered was required to submit (along with a box top) a picture he or she had drawn that depicted brand X cereal being eaten. The contest was run, the prizes awarded on the basis of artistic merit, and the brand manager turned his attention to other matters. A short time later a psychologist who worked for the company happened to see the pictures. He asked to be permitted to study them. He found that a sizable proportion of them showed a child eating cereal alone, often with no other dishes on the table. This suggested to him that cereal is often eaten by children as a between-meal snack. A later study by the company's marketing research department showed that cereals are eaten between meals by children in greater amounts than are eaten for breakfast. The advertising program of the company was subsequently changed to stress the benefits of its cereals as between-meal snacks.

SOME CONCLUDING COMMENTS

We have not discussed broader issues of overall questionnaire design, question sequencing, and so forth (see Table 7-5). This is not to say that these are not important issues.

TABLE 7-5   Major Aspects of Questionnaire Design

I.	Foundation of questionnaire: what information is needed from which respondents and how it is to be collected
II.	Content of questions
III.	Phrasing of each question
IV.	Response format: open-end or fixed number of alternatives
V.	Organization and sequencing of questions
VI.	Physical design of questionnaire
VII.	Pretesting and evaluation before final use

To the contrary, they are! For example, recent research has shown that questions appearing early in a questionnaire and early within their respective groups (when the questionnaire is so organized) are more likely to be answered than are questions placed elsewhere.[26] Similarly a well-known principle is that questionnaire design should follow a so-called funnel approach with respect to where variable kinds of questions should be placed (e.g.,

TABLE 7-6 CAPPA's Question Types with Mnemonics

Statement—*info:* This is a statement of facts or instructions for the respondent to read. The response is simply an indication to go to the next question.

Select 1/r—*pick-1:* Here the respondent is given a list of r options and is required to choose one option only.

Select n/r—*pick-n:* Here the respondent gets a set of r options to select from but this time chooses up to n options ($n \leqslant r$).

Select n1/r and **Rank n2/n1—*pick-and-rank:*** This question type is similar to pick-n, but in addition to selecting n1 options from a list of r options, the respondent is then asked to rank n2 of those options selected.

Select n1/n2/r—*pick-and-pick:* Respondent is asked to select n1 options in category 1 and n2 options in category 2. Each option can be selected in only one of the two categories.

Rank n/r—*rank:* In this question the respondent gets r options and is asked to rank the top n ($n \leqslant r$).

Integer Rating—*integer-scale:* The respondent is asked to rate on a linear scale of 1 to n the description on the screen or accompanying prop card (for example, 1 for completely disagree to 5 for completely agree). Only integer responses are accepted.

Continuous Rating—*real-scale:* This is similar to integer rating, except that the response can be any number (not necessarily an integer number) within the range (for example, 5.2 on a scale of 0 to 10).

Constant Sum—*constant-sum:* The respondent is provided with a set of attributes (up to 15) and is asked to distribute a total of p points across those attributes.

Yes/No—*yes-no:* This type of question entails a yes/no answer.

Integer—*integer-#:* The respondent is asked for a fact that can be expressed in integer number form. A valid range can be provided for error checking. Example: Age.

Real—*real-#:* Similar to integer-# except that the answer expected is in the form of a real (not necessarily an integer) number. Example: Income. A valid range can be provided for error checking.

Character—*text:* The respondent types in a string of characters as a response. Example: Name. No error checking is done on this type of input.

Multiple Integer Ratings—*multi-integer-scale:* This question type is identical to integer-scale except that multiple questions (classified as "options") can appear on a single screen. Each question is answered and recorded separately.

Multiple Real Number Ratings—*multi-real-scale:* This question type is identical to real-scale except that multiple questions (classified as "options") can appear on a single screen. Each question is answered and recorded separately.

[26]J. P. Dickinson and E. Kirzner, "Questionnaire Item Omission as a Function of Within-Group Question Position," *Journal of Business Research,* 13 (February 1985), 71–75.

TABLE 7-7   Outline of CAPPA Questionnaire

  I. Title
    Initial Randomization Command
    Variable Prompts: This section is used for personalizing the questionnaire.
 II. Preinterview Section (Optional)
     This section has the interviewer answer questions before the main interview takes place.
III. Greeting and Main Interview Section
    Part
      Question
      Question
        .
        .
        .

    Part
      Question
      Question
        .
        .
        .

        .
        .

    Thank You Message
 IV. Postinterview Section (Optional)
     This section has the interviewer answer questions after the main interview has taken place.

sensitive, important, hard to answer, demographic, etc.). These issues are covered rather thoroughly in books that are more narrowly focused.[27]

A more recent phenomenon parallels the advances made in the use of microcomputers. There are software packages that allow researchers to develop their own questionnaires by using general formats and structures of questions. An example of one such package is CAPPA.[28] This software includes three programs that create the questionnaire (with the help of a text editor), prepare it for gathering data, and summarize the interviewees' responses. The researcher can select among 15 "built-in" types of questions, as shown in Table 7-6 (see page 273). The end result of using this software is a questionnaire structured as shown in Table 7-7.

Another interesting application of computers in question formulation and questionnaire design that has been reported is computer-assisted speech analysis. This process translates the vocabulary used by consumers into the firm's vocabulary, which is then used to write questionnaires adapted to the consumer's vocabulary.[29] There appears to

---

[27]See, for example, Payne, *Art of Asking Questions;* Sudman and Bradburn, *Asking Questions;* and J. Converse and S. Presser, *Survey Questions: Handcrafting the Standardized Questionnaire* (Beverly Hills, Calif.: Sage, 1986).

[28]P. Green, P. Kedia, and R. Nikhil, *Electronic Questionnaire Design and Analysis with CAPPA* (Palo Alto, Calif.: Scientific Press, 1985).

[29]G. Sauris, "Computer-Assisted Speech Analysis Can Improve Questionnaire Design, Ad Copy," *Marketing News,* 18 (May 25, 1984), Sec. 1, p. 17.

be an almost unlimited horizon for development of microcomputer software to aid i. questionnaire design and implementation.

SUMMARY

This chapter focused on general concepts of measurement. We discussed the role of definitions and made a distinction between constitutive and operational definitions.

We then turned to measurement and examined what it is and how measurement relates to development of scales. Also discussed, but rather briefly, were alternative sources that cause variations within a set of measurements derived from a single instrument. This was followed by a description of measurement validity and reliability, and the various types of each that are of concern to an investigator.

The last section of the chapter looked at issues involved in asking questions. The exposition was in the context of response error and what might be done to control and, it is hoped, eliminate as much of this error as possible. Finally, some general principles of question formation were presented.

ASSIGNMENT MATERIAL

1. Categorize each of the following measurements by the type of scale it represents:
   a. Determination of whether a sample of respondents have used instant coffee within the past four weeks
   b. The number of ounces of instant coffee a respondent has bought within the past four weeks
   c. Establishing preference among instant coffee brands A, B, C, and D
   e. A respondent's answer of "probably buy" to a question of purchase intention
   f. The use of the number 4 (from a scale of 1 to 5) by a respondent to indicate importance of good service by marketers

2. The number series, 1, 2, 3, 4, 5 and 1, 6, 14, 16, 28 could each be used equally well to denote the rank order assigned to a set of five objects. Explain why statistics like the arithmetic mean and the standard deviation should not be calculated from such a series.

3. It has been asserted that for decisional research purposes the investigator is interested in predictive validity to the exclusion of reliability or any other kind of validity. Do you agree? Explain.

4. Suppose that properly gathered and tabulated data show the same results over many replications. Are the results valid? Are they reliable? Explain.

5. The manufacturer of a certain brand of nationally advertised and distributed frozen fruit juices has retained you as a consultant to advise on a questionnaire that is being prepared. The purpose of the survey is to determine consumer

opinions and attitudes about frozen versus fresh fruit juices. Personal interviews are to be conducted on a randomly selected sample of families.

a. The questions listed below are being considered for the questionnaire. Comment on each, indicating whether you would leave the question as it is or would change it. If you think it should be changed, rewrite it as you believe it should be asked.

(1) Do you or any of your family drink fruit juices?

          Yes _____   *No* _____

If *Yes:*

(2) Is the juice drunk at a meal or between meals or both?

   At meal _____   *Between meals* _____   *Both* _____

(3) Do you prefer frozen or fresh juices?

         Frozen _____   *Fresh* _____

(4) What advantages, if any, do you believe using fresh juice has to using frozen juice?

(5) What advantages, if any, do you believe using frozen juice has to using fresh juice?

(6) What brand or brands of juice do you regularly buy?

   _____

   _____

   _____   *Don't know* _____

(7) On this card is a list of fruit juices. Tell me which are your family's first, second, and third choices.

      grape   _____

      tomato   _____

      lime   _____

      lemonade _____

      orange   _____

      V-8   _____

      other   _____

(8) What is the last brand of juice bought by your family?

   _____   Don't know _____

b. Classify each of the above questions by type (*free-answer, multiple-choice,* or *dichotomous*).

6. The No-Fault Insurance Company, a relatively small company specializing in insuring automobiles, was interested in learning in what proportion of automobile accidents, in which the police were not called, an insuree was involved who had been driving under the influence of alcohol or some form of drugs. A member of the company's marketing research department took a simple random sample of 100 accidents by their insurees over the past 12 months in which there was no police investigation. The insuree was interviewed personally and, after a

suitable introduction, handed a card with the following instructions printed on it:

PLEASE READ THIS CARD ALL THE WAY THROUGH
BEFORE DOING ANY OF THE THINGS REQUESTED

1. The interviewer will hand you a penny after you have finished reading the card and have asked any questions you may have.

   Please flip the penny and determine whether it came up HEADS or TAILS *without letting the interviewer know which it was.*

2. The side of the coin that came up will determine which of the two questions given below you will answer. Please *answer the question with "YES" or "NO" only and do not say anything else* as we do not want the interviewer to know which question you answer.

3. If a penny came up HEADS, answer "YES" or "NO" (*only*) to the question:

   "Was your mother born in August?"

4. If the penny came up TAILS, answer "YES" or "NO" (*only*) to the question:

   "Before your last automobile accident had you been drinking alcohol or taken any drugs (including tranquilizers) that *might* have caused you to be unable to drive as well as you usually do?"

5. If you have any questions about any of these instructions please ask the interviewer for an explanation before you flip the penny. If the instructions are followed properly ONLY YOU SHOULD KNOW WHICH QUESTION YOU ANSWERED.

Responses were obtained from 91 persons (4 had died or otherwise could not be contacted and 5 refused to answer). Twenty-four (24) of the respondents answered "Yes."
   a. What is the estimated proportion of respondents who answered "Yes" to the question concerning driving after drinking alcohol or taking drugs?
   b. What are the nonsampling errors that are actually or potentially present in this estimate?
   c. Should these nonsampling errors be reflected in the estimate? If so, how?
7. A United States senator sent the questionnaire reproduced below to a mailing list of his constituents. Comment on the questionnaire indicating
   a. Your evaluation of each question
   b. Your appraisal of the questionnaire as a device for informing the senator of his constituents' opinions

QUESTIONNAIRE

1. Under present law, families who run small businesses and farms are often forced to sell their holdings rather than pass them on to the next generation owing to the burden of estate taxes. Would you favor legislation to ease this burden?   yes___ no___

2. Of the following areas of federal spending choose *one* in which you would prefer to make a budget cut:
   a. Public welfare payments   ___
   b. Public works projects   ___
   c. Defense spending   ___
   d. Foreign assistance programs   ___
   e. Food stamps   ___
   f. Education   ___
   g. Other_____   ___

3. Do you believe that charitable organizations such as churches and nonprofit hospitals should remain tax-exempt?   yes___ no___

4. Which *one* of the following would you choose as the most important in solving the energy shortage over the next 20 years?
   a. Solar/geothermal power development   ___
   b. Nuclear power development   ___
   c. Conservation of present sources of energy   ___
   d. Expansion of domestic oil reserves   ___
   e. Increased use of coal   ___

5. Which *one* of the following would you say is the most important effort Congress could make to prevent crime?
   a. Enact harsher penalties to deter crimes   ___
   b. Reenact the death penalty for certain crimes   ___
   c. Enact restrictions on violence on television   ___
   d. Increase funding for the courts   ___
   e. Increase funding for law enforcement agencies   ___
   f. Reform the country's prison system   ___

6. Most of the economic indicators for the nation show positive signs of a recovery. Unemployment is down to 7.6%, personal incomes are up, and the prime lending rate is down.
   a. Do you feel that we are in a recovery?   yes _____   no _____
   b. Do you feel that the economy has stabilized?   yes _____   no _____
   c. Do you expect inflation to increase?   yes _____   no _____

    d. Do you believe that unemployment will   yes _____   no _____
       increase?

    e. Should Congress finance more jobs   yes _____   no _____
       producing programs with tax revenues?

7. In each of the following areas do you feel that
    Congress's efforts should be *increased?*

    a. Energy research and development   yes _____   no _____

    b. Health care and insurance   yes _____   no _____

    c. Crime control   yes _____   no _____

    d. Tax reform   yes _____   no _____

    e. Preservation of the environment   yes _____   no _____

    f. Other _____ yes _____   no _____

8

Measurement and Scaling in Marketing Research

INTRODUCTION

In the preceding chapter we established the fact that some sort of scale was necessarily involved every time a measurement was made. We discussed the four commonly used types of scales—the nominal, ordinal, interval, and ratio scales. It will be recalled that these scales reflect different levels of measurement, according to the number of characteristics of the real number series (order, distance, origin) possessed by a scale type.

In this chapter we continue our discussion of how scales are developed. In addition, we describe how some of the more common scaling techniques and models can be used. Our concern is with basic concepts of psychological scaling, as related primarily to the study of consumer perception, preference, and motivation. Broadly, this is known as attitude scaling. We begin with a discussion of various methods for collecting scaling data (e.g., paired comparisons, rankings, ratings, etc.) in terms of their mechanics and assumptions regarding their scale properties. These methods revolve around the *tasks* required of respondents.

We then discuss specific procedures for scaling stimuli and/or respondents. Techniques such as Thurstonian Case V scaling, the semantic differential, the Likert summated scale, and the Thurstone differential scale are illustrated. We conclude with some issues and limitations of scaling.

Attitude Measurement

All attitude (and other psychological) measurement procedures are concerned with having people—consumers, purchasing agents, marketing managers, or whatever—respond to certain stimuli according to certain sets of instructions. The stimuli may be alternative advertising copy themes, package designs, salespeople's presentations, and so on. The response may involve which copy theme is more pleasing than another, which package design is more appealing than another, which adjectives best describe each salesperson, and so on.

Other operations involving the application of some type of scaling model may then intervene before we finally get a scale along which the attitude is measured. Scaling procedures can be classified in terms of the measurement properties of the final scale (i.e., nominal, ordinal, interval, or ratio), the task that the subject is asked to perform, or in still other ways.

One important basis for classifying scaling methods is whether the emphasis is to be placed on subjects, stimuli, or both.[1] To illustrate, suppose that each member of a group of respondents has been asked independently to rate a set of dishwashing detergent brands (stimuli) with respect to "gentleness on the hands." Three types of scaling might be distinguished:

1. *Subject-centered approach,* in which the researcher examines systematic variation across respondents
2. *Stimulus-centered approach,* in which the researcher investigates systematic variation across stimuli (the brands)
3. *Response approach,* in which the researcher examines *both* subject and stimulus variation

In the subject-centered and stimulus-centered approaches, the experimenter chooses either stimuli or respondents whose variability is (at least roughly) controlled so as to emphasize variation in the other mode. For example, if one is interested in subject-centered variation, stimuli would be chosen so as to emphasize individual respondent differences. Similarly, in stimulus-centered cases a homogeneous group of subjects may be sought so as to reduce variation contributed by this source. In response methods, however, the researcher is interested in both sources of variability.

DATA COLLECTION METHODS

While we shall be emphasizing scaling methods that are stimulus-centered, it turns out that there is another (and independent) way to classify scaling techniques, and that is in

[1]This classification method—and other descriptors used later in the chapter—is discussed in W. S. Torgerson, *Theory and Methods of Scaling* (New York: John Wiley, 1958).

terms of whether variability or quantitative-judgment procedures are used to *collect* the data. In *variability* methods it is assumed that the basic data are only ordinal-scaled. Some type of model is then applied to transform the ordinal data into an interval scale. In *quantitative-judgment* methods, direct numerical judgments are made by the respondent and it is assumed that the original input data are either interval-scaled or ratio-scaled. In this method, use of a model is directed toward finding the scale values that are most consistent with the (errorful) input data. (Often the "model" will involve nothing more than a simple averaging of the original numerical responses.)

Variability Methods

Variability methods include paired comparison, ranking, ordered-category sorting, and rating techniques. We discuss each of these data collection procedures in turn.

Paired Comparisons

As the name suggests, *paired comparisons* require the respondent to choose one of a pair of stimuli that "has more of," "dominates," "precedes," "wins over," or "exceeds" the other with respect to some designated property of interest. If, for example, six dishwashing detergent brands are to be compared for "gentleness on the hands," a full set of paired comparisons (if order of presentation is not considered) would involve $(6 \cdot 5)/2$, or 15, paired comparisons.

Figure 8-1   Paired-Comparison Responses For a Single Subject*

	BRAND							
		1	2	3	4	5	6	
	1	x	0	1	1	1	1	
	2	1	x	1	1	1	1	
BRAND	3	0	0	x	0	0	0	(Original Data)
	4	0	0	1	x	0	0	
	5	0	0	1	1	x	1	
	6	0	0	1	1	0	x	

	BRAND								
		2	1	5	6	4	3	Sum	
	2	x	1	1	1	1	1	5	
	1	0	x	1	1	1	1	4	
BRAND	5	0	0	x	1	1	1	3	(Permuted Rows
	6	0	0	0	x	1	1	2	and Columns)
	4	0	0	0	0	x	1	1	
	3	0	0	0	0	0	x	0	

*A cell value of "1" implies that the row brand exceeds the column brand; "0," otherwise.

The upper panel of Figure 8-1 shows illustratively how paired-comparison responses may be recorded for a single female subject. As noted from the figure, brand 2 dominates all the other five brands. This is shown by the fact that all of its paired comparisons with the remaining stimuli involve 1's (arbitrarily letting row dominate column) in the table of original data. In the lower panel of Figure 8-1, rows and columns of the original table have been permuted to yield the stimulus rank order: 2, 1, 5, 6, 4, 3, from most gentle to least gentle. The total number of "votes" received by each brand appears in the last column.

These hypothetical data are characterized by the fact that the respondent was "transitive" in her judgments, leading (after row and column permutation) to the triangular response pattern of 1's shown in the lower panel of the figure.

But what does one do if the judgments are not transitive? For example, the respondent may say that brand 2 exceeds brand 1; brand 1 exceeds brand 5; and brand 5 exceeds brand 2, leading to what is called a *circular triad*. The presence of circular triads in a subject's data requires the researcher to examine two questions: (1) how serious are the subject's violations of transitivity, and (2) if not "too" serious, how can the data be made transitive with the fewest number of alterations in the original paired-comparisons table?

Kendall[2] has developed summary measures and statistical tests regarding the incidence of "tolerable" levels of intransitivity; one may compute his coefficient of consistency and test this measure against the null hypothesis that the respondent is responding randomly. Slater[3] and Phillips[4] have described ways of finding the "best" rank order (one that least disturbs the original paired-comparison judgments) in the presence of intransitive data. Of course, the motivation for using paired comparisons in the first place stems from the researcher's interest in the *consistency* of respondents' choices; otherwise, one might just as well have the respondent rank the six brands, thereby reducing labor (but *forcing* consistency within that set of choices).

Other than the transitivity issue for more than two alternatives there is a possibility that respondents' judgments are not consistent (i.e., stable) in that they prefer brand A to B on one trial but brand B to A on another. In this situation there exists an underlying preference probability distribution and replicated judgments are needed.[5]

Implicit in the preceding discussion has been the assumption that the respondent must force a choice between each pair of brands. Variations in the method of paired comparisons allow the subject to express indifference between members of the pair (i.e., to "tie" the stimuli with respect to the property level of interest) or, after having chosen between members of the pair, to indicate on an "intensity scale" *how much* the chosen member of the pair exceeds the other with regard to some designated property, such as "gentleness on the hands."

[2]M. G. Kendall, *Rank Correlation Methods* (New York: Hafner, 1962).

[3]Patrick Slater, "Inconsistencies in a Schedule of Paired Comparisons," *Biometrica*, 48 (1961), 303–12.

[4]J. P. N. Phillips, "A Procedure for Determining Slater's *i* and All Nearest Adjoining Orders," *British Journal of Mathematical and Statistical Psychology,* 20 (1967), 217–25.

[5]See Morris J. Gottlieb, *A Modern Marketing Approach in Measuring Consumer Preference* (New York: Audits and Surveys, Inc.), Modern Marketing Series Number 4.

Exhibit 8-1   Method of Choices

This method provides a procedure for *indirectly* arriving at paired-comparison proportions of the form $p(B > A)$. Each respondent is presented with a set of n stimuli and is asked to indicate which one appears greatest or largest on, or has the most of, the attribute or characteristic being studied. The resulting data are the frequency with which each stimulus was the first choice. For any two stimuli, X and Y, the sum of the two frequencies gives the total number of observations in which we know the result of comparing the two stimuli. The proportion of times that X appeared greater than Y is given by

$$p(X > Y) = \frac{f(X)}{f(X) + f(Y)}$$

where

    $f(X)$ is the number of times X was first choice,
    $f(Y)$ is the number of times Y was first choice.

For example, if stimulus X was the first choice of 10 respondents and stimulus Y the favored choice of 15 respondents,

$$p(X > Y) = \frac{10}{10 + 15} = .40$$

All pairs of the stimuli can be analyzed in this manner to arrive at a matrix of preference proportions.

    This method has some deficiencies. In the first place, full use is not made of the ranked data that may be available—only top rankings are considered. Second, each proportion is based on different subsets of respondents. In addition, the number of observations upon which each proportion is based will differ. Third, those stimuli that never receive a first choice cannot be scaled. Finally, this method does not provide for appropriate goodness-of-fit tests.*

    *W Torgerson, *Theory and Methods of Scaling* (New York: John Wiley, 1958), p. 194.

Ranking Methods

Ranking procedures require the respondent to order stimuli with respect to some designated property of interest. For example, instead of using the paired-comparison technique for determining the perceived order of six dishwashing detergents with respect to "gentleness on the hands," each respondent might have been asked to *rank* the detergents with respect to that property. Similarly, ranking can be used to determine key attributes for services. The Travelers Companies had a study done in the mid-1980s in which 1,100 people (representing six key customer groups) were asked to list the most important attributes among a set of characteristics describing insurance and financial services companies. From this study Travelers was able to show the importance of product quality and basic fairness in dealing with people as well as the eroding appeal of technological leadership.[6]

A variety of ordering methods may be used to order k items from a full set of n items. These procedures, denoted by Coombs[7] as "order k/n" (k out of n), expand the repertory of ordering methods quite markedly. At the extremes, "order 1/2" involves a paired comparison, while "order $(n - 1)/n$" involves a full rank order.

The various ordering methods may prespecify the value of k ("order the top three out of six brands with respect to gentleness on the hands") or allow k to be chosen by the respondent ("select those of the six brands that seem to exhibit the most gentleness on the hands, and rank them").

Variations on the paired-comparison procedure have been developed so as to effect a compromise between the greater time and effort associated with the "order 1/2" procedure versus the additional information it provides for checking on a subject's consistency. A number of statistical design methods are available.[8] Generally speaking, these designs reduce the number of comparisons per respondent but provide a type of balancing across stimulus pairs and subjects. To date most marketing researchers have not taken advantage of these special designs, but we suspect that the situation will change as information about them receives wider dissemination.

Ordered-Category Sorting

Various data collection procedures are available that have as their purpose the assignment of a set of stimuli to a set of *ordered categories*. For example, if 15 varieties of dishwashing detergents represented the stimulus set, the respondent might be asked to sort them into three ordered categories: (1) highly gentle on the hands, (2) moderately gentle, and (3) not gentle at all.

Sorting procedures vary with regard to

1. The free versus forced assignment of so many stimuli to each category
2. The assumption of equal intervals between category boundaries versus the weaker assumption of category boundaries that are merely ordered with regard to the attribute of interest

In variability methods one assumes only an *ordering* of category boundaries. (The assumption of equal intervals separating boundaries is part of the quantitative-judgment set of methods.) Ordered-category sorting appears especially useful when the researcher is dealing with a relatively large number of stimuli (e.g., over 15 or so) and it is believed

---

[6]Reported in "Basic Research Uncovers Fairness as a Critical Component in Positioning of Financial Services," *Marketing News,* 18 (November 23, 1984), 8.

[7]C. H. Coombs, *A Theory of Data* (New York: John Wiley, 1964), Chap. 2, pp. 32–58.

[8]R. E. Kirk, *Experimental Design: Procedures for the Behavioral Sciences* (Belmont, Calif.: Wadsworth, 1968), Chap. 11, "Incomplete Block Designs"; and H. A. David, *The Method of Paired Comparisons* (New York: Hafner, 1963), p. 62.

that a subject's discrimination abilities do not justify a strict (no ties allowed) ranking of the stimulus objects.

If the equal-intervals assumption is not made, it then becomes the job of the researcher to scale these responses (by application of various models) to achieve "stronger" scales, if so desired.

Some data collection methods, most notably rating scales, are ambiguous. In some cases, the responses may be considered by the researcher to be only ordinal, while, in

Figure 8-2   Examples of Rating Scales Used in Marketing Research

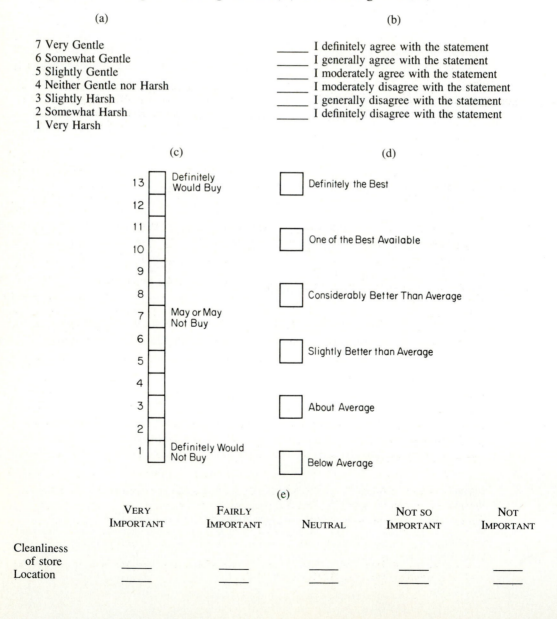

(a)

7 Very Gentle
6 Somewhat Gentle
5 Slightly Gentle
4 Neither Gentle nor Harsh
3 Slightly Harsh
2 Somewhat Harsh
1 Very Harsh

(b)

_____ I definitely agree with the statement
_____ I generally agree with the statement
_____ I moderately agree with the statement
_____ I moderately disagree with the statement
_____ I generally disagree with the statement
_____ I definitely disagree with the statement

(c)

13 Definitely Would Buy
12
11
10
9
8
7 May or May Not Buy
6
5
4
3
2
1 Definitely Would Not Buy

(d)

Definitely the Best

One of the Best Available

Considerably Better Than Average

Slightly Better than Average

About Average

Below Average

(e)

	VERY IMPORTANT	FAIRLY IMPORTANT	NEUTRAL	NOT SO IMPORTANT	NOT IMPORTANT
Cleanliness of store	_____	_____	_____	_____	_____
Location	_____	_____	_____	_____	_____

other cases, the researcher may treat them as more strongly (interval or ratio) scaled. As such, rating procedures can be appropriate for *either* the variability or quantitative-judgment data collection methods.

Rating Methods

Rating methods, as used in both marketing research and the behavioral sciences, represent one of the most popular and easily applied data collection methods. The task involves having a respondent place that which is being rated (e.g., a person, object, or concept) along a continuum or in one of an ordered set of categories. Rating allows a respondent to register a degree (or an amount) of a characteristic or attribute *directly* on a scale. In addition, the task of rating is used in other scaling approaches such as the semantic differential and the Likert summated scale.

Rating methods can take several forms: (1) numerical, (2) graphic, or (3) verbal. Often two or more of these formats appear together, as illustrated in Figure 8-2. As shown in Panel (a) of the figure, the respondent is given both a series of integers (1 through 7) and verbal descriptions of the degree of "gentleness-harshness." The respondent would then be asked to circle the number associated with the descriptive statement that comes closest to his or her feelings about the gentleness-harshness of the brand(s) being rated. In Panel (b) of Figure 8-2 the need is only to check the category appropriate for expressing feelings about some attitude statement regarding dishwashing detergents, whereas in Panel (e) the category checked represents the importance of characteristics of a retail store.

In Panel (c) of the figure a graduated thermometer scale with both numerical assignments and a (limited) set of descriptive statements illustrates another type of rating device (also see Exhibit 8-2). A pure numerical version would be to ask respondents to rate objects on some characteristic using a scale of 1 to 10 where the number 10 represents the most favorable (or most unfavorable) position. It is assumed that this numerical scale has more than ordinal properties. This scale may properly be viewed as a quantitative judgment method. Panel (d) attempts to "anchor" the scale in comparison to "average-type" brands. Many other types of rating methods are in use.[9]

In many instances where rating scales are used, the researcher assumes not only that the items are capable of being ranked but also that the descriptive levels progress in *equal-interval* steps psychologically. That is, the numerical correspondences shown in Panels (a) and (c) may be treated—sometimes erroneously—as interval- or ratio-scaled data. Even in cases represented by Panels (b), (d), and (e), it is not unusual to find that the researcher assigns successive integer values to the various category descriptions and subsequently works with the data as though the responses *were* interval-scaled.

In the preceding chapter we illustrated some of the problems associated with treating ordinal data as interval- or ratio-scaled data. Although methods are available for scaling the stimuli under weaker assumptions about the intervals that separate category labels (as mentioned earlier under ordered-category sorting), in practice these methods are often

---

[9]See, for example, R. Haley and P. Case, "Testing Thirteen Attitude Scales for Agreement and Brand Determination," *Journal of Marketing,* 43 (Fall 1979), 20–32.

Exhibit 8-2   A Rating Thermometer

We'd also like to get your feelings about some groups in American society. When I read the name of a group, we'd like you to rate it with what we call a feeling thermometer. It is on Page 19 of your booklet. Ratings between 50 and 100° mean that you feel favorably and warm toward the group; ratings between 0° and 50° mean that you don't feel favorably toward the group and that you don't care too much for that group. If you don't feel particularly warm or cold toward a group, you would rate them at 50°. If we come to a group you don't know much about, just tell me and we'll move on to the next one. Our first group is Big Business—how warm would you say you feel toward them? (*Write number of degrees or DK [don't know] in boxes provided below.*)

A. Big business ☐ ☐ ☐	S. Labor unions ☐ ☐ ☐
B. Poor people ☐ ☐ ☐	T. Young people ☐ ☐ ☐
C. Liberals ☐ ☐ ☐	U. Conservatives ☐ ☐ ☐
D. Southerners ☐ ☐ ☐	V. Women's Liberation
E. Chicanos,	movement ☐ ☐ ☐
Mexican-Americans ☐ ☐ ☐	W. People who use
F. Catholics ☐ ☐ ☐	marijuana ☐ ☐ ☐
G. Radical students ☐ ☐ ☐	X. Black militants ☐ ☐ ☐
H. Policemen ☐ ☐ ☐	Y. Jews ☐ ☐ ☐
J. Older people ☐ ☐ ☐	Z. Civil rights leaders ☐ ☐ ☐
K. Women ☐ ☐ ☐	AA. Protestants ☐ ☐ ☐
M. The military ☐ ☐ ☐	BB. Workingmen ☐ ☐ ☐
N. Blacks ☐ ☐ ☐	CC. Whites ☐ ☐ ☐
P. Democrats ☐ ☐ ☐	DD. Men ☐ ☐ ☐
Q. People on welfare ☐ ☐ ☐	EE. Middle-class people ☐ ☐ ☐
R. Republicans ☐ ☐ ☐	FF. Businessmen ☐ ☐ ☐

100° Very warm or favorable feeling
85°   Quite warm or favorable feeling
70°   Fairly warm or favorable feeling
60°   A bit more warm or favorable than cold feeling
50°   No feeling at all
40°   A bit more cold or unfavorable feeling
30°   Fairly cold or unfavorable feeling
15°   Quite cold or unfavorable feeling
0°   Very cold or unfavorable feeling

Source: S. Sudman and N. Bradburn, *Asking Questions* (San Francisco: Jossey-Bass, 1983), p. 159.

cumbersome to use and, accordingly, may not justify the time and effort associated with their application. However, this should not negate the importance of being aware of the implicit assumptions that one makes about the scale properties of rating instruments when certain statistical techniques are used to summarize and interrelate the response data.

Volumes have been written on various aspects of rating scales.[10] To illustrate:

1. Should negative numbers be used?
2. How many categories per se should be included?

[10]For a discussion of procedures for developing valid rating scales, see G. A. Churchill, Jr., "A Paradigm for Developing Better Measures of Marketing Constructs," *Journal of Marketing Research,* 16 (February 1979), 64–73.

3. Related to the number of categories is: Should there be an odd number or an even number? That is, should a neutral alternative be provided?

4. Should the scale be balanced or unbalanced?

5. Is it desirable to not force a "substantive" response by giving an opportunity to indicate "don't know," "no opinion," or something similar?

6. What does one do about "halo" effects—that is, the tendency of raters to ascribe favorable property levels to all attributes of a stimulus object if they happen to like a particular object in general?

7. How does one examine raters' biases—for example, the tendency to use extreme values or, perhaps, only the middle range of the response scale, or to overestimate the desirable features of the things liked (i.e., the *generosity* error)?

8. How should descriptive adjectives for rating categories be selected?

9. How should anchoring phrases for the scale's origin be chosen?

Guilford,[11] among others, lists a large number of "do's and don't's" regarding rating scales, which the interested reader might examine.[12]

In summary, rating methods—depending on the assumptions of the researcher—can be considered to lead to ordinal-, interval-, or even ratio-scaled responses. The latter two scales are taken up next in the context of quantitative-judgment methods. We shall see that rating methods figure prominently in the development of quantitative-judgment scales.

Quantitative-Judgment Methods

Direct-judgment estimates, fractionation, constant sum—indeed, rating methods also, if the researcher wishes to assume more than ordinal properties about respondents' judgments—are all variants of *quantitative-judgment methods*.

Direct-Judgment Methods

In *direct-judgment methods* the respondent is asked to give a *numerical* rating to each stimulus with respect to some designated attribute. In the *unlimited-response category* subcase, the respondent is free to choose his or her own number or, in graphical methods, to lay off a tick mark along some line that reflects his or her judgment about the magnitude of the stimulus relative to some reference points. This is illustrated in Panel (a) of Figure 8-3 for the rating of brand A.[13] The *limited-response category* subcase is illustrated by

---

[11]J. P. Guilford, *Psychometric Methods* (New York: McGraw-Hill, 1954). Also see S. Sudman and N. Bradburn, *Asking Questions* (San Francisco: Jossey-Bass, 1983).

[12]The effects of research design on reliability and validity of rating scales are discussed in two excellent review papers: G. A. Churchill, Jr., and J. P. Peter, "Research Design Effects on the Reliability of Rating Scales: A Meta-Analysis," *Journal of Marketing Research,* 21 (November 1984), 360–75; and J. P. Peter and G. A. Churchill, Jr., "Relationships among Research Design Choices and Psychometric Properties of Rating Scales: A Meta-Analysis," *Journal of Marketing Research,* 23 (February 1986), 1–10.

[13]This is a simplified version of *magnitude scaling,* which is based on psychophysical scaling. See M. Lodge, *Magnitude Scaling: Quantitative Measurement of Opinions* (Beverly Hills, Calif.: Sage, 1981). This method has been studied for use in a semantic differential context (to be discussed later in this chapter) and was found to have advantages in individual measurement without affecting aggregate properties of the measurement (See G. Albaum, R. Best, and D. Hawkins, "Continuous vs. Discrete Semantic Differential Rating Scales," *Psychological Reports,* 49 (1981), 83–86.

Figure 8-3   Some Illustrations of Quantitative-Judgment Methods

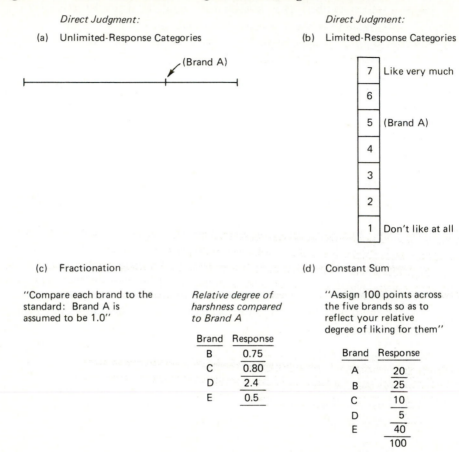

Direct Judgment:

(a)   Unlimited-Response Categories

Direct Judgment:

(b)   Limited-Response Categories

7	Like very much
6	
5	(Brand A)
4	
3	
2	
1	Don't like at all

(c)   Fractionation

"Compare each brand to the standard: Brand A is assumed to be 1.0"

Relative degree of harshness compared to Brand A

Brand	Response
B	0.75
C	0.80
D	2.4
E	0.5

(d)   Constant Sum

"Assign 100 points across the five brands so as to reflect your relative degree of liking for them"

Brand	Response
A	20
B	25
C	10
D	5
E	40
	100

Panel (b) in Figure 8-3. Here the respondent is limited to choosing one of seven categories. We note that in this instance the direct-judgment method is nothing more than a straight rating procedure, with the important addition that the ratings are now treated as either interval- or ratio-scaled data (depending on the application) rather than as simple rankings.

If the respondent has several items to rate, either the unlimited- or limited-response category procedures can also be employed. In the former case, the respondent arranges the stimuli (usually described on small cards) along some sort board, provided by the researcher, so that each appears approximately separated according to subjective distance relative to the others. In the latter case, one assigns cards to the designated category on the sort board that best matches one's evaluation of the stimulus.

Fractionation

Fractionation is a type of quantitative-judgment procedure in which the respondent is given two stimuli at a time (e.g., a standard dishwashing detergent and a test brand)

and asked to give some *numerical* estimate of the ratio between them, with respect to some attribute, such as "harshness on the hands."

The respondent may answer that the test brand, in his or her judgment, is three-fourths as harsh as the standard. After this is done, a new test brand is compared with the same standard, and so on, until all test items are judged. Panel (c) in Figure 8-3 illustrates this procedure.

In other cases—where the test item can be more or less continuously varied by the respondent—the respondent is asked to vary the test item so that it represents some designated ratio of the standard. For example, if the attribute is sweetness of lemonade, the respondent may be asked to add more sweetener until the test item is "twice as sweet" as the standard.

Constant Sum

Constant-sum methods, primarily because of their simplicity and ease of instructions, have become quite popular in marketing research. In constant-sum methods the respondent is given some number of points—typically 10 or 100—and asked to distribute them over the alternatives in a way that reflects their relative magnitude regarding some attitudinal characteristic.

Panel (d) of Figure 8-3 shows an illustration of the constant-sum procedure. Constant sum forces the respondent to "allocate" his or her evaluations and has the effect of standardizing each scale across persons, since all scores must add to the same constant (e.g., 10 or 100). As such, the constant-sum procedure requires the respondent to make a comparative evaluation of the stimuli. Generally, it is assumed that a subjective ratio scale is obtained by this method.

Summary

Unlike variability methods, the major assumption underlying quantitative-judgment methods is that a unit of measurement can be constructed *directly* from respondents' estimates about scale values associated with a set of stimuli. The subject's report is taken at face value and any variation in repeated estimates (over test occasions within respondent or over respondents) is treated as error; repeated estimates are usually averaged over persons and/or occasions.

The problems associated with quantitative-judgment methods include the following:

1. Respondents' subjective scale units may differ across each other, across testing occasions, or both.
2. Respondents' subjective origins (zero points) may differ across each other, across occasions, or both.
3. Unit and origin may shift over stimulus items *within* a single occasion.

These problems should not be treated lightly, particularly when data for several subjects are being averaged.

In addition, researchers should be aware of the constraints placed on the subject's response format. For example, if the respondent is asked to rate dishwashing detergents on a 5-point scale, ranging from 1 ("gentlest"), to 3 ("neither harsh nor gentle"), to 5 ("harshest"), the task, in a sense, may not be capable of being carried out. That is, one's *subjective* distance between the harshest detergent and the neutral detergent(s) may not equal one's perception of the distance between the neutral detergent(s) and the gentlest detergent.

Most quantitative-judgment methods have the virtue of being easy to apply. Moreover, little additional work beyond averaging is required to obtain the unit of measurement directly. Indeed, if a unique origin can be established (e.g., a zero level of the property), then the researcher obtains both an "absolute" origin and a measurement unit. As such, a subjective ratio scale is obtained.

TECHNIQUES FOR SCALING STIMULI

Any of the data collection methods just described—whether of the variability class or the quantitative-judgment class—produce a set of raw-data responses. In the case of variability methods, the raw data, describing *ordinal-scaled* judgments, usually undergo a further transformation, via a *scaling model,* into a set of scale values that are *interval-scaled*.

Technically speaking, the raw data obtained from quantitative-judgment procedures also require an intervening model. However, in this case the "model" may be no more elaborate than averaging the raw data across respondents and/or response occasions.

Thurstone's Case V method is a popular model for dealing with ordinal data obtained from variability methods. Osgood's semantic differential is an illustration of a procedure for dealing with raw data obtained from quantitative-judgment procedures. We consider each of these techniques in turn.

Case V Scaling

Thurstone's Case V Scaling model, based on his Law of Comparative Judgment, permits the construction of a unidimensional interval scale using responses from variability data collection procedures, such as paired comparisons.[14] Several subcases of Thurstone's model have been developed. We shall first describe the general case and then concentrate on Case V, a special version that is particularly amenable to application.

Essentially, Thurstone's procedure involves deriving an interval scale from comparative judgments of the type "A is fancier than B," "A is more prestigious than B," "A is preferred to B," and so on. Scale values may be estimated from data in which one individual makes many repeated judgments on each pair of a set of stimuli or from data obtained from a group of individuals with few or no replications per person.

---

[14]While illustrated here in the context of paired comparisons, Thurstone's model can be used to scale ranked data or ordered-category sorts. Thurstone's model is described in L. L. Thurstone, *The Measurement of Values* (Chicago: University of Chicago Press, 1959).

The concept that underlies the model of comparative judgment on which Case V scaling is based is simple to describe. Suppose that we have a group of subjects, almost all of whom prefer A to B. Then the proportion of total comparisons (no ties allowed) in which A is preferred to B will be close to 100%. Suppose, however, that when B is compared with C, only 55% of the group prefers B to C. Intuitively, we might think that the difference between the scale values associated with A and B should be much larger than the difference between the scale values associated with B and C. Under certain assumptions Thurstone's model of comparative judgment provides a means for developing an interval scale from these stimulus-comparison proportions. The test of the theory is how well scale values can be used to work backward, that is, to predict the original proportions.

The psychological process by which a person reacts to a stimulus is called the person's *discriminal process*. Since the same individual, on another occasion, may react differently to the same stimulus, we must consider a *modal* discriminal process that represents the sensory response that occurs most often when a particular stimulus is presented. The scale distance between the modal discriminal processes for any two stimuli represents the degree of separation assumed to be present on the individual's psychological scale and is called the *discriminal difference*. If each discriminal process is normally distributed—as assumed by Thurstone—the discriminal differences between pairs of stimuli are also normally distributed. Also, the mean of each discriminal process (as well as the median) will equal the mode. The same will be true of the discriminal differences.

Figure 8-4   Illustration of Response Differences Under Thurstone's Model of Comparative Judgment

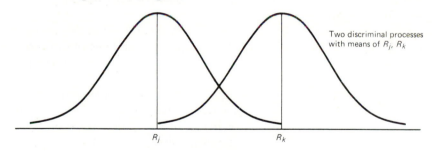

Two discriminal processes with means of R_j, R_k

R_j R_k

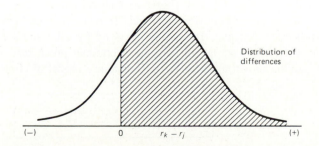

Distribution of differences

$(-)$ 0 $r_k - r_j$ $(+)$

Figure 8-4 (p. 293) illustrates this situation for a particular stimulus pair j and k. In the upper panel of the figure we note that each discriminal process is assumed to be normally distributed with mode (and mean) R_j and R_k, respectively. If stimuli j and k are presented for comparison, the subject is figuratively assumed to draw some value from each of his or her (subjective) distributions of discriminal processes. Most of the time the value r_k will exceed r_j (see shaded area in the lower panel of the figure) and the subject will report that stimulus k exceeds stimulus j with respect to some predesignated attribute. However, some of the time (unshaded area) r_j will exceed r_k, and hence the opposite will be reported.

The variability of the scale differences depends on both the intercorrelations between the discriminal processes and the possibility that their respective variances are unequal. We let R_j, R_k stand for mean values of the discriminal process j and k and σ_j^2, σ_k^2 stand for their variances; ρ_{jk} denotes their correlation coefficient.

What the researcher *observes*, however, is the proportion of times that stimulus j is preferred to stimulus k. The task is to *infer* scale values from the frequency data developed on each pair of stimuli.

Thurstone's most general model of comparative judgment is stated as

$$R_j - R_k = Z_{jk} \sqrt{\sigma_j^2 + \sigma_k^2 - 2\rho_{jk}\sigma_j\sigma_k}$$

where

$R_j - R_k = $ linear distance (on the subject's psychological scale) between stimulus j and stimulus k

$Z_{jk} = $ standard (unit normal) variate associated with the observed proportion of cases in which stimulus j is preferred to stimulus k

σ_j^2, $\sigma_k^2 = $ discriminal dispersion (variance) of stimulus j and k, respectively

$\rho_{jk} = $ coefficient of correlation between the discriminal processes associated with stimulus j versus stimulus k judgments

A particularly simple form of Thurstone's model can be stated if one assumes that (1) the discriminal dispersions are equal and (2) the correlation between each pair of discriminal processes is equal. By setting $\sigma_j^2 = \sigma_k^2$ for all j and k and letting ρ denote the *common* correlation across all pairs of discriminal processes, we obtain the following simplification, known as Case V, of Thurstone's model of comparative judgment:

$$R_j - R_k = Z_{jk} \sqrt{2\sigma^2(1 - \rho)}$$

However, it turns out that we can simplify things even more. This is because $\sqrt{2\sigma^2(1 - \rho)}$ is a *constant*. Since we plan to obtain an interval scale, we are free to choose the *unit of measurement* (and the origin or zero point as well). This being the case, we can set $\sqrt{2\sigma^2(1 - \rho)}$ equal to 1 and thus obtain the further simplication:[15]

$$\boxed{R_j - R_k = Z_{jk}}$$

Thus, Z_{jk} equals the standard unit normal variate, Z.

An example should make the Case V procedure easier to follow. Assume that 100 housewives were asked to compare five brands of canned tomato juice with respect to "overall goodness of flavor." Each housewife sipped a sample of each brand paired with a sample of every other brand (a total of ten pairs) from paper cups that were marked merely with identifying numbers. Table 8-1 shows the empirically observed proportion for each comparison.

From this table we see, for example, that 69% of the respondents preferred juice C to juice A and the remainder, 31%, preferred juice A to juice C (if we arbitrarily let column dominate row).[16] From the data of this table we next prepare Table 8-2, which summarizes the Z values appropriate for each proportion. (These Z values were obtained from Table A-1 in Appendix A at the end of this book.) If the proportion is less than 0.5, the Z value carries a negative sign; if the proportion is greater than 0.5, the Z value carries a positive sign. The Z values are standard unit variates that are associated with a given proportion of total area under the normal curve. (We recall that the Thurstonian model assumes normally distributed scale differences.)

For example, from Table 8-1 we note that the proportion of respondents preferring juice B over juice A is 0.82. We wish to know the Z value appropriate thereto. This value (labeled Z in the standard unit normal table of Table A-1) is 0.92. That is, 82% of the total area under the normal curve is between $Z = -\infty$ and $Z = 0.92$. All entries

TABLE 8-1 Observed Proportions Preferring Brand X (Top of Table) to Brand Y (Side of Table)

	PREFERRED BRAND				
BRAND	*A*	*B*	*C*	*D*	*E*
A	0.50	0.82	0.69	0.25	0.35
B	0.18	0.50	0.27	0.07	0.15
C	0.31	0.73	0.50	0.16	0.25
D	0.75	0.93	0.84	0.50	0.59
E	0.65	0.85	0.75	0.41	0.50

[15]A variation of this is based on setting $\rho = 0$ and $\sigma_j^2 = \sigma_k^2 = 1$. This results in $R_j - R_k = Z_{jk}\sqrt{2}$.
[16]It is customary to set self-comparisons (the main-diagonal entries of Table 8-1) to 0.5; this has no effect on the resulting scale values. See A. L. Edwards, *Techniques of Attitude Scale Construction* (New York: Appleton-Century-Crofts, 1957) for a discussion of this approach.

TABLE 8-2 Z Values Related to Preference Proportions in Table 8-1

BRAND	A	B	C	D	E
			BRAND		
A	0	0.92	0.50	-0.67	-0.39
B	-0.92	0	-0.61	-1.48	-1.04
C	-0.50	0.61	0	-0.99	-0.67
D	0.67	1.48	0.99	0	0.23
E	0.39	1.04	0.67	-0.23	0
Total	-0.36	4.05	1.55	-3.37	-1.87
Mean ($\bar{Z}$)	-0.072	0.810	0.310	-0.674	-0.374
R*	0.602	1.484	0.984	0	0.300

in Table 8-2 are obtained in a similar manner, a minus sign being prefixed to the Z value when the proportion is *less* than 0.5.

Column totals are next found for the entries in Table 8-2. Scale values are obtained from the column sums by taking a simple average of each column's Z values. For example, from Table 8-2, we note that the sum of the Z's for the first column (juice A) is -0.36. The average Z_A is simply:

$$\bar{Z}_A = -\frac{0.36}{5} = -0.072$$

This scale value expresses brand A as a *deviation from the mean* of all five scale values. The mean of the five values, as computed from the full row of $\bar{Z}$'s, will always be zero under this procedure.

Similarly, we find the average Z value for each of the remaining four columns of Table 8-2. Next, since the zero point of an interval scale is arbitrary, we can let the scale value for juice D ($R_D = \bar{Z}_D = -0.674$) be the reference point (or origin) of zero. We then simply add 0.674 to each of the other $\bar{Z}$ values to obtain the Case V scale values of the other four brands. These are denoted by $R*$ and appear in the last row of Table 8-2.

The scale values of brands A through E indicate the preference ordering

$$B > C > A > E > D$$

Moreover, assuming that an interval scale exists, we can say, for example, that the difference in "goodness of flavor" between brands B and A is 2.3 times the difference in "goodness of flavor" between brands C and A, since

$$1.484 - 0.602 = 2.3(0.984 - 0.602)$$

$$0.882 = 2.3(0.382)$$

(within rounding error).

One of the nice features of the Thurstonian Case V model is that we can find out how well this model fits the original proportions data. To do this, we simply work backward from the scale values shown in the last row of Table 8-2 to find the estimated proportions.

For example, assume that we wanted to find the *predicted* proportion of respondents preferring brand A to brand B. We first find the scale difference:

$$R_A^* - R_B^* = 0.602 - 1.484$$
$$= -0.882$$

We then find from Table A-1 that the proportion of area under the standard unit normal curve corresponding to a Z of -0.882 (on an interpolated basis) is $1 - 0.81 = 0.19$. That is, the Case V model estimates that 19% of the respondents would prefer brand A to brand B.

Table 8-1 shows, in fact, that 18% of the respondents preferred A to B, a discrepancy of only 1 percentage point. Similarly, we can find predicted proportions for all the remaining pairs of brands and compare these with the actual proportions of Table 8-1.

Table 8-3 shows the results of this comparison. As noted from the table, the Case V model appears to fit the original proportions data quite well. For any specific brand, the highest mean absolute discrepancy is 0.025 (brand A). Moreover, the overall mean absolute discrepancy is only 0.0198.[17]

TABLE 8-3   Actual Proportions Versus Proportions Predicted by the Case V Model

Row Brand Preferred to Column Brand	Brand				
	A	*B*	*C*	*D*	*E*
A (actual)	—	0.18	0.31	0.75	0.65
A' (predicted)	—	0.19	0.35	0.73	0.62
B	0.82	—	0.73	0.93	0.85
B'	0.81	—	0.69	0.93	0.88
C	0.69	0.27	—	0.84	0.75
C'	0.65	0.31	—	0.84	0.75
D	0.25	0.07	0.16	—	0.41
D'	0.27	0.07	0.16	—	0.38
E	0.35	0.15	0.25	0.59	—
E'	0.38	0.12	0.25	0.62	—
Mean absolute discrepancy	0.025	0.020	0.020	0.012	0.022
Overall mean absolute discrepancy					0.0198

[17]Although not demonstrated here there is a chi-square test for determining if the model represents a satisfactory description of the data. See F. Mosteller, "A Test of Significance for Paired Comparisons When Equal Standard Deviations and Equal Correlations Are Assumed," *Psychometrika,* 16 (1959), 207–8.

Figure 8-5   Plot of the Z Values (Table 8-2) Versus Proportions (Table 8-1)

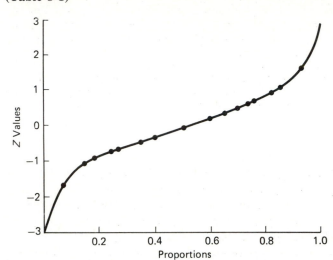

Thus, even the simplest version (Case V) of the Thurstonian model leads to fairly accurate predictions. Now that the model has been illustrated, we can examine the nature of the function that links the proportions data of Table 8-1 to the Z values of Table 8-2. Figure 8-5 shows this plot for the sample problem. As can be observed, the Z's (and, hence, the R^* scale values of the Case V model) follow a rank-preserving function of the original proportions data. As a matter of fact, over the proportions range of 0.15 to 0.85, the Case V function does not depart much from linearity. Only when the proportions are either very small or very large (e.g., less than 0.05 or more than 0.95) do we note a rapid change in the function.[18]

Another approach to obtain numerical scores from rankings is shown in Exhibit 8-3.

The Semantic Differential

The *semantic differential* is a type of quantitative-judgment method that results in (assumed interval) scales that are often further analyzed by such techniques as factor analysis (see Chapter 14).[19] Unlike the Case V model, the semantic differential provides no way to test the adequacy of the scaling model itself. That is, it is *assumed* that the raw data are interval-scaled; the intent of the semantic differential is to obtain these raw data for later processing by various multivariate models.

Essentially, the semantic differential procedure enables the researcher to probe into *both the direction and the intensity* of respondents' attitudes (i.e., measure psychological

---

[18]Theoretically, Z goes to $-\infty$ or $+\infty$, respectively, for proportions that approach zero or one. In practice, zero proportions are often set equal to 0.025 and proportions of one are set equal to 0.975.

[19]C. E. Osgood, G. J. Suci, and P. H. Tannenbaum, *The Measurement of Meaning* (Urbana: University of Illinois Press, 1957).

Exhibit 8-3   Converting Ranks Into Scale Values

Another approach to convert ranks into numerical scores is based on the assumption that true differences between adjacent objects ranked near the extremes tend to be larger than differences between objects falling near the middle in rank. Specifically, we can view relative differences among ranked objects as being similar to differences between the standardized or Z values falling at the boundary points of $N-1$ equally probable intervals falling in the midrange of a normal distribution. We would like the interval between each adjacent pair of ranks (e.g., 1 and 2, 7 and 8) to define an interval corresponding to $100/N$ of cases in a normal distribution. Finally, we arbitrarily set $100/2N$ as the percentage of cases in a normal distribution to be cut below the value of the object ranked 1 and above the value of the object ranked N. As shown in the figure for $N=10$, differences at the extremes are greater than those in the middle.

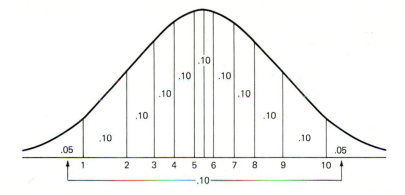

We can proceed as follows. For any stimulus object, such as a brand of soap, which has been ranked j, we find from the normal tables the Z score cutting off the lower $(j-.5)/N$ proportion of the area under the normal curve. Using this procedure we determine the Z values for 10 brands of soap (A–J) as follows:

BRAND	RANK	PERCENTILE	Z VALUE
C	1	5	−1.65
E	2	15	−1.04
A	3	25	−.67
D	4	35	−.39
F	5	45	−.13
H	6	55	.13
G	7	65	.39
J	8	75	.67
I	9	85	1.04
B	10	95	1.65

For brand E, for example, we find that the lower $(2-.5)/10$ or .15 proportion of the area under the normal curve corresponds to a Z value of -1.04. The end result is that the original ranks have been transformed into scale values, which can then be treated as if they were intervally-scaled.

This exposition has assumed a single evaluator. More realistically, a sample of people will do the rankings, thus creating for each brand a distribution of ranks. Each brand's scale value will then be an average Z value, as shown below:

Rankings Given to Ten Objects by Fifty Judges

BRAND	A	B	C	D	E	F	G	H	I	J	z
Rank											
1	20	6	2	12	0	0	0	10	0	0	-1.65
2	6	5	27	10	2	0	0	0	0	0	-1.04
3	2	27	15	6	0	0	0	0	0	0	$-.67$
4	12	10	6	7	15	0	0	0	0	0	$-.39$
5	10	0	0	15	17	8	0	0	0	0	$-.13$
6	0	0	0	0	10	17	21	2	0	0	.13
7	0	0	0	0	0	10	7	33	0	0	.39
8	0	0	0	0	6	0	10	5	27	2	.67
9	0	0	0	0	0	15	12	0	23	0	1.04
10	0	2	0	0	0	0	0	0	0	48	1.65
	$-.931$		$-.875$		$-.096$		.493		.840		
		$-.676$		$-.778$		.413		$-.0004$		1.61	
										scale =	average z
										value	value

Although perhaps not as refined a technique as the Thurstone law of comparative judgment, this technique is computationally simpler and gives results comparable with paired-comparison methods. The objects judged by this method can be viewed as being intervally-scaled where the unit is one standard deviation in the distribution of true values over all possible objects on this scale.

Source: Adapted from W. L. Hays, *Quantification in Psychology* (Belmont, Calif.: Brooks/Cole, 1967), pp. 35–39.

meaning) toward such concepts as corporate image, advertising image, brand or service image, and country image. One way this is done is to ask the respondent to describe the company by means of ratings on a set of bipolar adjectives, as illustrated in Figure 8-6.

As shown in Figure 8-6, the respondent may be given a set of pairs of antonyms, the extremes of each pair being separated by seven, say, (assumed equal) intervals. For each pair of adjectives (e.g., powerful–weak) the respondent is asked to judge the corporation along the seven-point scale with descriptive phrases such as

- Extremely powerful
- Very powerful
- Slightly powerful
- Neither powerful nor weak
- Slightly weak

- Very weak
- Extremely weak

In Figure 8-6, the subject scored the company as (1) extremely powerful, (2) slightly reliable, (3) slightly modern, (4) slightly cold, and (5) very careful. In practice, however, profiles would be built up for a large sample of respondents, with many more bipolar adjectives being used than given here.

By assigning integer values, such as $+3, +2, +1, 0, -1, -2, -3$, to the seven gradations of each bipolar scale in Figure 8-6, the responses can be quantified under the assumption of equal-appearing intervals. These scale values, in turn, can be averaged across respondents to develop semantic differential profiles. For example, Figure 8-7 shows the average-respondent profiles of two companies: X and Y. We note that company X is perceived as very weak, unreliable, old-fashioned, and careless, but rather warm. Company Y is perceived as powerful, reliable, and careful, but rather cold as well; it is almost neutral with respect to the modern–old-fashioned scale.

In marketing research applications the semantic differential often uses bipolar descriptive phrases rather than simply adjectives. Because of this, so-called tailor-made scales should be developed for particular context areas. When this is done, the scales have more meaning to respondents, thus leading usually to a high degree of reliability.[20]

The same types of questions that we presented earlier in this chapter as being applicable to rating scale use also apply to using the semantic differential. In addition, the researcher must select an overall format for presentation of the scales. Figure 8-8 illustrates (in the context of evaluating national retailers in the U.S.) the four major approaches, from which there are many specific variations.

The *traditional* approach is shown in Panel (a) of Figure 8-8. The object of concern, K-Mart, is rated on all attribute dimensions before the next object, Ward's, is rated on these dimensions. Next, Panel (b) illustrates a *modified traditional* format in that both

Figure 8-6 Corporate Profile Obtained by Means of the Semantic Differential

Powerful	_x_ :	____ :	____ :	____ :	____ :	____ :	____ Weak
Reliable	____ :	____ :	_x_ :	____ :	____ :	____ :	____ Unreliable
Modern	____ :	____ :	_x_ :	____ :	____ :	____ :	____ Old-fashioned
Warm	____ :	____ :	____ :	____ :	_x_ :	____ :	____ Cold
Careful	____ :	_x_ :	____ :	____ :	____ :	____ :	____ Careless

[20]J. Dickson and G. Albaum, "A Method for Developing Tailor-Made Semantic Differentials for Specific Marketing Content Areas," *Journal of Marketing Research*, 14 (February 1977), 87–91.

Figure 8-7   Average-Respondent Profile Comparisons of Companies
X and Y Via the Semantic Differential

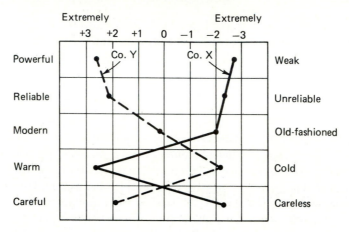

K-Mart and Ward's are evaluated on a single attribute (dull/exciting) before the next attribute (high quality/low quality) is introduced into the measurement process. Panel (c) illustrates what is called the *graphic positioning scale,*[21] in which all objects (i.e., Sears, K-Mart and Ward's) are evaluated on the same scale by some graphical means (usually

Figure 8-8   Formats of the Semantic Differential

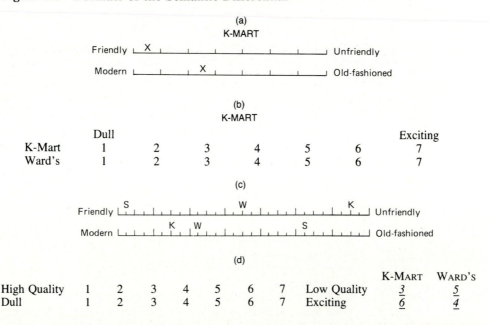

[21]C. Narayana, "Graphic Positioning Scale: An Economical Instrument for Surveys," *Journal of Marketing Research,* 14 (February 1977), 118–22.

Figure 8-9   A Stapel Scale

High Quality

```
(   ) + 5
(   ) + 4
(   ) + 3
(   ) + 2
(   ) + 1
(   ) − 1
(   ) − 2
(   ) − 3
(   ) − 4
(   ) − 5
```

letters) to reflect relative perceptual placement. Finally Panel (d) illustrates the *numerical comparative scale*.[22] Respondents make their judgments for both K-Mart and Ward's on one attribute before moving to the next one.

The number and type of stimuli to evaluate and the method of administration (personal interview, mail, telephone) should at the very least determine which format the researcher should use. Comparative studies of these formats are inconclusive and seem to indicate small differences in the content provided in the quality, including reliability, of the data obtained.[23] Therefore, choice of a format may be appropriately made on the basis of other considerations such as ease of subject understanding, ease of coding and intepretation for the researcher, ease of production and display, and cost.

Stapel Scale

A modification of the semantic differential is the Stapel scale.[24] This scale is an even-numbered nonverbal rating scale that is used in conjunction with single adjectives or phrases, rather than bipolar opposites, to rate an object, concept, person, and so on. Figure 8-9 shows the format of this scale, although it is not necessary that the scale be ten-point. Both intensity and direction are measured at the same time. It cannot be assumed that the intervals are equal and that ratings for a respondent are additive. Research has shown no differences in reliability and validity between this scale and the semantic differential.[25]

---

[22]L. Golden and G. Albaum, "An Analysis of Alternative Semantic Differential Formats for Measuring Retail Store Image," Proceedings of the Annual Meetings of Western AIDS, 1984, pp. 222–24.

[23]See E. D. Jaffe and I. D. Nebenzahl, "Alternative Questionnaire Formats for Country Image Studies," *Journal of Marketing Research*, 21 (November 1984), 463–71; and Golden and Albaum, "Analysis of Alternative Semantic Differential Formats."

[24]I. Crespi, "Use of a Scaling Technique in Surveys," *Journal of Marketing*, 25 (July 1961), 69–72.

[25]D. Menzes and N. F. Elbert, "Alternative Semantic Scaling Formats for Measuring Store Image: An Evaluation," *Journal of Marketing Research*, 16 (February 1979), 80–87; and D. Hawkins, G. Albaum, and R. Best, "Stapel Scale or Semantic Differential in Marketing Research?" *Journal of Marketing Research*, 11 (August 1974).

Multiattribute Modeling

Attitude researchers have incorporated the semantic differential into various models of attitude. As an illustration, Martin Fishbein[26] has proposed the following attitude model:

$$A_O = \sum_{i=1}^{n} B_i \alpha_i$$

where A_O denotes a respondent's overall attitude toward some object, B_i denotes the respondent's strength of belief that the object is associated with some attribute x_i, and α_i denotes the respondent's evaluation of x_i.

For example, suppose that a researcher were measuring psychiatrists' attitudes toward five leading antidepressant drugs in terms of the attributes:

x_1: effective in controlling hallucinations and delusions

x_2: effective in controlling paranoid behavior

x_3: effective in treating withdrawn/apathetic patients

x_4: exhibits rapid onset of action

x_5: safe for use in long-term therapy

The semantic differential is frequently employed to measure both the strength of belief of object–attribute association:

• How strongly do you believe that drug __exhibits attributes x_i?

and the evaluation of the attribute:

• How desirable is it that a drug possess attribute x_i?

Each drug would be evaluated separately on each of the five attributes in terms of the physician's belief that it possesses each attribute and his or her rating of the attribute's desirability. The physician's overall attitudinal score A_O is found (for each drug separately) by summing up the separate products of belief times value for each respective drug.

A Concluding Remark

Currently the semantic differential technique is being used in such applications as

• Comparing corporate images, both among suppliers of particular products and against an "ideal" image of what respondents think a company *should* be

---

[26]See Martin Fishbein, "A Behavioral Theory Approach to the Relations between Beliefs about an Object and the Attitude toward the Object," in *Readings in Attitude Theory and Measurement,* ed. M. Fishbein (New York: John Wiley, 1967), pp. 389–400.

- Comparing brands and services of competing suppliers
- Determining the attitudinal characteristics of purchasers of particular product classes or brands within product class, including perceptions of the country of origin for imported products
- Analyzing the effectiveness of advertising and other promotional stimuli toward changing attitudes

The comparatively widespread use of the semantic differential by marketing researchers suggests that this method provides a convenient and reasonably reliable way for developing consumer attitudes on a wide variety of topics. The semantic differential has enjoyed a popularity in marketing research that is unmatched by any other psychological scaling procedure.

TECHNIQUES FOR SCALING RESPONDENTS

Thurstone's Case V model and Osgood's semantic differential are primarily designed for scaling stimuli—tomato juices, brands of toothpaste, corporate images, retailing services, and the like. Behavioral scientists have also proposed techniques whose primary purpose is to scale *respondents* along some attitude continuum of interest. Three of the better-known procedures for doing this are

1. The summated scale
2. The Q-sort technique
3. The differential scale

Each of these is described in turn.

The Summated Scale

The *summated scale* was originally proposed by Rensis Likert, a psychologist.[27] To illustrate, assume that the researcher wishes to scale some characteristic, such as the public's attitude toward travel and vacations. In applying the Likert summated-scale technique, the following steps are typically carried out:

1. The researcher assembles a large number (e.g., 75 to 100) of statements concerning the public's sentiments toward travel and vacations.
2. Each of the test items is classified by the researcher as generally "favorable" or "unfavorable" with regard to the attitude under study. No attempt is made to

---

[27]A complete discussion of this scale appears in F. N. Kerlinger, *Foundation of Behavioral Research*, 2nd ed. (New York: Holt, Rinehart & Winston, 1973). Also see R. Likert, "The Method of Constructing an Attitude Scale," in *Readings in Attitude Theory and Measurement*, ed. M. Fishbein (New York: John Wiley, 1967), pp. 90–95.

scale the items; however, a pretest is conducted that involves the full set of statements and a limited sample of respondents.

3. In the pretest the respondent indicates approval (or not) with *every* item, checking one of the following direction–intensity descriptors:
    a. Strongly approve
    b. Approve
    c. Undecided
    d. Disapprove
    e. Strongly disapprove
4. Each response is given a numerical weight (e.g., $+2$, $+1$, 0, -1, -2).
5. The individual's *total-attitude score* is represented by the algebraic summation of weights associated with the items checked. In the scoring process, weights are assigned such that the direction of attitude—favorable to unfavorable—is consistent over items. For example, if a $+2$ were assigned to "strongly approve" for favorable items, a $+2$ should be assigned to "strongly disapprove" for unfavorable items.
6. After seeing the results of the pretest, the analyst selects only those items that appear to discriminate well between high and low *total* scorers. This may be done by first finding the highest and lowest quartiles of subjects on the basis of *total* score. Then, the mean differences on each *specific* item are compared between these high and low groups (excluding the middle 50% of subjects).
7. The 20 to 25 items finally selected are those that have discriminated "best" (i.e., exhibited the greatest differences in mean values) between high versus low total scorers in the pretest.
8. Steps 3 through 5 are then repeated in the main study.

Many users of the "final" Likert summated scale (the one developed after the pretest) assume only ordinal properties regarding the placement of respondents along the attitude continuum of interest. Nonetheless, two respondents could have the same total score even though their response patterns to individual items were quite different. That is, the process of obtaining a single (summated) score ignores the details of just which items were agreed with and which ones were not. Moreover, the total score is sensitive to how the respondent reacts to the descriptive intensity levels. (Some respondents tend to use the extreme ends of an intensity scale, while others tend to use the middle gradations.) For these (and other) reasons, the Likert summated scale should be used with more than the usual amount of attention to details. In particular, the classifying of items as favorable or unfavorable should be checked across several judges.

To further illustrate the use of this scale, a set of seven statements regarding travel and vacations are shown in Figure 8-10. Assume now that each of the seven test items has been classified as "favorable" (items 1, 3, and 7) or "unfavorable" (items 2, 4, 5, and 6). Each subject would be asked to circle the number that most represents his or her feeling toward the statement. We may use the weights $+2$ for "strongly agree," $+1$ for "agree," 0 for "neither," -1 for "disagree," and -2 for "strongly disagree." Since, by previous classification, items 1, 3, and 7 are "favorable" statements, we would use the

Figure 8-10   A Direction-Intensity Scale for Measuring Attitudes Toward Travel and Vacations

In this part of the questionnaire we are interested in your opinions about certain things. There are no right or wrong answers to any of these statements. What we would like you to do is simply read each statement as it appears. Then indicate the extent of your agreement or disagreement by circling the number that best describes your reaction to the statement: strongly agree (5), agree (4), neither agree nor disagree (3), disagree (2), strongly disagree (1).

		Strongly Agree	*Agree*	*Neither Agree nor Disagree*	*Disagree*	*Strongly Disagree*
1.	In the winter I need to go south to the sun.	5	4	3	2	1
2.	When you take trips with the children you're not really on vacation.	5	4	3	2	1
3.	I look for travel bargains.	5	4	3	2	1
4.	I "hate" to spend money.	5	4	3	2	1
5.	I do not like the fresh air and out-of-doors.	5	4	3	2	1
6.	I would feel lost if I were alone in a foreign country.	5	4	3	2	1
7.	A good vacation shortens the year and makes life longer.	5	4	3	2	1

PLEASE CIRCLE THE NUMBER THAT BEST DESCRIBES YOUR REACTION

preceding weights with no modification. On items 2, 4, 5, and 6 ("unfavorable" statements), we would reverse the order of the weights so as to maintain a consistent direction. Thus, in these items, +2 would stand for "strongly disagree," and so on.

Suppose that a subject evaluated the seven items in the following way:

ITEM	RESPONSE	
1	Strongly agree	+2
2	Disagree	+1
3	Agree	+1
4	Strongly disagree	+2
5	Disagree	+1
6	Strongly disagree	+2
7	Strongly agree	+2

The subject would receive a total score of

$$+ 2 + 1 + 1 + 2 + 1 + 2 + 2 = 11$$

Suppose that another subject responded to the seven items with (1) strongly disagree, (2) neither, (3) disagree, (4) strongly agree, (5) strongly disagree, (6) strongly agree, and (7) neither. This person's score would be

$$- 2 + 0 - 1 - 2 - 2 - 2 + 0 = -9$$

This listing indicates that the second subject would be ranked "lower" than the first— that is, as having a less-favorable attitude regarding travel and vacations. However, as indicated earlier, a given total score may have different meanings.

A final comment is in order. When using this format, Likert stated that a key criterion for statement preparation and selection should be that all statements be expressions of *desired behavior* and not statements of fact.[28] In practice this has not always been done. The problem seems to be that two persons with decidedly different attitudes may agree on fact. Thus, their reaction to a statement of fact is no indication of fact. Pragmatically a researcher may use this approach for fact so long as it is recognized that direction is the only meaningful measure obtained.

The Q-Sort Technique

The *Q-sort technique*, which was originally proposed by William Stephenson, has aspects in common with the summated scale.[29] Very simply, the task required of a respondent is to sort a number of statements (usually on individual cards) into a predetermined number of categories (usually 11) with a specified number having to be placed in each category.

In illustrating the Q-sort technique, assume that four subjects evaluate the test items dealing with travel and vacations. For purposes of illustration, only 3 piles will be used. The subjects are asked to sort items into:

MOST AGREED WITH (TWO ITEMS)	NEUTRAL ABOUT (THREE ITEMS)	LEAST AGREED WITH (TWO ITEMS)
+1	0	-1

[28]Likert, "Method of Constructing," p. 90.

[29]A discussion of this technique appears in Kerlinger, *Foundations of Behavioral Research*, Chap. 34. Also see G. D. Hughes, *Attitude Measurement for Marketing Strategies* (Glenview, Ill.: Scott, Foresman, 1971) for a general discussion of this and related techniques.

The numbers above the horizontal line represent the number of items that the subject *must* place into piles 1, 2, and 3, respectively. That is, the subject may first select the two items that he or she *most* agrees with; these go in pile 1. Next, the subject selects the two statements that he or she *least* agrees with; these go in pile 3. The remaining three items are placed in pile 2. The numbers below the line represent scale values. Suppose that the responses of the four subjects, A, B, C, and D, result in the following scale values:

	SUBJECT			
ITEM	A	B	C	D
1	+1	+1	−1	−1
2	0	0	0	0
3	+1	0	0	−1
4	−1	−1	+1	+1
5	0	0	0	0
6	−1	−1	+1	+1
7	0	+1	−1	−1

As can be noted, the subject pair A and B and the subject pair C and D seem "most alike" of the six distinct pairs that could be considered. We could, of course, actually correlate each subject's scores with every other subject and, similar to semantic differential applications, conduct factor or cluster analyses (see Chapter 14) on the resultant inter-correlations. Typically, these additional steps *are* undertaken in Q-sort studies.

The Differential Scale

When using a differential scale, it is assumed that a respondent will agree with only a subset, say one or two, of the items presented him or her concerning an object, a concept, a person, and so forth. The items agreed with correspond to the respondent's position on the dimension being measured, while the items disagreed with are on either side of those selected. This means that the respondent localizes his or her position.

Each of the items or statements used to construct a differential scale has attached to it a score (that is, a position on the scale) determined by outside judges. Judgments of scale position can be made by one of the following methods: paired-comparisons, equal-appearing intervals, or successive intervals. The most commonly used method is *equal-appearing intervals*, and it is this approach that we discuss in the framework of the model developed by L. L. Thurstone.

To develop this type of scale, the researcher starts with a large number of statements related to the attitude under study. These statements are given to a number of judges who are asked to sort independently each one into one of a specified number (often 11) of piles, ranging from most strongly positive or favorable to most strongly negative (i.e., least favorable). The scale value for each statement is usually computed as the *median* pile to which it is assigned by the judges, although in some cases the *mean* is used. A final list of statements consists of statements whose dispersion across judges is relatively small and which covers the range of attitude values. A respondent's attitude score (i.e., scale value) is the mean (or median) of the scale values of the statements with which he or she agrees. By using this procedure, respondents can be rank-ordered according to positiveness of attitude.

SCALING BOTH STIMULI AND RESPONDENTS

When both stimuli and respondents can be scaled, this is called the *response approach* to scaling. One approach to this involves cumulative scales.

Cumulative scales are constructed of a set of items with which the respondent indicates agreement or disagreement. If a cumulative scale exists, the items included are unidimensional. This means that they are related to each other such that (in the ideal case) a respondent who responds favorably to item 2 also responds favorably to item 1; one who responds favorably to item 4 also responds favorably to items 1, 2, and 3, and so on. This scale is based on the cumulative relation between items and the total scores of individuals. An individual's score is calculated by counting the number of items answered favorably. The basic idea is that if individuals can be ranked along a unidimensional continuum, then if A is more favorably inclined than B, he or she should endorse all the items that B does plus at least one other item. There is a *pattern* of item responses that is related to total score. If the scale is truly cumulative, when we know a person's total score we can predict his or her pattern.

In addition, if we know responses to "harder" items, we can predict the response to the easier items. For instance, if we gave a male respondent three mathematical problems to solve, each of differing difficulty, if he correctly answered the most difficult one he is likely to answer the other two correctly. On the other hand, a respondent who incorrectly solves the most difficult problem but correctly solves the next most difficult one will most likely answer the least difficult one correctly. In a similar manner, people can be asked attitudinal-oriented questions, and if the patterns of response arrange themselves similarly to the mathematical problem situation, then the questions are unidimensional. Consequently, people can be *ranked* on the basis of their scale responses. The resulting scale is ordinal.

One of the best-known approaches to cumulative scaling is *scalogram analysis*, developed by Louis Guttman.[30] The technique is designed to determine whether the items used to measure an attitude form a unidimensional scale. That is, if we know a person's rank order on a set of questions, can we predict his or her response to each question in some area of content? Both items and people can be scaled. A so-called universe of content is unidimensional, using the Guttman approach, if it yields a perfect or almost

---

[30]See L. Guttman, "Measuring the True-State of Opinion," in *Motivation and Market Behavior*, ed. R. Ferber and H. Wales (Homewood, Ill.: Richard D. Irwin, 1958), pp. 393–15. Also see Manual N. Manfield, "The Guttman Scale," in *Scientific Marketing Research*, ed. Gerald Albaum and M. Venkatesan (New York: Free Press, 1971), pp. 167–78.

TABLE 8-4   Ideal Pattern from Scalogram Analysis

Type of Respondent	"Yes" Answers				"No" Answers				Scale Score
	3	*1*	*4*	*2*	*3*	*1*	*4*	*2*	
1	X	X	X	X					(4)
2		X	X	X	X				(3)
3			X	X	X	X			(2)
4				X	X	X	X		(1)
5					X	X	X	X	(0)

perfect cumulative scale. Unfortunately, scalogram analysis is useful ex post and does not help in selecting items that are likely to form a cumulative scale.

To illustrate this approach we will present a highly simplified example. Assume our interest is in obtaining a measurement of an advertisement's ability to stimulate a consumer to some kind of action. We select four items representing actions that might occur, and we transform these actions into questions that call for a yes–no answer:

- Would you go out of your way to look at this product in a store? (2)
- Would you stop to look at this ad in a magazine? (4)
- Would you buy this product after reading this ad? (1)
- Would you want to show the ad to a friend or a neighbor? (3)

We present this set of questions to a group of respondents, whose task is to indicate "Yes" or "No" to each one. Their responses indicate the relative difficulty of answering "Yes." Assume the ranking of difficulty from most to least is shown by the numbers in parentheses. To determine whether the questions form a cumulative scale, we look at whether a pattern exists such that a respondent who answers "Yes" to a difficult question also answers "Yes" to the less-difficult ones. If a scale exists, then a respondent can be classified into one of five types of respondents depending on his or her response pattern. Table 8-4 shows the response patterns for an ideal cumulative scale. In practice this perfect pattern will not exist. Experience has shown that a cumulative scale will exist if no more than 10% of the answers vary from this geometric pattern.[31]

Our discussion so far has been concerned with unidimensional scales in which stimuli and respondents can be placed along a linear continuum. In *multidimensional scaling models*, the existence of an underlying multidimensional space is assumed. The stimuli in such models are represented by points in a space of several dimensions. Both stimuli and respondents can be scaled. The dimensions of this space represent attributes that are perceived to characterize the stimuli or respondents.

Multidimensional scaling is characterized by respondent judgments concerning the degree of similarity of *pairs* of stimuli on a similarity or distance basis. The scale value

---

[31]We have discussed only the content component of the Guttman scale. There are also components concerned with *intensity* and *location of origin*. These are discussed in Guttman, "Measuring the True-State"; Manfield, "Guttman Scale"; and Torgerson, *Theory and Methods of Scaling*.

TABLE 8-5   Basic Forms of Multidimensional Scaling

	ASSUMPTION	INPUT	OUTPUT
Fully metric	Respondent can provide a rank order of all stimulus pairs and these ranks represent ratio scaled distances between the stimuli	Ratio scaled (metric)	Ratio scaled (metric)
Fully nonmetric	Respondent can provide a rank order of all stimulus pairs	Ordinal scaled (nonmetric)	Ordinal scaled on each dimension (nonmetric)
Nonmetric	Respondent can provide a rank order of all stimulus pairs	Ordinal scaled (nonmetric)	Interval scaled (metric)

assigned each stimulus pair may be either *metric*, that is, interval or ratio scaled, or *nonmetric*, that is, ordinally scaled. In either case, the scale value reflects the psychological similarity (or dissimilarity) of each stimulus pair. And this concept of psychological distance is central to the theory behind multidimensional scaling as a measurement technique.

Multidimensional scaling can take three basic forms: (1) fully metric, (2) fully nonmetric, or (3) nonmetric. The assumptions required, the input data form, and the output form for each of these are displayed in Table 8-5. These techniques are presented in more depth in Chapter 15.

LIMITATIONS OF SCALING PROCEDURES

Although psychological measurement offers an interesting and potentially rewarding area of study by the marketing researcher, the reader should also be made aware of the limitations of current scaling techniques from the standpoint of their applicability to marketing problems.

First, it is apparent that more progress has been made in the construction of scales for measuring attitudes along a *single dimension* than in dealing with the more complex cases of *multidimensional* attitudes. A person's decision to purchase a particular brand, however, usually reflects a response to a variety of stimuli—for example, the brand's functional features, package design, advertising messages, corporate image, and so on. Much work still remains to be done on the development of scales to measure multidimensional stimuli. Accordingly, the nature of the progress that has been made in multidimensional scaling is a subject of later chapters, particularly Chapter 15.

Second, relatively little has been done on the development of anything like a general theory of individual buyer behavior that is *testable* in terms of empirical findings from psychological and sociological studies. In addition to consumer perception and preference studies, we still need to know much more about the influence of other persons (peers, superiors, subordinates) on the buyer decision process, consumer habit formation, and so on. The development of anything close to a general, operationally based, theory will require—at the least—validation of scaling techniques by behavioral-type measures under experimentally controlled conditions.

Finally, predictions from attitude scales, preference ratings, and the like still need to be transformed into measures (sales, market share) of more direct interest to the marketer. We still do not know, in many cases, how to translate verbalized product ratings, attitudes about corporations, and so on into the behavioral and financial measures required to evaluate the effectiveness of alternative marketing actions.

SUMMARY

In this chapter our major objective has been to discuss some of the fundamental concepts of measurement and psychological scaling and their relationship to the gathering and analysis of behavioral data.

We first discussed variability and quantitative-judgment methods of data collection.

Scaling procedures were next commented upon within the framework of stimulus-centered and subject-centered methods. As examples of stimulus-centered techniques, Thurstone's Case V model and Osgood's semantic differential were described in a marketing research context. Subject-centered scaling techniques—the Likert summated scale, Stephenson's Q-sort technique, and Thurstone's differential scale—were also described and illustrated by numerical examples. Next we covered techniques for scaling both stimuli and respondents. Guttman's scalogram analysis and an introduction to multidimensional scaling were presented.

The chapter concluded with a discussion of some of the difficult problems associated with testing the validity and reliability of psychological scales.

ASSIGNMENT MATERIAL

1. Take an article from a current marketing journal and do the following:
   a. Define key terms from an operational standpoint.
   b. Examine the author's justification for the type of measurement scale(s) used.
   c. Criticize the article from the standpoint of its operational usefulness to marketing management.

2. Design and administer a short questionnaire on the topic of student attitudes toward the teaching competence of your university's faculty members. Include questions dealing with paired comparisons, agree–disagree responses, and rating-type scales.

a. Apply Thurstone's Case V procedure to the paired-comparisons data. Apply also the method of Exhibit 8-3. What can your conclude about these approaches?

b. Summarize the rating-scale patterns in terms of a semantic differential profile.

c. Evaluate the usefulness of these procedures in the context of your problem.

3. The Grandma's Own Soup Company was considering the possibility of changing the consistency of its famous tomato soup. Five test soups were prepared, ranging from "very light" to "very heavy" consistency. A consumer clinic was held in which 15 housewives ranked each soup (no ties allowed) from 1 (liked best) to 5 (liked least). The data for this test are as follows:

	Subject														
Soup	1	2	3	4	5	6	7	8	9	10	11	12	13	14	15
A	2	4	3	2	2	1	2	2	2	2	3	1	2	3	2
B	1	2	1	1	1	2	1	3	1	1	1	2	1	2	4
C	4	1	4	5	4	5	3	1	5	3	4	4	5	4	5
D	3	3	2	3	3	3	5	4	3	4	2	3	3	1	3
E	5	5	5	4	5	4	4	5	4	5	5	5	4	5	1

a. On the basis of a composite (sum of the ranks), what is the rank order of the soups—from best liked to least liked?

b. What, if anything, can be said about how much better soup B is than soup E?

c. By going across rows of the above table one can count the number of times one soup of each possible pair is ranked higher than the other soup in the pair. Prepare a table of paired comparisons as derived from the ranked data, express the table entries in terms of proportions, and construct an interval scale, using Thurstone's Case V scaling.

d. What major assumption are we making abut the sample of subjects when we construct the interval scale above? Criticize this type of application of the Thurstone comparative judgment technique.

e. Apply the method described in Exhibit 8-3 to the rankings above. What can you conclude about this approach and that of Thurstone Case V?

4. Using the *method of choices*, construct an interval scale using Thurstone Case V scaling of the data shown in question 3 above. Evaluate the scale you have just derived from the standpoint of efficient use of data.

5. Assume that two groups—a group of housewives and a group of small businessmen—are asked to rate the Mighty Electric Company on the basis of the bipolar adjective pairs:

- Powerful—weak
- Reliable—nonreliable
- Modern—old-fashioned

The frequencies of each group of 100 respondents are shown below (numbers above the horizontal lines refer to housewives' responses; numbers below refer to businessmen's responses):

Powerful	$\dfrac{20}{40}$:	$\dfrac{42}{30}$:	$\dfrac{10}{15}$:	$\dfrac{5}{5}$:	$\dfrac{4}{5}$:	$\dfrac{12}{5}$:	$\dfrac{7}{0}$	Weak
Reliable	$\dfrac{52}{10}$:	$\dfrac{12}{15}$:	$\dfrac{8}{12}$:	$\dfrac{10}{22}$:	$\dfrac{8}{35}$:	$\dfrac{5}{6}$:	$\dfrac{5}{0}$	Nonreliable
Modern	$\dfrac{5}{6}$:	$\dfrac{14}{20}$:	$\dfrac{21}{25}$:	$\dfrac{25}{20}$:	$\dfrac{20}{12}$:	$\dfrac{10}{9}$:	$\dfrac{5}{8}$	Old-fashioned

a. Using a 7-point scale (where, for example, 7 = extremely powerful and 1 = extremely weak), find a summary rating index for each group of raters for each set of adjective pairs.

b. What assumptions are made by using the integer weights, 7, 6, . . . , 1?

c. In which adjective pairs are the rating indexes between the groups most similar; most dissimilar?

d. How would your answer to part (a) change if the weights $+3$, $+2$, $+1$, 0, -1, -2, and -3 were used instead of the weights, 7, 6, . . . , 1? Would rank order between pairs of summary indexes (for each adjective pair) be affected, and if so, how?

6. Select the scaling technique you would recommend be used to obtain measurements for the situations described below. Explain why you chose each.

a. Measurement of price elasticity of demand for a new product

b. Determination of preference of three levels of sweetness for a new product

c. Measurement of change of attitude toward a product as the package is changed

d. Determination of which respondents have tried a particular brand of product

e. Measurement of which of three advertisements has the greatest readership

f. Comparison of three retail stores on 15 attributes

g. Measurement of the proportion of "triers" who make repeat purchases of a new product

9

Sampling Procedures in Marketing Research

INTRODUCTION

There are many questions that marketing researchers must answer when considering a project to collect additional information about some population of interest. The following questions involve sampling:

- Should we take a census (i.e., a complete canvas) or a sample?
- What kind of sample should we take?
- What size should the sample be?

The answers to these questions depend on the application of statistical inference. We first consider the decision concerning the type of sample to take and the process of sample planning. Following this the various kinds of samples are described.

The final section of the chapter is concerned with the question of sample size. A brief review of the basic statistical models that underlie probability sampling—that is, the sampling distributions of the mean and proportion—is followed by a description of the rationale and procedures for determining sample size using traditional inferential methods. After discussing the limitations of these more commonly applied methods, we briefly describe the logic involved in determining sample size by means of the Bayesian approach.

THE DECISION CONCERNING WHAT TYPE OF SAMPLE TO TAKE

Underlying the use of samples in research projects are one or both of two broad objectives—*estimation* and *testing of hypotheses*. Each of these involves making inferences about a population on the basis of information from a sample.

The precision and accuracy of survey results are affected by the manner in which the sample has been chosen. Consequently, strict attention must be paid to the planning of the sample. It must also be recognized that sample planning is really part of the total planning of the survey. Regardless of the type of project to be conducted, the process of selecting a sample follows a well-defined progression. The major steps are shown in Figure 9-1.

Defining the Population

The first thing that the sample plan must include is a definition of the population to be investigated. While seemingly an easy task, defining the population is often one of the most difficult things to do in sampling. The greatest difficulty that arises in population definition is due to imprecise research problem definition. Imprecision of problem definition in turn is often the result of the fact that the purpose or objectives of the study,

Figure 9-1   Steps in Sample Planning

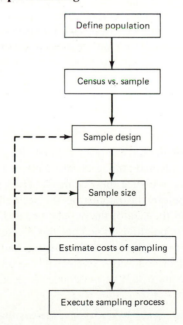

which are based on the decision problem of concern, are not clearly transmitted from the decision maker to the investigator.

Specification of a population involves identifying *which elements* (in terms of kind) are included, as well as *where* and *when*. For example, a financial institution considering making available a new type of loan plan might acquire information from any or all of the following groups:

WHICH ELEMENTS	WHERE	WHEN
All depositors	Designated bank	Last 12 months
Depositors who have borrowed money	Designated bank	Last 12 months
All people	Specified geographic area	Last 12 months
All people who have borrowed money	Specified geographic area	Last 12 months

From a research point of view, each group represents a distinct population with corresponding implications for the interpretation of any information obtained.

The population element is the unit of analysis and may be defined as an individual, household, institution, loan transaction, and so on.

The "where" and the "when" represent dimensions that are designed to define the population more precisely in terms of its extent and time. As such, these dimensions also define which units are to be excluded. It is clear that the population should be defined as precisely as possible. One useful approach is to first define the population as the *ideal* one to meet study objectives. Practical constraints then enter to define the *study population*. The advantage of starting with an ideal population is that exclusions are made explicit.[1] At the same time, however, overdefining the population should be avoided unless it is absolutely necessary. Overdefining can limit the extent to which findings can be generalized and operationally greatly increase the cost and difficulty of finding population elements.[2]

Census or Sample

Once the population has been defined, the investigator must decide whether the survey is to be conducted among all members of the population or only a subset of the population. That is, a choice must be made between census and sample. Obviously, this cannot be done before the population is specified, since the choice between the two depends largely on the size of the population, and the size is determined by the precise boundaries of the population. In practice this is often done in advance, as the investigator usually has some conception of the population and its approximate size.

Although ideal conditions (collect all needed information with little cost) might indicate that a census would be preferable, such ideal conditions rarely exist in the real

[1]Graham Kalton, *Introduction to Survey Sampling* (Beverly Hills, Calif.: Sage, 1983), pp. 6–7.
[2]Seymour Sudman, *Applied Sampling* (New York: Academic Press, 1976), p. 14.

world. A census may just not be feasible. In most instances, samples are used. The desirability and advantages of using a sample rather than a census depend on the absolute size of the population as well as the relative proportion of the population that will have to be used as the sample so as to provide results sufficiently accurate for the purposes for which they are required.

Two of the major advantages of using a sample rather than a census are *speed* and *timeliness*. A survey based on a sample takes much less time to complete than one based on a census. Moreover, in certain instances a complete count may require such a long time that, because of changes in conditions, it becomes a historical record by the time it is completed and available for use.

Another consideration in deciding whether to use sampling is the *relative cost* and *effort* that will be involved. The amount of effort and expense required to collect information is always greater per unit for a sample than for a complete census, but if the size of the sample needed to give the required accuracy represents only a small fraction of the whole population, the total effort and expense required to collect the information by sampling methods will be very much less than that required for a census of the entire population.[3] For example, even if possible, a census of all U.S. automobile owners regarding the type of wheels on their cars would hardly be economically practical for a manufacturer of magnesium wheels.

Often, administrative considerations dictate that sampling be used, particularly when a census would necessitate the hiring, training, and supervising of a large number of people. In many situations, therefore, the use of a sample results in notable economy of effort. This is particularly true when the experimental method is used.

In other situations, a sample is necessary because of the *destructive nature of the measurement,* such as the testing of matches or paint. This can be a serious problem in surveys of human populations when there is need for many different surveys to be conducted on the same population within a relatively short period of time. If such is the case and a census is used, there is a great risk that many of the individual members of the population will react negatively to being asked to participate in more than one study during a given time period. The chance that this can occur when sampling techniques are used is low if the sample is a small proportion of the total population and probability techniques are used for selecting the individual sample elements. When nonprobability techniques are used for selection, the problem can be protected against explicitly.

In still other situations, a sample may be desirable for controlling *nonsampling errors*. The smaller-scale aspects of taking a sample may permit tighter control of the measuring operations (better interviewing, less nonresponse through more call-backs, and so forth) to a point where the total amount of sampling and nonsampling error is actually less for the sample than the nonsampling error alone would be for a census.

A sample may be necessary to enable one to *concentrate attention on individual cases*. For example, in-depth studies of why a product is bought and how it is consumed may not be feasible to carry out on other than a sample basis. Closely related to this characteristic is that *it is possible to obtain more-detailed information* from a sample.

[3] Frank Yates, *Sampling Methods for Censuses and Surveys*, 3rd ed. (London: Charles Griffin, 1971), p. 63.

The reason is that the individuals concerned may be more willing to provide more-detailed information if they know they represent only a small proportion of the population.

Finally, a sample may be necessary simply because *there is no other alternative available* except to collect no information at all. The entire population may not be available for measurement at the time the study must be made.

Under certain conditions, however, a census may be preferable to a sample. When *the population is small, the variance in the characteristic being measured high, the cost of error high, and/or the fixed costs of sampling high, sampling may not be useful.* If one were doing a study to determine the acceptability to U.S. original equipment manufacturers of a new drive mechanism for snowmobiles, one might be well advised to conduct a census of the seven manufacturers involved. In addition, if the characteristic or attribute of interest occurs only rarely in the population, then a census might be desirable, since a relatively large sample would be necessary to provide information that is statistically reliable. Another alternative, however, would be to use a type of sampling known as *snowball*, particularly when the size of the population is large.

Sample Design

Operationally, *sample design* is the heart of sample planning. Specification of sample design, which includes the method of selecting individual sample members, involves both theoretical and practical (e.g., cost, time, labor involved, organization) considerations.

Typical questions to be answered include

- What type of sample to use?
- What is the appropriate sampling unit?
- What frame (that is, list of sampling units from which the sample is to be drawn) is available for the population and what problems might arise in using it for the particular design and unit decided upon?
- How are refusals and nonresponse to be handled? (See Exhibit 9-1.)

Type of Sample

Much of the sampling in marketing research is nonprobability in nature. That is, samples are selected on the basis of the judgment of the investigator, convenience, or by some other nonrandom process rather than by the use of a table of random numbers or some other randomizing device.

The advantages of probability sampling are that, if done properly, it provides a *bias-free method of selecting sample units and permits the measurement of sampling error*. Nonprobability samples offer neither of these features. In nonprobability sampling one must rely on the expertise of the person taking the sample, whereas in probability sampling the results are independent of the investigator.[4]

---

[4]It will be recalled that a method for estimating error from a nonprobability sample was presented in the appendix to Chapter 4.

Exhibit 9-1   Possible Answers to Reasons for Refusals

REASONS FOR REFUSING	. . . AND POSSIBLE RESPONSES
TOO BUSY	This should only take a few minutes. Sorry to have caught you at a bad time; I would be happy to call back. When would be a good time for me to call in the next day or two?
BAD HEALTH	I'm sorry to hear that. Have you been sick long? I would be happy to call back in a day or two. Would that be OK? (IF LENGTHY OR SERIOUS ILLNESS, substitute another member of household. IF THAT ISN'T POSSIBLE, excuse yourself and indicate they will *not* be called again.)
TOO OLD	Older people's opinions are just as important in this particular survey as anyone else's. In order for the results to be representative for all residents of the city, we have to be sure that older people have as much chance to give their opinion as anyone else does. We really do want *your* opinion.
FEEL INADEQUATE: DON'T KNOW ENOUGH TO ANSWER	The questions are not at all difficult. They mostly concern your attitudes about local recreation areas and activities rather than how much you know about certain things. Some of the people we have already interviewed had the same concern you have, but once we got started they didn't have any difficulty answering the questions. Maybe I could read just a few questions to you and you can see what they are like.
NOT INTERESTED	It's awfully important that we get the opinions of everyone in the sample, otherwise the results won't be very useful. So, I'd really like to talk with you.
NO ONE ELSE'S BUSINESS WHAT I THINK	I can certainly understand, that's why all of our interviews are confidential. Protecting people's privacy is one of our major concerns, and to do it people's names are separated from the answers just as soon as the interview is over. And, all the results are released in such a way that no single individual can ever be identified.
OBJECTS TO SURVEYS	We think this particular survey is very important because the questions are ones that people in parks and recreation want to know answers to, so we would really like to have your opinion too.
OBJECTS TO TELEPHONE SURVEYS	We have just recently started doing our surveys by telephone because this way is so much faster and it costs a lot less, especially when the survey is not very long, as this survey is not very long.

One should not conclude that probability sampling always yields results that are superior to nonprobability sampling, nor that the samples obtained by nonprobability methods are necessarily less "representative" of the populations under study. For example, a marketing researcher working for a drug firm may develop an index of salespeople's performance by measuring such items as doctor calls completed per week, number of new drugs promoted during call, and length of call. A particular item is included in the index because the marketing researcher feels that it is representative of something called "performance." And the researcher's nonprobability sampling may indeed be a better way to achieve a representation of the population than dropping a bunch of cards (on which are written possible characteristics of sales performance) in a hat and selecting five or six of the cards, blindfolded.

On the other hand, a cosmetics manufacturer may test consumer reactions to a new lipstick by giving samples of the product to the female members of his family and eliciting their responses a week or so later. In both cases, the samples are "biased" in the sense that they have been deliberately chosen to conform to the selector's idea of what the population does—or perhaps should—look like. In the first case we might argue that the marketing researcher's choice of characteristics is a reasonable one, in view of the purposes for which the index is being prepared. In the second case, assuming that the cosmetics manufacturer is attempting to infer "typical" consumer reaction to the lipstick, we might question the relevance of the reactions of his family members, independent of the fact that the sample size is small.

The choice between probability and nonprobability sampling ultimately turns on a judgment of the relative size of the sampling error of the probability sample versus the combined sampling error and selection bias of a nonprobability sample. For a given cost, one will normally be able to select a larger nonprobability sample than probability sample. This means that the sampling error should be lower in the nonprobability sample. However, a selection bias will have been introduced by the nonrandom process used for selecting the sample.

Sampling Unit

The sampling unit forms the basis of the actual sampling procedure. It is that which is actually chosen by the sampling process. The sampling unit may contain one or more population elements. That is, these units may be individual elements or aggregates of individual elements. For instance, in the new loan plan problem the financial institution may be interested in past loan behavior of the male wage earner or his entire household. In either case, it may be preferable to select a sample of households as sampling units.

Sample Frame

In Chapter 4 we defined a *sampling* (or sample) *frame* as a means of accounting for the elements in the population. The sampled elements are selected from the frame. In some cases, however, the frame consists of sampling units that are aggregates because the individual elements are not known. The sampling frame is usually a physical listing of the population elements. In those instances where such a listing is not available, the frame is a procedure that produces a result equivalent to a physical listing.[5] For instance, in a consumer survey where personal interviews are conducted with a sample of people "on-the-street" who pass by the interviewer, the frame might be defined as a "listing" of those people who might reasonably be expected to pass by the interviewer during some specified time period.

Ideally, the sample frame should identify each population element once, but only once, and should not include elements not in the defined population. Such a perfect frame is seldom available for marketing research purposes. As shown in Figure 9-2, a sampling

Figure 9-2   Sampling Frame–Population Relationships

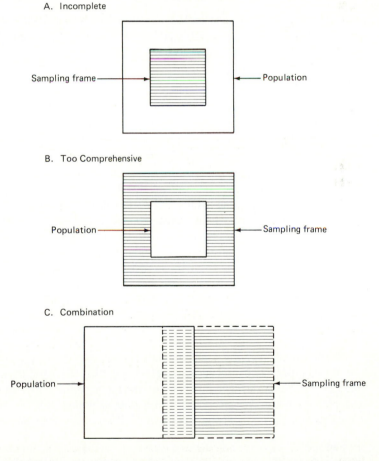

[5]William P. Dommermuth, *The Use of Sampling in Marketing Research* (Chicago: American Marketing Association, 1975), p. 11.

frame may be incomplete, too comprehensive, or a combination. In addition, the frame may include some individual population elements *more than once*. Each of these situations can lead to *coverage error*.[6]

Perhaps the most widely used frame in survey research for sampling human populations is the telephone directory. Use of such a frame, however, may lead to frame error that can arise from the exclusion of nonsubscribers, voluntary unlisted subscribers, and involuntary unlisted subscribers. For example, for many of the large metropolitan areas the proportion of subscribing households who are listed ranges from 70% to 90%.[7] Similar-type frame errors can arise from other sampling frames such as city directories, maps, trade association membership lists, or any other incomplete or dated listing or representation of a population.

Refusals and Nonresponse

The sample plan must include provision for how refusals and nonresponse are to be handled. Of concern is whether additional sampling units are to be chosen as replacements and, if so, how these are to be selected.

Sample Size

Somewhat related to sample design, but in many ways a separate decision area for the investigator, is the determination of the sample size. In general, size of sample is directly related to precision. There are four general traditional approaches to determining the size of the sample to be used in any given research project. The first three are (1) *arbitrarily* or *judgmentally* determined, (2) *minimum cell size* needed for analysis, and (3) *budget-based*. After the results of the study have been compiled for all of these, then, if a probability design is being used, the precision can be measured by applying the appropriate standard error formula or formulas. The fourth approach involves the opposite procedure. That is, by specifying a desired precision in advance, and by applying the appropriate standard error formula, sample size can be arrived at. Determining sample size will be discussed in more depth later in this chapter.

Costs of Sampling

The sample plan must take into account the estimated costs of sampling. Such costs are of two types: (1) overhead costs, which are relatively fixed for a sampling procedure, and (2) variable costs, which depend on the scope of the study. In reality, it is difficult, and perhaps not even reasonable, to separate sampling costs from overall study costs. Consequently, in a typical study costs from all aspects of the study are usually considered

---

[6]Interestingly, coverage error may also arise from survey definitions—e.g., what is a housing unit. See H. R. Hogan, J. K. Garrett, and C. P. Pautler, "Coverage Concepts and Issues in Data Collection and Data Presentation," paper presented at the Bureau of the Census Second Annual Research Conference, March 23–26, 1986.

[7]Sudman, *Applied Sampling*, p. 64.

together. Note that there is a dashed line in Figure 9-1 that relates this aspect of the plan to sample design and sample size. This means that the estimated costs may be so great that the investigator may want to consider using other sample designs and/or smaller-sized samples.

Execution of the Sampling Process

The last step in sample planning is the execution of the sampling process. In short, the sample is actually chosen. There are two basic requirements for the sampling procedure to fulfill.

A sample must be *representative* and it must be *adequate*. When it is representative, a sample will be a relatively small piece of the population that mirrors the various patterns and subclasses of the population. A sample is adequate when it is of sufficient size to provide confidence in the stability of its characteristics. This, in turn, requires a measure of precision, which requires the use of a probability-based design. From this discussion, one might conclude that the ideal sample is obtained by a probability process. In general, this is preferable. However, it should be recognized that it is more important to avoid distorted samples than to be able to measure sampling error. There may be a tendency to ignore the existence of potential bias when using probability designs.

In this chapter we shall be primarily concerned with probability sampling. However, before discussing this topic it is useful to describe some of the procedures by which nonprobability samples are selected in marketing research.

NONPROBABILITY SAMPLING PROCEDURES

Quota Sampling

Perhaps the most commonly employed nonprobability sampling procedure in marketing research is the *quota sample*.[8] Roughly described, in quota sampling the sizes of various subclasses (or strata) in the population are first estimated from some outside source, such as from Bureau of the Census data. For example, one may use census data to find out the proportion of the adult population who fall into various age-by-sex-by-education classes.

Next, if an interviewer has a total number of, say, 100 interviews to obtain, the age–sex–education proportions in the population are applied to the 100 total interviews to determine the appropriate quotas. This could lead, for example, to 4 interviews of respondents who are between 18 and 30 years of age, female, with some college (or above) and 9 interviews of respondents who are over 30 years of age, male, with high school (or below) education. Another illustration is presented in Exhibit 9-2.

---

[8]Quota sampling is discussed rather extensively in F. J. Stephan and P. J. McCarthy, *Sampling Opinions* (New York: John Wiley, 1958). A critique of the method is offered by W. E. Deming, *Sample Designs in Business Research* (New York: John Wiley, 1960).

Exhibit 9-2   Instructions for a Quota Sample

In a recent consumer study of fast-food restaurants the following instructions were given for the sample:

There are to be 200 completed interviews. To the extent possible, the sample should be as follows:

Area

      25–30% from Springfield
      70–75% from Greater Eugene

Sex

      60% males
      40% females

Age

      40% between 16 and 24
      40% between 25 and 50
      20% to be under 16 and over 50

Occupation

      20% university students
      80% non-students

The interviews should be conducted in the following areas:

(a)   Valley River Shopping Center
(b)   Downtown Springfield
(c)   Big M-Marks Shopping Center
(d)   Willamette Plaze
(e)   Downtown Eugene
(f)   University campus

The number of people who might have to be contacted will depend upon the incidence or rate of occurrence of persons eligible to fill each of the 24 cells.

Obviously, low incidence rates can lead to a greater number of needed contacts, which then leads to greater costs.*

*See, for example, K. G. Lee, "Incidence Is a Key Element," *Marketing News,* 19 (September 13, 1985), 50–52.

So far, this approach to stratification is quite sound, statistically. Indeed, as will be discussed later, this same initial step is employed in proportionate stratified random sampling. However, in quota sampling the interviewer is *not* required to select the respondents necessary to fill each quota on a random basis. This is the major distinction between quota sampling and stratified random sampling.

Since the interviewer's judgment is relied upon to select actual respondents within each quota, many sources of selection bias are potentially present. For example, the interviewer may not bother to call back if the first call results in a not-at-home. Interviewers may go to selected areas where the chances are good that a particular type of respondent is available. Certain houses may be skipped because the interviewer does not like the appearance of the property. Still other ways exist in which the habits and biases of interviewers can influence their selection of respondents within quota.

The advantages of quota sampling are, of course, the lower costs and greater convenience provided to the interviewer in selecting respondents to fill each quota. More recently, tighter controls have been established on the permissible travel patterns of interviewers, thus tending to reduce this potential source of selection bias. In fact, it has been shown that quota sampling is quite close to traditional probability sampling under certain conditions.[9]

Judgment Sampling

A somewhat representative sample may be provided by the use of *purposive* or *judgment sampling*. The key assumption underlying this type of sampling is that, with sound judgment or expertise and an appropriate strategy, one can carefully and consciously choose the elements to be included in the sample so that samples can be developed that are suitable for one's needs. The intent is to select elements that are believed to be typical or representative of the population in such a way that errors of judgment in the selection will cancel each other out. One weakness of this approach is that without an objective basis for making the judgments or without an external check, there is no way of knowing whether the so-called typical cases are, in fact, typical.[10]

The relative advantages of judgment sampling are claimed to be that it is low cost, convenient to use, less time-consuming, and as good as probability sampling.[11] However, its value depends entirely on the expert judgment of the researcher. An example of the use of this type of sampling is provided by the company that wanted to know why new products fail, so it conducted surveys on competitors whose products were similar or related to those it produced.

Convenience Sampling

Convenience sampling is a generic term that covers a wide variety of ad hoc procedures for selecting respondents. For example, some cities, such as Fort Worth, Texas, and Syracuse, New York, are viewed as "typical" cities whose demographic makeups are close to the national average. In market tests of new products it is not unusual to select such cities to obtain consumer evaluations that are believed to reflect "national" tastes. As in any other nonprobability procedure, however, there is no sound basis for estimating statistical confidence intervals around the sample statistics of interest.

Other forms of convenience sampling are prevalent. Many firms conduct "intercept" interviews among shopping-mall customers or in other areas where large numbers of consumers may congregate.[12] Firms may also authorize samples to be taken from such

---

[9]See Sudman, *Applied Sampling*, pp. 191–200.

[10]Claire Selltiz, Lawrence S. Wrightsman, and Stuart W. Cook, *Research Methods in Social Relations,* 3rd ed. (New York: Holt, Rinehart & Winston, 1976), p. 521.

[11]Robert P. Vichas, *Complete Handbook of Profitable Marketing Research Techniques* (Englewood Cliffs, N.J.: Prentice-Hall, 1982), p. 298.

[12]It is possible to use other types of sampling, and even probability sampling similar to a multistage area probability sample. See Patricia M. Reid, " 'Purists' May Disagree, but Almost All Types of Surveys Can Be Conducted in Malls," *Marketing News,* 18 (January 6, 1984), Sec. 1, p. 5; and Seymour Sudman, "Improving the Quality of Shopping Center Sampling," *Journal of Marketing Research,* 17 (November 1980), 423–31.

intact groups as Parent–Teacher Associations, church groups, and philanthropic organizations. Again, the purpose is to obtain a relatively large number of interviews quickly from a cooperating group of respondents. Usually the sponsoring organization receives a donation from the interviewing firm for the help and cooperation of the organization's members.

Surveys based on convenience sampling are also carried out by various magazines and newspapers (using subscriber lists and/or a pull-out or tear-out questionnaire included in the publication), department stores (using charge account lists), or gasoline companies (using credit card lists). Again, many potential sources of selection bias are present, assuming that the population under study is larger than the members of the various lists. For instance, research has shown that newspaper and magazine surveys do suffer from sampling bias in that less than 10% of readers return the questionnaires and that respondents tend to be disproportionately white, educated, and affluent.[13]

Convenience sampling means that the sampling units are accessible, convenient and easy to measure, cooperative, or articulate. New-product testing provides an illustration of the use of this type of sampling. A toy manufacturer invited a number of parents to "lend" their children to the company for a few hours of play with some new toys. Based on observations through one-way mirrors, redesigns for some toys were made. Wheels were added to a particular toy when it was observed that the children pulled it around.[14]

Snowball Sampling

Snowball sampling (also known as multiplicity sampling) is the rather colorful name given to a procedure in which initial respondents *are* selected randomly but where additional respondents are then obtained from referrals or by other information provided by the initial respondents. One major purpose of snowball sampling is to estimate various characteristics that are rare in the total population.[15]

For example, in a study of international tourism, the researchers were required to interview respondents in the United Kingdom, France, and Germany who visited the United States during the Bicentennial year. As might be expected, in most areas of these three countries, the likelihood of finding a qualified adult respondent was less than 2%. Accordingly, stratified probability methods were used to select initial respondents. Then a referral procedure (up to two referrals per qualified respondent) was used to obtain a second group of qualified respondents. (However, subsequent referrals were *not* obtained from this second group of respondents, in this particular study.)

Another example is the research company that uses the telephone to obtain referrals.

[13]Phillip Shaver and Carin Rubenstein, "Research Potential of Newspaper and Magazine Surveys," in *Naturalistic Approaches to Studying Social Interaction,* ed. Harry T. Reis (San Francisco: Jossey-Bass, 1983), pp. 75–91.

[14]Reported in Vichas, *Complete Handbook,* p. 300.

[15]For a more complete discussion of this technique, see George M. Zinkham, Scot Burton, and Melanie Wallendorf, "Marketing Applications for Snowball Sampling: Potential Benefits and Problems," in *Research Methods and Causal Models in Marketing,* ed. William R. Darden et al. (Chicago: American Marketing Association, 1983), pp. 5–8.

Random telephone calls are made, and regardless of whether the persons answering the telephone are qualified respondents, they are asked if someone else they know meets the study's respondent qualifications. If they do, the interviewer tries to get that person's name.[16]

In other types of snowball sampling, referrals from referrals are obtained, and so on, thus leading to the term "snowballing." Even though some probability-based procedure may be used to select the initial group of respondents, the overall sample is a nonprobability sample. For example, referrals will tend to exhibit demographic profiles that are more similar to those of the persons referring them than would be expected by chance.

In general, the sampling of rare characteristics is often aided by the employment of short and inexpensive *screening interviews* (usually by telephone), whose major purpose is to locate the subpopulation of interest for a subsequent personal interview that is more extensive.[17] Finally, it should be mentioned that, in the case of rare characteristics, it is not unusual to *oversample* some of the subgroups so as to obtain a sample size that is adequate in terms of the actual number of respondents to produce reasonably stable estimates. That is, in sampling various rare characteristics, the allocation of interviews may *not* be in direct proportion to the relative size of the strata if this leads to too few respondents in the smaller strata.

Major advantages of this type of sampling over conventional methods are that it substantially increases the probability of finding the desired characteristic in the population and lower sampling variance and costs.[18]

PROBABILITY SAMPLING DESIGNS

The best-known type of probability sample is no doubt the simple random sample. However, in marketing research many occasions exist for more specialized sampling procedures than those that can be met by simple random-sampling methods. Statisticians have developed a variety of specialized probability-sampling designs that, although derived from simple random-sampling principles, can be used to gain lower sampling error for a given cost or equal sampling error for a lower cost. Five major modifications can be made to the basic selection process, as shown in Table 9-1. Conceptually, these five dimensions allow for a total of 32 possible probability samples. However, some designs are used more widely and are of greater interest than others. Designs of particular interest

---

[16]Richard N. Frost, " 'Referral' Sampling Technique Finds Hard-to-Find Respondents," *Marketing News*, 16 (May 14, 1982), Sec. 1, p. 24.

[17]For a rare population, screening costs may be large when working with *special populations* for which no complete list exists. There are, however, rigorous methods for obtaining careful probability samples, although screening costs may still be significant. See Seymour Sudman, "Efficient Screening Methods for the Sampling of Geographically Clustered Special Populations," *Journal of Marketing Research*, 22 (February 1985), 20–29.

[18]"Select Rare Populations with Low-Cost Statistically Efficient Multiplicity Sampling," *Marketing News* 17 (May 13, 1983), Sec. 1, p. 21. Also see S. Dutka, *Sampling Rare Populations: An Alternative Method* (New York: Audits & Surveys, n.d.).

TABLE 9-1   Selection Methods for Probability Samples

I. *Equal probability* for all elements	*Unequal probabilities* for different elements; ordinarily compensated with inverse weights

a. Equal probabilities at all stages
   b. Equal overall probabilities for all elements obtained through compensating unequal probabilities at several stages
	a. Caused by irregularities in selection frames and procedures
	   b. Disproportionate allocation designed for optimum allocation

II. *Element Sampling:* single stage, sampling unit contains only one element	*Cluster Sampling:* sampling units are clusters of elements

	a. One-stage cluster sampling
	   b. Subsampling or multistage sampling
	   c. Equal clusters
	   d. Unequal clusters

III. *Unstratified Selection:* sampling units selected from entire population	*Stratified Sampling:* separated selections from partitions, or strata, of population
IV. *Random Selection* of individual sampling units from entire stratum or population	*Systematic Selection* of sampling units with selection interval applied to list
V. *One-Phase Sampling:* final sample selected directly from entire population	*Two-Phase (or Double) Sampling:* final sample selected from first-phase sample, which obtains information for stratification or estimation

Source: Adapted from Leslie Kish, *Survey Sampling* (New York: John Wiley, 1965), p. 20.

to the marketing researcher are systematic sampling, stratified sampling, cluster sampling, area sampling, and multistage sampling.

These techniques are discussed in turn, following a review of simple random sampling. Our purpose is to describe the major characteristics of each technique rather than to present a detailed mathematical exposition of these procedures.[19]

Simple Random Sampling

A *simple random sample* is one in which each sample element has a known and equal probability of selection, and each possible sample of *n* elements has a known and

---

[19]A brief review of the mathematical aspects of each of these sampling techniques is given in Martin Frankel, "Sampling Theory," in *Handbook of Survey Research,* ed. Peter H. Rossi, James D. Wright, and Andy B. Anderson (New York: Academic Press, 1983), pp. 21–67; and M. R. Frankel and L. R. Frankel, "Probability Sampling," in *Handbook of Marketing Research,* ed. R. Ferber (New York: McGraw-Hill, 1974), pp. 2-230–2-246. For a more extensive treatment, see M. H. Hansen, W. N. Hurwitz and W. G. Madow, *Sample Survey Methods and Theory* (New York: John Wiley, 1953), Vols. 1 and 2.

equal probability of being the sample actually selected. It is drawn by a random procedure from a sample *frame*, which is a list containing an exclusive and exhaustive enumeration of all sample elements.

Simple random samples are *not* widely used in marketing research, and especially so in consumer research, for two reasons. The first is that it is often difficult to obtain a sampling frame that will permit a simple random sample to be drawn. Consumer research usually requires that either *people, households, stores,* or *areas* be the basic sampling units. While a complete representation of areas is available through maps, there normally is no complete listing of persons (or the households in which they live) or of the stores available. When persons, households, or stores are to be sampled, therefore, some other sample design must be used.

However, in industrial marketing research, there is a greater opportunity for the application of simple random sampling. In this case, *people* (e.g., purchasing agents), *companies,* or *areas* are the usual sampling units. Since the population under study is often relatively small, one is in a better position to develop a complete respondent list or sample frame.

Industrial marketing research, however, provides a second reason for not using simple random sampling—that is, one may not want to have an *equal* probability of selection of all sample units. Most industries are characterized by a wide variation in the size of the firms that comprise them. One is likely to want to design the sample so that the larger firms have a considerably greater chance of being selected than the smaller firms.

Systematic Sampling

Systematic sampling involves only a slight variation from simple random sampling. A *systematic sample* is one in which each sample element has a known and equal probability of selection. The permissible samples of size *n* that are possible to be drawn have a known and equal probability of selection, while the remaining samples of size *n* have a probability of zero of being selected.

The mechanics of taking a systematic sample are rather simple. If the population contains *N* ordered elements and a sample size *n* is desired, one merely finds the ratio of these two numbers *N/n* and rounds to the nearest integer to obtain the sampling interval. For example, if there are 600 members of the population and one desires a sample of 60, the sampling interval is 10. A random number is then selected between 1 and 10, inclusively; suppose the number turns out to be 4. The analyst then takes as the sample elements 4, 14, 24, and so on.

Essentially, systematic sampling assumes that the population elements are ordered in some fashion—names in a telephone directory, a card index file, or the like. Some types of ordering, such as an alphabetical listing, will usually be uncorrelated with the characteristic (say, income level) being investigated. In other instances, the ordering of the elements may be directly related to the characteristic under study, such as a customer list arranged in decreasing order of annual purchase volume.

If the arrangement of the elements of the sample is itself random with regard to the characteristic under study, systematic sampling will tend to give results close to those provided by simple random sampling. We say "close" for the reason that, in systematic sampling, all combinations of the characteristic do *not* have the same chance of being included. For example, it is clear that, in the preceding example, the fifth, sixth, and so on items have zero chance of being included in the *particular* sample chosen.

Systematic sampling may, however, *increase* the sample's representativeness when the items are ordered with regard to the characteristic of interest. For example, if the analyst is sampling a customer group by decreasing order of purchase volume, a systematic sample will be sure to contain some high-volume customers and some low-volume customers. On the other hand, the simple random sample may yield, say, only low-volume customers, and may thus be unrepresentative of the population being sampled if the characteristic of interest is related to purchase volume.

It is also possible that systematic sampling may *decrease* the representativeness of the sample in those instances where the items are ordered in such a way as to produce a cyclical pattern. For example, if a marketing researcher were to use systematic sampling of daily retail-store sales volume, and were to choose a sampling interval of seven days, his or her choice of day would result in a sample that would not reflect day-of-the-week variations in sales.

Although systematic sampling can lead to greater reliability (lower sampling error) than simple random sampling, the major difficulty with this technique is the problem of estimating the variance of the universe from the variance of the sample. For example, if in the preceding example we happened to sample all "Tuesdays," we would probably find that we have seriously underestimated the variance across all seven days in the week. If we have prior knowledge about the characteristics of the groups making up the population, however, we may be able to use this information to select our sample in such a way as to increase the reliability of the sample over that obtained by simple random-sampling methods.

Stratified Sampling

It is sometimes desirable to break the population into different strata based on one or more characteristics such as the frequency of purchase of a product, type of customer (e.g., credit card versus non-credit card), or the industry in which a company competes. In such cases a separate sample is then taken from each stratum. Technically, a *stratified random sample* is one in which a simple random sample is taken from each stratum of interest in the population. (In practice, however, systematic and other types of random samples are sometimes taken from each of the strata and the resulting design is still referred to as a stratified sample.)

Stratified samples have the following general characteristics:

- The entire population is first divided into an exclusive and exhaustive set of strata, using some external source, such as census data, to form the strata.
- Within each stratum a separate random sample is selected.
- From each separate sample, some statistic (e.g., a mean) is computed and properly weighted to form an overall estimated mean for the whole population.

- Sample variances are also computed within each separate stratum and appropriately weighted to yield a combined estimate for the whole population.

Two basic varieties of stratified samples are proportionate and disproportionate. In *proportionate stratified sampling,* the sample that is drawn from each stratum is made proportionate in size to the relative size of that stratum in the total population. In *disproportionate stratified sampling* one departs from the preceding type of proportionality by taking other circumstances, such as the relative size of stratum variances, into account.

The decision concerning whether to use proportionate or disproportionate stratified sampling among strata rests on whether or not the variances among the strata are (approximately) equal. Suppose that a marketing researcher is interested in estimating the average purchases of consumers of hot cereal. The researcher may be willing to assume that, although average consumption would vary markedly by family size, the variances around the means of the strata would be more or less equal among family sizes. If so, the researcher would make use of proportionate stratified sampling.

More generally, however, both means and variances will differ among strata. If this is the case, the researcher would make use of disproportionate stratified sampling. In this instance the number of families included in each stratum would be proportionate to (the product of) the relative size of the different family-sized strata in the population and the standard deviation of each family class. This requires, of course, that the researcher be able to estimate (from past studies) the within-group standard deviation around the average purchase quantity of each purchasing stratum.[20]

As intuition would suggest, the increased efficiency of stratified sampling over simple random sampling depends on how different the means (or some other statistic) really are among strata, relative to the within-stratum variability. What is desired are strata whose within-stratum variation is small but whose among-strata differences are large. That is, the greater the within-stratum *homogeneity* and the among-strata *heterogeneity,* the more efficient stratified sampling is relative to simple random sampling.

Cluster Sampling

Although the researcher will ordinarily be interested in the characteristics of some elementary element in the population (e.g., individual family attitudes toward a new product), he or she may wish to select primary sampling units on a larger than individual family basis. The researcher may choose to sample city blocks and interview *all* the individual families residing therein. The *blocks,* not the individual families, would be selected at random. Each block consists of a cluster of respondents. Formally, a *cluster sample* is one in which a simple random or stratified random sample is selected of all primary sample units, each containing more than one sample element. Then, all elements within the selected primary units are sampled.

The main advantage of a cluster sample relative to simple random sampling is in lower interviewing costs rather than in greater reliability. One of the authors participated in a survey of salespeople's attitudes toward management policies of a large drug firm

---

[20]Formulas for computing sampling errors in stratified samples can be found in W. G. Cochran, *Sampling Techniques,* 2nd ed. (New York: John Wiley, 1963).

in which sales districts were the primary units that were sampled and all salespeople of the sampled districts were interviewed. As might be surmised, the attitudes of a given district's salespeople tended to be positively correlated among salespeople, resulting in greater sampling variance than would have been attained if random sampling (with the same sample size) had been performed at the individual salesperson level. On the other hand, the expense of transporting interviewers to various parts of the firm's overall marketing territory would have added substantially to the costs of the study.

Area Sampling—Single Stage and Multistage

As the name suggests, *area sampling* pertains to primary sampling of geographical areas—for example, counties, townships, blocks, and other area descriptions. If only one level of sampling takes place (e.g., a sampling of blocks) before the basic elements are sampled (e.g., the households), it is a *single-stage area sample*. If one or more successive samples within the larger area are taken before settling on the final clusters, the resulting design is usually referred to as a *multistage area sample*.

An example of multistage sampling is the sample design used by the Gallup Organization, Inc., in taking a nationwide poll. A random sample of approximately 300 locations is drawn as the first stage of the sampling process. Blocks or geographic segments are then randomly sampled from each of these locations in a second stage, followed by a systematic sampling of households within the blocks or segments. A total of about 1,500 persons are usually interviewed in the typical Gallup poll. Another example is provided by the Opinion Research Corporation (ORC) sampling for studies of the general public or defined segments of it. The ORC master sample consists of 360 communities arranged in six blocks. Each block is a random sample of communities, selected with probability proportioned to population. The 60 communities within each block are distributed further into six national probability replications of 10 communities each. For any given study, therefore, one or more blocks provide a national probability sample.[21]

A Final Comment

Our discussion of probability sampling designs has been general and is applicable to all methods of data collection. In some ways, sampling for telephone surveys is unique. A description of techniques specifically applicable to telephone surveys is in the appendix to this chapter.

THE DECISION CONCERNING WHAT SIZE SAMPLE TO TAKE

There are several ways to classify techniques for determining sample size. Two that are of primary importance here are whether the technique deals with fixed or sequential

---

[21]The descriptions for Gallup and ORC are contained in materials provided by these organizations.

sampling and whether its logic is based on traditional or Bayesian inferential methods. Other than for the brief discussion of sequential sampling that follows, this section is concerned with the determination of a *fixed* sample size with emphasis on *traditional* (i.e., Neyman–Pearson) inference rather than Bayesian inference. Although the discussion will focus on the statistical aspects of setting sample size, it should be recognized that nonstatistical dimensions may very well affect the value of a research project. Such things as the length of a questionnaire, budget, and time schedule, as well as attitudes, opinions, and expectations, all have a direct effect upon sample-size decisions.

Fixed versus Sequential Sampling

As the name implies, in *fixed-size sampling* the number of items is decided upon in advance. The size of the sample is chosen in such a way as to achieve some type of balance between sample reliability and sample cost. In general, all observations are taken before the data are analyzed.

In *sequential sampling,* however, the number of items is not preselected. Rather, the analyst sets up in advance a decision rule that includes not only the alternative of stopping the sampling process (and taking appropriate action, based on the sample evidence already in hand) but also the possibility of collecting more information before making a terminal decision. Observations may be taken either singly or in groups, the chief novelty being that the data are analyzed as they are assembled and sample size is not predetermined.

In general, sequential sampling will lead to smaller sample sizes, on the average, than those associated with fixed-size samples of a given reliability. The mathematics underlying sequential sampling are, however, more complex and time-consuming. In addition, the problem may be such that it is less expensive to select and analyze a sample of many items at one time than to draw items one at a time (or in small groups) and analyze each item before selecting the next.

Sampling Distributions and Standard Errors

Intuitively we might expect that when we increase the size of the sample, our estimate of the population parameter should "get closer" to the true value. Also, we might expect that the less dispersed the population's characteristics are, the closer our sample estimates should be to the "true" parameter. After all, the reason why we sample in the first place is to make some *inference* about the population. These inferences should be more reliable the larger the sample on which they are based and the less variable the items of the population are to begin with.

The reader will recall from elementary statistics the concept of a sampling distribution. A *sampling distribution* is the probability distribution of a specified sample statistic (e.g., the sample mean) for all possible random samples of a given size n drawn from the specified population. The *standard error* of the statistic is the standard deviation of the specified sampling distribution. We shall use the following symbols in our brief review of the elementary formulas for calculating the standard error of the mean and proportion (under simple random sampling):

μ = population mean

π = population proportion regarding some attribute

σ = standard deviation of the population

s = standard deviation of the sample, adjusted to serve
     as an estimate of the standard deviation of the population

$\overline{X}$ = arithmetic mean of a sample

p = sample proportion

n = number of items in the sample

As the reader will recall from elementary statistics, there are some important properties associated with sampling distributions:

1. The arithmetic mean of the sampling distribution of the mean ($\overline{X}$) or of the proportion (p) for any given size sample, equals the corresponding parameter value, μ and π, respectively.

2. The sampling distribution of the means of random samples will tend toward the *normal distribution* as sample size n increases, regardless of the original form of the population being sampled.

3. For large samples (e.g., $n \geq 100$ and for π fairly close to 0.5) the normal distribution also represents a reasonable approximation to the binomial distribution for dealing with sample proportions.

4. In the case of finite universes, where the sample size n is some appreciable fraction of the total number N of items in the universe, the standard error formulas should be adjusted by multiplication by the *finite multiplier,*

$$\sqrt{\frac{N-n}{N-1}}$$

For practical purposes, however, use of the finite multiplier is not required unless the sample contains an appreciable fraction, say 10% or more, of the population being sampled.

5. Probabilities of normally distributed variates depend only on the distance (expressed in multiples of the standard deviation) of the value of the variable from the distribution's mean. If we subtract a given population mean μ from a normally distributed variate X_i and divide this result by the original standard deviation σ, we get a *standardized* variate Z_i that is also normally distributed but with zero mean and unit standard deviation. In symbols,

$$Z_i = \frac{X_i - \mu}{\sigma}$$

Table A-1 in Appendix A at the end of this book presents the standardized normal distribution in tabular form. Note further that the original variate may be a sample mean, $\overline{X}$. If so, the denominator is the *standard error* (i.e., standard deviation of the sampling distribution). We can then define Z as some number of standard errors away from the mean of the sampling distribution

$$Z = \frac{\overline{X} - \mu}{\sigma_{\overline{x}}}$$

where $\sigma_{\overline{x}}$ denotes the standard error of the mean. (A similar idea is involved in the case of the standard error of the proportion.)

6. The formulas for the standard error of the mean and proportion of simple random samples are, respectively,

Mean	*Proportion*
$$\sigma_{\overline{x}} = \frac{\sigma}{\sqrt{n}}$$	$$\sigma_{\overline{p}} = \sqrt{\frac{\pi(1 - \pi)}{n}}$$

7. If the population standard deviation σ is not known, which is often the case, we can *estimate* it from the sample observations by use of the formula

$$s = \sqrt{\frac{\sum_{i=1}^{n} (X_1 - \overline{X})^2}{n - 1}}$$

We can consider s to be an *estimator* of the population standard deviation σ. In small samples (e.g., less than 30), the t distribution of Table A-2 in Appendix A is appropriate for finding probability points in this case. However, if the sample size exceeds 30 or so, the standardized normal distribution of Table A-1 is a good approximation to the t distribution.

In cases where σ is estimated by s, the standard error of the mean becomes

$$\text{est. } \sigma_{\overline{x}} = \frac{s}{\sqrt{n}}$$

where est. $\sigma_{\overline{x}}$ denotes the fact that σ is estimated from s, as defined above.

8. Analogously, in the case of the standard error of the proportion, we can use the sample proportion p as an estimator of π to obtain

$$\text{est. } \sigma_{\bar{p}} = \sqrt{\frac{p(1-p)}{n}}$$

as an estimated standard error of the proportion.[22]

ESTIMATING SAMPLE SIZE BY TRADITIONAL METHODS

In our discussion of sample planning we pointed out that there are four traditional approaches to determining sample size. First, the analyst can simply select a size either *arbitrarily* or on the basis of some *judgmentally based* criterion. Similarly, there may be instances where the size of sample represents all that were available at the time—e.g., when a sample is composed of members of some organization and data collection occurs during a meeting of the organization. Second, analysis considerations may enter and the sample size is determined from the *minimum cell size* needed. For example, if the critical aspect of the analysis required a breakdown (e.g., for a cross-tabulation) on three variables which created 12 cells, and it was felt that there should be at least 30 observations in a cell, then the absolute minimum sample size needed would be 360. Third, the *budget* may determine the sample size. If, for example, the research design for a survey called for personal interviews, the cost of each interview was estimated to be $50, and the budget allotted to data collection was $10,000, the sample size would be 200.

It may appear that these methods are for nonprobability samples. While this certainly is true, these methods are also applicable to probability samples and have occasionally been used for such samples. For probability samples, the precision must be determined after the fact.

The fourth approach to sample size determination is based on specifying the desired precision in advance and then applying the appropriate standard error formula to calculate the sample size. This is the approach of traditional inference. Two major classes of procedures are available for estimating sample sizes within the context of traditional (Neyman–Pearson) inference. The first, and better known, of these is based on the idea of constructing confidence intervals around sample means or proportions. This can be called the *confidence-interval approach*. The second approach makes use of both type I (rejecting a true null hypothesis) and type II (accepting a false null hypothesis) error risks and can be called the *hypothesis-testing approach*. We discuss each of these approaches in turn.

Before doing this, however, two points must be made. First, as with the other approaches, the analyst must still calculate the standard error after data collection in order

---

[22]Strictly speaking, $n - 1$ should appear in the denominator. However, if n exceeds about 100 (which is typical of the samples obtained in marketing research), this adjustment makes little difference in the results.

to know what it is for the actual sample that provided data. Second, the size of sample that results from traditional inference refers to the *obtained* (or *resultant*) *sample*. Depending on the data collection method used, the original sample may have to be much larger. For example, suppose that the size of the desired sample was 582. A mail survey is used for data collection and past experience has shown that the response rate would be around 25%. The original sample size in this case would have to be 2,328 in order that 582 responses would be obtained.

The Confidence-Interval Approach

As will be recalled from introductory statistics, it is not unusual to construct a confidence interval around some sample-based mean or proportion. The standard error formulas are employed for this purpose. For example, a researcher may have taken a sample of 100 consumers and noted that their average per capita consumption of orange juice was 2.6 pints per week. Past studies indicate that the population standard deviation σ can be assumed to be 0.3 pint.

With this information, we can find a range around the sample mean level of 2.6 pints for which some prespecified probability statement can be made about the *process underlying the construction of such confidence intervals*.

For example, suppose that we wished to set up a 95% confidence interval around the sample mean of 2.6 pints. We would proceed by first computing the standard error of the mean:

$$\sigma_{\bar{x}} = \frac{\sigma}{\sqrt{n}} = \frac{0.3}{\sqrt{100}} = 0.03$$

From Table A-1 in Appendix A we can find that the central 95% of the normal distribution lies within ± 1.96 Z variates (2.5% of the total area is in each tail of the normal curve).

With this information we can then set up the 95% confidence interval as

$$\bar{X} \pm 1.96\sigma_{\bar{x}} = 2.6 \pm 1.96(0.03)$$

and we note that the 95% confidence interval ranges from 2.54 to 2.66 pints.

Thus, the *preassigned* chance of finding the true population mean to be within 2.54 and 2.66 pints is 95%.

This basic idea can be adapted for finding the appropriate *sample size* that will lead to a certain desired confidence interval. To illustrate, let us now suppose that a researcher is interested in estimating annual per capital consumption of domestic wines for adults living in a particular area of the United States. The researcher knows that it is possible to take a random sample of respondents in the area and compute a sample mean. However, what the researcher really wants to do is be able to state with, say, 95% confidence that the *population* mean falls within some *allowable* interval, computed about the sample mean. The researcher wants to find a sample size that will permit this kind of statement.

The Case of the Sample Mean

Let us first assume that the allowable error is 0.5 gallon per capita and the level of confidence 95%. With this in mind, one goes through the following checklist:

1. *Specify the amount of error (E) that can be allowed.* This is the maximum allowable difference between the sample mean and the population mean. $\overline{X} \pm E$, therefore, defines the interval within which μ will lie with some prespecified level of confidence. In our example, the allowable error is set at $E = 0.5$ gallon per year.

2. *Specify the desired level of confidence.* In our illustrative problem involving domestic wine consumption, the confidence level is set at 95%.

3. *Determine the number of standard errors (Z) associated with the confidence level.* This is accomplished by use of a table of probabilities for a normal distribution. For a 95% confidence level, reference to Table A-1 indicates that the Z value that allows a 0.025 probability that the population mean will fall outside *one* end of the interval is $Z = 1.96$. Since we can allow a *total* probability of 0.05 that the population mean will lie outside *either* end of the interval, $Z = 1.96$ is the correct value for a 95% confidence level.

4. *Estimate the standard deviation of the population.* The standard deviation can be estimated by judgment, by reference to other studies, or by the use of a pilot sample. Suppose that the standard deviation of the area's population for domestic wine consumption is assumed to be 4.0 gallons per capita per year.

5. *Calculate the sample size using the formula for the standard error of the mean.* One standard error of the mean is to be set equal to the allowable error ($E = 0.5$) divided by the appropriate Z value of 1.96.

$$\sigma_{\overline{x}} = \frac{E}{Z} = \frac{0.5}{1.96} = 0.255$$

This will assure us that the interval to be computed around the to-be-found sample mean will have a 95% preassigned chance of being ± 0.5 gallon away from the population mean.

6. Neglecting the finite multiplier, we then solve for n in the formula

$$\sigma_{\overline{x}} = \frac{E}{Z} = \frac{\sigma}{\sqrt{n}}$$

or

$$\sigma_{\overline{x}} = 0.255 = \frac{4.0}{\sqrt{n}}$$

Hence,

$$n \cong 246 \ (\text{rounded})$$

7. In general, we can find n directly from the formula

$$n = \frac{\sigma^2 Z^2}{E^2} = \frac{16(1.96)^2}{(0.5)^2} \cong 246$$

If the resulting sample size represents a significant proportion of the population, say 10% or more, the finite population multiplier is required and the sample size must be recalculated using the following formula:

$$n = \frac{N(\sigma^2 Z^2)}{NE^2 + \sigma^2 Z^2}$$

where N is the size of the population.

The relationship between sample size and variability in the population may not be clear. Consider the problem of estimating the mean salary earned by educators where salary level is a function only of years teaching. For one group of teachers (A) the range in years is very narrow (e.g., 5 years). For another group (B) the range is wide (e.g., 25 years). Both groups have the same population mean. A smaller sample size would be needed for Group A than for Group B. The reason for this is simply that the variance around the mean is less in Group A than in Group B.

The Case of the Sample Proportion

Suppose that, in addition to estimating the mean number of gallons of domestic wine consumed per capita year year, the researcher is also concerned with estimating the proportion of respondents using one or more domestic wines in the past year. How should the sample size be determined in this case?

The procedures for determining sample size for interval estimates of proportions are very similar to those for interval estimates of means. In this case the following checklist would be used:

1. *Specify the amount of error that can be allowed.* Suppose that the desired reliability is such that an allowable interval of $p - \pi = \pm 0.05$ is set; that is, the allowable error E is 0.05, or 5 percentage points.
2. *Specify the desired level of confidence.* Suppose that the level of confidence here, as in the preceding problem, is set at 95%.

3. *Determine the number of standard errors Z associated with the confidence level.* This will be the same as for the preceding estimation; $Z = 1.96$.

4. *Estimate the population proportion (π).* The population proportion can again be estimated by judgment, by reference to other studies, or by the results of a pilot sample. Suppose that π is assumed to be 0.4 in this case; that is, the researcher assumes that 40% of the population used one or more domestic wines last year.

5. *Calculate the sample size using the formula for the standard error of the proportion.* One standard error of the proportion is to be set equal to the allowable error ($E = 0.05$) divided by the appropriate Z value of 1.96.

$$\sigma_{\bar{p}} = \frac{E}{Z} = \frac{0.05}{1.96} = 0.0255$$

6. Neglecting the finite multiplier, we then solve for n in the formula

$$\sigma_{\bar{p}} = \frac{E}{Z} = \sqrt{\frac{\pi(1 - \pi)}{n}}$$

$$= 0.0255 = \sqrt{\frac{0.4(0.6)}{n}}$$

Hence,

$$n \cong 369 \text{ (rounded)}$$

7. In general, we can find n directly from the formula

$$n = \frac{\pi(1 - \pi)Z^2}{E^2} = \frac{0.4(1 - 0.4)(1.96)^2}{(0.05)^2} \cong 369$$

Once again, if the resulting n is 10% or more of the population size, the finite population multiplier is required and the sample size can be computed from

$$n = \frac{N\pi(1 - \pi)Z^2}{NE^2 + \pi(1 - \pi)Z^2}$$

Determining Sample Size When More Than One Interval Estimate Is to Be Made from the Same Sample

The usual case when collecting sample data for estimation of various parameters is that more than one estimate is to be made. The sample size for each of the estimates will usually be different. Since only one sample is to be chosen, what size should it be?

A strict adherence to the allowable error and the confidence levels specified in the calculation of the sample sizes for the individual estimation problems leaves no choice but to take the *largest* sample size calculated. This will give more precision for the other estimates than was specified but will meet the specification for the estimate for which the size of sample was calculated. In the domestic wine consumption problem, for example, the sample size would be 369 (the sample size calculated for estimating the proportion of users) rather than 246 (the sample size calculated for estimating the mean amount used).

In practice, some devices can be used as shortcuts to determine a sample size that will provide sufficient accuracy helpful in rough-guide situations where the researcher is not sure of either allowable error levels or population standard deviations. One such device is the *nomograph,* which is a graphic instrument relating allowable error, confidence level, mean or proportion, and standard deviation.[23] In addition, there are numerous sample-size calculators available, which are similar to slide rules. All of these are based, however, on the formulas discussed above or some modification of the formulas. Many marketing research firms use these kinds of devices on a routine basis.

The Hypothesis-Testing Approach

As indicated earlier, sample sizes can also be determined (within the apparatus of traditional statistical inference) by the hypothesis-testing approach. In this case the procedures are more elaborate. We shall need both an assumed probability of making a type I error—called the *alpha risk*—and an assumed probability of making a type II error—called the *beta risk*. These risks are, in turn, based on two hypotheses:

> H_0: the null hypothesis
> H_1: the alternate hypothesis

As recalled from basic statistics, in hypothesis testing the sample results sometimes lead us to reject H_0 when it is true. This is a type I error. On other occasions the sample findings may lead us to accept H_0 when it is false. This is a type II error. The nature of these errors is shown in Table 9.2.

TABLE 9-2 Types of Error in Making a Wrong Decision

Act	H_0 Is True	H_0 Is False
Accept H_0	No error	Type II error (β)
Reject H_0	Type I error (α)	No error

[23]See Donald S. Tull and Del I. Hawkins, *Marketing Research: Measurement and Method,* 4th ed. (New York: Macmillan, 1987), pp. 409–13.

A numerical example should make this approach clearer. We first consider the case for means and then the case for proportions.

The Case Involving Means

As an illustrative example, let us assume that a store test of a new bleaching agent is to be conducted. It has been determined earlier that if the (population) sales per store average only 7 cases per week, the new product should not be marketed. On the other hand, a mean sales level of 10 cases per week would justify marketing the new product nationally. Using methods of traditional inference, how should the number of sample stores for the market test be determined?

The procedures are similar to those for interval estimation problems but are somewhat more complicated. Specifically, we go through the following checklist:

1. *Specify the values for the null (H_0) and the alternate (H_1) hypotheses to be tested in terms of population means, μ_0 and μ_1, respectively.* (By convention, the null hypothesis is the one that would result in no change being made, if accepted.) In the bleach-market-introduction problem, the values are set at H_0: $\mu_0 = 7$ cases per week, and H_1: $\mu_1 = 10$ cases per week.
2. *Specify the allowable probabilities (α and β, respectively) of a type I and type II error.* The type I error is the error of rejecting a true null hypothesis. The type II error is made when the alternate hypothesis is rejected when it is true. α and β are the allowable *probabilities* of making those two types of errors, respectively. They are shown graphically in Figure 9-3, where we assume that

Figure 9-3   Alpha and Beta Risks in the Hypothesis-Testing Approach

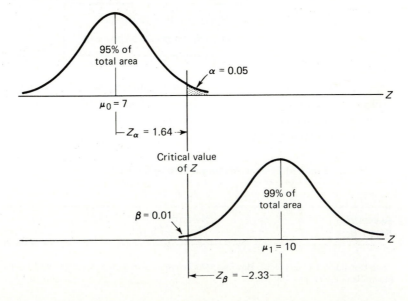

in the bleach-introduction problem the allowable probabilities of error are assigned as $\alpha = 0.05$ and $\beta = 0.01$.

3. *Determine the number of standard errors associated with each of the error probabilities α and β.* For a one-tailed test the Z values for the 0.05 and 0.01 risks, respectively, are found from Table A-1 in Appendix A to be $Z_\alpha = 1.64$ and $Z_\beta = 2.33$. These are shown in Figure 9-3. Note that in the figure we affix a *minus sign* to the value of Z_β since the critical value lies to the left of $\mu_1 = 10$.

4. *Estimate the population standard deviation σ.* In the case of the new bleach the standard deviation of cases sold per store per week is assumed to be 5 cases.

5. *Calculate the sample size that will meet the α and β error requirements.* Since *two* sampling distributions are involved, a simultaneous solution of two equations is required to determine the sample size and critical value that will satisfy both equations. These equations are:

$$\text{critical value} = \mu_0 + Z_\alpha \frac{\sigma}{\sqrt{n}}$$

$$\text{critical value} = \mu_1 - Z_\beta \frac{\sigma}{\sqrt{n}}$$

6. Setting the right-hand side of these two equations equal and solving for n gives

$$n = \frac{(Z_\alpha + Z_\beta)^2 \sigma^2}{(\mu_1 - \mu_0)^2}$$

In the bleach problem the desired sample size is

$$n = \frac{(1.64 + 2.33)^2 5^2}{(10 - 7)^2} \cong 44 \text{ stores (rounded)}$$

Having solved for n, the sample size, we can then go on to solve for the critical value for the mean number of cases, by means of the substitution[24]

$$\text{critical value} = \mu_1 - Z_\beta \frac{\sigma}{\sqrt{n}}$$

$$= 10 - (2.33)\frac{5}{\sqrt{44}}$$

$$= 8.24 \text{ cases}$$

[24]Alternatively, we could find the critical value from the first of the two equations:

$$\text{critical value} = 7 + (1.64)\frac{5}{\sqrt{44}} = 8.24$$

The decision rule then becomes: "Take a sample of 44 stores for the controlled store test. If the mean number of cases of the new bleach sold per week in the sample stores is less than or equal to 8.24 cases, do not introduce the product. If the mean number of cases of bleach sold per week is greater than 8.24 cases, introduce the product."

The Case Involving Proportions

For sample-size determination involving proportions, the following analogous steps are required:

1. *Specify the values of the null (H_1) and the alternate (H_1) hypotheses to be tested in terms of population proportions, π_0 and π_1, respectively.*
2. *Specify the allowable probabilities (α and β, respectively) of type I and type II errors.*
3. *Determine the number of standard errors associated with each of these error probabilities (Z_α and Z_β).*
4. *Calculate the desired sample size n from the formula:*

$$n = \left[\frac{Z_\alpha \sqrt{\pi_0(1 - \pi_0)} + Z_\beta \sqrt{\pi_1(1 - \pi_1)}}{\pi_1 - \pi_0} \right]^2$$

This formula is appropriate for relatively large samples ($n \geq 100$) where the normal distribution is a good approximation to the binomial. To illustrate its application, suppose that a researcher is interested in the true proportion of residents in a large city who would be willing to pay over \$200 for a portable refrigerator–bar combination if it were commercialized.

Assume that the marketing researcher would recommend commercialization of the firm's refrigerator–bar combination if the true proportion of consumers who would pay over \$200 for this class of goods is 70%. If the proportion is only 60%, the researcher would not recommend commercialization. The researcher then sets up the hypotheses:

$$H_0: \pi_0 = 0.6$$
$$H_1: \pi_1 = 0.7$$

The alpha risk associated with the null (status quo) hypothesis is selected by the researcher to be 0.05 *if* the true proportion π is equal to 0.6. Moreover, the researcher is willing to assume a beta risk of 0.1 if the true proportion is equal to 0.7. With these assumptions it is possible to obtain the approximate sample size by using the formula above:

$$n = \left[\frac{Z_\alpha \sqrt{\pi_0(1 - \pi_0)} + Z_\beta \sqrt{\pi_1(1 - \pi_1)}}{\pi_1 - \pi_0} \right]^2$$

where $Z_\alpha = Z_{0.05} = 1.64$, $Z_\beta = Z_{0.1} = 1.28$, $\pi_0 = 0.6$, and $\pi_1 = 0.7$. The solution is

$$n = \left[\frac{1.64\sqrt{0.6(0.4)} + 1.28\sqrt{0.7(0.3)}}{0.7 - 0.6} \right]^2$$

$$\cong 193 \text{ (rounded)}$$

Accordingly, in this example the sample size to take is 193.

The critical value can be found analogously as

$$\text{critical value} = \pi_1 - Z_\beta \sqrt{\frac{\pi_1(1 - \pi_1)}{n}}$$

$$= 0.7 - (1.28)\sqrt{\frac{0.7(0.3)}{193}}$$

$$= 0.658$$

In this case the decision rule is: "Take a sample of 193 residents. If the sample proportion who would pay over \$200 is less than or equal to 0.658, do not commercialize the refrigerator–bar combination. If the sample proportion exceeds 0.658, commercialize the product."

Determining Sample Size for Other Probability-Sample Designs

Thus far we have discussed only the determination of *simple* random-sample sizes using the methods of traditional statistical inference. How are the sizes for other types of random-sample designs—systematic, stratified, cluster, area, and multistage—determined?

The answer to this question is that the same *general* procedures are used to determine the overall sample size, but the formulas for the standard errors differ. The formulas become more complex and difficult to estimate as one considers stratified sampling, cluster sampling, or the other more elaborate designs. This is because the standard error for these designs is partially a function of the standard deviation (or proportion) of each stratum or cluster included in the design. For a multistage sample consisting of several strata in one stage followed by clusters in another and systematic sampling in a third, the standard error formula can become very complex indeed. And once the overall sample size is determined, it must be apportioned among the strata and clusters, which also adds to the complexity.

Appropriate formulas for estimating standard errors and sample sizes for other random-sample designs are available elsewhere.[25] In general, as compared with the size of simple-random samples, systematic samples may be the same (since, for purposes of calculating the standard error, the assumption is typically made that the systematic sample *is* a simple random sample). Stratified samples are usually smaller, and cluster samples will usually be larger in size to provide the same reliability as a simple random sample.

THE BAYESIAN APPROACH TO SAMPLE-SIZE DETERMINATION

In the treatment of the traditional approach to sample-size determination the underlying concepts were discussed and formulas were then developed. Here we shall describe the concepts on which the Bayesian procedures are based, but no attempt will be made to develop formulas. The reason for this is that calculating optimal sample sizes is much more difficult under the Bayesian approach.

Bayesian procedures are based on the central principle (first described in Chapter 3) that one should

select that sample size that results in the largest positive difference between the expected payoff of sample information and the estimated cost of sampling.

The difference between the expected payoff of sample information and the estimated cost of sampling is frequently referred to as the *expected net gain from sampling.* An equivalent way of stating the principle above is that one should *select the sample size that leads to the largest expected net gain from sampling.*

In a decisional situation in which one of the primary objectives is to maximize payoff, this rule is a sound prescription. The general approach to applying it requires the decision maker to

1. *Determine the expected value of sample information for a given sample size.*
2. *Estimate the sampling cost for that specific option.*
3. *Find the expected net gain from sampling under that option.*
4. *Search through other sample sizes to find the one that leads to the highest expected net gain from sampling.*

While logically sound and intuitively appealing in concept, the Bayesian approach is difficult to implement. The primary problem comes in operationalizing the first of the steps stated above. In order to determine the expected value of sample information for a given sample size, one must relate the sample size being considered to the *conditional probabilities of making errors,* including the effects of *nonsampling errors.* In realistic sampling situations, this can become very difficult to do. (The accurate estimation of nonsampling errors, in particular, is not an easy task.)

---

[25]See, for example, Kish, *Survey Sampling,* and Sudman, *Applied Sampling.*

Exhibit 9-3   The Standard Error for a Stratified Sample

The formulas for determing sample size for a stratified sample are basically the same as those used for a simple random sample. What is different, however, is the formula for the standard error.

General Stratified Sampling. The standard error of the mean for this type of sample is

$$\sigma_{\bar{X},s} = \sqrt{\sum_{i=1}^{m} W_i^2 \frac{\sigma_i^2}{n_i}}$$

where

$$W_i = \frac{N_i}{N}, \quad \sum_{i=1}^{m} N_i = N, \quad \sum_{i=1}^{m} W_i = 1$$

and

N_i = size of *i*th stratum
N = population of size
σ_i^2 = variance of the *i*th stratum
n_i = sample size of the *i*th stratum

The standard error of a proportion is

$$\sigma_{p,s} = \sqrt{\sum_{i=1}^{m} W_i^2 \frac{\pi_i (1 - \pi_i)}{n_i}}$$

where π_i = proportion in the *i*th stratum

Disproportionate Stratified Sampling. In disproportionate stratified sampling, both the relative size of each stratum and the within-stratum variance is taken into account. Thus, the rule for sample allocation is

$$n_i = \frac{W_i \sigma_i n}{\sum_{i=1}^{m} W_i \sigma_i}$$

The formula for the standard error of the mean of a disproportionate stratified sample becomes

$$\sigma_{\bar{X},s} = \sqrt{\frac{\left(\sum_{i=1}^{m} W_i \sigma_i\right)^2}{\sum_{i=1}^{k} n_i}}$$

When the cost of selecting sample members from one stratum is not necessarily the same as that from another stratum, the allocation rule must be modified:

$$n_i = \frac{W_i\sigma_i n/C_i}{\sum\limits_{i=1}^{m}(W_i\sigma_i/C_i)}$$

where C_i is the cost of selecting an individual from the ith stratum.

Proportionate Stratified Sampling. In contrast to disproportionate sampling, in proportionate stratified sampling the same sampling fraction is used throughout all population strata and

$$\frac{n_i}{n} = \frac{N_i}{N}$$

In this type of stratified sampling, only the size of the stratum is used as the guide for determining allocation of the total sample. Thus,

$$n_i = \frac{W_i n}{\sum\limits_{i=1}^{m} W_i}$$

The standard error of the mean for a proportionate stratified sample is

$$\sigma_{\bar{x},s} = \sqrt{\frac{\sum\limits_{i=1}^{m} W_i\hat{\sigma}_i^2}{\sum\limits_{i=1}^{m} n_i}}$$

Once the conditional probabilities of making errors are determined, one goes through the procedures described in Chapter 3 for determining the expected value of the sample information. That is, estimates of the *conditional costs of errors* (the payoffs) and the *prior probabilities* of the decision maker are obtained, and the difference in the expected value, with and without the sample information, is calculated. This is the *expected value of sample information* for the size and design of the sample being considered (step 1 above).

It is then necessary to estimate the *cost of sampling* for that option (step 2).[26] Subtracting the estimated sampling cost from the expected value of sample information (step 3) gives the *expected net gain from sampling* (ENGS).

ENGS is computed for each of the potential sample sizes to find the one that provides the highest ENGS (step 4). The necessity to search through the entire range of potential sample sizes usually dictates the use of computer programs for problems of realistic size and complexity.[27] Owing to the general complexity of the technique, this section has provided only a brief overview of the Bayesian approach to sample-size determination.

---

[26]For a discussion of estimating sampling costs see Seymour Sudman, *Applied Sampling,* Chap. 5; and Kish, *Survey Sampling,* Chap. 8.

[27]See Robert Schlaifer, *Computer Programs for Elementary Decision Analysis* (Cambridge, Mass.: Division of Research, Graduate School of Business Administration, Harvard University, 1971).

The reader interested in more-detailed exposition of the underlying theory and of the specific procedures is advised to examine material by Sudman, Brown, and Mayer.[28]

EVALUATION OF THE TRADITIONAL AND BAYESIAN APPROACHES

If one were to devise the ideal method of determining sample size, as a minimum one would want it to meet the criteria of being (1) logically complete, (2) adaptable to a wide range of sampling situations, and (3) simple to use. If the traditional (Neyman–Pearson) approach to sample-size determination were to be rated on these criteria, the rating would be *low* for logical completeness and *high* for both adaptability and simplicity. By contrast, the Bayesian approach would rate *high* on logical completeness but *low* on adaptability and simplicity of use.

The traditional approach is logically *in*complete since sample size is specified as being a function only of the conditional probabilities of making errors. Consideration of the conditional costs of wrong decisions, prior probabilities, nonsampling errors, and the cost of sampling are not included in the model.[29]

The fact that these variables are excluded implies that somehow they must be taken into account *outside* the model. However, the only way that accommodation can be made is through adjustment of either the specified confidence level or the assigned alpha and beta risks.

Despite the fact that the Bayesian approach is a logically complete model for determining sample size in a decisional situation, its lack of adaptability and its complexity of use have resulted in only limited application. It is ironic that a methodology that is statistically sound and includes all the relevant variables also becomes so unwieldy that it is seldom used.

The traditional approach has been under development and use for more than 85 years. The (modern form of the) Bayesian model is much newer, having been developed in the late 1950s. With the advent of new computer programs and greater dissemination of the basic methodology, the Bayesian approach could become much more widely used in the future.

SUMMARY

In this chapter we have been concerned with the questions of whether to take a census or a sample and, when sampling, what type and size of sample to take.

We first considered the question of when a sample, rather than a census, should

---

[28]Sudman, *Applied Sampling*, Chap. 5; R. V. Brown, "Evaluation of Total Survey Error," *Journal of Marketing Research*, 4 (May 1967), 117–27; Charles Mayer, "Assessing the Accuracy of Marketing Research," *Journal of Marketing Research*, 7 (August 1970), 285–91.

[29]More advanced texts, however, do consider traditional sample-size determination by means of formulas that include the costs of sampling. For example, see Cochran, *Sampling Techniques*, Chap. 4.

be taken, followed by a discussion of sample planning. Next, the various kinds of samples and the decisions concerning which kind to choose were discussed.

One of the most difficult problems in research design is the one concerned with the *size* of sample to take. We discussed the determination of sample size from the standpoint of traditional inferential methods and then considered the rationale of sample-size determination from the Bayesian point of view. We concluded the chapter with an evaluation of the two approaches to determining sample size.

Appendix 9-1

SAMPLING FOR TELEPHONE SURVEYS

Creating probability samples for telephone surveys is not an easy task. Although the general approaches to sample design can be used (i.e., simple random, systematic, stratified, cluster, etc.), there are some unique differences. The most commonly used methods are summarized in Table 1.[30]

Methods for telephone sampling can be categorized as *directory-based* or *random-digit dialing*. In all cases the result is a probability sample, although the actual probability of inclusion and even the extent of knowing this probability varies among the methods. In general, all directory-based approaches have limitations in that there is related high frame error due to exclusion of nonsubscribers and the generating of large numbers of unproductive telephone numbers (nonpopulation elements and nonworking numbers). In contrast, costs are relatively low. Random-digit dialing, on the other hand, tends to have lower frame error but higher costs. Primarily because of the frame error, major criticisms of directory-based samples have tended to be statistical in nature. Random-digit dialing methods are designed to overcome these statistical problems. However, some researchers believe that directory-based samples are just as representative and proportionate as those derived from random-digit dialing.[31]

Regardless of the method used to draw the sample, for a consumer study this sample is one of households. Thus, there still remains the problem of selecting a respondent. One option, of course, is to use the person answering the telephone if that person meets the eligibility requirements—e.g., minimum age. Technically speaking, this approach may produce essentially a nonprobability sample. A probability-based approach that is in general use is one developed by Kish.[32] This method requires that all eligible respondents within a household be listed by sex and within sex groupings by age from oldest

---

[30]For a more-detailed discussion, see Martin R. Frankel and Lester R. Frankel, "Some Recent Developments in Sample Survey Design," *Journal of Marketing Research,* 14 (August 1977), 280–93; and E. Laird Landon, Jr., and Sharon K. Banks, "Relative Efficiency and Bias of Plus-One Telephone Sampling Offers Efficiency and Minimal Bias," *Marketing News,* 17 (May 13, 1983), Sec. 2, pp. 2–3.

[31]See, for example, Peter C. Ellison, "Phone Directory Samples Just as Balanced as Samples from Computer Random Digit Dialing," *Marketing News,* 14 (January 11, 1980), 8.

[32]Leslie Kish, "A Procedure for Objective Respondent Selection within the Household," *American Statistical Association Journal,* September 1949, pp. 380–87.

TABLE 1   Telephone Sampling Methods

METHOD	SYNOPSIS OF PROCEDURE
Directory Assisted	
Selection of Listings	Systematic or simple random selection procedures are used to select a sample of directory lines. In some cases the selected line is used as a starting point for a cluster of k lines.
Add-a-Digit	Numbers are selected from the directory, and an integer (between 0 and 9) is added to the number.
Randomization of the r Last Digits	Numbers are selected from the directory. The r last digits (2, 3, or 4) are replaced by random selection of numbers.
Sudman's Method	This is a two-stage procedure. Numbers are selected from the directory. The last three digits are removed, leaving the central office code and the thousands digit. A group of three-place random digits is selected and added to the directory.
Random-Digit Dialing (RDD)	
Pure RDD	All numbers are generated at random and with equal probability.
Two-Stage RDD	This procedure uses known working prefixes (first three digits of the seven-digit number). After these are chosen, there are different ways to select the four-digit number to be attached.
Waksburg's Procedure	This is a two-stage method. All working three-digit prefixes in an area are identified. To each of these, all possible two digits are added. This process defines all banks of 100 numbers in the area. One of the five-digit numbers is selected at random (forming a primary sampling unit), and a randomly selected two-digit number is added. This number is called and if it is a residence, the bank of 100 that was selected is retained, and other numbers formed by adding sets of last two digits. If it is not a residence, the primary sampling unit is rejected. This procedure can be expanded to a national sample by defining the primary sampling unit as area code + prefix + first two digits.

to youngest. After all eligible respondents are identified, the respondent to be interviewed is selected by using a random number table.

The Kish technique requires much time at the beginning of the interview. To overcome this, Troldahl and Carter developed a method that requires that only two questions be asked: (1) the number of people 18 years of age or older and (2) the number of men. Using previously developed selection matrices rotated randomly over the sample, the proper selection can easily be made (see Table 2).[33] Another technique which is even

TABLE 2   Versions of Selection Matrices

TOTAL NUMBER OF MEN IN HOUSEHOLD	TOTAL NUMBER OF ADULTS IN HOUSEHOLD			
	1	*2*	*3*	*4 or more*
Version I				
0	Woman	Oldest woman	Youngest woman	Youngest woman
1	Man	Man	Man	Oldest woman
2		Oldest man	Youngest man	Youngest man
3			Youngest man	Oldest man
4+				Oldest man
Version II				
0	Woman	Youngest woman	Youngest woman	Oldest woman
1	Man	Man	Oldest woman	Man
2		Oldest man	Woman	Oldest woman
3			Youngest man	Woman or oldest woman
4+				Oldest man
Verison III				
0	Woman	Youngest woman	Oldest woman	Oldest woman
1	Man	Woman	Man	Youngest woman
2		Youngest man	Oldest man	Oldest man
3			Oldest man	Youngest man
4+				Youngest man
Version IV				
0	Woman	Oldest woman	Oldest woman	Youngest woman
1	Man	Woman	Youngest woman	Man
2		Youngest man	Woman	Youngest woman
3			Oldest man	Woman or youngest woman
4+				Youngest man

Source: Verling C. Troldahl and Roy E. Carter, Jr., "Random Selection of Respondents within Households in Phone Surveys," *Journal of Marketing Research,* 1 (May 1964), 73.

[33]Verling C. Troldahl and Roy E. Carter, Jr., "Random Selection of Respondents within Households in Phone Surveys," *Journal of Marketing Research,* 1 (May 1964), 71–76. A modification of this technique would be to ask for the number of women. Another modification has been proposed to account for changing patterns in household composition and for the higher refusal rates among men. See Barbara E. Bryant, "Respondent Selection in a Time of Changing Household Composition," *Journal of Marketing Research,* 12 (May 1975), 129–35.

simpler than Troldahl–Carter is the "birthday" method.[34] The one question asked is to speak to the adult who had the most recent birthday or the one who has the next birthday. There is no evidence that any one of these methods is universally better than the others. In fact, in a study comparing the Kish, Troldahl–Carter, and a modification of Troldahl–Carter, few differences were found in the cooperation rates and demographic characteristics of the respondents.[35]

In some instances the researcher may find it beneficial to use a *crisscross* or *cross-reference* directory.[36] These directories, which are published by private companies, typically list numbers numerically and also list subscribers geographically by alphabetical and numerical street address within each zip code. An example of the use of this type of directory is a study conducted in a medium-sized community to ascertain the attitudes and behavior of residents regarding parks and recreation. Due to budget constraints, the client specified a telephone survey and also wanted representation from the five park districts within the community. Since telephone exchanges were not area-based, random-digit dialing would have been too cumbersome and time-consuming. Other methods would also have required sequential sampling. Fortunately, a cross-reference directory was available, and once the park districts were outlined on a map, the sample was selected using systematic random sampling.

ASSIGNMENT MATERIAL

1. The founder of a well-known consulting firm specializing in consumer research once stated that the way he would select a sample of housewives to obtain information to be used for redesigning a line of refrigerators would be to "start talking to housewives I happen to know, ask them to refer me to others they know, and keep talking to additional ones until I found one *who really knows how a refrigerator should be designed.*"

   a. What kind of a sampling procedure has he described?

   b. What are its advantages? Disadvantages?

2. Explain the tradeoffs that may be necessary between reliability and costs for the various probability sampling designs.

3. Annual incomes of the 900 salespeople employed by the Lodish Hide Company are known to be approximately normally distributed. Last year the mean income of the group was $8,000 and the standard deviation of incomes was $1,000. Using Table A-1 in Appendix A:

   a. This year (based on nine months' experience extrapolated to a one-year basis), a random sample of 49 of Lodish's salespeople was selected. What is the

---

[34]Diane O'Rourke and Johnny Blair, "Improving Random Respondent Selection in Telephone Surveys," *Journal of Marketing Research,* 20 (November 1983), 428–32; and Charles T. Salmon and John Spicer Nichols, "The Next-Birthday Method of Respondent Selection," *Public Opinion Quarterly,* 47 (1983), pp. 270–76.

[35]Ronald Czaja, Johnny Blair, and Jutta P. Sebestik, "Respondent Selection in a Telephone Survey: A Comparison of Three Techniques," *Journal of Marketing Research,* 19 (August 1982), 381–85.

[36]See A. B. Blankenship, *Professional Telephone Surveys* (New York: McGraw-Hill, 1977), pp. 70–73.

probability that the sample arithmetic mean would differ from last year's population mean by more than $150 (assuming no change in parameter values and neglecting the finite multiplier)?

b. Now assume that the sample mean indicated $8,100 with a sample standard deviation (computed with $n - 1$ in the denominator) of $900. What is the probability of getting at least this large a sample mean given no change in last year's population mean of $8,000?

c. If the company wants to be 95% "confident" that the true mean of this year's salespeople's income does not differ by more than 2% of last year's mean of $8,000, what size of sample would be required (assuming a population standard deviation of $1,000 and neglecting the finite multiplier)?

4. Past information about the proportion of shoppers in a large city who would be receptive to saving trading stamps indicates a figure of somewhere around 80%. Suppose that a supermarket chain would adopt a trading stamp plan if the *true* proportion were 80%; if the true proportion were only 70%, it would not. The null and alternative hypotheses are as follows:

$$H_0: \pi_0 = 0.7$$
$$H_1: \pi_1 = 0.8$$

Assuming an alpha risk of 0.1 if $\pi_0 = 0.7$ and a beta risk of 0.2 if the true proportion were 0.8, what is the appropriate sample size (using traditional methods)?

5. The Wind Power and Light Company has recently launched a public relations campaign to persuade its subscribers to reduce the wasteful use of electricity. The firm's marketing research codirectors, Frank Carmine and Douglas Karrell, believe that about 40% of the subscribers are aware of the campaign. They wish to find out how large a sample would be needed to be 95% confident that the true proportion is within ±3% of the sample proportion.

a. Solve the problem analytically via the confidence-interval approach.

b. If one sets up the hypotheses:

$$H_0: \pi_0 = 0.4$$
$$H_1: \pi_1 = 0.5$$

with an alpha risk of 0.1 and a beta risk of 0.05 if $\pi_1 = 0.5$, what is the appropriate sample size under the hypothesis-testing approach?

6. An international airline is considering adding an "economy plan" on its Seattle-Copenhagen-Amsterdam flights. All passengers who travel on this plan must buy a round-trip fare, which will be 40% less than the regular fare, and fly on a space-available basis. The company's research director, Charlie Shue, and his assistant, Bill Bohen, decide to conduct an in-flight survey of passengers traveling under the existing fares. Among the informational items they will seek

from this survey are the mean number of flights taken per year and the proportion originating in Seattle. They estimate the standard deviation of the number of flights per year at $\hat{\sigma} = 2.0$. They decide they need a 95.4% level of confidence and can allow a difference of sample mean and population mean of $\pm .10$ flight.

Shue and Bohen estimate the proportion originating in Seattle at .10. They require that the sample proportion be within $\pm .02$ of the population proportion, and they would like a confidence level of 95.4% for the proportion estimate.

What sample size should they take if it is to be a simple random sample and the traditional method of determining sample size is used?

7. If $n = 100$ and $N = 10,000$ and it is assumed that $\sigma = 2$, compute the standard error of the mean, first using the finite multiplier and then without. How large would the sample size n have to be (given $N = 10,000$) to make the standard error of the mean equal to 0.05?

8. Discuss how one might modify quota sampling to make it more closely approximate stratified random sampling.

CASES FOR PART II

II-1

SYD COMPANY (B)

FC Associates, a group of students attending the Wharton School, University of Pennsylvania, had agreed to do an exploratory study for the Syd Company. Syd was a large packaged consumer goods company.

The project related to whether Syd should enter the women's shampoo market, a market for which it did not at present have a product. The study was to be concentrated among young female adults aged 18 through 30.

The concerns of Syd management and the overall design selected by FC Associates were discussed in the (A) case. For clarification, primary research questions are repeated here:

1. How do consumers of hair shampoos perceive various benefits as commonly (or rarely) available in shampoos *currently* on the market?

2. Given freedom to make up her own "ideal" shampoo, what "bundles" of benefits do consumers want? Specifically, how often is "body" included in their ideal benefit bundles?

3. Assuming that a consumer desired and could get a shampoo that delivered "body," what *other* benefits are also desired in the same brand?

4. What is conjured up by the phrase "shampoo body" and its various connotations—that is, what words are elicited on a free-association basis?

5. How do preferences for "body" in shampoos relate to
   a. Frequency of hair shampooing (i.e., heavy versus light users of shampoos)?
   b. Perceptions of its availability in current shampoos?
   c. Preference for other benefits in addition to "body"?

    d. Hair physiology and wearing style?

    e. Demographics (e.g., age, marital status, education, etc.)?

With these questions in mind, FC Associates designed the questionnaire shown in Figure 1. (pp. 359–362). The personal interview was selected as the mode of data collection because the number of questions raised meant that various interviewer "props" would be needed.

Note that the first two questions serve as screening criteria; in other words, to qualify for inclusion the respondent must (1) shampoo her hair at home at least twice a month on the average and (2) be between 18 and 30 years of age.

Part A of the questionnaire first attempts to measure respondents' perceptions of the prevalence of each shampoo benefit in brands currently on the market. Then, respondents are allowed to choose from the total set of 16 benefits [see the Syd (A) case] those 4 benefits that they would most like to have in an "ideal" shampoo. Part B—using the first 10 benefits in Table 1 of the Syd (A) case—examines respondents' benefit preferences in a conditional sense, assuming that they could obtain a shampoo that delivered "body."

Part C deals with free-association data, whereas Part D requests information on hair style and hair problems. Part E is devoted to more or less standard questions dealing with demographic variables.

1. Critically evaluate this questionnaire in the context of proper questionnaire design.

2. How would you approach the same (shampoo-benefits) problem if you were
   a. Developing a mail questionnaire?
   b. Developing a telephone questionnaire?

3. Suppose that you wished to add a section to the questionnaire that dealt with general attitudes toward hair and personal grooming.
   a. Prepare a set of sample statements that ask for the respondent's degree of agreement/disagreement.
   b. What other aspects of life-style might be worthwhile to include?

4. What kinds of questions should be added regarding
   a. Other types of hair-grooming products, such as rinses and setting gels?
   b. Current brand usage and preference?

II-2

RAP FOOD STORES

RAP Food Stores is a chain of large food stores that operate as supermarkets. The management of the chain has decided to expand to a new market area. At present, the company has stores located throughout the Midwest. The area for expansion includes the northwestern states of Washington, Oregon, and Idaho.

Figure 1   Questionnaire Used in Hair Shampoo Study

```
                    Time Interview Started_____
                                     Ended_____
Respondent Name_____   Respondent No._____
Address_____
City_____   State_____
Telephone No._____
Interviewer Name_____
Interview Date_____
Screening Questions (Part S)
```

Hello, I'm_____of the Wharton School, University of Pennsylvania. We're conducting a survey on women's attitudes and opinions about hair care products.

1. On the average, how often do you shampoo your hair at home?

```
    More than twice a week            _____
    Once or twice a week              _____
    Once or twice every two weeks     _____
    Once or twice every three weeks   _____
    Twice a month                     _____
    Less than twice a month           _____
```

IF LESS THAN TWICE A MONTH, TERMINATE

2. What is your age? _____
   (IF UNDER 18 OR OVER 30 TERMINATE)

PART A

First I'm going to show you a set of 16 cards. Each card contains the name of a benefit that a hair shampoo might provide. (PLACE SET OF WHITE CARDS ON TABLE IN FRONT OF RESPONDENT.) Please take a few moments to look over these benefits. (ALLOW TIME FOR RESPONDENT TO STUDY THE CARDS.)

Now, thinking about various brands of hair shampoo that you have tried or heard about, pick out those benefits that you think are most likely to be found in almost any hair shampoo that one could buy today. (RECORD CARD NUMBERS IN FIRST COLUMN OF RESPONSE FORM A AND TURN SELECTED CARDS FACE DOWN.)

Next, select all of those remaining benefits that you think are available in at least some hair shampoo—but not necessarily all in a single brand—that's currently on the market. (RECORD CARD NUMBERS IN SECOND COLUMN OF RESPONSE FORM A. RECORD REMAINING

Figure 1   **(cont.)**

CARD NUMBERS IN THIRD COLUMN. THEN RETURN ALL CARDS
TO TABLE.

Next, imagine that you could make up an ideal type
of shampoo—one that might not be available on today's
market. Suppose, however, that you were restricted
to only four of the sixteen benefits shown on the
cards in front of you. Which four of the sixteen benefits would you most like to have? (RECORD CARD NUMBERS
IN FOURTH COLUMN OF RESPONSE FORM A.)

RESPONSE FORM A

(1)	(2)	(3)	(4)
Benefits Most Likely to be Found in Almost Any Hair Shampoo—Card Numbers	Benefits Available in Some Shampoo—Card Numbers	Remaining Benefits—Card Numbers	Four-Benefit Ideal Set—Card Numbers

PART B

Now, let's again return to some of the shampoo bene-
fits you have already dealt with. (SELECT WHITE CARD
NUMBERS 1 THROUGH 10; PULL OUT CARD 4 AND PLACE IT IN
FRONT OF RESPONDENT.)

Suppose a shampoo were on the market that primarily
stressed this benefit—"Produces Hair that Has Body."
If you could get a shampoo that made good on this
claim, which one of the remaining nine benefits would
you most like to have as well? (RECORD NUMBER IN
RESPONSE FORM B.) Which next most? (RECORD.) Please
continue until all of the 9 benefits have been ranked.

Figure 1 (cont.)

RESPONSE FORM B

(Enter Card Numbers 1 Through 10 Excluding Card #4)
( ) Most Like to Have   ( )
( ) Next Most   ( )
( )   ( )
( )   ( ) Least Most
( )

PART C

Now, I am going to read to you some short phrases about hair. Listen to each phrase carefully and then tell me what single words first come to your mind when you hear each phrase? (RECORD UP TO THE FIRST THREE "ASSOCIATIVE-TYPE" WORDS THE RESPONDENT SAYS AFTER EACH PHRASE IN RESPONSE FORM C.)

RESPONSE FORM C

(a) Hair that has body

_____   _____   _____

(b) Hair with fullness

_____   _____   _____

(c) Hair that holds a set

_____   _____   _____

(d) Bouncy hair

_____   _____   _____

(e) Hair that's not limp

_____   _____   _____

(f) Manageable hair

_____   _____   _____

(g) Zesty hair

_____   _____   _____

(h) Natural hair

_____   _____   _____

PART D

At this point I would like to ask you a few questions about your hair.

1. Does your hair have enough body?

            Yes_____   No_____

Figure 1 (cont.)

2. Do you have any special problems with your hair?

Yes_____   No_____

If yes, what types of problems?

_____

_____

_____

How would you describe your hair?

3. My hair type is:

Dry_____   Normal_____   Oily_____

4. The texture of my hair is:

Fine_____   Normal_____   Coarse_____

5. My hair style (the way I wear my hair) is:

Straight_____

Slightly wavy or curly_____

Very wavy or curly_____

6. The length of my hair is:

Short (to ear lobes)_____

Medium (ear lobes to shoulder)_____

Long (below shoulder)_____

7. How would you describe the thickness of your hair?

Thick_____   Medium_____   Thin_____

PART E

Now I would like to ask you a few background questions.

1. Are you working (at least twenty hours per week, for compensation)?

Yes_____   No_____

2. Are you married?

Yes_____   No_____

3. What is your level of education?

Some high school_____   Completed high school_____   Some college_____

Completed college_____

4. (HAND RESPONDENT INCOME CARD.) Which letter on this card comes closest to describing your total annual family income before taxes? (CIRCLE APPROPRIATE LETTER.)

A. Under $3,000   E. $10,001–15,000
B. $3,000– 5,000   F. 15,001–20,000
C. 5,001– 7,000   G. Over $20,000
D. 7,001–10,000

(THANKS VERY MUCH FOR YOUR HELP)

One of the management group has suggested that the company take a thorough look at the store design. This manager feels that store design and layout that have been appropriate for the Midwest may not be so for the Northwest. The marketing research group at the corporate level has been asked to look at this issue for the stores that are to be opened in the new market area.

Ms. Panda Beaver has been appointed as the project director. Ms. Beaver has been with the company for about two years, having joined RAP upon receiving an M.B.A. degree from a leading midwestern university. In thinking about the problem posed by management, Ms. Beaver came to the conclusion that some form of qualitative research would be most appropriate. She also believed that whatever research was conducted should be done directly with potential consumers in the targeted market area.

Remembering what she learned in graduate school, Ms. Beaver is considering using *focus groups* and/or some form of *projective* technique. If focus groups are to be used, the question arises regarding who should conduct them, how many should be used, where they should be done, and similar methodological issues. Ms. Beaver has had experience with focus groups, having moderated some for one of her instructors in graduate school.

Selecting an appropriate projective technique would be difficult because of the many alternatives available. For example, Ms. Beaver believes that such techniques as the TAT, story completion, third-person approach, and others might be appropriate. In addition, Ms. Beaver remembers an unusual technique mentioned by a speaker in one of her marketing research courses. This speaker discussed an approach developed in clinical psychology—the "draw a supermarket" technique. Although the technique is mentioned in several marketing research texts, it has seen only limited application.

The "draw a supermarket" technique involves having a sample of people draw a picture of the interior of a supermarket in a simple rectangle on a blank piece of paper. These drawings are then analyzed with regard to the departments omitted, the order in which the departments are drawn, and the space allocated to each department. In addition to sketches, Ms. Beaver thought it would be helpful to get additional information from the members of the sample. Thus, sample members would be asked to indicate (a) the supermarket where most of the family groceries were purchased, (b) the supermarket department considered most important, and (c) the supermarket department considered least important.

Evaluate the potential use of qualitative techniques by RAP Food Stores in providing information to aid in the design and layout of supermarkets in the targeted market area.

Which technique(s) should Ms. Panda Beaver use, and why?

II-3

UNITED AIRLINES

United Airlines conducts in-flight passenger surveys periodically. United views these surveys as providing information, current and trends, relevant to three major areas:

1. Attitudes toward ground and in-flight services
2. Behavior associated with air travel
3. Characteristics of United Airlines passengers

A preferred approach to data collection is to prepare a questionnaire such that responses to the questions can be machine-read directly from the form. For convenience in administration, the length of the questionnaires is limited to four letter-size pages (8 1/2 × 11 inches). One oversized sheet of paper (11 × 17 inches) is folded to give four pages.

Often, the needs of a particular survey require a series of questions that exceed the four-page format. Alternative data collection methods for this situation are to *expand the length* of the questionnaire or use a *split-ballot* approach. When a split ballot is used, flight attendants randomly distribute the forms to passengers in flight and passengers self-report.

Representative of the split-ballot approach is the questionnaire shown in Exhibits I and II. Three versions were used, with only questions 1 through 10 and questions 28 through 33 common to all three. A couple of other questions were used on two of the three questionnaire forms.

1. Should United Airlines use the split-ballot approach for collecting data? What alternatives might have been used?
2. Evaluate any one of the questionnaire versions on the basis of questionnaire development criteria. In which ways, if any, is the questionnaire not "sound"?
3. Identify the various types of scales used by the United Airlines in-flight survey questionnaire. Could other types have been used to obtain the information?

Exhibit I   Questions Common to All Versions

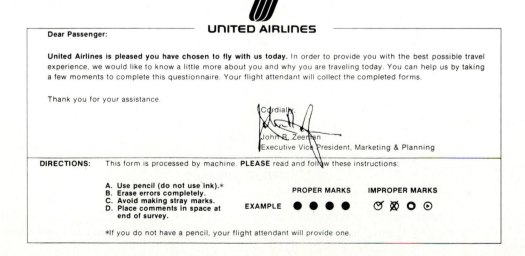

THE QUESTIONS BELOW PERTAIN TO THE TRAVEL PLANS AND EXPERIENCES FOR <u>THE FLIGHT YOU ARE ON RIGHT NOW.</u> PLEASE THINK ABOUT THIS PARTICULAR FLIGHT WHEN ANSWERING THE FOLLOWING QUESTIONS:

1a. What is your flight number?

1b. Today's date:

1c. In what city did you board this flight? →

2. How close to the scheduled departure time did this flight leave?

- ○ On time
- ○ 1-5 minutes late
- ○ 6-15 minutes late
- ○ 16-30 minutes late
- ○ 31-60 minutes late
- ○ Over 60 minutes late

3. Please indicate the type of fare you are using for this flight.

- ○ Full First Class Fare
- ○ Full Coach Fare
- ○ Discount Fare
- ○ Airline Employee/Travel Agent Fare
- ○ *Mileage Plus* Upgrade to First Class
- ○ *Mileage Plus* Free/Reduced Fare
- ○ Not sure/don't know

4. Printed below is a sample of a typical ticket (yours may vary slightly). Locate your ticket number in the upper right corner of your ticket or voucher (as illustrated). Please copy THE LAST 6 DIGITS of your ticket or voucher number in the appropriate spaces provided and fill in the matching circles below each number, as shown in the example below. The ticket number will provide information about your exact fare and itinerary but will not reveal your identity.

AIRLINE   FORM   SERIAL NUMBER
016 4452 123456

COPY: Last 6 digits of your Ticket No. here

5. Including today's trip, how many total _air round trips_ have you made in the last 12 months in the following categories?

EXAMPLE (10 Round Trips)

| / | 0 |

Total # Trips US (50 states)

Total # Trips International

FILL IN MATCHING CIRCLES BELOW

Where are you seated on today's flight?

6a. Cabin
- ○ First Class
- ○ Business
- ○ Coach

6b. Section
- ○ Smoking
- ○ Non-Smoking

6c. Seat
- ○ Window
- ○ Aisle
- ○ Other

7. Do you participate in United's *Mileage Plus* program?
- ○ Yes   ○ No

8. Are you a member of United's Red Carpet Club?
- ○ Yes   ○ No

9. What is your main purpose in taking this trip? (Please check only one answer.)
- ○ Business   ○ Pleasure/Personal

10. Which of the following phrases best describes this trip? (Fill in any that apply)

- ○ Internal company business (visit home office/branch)
- ○ Attend a company meeting (sales, training)
- ○ External company business (sales call, visit customer/vendor)
- ○ Official government/military business
- ○ Attend industry meeting/trade show
- ○ Attend convention
- ○ Accompany family member on business/convention
- ○ Other business (not described above)

- ○ Vacation
- ○ Incentive travel (company-paid pleasure trip)
- ○ Visit friends/relatives
- ○ Visit resort
- ○ My trip will (did) include the following activities:
  - ○ cruise   ○ ski   ○ golf   ○ tennis
- ○ Personal affairs (moving, to/from school)
- ○ Personal/family emergency
- ○ Other pleasure/personal reason

28. What is your occupation?
- ○ Executive/Managerial
- ○ Professional/Technical
- ○ Teacher/Professor
- ○ Salesperson/Buyer
- ○ Secretary/Clerk/ Office Worker
- ○ Government/Military
- ○ Craftsman/Laborer
- ○ Airline Employee/ Travel Agent
- ○ Self-Employed
- ○ Homemaker
- ○ Not Employed
- ○ Student
- ○ Retired
- ○ Other

29a. What is the approximate annual income, before taxes, for yourself and for your entire household?

	Your-self	Total house-hold
No income	○	○
Under - $10,000	○	○
10,000 - 19,999	○	○
20,000 - 29,999	○	○
30,000 - 39,999	○	○
40,000 - 49,999	○	○
50,000 - 59,999	○	○
60,000 - 74,999	○	○
75,000 - 100,000	○	○
Over $100,000	○	○

29b. How many wage earners?
- ○ 1
- ○ 2
- ○ 3
- ○ 4 or more

30. What is the highest level of formal education you have completed?
- ○ Less than high school graduate
- ○ High school graduate
- ○ Vocational/Trade school
- ○ Some college
- ○ College graduate
- ○ Post graduate degree

31. What age group are you in?
- ○ 12-17
- ○ 18-21
- ○ 22-29
- ○ 30-39
- ○ 40-49
- ○ 50-59
- ○ 60-64
- ○ 65 & over

32a. Are you:
- ○ Male
- ○ Female

32b. Are you:
- ○ Married   ○ Single
- ○ Widowed   ○ Divorced

33. Where do you live?
- ○ USA
- ○ Canada
- ○ Mexico
- ○ Europe
- ○ Orient
- ○ South America
- ○ Other

Fill matching circles below

(0) (0) (0) (0) (0) (0)
(1) (1) (1) (1) (1) (1)
(2) (2) (2) (2) (2) (2)
(3) (3) (3) (3) (3) (3)
(4) (4) (4) (4) (4) (4)
(5) (5) (5) (5) (5) (5)
(6) (6) (6) (6) (6) (6)
(7) (7) (7) (7) (7) (7)
(8) (8) (8) (8) (8) (8)
(9) (9) (9) (9) (9) (9)

If USA, what is ZIP Code?

ANY ADDITIONAL COMMENTS? (Please do NOT write outside this box.)

B/09871-001

Exhibit II   Other Questions

Version A

11. How did you get the information about schedules and fares for today's flight? (Fill in as many as apply)
- ○ I contacted United Airlines myself
- ○ I contacted another airline myself
- ○ I looked it up in the Official Airline Guide (OAG) or a printed airline timetable
- ○ I personally contacted a travel agent/tour operator
- ○ I used a personal computer terminal
- ○ I personally contacted my company/ Government/Military travel department
- ○ I used a self-service ticket machine
- ○ My secretary got the information
- ○ A friend/relative/spouse got the information
- ○ Someone else (not listed above) got the info.

12. Who actually made your airline reservation for this flight? (Fill in one)
- ○ I did, through a travel agent/tour operator
- ○ I contacted the airline myself
- ○ A friend/relative/spouse
- ○ My Company/Government/Military travel office
- ○ My secretary
- ○ An organized group
- ○ Other

13. How many days before starting this trip did you . . . ? (Please complete a, b & c)

	2 or less	3-6	7-13	14-20	21-29	30-59	60-89	90+
a. Decide to visit the destination	○	○	○	○	○	○	○	○
b. Make air reservations	○	○	○	○	○	○	○	○
c. Purchase tickets	○	○	○	○	○	○	○	○

14a. Who is actually paying for your ticket? (Fill in one)
- ○ I am personally
- ○ Friend/relative
- ○ Company/Employer
- ○ Government/Military
- ○ United (Mileage Plus ticket)
- ○ Other/Don't know

14b. Where was your ticket purchased or obtained?
- ○ United ticket counter
- ○ United ticket office (Not at airport)
- ○ United, by mail
- ○ Another airline
- ○ Travel agent/tour operator
- ○ Company/Gov't/Mil. office
- ○ Self-service ticket machine
- ○ Other/Don't know

15a. How many nights in total will you (did you) spend away from home on this trip?

- ○ None, same day return or one-way only
- ○ 1　○ 5　○ 9　○ 31-60
- ○ 2　○ 6　○ 10-14　○ over 60
- ○ 3　○ 7　○ 15-21
- ○ 4　○ 8　○ 22-30

15b. On which day of the week did you (will you) begin and end the <u>air travel</u> portion of your trip?

	SUN	MON	TUE	WED	THU	FRI	SAT
BEGIN TRIP	○	○	○	○	○	○	○
END TRIP	○	○	○	○	○	○	○

16. How many people (including yourself) are in your total travel party?

- ○ I am traveling alone **(Skip to question #17b)**
- ○ 2 people　○ 3 people　○ 4 people　○ 5-9 people　○ 10-19 people　○ 20 or more

17a. How many children, in these age groups, are traveling with you today?

2-11 years old
○ None　○ 2　○ 4
○ 1　○ 3　○ 5+

12-17 years old
○ None　○ 2　○ 4
○ 1　○ 3　○ 5+

17b. Will you (did you) rent a car on this trip?
○ Yes　○ No

17c. If so, which rental car company?
- ○ Alamo　○ Budget　○ National
- ○ Avis　○ Hertz　○ Other

18a. Where are you staying (or did you stay) on this trip?

- ○ Hotel/Motel　○ Friends/relative
- ○ Condo (Rent)　○ Cruise Ship
- ○ Condo (Own)　○ Other

18b. Including this trip, how many times have you been to the destination of this trip in the . . .

Past 12 months
○ 1　○ 4-6
○ 2　○ 7-9
○ 3　○ 10+

Past 4 years
○ 1　○ 4-6
○ 2　○ 7-9
○ 3　○ 10+

19. Please tell us how important each of the following was in making your decision to choose United for today's flight.

	Very Important	Somewhat Important	Not at all Important
United's departure and/or arrival time was more convenient	○	○	○
United's flight had fewer stops or better connections	○	○	○
United's air fare was better	○	○	○
United's Mileage Plus program	○	○	○
United's inflight services are better (meals, movies, flight attendants, etc.)	○	○	○
United's ground services are better (ticketing, baggage handling, check-in, etc.)	○	○	○
Personal preference for United Airlines	○	○	○
United was the only airline with seats available	○	○	○
Travel agent/Company travel department recommendation of United Airlines	○	○	○
Aircraft preference	○	○	○

20. Please answer Yes, No or Not Sure to the following statements about the air fare (price of ticket) for the trip you are taking today:

	Yes	No	Not Sure
I was planning this trip to this destination at this time regardless of the fare	○	○	○
I was planning this trip on another airline, but switched to United because of the fare	○	○	○
I was planning this trip with no particular airline in mind and selected United because of the fare	○	○	○
I was planning a trip to another destination, but switched to this destination because of the fare	○	○	○
I was planning this trip at a later or earlier time, but changed my plans to go now because of the fare	○	○	○
I was planning to drive or take the bus/train to this destination, but decided to fly because of the fare	○	○	○
I was not planning to take this trip at all, but decided to go because of the fare	○	○	○

21. What did you HAVE TO DO in order to get this air fare? Please answer Yes, No or Not Sure to each of the following statements.

	Yes	No	Not Sure
I had to purchase my ticket(s) a specific number of days in advance	○	○	○
I had to travel at a different time of day than I would have otherwise	○	○	○
I had to travel on a different day of the week than I would have otherwise	○	○	○
I had to stay away longer than I would have otherwise	○	○	○
I had to return sooner than I would have otherwise	○	○	○
I had to depart from a less convenient airport than I normally would have	○	○	○
I had to travel on a flight with more stops or connections than I would have	○	○	○
I had to travel via a different routing than I would have otherwise	○	○	○
I had to purchase a package deal (example: includes hotel, car, tour, etc.)	○	○	○

22. In which of the following "Frequent Flyer" programs do you participate? (Fill in all that apply)

- ○ None **(Skip to question #25)**
- ○ American AAdvantage
- ○ Continental Flight Bank
- ○ Delta Frequent Flyer
- ○ Eastern Frequent Traveler Bonus
- ○ Northwest Airlines
- ○ Pan Am World Pass
- ○ TWA Frequent Flight Bonus
- ○ United Airlines Mileage Plus
- ○ Other

23. Which "Frequent Flyer" program do you use most actively? (Fill in only one)

- ○ None
- ○ American AAdvantage
- ○ Continental Flight Bank
- ○ Delta Frequent Flyer
- ○ Eastern Frequent Traveler Bonus
- ○ Northwest Airlines
- ○ Pan Am World Pass
- ○ TWA Frequent Flight Bonus
- ○ United Airlines Mileage Plus
- ○ Other

24. How many times in the past 12 months have you selected an airline because you were a member of their "Frequent Flyer" program?

○ None　　○ 1-2　　○ 3-5　　○ 6-9　　○ 10 or more　　○ Not sure/Don't know

---

25. Please divide 10 points among the four items listed below to indicate how important each of these was to you in selecting today's flight. The more important one of these items was to you in selecting your flight, the more points you should give it. You may give any statement all or none of the 10 points, or as many or as few as you like, but please remember, **THE TOTAL NUMBER OF POINTS YOU GIVE MUST ADD TO 10.**

	NUMBER OF POINTS	Fill in the circle that matches the points you assign to each item. If no points are assigned to an item, fill in the zero.
Schedule Convenience	____	⓪ ① ② ③ ④ ⑤ ⑥ ⑦ ⑧ ⑨ ⑩
Price of the ticket	____	⓪ ① ② ③ ④ ⑤ ⑥ ⑦ ⑧ ⑨ ⑩
Frequent Flyer/Mileage Program . . .	____	⓪ ① ② ③ ④ ⑤ ⑥ ⑦ ⑧ ⑨ ⑩
Airline Preference	____	⓪ ① ② ③ ④ ⑤ ⑥ ⑦ ⑧ ⑨ ⑩
Must add to 10		
EXAMPLE 6		⓪ ① ② ③ ④ ⑤ ● ⑦ ⑧ ⑨ ⑩

Version B

11. Would you say the plane was: (Please answer one)

○ Full　　○ Three-quarters full　　○ Half full　　○ Less than half full

12a. Please rate the cleanliness of each of the following areas of the aircraft:

	Extremely Clean	Fairly Clean	Somewhat Dirty	Quite Dirty	Didn't Notice
Carpets	○	○	○	○	○
Seats	○	○	○	○	○
Seat Pockets	○	○	○	○	○
Walls	○	○	○	○	○
Tray Tables	○	○	○	○	○
Ash Trays	○	○	○	○	○
Lavatories	○	○	○	○	○
Overall Appearance	○	○	○	○	○

12b. Please rate the condition of each of the following areas of the aircraft:

	Excellent Condition "Like New"	Satisfactory Condition	Poor Condition "Old & Worn"	Didn't Notice
Carpets	○	○	○	○
Seats	○	○	○	○
Seat Pockets	○	○	○	○
Walls	○	○	○	○
Tray Tables	○	○	○	○
Ash Trays	○	○	○	○
Lavatories	○	○	○	○
Overall Condition	○	○	○	○

13. Please indicate if the following items did or did not work properly on today's flight:

	Worked Properly	Did not work Properly	Didn't Use or Notice
Seat Recline	○	○	○
Tray Tables	○	○	○
Ash Trays	○	○	○
Lavatories	○	○	○
Reading Light	○	○	○
Cabin Temperature	○	○	○
Fresh Air Circulation	○	○	○
Audio Entertainment System	○	○	○
Video Entertainment System	○	○	○

14. Is your seat on this flight comfortable?

○ Yes
○ No . . . **IF NO, WHY NOT?**   ○ Not enough leg room   ○ Not enough seat cushioning
                                  ○ Not enough seat width   ○ Not enough seat recline

15. How did the flight attendants on this flight perform the following tasks?

	Graciously	Adequately, Appropriately	Mechanically	Poorly, Rudely	Didn't Perform	Didn't Notice
Help passengers during boarding (seating, carry-ons, etc.)	○	○	○	○	○	○
Perform safety check (seat belts, tray tables, etc.)	○	○	○	○	○	○
Assist passengers with special needs (small children, elderly, disabled, etc.)	○	○	○	○	○	○
Offer food and/or beverages	○	○	○	○	○	○

16. Please rate the flight attendants on this flight for each of the following statements:

	Among the Best	Better than Most	About the same as Most	Not as good as Most	Among the Worst
Friendly, polite	○	○	○	○	○
Available for passenger needs	○	○	○	○	○
Worked well together	○	○	○	○	○
Responsive to passenger inquiries and requests	○	○	○	○	○
Neat and well-groomed	○	○	○	○	○
Efficient, well-trained	○	○	○	○	○
Served beverages/food as leisurely as flight time permitted	○	○	○	○	○

17. Overall, would you say that the flight attendants on this flight are. . .

○ Among the best   ○ About the same as most   ○ Among the worst
○ Better than most   ○ Not as good as most   ○ Can't say

18a. Were you served a meal on today's flight?   ○ Yes   ○ No (Skip to Question 23)

18b. If yes, overall, how would you compare this meal with other airline meals you have had on similar flights?

○ One of the best   ○ About the same as most   ○ One of the worst
○ Better than most   ○ Not as good as most   ○ Cannot say, no similar flights

19. Was the food you received today appropriate for the time of day?   ○ Yes   ○ No

20. How would you rate the quality of the food you received today?

○ Excellent   ○ Good   ○ Fair   ○ Poor

21. How would you rate the quantity of the food you received today?

○ Too Much   ○ Just Right   ○ Not Enough

22. If there was a choice of meals today, did you receive your choice?   ○ Yes   ○ No

23. How would you describe the overall quality of the following services provided on this flight?

	Among the Best	Better than Most	About the same as Most	Not as good as Most	Among the Worst	Not Offered/ Didn't Notice
Safety announcements	○	○	○	○	○	○
Information announcements	○	○	○	○	○	○
Audio programs	○	○	○	○	○	○
Movie/video programs	○	○	○	○	○	○
Beverage service	○	○	○	○	○	○
Meal/snack service	○	○	○	○	○	○

24a. For each of these areas that you used at the airport just departed, please indicate how long you waited in line . . . . and →   **24b. Was this wait acceptable or not?**

	Didn't Use	No Wait	5 min. or less	6-10 min.	11-20 min.	21+ min.	Yes	No
Curbside baggage check	○	○	○	○	○	○	○	○
Ticket counter	○	○	○	○	○	○	○	○
Express baggage/seat check-in counter	○	○	○	○	○	○	○	○
Security checkpoint	○	○	○	○	○	○	○	○
Red Carpet Room check-in desk	○	○	○	○	○	○	○	○
Boarding gate counter	○	○	○	○	○	○	○	○
Aircraft boarding	○	○	○	○	○	○	○	○

25. Overall, how courteous and helpful were United's personnel at the airport you just departed? . . . .

Among the Best	Better than Most	About the same as Most	Not as good as Most	Among the Worst
O	O	O	O	O

26. Now, thinking about the whole experience with this flight—from the time you arrived at the airport until now—would you say that this flight is . . . (Please fill in only one response)

- O One of the best
- O Better than most
- O About the same as most
- O Not as good as most
- O One of the worst
- O Cannot say

Version C

11. Did you **yourself** call United Airlines reservations to make the arrangements for this flight?

O Yes   O No . . . **(If NO, please skip to question #13)**

12. Please rate the pre-flight services you received from the United reservation agent when making your travel arrangements for this flight.

	Among the Best	Better than Most	About the same as Most	Not as good as Most	Among the Worst	Don't Know/ Don't Recall
Speed in getting through to Agent	O	O	O	O	O	O
Helpfulness of Agent	O	O	O	O	O	O
Courtesy of Reservation Agent	O	O	O	O	O	O
Accuracy of flight information	O	O	O	O	O	O
Accuracy of fare information	O	O	O	O	O	O

13. When did you receive your **seat assignment** (row and seat number) for today's flight?

Today:
- O At the airport just departed
- O At another airport

Prior to arriving at the airport today from:
- O Travel agent
- O United reservation agent
- O United ticket office
- O Company travel department
- O Government/Military
- O Other/don't know

14. When did you receive your **boarding pass** for today's flight?

Today:
- O At the airport just departed
- O At another airport

Prior to arriving at the airport today from:
- O Travel agent
- O United reservation agent
- O United ticket office
- O Company travel department
- O Government/Military
- O Other/don't know

15. How satisfactory was the seat assignment and boarding procedure on today's flight?

- O Very satisfactory
- O Somewhat satisfactory
- O Not satisfactory

16a. Did you check bag(s) today?
- O With United at the airport just departed
- O With United at another airport
- O At another airline
- O I did not check bags today **(Skip to question #17)**

16b. With whom did you check your bag(s) today?
- O With the Sky Cap at curbside
- O With the agent at the ticket counter
- O With the express baggage agent in the lobby
- O With the agent at the gate

17. Is there enough room for your carry-on baggage?
- O Enough room and convenient for me
- O Enough room but not convenient for me
- O Not enough room
- O Did not have carry-on baggage

18. How many pieces of baggage did you personally:

	0	1	2	3	4	5 or more
a. **Check** on today's flight?	O	O	O	O	O	O
b. **Carry on board?** (Not including purses)	O	O	O	O	O	O

19. Please rate the flight attendants on this flight for each of the following statements:

	Among the Best	Better than Most	About the same as Most	Not as good as Most	Among the Worst
Friendly, polite	O	O	O	O	O
Available for passenger needs	O	O	O	O	O
Worked well together	O	O	O	O	O
Responsive to passenger inquiries and requests	O	O	O	O	O
Neat and well-groomed	O	O	O	O	O
Efficient, well-trained	O	O	O	O	O
Served beverages/food as leisurely as flight time permitted	O	O	O	O	O

20. Overall, would you say that the flight attendants on this flight are . . .

O Among the best   O About the same as most   O Among the worst
O Better than most   O Not as good as most   O Can't say

21. Where did you begin your air travel today?

O At airport just departed   O At another airport (If so, please skip to question #27)

22a. For each of these areas that you used at the airport just departed, please indicate how long you waited in line . . . . and ⟶   22b. Was this wait acceptable or not?

	Didn't Use	No Wait	5 min. or less	6-10 min.	11-20 min.	21+ min.	Yes	No
Curbside baggage check	O	O	O	O	O	O	O	O
Ticket counter	O	O	O	O	O	O	O	O
Express baggage/seat check-in counter	O	O	O	O	O	O	O	O
Security checkpoint	O	O	O	O	O	O	O	O
Red Carpet Room check-in desk	O	O	O	O	O	O	O	O
Boarding gate counter	O	O	O	O	O	O	O	O
Aircraft boarding	O	O	O	O	O	O	O	O

23. Overall, how courteous and helpful were United's personnel at the airport you just departed?

	Among the Best	Better than Most	About the same as Most	Not as good as Most	Among the Worst
	O	O	O	O	O

24. If you were particularly dissatisfied with any of United's personnel at the airport you just departed, please indicate which personnel.

O Sky Cap
O Ticket Counter Agent
O Express Baggage Agent
O Security Checkpoint Personnel

O Red Carpet Room Receptionist
O Boarding Gate Agent
O Flight Attendant (during boarding)

25. Please indicate how well you were kept informed about the status of your flight today (departure/arrival times, gate information, delays, etc.).

O Very well   O Adequately   O Poorly

26. Overall, how would you compare United's preflight services at the airport today with other trips you have taken?

O Among the best   O Not as good as most
O Better than most   O Among the worst
O About the same as most   O Don't know

371

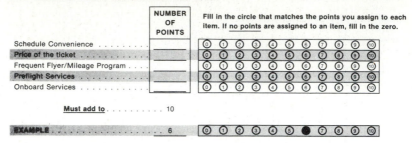

27. **Please divide 10 points among the five items listed below to indicate how important each of these was to you in selecting today's flight. The more important one of these items was to you in selecting your flight, the more points you should give it. You may give any statement all or none of the 10 points, or as many or as few as you like, but please remember, THE TOTAL NUMBER OF POINTS YOU GIVE MUST ADD TO 10.**

II-4

CHRYSLER CORPORATION: CONSUMER TESTING OF TURBINE-POWERED CAR

The Chrysler Corporation, in pioneering the development of the turbine-powered car, had an obvious interest in obtaining consumer evaluations and reactions before making the final decision to introduce it. There were substantial uncertainties as to how the consumer would react to the different operating characteristics and the product image associated with a turbine engine. These uncertainties, when coupled with the sizable outlays required for production tooling and the introduction of the car, made it highly desirable to obtain information from consumers who had actually used the car under conditions approximating normal car usage. The question was, How should such information be obtained?

Conventional market testing, such as that used in grocery products and drug sundries, has never been practical for use with new automobiles. It is far too costly to tool up for the quantity of cars required, there are serious morale problems in dealer selection, and the cars tend to be bought by customers who are not representative of the prospective market. Such market tests have been used only in testing the market for an existing model car in a foreign market.

It was evident that some sort of consumer use test would have to be conducted, however. The method decided upon to obtain the desired information was to place the turbine-powered car with selected users under a no-charge user agreement. Each selected user was to drive the car for a period of three months and agreed to furnish Chrysler with the information required for the market evaluation program.

It was decided that 50 prototype cars would be built and placed with users at a rate of one per week beginning in late October. The test was to be continued until evaluations had been received from a total of 200 users.

A news release of the program was made in midyear. Over a period of a few weeks Chrysler received some 20,000 unsolicited requests to participate in the evaluation program. It was decided that participants would be selected from among these 20,000 persons. Eligibility for participation would be limited to those candidates who owned a car (or were a member of a household in which a car was owned by the head of the household) and who had a valid driver's license. The candidate also had to be a resident of a major population center in one of the 48 continental United States. This stipulation was made to ensure a high degree of market exposure to the car and to test it under a variety of weather and terrain conditions. The users were then selected randomly from among the remaining candidates who had been grouped according to the make, price category, and age of the new and used cars owned. The intent was to select users whose car ownership pattern was representative of the population car-ownership pattern at that time.

Each candidate was asked to complete the questionnaire reproduced below. The completed questionnaire, along with the original correspondence, was forwarded to the public accounting firm of Touche, Ross, Bailey, and Smart, who made the final selection of users.

1. Evaluate the questionnaire in terms of
   a. The information requested versus that needed for selection of users
   b. The types and degree of potential errors in the information obtained
2. From the information given, would you conclude that a random sample of the population of prospective buyers of the turbine-powered car was taken? Why or why not?

QUESTIONNAIRE

Thank you for your request to test the Chrysler Corporation turbine car. Since we first announced our turbine evaluation program, we have been complimented with thousands of such requests which demonstrate the enthusiasm for this new automotive power concept. As you know from information already published, the program was successfully launched on October 20 of this year with the assignment of the first turbine car to a Chicago user for a three-month trial period. We expect to continue placing turbine cars with users at the rate of about one a week, until the 50 cars we are building have provided us with a sample of 200 turbine users.

A brochure explaining the selection process is enclosed. This was previously sent to those who are presently part of the active inquiry file. In addition, we have also included an interesting booklet about the turbine car.

The questionnaire included with this letter asks for certain information which would be helpful to us. Naturally, its return in no way obligates you and, likewise, our request for this information does not mean that you will be selected as a turbine car user.

Your interest is appreciated, and we hope that you will forward the filled-in questionnaire to us within the next two weeks if convenient. When we receive it, we will send your original correspondence and the questionnaire to the independent accounting firm of Touche, Ross, Bailey, and Smart. They have been engaged by us to select the participants in this program. It will not be necessary for you to supply us with any further data except, of course, a change of address, if it occurs.

1. In all, how many miles do you travel a year for both business and pleasure?
   _____ miles per year
2. How much of this traveling is by automobile?
   _____ miles per year
3. How large an area do you normally cover in your routine driving?
   _____ 50 mile radius _____ 300 mile radius _____ 1000 mile radius
   _____ 100 mile radius _____ 400 mile radius   if more, specify
   _____ 200 mile radius _____ 500 mile radius   _____
4. In routine driving do you normally travel alone or with someone else
   _____ alone _____ with someone else
   If not alone, how many others usually? _____
5. What portion of your driving is done:
   _____ % at low speeds (under 50 m.p.h.)
   _____ % at highway speeds (over 50 m.p.h.)
6. What make of car(s) do you own?
   1. _____ Year _____ Body Style _____
   2. _____ Year _____ Body Style _____
   3. _____ Year _____ Body Style _____
7. May we know your age? _____
   Education:
   _____ Grade school   _____ Completed high school
   _____ Some high school   _____ Some college
                                        _____ College graduate

   Marital status: _____ Married _____ Single
   Children: How many? _____
8. Do you have any hobbies? If so, would you please tell us what they are?

   _____
9. How are you employed? _____
   _____ self employed _____ employee of a company
   If self employed:
     What is the name of your business and the business address?

     _____
     What is the nature of your business? (For instance what do you manufacture,
     sell, or what service do you provide?)

     _____
     How long have you been in business for yourself?
     _____ years
   If employee of a company:
     What is the name of the company, and the business address where you are
     located?

     _____
     In what capacity are you employed? _____
     How long have you been employed by this company?
     _____ years
10. Additional comments:

    _____

    _____

QUESTIONNAIRE

II-5

TRAVEL & LEISURE

Travel & Leisure, a consumer magazine devoted to travel and the travel industry, is published by the American Express Publishing Corporation, which is a subsidiary of American Express Travel Related Services. The magazine is published monthly and contains extensive advertising in addition to articles about places around the world.

The magazine often utilizes marketing research to aid in article preparation as well as selling advertising. For example, the company has used full-service marketing research agencies such as Erdos and Morgan, Inc., to conduct surveys. The purpose of such surveys has been to bring subscribers' demographic data up to date. One approach has been to survey American Express Money Cardmembers. A typical survey of this type involves a data collection procedure consisting of preliminary notification post card, questionnaire mailing (with a $1.00 monetary incentive), and follow-up letter. A study using this approach generates, on the average, a total response rate of between 55% and 65%.

The research department at *Travel & Leisure* decided to try another approach to obtain information about travelers and travel behavior. The questionnaire shown below was run in the early pages of the June 1985 issue of the magazine.

1. Will the research being done by *Travel & Leisure* provide the necessary information for selling advertising and deciding upon articles for publication?
2. Evaluate the use of media for conducting surveys.

A TRAVEL & LEISURE QUESTIONNAIRE

How Do You Travel?

What kind of traveler are you? When you fly off to Paris, is it for the weekend or for a week? On business or pleasure—or both? Do you fly coach, business or first class? What do you look for in your hotel accommodations? These are the kinds of questions we'd like you to answer. Please take a minute to check the boxes on this and the backing page, and then tear out and return to us—see address at the end. We will share the results with all readers in a future issue. Thank you in advance for your time.

—THE EDITORS

ABOUT VACATION PLANNING & TRAVEL

1. When planning a vacation trip, which of the following do you generally do? (Please check all that apply.)
   Consult a travel agent . . . . ☐-1   5.
   Seek friends' advice . . . . ☐-2
   Plan independently . . . . ☐-3
   Refer to magazine/newspaper articles . . . . ☐-4
   Let someone else handle all arrangements . . . . ☐-5

2. Who in your family actually decides where to go on vacation? (Please check only *one*.)
   You alone . . . . ☐-1   Children . . . . ☐-3   6.
   Spouse or companion . . . . . ☐-2   Joint decision . . . . ☐-4

3. How long does your typical vacation trip usually last?
   Weekend . . . . ☐-1   2 weeks . . . . ☐-3   7.
   1 week . . . . ☐-2   3 weeks or more . . . . . ☐-4

4. Who makes most of the specific arrangements for your vacation? (Please check only *one*.)
   You alone . . . . ☐-1   Travel agent . . . . ☐-3   8.
   Spouse or companion . . . . . ☐-2   Secretary . . . . ☐-4

5a. On a vacation trip, where do you prefer to stay overnight when you're in an American city?
   At the first comfortable motel on the way into town . . . . . . ☐-1   9.
   At the last motel on the other side of town . . . . ☐-2
   In the center of the city . . . . ☐-3
   In a landmark hotel . . . . ☐-4
   Bed and breakfast inn . . . . ☐-5

   b. Do you usually make advance reservations?
   Yes . . . . ☐-1   No . . . . ☐-2   10.

6. How far ahead do you plan a vacation of a week or more?
   Spontaneously . . ☐-1   2-3 months . . . . . ☐-3   A year . . . . ☐-5   11.
   A month . . . . ☐-2   6 months . . . . ☐-4

7. How do you usually pay for these five aspects of travel?

	Plane	Car Rental	Hotel	Meals	Shopping
Cash	☐ 12-1	☐ 13-1	☐ 14-1	☐ 15-1	☐ 16-1
Personal check	☐-2	☐-2	☐-2	☐-2	☐-2
Charge card	☐-3	☐-3	☐-3	☐-3	☐-3
Travelers cheques . .	☐-4	☐-4	☐-4	☐-4	☐-4
Money order	☐-5	☐-5	☐-5	☐-5	☐-5

8. For a long-weekend getaway, which of the following destinations appeals to you most?
   Full-service resort hotel . . . ☐-1   Driving/Sightseeing . . . . ☐-3   17.
   City weekend in a hotel . . . ☐-2   Secluded motel/hotel . . ☐-4

9. If time and money were no consideration, how would you prefer to spend a 2-week vacation?
   Driving in the U.S./
   Sightseeing . . . . ☐-1   At a spa . . . . ☐-5   18.
   Driving in a foreign country ☐-2   Staying in *one* big city
   Being active—skiing, etc. . . ☐-3   —London, Rome,
   In a resort . . . . ☐-4   New York, etc. . . . . . . ☐-6
                                         Off-the-beaten-track . . . ☐-7

10. Are your vacation plans most influenced by: (Please check all that apply.)
    Work/Office schedules . . . . ☐-1   Season . . . . ☐-4   19.
    Family obligations . . . . ☐-2   Holiday periods (Christmas,
    Personal preferences . . . . . . ☐-3   July 4th, etc.) . . . . ☐-5

11. How do you choose a new destination for a vacation?
    Magazines/   Trends . . . . ☐-3   20.
    Newspapers . . . . ☐-1   Travel agents . . . . ☐-4
    Word of mouth . . . . ☐-2   Movies/TV . . . . ☐-5

12. When you travel, do you prefer to:
    Have a detailed itinerary . . . . ☐-1   21.
    Have a moderately structured itinerary . . . . ☐-2
    Have no itinerary . . . . ☐-3

13. Which of the following problems, if any, do you worry about when you plan a foreign trip? (Check all that apply.)
    Forgetting or losing   Getting to and from
    your passport . . . . ☐-1   the airport . . . . ☐-6   22.
    Dealing with   Luggage problems . . . . ☐-7
    foreign currency . . . . . . ☐-2   Language problems . . . ☐-8
    Tipping . . . . ☐-3   Protecting money
    Flight delays . . . . ☐-4   and valuables . . . . . . ☐-9
    Settling into a new   Jet lag . . . . ☐-0
    environment . . . . ☐-5

14a. How much vacation time do you usually have? (employed or self-employed)
    1 week . . . . ☐-1   4 weeks . . . . ☐-4   23.
    2 weeks . . . . ☐-2   4-6 weeks . . . . ☐-5
    3 weeks . . . . ☐-3   Over 6 weeks . . . . ☐-6

    b. Do you generally take all of your vacation time?
    Yes . . . . ☐-1   No . . . . ☐-2   24.

15. When you travel on vacation, what grade or class do you usually use in planes, in hotels, and in restaurants?
    Flights: Economy . . . . ☐-3   25.
    First class . . . . ☐-1   Promotional (APEX,
    Business class . . . . ☐-2   Supersaver, etc.) . . . . ☐-4
    Hotels:
    Deluxe . . . . . . ☐-1   First class . . . . . . ☐-2   Economy . . . ☐-3   26.
    Restaurants:
    Expensive . . . . ☐-1   Moderate . . . . ☐-2   Economical . ☐-4   27.

16. If you have ever had a poor or bad experience while on a vacation, which of the following has particularly bothered you? (Please check all that apply.)

Hotel	*Transportation*
Rude staff . . . . ☐ 28-1	Rude airline personnel . . ☐ 29-1
Room not available	Cancellation of flight/
on arrival . . . . ☐-2	transportation . . . . ☐-2
No record of reservation . . ☐-3	Missed connection . . . . . ☐-3
Room too small or noisy . . ☐-4	Overbooked flight . . . . . ☐-4
Room not clean . . . . ☐-5	Excessive delays . . . . . . ☐-5
Poor room service . . . . . . ☐-6	Smoking . . . . ☐-6
Room overpriced . . . . . . ☐-7	Taxi rip-offs . . . . ☐-7
Security . . . . ☐-8	

continued

ABOUT TRANSPORTATION

1. Given a choice, what means of long-distance vacation travel do you prefer? (Please check only *one*.)
   Air . . . . ☐-1   Train . . . . ☐-3   Rental car . . ☐-5   30.
   Ship . . . . ☐-2   Personal car . . . . ☐-4   Tour bus . . . ☐-6

2. How many times have you or other members of your household flown on a commercial airline either for business, pleasure or both during the past 12 months? (Count each round trip as two.)

	U.S. Travel	Foreign Travel
Business trip	———31	———37
Pleasure trip	———33	———39
Business/pleasure combined	———35	———41

3. How did you feel about the following during your *last* flight?

	(1.) Very Satisfied	(2.) Somewhat Satisfied	(3.) Somewhat Dissatisfied	(4.) Very Dissatisfied
Service	☐	☐	☐	☐	43
Comfort	☐	☐	☐	☐
Food/Drink	☐	☐	☐	☐
Convenient flying time . .	☐	☐	☐	☐
Luggage retrieval	☐	☐	☐	☐
Delays in takeoff/landing	☐	☐	☐	☐	48

4. Have you rented a car for vacation purposes in the past 12 months?
   Yes . . . . ☐-1   No . . . . ☐-2   49.

3. How important is each of the following in making your stay in a hotel pleasant?

	(1.) Very Important	(2.) Slightly Important	(3.) Not At All Important
Courteous staff	☐	☐	☐	5.
Comfortable/Spacious/			
Attractive room	☐	☐	☐
Comfortable bed	☐	☐	☐
Quiet	☐	☐	☐
Well-equipped bathroom	☐	☐	☐	9.
Generous giveaways			
(soaps, shampoos, etc.)	☐	☐	☐	10.
Prompt room service	☐	☐	☐
High-tech phone systems	☐	☐	☐
Cable TV	☐	☐	☐	13.
In-house movies	☐	☐	☐
Alarm clocks/radios	☐	☐	☐
Minibars	☐	☐	☐	16.

4. What safety features, if any, do you look for in a hotel?   17.
   Sophisticated door locks . . . ☐-1   Wall safes . . . . ☐-4
   In-room sprinklers . . . . ☐-2   Fire exit directions . . . . . ☐-5
   In-room smoke alarms . . . . . ☐-3   None of the above . . . . . ☐-6

5a. Do you use hotel concierge services?
   Yes . . . . ☐-1   No . . . . ☐-2   18.

   b. If "Yes," for what do you use them? (Check all that apply.)
   Theater tickets . . . . ☐-1   Tour information . . . . . . ☐-3   19.
   Restaurant reservations . . . ☐-2   General information . . . ☐-4

ABOUT HOTELS

1. How many trips have you made in the past 12 months where you stayed at a hotel or resort for business, pleasure, or both?

	Number of Trips
Business	_____ 50.
Pleasure	_____ 52.
Business/pleasure combined	_____ 54.

2. On vacation, how important are each of the following when you choose a resort hotel, big-city hotel, or country inn?

Resort Hotel	(1.) Very Important	(2.) Slightly Important	(3.) Not At All Important
Location	☐	☐	☐ 56.
Health/Sports facilities	☐	☐	☐
Beach/Pool	☐	☐	☐
Air conditioning	☐	☐	☐ 59.
Part of a package	☐	☐	☐
Good food on premises	☐	☐	☐
Gambling	☐	☐	☐
Nightlife	☐	☐	☐ 63.

Big-City Hotel	(1.) Very Important	(2.) Slightly Important	(3.) Not At All Important
Location	☐	☐	☐ 64.
Sleek/Modern	☐	☐	☐
Old/Charming	☐	☐	☐
Good restaurants	☐	☐	☐
Health/Sports facilities	☐	☐	☐
24-hour room service	☐	☐	☐ 69.

Country Inn	(1.) Very Important	(2.) Slightly Important	(3.) Not At All Important
Location	☐	☐	☐ 70.
Private bath	☐	☐	☐
Food other than breakfast	☐	☐	☐
Takes credit cards	☐	☐	☐
Surrounding sights	☐	☐	☐
Charm	☐	☐	☐ 75.
			80-1.

THANK YOU FOR YOUR TIME AND HELP.

ABOUT YOU AND YOUR FAMILY

(Confidential information for the statistical analysis of previous data.)

1. Your sex:
   Male ☐1   Female ☐2   20.

2. What is your marital status?
   Married ☐1   Single ☐2   21.
   Widowed/Separated/Divorced ☐3

3. Your age:
   Under 25 ☐1   40 – 44 ☐5   60 – 64 ☐9 22.
   25 – 29 ☐2   45 – 49 ☐6   65 and over ☐0
   30 – 34 ☐3   50 – 54 ☐7
   35 – 39 ☐4   55 – 59 ☐8

4. Please check the highest level of education you completed.
   Postgraduate degree ☐1   1 – 3 years college ☐4 23.
   Some postgraduate   High school graduate ☐5
   schooling ☐2   Some high school
   College graduate ☐3   or less ☐6

5a. Are you employed (or self-employed)?
   Full-time ☐1   Not at all ☐3 24.
   Part-time ☐2   Retired ☐4

b. What is your occupation? (Please check only *one*.)
   Professional ☐1   Sales/Clerical ☐4 25.
   Business executive/   Homemaker ☐5
   managerial ☐2
   Owner/Proprietor ☐3   Other: _____ 26.
                        (Please Specify)

5. What was your total family income before taxes last year? (Please include income from all household members and from all sources, such as salaries or wages, bonuses dividends, etc.)
   Under $20,000 ☐1 $75,000 – $99,999 ☐6 27.
   $20,000 – $24,999 ☐2 $100,000 – $149,999 ☐7
   $25,000 – $34,999 ☐3 $150,000 – $199,999 ☐8
   $35,000 – $49,999 ☐4 $200,000 or Over ☐9
   $50,000 – $74,999 ☐5

   CITY: _____   STATE: _____ 28.
   ZIP CODE: _____ 80-2.

PLEASE TEAR OUT PAGE AND MAIL TO:

Pamela Fiori, Editor-in-Chief
TRAVEL & LEISURE—Research Dept.
516 Fifth Avenue, Suite 605, New York, N.Y. 10036

II-6

MERCHANT'S ASSOCIATION SHOPPER SURVEY

A merchant's association for a relatively small shopping center located in a metropolitan area of 150,000 population conducted a survey of shoppers. The survey used a self-report questionnaire and there were no interviewers present. Rather, the questionnaires were placed on a table in the mall with a sign asking people to participate. The accompanying questionnaire was used.

1. What response errors are likely to arise? Explain.
2. Evaluate this survey and the questionnaire used as decisional research.
3. Revise the questionnaire to better obtain the information being sought.

MARTIN MALL—QUICK ROAD MERCHANTS ASSOCIATION
SHOPPER'S SURVEY

In an attempt to serve you better, the Martin Mall–Quick Road Merchant's Association requests that you complete this questionnaire and deposit it in the special container marked *"Deposit Shopper's Survey Here"* located in the Mall. All information is strictly confidential and *you need not sign the Survey*. Your cooperation will be sincerely appreciated.

Check one: Male _____   Female _____

1. Name of city or town in which you live _____
2. How long have you lived there? _____
3. Are you buying or renting a home? _____
4. How many automobiles in your household? _____
5. Husband's occupation? _____
6. Wife's occupation? _____
7. What is your annual income? (If both husband and wife work, please indicate total.) _____
8. What is your age? _____
9. Number of children in your family? _____
10. What are the ages of your children? _____
11. What radio station do you listen to most? _____
12. How often do you shop the Martin–Quick area? (Check one.)
    Weekly _____   Once or twice a month _____
    1–6 times a year _____   Only during special sales or events __
13. Do you enjoy shopping the Martin–Quick area? Yes __ No __
14. In general, how would you rate the people who work the Martin–Quick shopping area on courtesy?
    Excellent _____   Good _____   Fair _____   Poor _____
    Very poor _____
15. In general, are you able to find what you are shopping for in the Martin–Quick area? _____
16. How much time per shopping trip do you spend in the Martin Mall–Quick Road shopping area? _____

10

The Analysis Process—Basic Concepts and Analyzing Associative Data

INTRODUCTION

From a managerial perspective, *information* can be viewed as *recorded experience useful for making decisions*. Responses on measurement instruments (words, check marks, etc.) convey little information as such. These raw data must be compiled, analyzed, and interpreted carefully before their complete meanings and implications can be understood.

Analysis can be viewed as the ordering, the breaking down into constituent parts, and the manipulating of data to obtain answers to the research question or questions underlying the research project. Tightly interwoven with analysis is interpretation; it is so closely related to analysis that it is a special aspect of analysis rather than a separate activity. The process of interpretation involves taking the results of analysis, making inferences relevant to the research relationships studied, and drawing conclusions about these relationships. Since analysis represents the end of the research process (short of writing the report), everything done prior to this stage has been done for the sole purpose of analysis. From a decisional context, all conclusions, recommendations, and decisions are based on the analysis of the raw data obtained from the research project. This points to the need for considering analysis, or potential analysis, when planning and designing the project.

The competent analysis of research-obtained data requires a blending of art and science, of intuition and informal insight, of judgment and statistical treatment, combined with a thorough knowledge of the context of the problem being investigated. Some of these qualities can only be acquired by experience, while others are heavily dependent on the native abilities of the analyst. Still others can be acquired through education and training.

This chapter examines the major basic processes and concepts pertaining to how the meanings and interpretations of research data can best be extracted. After a brief discussion of the overall analysis process, some fundamental characteristics of data coding and tabulation are presented, with emphasis on cross-tabulation. The next section of the chapter considers some of the techniques for analyzing associative data. The concluding section of the chapter provides a brief overview of multivariate analysis. The central idea of a data matrix is introduced first. We then present a system for classifying multivariate techniques that is based on alternative ways of operating on the original data matrix. This classification system serves to organize the presentation of multivariate methods in subsequent chapters.

MAJOR STEPS IN THE ANALYSIS PROCESS

The overall process of analyzing sample data and making inferences from them can be viewed as involving a number of separate and sequential steps:

1. *Tabulation*. Establishing appropriate categories for the information desired, sorting the data into them, making the initial counts of responses, and using summarizing measures to provide economy of description and so facilitate understanding.
2. *Formulating additional hypotheses*. Using the inductions derived from the data concerning the relevant variables, their parameters, their differences, and relationships to suggest working hypotheses not originally considered.
3. *Making inferences*. Reaching conclusions about the variables that are important, their parameters, their differences, and the relationships among them.

While these steps have been shown as separate procedures and there is an implication that they are sequential, in practice they sometimes tend to merge or they do not always follow in sequence. For example, the initial sorting of the data may suggest additional hypotheses that in turn require more and different sorting. Nor are all of the steps always required in a particular project; the study may be exploratory in nature, which means that it is designed to formulate hypotheses to examine in a later, full-scale project.

Since a major part of this chapter deals with what tabulation involves, we will defer discussion until then. We now turn to the other major steps in the analysis process.

Formulating Additional Hypotheses

The objectives of the study and the hypotheses to be examined should be—to the extent feasible—clearly stated and agreed upon at the outset. These objectives and hypotheses shape and mold the study; they determine the kind of information that is required, the specific data that are to be collected, and the kind of analysis that will be necessary. However, a project will usually turn up new hypotheses, regardless of the rigor with which it was thought through and planned. New hypotheses are suggested at many stages of the project, ranging from data collection through the final interpretation of the findings.

In Chapter 2 it was pointed out that when the scientific method is used as the research process, hypothesis formulation precedes the collection of data to test it. Rigorous standards of investigation require that this be the case. Thus, the data that suggest an hypothesis should *not* be used to test it.

When new hypotheses are formulated during the project, it is desirable to expand the analysis to examine them to the extent that the data permit. At one extreme, it may be possible to show that the new hypothesis is not supported by the data and that no further investigation should be considered. At the other extreme, it may turn out that strong supportive evidence is provided by other portions of the data and that a high prior probability of its being correct will result. Between these extremes may be the outcome that the new hypothesis is neither supported nor rejected by the data. In this event additional collection of information may be indicated.

A more extreme position is taken by Selvin and Stuart, who feel that in survey research, it is rarely possible to formulate precise hypotheses independently of the data.[1] This means that most survey research is essentially exploratory in nature. Rather than having a single predesignated hypothesis in mind, the analyst works with many diffuse and ill-defined hypotheses. The added cost of an extra question is so low that the same survey can be used to investigate many problems without increasing the total cost very much. On a typical survey project, therefore, the analyst alternates between analyzing the data and formulating hypotheses. Obviously, there are exceptions to all general rules and phenomena. Selvin and Stuart, therefore, designate three practices of survey analysts:

1. *Snooping.* The process of testing from the data all of a predesignated set of hypotheses
2. *Fishing.* The process of using the data to choose which of a number of pre-designated variables to include in an explanatory model
3. *Hunting.* The process of searching through a body of data and looking at many relations in order to find those worth testing (that is, there is no predesignation)

The position taken by Selvin and Stuart may be reasonable for basic research but may not be practical for decisional research. Time and other pressures seem to require that snooping and perhaps fishing are useful in decision research. Rarely can the decision maker afford the luxury of hunting. Again, it simply reduces to the question of cost versus value. Moreover, overall value may be adversely effected when "one more question" is added to the measurement instrument.

---

[1]Hanan C. Selvin and Alan Stuart, "Data-Dredging Procedures in Survey Analysis," *The American Statistician,* June 1966, pp. 20–23.

Making Inferences

Once the data have been tabulated and summary measures calculated, it may be desirable to analyze them to determine whether observed differences between categories are indicative of actual differences or whether they occurred as the result of chance variation in the sample. In some studies, on the other hand, it may be sufficient simply to know the value of certain parameters of the population, such as the mean usage of our product per consuming unit, or the proportion of stores carrying our brand, or the preferences of housewives concerning alternative styles or designs of a new product. Even in these cases, however, it is desirable that the decision maker know about the underlying associated factors involved, if not for purposes of the immediate problem, then for use in solving later problems. In other cases, it is necessary to analyze the relationships of the variables and attributes involved to determine behavioral correlates and causal relationships. Knowledge of these relationships will enhance the ability to make reliable predictions of the results of decisions involving changes in controllable variables.

The broad objective of *testing of hypotheses* underlies all decisional research. Often this can be done directly. At times, however, *estimation* may be necessary. Thus, while estimation may be useful in itself in basic research, in decisional research it is done only when necessary for the testing of a hypothesis. In both estimation and hypothesis testing, *inferences* are made about the population of interest on the basis of information from a sample.

A question that continually plagues analysts is, What should be the significance level used in hypothesis testing? This involves specifying the value of α, which is the allowable amount of type I error (or the probability that we will incorrectly reject H_0).

Significance levels are—or should be—set as a result of (a) cost of error and (b) decision rule used.[2] There are substantial differences between basic and decisional research in assignment of error costs, and there *may* be differences in choice of decision rule as well. The result is that the levels of significance used in a basic research project may be entirely inappropriate for those in a decisional research project dealing with the same problem.

There is a tradition of conservatism in basic research. This conservative tradition has resulted in the practice of keeping the error of falsely rejecting the null hypothesis at a low level. This is to say that the type I error has been traditionally considered to be more important than the type II error and, correspondingly, that it is more important to have a low α than a low β. The basic researcher typically assigns higher costs to a type I than to a type II error.

In decisional research, the costs are assigned by the consequences of the errors. The cost of foregoing gain as a result of a type II error may be even greater than the loss from making a type I error, depending on the situation and the decision rule being used.

---

[2]For a somewhat "classic" paper dealing with criteria relevant for this question, see S. Labovitz, "Criteria for Selecting a Significance Level: A Note on the Sacredness of .05," *The American Sociologist,* 3 (August 1968), 220–22.

Of course not all decision situations have errors leading to such consequences. In some situations, making a type I error may lead to an opportunity cost (for example, a forgone gain) and a type II error may create a direct loss. For example, suppose an investigator had to decide which of two alternative measuring instruments to use in a study. One instrument was a "proven" one, with a reasonably high degree of pragmatic validity. The other instrument was newly developed, but the cost of administering it was less than the "proven" one. In this type of decisional situation, and a hypothesis of no difference, a type I error could lead to an opportunity cost, since the investigator would have decided to keep using the higher-cost instrument. On the other hand, a type II error could create direct monetary loss depending on the management decisions made on the basis of data provided by an "invalid" instrument.

GENERAL COMMENTS ON DATA TABULATION

Complete books could be written on various problems associated with data tabulation. Our discussion here will be comparatively brief. We consider basic aspects of the task: (1) the establishment of response categories, (2) editing and coding, and (3) tabulation. As simple as these steps are from a technical standpoint, they merit introductory discussion.

The Establishment of Categories

Analysis of any sizable array of data often requires that it be grouped into categories or classes. The early establishment of response categories has several advantages. It forces the analyst to consider alternative responses in more detail and often leads to improvements in the questionnaire or observation forms. It permits more-detailed instruction of interviewers with a resulting higher consistency of interpretation and reduction in editing problems. Precoding of collection forms is often possible and has the advantage of reducing the amount of transcription required, with a decrease in both processing errors and costs.

As desirable as the early establishing of categories is, it can sometimes be done only after the data have been collected. This is usually the case when free-answer, or open-end, questions, unstructured interviews, and projective techniques are used. The varieties of responses to questions such as "Why do you prefer brand X cooking sherry?" have startled many a researcher. Some of the classes of responses to questions such as these are unlikely to be anticipated, even by the experienced analyst.

The selection of categories is controlled by both the purposes of the study and the nature of the responses. Useful classifications meet the following conditions:

1. *Similarity of responses within categories.* Each category should contain responses that, for purposes of the study, are sufficiently similar that they can be considered homogeneous.

2. *Differences of responses between categories*. Differences in category descriptions should be great enough to disclose any important distinctions in the characteristic being examined.

3. *Mutually exclusive categories*. There should be an unambiguous description of categories, defined so that any response can be placed in only one category.

4. *Categories should be exhaustive*. The partitioning should provide categories for all responses.

The use of extensive open-end questions is a practice often associated with fledgling researchers. Open-end questions, of course, have their place in marketing research. However, the researcher should be aware of the difficulties that they can make for questionnaire coding and tabulation, not to mention their tendency to be more burdensome to the respondent. All of this is by way of saying that any open-end question should be carefully checked to see if a closed-end question (i.e., "check the appropriate box") can be substituted without doing violence to the intent of the question.

Editing and Coding

Editing

Editing is the process of reviewing the data to ensure maximum accuracy and unambiguity. Editing should be conducted as quickly as possible after the data have been collected. This applies to the editing of the collection forms used for pretesting as well as those for the full-scale project. Careful editing early in the collection process will often catch misunderstandings of instructions, errors in recording, and other problems at a stage when it is still possible to eliminate them from the later stages of the study. Early editing has the additional advantage of permitting the questioning of interviewers while the material is still relatively fresh in their minds.

Editing is normally centralized so as to ensure consistency and uniformity in treatment of the data. If the sample is not large, a single editor usually edits all the data to reduce variation in treatment. In those cases where the size of the project makes the use of more than one editor mandatory, it is usually best to assign each editor a different portion of the collection form to edit. In this way the same editor edits the same items on all forms, an arrangement that tends to improve both consistency and productivity.

Each collection form should be edited to ensure that the following requirements are fulfilled:

1. *Legibility of entries*. Obviously the data must be legible in order to be used. If an entry cannot be deciphered, and clarification of it cannot be obtained from the interviewer, it is sometimes possible to infer what it should be from other data on the form. In cases where any real doubt exists about the meaning of the entry, however, it should not be used.

2. *Completeness of entries*. On a fully structured collection form, the absence of an entry is ambiguous. It may mean that the interviewer failed to attempt to

obtain the data, that the respondent could not or would not provide it, or that there was a failure to record collected data. If the omission was the result of the interviewer's not recording the data, prompt questioning of the interviewer may provide the missing entry. If the omission was the result of either of the first two possible causes, it is still desirable to know which was the case.

3. *Consistency of entries.* As is the case with two watches that show different times, an entry that is inconsistent with another raises the question of which is correct. (If a respondent family is indicated as being a "nonuser" of cooking sherry, for example, and a later entry indicates that they purchased six bottles during the past month, an obvious question arises as to which is correct.) Again, such discrepancies should be cleared up by questioning of the interviewer, if it is possible to do so. When they cannot be resolved, discarding both entries is usually the wisest course of action.

4. *Accuracy of entries.* An editor should keep an eye out for any indications of inaccuracies of the data. Of particular importance is the detecting of any repetitive response patterns in the reports of individual interviewers. Such patterns may well be indicative of systematic interviewer bias or dishonesty.

Coding

Coding is the process by which responses are assigned to data categories and symbols (usually numbers) are assigned to identify them with the categories. *Precoding* results when codes are assigned to categories on structured questionnaires and observation forms *before* the data are collected. The interviewer, in effect, does the coding in this situation when interpreting the response and deciding into which category it should be placed.

Postcoding, the assignment of codes to responses *after* the data are collected, is required for responses reported on unstructured forms. The assignment of codes to responses is normally done at the same time that the data are edited. Careful interpretation and good judgment are required to ensure that the meaning of the response and the meaning of the category are consistently and uniformly matched.

An example of a simple and prevalent response that is often miscoded is the familiar "Don't Know" (DK). A respondent may give this reply for a variety of reasons; it may actually mean that the answer to the question is not known. On the other hand, the respondent may be confused as to the meaning of the question, or the reply is used to avoid giving an explicit answer. Good question construction and interviewing can do much to reduce the ambiguity of "Don't Know" answers. Careful coding can also assist in reducing this mismatching of response and category meaning.

Good coding requires training and supervision. The editor–coder should be provided with written instructions, including examples. He or she should be exposed to the interviewing or observing of respondents (whichever procedure is being used to collect the data) to become acquainted with the process and problems of collecting the data, thus providing aid in its interpretation. The coder also should be aware of the computer routines that are expected to be applied, insofar as they may require certain kinds of data formats.

Coding is an activity that should not be taken lightly. Improper coding can lead to poor analyses. Whenever possible (and cost allows) more than one person should do the coding, specifically the postcoding. By comparing the results of the various coders, a process known as determining *intercoder reliability,* any inconsistencies can be brought out into the open. In addition to the obvious purpose of eliminating them, the discovery of inconsistencies sometimes points to the need for additional categories for data classification and may sometimes mean that there is need to combine some of the categories.

Tabulation

Tabulating is the final step in the process. Tabulating is simply the counting of the number of responses in data categories.

The basic tabulation is the *simple tabulation,* often called the *marginal tabulation,* and familiar to all students of elementary statistics as the *frequency distribution.* A simple tabulation consists of a count of the number of responses that occur in each of the data categories that comprise a variables. An example is given in Table 10-1.

A *cross tabulation* is one of the more commonly employed and useful forms of tabulation for analytical purposes. A *cross tabulation involves the simultaneous counting of the number of observations that occur in each of the data categories of two or more variables.* An example is given in Table 10-2. We shall examine the use of cross tabulations in detail later in the chapter.

Tabulation can be done either by hand or by one of several mechanical methods. The choice of the method of tabulation to be used in a particular case is a function of the number of categories of data, the size of the sample, and the amount and kind of analyses to be performed. With few categories, a small sample, and limited analysis, hand tabulation is the fastest and least expensive method. As the number of categories, the size of the sample, and the amount and complexity of analysis required increase, a point is reached at which machine tabulation becomes more efficient. (In large-scale survey firms, programs for performing cross tabulation are a highly valued resource.)

Machine tabulation requires that the data be translated into machine language and transposed onto an input medium—disks, magnetic tape, paper tape, etc.—that the machine will accept. Preparation of the data is more expensive and time-consuming and must be carefully checked and rechecked at various stages to keep errors at a minimum. Once prepared, however, the tabulation and running of analytic calculations can be done quickly.

TABLE 10-1   Simple Tabulation: Cooking Sherry Purchased in Past Three Months*

NUMBER OF QUARTS	NUMBER OF RESPONDENTS
0	350
1	75
2	50
3 or more	25
Total	500

*Hypothetical data.

TABLE 10-2 Cross Tabulation: Cooking Sherry Purchased in Past Three Months by Income Classes of Respondents*

	NUMBER OF QUARTS PURCHASED				
INCOME CLASS	*Zero*	*One*	*Two*	*Three or More*	*Total*
Less than $5,000	160	25	15	0	200
$5,000–$7,499	120	15	10	5	150
$7,500–$9,999	60	20	15	5	100
$10,000–$14,999	5	10	5	5	25
$15,000 and over	5	5	5	10	25
Total	350	75	50	25	500

*Hypothetical data.

Although the use of machine tabulation provides added flexibility and ease of manipulation of data, these very features require that judgment and restraint be exercised in planning the tabulations to be made. There is a common tendency for the researcher to decide that, since cross tabulations (and correlations) are so easily obtained, large numbers of tabulations should be run. Not only is the way in which these tabulations are used frequently methodologically unsound, but it is costly in machine time and the time of the analyst as well. For 50 variables there are 1,225 different two-variable cross tabulations that can be made. Only a relatively few of these are potentially useful in a typical study.

Summarizing Data

Summarization so as to facilitate the understanding and analysis of data is only partly accomplished by their tabulation into frequency distributions. It is also desirable to summarize data further by computing descriptive measures of them: *relative* measures such as the percentage of people who have purchased cooking sherry; *averages,* such as the mean amount of sherry purchased; and the amount of *variation* in the distribution, such as the range or standard deviation of the amount of sherry purchased.

The use of the word *descriptive* for these measures is somewhat misleading because it implies that their only role is to describe the distribution from which they were computed. While this is one of the roles they occupy, they are also used for drawing inferences and making decisions. That is, in many instances they are crucial for testing hypotheses. For example, the appendix to this chapter discusses analyzing differences in means and proportions. In a more general context, it has been pointed out that the "major results of any empirical study, regardless of whether the prime purpose is description, prediction, or explanation, are the descriptive statistics that indicate the nature and size of any obtained effects."[3]

When used properly, descriptive statistical measures reduce a set of data into simple,

[3]A. G. Sawyer and J. P. Peter, "The Significance of Statistical Significance Tests in Marketing Research," *Journal of Marketing Research*, 20 (May 1983), 125.

precise, and meaningful figures. Occasionally it is possible to reduce a distribution of data into summary measures that, for purposes of decision making, can be substituted for the entire distribution.

BASIC CONCEPTS OF ANALYZING ASSOCIATIVE DATA

The brief discussion of cross tabulations in the previous section marked the beginning of a major topic of this book—the analysis of associative data. Although we shall continue to be interested in the study of variation in a single variable (or a composite of variables), a large part of the rest of the book will focus on methods for analyzing how this variation is associated with variation in *other* variables.

One of the most striking trends that has taken place in marketing research methodology over the past decade is the attention accorded to *multivariate* statistical procedures. Today an imposing array of such procedures—multiple regression, analysis of variance, discriminant analysis, cluster analysis, multidimensional scaling—is being used in the description and analysis of associative data. The next section has been prepared as a bridge between the comparatively simple marginal and cross tabulations already discussed and the more sophisticated multivariate techniques that will command our attention in later chapters.

The computation of row or column percentages in the presentation of cross tabulations is taken up first. We then show how various insights can be obtained as one goes beyond two variables in a cross tabulation to three (or more) variables. In particular, examples are presented of how the introduction of a third variable can often refine or explain the observed association between the first two variables.

Chi-square analysis is the central technique for testing the *statistical significance* of association in cross-tabulated frequency data. This method is illustrated by means of several numerical examples. Related descriptive indexes for summarizing the *degree of agreement* between two categorical (nominal-scaled) variables are also described.

MORE ON CROSS TABULATION

Cross tabulation represents the simplest form of associative data analysis. At the minimum we can start out with only two variables, such as occupation and education, each of which is discretized into a set of exclusive and exhaustive categories. Such data are called *qualitative* or *categorical,* since each variable is assumed to be only nominal-scaled, and the analysis is known as *bivariate cross tabulation.* Bivariate cross tabulation is widely used in marketing applications to analyze variables at all levels of measurement. In fact it is the single most widely used bivariate technique in applied settings. Reasons for the continued popularity of bivariate cross tabulation include the following:[4]

    1. They provide a means of data display and analysis that is clearly interpretable even to the less statistically inclined researcher or manager.

[4]Lawrence F. Feick, "Analyzing Marketing Research Data with Association Models," *Journal of Marketing Research,* 21 (November 1984), 376.

2. A series of bivariate tabulations provides insights into complex marketing phenomena that might be lost in a single multivariate analysis.

3. The clarity of interpretation affords a more readily constructed link between market research and market action.

4. Consideration of bivariate cross tabulations may lessen the problems of sparse cell values, which can plague the interpretation of discrete multivariate analyses.

The entities being cross-classified are often called *units of association*. Usually they will be people, objects, or events. The cross tabulation, at its simplest, consists of a simple count of the number of entities that fall into each of the possible categories of the cross-classification.[5]

However, we usually want to do more than show the raw frequency data. At the very least, row or column percentages (or both) are usually computed. Indeed, most computerized tabulation programs perform this step on a routine basis.

Percentages

The simple mechanics of calculating percentages are known to all of us. We are all also aware that the general purpose of percentages is to serve as a relative measure; that is, they are used to indicate more clearly the relative size of two or more numbers.

The ease and simplicity of calculation, the general understanding of its purpose, and the near universal applicability of the percent statistic have made it the most widely used statistical tool in marketing research. Yet its simplicity of calculation is sometimes deceptive, and the understanding of its purpose is frequently insufficient to ensure sound application and interpretation. The result is that the percent statistic is often the source of misrepresentations, either inadvertent or intentional.

Two problems in using percentages often crop up: (1) the direction in which percentages should be computed and (2) the interpretation of percentage change. Both these problems can be illustrated by a small numerical example.

Let us assume that an advertiser of salad dressings was interested in testing the effectiveness of spot TV ads in increasing consumer *awareness* of one of its brands—called *Gala*—that had been on the market for only four months. Two geographic areas were chosen for the test: (1) test area A and (2) control area B. The test area received a media weight of five 15-second television spots per week over an eight-week period, whereas the control area received no spot TV at all. (Other forms of advertising were equal between areas.)

Telephone interviews were conducted before and after the test in each of the areas. Respondents were asked to state all the brands of salad dressing they could think of, on an unprompted basis. If Gala was mentioned, it was assumed that this constituted consumer awareness of the brand. However, as it turned out, sample sizes differed across all four

---

[5]Excellent discussions of ways to analyze cross tabulations can be found in O. Hellevik, *Introduction to Causal Analysis: Exploring Survey Data by Crosstabulation* (Beverly Hills, Calif.: Sage, 1984); J. A. Davis, *Elementary Survey Analysis* (Englewood Cliffs, N.J.: Prentice-Hall, 1971); and Hans Zeisel, *Say It with Figures*, 4th ed. (New York: Harper & Row, 1957). This section of the chapter is based on Ziesel's discussion.

TABLE 10-3   Aware of Gala Salad Dressing—Before and After Spot TV

	BEFORE SPOT TV			AFTER SPOT TV		
	Aware	*Not Aware*	*Total*	*Aware*	*Not Aware*	*Total*
Test area	250	350	600	330	170	550
Control area	160	240	400	160	220	380
Total	410	590	1,000	490	390	880

sets of interviews. (This common fact of survey life increases the value of computing percentages.)

Table 10-3 shows the original frequency tables that were compiled on a before-and-after-test basis. (All four samples were independent samples.) Interpretation of Table 10-3 is hampered because the data are expressed as raw frequencies and different bases are involved. Accordingly, Table 10-4 shows the data in percentages based on column totals while Table 10-5 shows percentages based on row totals. Which of these tables— Table 10-4 or Table 10-5—is the more useful for analytical purposes?

Direction in Which to Compute Percentages

In examining the relationship between two variables, it is often clear from the context that one variable is more or less the independent or control variable while the other is the dependent or criterion variable. In cases where this distinction is clear, the rule is to *compute percentages across the dependent variable*.

In the example of Table 10-3 we would expect that experimental area (test versus control) is the control variable and awareness the dependent variable. Accordingly, Table 10-5 is the preferred way to express the percentages. We note that, before the spot TV campaign, the percentage of respondents who are aware of Gala is almost the same between test and control areas: 42% and 40%, respectively.

However, after the campaign, the test-area awareness level moves up to 66%, while the control-area awareness (42%) stays almost the same. (Presumably the small increase of 2 percentage points reflects either sampling variability or the effect of other factors that might be serving to increase awareness of Gala in the control area.)

On the other hand, computing percentages across the independent variable in Table

TABLE 10-4   Aware of Gala—Test versus Control, Percentages of Column Totals

	BEFORE SPOT TV			AFTER SPOT TV		
	Aware	*Not Aware*	*Total*	*Aware*	*Not Aware*	*Total*
Test area	61	59	60	67	44	57
Control area	39	41	40	33	56	43
Total	100	100	100	100	100	100

TABLE 10-5   Aware of Gala—Test versus Control, Percentages of Row Totals

| | BEFORE SPOT TV | | | AFTER SPOT TV | | |
	Aware	*Not Aware*	*Total*	*Aware*	*Not Aware*	*Total*
Test area	42	58	100	66	34	100
Control area	40	60	100	42	58	100

10-4 makes little sense. We note that 61% of the aware group (before the spot TV campaign) originates from the test area; however, this is mainly a reflection of the differences in total sample sizes between test and control areas.

After the campaign we note that the percentage of aware respondents in the control area is only 33%, versus 39% before the campaign. This may be erroneously interpreted as indicating that spot TV beamed to the test area *depressed* awareness in the control area. But we know this to be false from our earlier examination of Table 10-5.

It is not always the case that one variable is clearly the independent or control variable while the other is the dependent or criterion variable. This should pose no particular problem as long as we agree, for analysis purposes, which variable is to be considered the control variable. Indeed, cases often arise in which each of the variables in turn serves as the "independent" and "dependent" variable.

A useful aid to thinking about which way to compute percentages is to consider the problem in *conditional probability* terms. In Table 10-5 we are appropriately interested in the estimated conditional probabilities:

	BEFORE	AFTER
$P(\text{aware} \mid \text{test})$	0.42	0.66
$P(\text{aware} \mid \text{control})$	0.40	0.42

On the other hand, it makes little sense to be interested in the estimated conditional probabilities:

$$P(\text{test} \mid \text{aware}) \text{ or } P(\text{control} \mid \text{aware})$$

since respondents are assigned to test or control groups before (and independently of) their measurement on product awareness.

Interpretation of the Percentage Change

A second problem that arises in the use of percentages in cross tabulations is choosing the method to be used in measuring *differences* in percentages. Three principal ways for portraying percentage change are:

1. The absolute difference in percentages
2. The relative difference in percentages
3. The percentage of possible change in percentages

The same example can be used to illustrate the three methods.

Table 10-6 shows the percentage of respondents who are aware of Gala before and after the spot TV campaign in the test and control areas. First, we note that the test-area respondents displayed a greater *absolute* increase in awareness. The increase for the test-area respondents is 24 percentage points, while that for the control-area respondents is only 2 percentage points.

The *relative* increase in percentage is $[(66 - 42)]/42] \times 100 = 57\%$ and $[(42 - 40)/40] \times 100 = 5\%$, respectively, for test- and control-area respondents.

The *percentage of possible* increase for the test area is computed by first noting that the maximum percentage-point increase that could have occurred is $100 - 42 = 58$ points. The increase actually registered is 24 percentage points, or $100(24/58) = 41\%$ of the maximum possible. That of the control area is $100(2/60) = 3\%$ of the maximum possible.

In terms of the illustrative problem all three methods give consistent results in the sense that the awareness level in the test area undergoes greater change than that in the control area. However, in other situations conflicts among the measures may arise.

The *absolute difference* method is simple to use and requires only that the distinction between percentage and percentage points be understood. The *relative differences* method can be misleading, particularly if the base for computing the percentage change is small. The *percentage of possible difference* takes cognizance of the greater difficulty associated with obtaining increases in awareness as the difference between potential-level and realized-level decreases. In some studies all three measures are used, inasmuch as they emphasize different aspects of the relationship.

Introducing a Third Variable into the Analysis

Cross tabulation of marketing research data need not stop with two variables. Often much can be learned about the original two-variable association through the introduction of a third variable. As we shall illustrate, the third variable may refine or explain the original relationship. In some cases, it may show that the two variables are related even though no apparent relationship exists before the third variable is introduced. These ideas are most easily explained by numerical examples.

TABLE 10-6   Aware of Gala—Percentages Before and After the Spot TV Campaign

	BEFORE THE CAMPAIGN	AFTER THE CAMPAIGN
Test area	42	66
Control area	40	42

TABLE 10-7   Adoption of Message Recorder—Percentage by Respondent Age

	<35 Years	*≥35 Years*
Adopters	37	23
Nonadopters	63	77
Total	100	100
Number of cases:	300	300

Consider the situation facing a marketing researcher who works for a company that specializes in telecommunications equipment for the residential market. The company had recently test-marketed a new device for the automatic recording of home telephone messages. Several months after introduction a telephone survey was taken in which respondents in the test area were asked whether they had adopted the innovation. The total number of respondents interviewed was 600.

One of the variables of major interest to the marketing researcher is the age of the respondent. Based on earlier studies of the residential market, it appeared that adopters of the firm's new products tended to be less than 35 years old. Accordingly, the marketing researcher decides to look at the current data by means of a cross tabulation between adoption and respondent age. Respondents are classified into the categories "under 35 years" (<35) and "equal to or greater than 35 years" ($≥35$) and then cross-classified by adoption or not. Table 10-7 shows the cross tabulation. As noted from Table 10-7, the total sample of 600 is split evenly between those who are <35 and those who are $≥35$ years of age. Younger respondents display a higher percentage of adoption (37%) than older respondents (23%).

Example 1

The researcher wonders whether this finding would differ if a third variable, such as sex of the respondent, were introduced into the analysis. As it turned out, 400 respondents in the total sample were men while 200 were women. To simplify the three-way table, the researcher decides to show only the percentage of adopters, since 100 minus this percentage equals the percentage of nonadopters.

Table 10-8 shows the results of introducing sex as a third classificatory variable. In the case of men, 50% of the younger men adopt compared with only 30% of the older men. In the case of women, the percentages of adoption are much closer. Even here,

TABLE 10–8   Adoption—Percentage by Sex and Age

	MEN		WOMEN	
	<35 Years	*≥35 Years*	*<35 Years*	*≥35 Years*
Adopters	50	30	11	9
Number of cases:	200	200	100	100

however, younger women show a slightly higher percentage of adoption (11%) than older women (9%).

The effect of sex on the original association between adoption and age is to *refine* that association *without changing its basic character:* younger respondents show a higher incidence of adoption than older respondents. However, what can now be said is: If the respondent is a man, the *differential* effect of age on adoption is much more pronounced than if the respondent is a woman.

Figure 10-1 shows the same type of information graphically. The height of the bars within each rectangle represents the percentage of respondents who are adopters. The relative width of the bars denotes the relative size of the categories—men versus women—representing the third variable, sex. The shaded portions of the bars denote the percentage adopting by sex, while the dashed line represents the weighted average percentage *across* the sexes. It is easy to see from the figure that adoption differs by age group (37% versus 23%). Furthermore, the size of the difference depends on the sex of the respondent: Men display a relatively higher rate of adoption, compared with women, in the *younger* age category.

Although not illustrated here, we could also have the cases where adoption is higher for men in the younger age group, while for women:

1. There is *no difference* in adoption by age group.
2. The adoption rate is *lower* for younger than for older women.

Any of these cases could be compatible with the general direction of the two-way summary in Table 10-7.

However, be that as it may, we do note from Table 10-7 that adoption and age are associated to begin with; that is, the rate of adoption *differs* between young and old respondents. Next, let us assume a case in which we first observe *no difference* between adoption and age.

Figure 10-1   Adoption—Percentage by Age and Sex

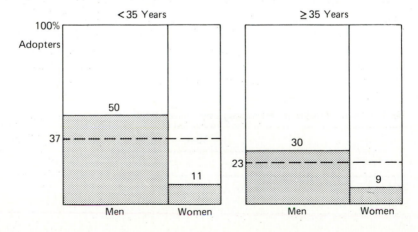

TABLE 10-9   Adoption—Percentage by Respondent Age

	<35 Years	*≥35 Years*
Adopters	50	50
Nonadopters	50	50
	100	100
Number of cases:	300	300

Example 2

In this second example assume that the association between adoption and age is now shown by Table 10-9. As noted, it would appear that the percentage of adopters is not affected by age. In each case the percentage of adoption is the same, namely 50%.

In this case let us assume that the effect of sex takes the form shown in Table 10-10 and Figure 10-2. As can be observed from either the table or the figure, the introduction of sex as a third variable shows that there is a strong association between adoption and age but that this association runs in *opposite directions* for men versus women. The overall effect is to suggest that adoption and age are *not* associated (when the effect of sex is not held constant).

Example 2 is an illustration of what is often called a *suppressor* effect. That is, failure to control on sex differences suppresses the relationship between adoption and age to the point where there appears to be no association at all. However, once we hold the level of sex constant—by tabulating adoption by age *within* the level of sex—the association becomes evident.

Example 3

As an additional illustration of what might happen when a third variable (sex) is introduced, consider the situation of Table 10-11. In this example we see that the association between adoption and age is not affected at all by the introduction of sex.

In this case sex is *independent* of the association between adoption and age. Although a figure is not shown for this simple case, it should be clear that the bars for the two age groups—within the separate men and women classes—will look exactly the same. Furthermore, the total-sample adoption percentage will be 60%. Tabulation of adoption by sex (across the two age categories) will show 50% adopters for both the men and women categories.

TABLE 10–10   Adoption—Percentage by Sex and Age

	MEN		WOMEN	
	<35 Years	*≥35 Years*	*<35 Years*	*≥35 Years*
Adopters	35	65	80	20
Number of cases:	200	200	100	100

Figure 10-2 Adoption—Percentage by Age and Sex

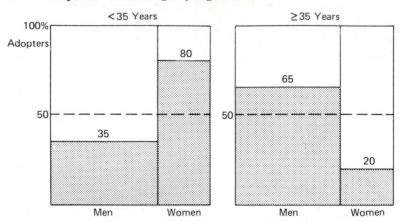

Our discussion so far about the various ways the original relationship can be modified has *assumed that sex was not related to the initial independent variable, age.* However, a fourth possibility exists in which the original relationship disappears upon the introduction of a third variable. Behavioral scientists often use the term *explanation* for this case. In order for the original association to vanish it is necessary that the third variable, sex, be *associated* with the original independent variable, age.

Example 4

To illustrate the idea of third-variable explanation, consider the new association between adoption and age that is shown in Table 10-12. Judging from this table it would appear to be the case that a higher percentage of adopters is drawn from the younger age group.

However, let us now consider introducing sex as the third variable. Table 10-13 shows the cross classification within each level of the third variable, men versus women. As can be observed, within each separate category of sex, there is *no difference* in the percentage of adopters. The apparent relationship between adoption and sex is due solely to the *difference in the relative size of the subsamples of men versus women within the two age categories.*

Figure 10-3 shows this effect graphically. In the case of the <35 age group there

TABLE 10–11 Adoption—Percentage by Sex and Age

	MEN		WOMEN	
	<35 Years	*≥35 Years*	*<35 Years*	*≥35 Years*
Adopters	60	40	60	40
Number of cases:	200	200	100	100

TABLE 10-12 Adoption—Percentage by Respondent Age

	<35 Years	≥35 Years
Adopters	50	35
Nonadopters	50	65
	100	100
Number of cases:	300	300

are 200 men and 100 women. However, in the ≥35 age group, there are 50 men and 250 women. These differences in subsample size affect the weighted-average percentages that are shown as dashed lines in the rectangles.

In the present case the sex variable is said to *explain* the (apparent) relationship between adoption and age. As observed from Table 10-13 and Figure 10-3, the percentage of adopters is *not* associated with age, once the data are examined separately for men and women.

Recapitulation

Representations of three-variable association can involve the following possibilities, as illustrated by the preceding adoption–age–sex example:

1. Adoption and age exhibit initial association; this association is still maintained in the aggregate but is *refined* by the introduction of the sex variable.
2. Adoption and age do not appear to be associated. However, controlling on the variable, sex, reveals *suppressed* association between the first two variables *within* the separate categories of men and women.
3. Adoption and age are not associated to begin with; furthermore, controlling on the *independent* variable, sex, does not change the situation.
4. Adoption and age exhibit initial association, which then disappears upon the introduction of the *explanatory* variable, sex.

Although the preceding examples were contrived to illustrate the concepts, none of these cases is all that unusual in practice. It goes almost without saying that the introduction of a third variable can often be useful in the interpretation of two-variable cross tabulations.

However, the reader should be aware of the fact that we have deliberately used the phrase *associated with*, not *caused by*. Association of two or more variables does *not*

TABLE 10–13 Adoption—Percentage by Sex and Age

	Men		Women	
	<35 Years	≥35 Years	<35 Years	≥35 Years
Adopters	60	60	30	30
Number of cases:	200	50	100	250

Figure 10-3   Adoption—Percentage by Age and Sex

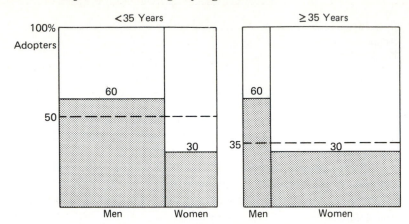

imply causation, and this statement is true regardless of our preceding efforts to refine some observed two-variable association through the introduction of a third variable.

In principle, of course, we could cross-tabulate four or even more variables with the possibility of obtaining further insight into lower-order (e.g., two-variable) associations. However, somewhere along the line, a problem arises in maintaining an adequate cell size for all categories. Unless sample sizes are extremely large in the aggregate and the number of categories per variable is relatively small, most cross tabulations rarely can deal with more than three variables at a time.[6] (Indeed, in practice most routine applications of cross tabulation involve only two variables at a time.)

As noted in Table 10-8, there are definite advantages associated with having a two-category criterion variable: adoption versus nonadoption. (In this case we can simplify the presentation by ignoring the complementary percentage of nonadoption.) In many applications, however, the criterion variable will have more than two categories. Cross tabulations can still be prepared in the usual manner, although they become somewhat more tedious to examine.

Up to this point we have considered cross tabulations at only a descriptive, content-oriented level. It is now time to consider ways to test whether the association observed in various cross tabulations is *statistically significant*. In many cases this involves testing hypotheses concerning the form of the population frequency distribution or hypotheses that involve comparing populations. Thus, nonparametric statistical methods, rather than parametric methods, must be used.

There are many nonparametric tests.[7] Which one is appropriate for analyzing a set of marketing research data depends on the level of measurement of the data, the number of samples that are involved, and, for multiple samples, whether they are independent or related (Exhibit 10-1).

---

[6]A further problem, independent of sample size, concerns the high degree of complexity of interpretation that is introduced by cross tabulations involving four or more variables.

[7]A classic exposition is presented in S. Siegel, *Nonparametric Statistics for the Behavioral Sciences* (New York: McGraw-Hill, 1956).

Exhibit 10-1   Selected Nonparametric Statistical Tests for One- and Two-Sample Cases

	LEVEL OF MEASUREMENT	
SAMPLE CASES	*Nominal*	*Ordinal*
One-sample	Binomial test χ^2 one-sample test	Kolmogorov–Smirnov one-sample test One-sample runs test
Two-sample Related samples	McNemar test for the significance of changes	Sign test Wilcoxon matched-pairs signed-ranks test
Independent samples	Fischer exact probability test χ^2 test for two independent samples	Median test Mann–Whitney U test Kolmogorov–Smirnov two-sample test Wald–Wolfowitz runs test

Source: Adapted from S. Siegel, *Nonparametric Statistics for the Behavioral Sciences* (New York: McGraw-Hill, 1956).

CHI-SQUARE TESTS

In addition to the substantive interpretation of cross-tabulation data, the marketing researcher is generally interested in two additional questions:

1. Is the observed association between the variables in the cross tabulation statistically significant?
2. How "strong" is this association?

Chi-square analysis is the technique that is typically used in answering the first question. The second question is answered by the computation of some type of *agreement index*.

Chi-square analysis can be used when the data consist of *counts or frequencies with which each category of a tabulation or cross tabulation appears*. Chi square is a useful technique for achieving the following objectives:

1. Determining the significance of sample deviations from assumed theoretical distributions; that is, finding out whether certain models fit the data. This is typically called a *goodness-of-fit test*.
2. Determining the significance of observed association in cross tabulations involving two or more variables. This is typically called a *test of independence*.

The procedure involved in chi-square analysis is basically quite simple. We compare the observed (frequency) data with another set of "data" based on a set of theoretical frequencies. These theoretical frequencies may result from application of some specific model of the phenomenon being investigated—objective 1 above. Or we might use the special model that the frequency of occurrence of two or more characteristics is mutually independent—objective 2 above. As an illustration of this second use, we may hypothesize that the presence of characteristic A (e.g., a consumer's purchase of a specific product) is unrelated to characteristic B (the consumer's occupational status).

In either case we compute a measure (chi square) of the variation between actual and theoretical frequencies, under the null hypothesis that the model fits the facts. If the measure of variation is "high," we reject the null hypothesis at some specified alpha risk. If the measure is "low," we accept the null hypothesis that the model's output is in agreement with the actual frequencies.

Single Classification

Suppose that we are interested in the frequency of selection of two test packages presented to a sample of respondents. Test package A contains an attached coupon involving so many cents off on a subsequent purchase of the brand by the respondent. Test package B is the same package but, rather than an attached coupon, it contains an attached premium (a ballpoint pen) that the respondent may keep. The packages are presented simultaneously to each of a sample of 100 respondents and each respondent is asked to choose one of the two packages.

The frequency of choice is presented in the first column (labeled "Observed") of Table 10-14. We see that 63 respondents out of 100 select package A. Suppose that the marketing researcher believes the "true" probability of selecting A versus B to be 50–50 and that the observed 63–37 split reflects sampling fluctuations. The researcher's model, then, would predict an estimated frequency of 50–50. Are the observed frequencies compatible with this theoretical prediction? In chi-square analysis we set up the null hypothesis that the observed (sample) frequencies are consistent with those expected under application of the model.

We use the following notation. Assume that there are k categories and a random sample of n observations; each observation must fall into one and only one category. The observed frequencies are

$$f_i(i = 1,2,...,k); \sum_{i=1}^{k} f_i = n$$

TABLE 10-14   Observed versus Theoretical Frequencies (Test-Package Illustration)

PACKAGE	f_i OBSERVED	F_i PREDICTED	$f_i - F_i$	$(f_i - F_i)^2/F_i$
A	63	50	13	$169/50 = 3.38$
B	37	50	−13	$169/50 = 3.38$
Total	100	100		6.76

The theoretical frequencies are

$$F_i(i = 1,2,\ldots,k); \sum_{i=1}^{k} F_i = n$$

In the problem above,

$$f_1 = 63, f_2 = 37, F_1 = 50, F_2 = 50, n = 100$$

We next compute the chi-square statistic:

$$\chi^2 = \sum_{i=1}^{k} \frac{(f_i - F_i)^2}{F_i}$$

In the one-way classification of the problem, the statistic above is approximately distributed as chi square with $k - 1$ degrees of freedom. In our problem we have only two categories and, hence, 1 degree of freedom. Table A-3 in Appendix A at the end of this book shows the appropriate distribution.

In Table A-3 the tabular chi-square value for $\alpha = 0.05$ and $k - 1 = 1$ is 3.84. If the null hypothesis is true, the probability of getting a chi-square value greater than 3.84 is 0.05. Since our computed chi-square value is 6.76 (see Table 10-14), we *reject* the hypothesis that the output of the theoretical model corresponds with the observed frequencies. In using the chi-square table we note that only k, the number of categories, is pertinent, rather than the sample size n. (Sample size *is* important to the quality of the approximation and the power of the test.) A good rule of thumb, however, is that chi-square analysis should be used only when the *theoretical* frequencies in each cell exceed five; otherwise, the distribution in Table A-3 will not be a good approximation. Pragmatically, the "risk" is that with a theoretical frequency less than five, a single cell's chi-square value may be unusually high and, thus, unduly influence the overall value.

Two-Way Classification

In marketing research, observations may be cross-classified as, for example, when we are interested in testing whether occupational status is *associated* with brand loyalty. Suppose, for illustrative purposes, that a marketing researcher has assembled data on brand loyalty by consumers of a particular product class and also data on occupational status—white collar, blue collar, and unemployed/retired. The data for our hypothetical problem appear in Table 10-15. (Tables such as these are often called *contingency tables.*)

Our sample of 230 consumers suggests that *occupational status* may be associated with the characteristic *loyalty status*. But is the observed association a reflection of sampling variation? Expressed in probability terms, are the conditional probabilities of

TABLE 10-15   Observed versus Theoretical Frequencies (Brand-Loyalty Illustration)

Occupational Status	Highly Loyal	Moderately Loyal	Brand Switchers	Total
White-collar	30 (30.5)	42 (34.1)	18 (25.4)	90
Blue-collar	14 (22.1)	20 (24.5)	31 (18.4)	65
Unemployed/retired	34 (25.4)	25 (28.4)	16 (21.2)	75
Total	78	87	65	230

being highly loyal, moderately loyal, and brand switcher, given the type of occupational status, equal to their respective marginal probabilities?

In analyzing the problem by means of chi square, we make use of the marginal totals (columns and rows) in computing theoretical frequencies, given (the hypothesized) independence between the attributes *loyalty status* and *occupational status*. For example, we note from Table 10-15 that 78 out of a total of 230 respondents are highly loyal. If possession of this characteristic is independent of occupational status, we would expect that 78/230 of the 90 respondents (i.e., 30.5) classified as white-collar workers would be highly loyal. Similarly, 87/230 of the 90 (34.1) would be moderately loyal, and 65/230 of the 90 (25.4) would be brand switchers. In a similar fashion we can compute theoretical frequencies for each cell on the null hypothesis that *loyalty status* is statistically independent of *occupational status*.

The theoretical frequencies (under the null hypothesis) are computed and appear in parentheses in Table 10-15. The chi-square statistic is then calculated as follows:

$$\chi^2 = \frac{(30 - 30.5)^2}{30.5} + \frac{(42 - 34.1)^2}{34.1} + \frac{(18 - 25.4)^2}{25.4}$$

$$+ \frac{(14 - 22.1)^2}{22.1} + \frac{(20 - 24.5)^2}{24.5} + \frac{(31 - 18.4)^2}{18.4}$$

$$+ \frac{(34 - 25.4)^2}{25.4} + \frac{(25 - 28.4)^2}{28.4} + \frac{(16 - 21.2)^2}{21.2}$$

$$= 21.1$$

The appropriate number of degrees of freedom to use in this example is 4. In general, if we have R rows and C columns, the degrees of freedom associated with the chi-square statistic are equal to the product

$$(R - 1)(C - 1)$$

If we use a significance level of 0.05, the tabular value of chi square (Table A-3) is 9.488. Hence, we reject the hypothesis of independence between the characteristics *loyalty status* and *occupational status*.

When the number of observations in a cell is less than 10 (or where a 2×2 contingency table is involved), a correction factor must be applied to the formula for chi square. The numerator within the summation sign becomes $(|f_i - F_i| - 1/2)^2$ where the value 1/2 is the Yates *continuity correction*. This correction factor adjusts for the use of a continuous distribution to estimate probability in a discrete distribution.

Chi-square analysis can be extended to deal with more classificatory variables than two. No new principles are involved, but the procedure naturally becomes more tedious. Two characteristics of the technique should be borne in mind, however. First, chi-square analysis deals with counts (frequencies) of data. If the data are expressed in percentage form, they should be converted to absolute frequencies. Second, the technique assumes that the observations are drawn independently.

Other Tests

One reason for the widespread use of chi square in cross-tabulation analysis is that most computer computational routines show the statistic as part of output, or at least it is an option that the analyst can choose. Sometimes the data available are stronger than simple nominal measurement and are ordinal. In this situation other tests are more powerful than chi square. Three regularly used tests are the *Wilcoxon Rank Sum* (T), the *Mann–Whitney U,* and the *Kolmogorov–Smirnov* test.

The Wilcoxon "T" test is used for dependent samples in which the data are collected in matched pairs. This test takes into account both the direction of differences within pairs of observations and the relative magnitude of the differences. The Wilcoxon matched-pairs signed-ranks test gives more weight to pairs showing large differences between the two measurements than to a pair showing a small difference. To use this test, measurements must at least be ordinally scaled within pairs. In addition, ordinal measurement must hold for the differences between pairs.

This test has many practical applications in marketing research. For instance, it may be used to test whether a promotional campaign has had an effect on attitudes. An ordinal scaling device, such as a semantic differential, can be used to measure attitudes toward, say, a bank. Then, after a special promotional campaign, the same sample would be given the same scaling device. Changes in values of each scale could be analyzed by this Wilcoxon test.

With ordinal measurement and two independent samples, the Mann–Whitney U test may be used to test whether the two groups are from the same population. This is a relatively powerful nonparametric test, and it is an alternative to the Student *t* test when the analyst cannot meet the assumptions of the *t* test or when measurement is at best ordinal. Both one- and two-tailed tests can be conducted.

The Kolmogorov–Smirnov two-sample test is a test of whether two independent samples come from the same population or from populations with the same distribution. This test is sensitive to any kind of difference in the distributions from which the two samples were drawn—differences in location (central tendency), dispersion, skewness, and so on. This characteristic of the test makes it a very versatile test. Unfortunately, the test does not by itself show what kind of difference exists. There is a Kolmogorov–

Smirnov one-sample test that is concerned with the agreement between an observed distribution of a set of sample values and some specified theoretical distribution. In this case it is a goodness-of-fit test similar to single-classification chi-square analysis.

INDEXES OF AGREEMENT

Chi-square analysis is appropriate for making statistical tests of independence in cross tabulations. Usually, however, we are interested in the *strength* of association as well as the statistical significance of association. This concern is for what is known as *substantive* or *practical* significance. An association is substantively significant when it is statistically significant and of sufficient strength. Unlike statistical significance, however, there is no simple numerical value to compare with and considerable research judgment is necessary. Although such judgment is subjective it need not be completely arbitrary. The nature of the problem can offer some basis for judgment, and common sense can indicate that the degree of association is too low in some cases and high enough in others.[8]

Statisticians have devised a plethora of indexes—often called *indexes of agreement*—for measuring the strength of association between two variables in a cross tabulation. The main descriptors for classifying the various indexes are

1. Whether the table is 2×2 or larger, $R \times C$
2. Whether one, both, or neither of the variables has categories that obey some natural order (e.g., age, income level, family size)
3. Whether association is to be treated symmetrically or whether we want to predict membership in one variable's categories from (assumed known) membership in the other variable's categories

Space does not permit coverage of even an appreciable fraction of the dozens of agreement indexes that have been proposed. Rather, we shall illustrate one commonly used index for 2×2 tables and two indexes that deal with different aspects of the larger $R \times C$ (row-by-column) tables.[9]

The 2 × 2 Case

The *phi correlation coefficient* is a useful agreement index for the special case of 2×2 tables in which both variables are dichotomous. Moreover, an added bonus is the fact that phi equals the product-moment correlation—a cornerstone of multivariate methods—that one would obtain if he or she correlated the two variables expressed in coded $0 - 1$ form.

---

[8]David Gold, "Statistical Tests and Substantive Significance," *American Sociologist,* 4 (February 1969), 44.

[9]The usefulness of some association models for ordered cross classifications are illustrated in Feick, "Analyzing Marketing Research Data," pp. 376–86.

TABLE 10-16 Does Hair Have Enough Body versus Body Inclusion in Ideal Set

	HAIR HAVE ENOUGH BODY?		
	No	*Yes*	*Total*
Body included in ideal set	26 (A)	8 (B)	34
Body excluded from ideal set	17 (C)	33 (D)	50
Total	43	41	84

To illustrate, consider the 2×2 cross tabulation in Table 10-16, taken from a study relating to shampoos. We wish to see if inclusion of the shampoo benefit of "body" in the respondent's ideal set is associated with the respondent's indication that her hair lacks natural "body." We first note from the table that high frequencies appear in the cells: (1) "body" included in ideal set and "no" to the question of whether her hair has enough (natural) body, and (2) "body" excluded from the ideal set and "yes" to the same question.

Before computing the phi coefficient, first note the labels, A, B, C, and D assigned to the four cells in Table 10-16. The phi coefficient is defined as

$$\phi = \frac{AD - BC}{\sqrt{(A + B)(C + D)(A + C)(B + D)}}$$

$$= \frac{26(33) - 8(17)}{\sqrt{(26 + 8)(17 + 33)(26 + 17)(8 + 33)}}$$

$$= 0.417$$

The value 0.417 is also what would be found if an ordinary product-moment correlation, to be described in Chapter 11, is computed across the 84 pairs of numbers where the code values

- Body included in ideal set $\Rightarrow 1$
- Body excluded from ideal set $\Rightarrow 0$
- Hair have enough body? $\begin{cases} \text{No} \Rightarrow 1 \\ \text{Yes} \Rightarrow 0 \end{cases}$

are used to identify the responses.[10]

The phi coefficient can vary from -1 to 1 (just like the ordinary product-moment correlation). However, in any given problem the upper limit of phi depends on the relationships among the marginals. Specifically, a phi coefficient of -1 (perfect negative

---

[10]This is a nice feature of phi in the sense that standard computer programs for calculating product-moment correlations can be used for dichotomous variables.

association) or 1 (perfect positive association) assumes that the marginal totals of the first variable are *identical* to those of the second.[11] The more different the marginals, the lower the upper limit that the (absolute) value of phi can assume.

The phi coefficient assumes the value of zero if the two variables are statistically independent (as would be shown by a chi-square value that is also zero). Indeed, the absolute value of phi is related to chi square by the expression

$$\phi = \sqrt{\frac{\chi^2}{n}}$$

where n is the total frequency (sample size). This is a nice feature of phi, in the sense that it can be computed quite easily after chi square has been computed. Note, however, that phi, unlike chi square, is *not* affected by total sample size, since we have the divisor n in the above formula to adjust for differences in sample size.

The R × C Case

One of the most popular agreement indexes for summarizing the degree of association between two variables in a cross tabulation of R rows and C columns is the *contingency coefficient*. This index is also related to chi square and is defined as

$$C = \sqrt{\frac{\chi^2}{\chi^2 + n}}$$

where n is again the total sample size. From Table 10-16 we can first determine that chi square is equal to 14.61, which, with 1 degree of freedom, is significant beyond the 0.01 level.

We can then find the contingency coefficient C as:

$$C = \sqrt{\frac{14.61}{14.61 + 84}}$$

$$= 0.385$$

As may be surmised, the contingency coefficient lies between zero and 1, with zero reserved for the case of statistical independence (a chi-square value of zero). However, unlike the phi coefficient, the contingency coefficient can never attain a maximum value

---

[11]Looking at the letters (A, B, C, D) of Table 10-16, assume that the row marginals equaled the column marginals; then, $\phi = 1$ if $B = C = 0$; similarly, $\phi = -1$ if $A = D = 0$.

of unity. For example, in a 2×2 table,[12] C cannot exceed 0.707. In a 4×4 table its upper limit is 0.87. Therefore, contingency coefficients computed from different-sized tables are not easily comparable.

However, like phi, the contingency coefficient is easy to compute from chi square; moreover, like phi, its significance has already been tested in the course of running the chi-square test.

Both phi and the contingency coefficient are symmetric measures of association. Occasions often arise in the analysis of $R \times C$ tables (or the special case of 2×2 tables) where we desire to compute an *asymmetric* measure of the extent to which we can reduce errors in predicting categories of one variable from knowledge of the categories of some other variable. Goodman and Kruskal's *lambda-asymmetric coefficient* can be used for this purpose.[13]

To illustrate the lambda-asymmetric coefficient, let us return to the cross tabulation of Table 10-16. Suppose that we wished to predict what category—"no" versus "yes"— a randomly selected person would fall in when asked the question, "Does your hair have enough body?" If we had no knowledge of the row variable (whether that person included "body" in her ideal set or not), we would have only the *column* marginal frequencies to rely on.

Our best bet, given no knowledge of the row variable, is always to predict "no," the *higher* of the column marginal frequencies. As a consequence we shall be wrong in 41 of the 84 cases, a probability error of $41/84 = 0.49$. Can we do better, in the sense of lower prediction errors, if we utilize information provided by the row variable?

If we know that "body" is included in the ideal set, we shall predict "no" and be wrong in only 8 cases. If we know that "body" is not included in the ideal set, we shall predict "yes" and be wrong in 17 cases. Therefore, we have reduced our number of prediction errors from 41 to $8 + 17 = 25$, a decrease of 16 errors. We can consider this error reduction *relatively*:

$$\lambda_{C|R} = \frac{\text{(number of errors in first case)} - \text{(number of errors in second case)}}{\text{number of errors in first case}}$$

$$= \frac{41 - 25}{41} = 0.39$$

In other words, 39% of the errors in predicting the column variable are eliminated by knowing the individual's row variable.

[12]As might be noticed by the reader, there is an algebraic relationship between phi and the contingency coefficient (if the latter is applied to the 2×2 table):

$$\phi^2 = \frac{C^2}{1 - C^2}$$

[13]See L. A. Goodman and W. H. Kruskal, "Measures of Association for Cross Classification," *Journal of the American Statistical Association*, 49 (December 1954), 732–64. However, the original development is contained in Louis Guttman, "An Outline of the Statistical Theory of Prediction," in *The Prediction of Personal Adjustment*, ed. Paul Horst, Social Science Research Council Bulletin 48 (New York, 1941).

A less cumbersome (but also less transparent) formula for lambda-asymmetric is

$$\lambda_{C|R} = \frac{\sum_{k=1}^{K} f_{kR}^* - F_C^*}{n - F_C^*} = \frac{(26 + 33) - 43}{84 - 43} = 0.39$$

where f_{kR}^* is the *maximum* frequency found within each subclass of the row variable, F_C^* is the *maximum* frequency among the marginal totals of the column variable, and n is the total number of cases.

Lambda-asymmetric varies between *zero,* indicating no ability at all to eliminate errors in predicting the column variable on the basis of the row variable, and 1, indicating an ability to eliminate all errors in the column variable predictions, given knowledge of the row variable.

Not surprisingly, we could reverse the role of criterion and predictor variables and find lambda-asymmetric for the row variable, given the column variable. In the case of Table 10-16, this is

$$\lambda_{R|C} = \frac{\sum_{l=1}^{L} f_{iC}^* - F_R^*}{n - F_R^*} = \frac{(26 + 33) - 50}{84 - 50} = 0.26$$

Note that in this case we simply reverse the roles of row and column variables.

Finally, if desired, we could find a *lambda-symmetric* index via a weighted averaging of $\lambda_{C|R}$ and $\lambda_{R|C}$. However, in the authors' opinion, lambda-asymmetric is of particular usefulness to the analysis of cross tabulations, since we often want to consider one variable as a predictor and the other as a criterion. Furthermore, lambda-asymmetric has a natural and useful interpretation as the percentage of total prediction errors that are eliminated in predicting one variable (e.g., the column variable) from another (e.g., the row variable). [14]

Computer Programs for Cross Tabulations

Virtually any computer installation has at least one program for constructing and analyzing cross tabulations from raw categorical data. This is true not only for the mainframe and minicomputer installation, but increasingly so for microcomputers (i.e., personal computers).

For microcomputers there are cross-tabulation programs that are included in a statistical package. In addition, there are programs that are designed primarily for cross

---

[14]Significance tests and confidence intervals are also available for either lambda-asymmetric or lambda-symmetric. See L. A. Goodman and W. H. Kruskal, "Measures of Association for Cross Classification: Appropriate Sampling Theory," *Journal of the American Statistical Association,* 88 (June 1963). 310–64.

tabulation and will present as output so-called report ready tables. In general, all these programs will include chi square for significance-testing purposes. However, the extent to which indexes of agreement are included varies widely. Since there are many software programs available and most of them are somewhat similar in type of output, it is difficult to state which one is "right" for a marketing researcher. At the very least this will depend on the hardware setup and the nature and size of data base to be analyzed. It will also be influenced by whether the researcher has access to a mainframe or minicomputer. Software packages including cross tabulations or basically only cross tabulations are available for these computers and are obviously more "powerful" and "versatile."

When it comes to computing agreement indexes, however, the major mainframe packages BMD, SPSS–X, and SAS (all of which have microcomputer versions) have few equals.[15] Their cross-tabulation programs can compute not only the measures discussed in this chapter but many others as well. A partial list of these is shown in Table 10-17.

The BMD–PIF program is designed basically for the analysis of two-way contingency tables. However, a special feature of the program allows the user to single out various third variables of interest and tabulate two-way tables for each category of any

TABLE 10-17   Some Agreement Indexes Obtained from Cross-Tabulation Programs of Mainframe Packages*

BMD–PIF:

For $R \times C$ tables with unordered categories: chi square; contingency coefficient; Cramer's V; maximum-likelihood chi square; Goodman and Kruskal's lambda, lambda-asymmetric, and tau-asymmetric; uncertainty coefficient

Additional outputs if the table is 2×2: phi; Yule's Q; Yule's Y; logarithm of the cross-product ratio; phi-max; C-max; Fisher's exact probability test

Additional measures if the rows and columns of $R \times C$ table are ordered: Spearman's rank correlation; Kendall's tau, Stuart's tau; Goodman and Kruskal's gamma, and gamma-asymmetric; Somer's d measure

SPSS^X CROSSTABS:

For $R \times C$ tables with unordered categories: chi square; contingency coefficients; Cramer's V; lambda (symmetric and asymmetric); uncertainty coefficient (symmetric and asymmetric)

Additional outputs if table is 2×2: phi; Fisher's exact probability test

For $R \times C$ tables with ordered categories: Kendall's tau-b, tau-c; gamma; Somer's d (symmetric and asymmetric); eta; Pearson's r

SAS FREQ

Essentially the same indexes as BMD–PIF

*Theoretical sources of indexes above are: L. A. Goodman and W. H. Kruskal, "Measures of Association for Cross Classification," *Journal of the American Statistical Association*, 49, (1954), 732–64; 58 (1963), 310–64; 67 (1972), 415–21; and Y.M.M. Bishop, S.E. Fienberg, and P.W. Holland, *Discrete Multivariate Analysis: Theory and Practice* (Cambridge, Mass.: MIT Press, 1975), Chap. 11.

[15]See W. J. Dixon, ed., *BMDP: Biomedical Computer Programs* (Berkeley: University of California Press, 1975); *SPSS^X User's Guide*, 2nd ed. (New York: McGraw-Hill, 1986); and *SAS User's Guide: Basics*, Version 5 ed. (Cary, N.C.: SAS Institute, 1985).

third variable that is selected. In contrast, the SPSS^X program CROSSTABS can provide a maximum of 8 or 10 dimensions per table depending on the command mode specified.

As noted from Table 10-17, several different indexes can be computed for the general $R \times C$ case. However, if the table also happens to be 2×2, additional indexes that are specific to this case can also be computed. Finally, if the categories of each variable follow some natural order, such as age, income, or family size, various *rank-correlation measures* can be computed as well.

In short, the mainframe programs provide a complete approach to all the topics considered in this chapter:

1. Computation of row and column percentages
2. Introduction of a third variable in describing association between some other pair of variables
3. Determining the statistical significance of the association observed in any cross tabulation of interest
4. Measuring the strength of that association by means of some type of agreement index

In practice, of course, the marketing researcher rarely needs to deal with more than one or two agreement indexes. Still it is comforting to know that these programs provide the flexibility for examining almost any kind of two-way table that one could find in marketing research applications, including tables with *ordered* classes.[16]

AN OVERVIEW OF MULTIVARIATE PROCEDURES

Chi square and the various agreement indexes discussed so far are typically used for analyzing association between two variables—what may be called bivariate data. In the remaining chapters of Part III and in Part IV, we shall be emphasizing *multivariate* data in which association among *three or more variables* is of primary interest. One of the first problems that crops up in analyzing association between variables concerns whether one variable *causes* another.

Association implies only that two or more variables tend to change together to a greater or lesser extent, depending on the degree of the association involved. If we measure the amount of mutual change and find it to be persistent in both direction and degree, we may *not* conclude that there is a necessary *causal* relationship such that one variable is dependent (effect) and the other variable, or variables, are independent (deterministic or probabilistic causes). It should be understood, then, that *association does not imply*

---

[16]For agreement measures involving (a) one nominal-scaled variable and one interval-scaled variable or (b) one nominal-scaled variable and one ordinal-scaled variable, the reader is referred to L. C. Freeman, *Elementary Applied Statistics* (New York: John Wiley, 1965).

causation.[17] (However, if a set of variables are causally related, they will be associated in some way.)

The Data Matrix

The raw input to any analysis of associative data consists of the *data matrix*. This is a rectangular array of entries whose informational content is to be summarized and portrayed in some way. For example, the computation of the mean and standard deviation of a single column of numbers is often done simply because we are unable to comprehend the meaning of the entire column of values. In so doing we often (willingly) forgo the full information provided by the data in order to understand some of its basic character-istics, such as central tendency and dispersion.

In virtually all marketing research studies we are concerned with variation in some characteristic, be it per capita consumption of coffee or TV viewing frequency. (If there is no variation in the characteristic under study, there is little need for statistical methods.) Our objective now, however, is to concentrate on accounting for the variation in one variable or group of variables in terms of *covariation* with other variables. When we analyze associative data, we hope to "explain" variation according to one or more of the following points of view:

1. Determination of the overall strength of association between the *criterion* and *predictor* variables (often called "dependent" and "independent" variables, re-spectively)
2. Determination of a function or formula by which we can estimate values of the criterion variable(s) from values of the predictor variable(s)
3. Determination of the statistical "confidence" in either or both of the above

In some cases of interest, however, we have no a priori basis for distinguishing between criterion and predictor variables. We may still be interested in their *interdependence* as a whole and the possibility of summarizing information provided by this interdependence in terms of other variables, often taken to be linear combinations of the original ones.

A Classification of Techniques for Analyzing Associative Data

The field of associative data analysis is vast; hence, it seems useful to enumerate various descriptors by which the field can be classified. The key notion underlying our classification is the data matrix. A conceptual illustration is shown in Table 10–18. We note that the table consists of a set of objects (the *n* rows) and a set of measurements on those

---

[17]Recently the field of causal-path analysis has been developed to aid in examining possible causal relations in correlational data. For an introduction to this field, see H. M. Blalock, Jr., *Causal Inferences in Nonexperimental Research* (Chapel Hill: University of North Carolina Press, 1962); R. Bagozzi, *Causal Models in Marketing* (New York: John Wiley, 1980); and Kent B. Monroe and Susan M. Petroshius, "Developing Causal Priorities in Marketing," Working Paper, Virginia Polytechnic Institute and State University, n.d.

TABLE 10-18 Illustrative Data Matrix

	VARIABLE						
OBJECT	1	2	3	$\cdots$	j	$\cdots$	m
1	X_{11}	X_{12}	X_{13}	$\cdots$	X_{1j}	$\cdots$	X_{1m}
2	X_{21}	X_{22}	X_{23}	$\cdots$	X_{2j}	$\cdots$	X_{2m}
3	X_{31}	X_{32}	X_{33}	$\cdots$	X_{3j}	$\cdots$	X_{3m}
.	.	.	.		.		.
.	.	.	.		.		.
.	.	.	.		.		.
i	X_{i1}	X_{i2}	X_{i3}	$\cdots$	X_{ij}	$\cdots$	X_{im}
.	.	.	.		.		.
.	.	.	.		.		.
.	.	.	.		.		.
n	X_{n1}	X_{n2}	X_{n3}	$\cdots$	X_{nj}	$\cdots$	X_{nm}

objects (the m columns). The objects may be people, things, concepts, or events. The variables are characteristics of the objects. The cell values represent the state of object i with respect to variable j. Cell values may consist of nominal-, ordinal-, interval-, or ratio-scaled measurements or various combinations of these as we go across columns.

There are many descriptors by which we can characterize methods for analyzing associative data.[18] Although not exhaustive (nor exclusive), the following represent the more common bases by which this activity can be classified:

1. Purpose of the study and the types of assertions desired by the researcher: What kinds of statements—descriptive or inferential—does the researcher wish to make?

2. Focus of research—emphasis on the objects (the whole profile or "bundle" of variables), the variables, or both.

3. Nature of the researcher's assumed *prior* judgments as to how the data matrix should be partitioned (subdivided) in terms of number of subsets of variables.

4. Number of variables in each of the partitioned subsets—the criterion versus predictor variables.

5. Type of association under study—linear, transformable to linear, or nonlinear.

6. Scales by which variables are measured—nominal, ordinal, interval, ratio, mixed.

All of these descriptors relate to certain decisions required of the researcher. Suppose there is interest in studying descriptive interrelationships among variables. If so, the researcher must make decisions about how to partition the set of columns (see Table 10-18) into subsets. He or she must also decide on the number of variables to include in

[18]An excellent classification, based on a subset of the descriptors shown here, has been provided by M. M. Tatsuoka and D. V. Tiedeman, "Statistics as an Aspect of Scientific Method in Research on Teaching," in *Handbook of Research on Teaching,* ed. N. L. Gage (Skokie, Ill.: Rand McNally, 1963), pp. 142–70.

each subset and on what type of relationship (linear, transformation to linear, nonlinear) is asserted to hold among the variables.

Most decisions about associative data analysis are based on the researcher's private model of how the data are interrelated and what features are useful for study. The choice of various public models for analysis (multiple regression, discriminant analysis, etc.) is predicted on prior knowledge of the characteristics of the statistical universe from which the data were obtained and knowledge of the assumption structure and objectives of each candidate technique.

Fortunately, we can make a few simplifications of the preceding descriptors. First, insofar as types of scales, all the multivariate techniques of this book require no stronger measurement than interval scaling. Second, except for Chapter 15 (which deals with various types of ordinal-scaling methods), we shall assume that (1) the variables are either nominal-scaled or interval-scaled, and (2) the functional form is linear in the parameters.[19] Even with these simplifying assumptions we shall be able to describe a wide variety of possible techniques, and these may vary from being relatively simple (Exhibit 10-2) to complex.

The principal descriptors of interest are now:

1. Whether the matrix is partitioned into subsets or kept intact
2. If partitioned into subsets of criterion and predictor variables, the number of variables in each subset
3. Whether the variables are nominal-scaled or interval-scaled

Analysis of Dependence

If we elect to partition the data matrix into criterion and predictor variables, the problem becomes one of analyzing *dependence structures*. This, in turn, can be broken down into two subcategories:

1. Single criterion/multiple predictor association
2. Multiple criterion/multiple predictor association

Multivariate techniques that deal with single criterion/multiple predictor association include such procedures as multiple regression, analysis of variance and covariance, two-group discriminant analysis, and automatic interaction detection.

Multivariate techniques that deal with multiple criterion/multiple predictor associ-

---

[19]While the original data may have been transformed by some nonlinear transformation (e.g., logarithmic), *linear in the parameters* means that all computed parameters *after* the transformation are of the first degree. For example, the function

$$Y = b_0 + b_1 X_1 + b_2 X_2 + \cdots + b_m X_m$$

is linear in the parameters. Note that b_0 is a constant, while the other parameters, $b_1, b_2, \ldots, b_m$ are all of the first degree. Moreover, none of the b_j's depends on the value of either its own X_j or any other X_k ($k \neq j$).

ation include such procedures as canonical correlation, multivariate analysis of variance and covariance, and multiple discriminant analysis.

Analysis of Interdependence

In some cases we may not wish to partition the data matrix into criterion and predictor subsets. If so, we refer to this case as analyzing *interdependence structures*.

Exhibit 10-2   Multivariate Analysis Can Be Simple

Not all multivariate analyses need to involve relatively complex and sophisticated statistical techniques. To illustrate, we consider an automobile dealer whose records indicated that less than 40 percent of its new car buyers remained loyal service customers after the 6,000 mile service. The company had hoped to increase this to at least 50 percent as a means of improving service department profits as well as stimulating repeat sales of new vehicles.

Fourteen attributes were identified as affecting service department patronage. A mail survey was conducted among new car purchasers between one and two years earlier. Respondents were asked two questions about each attribute: (1) how important is the feature, and (2) how well did the dealer perform. Mean importance and performance ratings from 284 respondents (45% return) are shown in the Table. These data were then plotted in two-dimensional space, as shown in the Figure.

Importance and Performance Ratings for Automobile Dealer's Service Department

ATTRIBUTE NUMBER	ATTRIBUTE DESCRIPTION	MEAN IMPORTANCE RATING*	MEAN PERFORMANCE RATING†
1	Job done right the first time	3.83	2.63
2	Fast action on complaints	3.63	2.73
3	Prompt warranty work	3.60	3.15
4	Able to do any job needed	3.56	3.00
5	Service available when needed	3.41	3.05
6	Courteous and friendly service	3.41	3.29
7	Car ready when promised	3.38	3.03
8	Perform only necessary work	3.37	3.11
9	Low prices on service	3.29	2.00
10	Clean up after service work	3.27	3.02
11	Convenient to home	2.52	2.25
12	Convenient to work	2.43	2.49
13	Courtesy buses and rental cars	2.37	2.35
14	Send out maintenance notices	2.05	3.33

*Ratings obtained from a four-point scale of "extremely important," "important," "slightly important," and "not important."
†Ratings obtained from a four-point scale of "excellent," "good," "fair," and "poor." A "no basis for judgment" category was also provided.

Importance-Performance Grid with Attribute Ratings for Automobile Dealer's Service Department

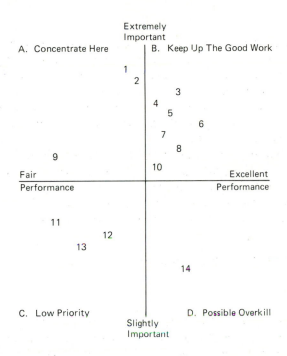

Interpretation of the importance-performance grid can be illustrated as follows:

    A.   **Concentrate here**   Customers feel that low service prices (Attribute 9) are very important but indicate low satisfaction with the dealer's performance.

    B.   **Keep up with the good work**   Customers value courteous and friendly service (Attribute 6) and are pleased with the dealer's performance.

    C.   **Low priority**   The dealer is rated low in terms of providing courtesy buses and rental cars (Attribute 13), but customers do not perceive this feature to be very important.

    D.   **Possible overkill**   The dealer is judged to be doing a good job of sending out maintenance notices (Attribute 14), but customers attach only slight importance to them. (However, there may be other good reasons for continuing this practice.)

Relatively simple analysis such as this can provide management with a useful focus for developing marketing strategies. This and similar techniques will be low-cost and easily understood by research information users.

Adapted from   J. A. Martilla and J. C. James, "Importance-Performance Analysis," *Journal of Marketing*, 41 (January 1977), 77–79.

TABLE 10-19 Multivariate Technique Classification

DEPENDENCE STRUCTURES		INTERDEPENDENCE STRUCTURES	
Single Criterion/ Multiple Predictor Variable	*Multiple Criterion/ Multiple Predictor Variables*	*Emphasis on Variables*	*Emphasis on Objects*
• Multiple regression (Chapter 11)	• Multiple discriminant analysis (Chapter 13)	• Factor analysis (Chapter 14)	• Cluster analysis (Chapter 14)
• Analysis of variance and covariance (Chapter 12)	• Canonical correlation (Chapter 13)		
• Two-group discriminant analysis (Chapter 13)	• Multivariate analysis of variance and covariance (Chapter 12)		
• Automatic interaction detection (Chapter 13)			
• LOGIT (Chapter 13)			
• PROBIT (Chapter 13)			

Techniques such as factor analysis are used in this case if our focus of interest is on the *variables* of the (intact) data matrix. Cluster analysis is relevant if we wish to focus on the grouping of *objects* in the data matrix (as based on their profile similarities).

Table 10-19 shows where each of the multivariate techniques considered in later chapters is classified. (The chapter references provide a guided tour for the reader interested in particular methods.)

Dummy Variables

Our discussion in this chapter has emphasized nominal-scaled (categorical) data. Moreover, we discussed methods for dealing with two types of nominal-scaled variables:

1. Dichotomies, where the variable consists of only two classes, such as male versus female
2. Polytomies, where the variable is comprised of three or more (assumed *unordered*) classes, such as Protestant denomination: Episcopalian, Baptist, Methodist, all other Protestants

A key concept in working with nominal-scaled variables in multivariate analysis is the *dummy variable*. If a nominal-scaled variable is a dichotomy, we can code one category (say, male) as 1 and the other category (female) as 0. The resulting variable is called a "dummy variable." From here on we can treat this variable as consisting simply of a string of 0's and 1's, depending on the sex of each person in that column.

The same idea holds for polytomies. However, in this case we are going to need more than a single dummy variable. If the polytomy consists of k classes, we shall need $k - 1$ dummy variables.

To illustrate, suppose that we had the nominal-scaled variable *occupation* expressed as a five-state polytomy. If so, we could set up four dummy variables, as follows:

OCCUPATIONAL CATEGORY	DUMMY VARIABLE			
	1	*2*	*3*	*4*
Professional	1	0	0	0
Clerical	0	1	0	0
Skilled laborer	0	0	1	0
Unskilled laborer	0	0	0	1
Other	0	0	0	0

As noted, if the person's occupation is Professional he or she receives a 1 on dummy variable 1 and zero on the other three dummies. The last category, Other, receives a zero on all four dummies. Notice that this is consistent with the dummy-variable coding of a dichotomy, since in this case we have a single dummy variable for two states. Furthermore, since the dichotomy or polytomy is unordered to begin with, it does not matter which category receives which coding.

As we shall see in subsequent chapters, the concept of dummy variable provides a very useful and flexible way to introduce nominal-scaled variables in multivariate methodology. Furthermore, it links the discussion of cross tabulations with the material of multivariate analysis.

SUMMARY

Analysis of associative data is the hallmark of modern marketing research. This chapter provides a bridge between the strictly descriptive treatment afforded by marginal and cross tabulations and the more highly sophisticated techniques of multivariate analysis.

Marginal and cross tabulations continue to represent major ways by which survey responses are summarized and analyzed. This chapter first discussed the topic from a general viewpoint and covered the major steps in the analysis process. Introductory comments were made regarding category definition, editing, coding, tabulation, and summarization.

We reviewed the computation of percentages in cross tabulations and then discussed the interpretive value of introducing a third variable into the original two-variable cross tabulation. The next main section of the chapter dealt with the analysis of contingency tables (cross tabulations of frequency data) via chi-square techniques. Agreement indexes for measuring the strength of association between two categorical variables were also illustrated.

The concluding section of the chapter dealt with introductory remarks on multivariate analysis, the principal topic of Parts III and IV. The data matrix is the grist of the multivariate analyst's mill. We described the various classes of multivariate techniques as consisting of

1. Single criterion/multiple predictor association
2. Multiple criterion/multiple predictor association
3. The analysis of interdependence

Although this chapter emphasized bivariate association between nominal-scaled variables, it should be mentioned that more-advanced techniques have extended chi-square analysis to multiway tables (involving three or more categorizations).[20] In particular, there is increasing interest in the development of new models for analyzing multiway contingency tables in marketing research and in the behavioral sciences generally.[21]

Appendix 10-1

DIFFERENCES IN MEANS AND PROPORTIONS

A great amount of marketing research is concerned with estimating parameters of one or more populations. In addition, many studies go beyond estimation and compare such population parameters by testing hypotheses about differences between them. Very often it is *means, proportions,* and/or *variances* that are the summary measures of concern. Our concern at this point is with differences in means and proportions. Direct comparisons of variances are a special case of the more general technique of analysis of variance, which is covered in Chapter 12.

Standard Error of Differences

In Chapter 9 we briefly discussed sampling distributions and standard errors as they apply to a single statistic. Appropriate formulas were presented. We extend this discussion to cover *differences* in statistics and show a traditional hypothesis test for differences.

---

[20]See H. O. Lancaster, *The Chi Squared Distribution* (New York: John Wiley, 1969).

[21]As examples from marketing research, see P. E. Green, F. J. Carmone, and D. M. Wachspress, "On the Analysis of Qualitative Data in Marketing Research," *Journal of Marketing Research,* 14 (February 1977), 52–59; and Feick, "Analyzing Marketing Research Data." As an example from behavioral science, see L. A. Goodman, "A General Model for the Analysis of Surveys," *American Journal of Sociology,* 77 (1971), 1035–86.

The starting point is the standard error of the difference. For samples that are independent and randomly selected, the standard error of the differences in means is calculated by

$$\sigma_{\bar{x}_A - \bar{x}_B} = \sqrt{\frac{\sigma_A{}^2}{n_A} + \frac{\sigma_B{}^2}{n_B}}$$

If the population standard deviations σ_i are not known, then we must estimate them in the manner shown in Chapter 9. The estimated standard error becomes

$$\text{est. } \sigma_{\bar{x}_A - \bar{x}_B} = \sqrt{\frac{s_A{}^2}{n_A} + \frac{s_B{}^2}{n_B}}$$

For relatively small samples the correction factor N_i/n_{i-1} is used and the resulting formula for the estimated standard error is

$$\text{est. } \sigma_{\bar{x}_A - \bar{x}_B} = \sqrt{\frac{s_A{}^2}{n_A - 1} + \frac{s_B{}^2}{n_B - 1}}$$

Turning now to proportions, the derivation of the standard error of the differences is somewhat similar. Specifically, for large samples

$$\text{est. } \sigma_{pA - pB} = \sqrt{\frac{p_A(1 - p_A)}{n_A} + \frac{p_B(1 - p_B)}{n_B}}$$

For small samples, the correction factor is applied resulting in

$$\text{est. } \hat{\sigma}_{pA - pB} = \sqrt{\frac{p_A(1 - p_A)}{n_A - 1} + \frac{p_B(1 - p_B)}{n_B - 1}}$$

Testing of Hypotheses

When applying the above formulas for hypotheses testing concerning parameters, the following conditions must be met:

1. Samples must be independent.
2. Individual items in samples must be drawn in a random manner.
3. The population being sampled must be normally distributed (or the sample of sufficiently large size).
4. For small samples, the population variances are equal.
5. The data must at least be intervally scaled.

When these five conditions are met, or can at least be reasonably assumed to exist, the traditional approach is as follows.

1. The null hypothesis (H_0) is specified that there is no difference between the parameters of interest in the two populations; any observed difference occurred solely because of sampling variation.
2. The alpha risk is established
3. A Z value is calculated by the appropriate adaptation of the Z formula. For the means, Z is calculated in the following way:

$$Z = \frac{(\overline{X}_A - \overline{X}_B) - (\mu_A - \mu_B)}{\sigma_{\overline{x}_A - \overline{x}_B}} = \frac{\overline{X}_A - \overline{X}_B) - 0}{\sigma_{\overline{x}_A - \overline{x}_B}}$$

and for proportions

$$Z = \frac{(p_A - p_B) - (\pi_A - \pi_B)}{\sigma_{pA - pB}} = \frac{(p_A - p_B) - 0}{\sigma_{pA - pB}}$$

For small samples, the Student t distribution must be used, and for means, t is calculated from

$$t = \frac{(\overline{X}_A - \overline{X}_B) - (\mu_A - \mu_B)}{\sigma_{\overline{x}_A - \overline{x}_B}} = \frac{(\overline{X}_A - \overline{X}_B) - 0}{\sigma_{\overline{x}_A - \overline{x}_B}}$$

4. The probability of the observed difference of the two sample statistics having occurred by chance is determined from a table of the normal distribution (Appendix A, Table A-1) (or the t distribution from Appendix A, Table A-2, interpreted with $[n_A + n_B - 2]$ degrees of freedom).
5. If the probability of the observed difference's having occurred by chance is *greater* than the alpha risk, the null hypothesis is accepted; it is concluded that the parameters of the two universes are not significantly different. If the probability of the observed differences having occurred by chance is *less* than the alpha risk, the null hypothesis is rejected; it is concluded that the parameters of the two populations differ significantly.

In a decisional situation, the procedure explained above will be modified. Strictly speaking, null hypotheses are not necessarily tested according to a predetermined alpha level. Rather, the value of α at which significance occurs is determined, and the decision maker balances this with the cost involved in making a type I error, taking into account the associated beta risk (if it is estimated) and the cost of making a type II error.

An example will illustrate the application of this procedure. Suppose that a survey of nonfood purchases from supermarkets has been made among urban (population A) and rural (population B) families. The average weekly amount spent by a random sample of 400 urban families (n_A) was found to be \$32 ($\overline{X}_A$) with a standard deviation (s_A) of \$10; for a random sample of 225 rural families (n_B) the average was \$30.80 ($\overline{X}_B$) with a standard deviation (s_B) of \$9. The question facing the researcher is, Do urban families spend more on nonfood items, or is the \$1.20 difference in means caused by sampling variations?

We proceed as follows. The hypothesis of no difference in means is established. We assume the alpha risk is set at .05. Since a large sample test is called for, the Z value is calculated by first estimating the standard error of differences in means:

$$\sigma_{\overline{x}_A - \overline{x}_B} = \sqrt{\frac{(10.0)^2}{400} + \frac{(9.0)^2}{225}} = \$0.78$$

The Z value is then determined to be

$$Z = \frac{(32.0 - 30.8) - 0}{.78} = +1.54$$

The probability of the observed difference in the sample means having been due to sampling is specified by finding the area under the normal curve that falls to the right of the point $Z = +1.54$. Consulting Table A-1 in Appendix A, we find this area to be $1.0 - .9382 = 0.0618$. Since this probability associated with the observed difference ($p = 0.06$) is greater than the preset alpha, a strict interpretation would be that there is no difference between the two types of families concerning the average expenditure on nonfood items. In a decision setting, however, the manager would have to determine whether this probability (0.06) is low enough to conclude, on pragmatic grounds, that the families do not differ in their behavior.

To illustrate the small sample case, let us assume that we obtain the same mean values and get values for s_A and s_B such that est. $\sigma_{\overline{x}_A - \overline{x}_B} = \$0.78$ from samples $n_A = 15$ and $n_B = 12$. With these data we calculate t as follows:

$$t = \frac{(32.0 - 30.8) - 0}{0.78} = 1.54$$

The critical value of t is obtained from Table A-2 of Appendix A. For, say, $\sigma = .05$, we determine the critical value of t for $(n_A + n_B - 2) = 25$ degrees of freedom to be

1.708 (one-tailed test). Since the calculated $t < 1.708$, we cannot reject the hypothesis of no difference in average amount spent by the two types of families.

When samples are not independent the same general procedure is followed. The formulas for calculating the test statistics differ, however.

ASSIGNMENT MATERIAL

1. The marketing research department of a prominent advertising agency decides to measure the sales response to the magazine advertising of brand S hand soap. The product is to be advertised initially in the July 4 issue of Magazine M, a magazine issued every two weeks. The agency selects a simple random sample of 200 subscribing families to Magazine M and interviews each of these sample families on July 19. The interview is designed to determine (1) whether the family shopper reads the soap advertisement, and (2) whether brand S soap was purchased within the period July 5 through July 18. The results are summarized in the accompanying table.

Reading of Brand S Advertisment in Magazine M versus Purchase of Brand S during Following Two Weeks

	NUMBER PURCHASING BRAND S JULY 5–JULY 18	NUMBER NOT PURCHASING BRAND S JULY 5–JULY 18	TOTAL
Subscribers who read the brand S advertisement in Magazine M issue of July 4	6	54	60
Subscribers who did *not* read the brand S advertisement in Magazine M issue of July 4	11	129	140
Total	17	183	200

   a. Calculate the percentage of difference between those subscribers who read the advertisement and purchased and those who did not read the advertisement and purchased by each of the following methods:
   (1) Absolute difference in percentages
   (2) Relative difference in percentages
   b. Which method(s) would you recommend that the agency use in preparing a report to the client?

2. A marketing researcher interested in the business-publication reading habits of purchasing agents has assembled the following data:

Business-Publication Preferences (First-Choice Mentions)

Business Publication	Frequency of First Choice
W	35
X	30
Y	45
Z	55
Total	165

a. Test the null hypothesis ($\alpha = 0.05$) that there are no differences among frequencies of choice for publications W, X, Y, and Z.

b. Suppose that the researcher had aggregated responses for the publication pairs W-Y and X-Z. Test the null hypothesis ($\alpha = 0.05$) that there are no differences among frequencies of choice for the two publication pairs.

3. In analyzing its sales records for a metropolitan area, the Scott Smath Company derives the following information concerning the size distribution of its customers, by locality:

Customer Size (Sales Volume)	Number of Central City Customers	Number of Suburban Customers
Under $250,000	20	30
$250,000 to $1,000,00	18	40
Over $1,000,000	40	52

To what extent are size and location related? Is this significant?

4. What are some marketing examples where we might be interested in
   a. Single criterion/multiple predictor association?
   b. Multiple criterion/multiple predictor association?
   c. Cluster analysis of consumers into relatively homogeneous groups?
   d. Introducing a third variable into a cross tabulation involving choice of our brand (versus others) and respondent income?

5. A manufacturer wants to determine whether a "new and improved" product appeals more to women than to men. L. Gilden Associates is hired to do a study on this question. A survey is conducted of a group of women ($n = 25$) and a group of men ($n = 25$) and each person is asked how many units he or she might purchase during a one-month time period. The samples are randomly selected. The following data are obtained:

	MEN	WOMEN
Total number of units expected to be bought	50	61
Sample standard deviation	0.6	0.8

a. Is there a significant difference between men and women in the mean number of expected purchases of the product?

b. How would your solution above differ according to whether you approached the study as basic or decisional research?

11

Multiple and Partial Regression

INTRODUCTION

In Chapter 10 we introduced multivariate procedures and briefly discussed analyses of dependence and independence. Which of the many multivariate techniques is most appropriate for a problem depends on the number of dependent and independent variables and the level of measurement of the variables. This is illustrated in Figure 11-1. Our concern in this chapter is *regression*. Other techniques are discussed in Chapters 12–15.

The multiple regression model is the prototype of single criterion/multiple predictor association, as described in the concluding section of Chapter 10. This chapter presents an introductory discussion of the topic. The case of one criterion and one predictor variable (called simple or bivariate regression) is discussed first. We then introduce a second predictor variable and describe the principal concepts of multiple and partial regression.

Inasmuch as virtually all regression problems of realistic size are solved by the computer, we next turn to a discussion of two widely used types of programs: an all-variable regression program and a stepwise regression program. The use of dummy-variable coding is also illustrated at this point.

The concluding section of the chapter deals with the important problem of multi-collinearity in which some or all of the predictor variables are highly correlated. Ways are discussed for coping with this problem, and caveats are presented regarding the interpretation of partial regression coefficients under these conditions.

Figure 11-1. Multivariate Analysis

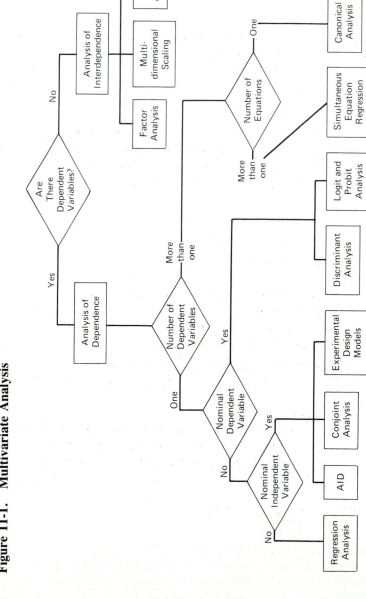

Source: D. A. Aaker, "Multivariate Analysis in Marketing," in *Multivariate Analysis in Marketing*, 2nd ed. (Palo Alto, Calif.: Scientific Press, 1981), p. 2.

SOME BASIC CONCEPTS

In the analysis of associative data the marketing researcher is almost always interested in *prediction* problems:

- Can we predict how much beer a consumer may purchase per week from that person's sex, age, income, and education level?
- Can we predict the dollar volume of purchase of our product by industrial purchasing agents as a function of our relative price, delivery schedules, product quality, and technical service?

The list of such problems is almost endless. Not surprisingly, the linear regression model—as applied in either the bivariate or multivariate form—is one of the most popular tools in the marketing researcher's kit.

Some Industry Examples

The regression model has been applied to problems ranging from estimating salespeople's quotas to predicting demand for new shopping centers.

As an illustration of an offbeat application, one of the leading ski resorts in northeastern Pennsylvania used a regression model to predict weekend attendance, based on such variables as

- Turnpike driving conditions
- Average temperature in the three-day period preceding the weekend
- Local weather forecast for the weekend
- Amount of newspaper space devoted to the resort's advertisements in surrounding city newspapers
- A moving average of the three preceding weekends' attendance

The model's accuracy was within ±6% of actual attendance throughout the season.

One firm used a regression model to predict physicians' readership of various medical journals as related to physician ratings of each journal's

- Writing style
- Quality of illustrations
- Informativeness of advertisements
- Relevance to physician needs
- Authoritativeness in the medical profession
- Frequency of issue

The model predicted actual readership in future time periods quite well. Moreover, it provided diagnostic information as to how various journals' editorial policy and advertising could be improved.

A bakery explored the use of a regression model to predict sales of hamburger buns as a guide to production policy. The factors included as independent variables were

- The weather
- The day of the month
- The proximity to a holiday

The model was able to predict reasonably well in that its use would have led to an average decrease in returned goods of four percentage points (from 10.4% to 6.4%).

In all these problems the researcher wishing to use multiple regression (or its special case, bivariate regression) is interested in four main questions:

1. Can we find a linear composite of the predictor variables that will compactly express the relationship between a criterion variable and the set of predictors?
2. If we can, how strong is the relationship; that is, how well can we predict values of the criterion variable from values of the linear composite?
3. Is the overall relationship statistically significant?
4. Which predictors are most important in accounting for variation in the criterion variable; in particular, can the original model be reduced to fewer variables that still provide adequate prediction of the criterion?

The basic ideas of multiple regression are most easily explained by a numerical example. We proceed one step at a time by first discussing bivariate regression (involving a single criterion and a single predictor) and then on to multiple regression.

A Numerical Example of Simple Regression

Suppose that a marketing researcher is interested in consumers' attitudes toward nutritional additives in ready-to-eat cereals. Specifically, a set of written concept descriptions of a children's cereal is prepared in which two characteristics of the cereal are varied:

X_1: the amount of protein (in grams) per 2-ounce serving, and
X_2: the percentage of minimum daily requirements of vitamin D per 2-ounce serving.

In the nature of a pretest, the researcher obtains consumers' interval-scaled evaluations of the ten concept descriptions, on a preference rating scale, ranging from 1, dislike extremely, up to 9, like extremely well.

TABLE 11-1   Consumer Preference Ratings of Ten Cereals Varying in Nutritional Level

(1)	(2)	(3)	(4)	(5)	(6)	(7)	(8)	(9)	(10)
Rater	Preference rating, Y	Protein, X_1	Vitamin D, X_2	Y^2	X_1^2	YX_1	X_2^2	YX_2	X_1X_2
1	3	4	2	9	16	12	4	6	8
2	7	9	7	49	81	63	49	49	63
3	2	3	1	4	9	6	1	2	3
4	1	1	2	1	1	1	4	2	2
5	6	3	3	36	9	18	9	18	9
6	2	4	4	4	16	8	16	8	16
7	8	7	9	64	49	56	81	72	63
8	3	3	2	9	9	9	4	6	6
9	9	8	7	81	64	72	49	63	56
10	2	1	3	4	1	2	9	6	3
Total	43	43	40	261	255	247	226	232	229
Mean	4.3	4.3	4.0						
Standard deviation	2.908	2.791	2.708						

Figure 11-2   Scatter Diagram and Least-Squares Regression Line—Preference Rating versus Grams of Protein

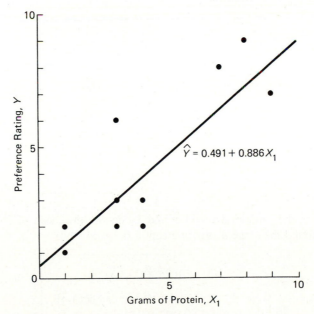

$\hat{Y} = 0.491 + 0.886 X_1$

The (hypothetical) data appear in Table 11-1. For the moment let us confine our attention to columns 2, 3, 5, 6, and 7, which pertain to the criterion variable Y and the first predictor variable X_1. We wish to see if we can predict values of Y from values of X_1.

One of the first things that is usually done in examining two-variable relationships is to prepare a *scatter diagram* in which the ten values of Y are plotted against their X_1 counterparts. Figure 11-2 shows this plot. It appears that there is a direct relationship between Y and X_1. Moreover, it would seem that a linear or straight-line relationship might describe the functional form rather well. A scatter diagram is a useful tool for aiding in *model specification*.

The linear model can be written

$$\hat{Y} = a + bX_1$$

where $\hat{Y}$ denotes values of the criterion that are predicted by the linear model; a denotes the intercept, or value of $\hat{Y}$ when X_1 is zero; and b denotes the slope of the line, or change in $\hat{Y}$ per unit change in X_1.

But how do we find the numerical values of a and b? The method used in this chapter is known as *least squares*. As the reader will recall from introductory statistics, the method of least squares finds that line whose sum of squared deviations of the observed values Y_i from their estimated counterparts $\hat{Y}_i$ (on the regression line) is a minimum.

Parameter Estimation

To compute the estimated parameters (a and b) of the linear model, we return to the data of Table 11-1. In the two-variable case the formulas are relatively simple:

$$b = \frac{\sum YX_1 - n\bar{Y}\bar{X}_1}{\sum X_1^2 - n\bar{X}_1^2}$$

$$= \frac{247 - 10(4.3)(4.3)}{255 - 10(4.3)^2}$$

$$= 0.886$$

where n is the sample size and $\bar{Y}$ and $\bar{X}_1$ denote the mean of Y and X_1, respectively. Having found the slope b, the intercept a is found from

$$a = \bar{Y} - b\bar{X}_1$$

$$= 4.3 - 0.886(4.3)$$

$$= 0.491$$

leading to the linear function

$$\hat{Y} = 0.491 + 0.886X_1$$

This function is plotted in Figure 11-2; it appears to fit the plotted points rather well, and the model seems to be well specified.

Assumptions of the Model

Underlying least-squares computations is a set of assumptions. Although least-squares regression models do not need to assume normality in the (conditional) distributions of the criterion variable, we shall make this assumption for our subsequent discussion of significance testing. With this in mind the assumptions of the regression model are as follows:[1]

1. For each fixed value of X_1 we assume a normal distribution of Y from which our particular sample has been drawn independently.[2]
2. The means of all of these normal distributions of Y—as conditioned by X_1—lie on a straight line with slope β.
3. The normal distributions of Y all have equal variances. This (common) variance does not depend on values assumed by the variable X_1.

Expressed algebraically, our model is

$$Y = \alpha + \beta X_1 + \varepsilon$$

where α = mean of Y population when $X_1 = 0$
β = change in Y population mean per unit change in X_1
ε = error term drawn independently from a normally distributed universe with mean $\mu(\varepsilon) = 0$ and variance $\sigma^2(\varepsilon)$; the error term is independent of X_1

Figure 11-3 illustrates the nature of these assumptions. The reader should note that each value of X_1 has associated with it a normal curve for Y. The means of all these normal distributions lie on the straight line shown in the figure.

In constructing the estimating equation by least squares we have computed a *sample* regression line,

$$\hat{Y} = a + bX_1$$

[1] Greek symbols α and β are used to denote universe counterparts of a and b.

[2] What is being described is the "classical" regression model. Modern versions of the model permit the predictors to be random variables, but their distribution is not allowed to depend on the parameters of the regression equation.

Figure 11-3   Two-variable Regression Model—Theoretical

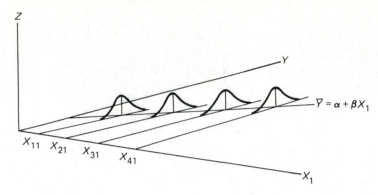

where $\hat{Y}$ is the estimated mean of Y, given X_1, and a, b are the sample estimates of α and β in the theoretical model. As already noted, this line appears in Figure 11-2 for the specific bivariate problem of Table 11-1.

However, functional forms other than the linear may be suggested by the preliminary scatter plot. Figure 11-4 shows various types of scatter diagrams and regression lines for

Figure 11-4   Illustrative Scatter Diagrams and Regression Lines

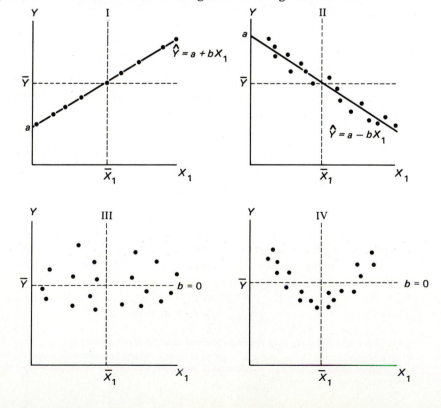

Figure 11-5 Scatter Diagram and Regression Line for Bakery Problem

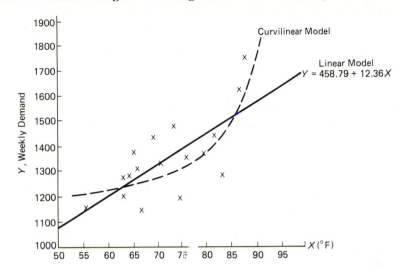

the two-variable case. Panel I shows the ideal case in which *all* the variation in Y is accounted for by variation in X_1. We note that the regression line passes through the mean of each variable and that the slope b happens to be positive. The intercept a represents the predicted value of $\hat{Y}$ when $X_1 = 0$. In Panel II we note that there is residual variation in Y, and, furthermore, that the slope b is negative. Panel III demonstrates the case in which no association between Y and X_1 is found. In this case the mean of Y is as good a predictor as the variable X_1 (the slope b is zero). Panel IV emphasizes that a linear model is being fitted. That is, no *linear* association is found ($b = 0$), even though a curvilinear relationship is apparent from the scatter diagram. Figure 11-4 illustrates the desirability of plotting one's data *before* proceeding to formulate a specific regression model.

Figure 11-5 shows a scatter plot for the bakery illustration mentioned earlier. Although a liner model was used to determine the relationship between average weekly temperature (X) and weekly demand for hamburger buns, it is clear that the curvilinear model (dashed line) gives a much better fit.

Strength of Association

It is one thing to find the regression equation (as shown in Figure 11-2), but at this point we still do not know how *strong* the association is. In other words, how well does X_1 predict Y?

The measure of strength of association in bivariate regression is denoted by r^2 and is called the *coefficient of determination*. This coefficient varies between 0 and 1 and represents the proportion of total variation in Y (as measured about its own mean Y) that is accounted for by variation in X_1.

If we were to use $\bar{Y}$ to estimate each separate value of Y, then a measure of our *inability* to predict Y would be given by the sum of the squared deviations $\sum_{i=1}^{n}(Y_i - \bar{Y})^2$. On the other hand, if we tried to predict Y by employing a linear regression based on X_1, we could use each $\hat{Y}_i$ to predict its counterpart Y_i. In this case a measure of our *inability* to predict Y_i is given by $\sum_{i=1}^{n}(Y_i - \hat{Y}_i)^2$. We can define r^2 as a function of these two quantities:

$$r^2 = 1 - \frac{\sum_{i=1}^{n}(Y_i - \hat{Y}_i)^2}{\sum_{i=1}^{n}(Y_i - \bar{Y})^2}$$

If each $\hat{Y}_i$ predicts its counterpart Y_i perfectly, then $r^2 = 1$, since the numerator of the second term on the right is zero. However, if using the regression equation does no better than $\bar{Y}$ alone, then the second term on the right is 1 and $r^2 = 0$, indicating no ability to predict Y_i (beyond the use of $\bar{Y}$ itself).[3] What this formula says, in words, is

$$r^2 = 1 - \frac{\text{unaccounted-for variance}}{\text{total variance}} = \frac{\text{accounted-for variance}}{\text{total variance}}$$

TABLE 11-2   Actual Y_i, Predicted $\hat{Y}_i$, and Residuals $Y_i - \hat{Y}_i$

RATER	ACTUAL, Y_i	PREDICTED,* $\hat{Y}_i$	RESIDUALS, $Y_i - \hat{Y}_i$
1	3	4.034	−1.034
2	7	8.464	−1.464
3	2	3.148	−1.148
4	1	1.377	−0.377
5	6	3.148	2.852
6	2	4.034	−2.034
7	8	6.692	1.308
8	3	3.148	−0.148
9	9	7.579	1.422
10	2	1.377	0.623
Mean	4.3	4.3	0

*From the equation $\hat{Y}_i = 0.491 + 0.886X_{i1}$.

[3]The use of X_1 in a linear regression can do no worse than $\bar{Y}$. Even if b turns out to be zero, the predictions are $\hat{Y}_i = a = \bar{Y}$, which are the same as using the mean of criterion values in the first place.

Table 11-2 (p. 433) shows the residuals obtained after using the regression equation to predict each value of Y_t via its counterpart $\hat{Y}_i$. We then find $r^2_{yx_1}$ (where we now show the explicit subscripts) by computing from the table:

$$\sum_{i=1}^{n}(Y_i - \hat{Y}_i)^2 = (-1.034)^2 + (-1.464)^2 + \cdots + (0.623)^2$$

$$= 21.09$$

This is the sum of squared errors in predicting Y_i from $\hat{Y}_i$. Next, we find:

$$\sum_{i=1}^{n}(Y_i - \bar{Y})^2 = (3 - 4.3)^2 + (7 - 4.3)^2 + \cdots + (2 - 4.3)^2$$

$$= 76.10$$

This is the sum of squared errors in predicting Y_i from $\bar{Y}$. Hence,

$$r^2_{yx_1} = 1 - \frac{21.09}{76.10}$$

$$= 0.723$$

and we say that *72% of the variation in Y has been accounted for by variation in X_1*. As might also be surmised, there is one more quantity of interest:

$$\sum_{i=1}^{n}(\hat{Y}_i - \bar{Y})^2 = (4.034 - 4.3)^2 + (8.464 - 4.3)^2 + \cdots + (1.377 - 4.3)^2$$

$$= 55.01$$

which is the accounted-for sum of squares due to the regression of Y on X_1.

Figure 11-6 puts all these quantities in perspective by first showing deviations of $Y_1 - \bar{Y}$. As noted above, the sum of these squared deviations is 76.10. Panel II shows the counterpart deviations of Y_i from $\hat{Y}_i$; the sum of these squared deviations is 21.09. Panel III shows the deviations of $\hat{Y}_i$ from $\bar{Y}$; the sum of these squared deviations is 55.01. We note that the results are additive: $21.09 + 55.01 = 76.10$.

The Product-Moment Correlation

Another quantity of interest in bivariate regression is the well-known *product-moment correlation*. The correlation between Y and X_1, denoted r_{yx1}, is defined most simply as the *average cross product*:

$$r_{yx_1} = \frac{1}{n}\sum_{i=1}^{n} Z_{y_i}Z_{x_{i1}}$$

where Z_{y_i} and $Z_{x_{i1}}$ are the standard unit variate forms of Y_i and X_{i1}, respectively. They are defined by

$$Z_{y_i} = \frac{Y_i - \overline{Y}}{s_y}; \quad Z_{x_{i1}} = \frac{X_{i1} - \overline{X}_1}{s_{x_1}}$$

Figure 11-6   Breakdown of Deviations $Y_i - \overline{Y}$ into Two Additive Parts

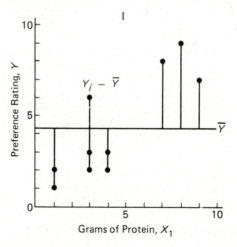

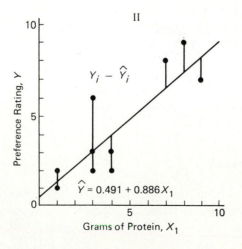

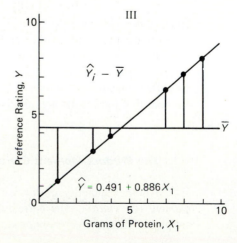

where s_y and s_{x1} are the standard deviations of Y and X_1, respectively. Thus, each Z value has a zero mean and unit standard deviation. Computationally, however, we can also obtain r_{yx1} from the regression coefficient b and the standard deviations of Y and X_1 (see Table 11-1 for the latter):

$$r_{yx_1} = b \frac{s_{x_1}}{s_y} = 0.886 \frac{2.791}{2.908}$$

$$= 0.850$$

The correlation coefficient $r_{yx}1$ varies between -1 for perfect negative correlation and 1 for perfect positive correlation. It is simply the regression of Y on X_1 when both are expressed in standard unit deviate form.[4] (In this case the intercept is zero, since the mean of both Y and X_1 is zero and the regression line will pass through their joint means.)

Exhibit 11-1   Effects of Scaling on the Correlation Coefficient

A number of researchers have investigated the effects of variable scaling or categorization on the correlation coefficient (and thus the coefficient of determination).[*] Most of the research concludes that as the number of scale points decreases, information loss increases and the correlation coefficient can become distorted. However, the loss of information does not seem to be significant when there are more than 10 scale points, a situation that is not common in marketing research studies. Moreover, until the number of categories reaches *five*, any such distortion may not be critical.

Other research has shown that when variables with 10 or fewer categories have unequal numbers of scale points, only the smaller number of scale points is influential in determining information loss.[†] The need to correct or adjust calculated correlation coefficients for possible scaling effects is evident. Different researchers have suggested various ways of dealing with the problem; these are summarized elsewhere.[‡] Any procedure for correction of r must explicitly incorporate the effect of rho, the true correlation.

[*]See, for example, W. S. Martin, "Effects of Scaling on the Correlation Coefficient: Additional Considerations," *Journal of Marketing Research*, 15 (May 1978), 304–8; and K. A. Bollen and K. H. Barb, "Pearson's R and Coarsely Categorized Measures," *American Sociological Review*, 46 (1981), 232–39.

[†]S. Sharma and R. A. Peterson, "Effects of Scaling on the Correlation Coefficient: Issues and Outlooks," paper presented at the 1982 Annual Conference of the American Institute for Decision Sciences.

[‡]See Martin, "Effects of Scaling on the Correlation Coefficient: Additional Considerations"; Sharma and Peterson, "Effects of Scaling on the Correlation Coefficient: Issues and Outlooks"; and R. A. Peterson and S. Sharma, "Adjusting Correlation Coefficients for the Effects of Scaling," *Proceedings,* Business and Economic Statistics Section, American Statistical Association, 1977, pp. 784–86.

[4]If we were to reverse the process and regress X_1 on Y, we would find that the slope was 0.816 and

$$r_{yx_1} = 0.816 \frac{2.908}{2.791} = 0.850$$

Either way, we get the same result. The product-moment correlation is a *symmetric* measure of association between Y and X_1.

Finally, we note that the coefficient of determination, $r^2_{yx_1}$, computed earlier, is simply the *square* of the product-moment correlation r_{yx_1}. That is, $0.723 = (0.85)^2$, even though each has been developed conceptually along somewhat different lines.

MULTIPLE AND PARTIAL REGRESSION

It is time to introduce the second predictor variable X_2, as shown in Table 11-1. The theoretical model now becomes

$$Y = \alpha + \beta_1 X_1 + \beta_2 X_2 + \varepsilon$$

with parameters estimated by

$$\hat{Y} = a + b_1 X_1 + b_2 X_2$$

All assumptions regarding the bivariate regression model continue to hold in the present case as well. However, it is important to remember that, in general, the current b_1—now

Figure 11-7   Scatter Plot and Fitted Regression Plane

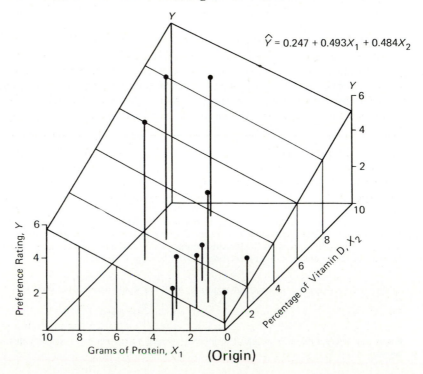

$\hat{Y} = 0.247 + 0.493X_1 + 0.484X_2$

called a *partial* regression coefficient with respect to X_1—will *not* equal its counterpart coefficient (b) obtained from the bivariate regression. This is because X_1 itself *will usually be correlated with* X_2. In the bivariate case X_2 was ignored and any of the variation in Y that was shared by X_1 *and* X_2 was credited solely to X_1. Such will no longer be the case.

In the case of only two predictors, X_1 and X_2, it is still possible to prepare a scatter plot. However, now the plot appears in terms of a *three-dimensional* space. In this case we fit a plane—that particular plane whose sum of squared deviations of the Y_i from their $\hat{Y}_i$ counterparts (on the plane) is a minimum. Figure 11-7 (p. 437) shows the original scatter and the fitted plane for the sample problem of Table 11-1. The estimated (least-squares) equation is

$$\hat{Y} = 0.247 + 0.493X_1 + 0.484 X_2$$

The first slope coefficient of 0.493 denotes the change in $\hat{Y}$ per unit change in X_1 when X_2 is held constant; similarly, 0.484 denotes the change in $\hat{Y}$ per unit change in X_2 when X_1 is held constant. We note that $0.493 \neq 0.886$, the slope obtained earlier in the bivariate case. This is because X_1 and X_2 are, themselves, correlated and X_1 is now forced to share some of its Y-variable association with the second predictor X_2.

Parameter Estimation

Finding the partial regression coefficients $b_1 = 0.493$ and $b_2 = 0.484$ and the intercept $a = 0.247$ is considerably more complicated in the case of multiple regression. Table 11-1 provides the various sums of squares and cross products that we need. Table 11-3 shows the results of solving the set of simultaneous equations to find b_1 and b_2. Following this, we compute the intercept value of $a = 0.247$ in the manner shown.

But what is the relationship of, say, $b_1 = 0.493$ to the case of simple regression? One way of thinking about the interpretation of b_1 is to imagine our first regressing X_1 on X_2 and then computing *residuals* $X_{i1} - \hat{X}_{i1}$ from this regression. If we then regress the original values of Y on the set of X_1 residuals, the "simple" regression coefficient in this situation turns out to be precisely the *partial regression coefficient, $b_1 = 0.493$*, that was obtained from Table 11-3. Interestingly enough, we could also get b_1 by regressing Y residuals on X_1 residuals, where *both* are net of their linear association with X_2. However, such a step is not needed to obtain the partial regression coefficient. Similar kinds of remarks pertain to b_2, but in this case it is X_2 whose linear association with X_1 is removed before regressing Y on the set of X_2 residuals.

The same general idea extends to three or more predictor variables. In the more general case, the appropriate residuals are found by regressing the particular X_j of interest on *all* the remaining predictors via a *multiple* regression. Then, we would regress Y on the set of X_j residuals to get the b_j of interest. While this procedure would be going about the calculation of partial regression coefficients the hard way, it does serve to show their conceptual linkage to simple (bivariate) regression coefficients.

TABLE 11-3   Computation of Partial Regression Coefficients and the Coefficient of Multiple Determination

From Table 11-1: mean corrected sums of squares and cross products:

$$\begin{aligned}
\Sigma\, y^2 &= \Sigma\, Y^2 - n\bar{Y}^2 &&= 261 - 10(4.3)^2 &&= 76.1 \\
\Sigma\, x_1^2 &= \Sigma\, X_1^2 - n\bar{X}_1^2 &&= 255 - 10(4.3)^2 &&= 70.1 \\
\Sigma\, x_2^2 &= \Sigma\, X_2^2 - n\bar{X}_2^2 &&= 226 - 10(4.0)^2 &&= 66.0 \\
\Sigma\, yx_1 &= \Sigma\, YX_1 - n\bar{Y}\bar{X}_1 &&= 247 - 10(4.3)(4.3) &&= 62.1 \\
\Sigma\, yx_2 &= \Sigma\, YX_2 - n\bar{Y}\bar{X}_2 &&= 232 - 10(4.3)(4.0) &&= 60.0 \\
\Sigma\, x_1x_2 &= \Sigma\, X_1X_2 - n\bar{X}_1\bar{X}_2 &&= 229 - 10(4.3)(4.0) &&= 57.0
\end{aligned}$$

Solving for the regression equation:

$$\begin{aligned}
\Sigma\, yx_1 &= \Sigma\, x_1^2 b_1 + \Sigma\, x_1x_2 b_2 \\
\Sigma\, yx_2 &= \Sigma\, x_1x_2 b_1 + \Sigma\, x_2^2 b_2 \\
62.1 &= 70.1 b_1 + 57.0 b_2 \\
60.0 &= 57.0 b_1 + 66.0 b_2 \\
b_1 &= 0.493; \qquad b_2 = 0.484 \\
a &= \bar{Y} - b_1\bar{X}_1 - b_2\bar{X}_2 \\
&= 4.3 - 0.493(4.3) - 0.484(4.0) \\
&= 0.247
\end{aligned}$$

Computing the coefficient of multiple determination:

$$R^2_{y \cdot x_1, x_2} = \frac{b_1\, \Sigma yx_1 + b_2\, \Sigma yx_2}{\Sigma y^2} = \frac{0.493(62.1) + 0.484(60.0)}{76.1} = 0.783$$

Coefficient of Multiple Determination

Finding the *coefficient of multiple determination* proceeds in just the same way as the bivariate case, although, as might be surmised, various computational shortcuts are available. Table 11-3 shows that application of a shortcut formula leads to

$$R^2_{y \cdot x_1, x_2} = 0.783$$

However, Table 11-4 shows that we can get the same thing through the more roundabout procedure of finding the predicted $\hat{Y}_i$ values from the *multiple* regression and then the residuals $Y_i - \hat{Y}_i$. This is the same approach as was followed in the bivariate case.

We note that the multiple regression equation does quite well at prediction, since 78% of the variation in Y is accounted for by variation in X_1 *and* X_2. However, we recall that, if only X_1 is employed, the (simple) coefficient of determination is 72%. Apparently, X_2 and X_1 are so highly correlated—their simple correlation is 0.838—that once X_1 is in the multiple regression equation there is little need for X_2 as well.

TABLE 11-4 Calculation of the Coefficient of Multiple Determination from the Regression Residuals

Rater	Y_i	$\hat{Y}_i$	$Y_i - \hat{Y}_i$	Rater	Y_i	$\hat{Y}_i$	$Y_i - \hat{Y}_i$
1	3	3.185	−0.185	6	2	4.152	−2.152
2	7	8.066	−1.066	7	8	8.048	−0.048
3	2	2.209	−0.209	8	3	2.692	0.308
4	1	1.707	−0.707	9	9	7.574	1.426
5	6	3.176	2.824	10	2	2.191	−0.191

Coefficient of multiple determination:

$$R^2_{y \cdot x_1, x_2} = \frac{\sum\limits_{i=1}^{n} (Y_i - \hat{Y}_i)^2}{\sum\limits_{i=1}^{n} (Y_i - \bar{Y})^2}$$

$$= 1 - \left[\frac{(-0.185)^2 + (-1.066)^2 + \cdots + (-0.191)^2}{76.10} \right]$$

$$= 1 - \frac{16.49}{76.10} = 0.783; \qquad R_{y \cdot x_1, x_2} = 0.885$$

What about the *square root* of $R^2_{y \cdot x_1, x_2}$? This is called the *coefficient of multiple correlation:*

$$R_{y \cdot x_1 x_2} = \sqrt{0.783} = 0.885$$

and is interpreted as the *simple correlation* (i.e., bivariate correlation) between Y_i and $\hat{Y}_i$ where, as we know, the $\hat{Y}_i$ are the *predicted* values obtained by the best linear composite of X_1 and X_2 in the least-squares sense; this composite is given by the multiple regression equation.

Other Coefficients of Interest

Computing the partial regression coefficients and the coefficient of multiple determination still does not exhaust the possible output coefficients in multiple regression. Marketing researchers frequently have interest in three other measures:

- The beta coefficients b^*_j
- The partial coefficients $r_{yx_j \cdot x_k, x_l \dots}$
- The part correlation coefficients $r_{yx_j \, (x_k, x_l \dots)}$

As it turns out, these three measures are not difficult to understand, once they are defined conceptually:

1. The beta coefficients b_j^* are the partial regression coefficients (b_j) that one gets if all variables (Y, X_1, X_2) entering the analysis are each standardized to zero mean and unit standard deviation *before* the multiple regression equation is computed.

2. The partial correlation coefficients $r_{yx_j \cdot x_k, x_l \ldots}$ are actually *simple* (two-variable) correlations between the *two sets of residuals* that remain after association of all other predictors is removed from Y and X_j separately.

3. The part correlation coefficients $r_{yx_j (x_k, x_l \ldots)}$ are also simple correlations, this time between the *original Y* variable and the set of X_j residuals that remain after removing only X_j's linear association with all other predictors.

We do not delve into computational formulas for the beta coefficients, partial correlation coefficients, and part correlation coefficients, since, in practice, these measures are calculated by various regression programs.[5] Of these, the partial correlation coefficient is generally viewed as the most important; we consider its use in a later section.

The beta coefficients b_j^* can be important when examining the question of which predictor variables are most important in accounting for variation in the dependent variable.

Recapitulation

Once we get used to the idea of drawing parallels between multiple and simple regression we see that

1. A partial regression coefficient is really a simple (bivariate) regression coefficient between the original Y and a set of X_j residuals that remain after X_j has been regressed on all the other predictors.

2. The multiple correlation coefficient is the simple correlation between the original criterion variable Y_i and $\hat{Y}_i$, where the latter is given by the least-squares multiple regression.

[5]However, a simple way to think about the (squared) *part* correlation is in terms of the change in R^2 before and after inclusion of, say, X_1. That is, the squared part correlation of Y with X_1 can be defined as

$$r^2_{yx_1(x_2, \ x_3, \ldots)} = R^2_{y \cdot x_1, x_2, x_3 \ldots} - R^2_{y \cdot x_2, x_3, \ldots}$$

Thus, the (squared) part correlation is simply the difference in R^2 between an equation that includes all predictors and one that omits the jth predictor of interest. Moreover, we can find the (squared) *partial* correlation of Y with X_1 from the *relative* measure:

$$r^2_{yx_1 \cdot x_2, x_3, \ldots} = \frac{R^2_{y \cdot x_1, x_2, \ x_3, \ldots} - R^2_{y \cdot x_2, x_3 \ldots}}{1 - R^2_{y \cdot x_2, x_3 \ldots}}$$

Similar remarks pertain to the (squared) partial correlation of Y with X_2 (or any other predictor X_j in the case of three or more predictors).

3. A partial correlation coefficient is the simple correlation between the set of Y residuals and the set of X_j residuals, where both are net of linear association with all other predictors.

4. The part correlation coefficient takes out the linear association of X_j (only) with the remaining predictors before finding its simple correlation with Y.

5. The beta coefficient is a partial regression coefficient that is obtained if all variables are previously expressed as standard unit variates before the multiple regression equation is computed.

At this point the reader should have some appreciation for the labor involved in computing multiple regression equations and related coefficients. Moreover, we still have not discussed questions of statistical significance and the possibility of finding regression models with fewer parameters than we begin with originally. These topics are best explored in the context of *computerized* regression procedures.

COMPUTERIZED REGRESSION

With the availability of a large variety of packaged programs, computation of multiple regressions is almost invariably carried out by the computer. (This is also the case for all the other multivariate techniques considered in this book.) For this reason, it is appropriate to describe the output that one obtains from such programs.

As shown in Table 11-5 there are many regression programs available in the major mainframe software packages—SPSS$^\text{x}$, SAS, and BMDP. Similarly, there are many such programs available for microcomputers. Within a package, individual programs may differ with respect to the criterion for including independent variables in the multiple regression, the ability to repeat the analysis on subgroups of the cases and compare these groups, the residual analyses available, the numerical precision used for the computations, and the linearity assumption used in the analysis. Some of these factors may also reflect differences between the packages.

The two most widely used approaches (available in all packages) are *all-variables* regression and *stepwise* regression. An example of each drawn from an earlier version of BMDP is discussed as a prototypical case. Many of the items shown on an output are common to all packages, although not necessarily presented in exactly the same format and/or sequence.

All-Variables Regression

An all-variables program is one in which the regression is computed across the full set of predictors, rather than on a one-at-a-time basis. Generally, a large number of predictors can be accommodated with a virtually unlimited number of cases. In order to

TABLE 11-5   Computer Programs for Regression and Correlation

SPSS[x]*

    SCATTERGRAM   prints bivariate plots where each point represents the values for one case on the two variables. An option provides for the statistics associated with the simple regression of one variable on the other.

    PEARSON CORR   produces Pearson product-moment correlations with significance levels. Univariate statistics, covariances, and cross-product deviations are an option.

    PARTIAL CORR   provides partial correlation coefficients that describe the relationship between two variables while adjusting for the effects of one or more additional variables.

    REGRESSION   calculates a multiple regression equation and associated statistics and plots. Several types of plots, including partial residual plots, can be displayed. Both stepwise and all-variables are possible as methods for building a model.

SAS†

    REG   performs general-purpose regression by fitting least-squares estimates to linear regression models.

    RSQUARE   performs all possible regressions for one or more dependent variables and a collection of independent variables. This procedure is useful for investigating the behavior of many regression models.

    STEPWISE   has five methods for stepwise regression, an approach that is useful for handling many independent variables and determining which of these should be included in a "final" regression model.

    NLIN   builds nonlinear regression models by least-squares.

    RSREG   fits a quadratic response-surface model, which is useful in searching for factor values that optimize a response.

BMDP‡

    P1R   estimates the multiple linear regression equation using all the independent variables. Options include covariance and correlation matrices and plotted residuals. Univariate statistics are provided for each variable.

    P2R   develops a multiple linear regression equation in a stepwise manner. At each step variables are entered or removed according to researcher-specified criteria. Statistics and options similar to those for P1R are available.

    P3R   is used to estimate parameters in nonlinear models by least squares.

There are other programs designed to handle special types of regression problems (e.g., polynomial regression, principal components, and all possible subsets).

*SPSS[x] User's Guide, 2nd ed. (New York: McGraw-Hill, 1986).
†*SAS User's Guide: Statistics,* Version 5 ed. (Cary, N.C.: SAS Institute, 1985).
‡W. J. Dixon and M. B. Brown, eds., *BMDP–79: Biomedical Computer Programs P Series* (Berkeley: University of California Press, 1979).

TABLE 11-6   Summary Output of Regression Analysis of Sample Data from Table 11-1*

Sample R^2	0.783
Adjusted R^2	0.721
Sample R (unadjusted)	0.885
SS due to regression	59.61
SS of deviations from regression	16.49
Variance of estimate	2.356
Standard error of estimate	1.535
Intercept: $a = 0.247$	

ANALYSIS OF VARIANCE FOR THE FULL REGRESSION

Source of Variation	Degrees of Freedom	Sum of Squares	Mean Square	F Ratio
Due to regression	2	59.61	29.805	12.652
Deviations about regression	7	16.49	2.356	
Total	9	76.10		

ADDITIONAL STATISTICS

Variable Number	Mean	Standard Deviation	Regression Coefficient	Standard Error of Regression Coefficient	Computed t Value	Partial Correlation Coefficient	Sum of Squares Added	Proportion Total of Variation
X_1	4.3	2.791	0.493	0.336	1.466	0.485	55.013	0.723
X_2	4.0	2.708	0.484	0.346	1.397	0.467	4.597	0.060
Y	4.3	2.908					59.610	0.783

*From BMD-03R.

show comparisons with our earlier computations, the same sample of data of Table 11-1 was run through a BMD program. Table 11-6 shows the output provided by this program. Most of the coefficients that were shown earlier appear here, along with some additional measures as well.

Starting at the top of the table we find the same coefficient of multiple determination that was computed in Table 11-3. However, we also note that an *adjusted* R^2 of 0.721 is printed out. This is computed from the same R^2 as follows:

$$R_2 \text{ (adjusted} = 1 - (1 - R^2)\frac{n - 1}{n - m - 1}$$

$$= 1 - \frac{0.217(9)}{7}$$

$$= 0.721$$

where m denotes the number of predictor variables. Adjusted R^2 is computed to reflect the fact that the sample R^2 capitalizes on chance variation in the *specific* data set under study. Adjusted R^2 provides a better estimate of the universe R^2 value.[6]

The quantities 59.61 (sum of squares due to regression), 16.49 (sum of squares of deviations from regression), and 76.10 (total sum of squares about the mean of Y) have all been discussed conceptually in Figure 11-6 (in the bivariate case) and numerically in Table 11-4.[7] What is new in Table 11-6, however, is the analysis of variance table in which the following (equivalent) hypotheses are tested:

$$R_p^2 = 0; \quad \beta_1 = \beta_2 = 0$$

where R_p^2 denotes the population coefficient of multiple determination.

The *F*-Ratio Test

The F ratio is the appropriate test for these hypotheses.[8] We first obtain the mean squares, 29.805 and 2.356, by dividing the corresponding sums of squares by their respective degrees of freedom. Then we find the F ratio of 12.652. This value, with 2 degrees of freedom for numerator and 7 degrees of freedom for denominator, is compared with a tabular F (see Table A-4 in Appendix A) of 3.26 with an (illustrative) significance level of 0.1. We reject the preceding null hypotheses and conclude that the *overall regression equation is statistically significant.*

Having satisfied ourselves that at least one β coefficient is significant, there are two additional questions to raise:

1. Does each predictor separately account for statistically significant variation in Y?
2. What does each predictor contribute in terms of total accounted-for variation in Y?

We discuss these questions next, in the context of Table 11-6.

---

[6]More precisely, even if the null hypothesis $H_0 : R_p^2 = 0$ is true, the expectation of R^2, denoted $E(R^2)$, does not equal zero. Rather, $E(R^2) = m/(n - 1)$ so that as m approaches n, the sample size, $E(R^2)$ approaches 1. The adjusted R^2 can actually decrease if a new predictor enters the regression equation, since the increase in accounted-for sum of squares may be more than counterbalanced by the loss of a degree of freedom in the denominator ($n - m - 1$). In contrast, unadjusted R^2 can never decrease as a new predictor is introduced into the regression equation.

[7]The quantity 2.356, called the *variance of the estimate,* is simply the sum of squared deviations from regression, 16.49, divided by 7, the associated degrees of freedom. It is analogous to the variance around a mean. Its square root is 1.535 and is called the *standard error of the estimate.* This later quantity is analogous to a standard deviation around a mean. The larger either of these two quantities is, the poorer the fit of the regression equation.

[8]This test is discussed in more detail in Chapter 12, in the context of analysis of variance. However, as recalled from basic statistics, the F distribution is the distribution followed by the ratio of two independent, unbiased estimates of the normal population variance σ^2. If R_p^2 is zero, then the sample R^2 reflects only sampling error and the F ratio will tend to be equal to unity.

Standard Errors and t Tests

While the preceding analysis has indicated that the full regression is significant, it does not follow that *both* b_1 and b_2 contribute significantly to overall accounted-for variance. It may be the case that a simpler model involving only X_1 (or one involving only X_2) would be sufficient. The standard error of each individual regression coefficient is shown in Table 11-6. This is a dispersion measure that reflects two main things:

1. How highly correlated X_j is with the other predictor(s)
2. How much variance in Y is still to be accounted for

To illustrate, the standard error (SE) of b_1 is computed as follows:

$$
\begin{aligned}
\text{SE}(b_1) &= \frac{S_y}{S_{x_1}} \sqrt{\frac{1}{n-m-1} \cdot \frac{1 - R^2_{y \cdot x_1, x_2, x_3, \ldots}}{1 - R^2_{x_1 \cdot x_2, x^3, \ldots}}} \\
&= \frac{2.908}{2.791} \sqrt{\frac{1}{7} \cdot \frac{0.217}{0.298}} \\
&= 0.336
\end{aligned}
$$

where n is the sample size and m is the number of predictors. The standard error is a measure of dispersion about the average partial regression coefficient over repeated samplings of Y for a fixed set of values on each of the predictors. The larger the standard error is, the less reliable b_1 is across repeated samplings from the same universe. Thus, we would like to see intuitively how SE (b_1) depends on the quantities to the right of the equals sign.

In particular, we note that $1 - R^2_{y \cdot x_1, x_2, x_3, \ldots}$ is the residual variance in Y after *all* predictors are considered; this is $1 - 0.783$, or 0.217. Other things equal, larger values of residual variance in Y (i.e., smaller R^2's) lead to higher standard errors.

Next, the value 0.298 in the denominator under the square-root sign is equal to the residual variance in X_1. The residual variance in X_1 is the variance of the X_1 residuals and, hence, that part of the X_1 that cannot be predicted by the other predictor variables. Other things equal, *smaller* values of residual variance in X_1 lead to *higher* standard errors.

What this latter statement means conceptually is that the standard error of b_1 increases as X_1 becomes *more completely accounted for by the remaining predictor variables*. That is, as X_1 becomes increasingly redundant with the remaining predictors, its standard error increases.

The t value of 1.466 in Table 11-6 is simply the ratio of b_1 to its own standard error SE(b_1). The test of significance of t_1 is carried out by finding the tabular value of the t distribution (Table A-2 in Appendix A) for 7 degrees of freedom. If we continue to use a significance level of 0.1, then the tabular value of t is 1.415 and b_1 is significant. However, b_2 (whose t value is 1.397) is *not* significant at the 0.1 level.

The t test for each individual partial regression coefficient tests whether the increment in R^2 produced by the predictor in question is significant when a model including the predictor (and all other predictors) is compared with a model including all predictors but the one being tested.

Contribution to Accounted-For Variation

The last column in the lower portion of Table 11-6, Proportion of Total Variation, still needs to be explained. First, we observe that the two contributory R^2's sum to the total sample R^2 of 0.783. However, the R^2 attributed to X_1 (0.723) is considerably greater than that (0.060) attributed to X_2.[9]

The reason is simple. This column of the output assigns any shared variation between X_1 and X_2 to X_1, *the predictor appearing first in the input data*. $R^2 = 0.723$ is actually the *simple* coefficient of determination between Y and X_1, ignoring X_2. On the other hand, $R_2 = 0.06$ is the squared part correlation of Y and X_2 *after* the linear association of X_1 has been removed from X_2 only. This is the association between X_2 and Y which is independent of X_1.

Which Variable To Retain?

At this point we observe from the separate t tests that b_1 is significant at the 0.1 level but b_2 is not. Moreover, the introduction of X_2 *after* X_1 accounts for relatively little variation in Y (actually, an incremental R^2 of only 0.06). However, entering X_1 before X_2 is largely an arbitrary decision. We might now ask, Suppose that X_2, rather than X_1, had been entered first? If X_2 is entered first, followed by X_1, we would find that the only values that change in the whole set of output statistics in Table 11-6 are the last two columns. These become:

Variable Number	Sum of Squares Added	Proportion of Total Variance
X_1	5.065	0.067
X_2	54.545	0.716
	59.610	0.783

[9]By way of general interest, note that the squared partial correlation of Y with X_2 can be found from the formula stated earlier

$$r^2_{yx_2 \cdot x_1} = \frac{R^2_{y \cdot x_1 x_2} - R^2_{y \cdot x_1}}{1 - R^2_{y \cdot x_1}}$$

$$= \frac{0.783 - 0.723}{1 - 0.723} = 0.217$$

We then find

$$r_{yx_2 \cdot x_1} = \sqrt{0.217} \cong 0.467$$

as shown in Table 11-6. To find the counterpart measure for X_1 we would need $R^2_{y \cdot x_2}$ or, in effect, the *simple* coefficient of determination of Y with X_2. While not computed in Table 11-6, this turns out to be 0.716 and $r^2_{yx_1 \cdot x_2}$ is then 0.236. Its square root, the partial correlation, is 0.485, and is shown in Table 11.6.

In practice, the question of which variables to retain is guided by substantive theory, assuming that the candidate predictors are statistically significant. Since the t value tests the *individual* significance of a partial regression coefficient (as though each variable being tested were the *last* to enter the regression), order does not matter in this case. Hence, we keep X_1 (at the 0.1 alpha level) and drop X_2, although the decision is a close one.

What *does* change by reversing the order of entry is the apportionment *between* X_1 and X_2 of accounted-for variation. Accordingly, it is good practice in using any program to include those predictor variables of most theoretical interest to the researcher *in front of those variables of less interest*. This prior ordering has no effect on anything except the last two columns of the lower portion of Table 11-6. Here, however, any variable entered earlier will receive sole credit for variation shared with those entered after it.

In summary, Table 11-6 shows that the program used provides the major output measures of interest in applied multiple regression studies:

1. The regression equation
2. R^2—both the sample-determined and the population-adjusted values
3. An F test for testing the significance of the overall regression (involving both X_1 and X_2)
4. Individual t tests and standard errors for testing each specific partial regression coefficient
5. Partial correlation coefficients
6. The accounted-for variance contributed by each predictor, where any shared variance of each predictor (beyond the first) is credited to the predictors that precede it, based on the researcher's order for including the predictor variables

In the sample problem R^2 was highly significant, but only the first variable X_1 was needed to account for most of the variance in Y. That is, the addition of X_2 accounted for an incremental variance of only 6 percentage points; moreover, the t test for b_2 was not significant at the 0.1 level. Therefore, in practice we would employ a *simple* regression of Y on X_1 alone. This has already been computed as $\hat{Y} = 0.491 + 0.886X_1$.

Some General Comments on R^2 and the b_j Values

Since multiple regression is the most often used technique of multivariate analysis, it is appropriate to add a few general comments regarding the key measure, R^2 and the b_j's. First, the coefficient of multiple determination R^2 cannot be lower than the highest simple r^2 with any single predictor variable. However, if all predictors correlate zero with the criterion variable, R^2 will also be zero.

When the predictors exhibit low intercorrelation among themselves, R^2 will tend to be larger; in the limit if all predictors are uncorrelated, R^2 equals the sum of the simple r^2 of each predictor, in turn, with the criterion variable. However, in the more usual case it is difficult to estimate R^2 from simple r^2's. Although rare, cases can exist where an r^2 with one predictor can be zero and yet R^2 can be substantially higher than the r^2 with the second variable; in this case the first predictor serves the function of a *suppressor* variable (a general concept that we described in Chapter 10 in the context of cross tabulations). Within the context of the present discussion we can define a suppressor variable as an independent variable (X_1) that has a zero (or relatively low) correlation with a dependent variable (Y) and a greater than zero (relatively high) absolute correlation with another independent variable (X_2) that has a greater than zero correlation with the dependent variable (Y).[10] Although not particularly prevalent in occurrence, suppressor variables have the potential for creating interpretation problems (i.e., having negative coefficients when positive ones are expected and vice versa), particularly in psychologically oriented marketing research. Yet it has been argued that a carefully constructed suppressor variable can be used advantageously for *prediction* but not for explanation.[11]

As additional predictor variables are added, R^2 cannot decrease, but usually diminishing returns set in, so that in most applications it is rare to find much increase in R^2 beyond the first several predictor variables. For example, in a recent study an analyst found that by increasing the number of predictor variables from 2 to 11 R^2 increased only .03 (from .41 to .44). The upper limit of this measure is unity, and we often find that the additional predictor variables are so highly correlated with ones already entered in the equation that little change is noted in total R^2 after their inclusion.

Finally, we should reiterate that R^2 is systematically biased upward; this was the reason for adjusting R^2 for degrees of freedom. However, when various computer programs using stepwise procedures (in which predictor variables are entered sequentially) are used to run multiple regressions, even adjusting R^2 for degrees of freedom in the final equation does not solve the "bias" problem. The reason is simple: With a large number of predictor variables it is quite easy in stepwise regression programs to take advantage of chance, not only by finding at least *some* variables that correlate highly with the criterion but also because of the freedom such programs provide for selecting various *combinations* of predictor variables.

Stepwise Regression

The stepwise regression program used in this discussion (BMD-02R) represents an excellent prototype of stepwise procedures in general. By "stepwise" is meant that the predictor variables enter the regression equation one at a time. The purpose of this approach is to be able to screen through a large number of predictors to find some smaller subset that accounts for most of the variation in the criterion variable. Typically, mainframe stepwise programs will accommodate a large number of predictors with a sample size that is virtually unlimited.[12]

---

[10]See J. C. Nunnally, *Psychometric Theory* (New York: McGraw-Hill, 1967), p. 162.

[11]T. C. Wilson, "Using Suppressor Variables in Marketing Research," paper presented at the 1980 annual meeting of Western AIDS.

[12]We should warn the reader at the outset that stepwise procedures do not produce "optimal" regression equations. Because of correlatedness among the predictors (to be considered later), it is possible for an important variable never to get into the equation. Conversely, a less important variable may enter because of its particular correlation pattern with other predictors.

In using the program for this illustration certain control parameters need to be set. For example, the user is asked to state an F ratio for inclusion, an F ratio for deletion, and a tolerance level. (The tolerance level is defined as the value $1 - R^2$ for the jth predictor, when it is regressed on all predictors then in the equation. As such, it is a measure of the *lack* of redundancy of X_j with predictors already in the equation.) The program's default values for the preceding three control parameters are, respectively, 0.01, 0.005, and 0.001. These are "loose" values in the sense of tending to include and retain all predictors.

As preliminary output the program prints means, standard deviations, and the correlation matrix of all variables (including the criterion). Then the following features of the program are implemented:

1. The predictor with the highest (squared) simple r with the criterion (or, equivalently, the one with the highest F ratio) is entered, assuming that it passes the F-ratio control value to enter.[13]

2. Any new predictor is added to the equation on the basis of its displaying the highest squared partial r (or, equivalently, the highest F value) with those predictors already in the equation, assuming that its F level and tolerance value exceed the control parameters.

3. A predictor can be deleted at any stage if its F value to remove drops below the control parameter. That is, at any given state beyond the first, each predictor in the equation is tested as though it were the last to enter. If any F values are less than the F for retention, the one with the lowest F value is deleted at that stage.

4. At each stage in the accretion of predictors a regression equation is computed (including intercept), as well as a multiple R, and an ANOVA table for testing R^2. In addition, the standard error of each predictor in the equation is computed, as well as the F value associated with the predictor-retention test.

5. Also at each stage, the partial r's of all predictors not in the equation, their tolerance levels, and F values to enter are computed and displayed.

6. At the end of the process, a summary table with R, R^2, incremental R^2, and the F values to enter (associated with the full sequence of entered predictors) is printed.

7. The program also provides a capability for listing and plotting residuals $Y_i - \hat{Y}_i$ versus specified predictors and versus $\hat{Y}_i$ itself.

---

[13]We say "equivalently" in the sense that both measures give the same rank order of variables. The relationship between F and the square of the partial correlation coefficient is

$$F = \frac{r^2_{yx_j \cdot x_k}}{1 - r^2_{yx_j \cdot x_k}} (n - m - 1)$$

where $r^2_{yx_j \cdot x_k}$ denotes the (squared) partial correlation of Y with X_1, conditioned on the rest of the predictors (generically denoted by k in this case).

After the regression run has been made, the user is free to go back to that step in the sequence in which R^2 and all individual F values for retention are significant. Since the equation for that subset of variables is already available, the program does not need to be rerun.

Of course, considerations other than significance levels should direct which equation is chosen. Moreover, there is *no guarantee* that the particular subset of $k(<m)$ predictors chosen by stepwise regression is the best possible subset of size k, in the sense of providing the largest (sample) R^2. One would have to compute all possible combinations of the predictors to see if this is so.

An Industry Application

In a recent study conducted for a large manufacturer of steel-belted radial tires, interest centered on whether consumer interest in the firm's new radial tire brand—after exposure to a set of TV commercials, including the firm's and competitive brands—could be predicted from

X_1: general interest in the product class of steel-belted radials;

X_2: whether the firm's old brand was chosen on the respondent's last purchase of replacement tires;

X_3: preexposure (before seeing the commercials) interest in the firm's new brand of steel-belted radials;

X_4: age;

X_5: family size;

X_6: years of education;

X_7: marital status;

$\left.\begin{array}{l} X_8: \\ X_9: \end{array}\right\}$ occupation; and

X_{10}: income.

A sample of 252 male adults, all of whom were responsible for purchasing replacement tires in their respective households, provided the input data.

Dummy Variables

Of additional interest in the study was that five of the predictors were dummy variables. In particular, the following predictors were coded as dummies:

X_1: Is the respondent interested in the product class of steel-belted radial tires? If yes, coded 1; if no, coded 0.

X_2: Was the firm's old brand chosen as the last purchase by the respondent? If yes, coded 1; if no, coded 0.

X_7: Is the respondent married? If yes, coded 1; if no, coded 0.

X_8: Is the respondent's occupation professional or white-collar? If yes, coded 1; if no, coded 0.

X_9: Is the respondent's occupation blue-collar? Is yes, coded 1; if no, coded 0.

The dummy variables X_1, X_2, and X_7 are each dichotomies and present no special problems. On the other hand, the dummy variables X_8 and X_9 are developed from an originally polytomous classification:

	DUMMY VARIABLE	
OCCUPATION CATEGORY	X_8	X_9
Professional or white-collar	1	0
Blue-collar	0	1
Other (including unemployed)	0	0

Note, then, that the third category does *not appear explicitly* in the regression. Its contribution will be buried in the intercept term of the regression equation, while the contributions of X_8 and X_9 will be expressed as *differential* contributions relative to the third, or base, category. As recalled, the intercept term is obtained when all predictors (including X_8 and X_9) assume the value zero.

Generally, however, we are interested in only *relative effects* compared with some (often arbitrary) base category. Any of the three classes of occupation could serve as this base category without affecting the relative contribution of the remaining two categories, since *differential* effects are not influences by which category serves as the reference class.

Stepwise Regression Results

The program produces a rather voluminous output, since summary statistics appear each time a new variable enters the regression equation. For this reason we show only two parts of the output:

1. The regression summary at step 3 of the analysis
2. Summary output at the end of the regression run[14]

Table 11-7 shows the step 3 results.

We note from Table 11-7 that the first three variables (of the ten candidate predictors) to enter are in order X_3, X_1, and X_2. The overall regression equation is "significant." (The F ratio, with 3 degrees of freedom for numerator and 248 degrees of freedom for denominator, is significant well beyond the 0.001 level.) The multiple R is 0.58; hence, the three-predictor regression is accounting for about 34% of the variance in Y.

---

[14]This run was made with a rather loose criterion value of 0.3 each for the: (a) F value for inclusion, (b) F value for retention, and (c) tolerance level.

TABLE 11-7   Step 3 in the Regression Analysis of Purchase Interest in the Firm's New Tire Brand*

Step 3:

Variable entered	2
Multiple R	0.580
Standard error of estimate	2.419

ANALYSIS OF VARIANCE

	Degrees of Freedom	Sum of Squares	Mean Square	F Ratio
Due to regression	3	735.82	245.27	41.91
Residual	248	1,451.57	5.85	
Total	251			

VARIABLES IN EQUATION				VARIABLES NOT IN EQUATION		
ORDER OF ENTERING VARIABLES	Partial Regression Coefficient	Standard Error	Variable	Partial Correlation	Tolerance	F to Enter
3	1.209	0.317	4	−0.079	0.980	1.534
1	0.585	0.402	5	0.000	0.997	0.000
2	0.434	0.050	6	0.006	0.989	0.009
Intercept	(2.957)		7	−0.036	0.979	0.321
			8	0.030	0.961	0.222
			9	−0.028	0.979	0.187
			10	0.078	0.985	1.526

*From BMD-02R.

Judging from the last column of the table, predictor X_4 (with an F value of 1.534) will be the next variable to enter. Equivalently, its partial correlation of −0.079 is the highest in absolute value of those variables not yet in the equation.

The regression equation is

$$\hat{Y} = 2.957 + 0.585X_1 + 0.434X_2 + 1.209X_3$$

Based on these partial regression coefficients, postexposure interest in the firm's new brand increases with

1. Interest in the product class of steel-belted radial tires
2. Purchase of the firm's old brand on the last purchase occasion
3. Preexposure interest in the firm's new brand

All three of these coefficients make sense from an interpretive point of view.

TABLE 11-8 **Summary Output of Stepwise Regression of Purchase Interest in the Firm's New Tire Brand**

Step Number	Variable Entered Removed	Multiple R	Multiple R^2	Increase in R^2	F Value to Enter
1	3	0.539	0.291	—	102.51
2	1	0.575	0.331	0.040	14.85
3	2	0.580	0.336	0.005	2.12
4	4	0.584	0.341	0.005	1.53
5	10	0.588	0.346	0.005	1.94
6	5	0.589	0.347	0.001	0.41

Judging from the small values of F to enter we would expect that not much is to be gained in going beyond three predictors. This hunch is borne out by the summary results appearing in Table 11-8.

We note from Table 11-8 that the program terminated after step 6, since the F values to enter (at step 7) were all less than 0.3.[15] Even with the three additional steps R^2 has only increased about 1 percentage point from that noted in step 3. We conclude that the demographic variables add little to accounted-for variation in Y. One may just as well stop with the three-predictor equation of Table 11-7. Although not shown here, it should be reiterated that the same level of output illustrated in Table 11-7 is printed out at *each step* in the stepwise run.

The sponsor of this study decided to use the three-predictor equation of Table 11-7 in further studies of TV commercial effectiveness. Although the R^2 was not outstanding, enough variation in Y was accounted for (and the equation made sense from a content viewpoint) to justify its use in further studies of TV commercial effectiveness.

We close this section with a technical caveat concerning the use of polytomous predictors (recorded as dummy variables) in stepwise regression: Arbitrariness of coding— in particular, assignment of one of the categories to be the kth class, consisting of all zeros in the $k - 1$ dummy-variable coding—can affect the results. This is because that kth class will *always* be in the regression (as part of the intercept value). Hence, if polytomies are used as predictors, it is advisable to make sure that *all* dummy-variable codes appear in the final regression equation. While variables X_8 and X_9 (the occupational dummies) never entered the regression, in other applications this problem may be encountered.[16]

MULTICOLLINEARITY AND RELATED PROBLEMS

Put rather simply, *multicollinearity* refers to an all-too-common problem in applied regression studies in which the *predictor variables exhibit excessively high correlation among*

---

[15]As it turned out, no predictors were deleted once they entered the regression; that is, their F values for deletion all exceeded the control value of 0.3.

[16]Fortunately, the program used has a "forcing-variables" option by which the user can make sure that certain predictors enter and remain in the equation, regardless of the standard F-value criteria.

themselves. This problem has a bearing on two topics discussed earlier: (1) dummy-variable coding and (2) computing standard errors of the regression coefficients (as illustrated in Table 11-6).

In our use of dummy-variable regression[17] we made sure that the k-class polytomy was recoded into $k - 1$ dummy variables. Failure to have done this would have led to *perfect* multicollinearity—that is, the complete dependence of values in the kth class on values taken on by the other $k - 1$ dummies. If three classes and three dummies are involved, knowledge that no "1" appears in the first two dummies enables us to predict the appearance of a "1" in the third dummy variable with certainty. However, by choosing only two dummies and coding the third class (0,0), we guard against this type of redundancy.

Once one remembers to code k-class polytomies into $k - 1$ dummy variables, the potential problem of perfect multicollinearity in the case of polytomies disappears. However, the more subtle cases involve predictors that just happen to be highly (but not necessarily perfectly) correlated in the first place. As Johnston[18] points out, the *effects* of this more insidious problem may involve any of the following:

1. A reduction in the precision of estimating the coefficient of the regression equation and the difficulty, if not impossibility, of disentangling the separate effects of each predictor variable on the criterion variable.
2. Predictor variables may be dropped incorrectly (perhaps mechanically so in stepwise regression procedures) because of the high standard errors.
3. Estimation of partial regression coefficients may become highly sensitive to the specific sample; addition or deletion of a few observations may produce marked differences in the values of the coefficients, including even changes in algebraic sign.

Unless one is dealing with experimental design data, it is almost always the case that predictor variables in multiple regression will be correlated to some degree. The question is, How much multicollinearity can be tolerated without seriously affecting the results? Unfortunately there is no simple answer to this question.

The study of multicollinearity in data analysis evolves around two major problems: (1) How can it be detected? and (2) what can be done about it? These problems are particularly relevant to marketing research, where one often faces the dilemma of needing a large number of variables to achieve accuracy of predictors yet finding that as more predictors *are* added to the model, their intercorrelations become larger.

As indicated above, what constitutes "serious" multicollinearity is ambiguous. Some researchers have adopted various rules of thumb: For example, any pair of predictor variables must not correlate more than 0.9; if so, one of the predictors is discarded. While looking at simple correlations between pairs of predictors has merit, it can miss more subtle relationships involving three or more predictors.

[17]Dummy-variable regression is not the same as *binary* regression. Although closely related to standard regression analysis, binary regression is useful when the dependent variable is a dummy variable taking only the values 0 and 1: See B. B. Jackson, *Multivariate Data Analysis: An Introduction* (Homewood, Ill.: Richard D. Irwin, 1983), Chap. 4.

[18]J. Johnston, *Econometric Methods*, 2nd ed. (New York: McGraw-Hill, 1972).

The above rule can be extended, of course, to the examination of *multiple* correlations between each predictor and all other predictors. Usually one would want to guard against having any of these multiple correlations exceed the multiple correlation of the *criterion* variable with the predictor set.

Another test for multicollinearity provided in many regression programs involves examining the determinant[19] of the correlation matrix. As the value of the determinant approaches zero, extreme multicollinearity is the case; it approaches unity as the predictor variables become mutually uncorrelated. Unfortunately, it is not clear what a "reasonable" value of the determinant should be. However, research activity is being devoted to the development of more rigorous measures of multicollinearity and, in particular, to ways of pinpointing its presence in specific subsets of the predictor variables.

Procedures for Coping with Multicollinearity

Essentially there are three procedures for dealing with multicollinearity: (1) ignore it, (2) delete one or more of the offending predictors, and (3) transform the set of predictor variables into a new set of predictor-variable combinations that are mutually uncorrelated.

Ignoring multicollinearity need not be as cavalier as it might sound. First, one can have multicollinearity in the predictor variables and still have strong enough effects that the estimating coefficients remain reasonably stable. Second, multicollinearity may be prominent in only a subset of the predictors, a subset that may not contribute much to accounted-for variance anyway. A prudent procedure in checking one's predictor set for multicollinearity is to examine the standard errors of the regression coefficients (which will tend to be large in the case of high multicollinearity). Second, one may randomly drop some subset of the cases (perhaps 20% or so), rerun the regression, and then check to see if the signs and relative sizes of the regression coefficients are stable. Third, a number of recently developed regression routines incorporate checks for serious multicollinearity; if the program does not indicate this condition, the researcher can generally assume that the problem is not acute.

If multicollinearity is "severe," one rather simple procedure is to drop one or more predictor variables that represent the major offenders. Usually, because of their high intercorrelations with the retained predictors, the overall fit will not change markedly. (Pragmatically, if a particular pair of predictors are highly collinear, one would retain that member of the pair whose measurement reliability and/or theoretical importance is higher in the substantive problem under study.)

Methods also exist (e.g., principal components analysis) for transforming the orig-

---

[19]The determinant of a (square) matrix is a single number that represents the sum of alternately signed products of matrix elements. In the 2×2 case the determinant is computed as

$$|A| = \begin{vmatrix} a_{11} & a_{12} \\ a_{21} & a_{22} \end{vmatrix}$$

$$= a_{11}a_{22} - a_{12}a_{21}$$

If the determinant A is zero, the matrix is called *singular*; such would be the case under conditions of perfect multicollinearity.

inal set of predictors to a mutually uncorrelated set of linear composites. If these components (linear composites) are interpretable in themselves, the researcher may use *these* in the regression analysis rather than the original variables. If *all* components are retained, the predictive accuracy will be precisely the same as that obtained from the original set of predictors. However, the problem here is that the components may *not* be interpretable in their own right. We discuss this approach in more detail in Chapter 14. Another possibility, of course, is to use only one of the variables for each component to represent that component in the regression analysis.

Cross Validation

Probably the safest procedure for coping with a variety of problems in multiple regression, including multicollinearity, is to use *cross validation*. We have frequently commented in this chapter on the tendency of regression models (and the same is true of other multivariate techniques as well) to capitalize on chance variation in the sample data. Since these techniques are optimizing methods, they find the best possible fit of the model to the *specific* data at hand. When the regression function is tried out on fresh data, one almost invariably finds a poorer fit.

Cross validation is a simple procedure for examining whether the regression equation holds up beyond the data on which its parameters are based. The researcher simply takes part of the data (perhaps a quarter to a third) and puts it aside. The regression equation is then computed from the remaining data. Following this, the researcher takes the held-out data and computes a set of $\hat{Y}_i$, using the earlier-computed regression equation and the predictor-variable values of the held-out sample. The researcher then finds the simple coefficient of determination between the Y_i in the held-out sample and their predicted $\hat{Y}_i$ counterparts. This coefficient is compared with the R^2 obtained from the original analysis to see what the degree of "shrinkage" is.

An even better procedure is to *doubly cross-validate*. This is carried out by the following steps:

1. Split the cases randomly into halves.
2. Compute *separate* regression equations for each half.
3. Use the first-half equation to predict the second-half Y_i values.
4. Use the second-half equation to predict the first-half Y_i values.
5. Examine each partial regression coefficient across split halves to see if agreement is obtained in both directions (algebraic sign) and in magnitude.
6. Compute a regression equation for the entire sample, using only those variables that show stability in the preceding step.

Since high multicollinearity will make sample-to-sample regression coefficients unstable, double cross validation can help the researcher find out which coefficients exhibit stability across split halves.

Depending on the sample size, of course, one could split the sample into thirds, quarters, and so on. Usually, however, there are sufficient constraints on sample size, relative to the number of predictors, that split-half testing is about all that gets done. Even so, single or double cross validation is an extremely useful undertaking and, in the age of computer programs, not that difficult to implement.

Importance of Predictor Variables

In almost any applied regression problem there is an urge to use such measures as squared partial correlations or squared beta coefficients to rank predictors in order of importance in accounting for variation in the criterion. If the predictors are uncorrelated, this is a perfectly sensible thing to do.[20] If not, the urge should be tempered. This is simply because, in the case of correlated predictors, *there is no unambiguous measure of relative importance of predictor variables.*

Figure 11-8   Procedures for Dealing with Overlapping Variance

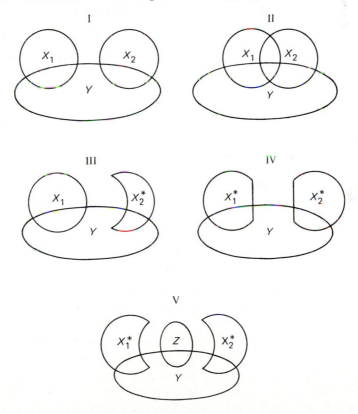

---

[20]If the predictors are uncorrelated, (squared) simple correlations, (squared) partial correlations, and (squared) betas will *all* be equal and, obviously, will rank the variables the same way. However, unless one is dealing with a designed experiment, such occasions are rare.

The problem of relative importance of predictors is illustrated compactly in Figure 11-8, showing five cases of interest, as described by Gorsuch.[21] In Panel I, no problem arises; although X_1 and X_2 both contribute to variance in Y, their contributions are separate. This is the type of situation that arises in designed experiments and leads to an *unambiguous allocation* of criterion-variable variance across the predictors.

Panel II, however, is the more usual situation encountered in multiple regression and other instances in which the predictors exhibit multicollinearity. Here we note that X_1 and X_2 each contribute to accounted-for variance in Y but also share some of this accounted-for variance.

Panel III illustrates the case in which X_1 is credited not only with its unique variance but also with all that it shares with X_2. Panel IV splits, often in a rather arbitrary way, the shared variance between X_1 and X_2. Panel V shows the least common case (illustrated by Gorsuch) in which a new composite variable Z is created to represent shared variance in X_1 and X_2.

No firm recommendations can be made regarding which strategy to adopt in selecting an importance measure, since, obviously, the strategy will depend on the researcher's objective. It is worth repeating, however, that in the stepwise regression programs—even though variables to be included are selected on the basis of highest incremental contribution to accounted-for-variance—the contributions ascribed to new variables to be added are conditioned by predictors already in the equation.[22] (This is the situation of Panel III in Figure 11-8.)

RANK CORRELATION

Our discussion in this chapter is based on the premise that the dependent variable is at least intervally scaled or can be treated as such with little error. There are marketing problems, however, where the "dependent" and "independent" variables are rank orders or are best transformed into such rankings. In this situation *rank correlation* techniques can be used to estimate the association between sets of data.

For two variables the best-known and easiest technique is that involving use of the Spearman rank correlation coefficient, r_s.[23] We show the use of this measure by an example. Suppose a sales manager evaluates salespersons by two different methods (performance index and a new method). Since the new method is easier to use, the manager wants to know if it will yield the same relative results as the "proven" existing method. The scores have been transformed into rankings so that each salesperson has two rankings. Table 11-9 shows the rankings.

---

[21]Figure 11-8 has been adapted from R. L. Gorsuch, "Data Analysis of Correlated Independent Variables," *Multivariate Behavioral Research,* 8 (January 1973), 89–107.

[22]In all-variables programs the same idea holds except for the fact that a prior ordering of the variables is implicitly established by the researcher by the manner in which he or she enters the predictor variables.

[23]Another measure that gives comparable results is the Kendall rank correlation coefficient, τ (tau). One advantage to τ is that it can be generalized to a partial correlation coefficient. See S. Siegel, *Nonparametric Statistics for the Behavioral Sciences* (New York: McGraw-Hill, 1957), pp. 213–29.

TABLE 11-9 Ranks on Two Methods of Salesperson Evaluation

	RANK			
SALESPERSON	*Performance Index* (X)	*New Method* (Y)	d_i	d_i^2
A	8	6	2	4
B	4	7	−3	9
C	1	2	−1	1
D	6	3	3	9
E	2	1	1	1
F	10	8	2	4
G	5	5	0	0
H	3	9	−6	36
I	7	4	3	9
J	9	10	1	1
			$\Sigma d_i^2 =$	74

To measure the extent of rank correlation we use the statistic

$$r_s = 1 - \frac{6 \sum_{i=1}^{N} d^2}{N(N^2 - 1)}$$

where N is the number of pairs of ranks and d is the difference between the two rankings for an individual (that is, $X - Y$). Applying this formula to our example, we get

$$r_s = 1 - \frac{6(74)}{10(100 - 1)} = .55$$

If the subjects whose scores were used in computing r_s were randomly drawn from a population, we can test the significance of the obtained value. The null hypothesis is that the two variables are not associated, and thus the true value of ρ is zero. Under H_o any observed value would be due to chance. When $N \geq 10$, significance can be tested using the statistic

$$t = r_s \sqrt{\frac{N - 2}{1 - r_s^2}}$$

which is interpreted from Table A-3 of Appendix A with $(N - 2)$ degrees of freedom. For our example, we calculate

$$t = .55 \sqrt{\frac{10 - 2}{1 - (.55)^2}} = 1.870$$

Looking at the table of critical values of *t*, we find that $p > .10$ (two-tailed test) for $(10 - 2 = 8)$ degrees of freedom. Thus, if a strict α level is to be adhered to (.10 or less), we accept H_0 and conclude that it is unlikely that a correlation exists between the scores from the two evaluation methods.

One final point concerning the use of the Spearman rank correlation coefficient is warranted. At times, tied observations will exist. When this happens, each of them is assigned the average of the ranks that would have been assigned in the absence of ties. If the proportion of ties is small, the effect on r_s is minute. If large, however, a correction factor must be applied.[24]

The Spearman rank correlation coefficient is limited to measuring correlation between only two sets of rankings. If an analyst wants to measure the relationship between three or more rankings of *N* things, the nonparametric *Kendall coefficient of concordance, W,* can be used. This measure is useful in looking at the extent of agreement among several sets of judges, such as used in developing scaling instruments, or simply the association among many variables, which are at best ordinally scaled. We shall not discuss this measure further but refer the reader to the writings of Siegel.[25]

SUMMARY

Our discussion of multiple and partial regression has been more detailed than will be the description of other multivariate techniques in subsequent chapters. This has been deliberate: multiple regression is not only the best known of these techniques but a grasp of its essentials markedly facilitates understanding of more-advanced procedures.

We started the chapter with a discussion of simple (bivariate) regression and described such measures as regression coefficients, the coefficient of determination, and the product-moment correlation. Graphical aids were employed wherever possible.

We next considered the multiple regression case and showed how its measures could be given interpretations in terms of counterpart simple coefficients.

Since nowadays almost all multiple regressions are carried out by computer, we discussed two programs—an all-variables program and a stepwise program—and illustrated their application numerically. Each aspect of their outputs was described conceptually and numerically.[26]

The concluding parts of the chapter dealt with the problems of multicollinearity,

---

[24]See Siegel, *Nonparametric Statistics for the Behavioral Sciences,* pp. 206–10.

[25]Ibid., pp. 229–38.

[26]More-advanced material on multiple regression, including computer-based procedures, can be found in N. R. Draper and H. Smith, *Applied Regression Analysis* (New York: John Wiley, 1966); and J. Cohen and P. Cohen, *Applied Multiple Regression/Correlation Analysis for the Behavioral Sciences,* 2nd ed. (Hillsdale, N.J.: Lawrence Erlbaum Associates, 1983).

cross validation, the determination of the relative importance of predictor variables, and the case where the data are rankings. As stressed throughout, in the case of correlated predictors relative importances are, at best, ambiguous and can be misleading. Only in designed experiments involving uncorrelated predictors do we find unequivocal measures of relative importance.

ASSIGNMENT MATERIAL

1. A sample survey of home swimming pool owners in southeastern Pennsylvania has yielded the following information regarding pool costs versus annual income.
   a. Using least squares, compute a linear regression of Y on X. How do you interpret the formula?
   b. Compute the coefficient of determination and the variance of the estimate. Interpret these measures.
   c. What applications would you suggest for the regression formula if you were employed by a Pennsylvania swimming pool builder?

Respondent	Pool Cost, Y (THOUSANDS OF DOLLARS)	Annual Income, X (THOUSANDS OF DOLLARS)
1	3.6	9.3
2	4.8	10.2
3	2.4	9.7
4	7.2	11.5
5	6.9	12.0
6	8.4	14.2
7	10.7	18.6
8	11.2	28.4
9	6.1	13.2
10	7.9	10.8
11	9.5	22.7
12	5.4	12.3

2. Assume next that the survey of swimming pool owners also yielded information on total size of the pool owner's lot. The data (expressed in thousands of square feet) appear as follows:

Respondent	1	2	3	4	5	6	7	8	9	10	11	12
Lot size, Z	30.2	40.1	35.3	45.1	38.0	50.1	60.2	100.4	25.1	40.7	68.4	60.3

   a. Using the data of the preceding problem, compute, by least squares, a linear multiple regression of Y on X and Z. How would you interpret this formula?

b. If you were told that a pool owner had an income of $12,500 annually and a lot size of 40,000 square feet, what pool cost would you predict?

c. Compute the coefficient of multiple determination R^2. What effect does knowledge of both annual income *and* lot size have on the "explanatory" power of the regression in contrast to knowledge only about annual income?

d. What are the assumptions underlying the least-squares regression model?

3. Apply a stepwise regression program to a data set of your choice:

a. Using the program's default values on variable inclusion and retention, run the analysis on the whole data set.

b. Next, split the data into halves by taking odd-numbered and even-numbered cases. Perform separate regressions. How do these split-half results compare with those obtained from the full sample?

4. Using the same data set as in question 3 above, do the same types of analyses but use an all-variables program. What can you conclude about the results from stepwise and all-variables programs?

5. Compare the advantages of partial regression coefficients versus partial correlation coefficients in representing the relative importance of predictor variables.

6. In what ways can multiple regression be used to forecast some industry's sales? A specific company's sales?

12

Analysis of Variance and Covariance

INTRODUCTION

In the preceding chapter we discussed the regression model and correlation analysis, techniques that are appropriate where the researcher investigates possible changes in the dependent variable that may accompany changes in the independent variable(s). In this situation all variables are at least interval-scaled, although one or more independent variables may sometimes be at a lesser level of measurement.

For a single dependent variable that is at least interval-scaled, there are two other possibilities. First, when the independent variable(s) is (are) at most ordinal-scaled, the researcher is usually concerned with differences in the average value of the dependent variable over the various categories of the independent variable(s). A technique of analysis appropriate for this situation is analysis of variance (ANOVA). Second, many research studies involve a set of independent variables that are mixed in level of measurement and range from nominal to ratio. When this type of situation exists, the researcher can select either analysis of covariance (ANCOVA) or regression analysis with dummy variables, two techniques that are statistically similar.

In this chapter our concern is with ANOVA primarily and ANCOVA to a very limited extent. Traditional use of analysis of variance has been with experimental designs such as those statistical, multivariable designs discussed previously in Chapter 6—completely randomized, randomized block, latin square, and factorial designs. However, it must be recognized that use of ANOVA is not limited to experimentation and that it is appropriate for survey designs and observational data. The appropriateness depends on the purpose of the analysis, the level of measurement of the variables, and certain assumptions about the nature of the errors. Research design per se is not necessarily a determinant of appropriateness. Similarly, analysis of covariance is useful for any type of research design, as it is essentially a combination of analysis of variance and regression analysis.

We start by looking at experimental design and analysis of variance. Our discussion of this technique (and that of covariance analysis) within the context of experimental research is appropriate because ANOVA is widely used for analyzing experimental research and because non-experimentally-obtained data are often analyzed as if they were obtained by experimental means. We can turn to single- and multiple-factor ANOVA designs. Selected computer routines for performing ANOVA and ANCOVA are presented as illustrations only. There are many such routines available from the mainframe statistical package, and many routines have been written for microcomputer use. The next section of this chapter concerns the interpretation of experimental results within the context of ANOVA. Relevant topics are the various types of interactions that may occur, the tests for multiple comparisons, and the way to ascertain the relative importance of independent variables in explaining the variation in the dependent variable. The final section contains a relatively brief discussion of basic concepts of multivariate analysis of variance and covariance.

EXPERIMENTAL DESIGN AND THE ANALYSIS OF VARIANCE

There are two principal aspects of experimental design: (1) the experimental layouts by which treatment levels are assigned to test objects and (2) the techniques that are used to analyze the results of the experiment. The first aspect was covered in Chapter 6, and we now turn to the techniques of analysis. The generic name for these techniques is *analysis of variance and covariance*. Let us first consider the analysis of variance (ANOVA).

At first glance, the phrase "analysis of variance" may give the impression that the technique is used to test for significant differences among the variances of two or more sample universes. Actually, however, the objective of ANOVA is to test the statistical significance of differences among *average responses* due to controlled variables, after allowance is made for influences on response due to uncontrolled variables (Exhibit 12-1). The label "analysis of variance" is appropriate because if the mean responses of the test objects are different *among* treatments, then the *variance of the combined groups will exceed the variances of the individual groups*.

An example should make this clear. Suppose that one universe of responses has, in fact, a mean of 4 and another universe of responses has a mean of 12, each with a variance of 1.

$$\mu_1 = 4, \qquad \sigma_1^2 = 1$$

$$\mu_2 = 12, \qquad \sigma_2^2 = 1$$

Exhibit 12-1   Determining When Means Are Significantly Different

As an illustration let us assume that we have measured the purchase of a new brand of ice cream at two food stores—a supermarket (SM) and a convenience store (CV). Observations have been made for five days at each store. This study could have been run as a rigorous controlled experiment or as a more loosely run observational study.

We are interested in determining whether the mean number of quarts sold at the two stores (Y_i) differed significantly. Graph I below shows that the means are numerically different, but we cannot tell whether they are significantly different.

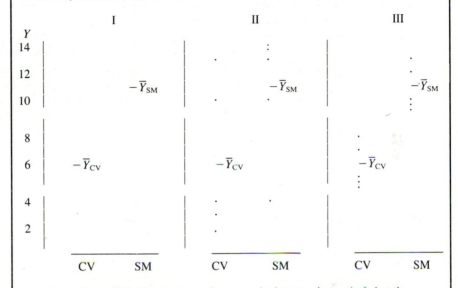

In Graph II the difference between the means is the same it was in I, but the difference is suspect because the individual observations are spread out. Within each group the variance is so great that the difference in the means is not convincing.

The situation differs considerably in Graph III where the difference between means is the same as in the two previous situations. However, the observations are clustered around the means for each store. This clustering now allows us to conclude that there is a statistically significant difference between the two means.

The problem is how to decide when means are different enough, relative to the spread of the observations (i.e., the variance) in each group, to conclude that there is a statistically significant difference between the means. Analysis of variance helps us answer the question.

Source: Adapted from Gudmund R. Iversen and Helmut Norpoth, *Analysis of Variance*, (Beverly Hills, Calif.: Sage, 1976), pp. 11–13.

Suppose that we sampled from each universe and then *combined* these two samples and calculated a grand mean (based on an equal number of observations from each group). This mean would be approximately equal to 8, but the *variance* of the combined sample would be "close to" $(4 - 8)^2 = (12 - 8)^2 = 16$, which is much larger than the variances ($\sigma_1^2 = \sigma_2^2 = 1$) of the individual populations. This illustrates the danger of combining observations into a single sample, since such a procedure is strictly correct only *if the means and variances of the two universes being combined are equal.* In the analysis of variance we take advantage of the principle illustrated above by separating the total variance of all observations into two parts: variance due to the *within* variability of the universes and variance due to differences *among* the means of the universes from which the sample was taken. The latter variance will be larger than the former *if differences among means exist.*

In essence, then, the analysis of variance is used as a test of *means* among two or more universes. The null hypothesis is typically that all means are equal, although the experimenter (through appropriate technique refinements) may sometimes compare the means of specific individual universes. Analysis of variance thus involves making statistical inferences from samples to universes just as any sampling problem does.

From a formal standpoint, analysis of variance is a type of multiple regression with dummy-valued predictor variables.[1] The elegant apparatus of ANOVA is based on the *maintenance of independence among the treatment variables.* That is, by designing experiments in which the treatment variable is independently varied (and by ensuring an equal number of response observations for each combination of treatment variables), special analytical procedures can be employed to assess the effect of each predictor, unconfounded with other effects.

Among and Within Sums of Squares

In Chapter 11 we described how r^2, the coefficient of determination, utilized two sums of squares in its calculation:

- The sum of squared errors in predicting each Y_i from $\hat{Y}_i$ (the latter computed from the regression equation).
- The sum of squared errors in predicting each Y_i from $\overline{Y}_i$, the criterion-variable mean.

Furthermore, Figure 11-6 showed how the deviations of $Y_i - \overline{Y}$ could be broken down into additive parts—a deviation of Y_i from $\hat{Y}_i$ and a deviation $\hat{Y}_i$ from $\overline{Y}$.

Similar ideas underlie analysis of variance. That is, an observation can be decomposed into three terms, which are additive:

> Observation = Overall mean + Deviation of group mean from
>
> overall mean + Deviation of observation
>
> from group mean

---

[1]We refer here to *fixed-effects* analysis of variance in which the levels of treatment variables are fixed and are the only levels of concern in a study. In contast is a *random-effects* analysis where random variables are involved and the treatment levels are a sample such that there will be inferences beyond those levels used in the study. While computations for the two models are similar, interpretations of results differ. A comparison of these approaches is found in J. Neter, W. Wasserman, and M. Kutner, *Applied Linear Statistical Models*, 2nd ed. (Homewood, Ill.: Richard D. Irwin, 1985).

The overall mean is a constant, common to all observations; the deviation of a group mean from the overall mean represents the effect on each observation of belonging to that particular group; and the deviation of an observation from its group mean represents the effect on that observation of all variables other than the group variable.[2] To illustrate, assume that we had responses to three treatment "levels," such as three magazine advertising copy themes: A, B, and C.

REPLICATION	THEME A	THEME B	THEME C
1	6	8	0
2	4	11	2
3	3	5	1
4	3	4	1
$\overline{X}_j$	4	7	1

Grand mean: 4

For illustrative purposes the responses are assumed to be ratings on a 0–11 purchase-interest scale (0 denoting no interest and 11 denoting very high interest in purchasing the advertised brand). Each copy theme is evaluated by four randomly chosen persons and no person evaluates more than one copy theme (this is a completely randomized design).

The *sample* means show that theme B is highest on the average, followed by A and then C. Are the universe means significantly different? Before trying to answer the statistical question, let us calculate three sums of squares:

- The pooled within-samples sum of squares
- The among-samples sum of squares
- The total-samples sum of squares

The within-samples sum of square is

Theme

A: $(6 - 4)^2 + (4 - 4)^2 + (3 - 4)^2 + (3 - 4)^2 = 6$

B: $(8 - 7)^2 + (11 - 7)^2 + (5 - 7)^2 + (4 - 7)^2 = 30$

C: $(0 - 1)^2 + (2 - 1)^2 + (1 - 1)^2 + (1 - 1)^2 = \underline{2}$

38

The among-samples sum of squares is

$$4(4 - 4)^2 + 4(7 - 4)^2 + 4(1 - 4)^2 = 72$$

The total-sample sum of squares is

$$(6 - 4)^2 + (4 - 4)^2 + \cdots + (1 - 4)^2 + (1 - 4)^2 = 110$$

[2]G. Iversen and H. Norpoth, *Analysis of Variance* (Beverly Hills, Calif.: Sage, 1976), p. 23.

As shown, each within-sample sum of squares is computed around that specific sample's mean. The results are then added to obtain the pooled value of 38. In the case of the among-samples sum of squares, each sample mean is based on four observations; hence, if *each case* in a particular sample were represented by that sample's mean, the sum of squares around the total-sample mean would be 72, as shown. Finally, we note that the within-samples sum of squares plus the among-samples sum of squares equals the total-sample sum of squares of 110.

The basic idea of ANOVA is to compare the among-samples sum of squares (after adjustment by degrees of freedom to get a *mean square*) with the (similarly adjusted) within-samples value. This is the F ratio, described earlier in Chapter 11. The *larger* the ratio of among to within, the more we are inclined to reject the null hypothesis that the

Figure 12-1   Breakdown of Deviations $Y_i - \bar{Y}$ into Two Additive Parts

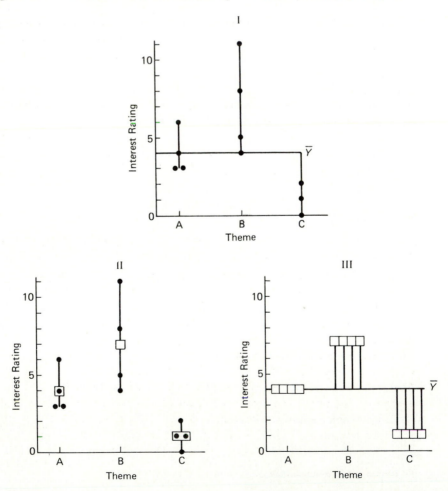

universe means μ_A, μ_B, and μ_C are equal.[3] Conversely, if the three sample means were very close to each other, the among-samples sum of squares would be close to zero and we would conclude that the universe means are not different, once we consider the variability of individual cases within each sample.

However, to make this comparison it is necessary to assume that the error-term distribution has constant variance over all observations. This is exactly the same assumption made in the regression model of Chapter 11.

Figure 12-1 (p. 469) represents the counterpart case of Figure 11-6. In Panel I of Figure 12-1 we show the deviations that would be obtained by trying to predict each individual observation by the total-sample mean. The sum of these squared errors is 110, as noted above. Panels II and III show how the errors break down into within and among portions.

Panel II shows the deviations obtained by trying to predict each case in a specific sample by that sample's mean (denoted by a small box in Panel II). The sum of these squared errors, added over the three samples, is 38, the within-samples sum of squares.

Panel III shows the deviations obtained by trying to predict each case—assuming it were equal to its respective sample's mean—by the total-sample mean. The sum of these squared errors is 72, the among-samples sum of squares. Thus, the analogy with regression is complete, once we get used to the idea that the predicted or $\hat{Y}_i$ values in ANOVA are the specific sample means (4, 7, or 1) for each of the four cases in that respective sample.

However, in the next section of the chapter we shall (1) use more efficient computational techniques, (2) consider the adjustment for degrees of freedom to obtain *mean squares*, and (3) show the case of the F ratio in testing significance. Still, the foregoing remarks represent the basic ANOVA idea of comparing among- with within-samples variability.

Single-Factor Analysis of Variance

As an illustration of analysis of variance in its simplest (single-factor) form, suppose that a marketer is interested in the effect of shelf height on supermarket sales of canned dog food. The marketer has been able to secure the cooperation of a store manager to run an experiment involving three levels of shelf height ("knee" level, "waist" level, and "eye" level) on sales of a single brand of dog food, which we shall call Arf. Assume further that our experiment must be conducted in a single supermarket and that our response variable will be sales, in cans, of Arf dog food for some appropriate unit of time. But what shall we use for our unit of time? Sales of dog food in a single store may exhibit week-to-week variation, day-to-day variation, and even hour-to-hour variation. In addition, sales of this particular brand may be affected by the price or special promotions of competitive brands, the store management's knowledge that an experiment is going on, and other variables that we cannot control at all or would find too costly to control.

We shall address ourselves to some of these questions (and others) in a later section

---

[3]As may be recalled from elementary statistics, the Student t test, it turns out, is just a special case of the F test when two samples are involved.

TABLE 12-1   Sales of Arf Dog Food (in Units) by Level of Shelf Height

		SHELF HEIGHT				
Knee Level		Waist Level		Eye Level		GRAND TOTAL
X_{11}	77	X_{12}	88	X_{13}	85	
X_{21}	82	X_{22}	94	X_{23}	85	
X_{31}	86	X_{32}	93	X_{33}	87	
X_{41}	78	X_{42}	90	X_{43}	81	
X_{51}	81	X_{52}	91	X_{53}	80	
X_{61}	86	X_{62}	94	X_{63}	79	
X_{71}	77	X_{72}	90	X_{73}	87	
X_{81}	81	X_{82}	87	X_{83}	93	
$X_{T1} = 648$		$X_{T2} = 727$		$X_{T3} = 677$		$X_{TT} = 2{,}052$
$\overline{X}_1 = 81.0$		$\overline{X}_2 = 90.9$		$\overline{X}_3 = 84.6$		$\overline{X}_{TT} = 85.5$

of this chapter, but for the time being, assume that we have agreed to change the shelf-height position of Arf three times per day and run the experiment over eight days. We shall fill the remaining sections of the particular gondola that houses our brand with a "filler" brand, which is not familiar to customers in the geographical area in which the test is being conducted. Furthermore, since our primary emphasis is on explaining the technique of analysis of variance in its simplest form (a single variable of classification), we shall assign the shelf heights at random over the three time periods per day and not deal explicitly with within-day and among-day differences. If so, our experimental results might look like those shown in Table 12-1. Here, we let X_{ij} denote the sales (in units) of Arf during the ith day under the jth treatment level. If we look at mean sales by each level of shelf height, it appears as though the waist-level treatment, the average response to which is $\overline{X}_2 = 90.9$, results in highest mean sales over the experimental period. However, we note that the last observation (93) under the eye-level treatment exceeds the waist-level treatment mean. Is this a fluke observation? We know that these means are, after all, *sample* means, and our interest lies in whether the *universe* means are equal or not.

Now assume for the moment that we possess omniscience and can look into the *underlying process* that produced our experimental results. Assume that the universe means are *really different* and are as follows:

$$\mu_1 = 80; \qquad \mu_2 = 90; \qquad \mu_3 = 85$$

If we wish, however, we can represent the three means as deviations from a grand mean $\mu = 85$; then $\mu_1 = \mu - 5$; $\mu_2 = \mu + 5$; $\mu_3 = \mu + 0$. Let us also assume that the error term ε_{ij} of each universe is normally distributed with a zero mean and a (common) variance:

$$\sigma_1^2 = 16; \qquad \sigma_2^2 = 16; \qquad \sigma_3^2 = 16$$

With these assumptions we can run a "dummy" experiment by drawing random normal numbers from a common probability distribution that we shall call the ε (epsilon) distribution. Then *any* observation X_{ij} can be looked upon as the sum of three numbers:

$$X_{ij} = \mu + \tau_j + \varepsilon_{ij}, \ \Sigma\tau_j = 0; \qquad i = 1, 2, \ldots, n_j, j = 1, 2, 3$$

$$n = \Sigma n_j$$

where μ = grand mean over the three universes

τ_j = effect due to treatment j, $j = 1, 2, 3$

ε_{ij} = effect due to uncontrolled variation; this variable is assumed to be normally and independently distributed with $\mu(\varepsilon) = 0$, and $\sigma^2(\varepsilon) = 16$; $\sigma(\varepsilon) = 4$

This is precisely what we have done in concocting the "data" of Table 12-1. To summarize, the parameter values are as follows:

$$\mu = 85$$

$$\tau_1 = -5, \tau_2 = +5, \tau_3 = 0$$

$$\mu(\varepsilon) = 0; \qquad \sigma(\varepsilon) = 4$$

For example, the first observation under the knee-level treatment column (77) was found by taking the random normal number -0.783 from a standard table[4] and multiplying this value by 4, the standard deviation of the error (epsilon) distribution, and rounding off the answer to the nearest integer: $4(-0.783) = -3.132 \cong -3$. Thus,

$$77 = 85 - 5 - 3$$

In a similar way, we developed the other entries of Table 12-1. Now we shall show what happens when one goes through typical analysis-of-variance computations for this problem. These calculations are shown in Table 12-2.

Table 12-2 shows the mechanics of developing the among-treatments, within-treatments, and total sums of squares, the mean squares, and the F ratio. Had the experimenter used an alpha risk of 0.01, the null hypothesis of no differences among treatment levels would have been rejected. (A table of F ratios is found in Table A-4, Appendix A.)

Note that Table 12-2 shows shortcut procedures for finding each sum of squares. For example, the total sum of squares is given by

$$\Sigma X_{ij}^2 - \frac{(X_{TT})^2}{n} = 688.0$$

[4]For an extensive list of random normal numbers, see Rand Corporation, *A Million Digits with 100,000 Normal Deviates* (New York: Free Press, 1955). For a short list of random normal numbers, see Table A-6 in Appendix A.

TABLE 12-2 Analysis of Variance—Arf Dog Food Experiment

Source of Variation	Degrees of Freedom	Sum of Squares	Mean Square	F Ratio
Among treatments	$t - 1 = 2$	399.3	199.7	14.6 ($p < 0.01$)
Within treatments	$n - t = 21$	288.7	13.7	
Total	$n - 1 = 23$	688.0		

Correction factor

$$C = \frac{(X_{TT})^2}{n} = \frac{(2,052)^2}{24} = 175,446.0$$

Total sum of squares

$$\Sigma X_{ij}^2 - C = (77)^2 + (82)^2 + \cdots + (87)^2 + (93)^2$$
$$- 175,466.0 = 688.0$$

Treatment sum of squares

$$\frac{\Sigma X_{Tj}^2}{n_j} - C = \frac{(648)^2 + (727)^2 + (677)^2}{8} - 175,446.0 = 399.3$$

Within treatment sum of squares

$$\Sigma X_{ij}^2 - \frac{\Sigma X_{Tj}^2}{n_j} = (77)^2 + (82)^2 + \cdots + (87)^2$$
$$+ (93)^2 - \frac{(648)^2 + (727)^2 + (677)^2}{8}$$
$$= 288.7$$

This is the same quantity that would be obtained by subtracting the grand mean of 85 from each original observation, squaring the result, and adding up the 24 squared deviations. This mean-corrected sum of squares is equivalent to the type of formula used in Table 11-3. Note also that the mean squares are *universe estimates,* since we have divided each sum of squares by its degrees of freedom.

Our purpose in this exposition, however, is to look behind the preceding calculations and consider what we know about the distributions from which the data in the dummy experiment were derived. First, we know that the grand mean of all three universes μ is equal to 85. If we let $K^2 = (\Sigma \tau_j^2)/(t - 1)$, the estimated "variance" among treatment ($t = 3$) means is

$$K^2 = \frac{(-5)^2 + (+5)^2 + (0)^2}{2} = \frac{50}{2} = 25$$

Also, note that each treatment effect is based on eight observations. The variance of the error distribution ε is, by design, equal to 16. The parameter that we have estimated by the among-treatments means square is

$$\sigma^2(\varepsilon) + 8K^2 = 16 + 8(25) = 16 + 200 = 216$$

The within-treatments mean square estimates just $\sigma^2(\varepsilon) = 16$. Now, if the null hypothesis were true (which we know is *not* the case), then K^2 would be equal to zero, since the treatment effects τ_j *would all equal zero* and $\mu_1 = \mu_2 = \mu_3 = 85$. If so, the among-treatments mean square (i.e., variance) would be an estimate of *only* $\sigma^2(\varepsilon) = 16$.

On the other hand, if the null hypothesis is *not* true and some of the μ_j's are unequal, then K^2 would be greater than zero and, *aside from sampling error,* we would expect the ratio of the among-treatments variance estimate to the within-treatments variance estimate to *exceed unity*. Thus, in Table 12-2 the mean square 199.7 estimates the number 216, and the mean square 13.7 estimates the number 16. Strictly speaking K^2 is a measure of the noncentrality of the treatment means—that is, the "spread" of these around the grand mean. It is *not* a variance in the usual sense of being a parameter of a probability distribution. However, the variance $\sigma^2(\varepsilon)$ *is* a parameter of the error distribution ε.

Statistical Assumptions

Now that we have looked behind the computations involved in single-factor analysis of variance, it is well to summarize the statistical assumptions made in this model.

1. In the "fixed effects" model, which we have assumed in the preceding example, the treatment set τ represents the *entire* set of (three) treatments of interest, not just a sample of treatments from some larger group.
2. The error distribution ε is normally distributed with $\mu(\varepsilon) = 0$ and $\sigma^2(\varepsilon)$ constant over all observations. Moreover, ε does not depend on any of the treatment levels.
3. The effects of treatment are additive.
4. Observations represent independent "draws" from the error distribution ε.

In commenting upon assumption 1 we should note that other models (so-called random-effects models) exist for dealing with cases where the treatments represent some sample from a universe of treatments.[5] A *mixed effects,* or *composite, model* is also available for dealing with both fixed- and random-sample interpretations of the group of experimental treatments.

In commenting upon assumption 2 we may note that research has indicated that moderate departures from normality and equality of variances (homoscedasticity) do not seriously affect the validity of the tests. Moreover, mathematical transformations (logarithmic, square root, arc sine) are available to achieve equal variances and/or normality. Transformations are also available to satisfy assumption 3. For example, if the effects due to treatments are multiplicative, the experimenter may use logarithms of the data.

Departures from the conditions of assumption 4 can distort seriously the appropriate F ratios. The researcher should attempt to design the experiment to avoid dependency among observations or else should use other types of analytical techniques.

---

[5]For an appropriate discussion, see Neter, Wasserman and Kutner, *Applied Linear Statistical Models*.

In addition to the assumptions noted above, the reader should observe that we have neglected mention of type II errors. Our null hypothesis of "no differences in mean response to treatments" used the standard F-ratio approach with an alpha risk of 0.01. Techniques are available for determining beta risks but, unfortunately, are seldom used in practice and are beyond the scope of this chapter.[6]

The important consideration to remember is that, aside from the statistical assumptions underlying the analysis of variance, the *variance of the error distribution* will influence markedly the significance of the results. That is, if the variance is *large* relative to differences among treatments, then the true effects may be swamped, leading to an acceptance of the null hypothesis when it is false. Chapter 9 has already indicated that increased sample size can reduce experimental error. In the next section we discuss more *specialized* experimental designs whose objective is to increase the efficiency of the experiment by reducing the error variance.

Finally, we should reiterate the connection between the analysis of variance carried out in Table 12-2 and the one conducted earlier in Table 11-7 (in the context of multiple regression). In both cases a *comparison of models* is involved where two independent sources of variance are compared to see whether the among-groups variation (analogous to variance due to regression) differs from within-groups variation (analogous to error variance after regression). The basic idea is the same.

MULTIPLE CLASSIFICATIONS

The preceding example dealt with the simplest of ANOVA designs—classification by a single factor. Suppose that our marketing researcher were interested in the effect of *other* point-of-purchase variables such as shelf "facings" (width of display) and shelf fullness on sales. Or, suppose that the researcher would like to generalize the results of the experiment to other sizes of stores in other marketing regions. It may be preferable to "ask many rather than few questions of nature" if the researcher would like to establish the most general conditions under which the findings are expected to hold. That is, not only may single-factor manipulation be difficult to do in practice, but it may be inefficient as well. In this section we discuss somewhat more specialized experimental designs, all of which are characterized by *two or more variables of classification.*

Factorial Designs

A *factorial experiment* is one in which an equal number of observations is made of all combinations involving at least two levels of at least two variables. This type of experiment enables the researcher to study possible *interactions* among the variables of interest. Suppose we return to our canned dog food illustration but now assume that the researcher is interested in studying the effects of *two* variables of interest: shelf height

---

[6]This issue is discussed in W. J. Dixon and F. J. Massey, *Introduction to Statistical Analysis,* 2nd ed. (New York: McGraw-Hill, 1957), pp. 256–59.

TABLE 12-3 Factorial Display—Arf Dog Food Experiment*

| | SHELF HEIGHT | | | |
FACINGS	Knee Level	Waist Level	Eye Level	TOTAL
Level 1	(70, 75, 79)	(85, 88, 93)	(77, 81, 78)	
(half width)	224	266	236	726
Level 2	(91, 90, 87)	(94, 97, 93)	(87, 90, 90)	
(full width)	268	284	267	819
Total	492	550	503	1,545

*Cell entries are sales in units.

(still at three levels) and shelf facing (at two levels—that is, at half the width of the gondola and at full width of the gondola). While the plan still is to use a single store for the experiment, the researcher intends to replicate each combination three times, leading to $3 \times 2 \times 3 = 18$ observations. Assume that the experiment results in the data shown in Table 12-3.

As noted in Table 12-3, for each combination of shelf height and shelf facing we have three observations. Again, we can set up a theoretical model for this experiment:

$$X_{ijk} = \mu + \alpha_i + \beta_j + (\alpha\beta)_{ij} + \varepsilon_{ijk}$$

where
μ = mean of universe

α_i = true effect of shelf facings, $i = 1, \ldots, a; a = 2$

β_j = true effect of shelf height, $j = 1, \ldots, b; b = 3$

(the terms α_i and β_j are usually called *main effects,* since they refer to responses that are averaged over the other variable of interest)

$(\alpha\beta)_{ij}$ = true interaction effect of ith level of α and jth level of β

ε_{ijk} = random effect from uncontrolled variation with $\mu(\varepsilon) = 0$

$\sigma^2(\varepsilon)$ is = constant over all observations, $k = 1, 2, \ldots, m; m = 3,$
and

$$\Sigma\alpha_i = \Sigma\beta_j = \Sigma(\alpha\beta)_i = \Sigma(\alpha\beta)_j = 0; \quad n = abm$$

In this model we are merely replacing the τ_j of our one-classification model with the symbols α_i and β_j standing for the effects of various levels of two factors.

As in Table 12-2 we need to compute the various sums of squares—in this case of treatments A, B, and A × B interaction, error, and total.[7] Each mean square is compared,

[7] Computing formulas can be found in Wayne W. Daniel and James C. Terrell, *Business Statistics: Basic Concepts and Methodology,* 4th ed. (Boston: Houghton Mifflin, 1986), pp. 336–44.

TABLE 12-4 Analysis of Variance, Factorial Display—Arf Dog Food Experiment

Source of Variation	Degrees of Freedom	Sum of Squares	Mean Square	F Ratio
Treatments				
A (facings)	1	480.5	480.5	54.6 ($p < 0.01$)
B (height)	2	316.3	158.2	18.0 ($p < 0.01$)
A × B	2	56.4	28.2	3.2 ($0.1 > p > 0.05$)
Error	12	105.3	8.8	
Total	17	958.5		

in turn, with the error mean square via the F ratio. The analysis-of-variance summary is shown in Table 12-4.

Looking at the F ratios of Table 12-4, we note that the AB interaction is insignificant at the 0.05 alpha level (but is significant at the 0.1 alpha level). Still, if the researcher were interested in the particular combination of shelf height and shelf facings that would produce highest sales, it would seem as though the combination full width, waist level is best (see Table 12-3).

One of the easiest ways to understand the nature of interaction is to plot the response variable against changes in one of the treatment variables at different levels of a second treatment variable. This is done for the averaged cell responses in Table 12-3 and the

Figure 12-2 Plot of the A × B (Shelf Height by Facings) Interaction

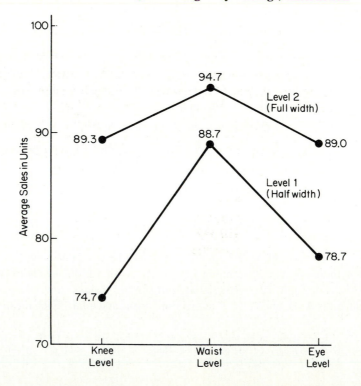

results are shown in Figure 12-2 (p. 477). The vertical axis of the chart shows average unit sales, whereas the horizontal axis shows levels of the shelf-height variable. Connecting lines between effects are shown strictly for visual purposes, since only discrete levels of A and B are involved.

For example, averaged unit sales when shelf height is at knee level and facings are at *half width* is 74.7 units, as shown on the chart. As can be seen, average sales increase (to 88.7) at waist level and then decline (to 78.7) at eye level. However, when we examine the average sales unit response to changes in shelf height when facings are *full width,* we see that the response *increments* differ; that is, the line segments are not parallel. That is, the response to changes in shelf height differs across the two levels of facings.

Another way of saying this is to note that the *differential effect of* moving from knee level to waist level depends on what the level of facings is. For facings at half width the difference is 88.7 − 74.7 = 14.0. When facings are at full width, the difference is 94.7 − 89.3 = 5.4; that is, the incremental effect is less pronounced. If the *observed* departures from parallelism in each of the line segment pairs cannot be ascribed to sampling fluctuations, then we say that a significant interaction exists.

Technically, what is shown here is an *ordinal* interaction. By this is meant that sales response to waist level is still higher than sales response to knee level, independent of facings level—it is the *incremental* difference that varies. Had average sales response to the combination of waist level and full-width facings been, say, only 72 units, then a *disordinal* interaction would be involved. The latter case is much more serious, since before we can specify what level of shelf height to consider from a marketing strategy standpoint, we must know what level of facings is involved. On the other hand, under ordinal interactions (assuming equal implementation costs for each alternative), waist level leads to highest sales at each level of facings.

In the case of quantitative factors, such as shelf height or facings, it is useful to distinguish between *interaction* and *nonlinearity*. For example, suppose we were to assume that the three levels of shelf height—knee level, waist level, and eye level—were equally spaced in inches. That is, waist level is halfway between knee level and eye level.

Figure 12-3 shows some hypothetical effects that might be obtained in an experiment of this type. As noted in Panel I, sales volume displays a linear relationship with shelf height (assuming that other experimental levels of shelf height would also lead to sales responses that fell on the same line connecting the three points). Moreover, the two lines are parallel for full-width versus half-width facings, suggesting no interaction between this factor and shelf height.

Panel II shows the presence of a nonlinear relationship between sales and shelf height. In this case sales volume tapers off in its rate of increase as shelf height increases. However, the parallelism of the line segments suggests no interaction between shelf height and facings.

Panels III and IV show the remaining two cases, both involving interaction. In Panel III the slopes of the linear functions differ; hence, interaction exists. In Panel IV the data are characterized by *both* nonlinearity *and* interaction. (We assume, of course, the associated statistical tests support the graphical results; that is, the observed effects are statistically significant as well.)

Note that in the factorial experiment we can test for all main effects, and in this

**Figure 12-3   Distinction Between Interaction and Nonlinearity
of Experimental Effects**

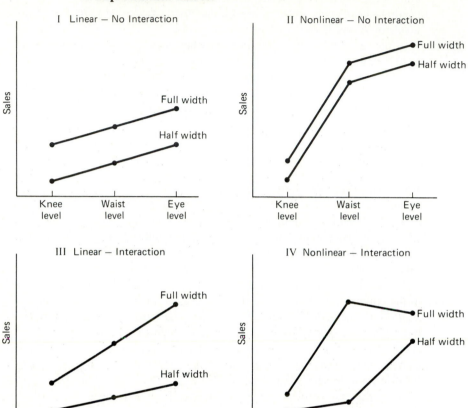

case, where we have replicated each combination, for the interaction of the variables as well. If the interaction term is significant, ordinarily the calculation of main effects is superfluous, since the experimenter will customarily be interested in the best *combination* of variables. In any event, we have included tests for main effects for the sake of illustration; as can be noted, both treatment effects *A* and *B* are significant at an alpha level of 0.01.

In summary, factorial experimentation permits the researcher to study the effect on response of several variables in *combination*. Not only may main effects be estimated but, more importantly, the researcher may study interaction effects as well. This latter advantage is particularly important in market experimentation where the researcher is typically interested in the combination of controlled variables that leads to the best payoff in terms of sales, cash flow, or some other measure of effectiveness. (We return to the topic of interaction later in the chapter.)

Other Multiple Classifications

Designs other than factorial designs can be used for dealing with multivariable classifications. Within the scope of this chapter we can only describe briefly the model underlying the analysis of data generated from such designs. Design characteristics per se were presented in Chapter 6.

Recall that a *latin-square* design is one that is used to reduce the number of observations that would be required in a full factorial design. Such a design is used when it is believed (or assumed) that interaction effects either do not exist or are negligible; in so doing, all main effects are estimated by this procedure.

As shown in Table 6-7 each level of the "main" treatment appears once in each row and each column (rows and columns represent other treatment or blocking variables). Also the number of levels is the same for all treatments (or blocking variables). The underlying model for analysis is

$$X_{ijk} = \mu + \alpha_i + \beta_j + \gamma_k + \varepsilon_{ijk}$$

where $i, j, k = 1, \ldots, a;$ $\mu(\varepsilon) = 0;$ $\sigma^2(\varepsilon)$ is constant; and

$$\Sigma\alpha_i = \Sigma\beta_j = \Sigma\gamma_k = 0$$

Notice that no interaction terms appear in this model.

Another often-used multivariable classification design is the *randomized-block* design. It will be recalled from Chapter 6 that this design typically is used when the experimenter wishes to eliminate one possible source of uncontrolled variation from the error term. One structure of this type of design was presented in Table 6-9. The general model for this design is

$$X_{ij} = \mu + \beta_i + \tau_j + \varepsilon_{ij}$$

where β_i represents the effect of block i $(i = 1, \ldots, n)$ and the other factors are interpreted similarly to designs already discussed. Computing formulas for this design and the latin square can be found in Daniel and Terrell.[8]

ANALYSIS OF COVARIANCE

Analysis of variance focuses (in an experimental situation) on the impact of manipulated variables on the dependent variable(s). Analysis of covariance (ANCOVA), on the other hand, is concerned with extraneous variables that may have an important effect and which the analyst wishes to account for or remove its (their) effect from the dependent measures.

[8]Ibid.

Applications in which ANCOVA is appropriate are characterized by the presence of a quantitative dependent variable, and both quantitative and qualitative independent variables. The principal uses of ANCOVA are to[9]

(1) Increase precision in randomized experiments,
(2) Remove bias which may result when random assignment of units cannot be done,
(3) Remove effects of disturbing variables in observational studies, and
(4) Fit regressions in the context of multiple classifications.

While space does not permit a detailed discussion of covariance, we can show the results of applying one of the BMD programs to the same type of data that were considered in Table 12-1. Let us now assume, however, that *traffic counts* of customers passing the dog food display can be made during the experiment. Although we cannot control this variable, we do suspect that store traffic affects dog food sales, and at least we are able to measure (if not control) its effect. Our primary interest still centers on the effect of shelf height on sales, but we would like to take into account the independent influence of store traffic on sales.

The covariance model for this experiment is very similar to the single-factor model described earlier:

Observed value of dependent variable	= Constant +	Effect of treatment level [shelf height]	+ Effect of covariate [traffic]	+ Residual effect

Algebraically, this is shown as

$$Y_{ij} = \mu + \tau_j + \beta X_{ij} + \varepsilon_{ij}$$
$$\Sigma \tau_j = 0; \qquad \mu(\varepsilon) = 0; \qquad \text{variance } (\varepsilon) = \sigma^2$$

First, since store traffic is going to be introduced as a covariate, we now let Y denote the response and X denote the covariate, similar to a regression model.

The principal novelty of the covariance model is the presence of a slope coefficient β denoting the (pooled) within-groups regression of Y on X, across all three groups. (Furthermore, for convenience we shall measure store traffic in terms of deviations from its own mean.) In brief, covariance is a combination of regression and analysis of variance. We are not interested in the regression as such; rather we wish to "net out" the influence of X on Y so that the effect of the treatments can be made more precise. Without covariance

---

[9]For a more-detailed discussion, see A. R. Wildt and O. T. Ahtola, *Analysis of Covariance* (Beverly Hills, Calif.: Sage, 1978), pp. 13–17.

TABLE 12-5   Covariance Problem—Arf Dog Food Experiment

SHELF HEIGHT—KNEE LEVEL		SHELF HEIGHT—WAIST LEVEL		SHELF HEIGHT—EYE LEVEL	
Sales	*Store Traffic*	*Sales*	*Store Traffic*	*Sales*	*Store Traffic*
87	5	92	2	93	4
94	6	96	1	103	9
92	3	99	3	111	12
82	2	98	4	85	2
95	7	105	7	86	3
102	8	106	6	83	6
87	5	98	4	107	10
93	6	91	2	109	8
$Y_{T1} = 732,$	$X_{T1} = 42,$	$Y_{T2} = 785,$	$X_{T2} = 29,$	$Y_{T3} = 777,$	$X_{T3} = 54$
$\bar{Y}_1 = 91.50,$	$\bar{X}_1 = 5.25,$	$\bar{Y}_2 = 98.13,$	$\bar{X}_2 = 3.63,$	$\bar{Y}_3 = 97.13,$	$\bar{X}_3 = 6.75$

Grand total $\quad Y_{TT} = 2,294, X_{TT} = 125$

adjustment the effect of X on Y would simply inflate the error term and reduce the sensitivity of the test.

Table 12-5 shows the input data for the covariance analysis. As shown, Y denotes the response variable and X denotes the covariate. Before carrying out the covariance analysis, Table 12-6 shows an ordinary analysis of variance that *ignores* the covariate. This analysis is just like that of Table 12-2 and was also carried out by a single-factor BMD program. We note that the F ratio is only 1.51 and is not significant at the $\alpha = 0.05$ level.

Table 12-7 shows what happens when BMD is used to analyze the data of Table 12-5 *including* the covariate. In this case each sum of squares in the response variable is *adjusted for linear association with the covariate X*. As a result of introducing the covariate, the *adjusted* sum of squares for Y decreases from a total of 1,621.83 (Table 12-6) to 853.15 (Table 12-7). Among- and within-treatment sums of squares decrease as well. The net effect is to produce an F ratio in Table 12-7 of 13.17 which, with 2 and 20 degrees of freedom, is *highly significant at the 0.05 level*. (One degree of freedom is lost within treatments by computing the pooled within-treatments regression between response and covariate.)

The upshot of all of this is that introduction of the covariate has made the experiment much more sensitive and we now find that the treatments produce significant differences in response.

TABLE 12-6   Preliminary Calculations—Arf Dog Food Experiment

SOURCE OF VARIATION	DEGREES OF FREEDOM	SUM OF SQUARES	MEAN SQUARE	F RATIO
Among treatments	$t - 1 = 2$	204.08	102.04	1.51 ($p > 0.05$)
Within treatments	$n - t = 21$	1,417.75	67.51	
	$n - 1 = 23$	1,621.83		

TABLE 12-7   Covariance Analysis—Arf Dog Food Experiment

	ADJUSTED DEGREES OF FREEDOM	ADJUSTED SUM OF SQUARES	MEAN SQUARE	F RATIO*
Among treatments	2	484.97	242.49	13.17 ($p < 0.05$)
Within treatments	20	368.18	18.41	
Total	22	853.15		

*Tabular F (see Table A-4 in Appendix A) for 2 and 20 degrees of freedom is only 3.49 for $\alpha = 0.05$.

In summary, covariance analysis offers a partial substitute for control in cases where it is suspected that some variable(s) not under control is affecting the response variable. The effect of the covariate is removed separately (by regression) from both the among-groups and the within-groups sums of squares. In this way the *residuals* (following the regression part) are net of the covariate. The influence of the covariate is no longer buried in the error variance and the effect is to increase the sensitivity of the F test.

Ideally, covariance analysis should be employed in cases where the covariate is (1) highly correlated with the response variable and (2) not correlated with the treatment variables. If correlation with the response variable is low, the sensitivity of the experiment is not appreciably increased. If the covariate is correlated with the treatment variables, removal of its effect also removes some of the variance that is shared with the treatment variable.

In this connection it should be noted that some researchers attempt to bypass the analysis of covariance entirely by performing a straight analysis of variance on a set of Y residuals found after regressing Y on X. This practice is not to be encouraged, since, in general, it overestimates the among-groups sum of squares when the covariate is correlated with the treatment variable. This is because the covariance model employs a pooled within-groups regression, *not* a total-sample regression. If treatment-level means differ on the covariate, the two regression slopes will not be the same. (Moreover, degrees of freedom for the error variance differ between the two approaches.)

COMPUTER ROUTINES FOR THE ANALYSIS OF VARIANCE AND COVARIANCE

As the reader has no doubt surmised by now, the analysis of variance and covariance is typically carried out by means of computer programs. Three widely used mainframe (and to an extent minicomputer and microcomputer) packages that include these programs are SPSS^{x}, SAS, and BMDP. The decision regarding which individual program is appropriate for the analysis must be based on a number of considerations, which include the nature of the research design used, the level of measurement of the independent variable(s), the number of measures, and the objectives of the analysis.

The main analysis of variance and analysis of covariance programs available are listed in Table 12-8. As will be noted, there are many similarities among the packages.

TABLE 12-8   Computer Programs for Analysis of Variance and Analysis of Covariance

SPSS^x *

ONEWAY
produces a one-way analysis of variance for an interval-level variable and one independent variable. Also, tests not available in the other SPSS^x programs can be run: (1) test for trends across categories, (2) specify contrasts, (3) range tests. Several range tests for multiple comparisons are available including least-square differences, Tukey, Duncan, Scheffé.

ANOVA
performs analysis of variance for factorial designs. Although covariates can be specified, a full analysis of covariance cannot be done. This program is not intended for comprehensive analyses of variance or analyses of covariance. The dependent variable is interval and one or more categorical variables (factors) can be used to define the groups. Multiple classification analysis can be requested.

MANOVA
is a generalized multivariate analysis of variance and covariance program. This procedure performs univariate and multivariate linear estimation. This program is appropriate for multiple dependent variables, repeated measures designs, factor-by-covariate interaction in the analysis of covariance, or nested or nonfactorial designs.

SAS†

GLM
performs analysis of variance, analysis of covariance, and multivariate analysis of variance. This procedure analyzes data with the framework of general linear models and is particularly useful for unbalanced designs (balanced designs can be analyzed). A number of multiple comparison tests can be made.

ANOVA
handles analysis of variance for balanced designs. Data from a wide variety of experimental designs can be analyzed by this procedure. Multiple comparison tests can be run.

NESTED
performs analysis of variance and analysis of covariance for purely nested (hierarchical) random models. This model is more efficient than others in this package for the type of design involved, especially when there are large numbers of levels and observations.

VARCOMP
estimates variance components in a general linear model and is designed to handle models that have random effects.

NPAR1WAY
performs nonparametric one-way analysis of variance on ranks and certain rank scores.

BMDP‡

P1V
is a program concentrating on single-factor designs. If covariates are specified an analysis of covariance is performed.

P2V
performs an analysis of variance or covariance for a wide variety of fixed effects models and for repeated measures models with equal or unequal cell sizes: Fixed effects models that can be analyzed include factorial designs, latin squares, incomplete blocks, and fractional factorials.

P3V
analyzes general mixed models using maximum likelihood estimation. Balance is not required.

P8V
performs an analysis of variance for any complete design with equal cell sizes. This includes nested, crossed, and partially nested and partially crossed designs for fixed-effects models, mixed models (including repeated measures), and random effects models.

SPSS^x User's Guide, 2nd ed. (New York: McGraw-Hill, 1986).

†*SAS User's Guide: Statistics,* Version 5 ed. (Cary, N.C.: SAS Institute, 1985).

‡W. J. Dixon and M. B. Brown, eds., *BMDP–79: Biomedical Computer Programs P Series* (Berkeley: University of California Press, 1979).

However, there also are differences, so potential users do have choices depending on need. The various programs may have varying limitations for such dimensions as maximum number of observations, factors, levels of a factor, and number of covariates. The output illustrated in Tables 12-2 and 12-4 was generated from applying earlier versions of BMD programs.

INTERPRETING EXPERIMENTAL RESULTS

Up to this point we have emphasized significance testing (via analysis of variance and covariance) and experimental layouts. Three other topics are central to the analysis of experimental data:

1. The varieties of interactions that may occur in experimental design work
2. Measuring the contribution of each experimental factor to accounted-for variance in the response variable, similar to the role that partial correlations play in multiple regression
3. Multiple comparison analysis

We discuss each of these topics briefly.

Varieties of Interactions

Figures 12-2 and 12-3 have already shown how one can examine two-factor interactions graphically. As indicated earlier, interactions occur when response functions depart from parallelism (beyond what might be expected by chance). As also pointed out, interactions are of two basic kinds: *ordinal* and *disordinal*. In the former case the rank order of effects due to one treatment variable is not changed across levels of some second treatment variable. (More generally, the rank order is unaffected by the *joint levels* assumed by *all* other treatment variables.) In disordinal interactions such is not the case.

Let us examine these concepts more closely. Assume that we have a two-variable factorial design with factor A at three levels and factor B at two levels. What are some of the ways that the response variable may be related to changes in factor A at each level of factor B?

Figure 12-4 shows some illustrative cases. Panel I illustrates the case of *no interaction* at all. All line segments are parallel and the joint effect of A and B is given by the sum of their separate main effects. Note that the *increment* of B_2 over B_1 remains constant across the three levels of A.

Panel II shows a case of *ordinal interaction*. At level B_1 the effect of A is in the rank order of A_2, A_1, and A_3, highest to lowest. At level B_2 the rank order of A effects is still A_2, A_1, and A_3. However, the line segments are not parallel. The difference in Y between B_2 and B_1 at level A_2 is much less than the difference noted at level A_3.

Panel III shows a case of *disordinal interaction*. Had only level B_1 been examined,

Figure 12-4 Alternative Patterns of Interaction

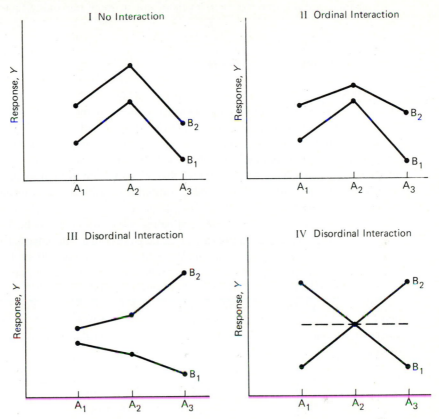

we would have concluded that the Y effects are in the order A_1, A_2, and A_3, highest to lowest. Had only B_2 been examined, we would have concluded that the Y effects are in the opposite order, A_3, A_2, and A_1, highest to lowest.

Panel IV shows an even more stringent case of *disordinal interaction*. In this case the Y effect is *all* interaction. That is, if we average over levels of B, the dashed line, denoting the effect due to A, is horizontal. However, separating effects by each level of B shows how strong the differences really are.

From a decision-oriented viewpoint the presence of disordinal interaction is much more serious than the case of ordinal interaction. In disordinal interaction it is equivocal as to which level of, say, factor A is best unless we know the level of B as well. In the ordinal interaction case this ambiguity does not arise; even though the superiority of one level of A over another may depend on B, the best level of A still remains the best over both levels of B.

A third type of interaction is *hybrid interaction*.[10] This differs from ordinal inter-

---

[10]See J. H. Leigh and T. C. Kinnear, "On Interaction Classification," *Educational and Psychological Measurement*, 40 (Winter 1980), 841–43.

action in that the rank order of treatment profiles is invariant between levels of one or more factors, and it varies between levels of one or more remaining factors.

Hays' Omega-Square Measure

Marketing researchers are finding it increasingly useful to go beyond significance testing of various treatment variables in order to ascertain the relative importance of each factor in contributing to variation in some response variable Y. As a matter of fact, the balance that is achieved by employing an equal number of cases in each cell of a factorial design leads to *uncorrelatedness* among the treatment variables. This is all to the good, since one does not have the ambiguity that is associated with measuring the relative importance of predictor variables under correlated conditions (as is usually the case in multiple regression).

This type of analysis involves estimating what has come to be known as *effect size*—i.e., the strength of a relationship or the magnitude of a difference between variables. Some have rightly argued that the "major results of any empirical study, regardless of whether the prime purpose is description, prediction, or explanation, are the descriptive statistics that indicate the nature and size of any obtained effects."[11]

Hays has proposed a useful descriptive measure of effect, called omega squared, that can readily be computed for various kinds of experimental designs in the course of carrying out analysis-of-variance correlations.[12] The measure is defined operationally as follows:

$$\hat{\omega}^2 = \frac{\text{SS among} - (\text{df among} \cdot \text{MS error})}{\text{SS total} + \text{MS error}}$$

where $\hat{\omega}^2$ denotes estimated (from the sample) omega square. The other quantities are obtained from the analysis-of-variance computations.

To illustrate, consider the analysis of the factorial design in Table 12-4. Suppose that we adopt an alpha risk of 0.1 so that all three effects are significant: A, B, and $A \times B$. If so, we can find the $\hat{\omega}^2$ for each contribution.

For example, let us take the case of factor A and substitute the appropriate quantities for SS (sum of squares) and MS (mean square) from Table 12-4:

$$\hat{\omega}_A^2 = \frac{480.5 - [1 \cdot (8.8)]}{958.5 + 8.8}$$

$$= 0.49$$

---

[11]A. Sawyer and J. P. Peter, "The Significance of Statistical Significance Tests in Marketing Research," *Journal of Marketing Research*, 20 (May 1983), 125.

[12]See W. L. Hays, *Statistics for Psychologists* (New York: Holt, Rinehart & Winston, 1963).

The quantity $\hat{\omega}_A^2$ bears a marked resemblance to R^2 in the context of multiple regression. Speaking *roughly*, the measure can be described in words as:

$$\hat{\omega}^2 = \frac{\text{Accounted-for variation due to factor } A}{\text{Total variation in the criterion variable}}$$

Similarly, we find the counterpart $\hat{\omega}^2$ measures for B and $A \times B$ to be 0.31 and 0.04, respectively. The three separate measures sum to 0.84. This last measure is analogous to R^2 in the context of multiple regression.

A theoretical rationale for omega squared can be found in Hays' book. The application of omega squared to marketing research is discussed by Green,[13] and its use (and lack of use) in consumer behavior experiments are discussed by Peterson et al.[14] The index is not only simple to compute,[15] but it is also useful in showing which factors are the most important in accounting for variation in the response variable. (Ordinarily, omega squared is computed only for those effects that are statistically significant.)

Experience has shown that in many areas of behavioral (and marketing) research, small effect sizes are typical. This is not necessarily a bad situation per se, since effects explaining as little as 5% (perhaps even 1%) of variance may well be considered either theoretically or practically important. Since large effect sizes are more likely to exist for relationships that are "obvious," it may be argued that these are situations whereby no new knowledge is contributed by the research.

Multiple Comparisons

The usual procedure in analysis of variance is to test the hypothesis that all treatment means are equal. If there is a significant difference among the means, interest will turn toward contrasts that are possible—i.e., what is the nature of the differences among the means.

The primary way in which this is done is by pairwise comparisons. That is, comparisons are made between all possible pairs of group means. There are a number of procedures available for these analyses, often called *range tests,* including Tukey's honestly significant difference test, Scheffé's test, Duncan's multiple range test, and the least significant difference. The types of data, research design, and statistical package (and program within the package) used are included among the determinants of which test should (or can) be used.

---

[13]P. E. Green, "On the Analysis of Interactions in Marketing Research Data," *Journal of Marketing Research,* 10 (November 1973), 410–20.

[14]R. A. Peterson, G. Albaum, and R. F. Beltramini, "A Meta-Analysis of Effect Sizes in Consumer Behavior Experiments," *Journal of Consumer Research,* 12 (June 1985), 97–103.

[15]General computational formulas are contained in D. H. Dodd and R. F. Schultz, Jr., "Computational Procedures for Estimating Magnitude of Effect for Some Analysis of Variance Designs," *Psychological Bulletin,* 79 (1973), 391–95.

BASIC CONCEPTS OF MULTIVARIATE ANALYSIS OF VARIANCE AND COVARIANCE

Multivariate analysis of variance (MANOVA) and covariance has received relatively little attention by marketing researchers. Our description of univariate analysis of variance (ANOVA) and covariance (ANCOVA) in this chapter provides the base for the present discussion. In recent years, statisticians have generalized these procedures to cases in which more than a single criterion variable is involved. For example, if a researcher were to set up a package-design experiment in which package shape, background color, and printing motif were the controllable variables, he or she might solicit subjects' responses on a variety of rating scales: (1) personal preferences, (2) judgments of the aesthetic beauty of each package, (3) how well each package seemed to describe the product contents, and so on. If so, the subject's responses would consist of *more than a single criterion variable*. Moreover, in all likelihood the set of criterion (response) variables would themselves be correlated. Another illustration of the use of a MANOVA design is provided by a study of salespersons where interest was in assessing the effects of career stages on job attitudes, facets of job satisfaction, and perceived work environment.[16] Other main effects were business strategy and company; age of salesperson was treated as a covariate.

Multivariate analysis of variance and covariance is analogous to its univariate counterpart. Once again we are testing for differences between two or more group means—in this case centroids, since more than a single criterion is involved. Analogous to the assumption of common variance in the ANOVA model, we assume in multivariate analysis of variance and covariance that the within-groups sums of squares and cross products of deviations from their respective means are equal across the groups. Separate tests are available to see if this assumption of common within-groups variability is justified.[17]

Analogous to univariate ANOVA, we now assume that the set of criterion (response) variables is *multinormally* distributed. In ANOVA we recall that an F ratio was computed for testing the equality of treatment means. This F ratio involved a ratio of the among-groups mean square to the within-groups mean square. In the multivariate variety a similar type of ratio is involved; in this case, however, it consists of a generalization of the univariate F ratio to a function of the within-groups and total-groups sums of squares and cross products.

While the procedures for multivariate analysis of variance and covariance are considerably more complicated than their univariate counterparts, the motivation is *precisely the same:* to test for equality of group means (actually centroids in the multivariate case) where the groups have been formed on some prior basis—for example, as "treatment" groups in the format of an experimental design.

Multivariate analyses of variance and covariance programs produce a rather voluminous output that includes a number of special-purpose measures whose description

---

[16]W. L. Cron and J. W. Slocum, Jr., "The Influence of Career Stages on Salespeople's Job Attitudes, Work Perceptions, and Performance," *Journal of Marketing Research*, 23 (May 1986), 119–29.

[17]See G. E. P. Box, "A General Distribution Theory for a Class of Likelihood Criteria," *Biometrica*, 36 (1949), 317–46.

would exceed the scope of this text. Therefore, we do not show a numerical illustration of this technique. Examples of the computer programs having wide applicability to multivariate analysis of variance and covariance were included in Table 12-8. The more technically trained reader is referred to books by Harris[18] and Green[19] on multivariate analysis per se. A less-technical presentation is found in the book by Bray and Maxwell.[20]

Multivariate analysis of variance represents a particularly useful tool for marketing research and decision making related to that research. Much research in marketing involves data on multiple variables, often more than one response from the same person, the correlations between which may not be known, and the most important variable is not always obvious. Under these conditions, MANOVA is extremely relevant because it does not force the researcher to determine *a priori* which variables are important, it allows the simultaneous use of all relevant variables in the analysis, and it accounts for the correlations that may exist among the relevant variables.[21]

SUMMARY

In this chapter our primary concern has been to develop the necessary statistical machinery (analysis of variance and covariance) to analyze experimental data. These techniques, however, are also useful for non-experimentally-obtained data. The first section of the chapter dealt with experimental design and the analysis of variance. We explained what goes on when one uses analysis of variance procedures. A simple numerical example was used to demonstrate the partitioning of variance into among- and within-components.

The assumptions underlying various ANOVA models were pointed out and a hypothetical data experiment was analyzed to show how the models operate. The topics of interaction plotting, effect size, and multiple comparisons were introduced to aid the researcher in interpreting the results of his or her analysis.

We concluded the chapter with a relatively brief overview of basic concepts of multivariate analysis of variance.

ASSIGNMENT MATERIAL

1. The marketing research department of the Gamma Adhesive Company is attempting to find some attribute of their gummed labels that can be merchandised as being superior to competitive products. The manager of the department, Mr.

---

[18]See R. J. Harris, *A Primer of Multivariate Statistics* (New York: Academic Press, 1975), for further details on this test.
[19]See P. E. Green, *Analyzing Multivariate Data* (Hinsdale, Ill.: Dryden Press, 1978).
[20]See J. H. Bray and S. E. Maxwell, *Multivariate Analysis of Variance* (Beverly Hills, Calif.: Sage, 1985).
[21]R. Redinger, "Multivariate Analysis of Variance," in *Multivariate Methods for Market and Survey Research,* ed. J. N. Sheth (Chicago: American Marketing Association, 1977), p. 95.

Beckwith, feels that the strength of their adhesive represents a good promotional point. Accordingly, samples of the company's adhesive and three other brands are tested by an independent research company. The "strength indexes" of the four products are as follows:

| | | COMPETITIVE ADHESIVE | | |
| | GAMMA | | | |
TRIAL	ADHESIVE	X	Y	Z
1	35	32	22	24
2	11	29	18	19
3	28	17	23	26
4	26	24	17	19
5	32	15	19	22

Assume that trials are merely replications of the same experiment (that is, that a one-way classification is appropriate) and a common error variance exists for all four "treatments."

a. Test the null hypothesis that the means of all treatments are equal (use an alpha risk of 0.05).

b. Assume now that the trials can be treated as "blocks" and perform a two-way analysis of variance. Compare your answer with part (a).

c. What additional statistical assumptions (other than equality of variance) are you making in using analysis of variance procedures in this problem?

2. Referring to the latin-square problem in Chapter 6, assume that a researcher has carried out the suggested experiment (dealing with shelf height A_i, number of facings B_j, and shelf fullness C_k), using the particular design shown in Table 6–7. The data are as follows (table entries are unit sales):

	B_1	B_2	B_3	B_4
A_1	$C_1 = 13$	$C_2 = 16$	$C_3 = 16$	$C_4 = 14$
A_2	$C_4 = 9$	$C_1 = 17$	$C_2 = 20$	$C_3 = 20$
A_3	$C_3 = 14$	$C_4 = 19$	$C_1 = 17$	$C_2 = 21$
A_4	$C_2 = 15$	$C_3 = 17$	$C_4 = 18$	$C_1 = 19$

a. Test the hypothesis that no significant differences exist among sales response due to shelf height, number of facings, and shelf fullness (use an alpha risk of 0.05).

b. Without carrying out statistical tests, do you notice any apparent trends in sales response for each treatment variable considered separately?

3. Consider the following factorial layout:

| | PERSONAL SELLING EFFORT | | |
DIRECT MAIL	*Level 1*	*Level 2*	*Level 3*
Level 1	40; 33	49; 47	56; 60
Level 2	37; 40	47; 51	62; 56
Level 3	51; 47	51; 60	73; 76

As noted, two replications of personal selling effort and direct mail, each at three levels, are made. This leads to 18 observations of sales response.

a. Test the null hypothesis (alpha risk at 0.05) of no difference in sales due to personal selling effort versus direct mail.

b. Does a significant interaction exist (alpha risk at 0.05) between personal selling effort and direct-mail advertising?

c. If, as a researcher, you had to recommend one particular combination of personal selling effort and direct-mail advertising, what kinds of additional information would you need before presenting your recommendation?

4. A company making cutlery products for consumers is about to embark on a study that will help it determine how it should sell its products. Alternatives to be considered are (1) one-on-one direct selling, (2) party plan direct selling, (3) mail order and telemarketing, and (4) regular retailers. Would analysis of covariance be appropriate for this study? If so, suggest some possible variables that might be covariates. If not, explain why it would not be appropriate.

CASES FOR PART III

III-1

OERLIKON SYNCHROMATIC WATCH

The Oerlikon Watch Company recently introduced a new type of wristwatch. Named the "Synchromatic," it operates on the principle of establishing a constant frequency in a tuning fork that is actuated by a small battery in the watch. The tuning fork vibrates at a frequency of 360 cycles per second and produces a slight humming sound instead of the ordinary ticking. The watch has very few moving parts and is highly accurate. It is shockproof, waterproof, and antimagnetic. The battery has a life expectancy of approximately one year.

Before the watch was introduced, a consumer use test was held in which a judgment sample of 25 men was selected to wear the watch. These men collectively represented a wide range of occupational and age groups. They each agreed to wear the watch at all times and under the same conditions they would normally wear a wristwatch. They also agreed to being interviewed at the end of a three-month period.

Two of the questions that each man was asked during the interview after having worn the watch were, "What did you find that you liked about the watch?" and "What did you find that you disliked about the watch?" The responses to these questions for each of the 25 respondents are given below.

Question: "What did you find that you liked about the watch?"

RESPONDENT NUMBER	RESPONSE
1.	"Most accurate watch I have ever worn." "Everyone at the plant was impressed."
2.	"I didn't have to wind it once."
3.	"Kept very good time." "I could see the dial at night."
4.	"I never had to worry about whether my watch was off and I would be late for an appointment."
5.	"I didn't miss a single train to work because my watch was wrong."
6.	"I work with a group of engineers, and they were all impressed with the watch."
7.	"I always forget to wind my watch, and since I am on the road driving a lot, this causes me a lot of trouble. I like this one because I didn't have to wind it."
8.	"I like to try new things. I don't understand how this watch works but I was talking to my doctor about it, and he said he would like to get one too."
9.	"I always like to know how things work. I got so interested in how a tuning fork could be used to keep time that I read all the company literature they would send me. I think the design is very clever."
10.	"I work around a lot of equipment that generates electrical fields. I found that the watch kept perfect time while my present watch, which is supposed to be antimagnetic, is pretty erratic."
11.	"I like a watch with a little heft to it that you don't have to worry about banging it up. This one I dropped at least three times on a hardwood floor, and it didn't affect it at all"
12.	"I don't know whether you have other doctors trying the watch or not, but we need watches that are accurate and dependable. I found this watch to be both highly accurate and always running." "Since I have to wash my hands a lot, I have to have a watch that is waterproof. This one seemed completely waterproof." "I need a watch that has a clean design that will not catch and hold dust and dirt. I like the design of this one, since it doesn't have a stem."
13.	"All my friends never heard of a watch like this before. The other guys kept asking me who I knew to get to wear a watch like this. This is the kind of a watch a man can be proud of."
14.	"This is the most accurate watch I have ever worn. It is even better than my pocket watch and I thought it was good."
15.	"Everything is electronic these days. An electronic watch is something that not very many people have, however."
16.	"We get time signals from the Naval Observatory at the radio station at which I work. I didn't believe that you could get a watch that was this accurate until I had tried it."
17.	"I skin-dive a lot and need a watch I can depend on so that I will know how long I have been down. This one worked well. I also need a watch that has a large luminous dial that I can read under water. I could read the time easily with this watch."

18.   "I sometimes have trouble getting to sleep and always wear my watch. The ticking often annoys me on my watch. I like the low hum of this one."

19.   "All the guys in the fraternity were pretty impressed. Even my physics prof thought it was a good watch. We checked out the frequency one day in class on a scope."

20.   "Riding in a cab over a diesel engine all day I get a lot of vibration. If this watch continues to keep as good time for the next year as it has for the last three months I would say you have a good product on your hands."

21.   "I always take off my watch at work and leave it on my desk. The self-winding watch I now have sometimes stops. I didn't have any trouble with this one."

22.   "I never placed much stock in this 'taste-maker' concept you read about, but I found that I enjoyed showing and telling people about this watch."

23.   "This is a watch that I would like to give my son for graduation, as I think he would be proud to own one."
        "I found I became more time-conscious as a result of wearing such an accurate watch."

24.   "The boss heard about me wearing this new kind of watch and called me in one day. We must have spent half an hour talking about it. It was the first time I ever knew he knew I even worked for him."

25.   "When are you going to start selling this watch? Everybody I talked with about it seemed very impressed."

Question: "What did you find that you disliked about the watch?"

RESPONDENT NUMBER	RESPONSE
1.	"The watch is too big. My sleeve is always getting hung on it."
2.	"The humming bothered me at night. When I put my arm under the pillow, it seemed to come right through."
3.	"I was annoyed that it tended to fray the cuff of the left sleeve on my shirts. You ought to do something about the sharp edges on the case."
4.	"I would imagine this is going to be a high-priced watch. I didn't like the styling at all. It looked like an inexpensive watch."
5.	"The watch is far too large."
6.	"I think the watch is too thick and big around even for a man's watch. I don't see how you ever sell a watch of this size to women."
7.	"It's a funny thing, but the humming bothered me when I was trying to get to sleep. I never noticed the ticking on my regular watch, but the humming noise kept me awake. I don't understand it, as I couldn't even hear the humming during the day."
8.	"It wore out the cuff on my sleeve."
9.	"I think you ought to make it look more expensive."
	"Something ought to be done about making it smaller. I suppose you have problems with the battery and all, but the watch is too big in my opinion."
10.	"I am a physicist and I noticed that the headboard of my bed tended to act as a sounding board for the humming. However, since I don't suppose many people tend to wear their watches at night, this wouldn't pose much of a problem generally."
11.	"I don't like the styling of the watch."
12.	"I prefer a thin case on a watch and one that has a contemporary design. This one looks like the old Ingersoll dollar pocket watch to me."

"I had a problem with this watch wearing the cuff on my shirt sleeve. I always wear starched cuffs and the watch tended to catch and pull threads in the cuff."

13.   "You should reduce the size of the watch."

14.   "This watch doesn't look like one an executive should be wearing."

15.   "I was bothered somewhat by the humming of the watch while I was trying to get to sleep."

16.   "The dial is apparently made out of plastic which scratches easily. This gives a very poor appearance to the watch."

17.   "I recognize some of the problems of miniaturizing a watch of this kind, but I think you are going to have to get it down to the size of a conventional watch before it will sell very well."

18.   "I don't know whether I happened to get a lemon or not, but it kept stopping on me. I notified the people you told me to and they adjusted it several times but it never did work right."

19.   "It got to the point where I began to roll back my shirt cuff at work because the edge of the case was wearing it out."

20.   "This watch isn't styled very well in my opinion. It looks like it was designed for installation in the instrument panel of a locomotive."

21.   "This watch is definitely too large."

"I don't like the styling at all. It looks cheap."

22.   "The crystal scratches awfully easily."

"I think you could improve on the way the watch looks."

23.   "You ought to do something about the crystal. It got so scratched that sometimes when the light was from a certain angle I couldn't see the hands."

24.   "The watch did a pretty good job on my shirt cuffs. It seemed as if every time I pulled the cuff up to see what time it was it wouild catch on the watch."

25.   "I didn't find anything I disliked about the watch."

1. a. Establish categories and tabulate the responses to the question "What did you find that you liked about the watch?"

   b. What conclusions could be drawn from the responses about the features that appealed to the wearers? Are these features the ones that should have been used in the appeals and copy of an introductory advertising campaign?

2. a. Establish categories and tabulate the responses to the question "What did you find that you disliked about the watch?"

   b. What conclusions could be drawn from the responses about the undesirable features or attributes of the watch? Which of these, in your judgment, should have been changed before the product was introduced?

III-2

MOUNT RUSHMORE INSURANCE COMPANY (A)

The management of the Mount Rushmore Insurance Company, a company specializing in automobile insurance, asked the marketing research manager to conduct a survey to determine consumer interest in a new auto insurance concept then under consideration.

The concept involved coverage for costs incurred as a result of a car breaking down while on a trip.

The marketing research manager designed and conducted a small telephone survey involving a sample of 60 respondents. Half the sample was drawn randomly from the company's present customer list, and half was drawn by means of random-digit dialing. In each interview the following statement describing the proposed insurance coverage was read to the respondent over the telephone:

> An insurance company is considering providing a policy that would pay toward expenses incurred when your car breaks down while you are driving more than 150 miles from home. It pays up to $500 toward such items as towing, repair costs, other transportation, rooms, and meals. Payments are subject to a $50 deductible amount. The policy will cost $15 a year.

Following the reading of this statement, the respondent was asked to state his or her degree of interest in the policy on a 5-point scale ranging from 1 (definitely not interested) to 5 (very much interested).

The respondent was then asked to supply a small amount of background data regarding

- Age
- Marital status
- Number of cars owned
- Average age of car(s)
- Number of trips taken by automobile (for any purpose whatsoever) over the past year that exceeded 300 miles on a round-trip basis

The data obtained from the survey are shown in Table 1.

1. Divide the sample into two groups:
   a. Those showing high interest—"4" or "5" ratings
   5. Those showing lower interest—"1," "2," or "3" ratings

   Cross-tabulate high versus low interest in Rushmore customers versus customers of other companies. How strong is the association between interest in the policy and current insurance supplier, and at what levels is it statistically significant?
2. What happens to the association observed in the preceding cross tabulation when older (40 years and over) versus younger respondents are introduced as a third two-category variable?
3. We can consider the concept rating as a criterion variable and the remaining six variables as predictor variables in a multiple regression. In the case of current insurance supplier, we can use the dummy-variable coding:

$$\text{If Rushmore customer} \Rightarrow 1$$
$$\text{If other company customer} \Rightarrow 0$$

TABLE 1 Telephone Survey Data*

Respondent	Concept Rating	Current Insurance Supplier	Age	Marital Status	Number of Cars	Average Age of Car(s)	Number of Trips
1	4	Rushmore	42	M	1	0.5	3
2	3	R	39	M	1	1.5	1
3	5	R	47	M	1	1	4
4	2	R	24	S	3	1	2
5	4	R	43	M	2	1.5	4
6	5	R	62	M	1	0.5	6
7	1	R	27	M	1	2	3
8	5	R	55	M	2	0.5	4
9	4	R	42	S	1	2	2
10	3	R	36	M	2	2.5	1
11	4	R	39	M	3	1.5	5
12	2	R	24	S	4	2	0
13	5	R	58	M	1	2	6
14	4	R	43	M	1	0.4	2
15	1	R	23	S	2	2.5	0
16	5	R	59	M	1	0.5	7
17	4	R	43	M	3	1.5	3
18	3	R	36	S	1	2	0
19	3	R	47	M	1	2	1
20	4	R	42	M	1	1.5	4
21	4	R	47	M	4	1.5	4
22	4	R	38	M	2	1	3
23	5	R	37	M	2	0.8	8
24	3	R	39	S	1	2	0
25	4	R	51	M	1	1	2
26	4	R	47	M	2	1.5	1
27	5	R	51	M	1	2	6
28	1	R	30	S	1	2	0
29	1	R	28	S	2	4.5	2
30	3	R	42	M	2	3.5	1
31	2	Other	32	M	3	3	0
32	4	O	29	M	1	2	3
33	2	O	32	M	1	1	0
34	1	O	37	M	1	1	0
35	3	O	24	S	4	2.5	1
36	2	O	41	M	1	2	3
37	3	O	23	M	1	2	0
38	1	O	34	M	5	3	1
39	2	O	38	M	2	2	0
40	4	O	47	M	2	1	5
41	5	O	24	M	1	0.5	9
42	3	O	32	M	1	1.5	0
43	1	O	22	S	1	3	1
44	2	O	27	S	1	2.5	0
45	2	O	29	M	3	2.5	0
46	4	O	43	M	2	1	2

TABLE 1 (*Continued*)

RESPONDENT	CONCEPT RATING	CURRENT INSURANCE SUPPLIER	AGE	MARITAL STATUS	NUMBER OF CARS	AVERAGE AGE OF CAR(S)	NUMBER OF TRIPS
47	5	O	48	S	1	0.5	3
48	3	O	36	M	1	1.5	0
49	4	O	42	M	3	1.5	2
50	2	O	26	S	2	2	2
51	2	O	29	S	1	2.5	1
52	1	O	23	S	1	3	0
53	3	O	34	M	1	1.5	0
54	4	O	37	S	1	1.5	2
55	2	O	24	S	2	3	0
56	3	O	32	M	2	2	1
57	5	O	44	M	1	0.5	7
58	1	O	28	M	1	2.5	0
59	1	O	22	S	2	3	1
60	2	O	26	S	1	2	1

*These data are contrived.

Similarly, in the case of marital status, we can use the dummy-variable coding:

$$\text{If single} \Rightarrow 1$$
$$\text{If married} \Rightarrow 0$$

Having done this, regress the column of concept ratings (criterion variable) on the six predictor variables:

a. Interpret the regression equation, and indicate the extent to which the variation in the predictor variables explain the variation in the criterion variable.

b. Is each separate predictor statistically significant at the 0.05 level?

c. Can a simpler model (involving fewer predictor variables) be developed? If so, how do the predictors enter such a simpler model?

4. Divide the sample into four groups: Rushmore, single; Rushmore, married; other company, single; and other company, married.

a. If we consider these four groups in a single-factor analysis of variance with the concept rating serving as a criterion variable, do we accept the null hypothesis that the four mean concept ratings are equal (at the 0.05 level)? If not, which group has the highest rating?

b. What are the assumptions about the error term in the single-factor ANOVA model?

c. Using the concept rating as a criterion variable, examine the significance of current insurance supplier and number of cars (1, more than 1) on ratings in a two-factor ANOVA.

III-3

SYD COMPANY (C)

The management of the Syd Company, a large packaged consumer goods company, was actively exploring whether the company should add a women's shampoo product to its product line. At the present time the company did not have an entrant in the women's shampoo market.

FC Associates was hired to conduct an exploratory study. The background of the research problem and the questionnaire designed for the project are discussed in the Syd Company (A) and (B) cases.

Data were to be collected by personal interview. After the usual type of pretest, the questionnaire was administered in the home to a convenience sample of residents in an area near the offices of FC Associates. Interview time averaged about 30 minutes; all data were collected over the span of one week. A total of 84 people agreed to be interviewed.

A coding system was developed for the questionnaire, which is shown in Syd Company (B). This coding is reproduced in Table 1. The coded data from the 84 respondents are shown in Table 2. All data have been coded except those from the free association questions of Part C.

TABLE 1   Coding Form for Shampoo Benefits Study

A. For *all* cards (three in number)

$\dfrac{cc}{1-3}$ Subject Number: 001, 002, . . . , 084

B. Card 1 (Usage, Hair Type, Demographics, Life-Style)

$\dfrac{cc}{4-5}$ 01 (Card number)

6   Blank

7–8

Q-1
- 12   (More than twice a week)
- 06   (Once or twice a week)
- 04   (Once or twice every two weeks)
- 03   (Once or twice every three weeks)
- 02   (Twice a month)

9

D-Q-1
- 1   (Yes)
- 0   (No)

10

D-Q-2
- 1   (Yes)
- 0   (No)

11

D-Q-3
- 1   (Dry)
- 2   (Normal)
- 3   (Oily)

TABLE 1 (*Continued*)

12			
	D-Q-4	1	(Fine)
		2	(Normal)
		3	(Coarse)
13			
	D-Q-5	1	(Straight)
		2	(Slightly wavy or curly)
		3	(Very wavy or curly)
14			
	D-Q-6	1	(Short)
		2	(Medium)
		3	(Long)
15			
	D-Q-7	1	(Thick)
		2	(Medium)
		3	(Thin)
16	Blank		
17			
	E-Q-1	1	(Yes, working)
		0	(No, not working)
18			
	E-Q-2	1	(Yes, married)
		0	(No, not married)
19–20	Q-2		(Enter age of respondent from screening question)
21			
	E-Q-3	1	(Some high school, or less)
		2	(Completed high school)
		3	(Some college)
		4	(Completed college)
22–25			
	E-Q-4	01.5	(If A)
		04.0	(If B)
		06.0	(If C)
		08.5	(If D)
		12.5	(If E)
		17.5	(If F)
		30.0	(If G)

C. Card 2 (Part A)

$\dfrac{cc}{4\text{–}5}$ 02 (Card Number)

7	Benefit 1	
8	Benefit 2	
9	Benefit 3	
10	Benefit 4	In each case, enter
11	Benefit 5	
12	Benefit 6	1 (If in most likely column)
13	Benefit 7	
14	Benefit 8	2 (If available in some shampoos)
15	Benefit 9	
16	Benefit 10	3 (If otherwise, i.e., uncommon)
17	Benefit 11	
18	Benefit 12	

TABLE 1   Coding Form for Shampoo Benefits Study (*Continued*)

19		Benefit 13 ⎤
20		Benefit 14 ⎥
21		Benefit 15 ⎥
22		Benefit 16 ⎦
23	Blank	
24		Benefit 1 ⎤
25		Benefit 2 ⎥
26		Benefit 3 ⎥
27		Benefit 4 ⎥
28		Benefit 5 ⎥
29		Benefit 6 ⎥ In each case, enter
30		Benefit 7 ⎥
31		Benefit 8 ⎥ 1 (If benefit is member of ideal
32		Benefit 9 ⎥ set of four)
33		Benefit 10 ⎥
34		Benefit 11 ⎥ 0 (If otherwise)
35		Benefit 12 ⎥
36		Benefit 13 ⎥
37		Benefit 14 ⎥
38		Benefit 15 ⎥
39		Benefit 16 ⎦
40	Blank	

Card 2 (Part B)

41–58   Enter card numbers, 01 through 10, from most to least desired

TABLE 2   Shampoo Benefits Study Data Set

1	1	060021232 0125408.5
1	2	3123213332313331 1010101000000000 010905030608071002
2	1	121032221 1125404.0
2	2	3232113233132233 1100010010000000 090201061003070508
3	1	121022223 1124406.0
3	2	2111211211322323 1101100000000000 010502091007030806
4	1	120121222 1124412.5
4	2	3113123131313311 0110010010000000 060209050308010710
5	1	061122131 0020330.0
5	2	3311123333233231 0111000100000000 080503020607100901
6	1	061021133 0021301.5
6	2	1133313321323323 1100010001000000 010209100605030807
7	1	060131133 0119317.5
7	2	1213313111323321 1001100010000000 050306011009080702
8	1	120121132 0019330.0
8	2	3122313311323332 1001101000000000 070501060309100802
9	1	061022222 0019312.5
9	2	2212132212222212 1100010010000000 010210090708060305
10	1	120131233 1123406.0
10	2	3223312222223222 1110010000000000 010602050907030810

TABLE 2 (*Continued*)

```
11   1   120122132 1021317.5
11   2   3212113222131223 1100101000000000 010705030206090810
12   1   040112213 0021230.0
12   2   3222322223223223 1110100000000000 010210090506070803
13   1   060121233 1128412.5
13   2   2233312233333333 1001110000000000 050306080701100902
14   1   061022232 0127312.5
14   2   2212212222223321 0100011001000000 051006020709010308
15   1   121121221 1024406.0
15   2   2313313333333332 0010111000000000 050603070110020908
16   1   060121133 0021430.0
16   2   1212321222333331 1001010100000000 060103080209071005
17   1   061123231 1027412.5
17   2   2121121312111132 1010010001000000 060310050107090208
18   1   120131133 1127317.5
18   2   3211112222321131 0001011010000000 060907030201050810
19   1   060131132 1123306.0
19   2   3112311211232221 1101010000000000 060201050307080910
20   1   060121233 1123408.5
20   2   3212313332223331 0011011000000000 060307010908051002
21   1   120021232 1023306.0
21   2   3213312222322332 0011101000000000 030605070208100901
22   1   060131323 0026430.0
22   2   2222222222221221 0000111010000000 060702050308010910
23   1   061112212 0123404.0
23   2   2222212222222321 0100111000000000 060209010508100703
24   1   060131223 0126408.5
24   2   3232313222323333 0011100010000000 090106030507080210
25   1   060121231 1124417.5
25   2   1213213221333321 0101011000000000 060207080501091003
26   1   061023221 0130430.0
26   2   3213233222333333 0100111000000000 020607030508091001
27   1   061123211 1126412.5
27   2   1212312111323321 1110010000000000 020103060509100807
28   1   061023231 0129417.5
28   2   1212213223333323 1110010000000000 010602030907050810
29   1   060121223 1128430.0
29   2   3213313222323331 0001111000000000 050607030209100801
30   1   061022222 0023401.5
30   2   3212113322332211 0110010000000000 060302011005080907
31   1   060121223 1125408.5
31   2   1211112222122221 0011000011000000 100305010609070208
32   1   121132231 1024408.5
32   2   3212313333333323 1000101001000000 010603050907020810
33   1   121122231 1120312.5
33   2   3332323233233222 1010110000000000 030201060507100908
34   1   060122222 1123408.5
34   2   3212212222222222 1001110000000000 010506030207080910
35   1   121122212 0024404.0
35   2   3212222212221222 1100110000000000 020103050609070810
```

TABLE 2   Shampoo Benefits Study Data Set (*Continued*)

36	1	120131113 0130401.5
36	2	1213311133323311 1110010000000000 010903060502080710
37	1	120131233 1024408.5
37	2	1223323222333322 1001011000000000 010609050307080210
38	1	120131133 1024412.5
38	2	2212112221213211 1100101000000000 010902070506030810
39	1	120112132 1126430.0
39	2	3232323213333323 0001111000000000 060507030801100209
40	1	120131132 1123408.5
40	2	3121311223313223 0100011010000000 060901050807020310
41	1	060111133 0027308.5
41	2	3232222222323233 0100010011000000 021007080901060305
42	1	061122132 0021312.5
42	2	3212211331223121 0101110000000000 020605090108100703
43	1	120022132 1120212.5
43	2	3112132233333233 1111000000000000 020107090503060810
44	1	120022132 1022306.0
44	2	3121122331331321 0110101000000000 010209050806070310
45	1	121112221 1124406.0
45	2	2211112211221222 0011010100000000 060807030502010910
46	1	121021231 0023301.5
46	2	2212223222223331 1000110001000000 060109031007080205
47	1	061122231 0124401.5
47	2	2212212222212331 0110011000000000 030209060708100501
48	1	061012131 0125404.0
48	2	3131313133131331 1110100000000000 030102051009060708
49	1	061023321 1023408.5
49	2	2222222222333333 0110000000100010 020308091007010506
50	1	060113122 0023401.5
50	2	3113121233333313 0100001100000010 080302050706100901
51	1	061133131 1122417.5
51	2	3332323332333333 0100001010010000 060102090910030508
52	1	061112131 1124306.0
52	2	3212113332331231 0100110100000000 020601050807031009
53	1	021013312 0019312.5
53	2	1211232123333121 0111000100000000 031001050806020709
54	1	060113312 1025412.5
54	2	1322322132322122 0101011000000000 020807030610050901
55	1	061122221 1130312.5
55	2	3211213322122121 0100110010000000 020509070306011008
56	1	060122132 1021306.0
56	2	3131312122223133 1001011000000000 010706020308051009
57	1	060021123 1120212.5
57	2	3111111132233223 0001011100000000 060802050703100901
58	1	061112231 0024430.0
58	2	1321233212111112 0100011001000000 020706100308050901
59	1	121011133 1126404.0
59	2	3233213111221212 1011001000000000 060301020705081009
60	1	061113321 0023430.0
60	2	3132211133121122 1010000011000000 030105100902070806

TABLE 2 (*Continued*)

61	1	061132132 1028412.5
61	2	3312213322222221 0110110000000000 020601030509071008
62	1	121031133 0020312.5
62	2	3232323232333213 0110010010000000 090201030506070810
63	1	120021112 1124406.0
63	2	3112213221223113 0011011000000000 030508070601090210
64	1	060021132 1123408.5
64	2	3213313322333313 0110110000000000 030605010209100708
65	1	060131213 0130430.0
65	2	2323313323333331 0001100000001010 090103050608070210
66	1	060131223 1029412.5
66	2	3312233222332311 0111100000000000 020905030601081007
67	1	060131132 0025406.0
67	2	3223332222333221 1100110000000000 050308061007020109
68	1	061023131 1123408.5
68	2	3212333332333211 1110100000000000 020305010607090810
69	1	061111232 1024408.5
69	2	1113323222333333 1000111000000000 050102070610090308
70	1	120122122 1125308.5
70	2	3213323221313331 0001111000000000 050603070809100201
71	1	060031132 0019301.5
71	2	3323123333311322 0110010000000000 090702030610050801
72	1	061023131 0123404.0
72	2	3233313332333333 1000011001000000 060107051002090308
73	1	120032321 1020306.0
73	2	2233311211223323 1100010010000000 020906010803050710
74	1	120121223 1023408.5
74	2	3111121331123133 0100111000000000 050307020610010908
75	1	121022222 0126417.5
75	2	1231321231122311 1100010001000000 051002090108060307
76	1	120131133 1125412.5
76	2	3213322322333331 1001001010000000 090107020508060310
77	1	121112331 0018101.5
77	2	1112223111333231 0010110001000000 060503080710010902
78	1	060021213 0128417.5
78	2	1232321222231332 0100101010000000 010205060709031008
79	1	061132222 1028304.0
79	2	2112212211222222 0110000110000000 080206050103090710
80	1	120121233 1025408.5
80	2	1111111111111111 0110100000000000 020803060507100901
81	1	061113221 1127212.5
81	2	2312313313112133 1110001000000000 020107030806051009
82	1	061123231 1126408.5
82	2	1223313333323331 0101110000000000 050206070809100103
83	1	061021322 1123430.0
83	2	2222222222222222 1000001101000000 010708090306100502
84	1	021023131 1126417.5
84	2	1111111111111111 0100011010000000 020109070306050810

1. How should FC first proceed in the analysis of the data?
2. Cross-tabulate the major variable (i.e., product benefit) of interest with other variables in the questionnaire. What conclusions do you reach?
3. Apply Thurstone's Case V scaling to the data obtained in Part B of the questionnaire. What is the ranking of the shampoo benefits and how is this interpreted?

13

Other Techniques for Analyzing Criterion–Predictor Association

INTRODUCTION

Multiple regression and the analysis of variance and covariance (Chapters 11 and 12, respectively) are both characterized by the fact that they deal with the analysis of *dependence* structures—a data structure that consists of a single criterion variable and multiple predictors.

Several other techniques are available for analyzing criterion–predictor association. In this chapter we describe the more important ones insofar as marketing research is concerned:

- Discriminant analysis: two-group and multiple-group
- Automatic interaction detection
- Probit and logit
- Canonical correlation
- Path analysis/causal modeling

These techniques are considerably more complex than those of Chapters 11 and 12. Accordingly, we do not delve deeply into technical details. Rather, our interest is applications oriented and our scope emphasizes the conceptual basis of each method.

Discriminant analysis is the most widely used of this group of techniques; hence, we start the discussion with an introduction to two-group discriminant analysis. A sample problem is described and solved numerically. We then describe the assumption structure of the technique and a computer program for performing two-group discriminant analysis. The multiple (three or more groups) case is discussed next, including an illustrative application of a stepwise multiple discriminant program.

We then turn to automatic interaction detection (AID), a procedure for systematically splitting a large sample of multivariate data into smaller, more homogeneous groups whose criterion-variable means are widely separated. We show how AID can be used as a preliminary data-combing procedure prior to the application of parameterized models, such as multiple regression and two-group discriminant analysis.

The last techniques to be discussed in this chapter—and briefly at that—are probit and logit, canonical correlation, and path analysis/causal modeling. Our presentation is descriptive in that the objectives of each technique and its application to marketing research are emphasized.

TWO-GROUP DISCRIMINANT ANALYSIS

As briefly described in Chapter 10, when dealing with associative data the marketing researcher may encounter cases where the criterion variable is categorical but where the predictor variables involve interval-scaled data. For example, one may wish to predict whether sales potential in a given marketing territory will be "good" or "bad," based on certain measurements regarding the territory's personal disposable income, population density, number of retail outlets, and the like.

Other potential applications also come to mind, such as

- How do consumers who are loyal to my brand differ in their demographic profiles from those who are not loyal?
- How do respondents who show high interest in a new set of concept descriptions differ in their readership levels of certain magazines from those who show low interest?
- How do homeowners who select a variable rate mortgage differ in their demographic profiles, mortgage shopping behavior and attitudes, and preferences for mortgage features from homeowners selecting a conventional fixed rate mortgage?

The classification need not be limited to two groups. For example:

- Are significant demographic differences observed among purchasers of Sears, Goodyear, Goodrich, and Firestone tires?
- How do doctors, lawyers, and bankers differ in terms of their preference ratings of eight different luxury automobiles?
- Do long-distance, local, and quasi-local/long-distance geographically mobile people differ in individual household demographic and economic characteristics?
- How can "loyal shoppers" of Lord and Taylor, Marshall Field, and Neiman-Marcus be distinguished on the basis of their attitudes about each retailer?

Still other such problems could be added to the list. However, each one has a common structure in which we assume that some test object (usually a person) falls into one of a set of categories. It is also assumed that we know that person's profile on a set of interval-scaled predictor variables, such as age, income, years of education, or other background variables.

The problem is to predict a person's category from some function of the predictor variables. Here we shall assume that the function is linear. If only two categories are involved, the problem is a *two-group* discriminant case; if three or more categories are involved, we are dealing with *multiple* (group) discriminant analysis. We first focus on the simple, two-group case and then consider the multiple-group version.

Objectives of Two-Group Discriminant Analysis

Two-group discriminant analysis (and classification) involves four main objectives:

1. Finding linear composites of the predictor variables that enable the analyst to separate the groups by maximizing among-groups relative to within-groups variation
2. Establishing procedures for assigning new individuals, whose profiles but not group identity are known, to one of the two groups
3. Testing whether significant differences exist between the mean predictor-variable profiles of the two groups
4. Determining which variables account most for intergroup differences in mean profiles

These objectives are the bases for the existence of the two major, and very distinct, purposes and procedures for conducting discriminant analysis. The first procedure, *discriminant predictive (or explanatory) analysis,* is used to optimize the predictive functions. The second procedure, *discriminant classification analysis,* uses the predictive functions derived in the first procedure to either classify fresh sets of data of known group membership, thereby validating the predictive function, or if the function has previously been validated, to classify new sets of observations of unknown group membership. The differences in the application and requirements for each are summarized in Table 13-1.

Geometric Representation

If we have n persons measured on m variables, the profile of each person can be portrayed as a point in m dimensions. If we *also* know the group to which each person belongs, and the groups differ in terms of average profiles, often called *centroids,* we might expect to find different groups occupying different regions of the space. The less overlap noted among intergroup profiles in that space, the more likely it is that discriminant analysis can help us separate the groups.

One way to show what happens when a two-group discriminant function is computed

TABLE 13-1   Stages of Discriminant Analysis

		STAGES		
	Predictive Discriminant Analysis	*Classification Analysis of Initial Data Set of Known Groupings*	*Classification Analysis of New Data Set of Known Groupings*	*Classification Analysis of New Data Set of Unknown Groupings*
Purpose	Derive discriminant function using initial data set: No classification involved	Determine how well discriminant function classifies (biased)	(1) Classify data using classification rule derived from predictive function (2) May be part of validation analysis of initial predictive function	(1) Classify data using classification rule derived from predictive function (2) May be part of validation analysis of initial predictive function
Requirements	Assumptions of linear discriminant model: No validation required	No validation required	Validation required	Initial predictive function must have been previously validated

Source: Scott Smith, "A Note on the Interpretation and Analysis of the Linear Discriminant Model for Prediction and Classification," Working Paper No. 127, College of Business Administration, University of Oregon, 1979, p. 16.

is provided by the scatter diagram and projection in Figure 13-1. Suppose that we had two groups, *A* and *B*, and two measures, X_1 and X_2, on each member of the two groups. We could plot in the scatter diagram the association of variable X_2 with X_1 for each group, maintaining group identity by the use of filled-in dots or open circles. The resultant ellipses enclose some specified proportion of the points, say 95% in each group. If a straight line is drawn through the two points where the ellipses intersect and then projected to a new axis *Z*, we can say that the overlap between the *univariate* distributions *A'* and *B'* (represented by the shaded area) is smaller than would be obtained by any other line drawn through the ellipses representing the scatter plots.[1]

---

[1] The shaded region under the curves can also be interpreted as representing the probabilities of mistakes when classification is done on the basis of likelihoods only.

Figure 13-1   Graphical Illustration of Two-Group Discriminant Analysis

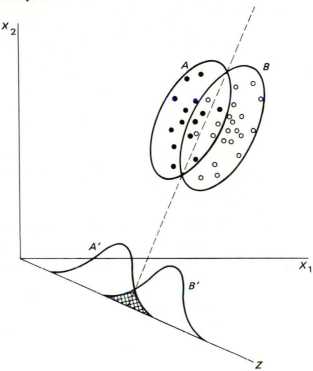

The important thing to note about Figure 13-1 is that the Z axis expresses the two-variable profiles of groups A and B as *single* numbers. That is, by finding a linear composite of the original profile scores we can portray each profile as a point on a line. Thus, the axis Z "condenses" the information about group separability (shown in the bivariate plot) into a set of points on a single axis. Z is the *discriminant* axis.

In most problems of realistic size, we have more than two predictor variables. If so, each predictor can represent a *separate* dimension (although we would be limited to three predictor variables if we wished to plot the data). In any case the basic objective is still to find one axis in the m-dimensional space that maximally separates the centroids of the two groups after the points are projected onto this new axis.

In our discussion of multiple regression analysis we noted that one finds a linear composite that maximizes the coefficient of multiple determination, R^2. Analogously, in two-group discriminant analysis we try to find a linear composite of the original variables that maximizes the *ratio* of among-to-within groups variability. It should be noted that if m, the number of predictor variables, is quite large, we shall be able to effect a great deal of parsimony by portraying among- to within-groups variation in many fewer dimensions (actually a *single dimension* in the two-group case) than found originally.

A Numerical Example

Let us return to the example involving ready-to-eat cereals that was first presented in Table 11-1 in the context of multiple regression. As recalled, we wished to see if amount of protein and vitamin D influenced consumers' evaluations of the cereals.

In the present case we shall assume that a different pretest has been run in which ten different test cereals are described. However, in the present case each of the ten consumer raters is simply asked to classify the cereal into one of two categories: *like* versus *dislike*. The (hypothetical) data appear in Table 13-2. The predictor variables are (again):

X_1: the amount of protein (in grams) per 2-ounce serving, and

X_2: the percentage of minimum daily requirements of vitamin D per 2-ounce serving.

Also shown in Table 13-2 are various sums of squares and cross products, the means on X_1 and X_2 of each group, and the total-sample mean. For example, the grand mean (i.e., grand centroid) is

$$\bar{X}_1 = 6.5; \quad \bar{X}_2 = 5.4$$

We first note from the table that the two groups are much more widely separated on X_1 (protein) than they are on X_2 (vitamin D). If we were forced to choose just one of

TABLE 13-2   Consumer Evaluations (Like Versus Dislike) of Ten Cereals Varying in Nutritional Content

PERSON	EVALUATION		PROTEIN X_1	VITAMIN D X_2		X_1^2	X_2^2	X_1X_2
1	Dislike		2	4		4	16	8
2	Dislike		3	2		9	4	6
3	Dislike		4	5		16	25	20
4	Dislike		5	4		25	16	20
5	Dislike		6	7		36	49	42
		Mean	4	4.4	Sum	90	110	96
6	Like		7	6		49	36	42
7	Like		8	4		64	16	32
8	Like		9	7		81	49	63
9	Like		10	6		100	36	60
10	Like		11	9		121	81	99
		Mean	9	6.4	Sum	415	218	296
	Grand mean		6.5	5.4				
	Standard deviation		3.028	2.011				

Figure 13-2   Scatter Plot of Two-Group Sample Data of Table 13-2

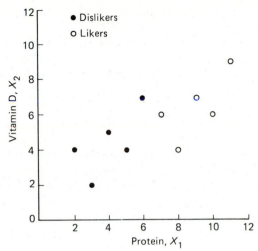

the axes, it would seem that X_1 is a better bet than X_2. However, there *is* information provided by the group separation on X_2, so we wonder if some linear composite of *both* X_1 and X_2 could do better than X_1 alone.

Figure 13-2 shows a scatter plot of the X_1 and X_2 data of Table 13-2. We note that perfect discrimination can be achieved with X_1 if we erected a line perpendicular to the horizontal axis between the scale values of 6 and 7. On the other hand, there is no way that the use of X_2 alone would enable us to separate the groups. Given this picture, we would not be surprised if the best linear composite turns out to favor X_1 with a considerably larger weight than X_2 receives.

Why not use X_1 alone, rather than a composite of X_1 and X_2? First, the data of Table 13-2 represent only a *sample;* it is quite possible that additional observations would show that X_1 alone would *not* effect perfect discrimination between the two groups. Second, we have not explicitly taken into consideration either the variability about X_1 versus X_2 or their correlation. One of the nice features of discriminant analysis is that all three aspects of the data—centroid, variance, and correlation—are considered in developing the linear composite that maximally separates the groups.

As noted earlier, the key problem of two-group discriminant analysis is to find a new axis so that projections of the points onto that axis exhibit the property of maximizing the separation between group means relative to their within-groups variability on the *composite*. This discriminant axis can be defined in terms of a set of weights—one for each predictor-variable axis—so that we have the following linear function:

$$Z = k_1 X_1 + k_2 X_2$$

where k_1 and k_2 are the weights that we seek.

But how shall we define variability? In discriminant analysis there are several ways to do this. However, the most straightforward way is to find the ratio of two sums of squares *after* the set of scores on the linear composite has been computed. One sum of squared deviations represents the variability of the two group means on the composite around their grand mean. The second sum of squared deviations represents the pooled variability of the individual cases around their respective group means—also on the linear composite. One can then find the ratio of the first sum of squares to the second. It is this ratio that is to be maximized through the appropriate choice of k_1 and k_2.

Finding the values of k_1 and k_2 in the first place also involves computing various sums of squares. However, in this case sums of cross products are required as well, since we have more than a single predictor variable. The reader should keep these two aspects straight. To find k_1 and k_2 we work with sums of squares *and* cross products. However, *after* k_1 and k_2 have been found and applied to X_1 and X_2, we have only a *single* variable, namely the linear composite. In this case we only need to talk about sums of squared deviations regarding various means on the linear composite, namely the grand mean or the separate group means.

Computing the Discriminant Weights

Solving for the *discriminant weights* (k_1 and k_2) that maximize the separation between the groups involves a procedure quite similar to that followed in Table 11-3 in the context of multiple regression. However, in the present case we shall want to find a set of sums of squares and cross products that relate to the variation *within* groups.[2]

Table 13-3 shows the computations required to solve for k_1 and k_2. Note that we first find mean-corrected sums of squares and cross products within each group separately. These are then summed across the two groups to obtain the pooled quantities shown in the last column. Then, similar to solving for the partial regression coefficients in Table 11-3, we solve the set of simultaneous equations for k_1 and k_2. In the present case the right-hand side of each equation is the difference in means between likers and dislikers on each variable separately:

$$\text{Protein: } \overline{X}_1 \text{ (likers)} - \overline{X}_1 \text{ (dislikers)} = 9 - 4 = 5$$

$$\text{Vitamin D: } \overline{X}_2 \text{ (likers)} - \overline{X}_2 \text{ (dislikers)} = 6.4 - 4.4 = 2$$

Solving the two simultaneous equations leads to the desired discriminant function:

$$Z = 0.368X_1 - 0.147X_2$$

---

[2]While the weights (k_1 and k_2) are developed here in the context of variation within groups, it should be mentioned that a proportional set of weights could be developed from variation across the *total* sample. Indeed, in the two-group discriminant case, multiple regression—in which the criterion variable is expressed as a 0–1 dummy variable—yields partial regression coefficients that are *proportional* to k_1 and k_2.

TABLE 13-3 Solving for the Discriminant Weights

FROM TABLE 13-2 MEAN CORRECTED SUMS OF SQUARES AND CROSS PRODUCTS

	Dislikers	Likers	Total
$\Sigma\, x_1^2 = \Sigma\, X_1^2 - n\bar{X}_1^2$	$90 - 5(4)^2 = 10$	$415 - 5(9)^2 = 10$	20
$\Sigma\, x_2^2 = \Sigma\, X_2^2 - n\bar{X}_2^2$	$110 - 5(4.4)^2 = 13.2$	$218 - 5(6.4)^2 = 13.2$	26.4
$\Sigma\, x_1 x_2 = \Sigma\, X_1 X_2 - n\bar{X}_1\bar{X}_2$	$96 - 5(4)(4.4) = 8$	$296 - 5(9)(6.4) = 8$	16

Solving for the discriminant weights:
  To find k_1 and k_2, we solve the simultaneous equations:

$$\Sigma\, x_1^2 k_1 + \Sigma\, x_1 x_2 k_2 = \bar{X}_1 \text{ (likers)} - \bar{X}_1 \text{ (dislikers)}$$
$$\Sigma\, x_1 x_2 k_1 + \Sigma\, x_2^2 k_2 = \bar{X}_2 \text{ (likers)} - \bar{X}_2 \text{ (dislikers)}$$

We make the appropriate numerical substitutions and then solve for k_1 and k_2:

$$20k_1 + 16k_2 = 5$$
$$16k_1 + 26.4k_2 = 2$$
$$k_1 = 0.368; \qquad k_1 = -0.147$$

Discriminant function:

$$Z = 0.368\, X_1 - 0.147\, X_2$$

The weights k_1 and k_2 are known and are shown on computer output as *unstandardized discriminant function coefficients*.[3] Having found the discriminant function, it is a straightforward procedure to apply it to each of the ten pairs of X_1, X_2 values in Table 13-2 to get the linear composite. For example, the discriminant score for the first case in the disliker group is

$$Z = 0.368(2) - 0.147(4)$$
$$= 0.148$$

We can also find discriminant scores for the centroids of the two groups and the grand mean:

$$\bar{Z} \text{ (dislikers)} = 0.368(4) - 0.147(4.4) = 0.824$$
$$\bar{Z} \text{ (likers)} = 0.368(9) - 0.147(6.4) = 2.368$$
$$\bar{Z} \text{ (grand mean)} = 0.368(6.5) - 0.147(5.4) = 1.596$$

Plotting the Discriminant Function

The original scatter plot of the ten observations is reproduced in Figure 13-3. However, this time we also show the discriminant axis (linear composite) by passing a

---

[3]The general form for a linear discriminant function is $Z = k_0 + k_1 X_1 + k_2 X_2$ where k_0 is the intercept or constant term in the function. Since the example used deviations for calculating the weights k_1 and k_2, the function goes through the origin and $k_0 = 0$.

Figure 13-3   Plot of the Discriminant Axis and Point Projections (see Figure 13-2)

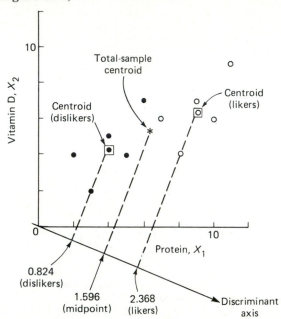

straight line through the point $(0.368, -0.147)$ and the intersection of the original axes.[4] The original points can then be projected onto this new axis.

    Illustratively, we show projections of the grand centroid and the centroids of the dislikers and likers, respectively. (Similarly, all of the ten original points could be projected onto the discriminant axis as well.) We note that the discriminant axis "favors" X_1 (as we guessed it would) by giving about 2.5 times the (absolute-value) weight ($k_1 = 0.368$ versus $k_2 = -0.147$) to X_1 as is given to X_2.

    The discriminant scores of each person are shown in Table 13-4. As illustrated earlier for the first person in the disliker group, each score is computed by application of the discriminant function to the person's original X_1 and X_2 values. We can now examine the criterion being optimized in solving for the discriminant weights.

The Discriminant Criterion

    As stated earlier, the discriminant function represents a linear composite of the original data that maximizes the ratio of among-groups variability to within-groups variability. Table 13-4 shows what this means. First, we compute a measure of between-

---

[4]Or one could use any point whose coordinates are proportional to $(0.368, -0.147)$. However, it should be noted that the *scale unit* on the discriminant axis in Figure 13-3 differs from the original unit in which X_1 and X_2 are expressed. To maintain the original unit, k_1 and k_2 would have to be normalized so that their sum of squares equals unity.

TABLE 13-4 Scores on Discriminant Axis and Values of the Discriminant Criterion

| | DISLIKERS | | | LIKERS | |
| | *Discriminant* | | | *Discriminant* | |
Person	*Score*		*Person*	*Score*	
1	0.148		6	1.691	
2	0.809		7	2.353	
3	0.735		8	2.279	
4	1.250		9	2.794	
5	1.176		10	2.721	
Mean	0.824		Mean	2.368	

$$\text{Grand mean} \quad 1.596$$

Between-groups variability:

$$5(0.824 - 1.596)^2 + 5(2.368 - 1.596)^2 = 5.96$$

Within-groups variability:

Dislikers: $(0.148 - 0.824)^2 + (0.809 - 0.824)^2 + \cdots + (1.176 - 0.824)^2 = 0.772$
Likers: $(1.691 - 2.368)^2 + (2.353 - 2.368)^2 + \cdots + (2.721 - 2.368)^2 = \underline{0.772}$
$$1.544$$

Discriminant criterion:

$$C = \frac{5.096}{1.544} = 3.86$$

groups variability by finding the deviation of each of the two group means from the grand mean on the discriminant function. These deviations are squared, multiplied by the number of persons in each group, and summed. Table 13-4 details the calculations, and we note that the between-groups variability is 5.96.

The within-groups variability is found in a similar manner except for the fact that squared deviations are taken about each group's own mean. The two separate measures are then summed to give 1.544 as a pooled within-groups sum of squares. Finally, the discriminant criterion being maximized is the ratio of the between-groups to the within-groups sum of squares:

$$C = \frac{5.96}{1.544} = 3.86$$

We can now see whether using X_1, while ignoring X_2, can produce a higher discriminant ratio. All the input data needed for these comparison calculations appear in Tables 13-2 and 13-3. The between-groups variability (from Table 13-2) is calculated as

$$5(4 - 6.5)^2 + 5(9 - 6.5)^2 = 62.5$$

The pooled within-groups variability on X_1 (from Table 13-3) is calculated from

$$\sum x_1^2 \ (\text{dislikers}) \ = \ 10$$

$$\sum x_1^2 \ (\text{likers}) \ = \ \underline{\ \ 10\ \ }$$
$$20$$

and the discriminant criterion in this case is

$$C \ = \ \frac{62.5}{20} \ = \ 3.125$$

which, of course, is *less* than that obtained from the (best) linear composite.

It is rather interesting that the optimal function,

$$Z \ = \ 0.368X_1 \ - \ 0.147X_2$$

is a *difference* function in which X_2 (vitamin D) receives a *negative* weight. However, as recalled, the two groups are *not* highly separated on X_2, even though the mean of the likers, 6.4, is somewhat higher than the mean of the dislikers, 4.4, on X_2.

More important is the fact that X_2 is *highly correlated* with X_1 and, hence, can account for some of the error variance in X_1. That is, X_2 serves as a *suppressor variable*. By giving X_2 a *negative* weight in the discriminant function in which X_1 has a positive weight, the predictability of the criterion is further enhanced. X_2 receives a negative weight because it does a better job of suppressing error variance in X_1 (through its high correlation with X_1) than it does in separating group means on its own account.

It is important to bring this point out because it is not unusual in various applied discriminant analyses to find evidence of suppressor effects. This is also true of applied regression analyses, as we showed in Chapter 11.

Classifying the Persons

It is all well and good to find the discriminant function, but the remaining three questions posed at the beginning of the chapter still remain to be answered:

1. How well does the function classify the ten cases?
2. Is the function statistically significant?
3. What is the relative importance of the predictor variables?

The classification problem, in turn, involves two additional questions: (1) how well does the function assign the known cases in the sample, and (2) how well does it assign new cases *not* used in computing the function in the first place?

These questions provide direct parallels to the topics of R^2 (strength of relationship) and cross validation in regression analysis. In the case of discriminant analysis we need an *assignment rule*. One rule that seems intuitively plausible is based on Figure 13-3. A *classification boundary* between the two groups, $Z_{crit.}$, can be identified as being midway between the means of the function for each of the two groups. To classify an individual, if $Z_i > Z_{crit.}$ the individual belongs in one group, while if $Z_i < Z_{crit.}$ the individual goes into the other group. As can be seen from Figure 13-3, no misassignments will be made if we adopt the rule:

- Assign all cases with discriminant scores that are on the left of the midpoint (1.596) to the *disliker* group.
- Assign all cases with discriminant scores that are on the right of the midpoint (1.596) to the *liker* group.

That is, all true dislikers will be correctly classified as such and all true likers will be correctly classified. This can be shown by a 2 × 2 table (known as a *confusion matrix*):

TRUE STATE	ASSIGNED BY RULE		TOTAL
	Disliker	*Liker*	
Disliker	5	0	5
Liker	0	5	5
Total	5	5	10

We see that all entries fall along the main diagonal. For example, had any of the five true dislikers been called likers, the first row and second column would contain not a 0 but, rather, the number of such misassignments.

Application of this rule can be stated in the equivalent terms:

- Substitute the centroid of each group in the discriminant function and find the respective group scores (in our case 0.824 for dislikers and 2.368 for likers).
- For any new case compute the discriminant score and assign the case to that group whose group score is closer.

This rule makes two specific assumptions: (1) the prior probability of a new case falling into each of the groups is equal across groups, and (2) the cost of misclassification is equal across groups.[5]

If a higher prior probability existed for likers, we could reduce the expected probability of misclassification by moving the cutting point of 1.596 to the left (closer to 0.824, the mean score for dislikers) so as to give a wider interval for the larger (likers) group. Similarly, if the cost of misclassifying a liker is higher than that for misclassifying

---

[5]There is a further assumption that is germane to linear discriminant functions: the predictors of each group must have equal variance-covariance matrices. These matrices are assumed to be based on multivariate normally distributed variables with known variances and covariances when the above rule is used for case assignments.

a disliker, the cutting point would also be moved closer to 0.824. More advanced procedures are available for determining just what the new cutting point should be, given differences in prior probabilities or misclassification costs.[6]

A second point of interest concerns the tendency for assignment tables (i.e., the confusion matrix) based on the calibration sample to show better results than would be found upon cross validation with new cases. That is, some capitalization on chance takes place in discriminant analysis and one needs a way to measure this bias of an inflated percentage of correctly classified observations, just as cross validation should be employed in multiple regression (as described in Chapter 11). Procedures are available to develop a truer summary of the degree of correct assignments that would be obtained from fresh data.[7] One procedure involves Monte Carlo generation of pseudo-observations composed of independent standard normal random variables. These observations are then arbitrarily assigned to groups and discriminant functions are derived. This approach probably is most useful for evaluating the work of others when the actual data are not available.

The most frequently suggested validation approach is the *holdout* method, in which the data set is randomly split into two subsamples. One subsample is used to develop the discriminant and the other subsample is used as "fresh data" to test the function. It is suggested that this split sample validation be replicated by using a different convention for the random assignment of the observations. Whether a researcher uses only one validation sample or replications, there may be problems associated with the sampling procedures used to arrive at the analysis and validation subsamples. These problems relate to the number of variables included in the discriminant function (when a stepwise procedure is used) and to the inference that the researcher might make concerning the classificatory power of resulting discriminant functions.[8] Table 13-5 reproduces the results from a study of the behavior of inventors receiving patents which looked at these problems. As these data show, there may be differing numbers of variables included on any given replication. Also, there was a wide range in the correct classification performance of the validation replications, although the analysis functions were quite stable.

The data in Table 13-5 also show another dimension to the validation process for discriminant analysis. For the analysis and validation samples there is a measure of the percentage of inventors who would have been correctly classified based on *chance* alone. Obviously, the researcher is interested in whether the discriminant function is a significant improvement over chance classification, and there are different measures of chance classification that can be used.[9]

For small sample studies different validation methods should be used. One approach that has been proposed is to randomly assign observations to groups and then compute

---

[6]See A. A. Afifi and S. P. Azer, *Statistical Analysis: A Computer Oriented Approach* (New York: Academic Press, 1972).

[7]For a general discussion of the topic, see P. A. Lachenbruch, *Discriminant Analysis* (New York: Hafner Press, 1975). Some specific procedures can be found in R. E. Frank, W. F. Massy, and D. G. Morrison, "Bias in Multiple Discriminant Analysis," *Journal of Marketing Research*, 2 (August 1965), 250–58.

[8]See G. Albaum and K. Baker, "The Sampling Problem in Validation of Multiple Discriminant Analysis," *Journal of the Market Research Society*, 18 (July 1976).

[9]See D. G. Morrison, "On the Interpretation of Discriminant Analysis," *Journal of Marketing Research*, 6 (May 1969), 156–63.

TABLE 13-5 Comparison of Analysis and Validation Sample Results—Inventor Study[a]

REPLICATION	NUMBER OF VARIABLES INCLUDED	ANALYSIS SAMPLE (N = 46)				VALIDATION SAMPLE (N = 41)		
		F	Percent correctly classified (P.C.C.)	Chance percent correctly classified (C_{pro})	t	Percent correctly classified (P.C.C.)	Chance percent correctly classified (C_{pro})	t
1	16	3.70†	89.1	50.0	5.28†	53.7	50.7	0.38
2	17	3.95†	93.4	50.0	5.86†	58.5	50.7	1.00
3	17	3.04†	95.7	50.0	6.18†	78.0	50.7	3.50†
4	17	1.84*	87.0	50.0	5.00†	73.2	50.7	2.88†
Average			91.3			65.8		
Standard error of the mean			1.9			5.8		

*$p < .10$, one-tailed test
†$p < .01$, one-tailed test
[a]Adapted from G. Albaum and K. Baker, "The Sampling Problem in Validation of Multiple Discriminant Analysis," *Journal of the Market Research Society*, 18 (July 1976).

discriminant scores. This procedure is replicated a number of times, and the results of these classifications can be compared with the true group results.[10] This approach, like that of the holdout method, does not allow the researcher to evaluate the discriminant function as a means of defining differences between groups. At the most basic level, the validity of discriminant function analysis lies in the stability of the coefficients derived. These coefficients are the basis of classifying, profiling, and evaluating the underlying discriminant dimensions. It would be valuable to have a validation procedure that uses all the sample data for evaluating the stability of parameter estimates while allowing unbiased estimation of error rates. The *jackknife statistic* and the *U–Method* have been proposed as such procedures.[11] When the number of groups is greater than two, the suggestion has been made that a combination of the U–Method and posterior probability estimator might be a viable method for estimating the classification accuracy of linear discriminant functions.[12] It is beyond the scope of this book to discuss these "specialized" techniques, and the reader is referred to the excellent references already cited.[13]

Testing Statistical Significance

While the discriminant function does perfectly in classifying the ten cases of the calibration sample in our cereal likes and dislikes illustration, we still have not tested whether the group centroids differ significantly. This is analogous to testing for the significance of R^2 in multiple regression. Tests of the equality of group centroids can also proceed on the basis of an F ratio that, in turn, is calculated from a variability measure known as *Mahalanobis squared distance*. This is illustrated by the column in Table 13-5 that shows an F value for each replication. We do not delve into the technical details of Mahalanobis squared distance other than to say that it is like ordinary (Euclidian) squared distance that is computed between two centroids in a space with correlated axes and different measurement units.[14] Mahalanobis squared distance can also be used for classification in that we can measure the squared distance from the individual case to each group centroid and classify the case into the group with the smallest squared distance. Finally, this distance measure is used in some stepwise programs as a criterion for variable inclusion.[15]

Two other measures are widely used for testing overall statistical significance related to a discriminant function. The *canonical correlation coefficient* is a measure of the

---

[10]See D. B. Montgomery, "New Product Distribution: An Analysis of Supermarket Buyer Decisions," *Journal of Marketing Research,* 12 (August 1975), 255–64.

[11]M. R. Crask and W. D. Perreault, Jr., "Validation of Discriminant Analysis in Marketing Research," *Journal of Marketing Research,* 14 (February 1977), 60–68.

[12]S. C. Hora and J. B. Wilcox, "Estimation of Error Rates in Several-Population Discriminant Analysis," *Journal of Marketing Research,* 19 (February 1982), 57–61.

[13]A review of nine different techniques developed for error rate estimation is found in W. R. Dillon, "The Performance of the Linear Discriminant Function in Nonoptimal Situations and the Estimation of Classification Error Rates: A Review of Recent Findings," *Journal of Marketing Research,* 16 (August 1979), 370–81.

[14]See J. E. Overall and C. J. Klett, *Applied Multivariate Analysis* (New York: McGraw-Hill, 1972), for details. In the present problem Mahalanobis squared distance is equal to 8(1.544) = 12.353, where 8 is the number of degrees of freedom and 1.544 is the pooled within-groups sum of squares from Table 13-4.

[15]F ratios based on other statistics may also be used for this purpose.

association that summarizes how related the discriminant function is to the groups. We discuss canonical correlation analysis later in this chapter. An indirect, and most widely used, approach to test for the statistical significance of the discriminant function examines the ability of the variables to discriminate among the groups beyond the information that has been extracted by the previously computed functions. This is known as *residual discrimination* and is measured by the statistic *Wilks' lambda* (also called the *U* statistic). Wilks' lambda is a multivariate measure of group differences over discriminating variables and can be calculated in several ways. In general, it is calculated such that values of lambda near zero indicate high discrimination, and when it equals its maximum value of 1.0 the group centroids are equal and there is no discrimination.

Fortunately, most measures of significance are routinely computed by computer programs, but not necessarily in the same format. Some, however, may be unique to a specific program. It is beyond the scope of this book to discuss these techniques further, although we will return to them when we discuss a computer illustration.[16] It is important to remember, however, that tests such as those discussed are used to indicate whether (1) overall discrimination exists among the groups and (2) if so, which and how many discriminant functions (one or more) are statistically significant.

The statistical significance of a discriminant analysis merely provides answers to such questions as

- Is there a relationship?
- Do the predictor variables discriminate among the groups?
- Does this particular discriminant function contribute to the relationship?

Statistical significance says nothing about *how strong* a relationship is, *how much* difference exists between the groups, or to *what extent* a function contributes to overall discrimination. Moreover, tests of statistical significance are sensitive to sample size. For example, with a large sample size it is not difficult to get a significant *F* ratio, even though classification accuracy is poor.

There is need to go beyond statistical significance and test for the *practical* (or substantive) significance. This, of course, is not limited to discriminant analysis. There is no single index of practical significance that is widely accepted. However, using a discrimination index based on omega-squared used in ANOVA (see Chapter 12) gives a measure of the amount of variance in the criterion variable accounted for by the predictor variables acting together as a set.[17] This index is analogous to R^2 for regression analysis.

Relative Importance of Predictor Variables

Recall that the discriminant weights of the sample problem were

$$k_1 = 0.368 \qquad k_2 = -0.147$$

[16]See W. R. Klecka, *Discriminant Analysis* (Beverly Hills, Calif.: Sage, 1980).

[17]R. A. Peterson and V. Mahajan, "Practical Significance and Partitioning Variance in Discriminant Analysis," *Decision Sciences,* 7 (October 1976), 649–58.

Since the original variables X_1 and X_2 were expressed in different units and display different standard deviations as well, the analyst generally *standardizes* the discriminant weights before assaying their relative importance.

Two standardization procedures are used. One of these multiplies each discriminant weight (unstandardized) by the *total sample standard deviation* of that variable:

$$k_j^{s(\omega)} = k_j \sigma_j$$

The other procedure multiplies the weight by *pooled within-groups standard deviation* of that variable.[18] These procedures are illustrated in Table 13-6. While the two methods yield different numerical values (and different ratios of standardized k_1 to standardized k_2), they *rank* the coefficients in the same way—and that ranking also agrees with the original ranking. That is, X_1 is "more important" than X_2. It is the absolute value of the standardized coefficient (i.e., the sign is ignored) which is the basis of the ranking.

It should be emphasized, however, that the same limitations regarding the relative importance of predictor variables apply here as applied in the case of correlated predictors in multiple regression. Even *after* standardization a certain degree of ambiguity remains as long as the predictors are correlated (which certainly is the case here).

Standardized coefficients allow only an ordinal interpretation of variable importance. These coefficients are not appropriate in assessing the relative discriminatory power of

---

TABLE 13-6   Calculating Standardized Discriminant Coefficients

Method 1:
From Table 13-2, the total-sample standard deviations are $s_{x1} = 3.028$ and $s_{x2} = 2.011$. The standardized discriminant weights are then:

$$k_1^{s(t)} = 3.028(\ 0.368) = \ \ \ 2.240$$
$$k_2^{s(t)} = 2.011(-0.147) = -0.296$$

Method 2:
From Table 13-3, we can find the pooled within-groups standard deviation of X_1 and X_2 from

$$s_{x1}^{(w)} = \sqrt{\frac{\Sigma\ x_1^2}{8}} = \sqrt{\frac{20}{8}} = 1.581; \quad s_{x2}^{(w)} \sqrt{\frac{\Sigma\ x_2^2}{8}} = \sqrt{\frac{26.4}{8}} = 1.817$$

where $8 = n - 2$, the degrees of freedom for the pooled groups (where n denotes the total-sample size). The standardized weights are then

$$k_1^{s(w)} = 1.581(\ 0.368) = \ \ \ 0.582$$
$$k_2^{s(w)} = 1.817(-0.147) = -0.267$$

---

[18]See Klecka, *Discriminant Analysis*, pp. 29–39.

the variables included in the analysis. An appropriate measure of relative discriminating power is[19]

$$I_j = \left| k_j \left(\overline{X}_{j1} - \overline{X}_{j2} \right) \right|$$

where

I_j = the importance value of the jth variable

k_j = unstandardized discriminant coefficient for the jth variable

$\overline{X}_{jk}$ = mean of the jth variable for the kth group

The relative importance weights may be interpreted as the portion of the discriminant score separation between the groups that is attributable to the jth variable. Since a relative importance value shows the value of a particular variable relative to the sum of the importance values of all variables, the relative importance of a variable (R_j) is given by[20]

$$R_j = \frac{I_j}{\sum\limits_{j=1}^{n} I_j}$$

The end result of using this procedure is shown in Table 13-7, which is taken from a study of fixed-rate and variable-rate mortgage holders in which one objective was to

TABLE 13-7   Relative Importance of Demographic and Socioeconomic Variables in Selecting Type of Mortgage*

STEP NO.	STANDARDIZED DISCRIMINANT FUNCTION COEFFICIENTS	VARIABLE DESCRIPTION	I_j	R_j
1	.655	Total household income	.147	30.8%
2	.384	Marital status	.080	16.7%
3	.475	Occupation	.066	13.8%
4	−.911	Date of birth	.157	32.8%
5	−.664	Age of youngest child	.028	5.9%
6	−.353	Total financial assets	.000	0.0%
			.478	

*Correctly classified 52.5%
Wilks' lambda = 0.9574, $p < .09$
Canonical correlation = .206
Source: G. Albaum and D. Hawkins, "An Analysis of Differences between Consumers of Variable-Rate and Fixed-Rate Residential Mortgages," paper presented at the 1979 annual conference of the Association for Consumer Research.

[19]F. Mosteller and D. F. Wallace, "Influence in an Authorship Problem," *Journal of the American Statistical Association,* 58 (June 1963), 275–309.
[20]R. W. Aw and D. Waters, "A Discriminant Analysis of Economic, Demographic, and Attitudinal Characteristics of Bank Charge-Card Customers," *Journal of Finance,* 29 (1974), 973–80.

see if demographic and socioeconomic variables could discriminate. As these data show, although six variables were included in the discriminant function, slightly less than two-thirds of the total discrimination was accounted for by only two variables. It will be noted that rankings based on the two criteria are not the same. The age of youngest child is the second most important variable based on standardized coefficients, but it is next to last on the basis of contribution to discrimination.

Determining relative importance of the predictor variables in discriminant analysis becomes increasingly difficult when more than two groups are involved. Although various coefficients and indices can be determined, interpretation becomes critical since more than one discriminant function may be involved. One approach to handling this situation is discussed by Peterson and Mahajan.[21]

Concluding Comments on Two-Group Discriminant Analysis

We can review the two-group model's assumptions as follows:

1. If interest rests solely on finding *linear* functions that maximize between-groups to within-groups variability, then we must assume that the within-groups sums of squares and cross products are equal (if unknown) across the groups.
2. If we are also concerned with statistical significance, then we add the assumption that the original profiles are multivariate normally distributed with unknown (but equal) sums of squares and cross products.
3. If we are further concerned with assigning cases to groups on the basis of which mean discriminant score is the closer, then the additional assumptions of (a) equal prior probabilities, (b) equal costs of misclassification, and (c) *known* sums of squares and cross-product matrices must be made.

If the first assumption of equality of within-groups variability is not met, other functions, such as quadratic discriminants, may still be applicable. Moreover, tests are available for checking on the equality of within-groups variability before applying discriminant analysis programs.[22]

MULTIPLE DISCRIMINANT ANALYSIS

All of the preceding discussion regarding objectives and assumption structure applies to multiple discriminant analysis as well. Accordingly, discussion of this section will be comparatively brief. What primarily distinguishes *multiple discriminant analysis* from the two-group case is that *more than one* discriminant function may be computed.

---

[21]Peterson and Mahajan, "Practical Significance and Partitioning Variance in Discriminant Analysis."

[22]A discussion of quadratic discriminants and tests of the equality of within-groups sums of squares and cross products can be found in M. G. Kendall, *A Course in Multivariate Analysis,* 2nd ed. (New York: Hafner, 1968).

TABLE 13-8 **Standardized Discriminant Function Coefficients for Geographic Mobility Study**

VARIABLE	FUNCTION 1*	FUNCTION 2†
Occupation of spouse	−.484	.132
Education of spouse	.474	−.211
Number of children at home	.465	−.537
Occupation of respondent	−.316	.454
Ethnic background	.313	−.115
Education of respondent	.271	.605
Characterize income	.195	.294
Age of respondent	−.115	−.687
Age of youngest child at home	−.046	.747

*Wilks' lambda = .868, $p < .001$
Canonical correlation = .307
†Wilk's lambda = .958, p < .03
Canonical correlation = .204

Source: G. Albaum and D. I. Hawkins, "Geographic Mobility and Demographic and Socioeconomic Market Segmentation," *Journal of the Academy of Marketing Science*, 11 (Spring 1983), 110.

For example, if we have three groups we can compute, in general, two nonredundant discriminant functions (as long as we also have at least two predictor variables). In general, with G groups and m predictors we can find up to the lesser of $G − 1$, or m, discriminant functions. Some intuitive flavor of why we need no more than $G − 1$ functions for G groups is obtained by recalling that we can code any G-state polytomy into $G − 1$ dummy variables. Each dummy variable qualifies for a discriminant function. Note also that for two groups we get one function, as already described in the preceding section.

Not all the discriminants may be statistically significant, however. Moreover, it turns out to be a characteristic of multiple discriminant analysis that the first function accounts for the highest proportion of the among- to within-groups variability; the second function, the next highest; and so on. Accordingly, we may want to consider only the first few functions, particularly when the input data are rather noisy or unreliable to begin with. There remains the "problem" of interpretation of the functions.

As an illustration, the data in Table 13-8 are taken from a study of geographic mobility of consumers. Mobility behavior was categorized into three types, and a discriminant analysis was conducted to determine if demographic and socioeconomic characteristics could explain differences in geographic mobility behavior. Since there were three groups, two functions were produced. The first function appears to primarily represent the spouse, while the second function represents the respondent and children.

Multiple discriminant analysis is considerably more detailed than might be surmised by this brief review. Interested readers should consult more extensive and advanced discussions of the subject.[23]

---

[23]For example, see R. A. Eisenbeis and R. B. Avery, *Discriminant Analysis and Classification Procedures* (Lexington, Mass.: Heath, 1972); and R. A. Johnson and D. W. Wichern, *Applied Multivariate Statistical Analysis* (Englewood Cliffs, N.J.: Prentice-Hall, 1982).

COMPUTERIZED ANALYSIS

Virtually all discriminant analyses of any appreciable size are carried out by the computer. This is as true of two-group as it is of multiple discriminant analysis. Computer programs are available for all sizes of computers from the mainframe down to the microcomputer. The major mainframe programs, most of which also are available for the microcomputer, are described briefly in Table 13-9. It is clear that both SPSS^x and BMDP have general programs, although BMD-P7M seems to provide a somewhat more limited output. In contrast, SAS offers a variety of programs that tend to be more specialized.

Each program has its own limitations for the maximum number of groups, predictor variables, and observations that can be handled. Maximum size of problem may be determined by a mathematical combination of these three dimensions. In addition, the

TABLE 13-9   Computer Programs for Discriminant Analysis

SPSS^x*

DISCRIMINANT — is a general program that handles two or more groups in computing a canonical discriminant function. Direct entry of all variables and stepwise entry of variables are possible. There are five alternative methods of variable selection for the stepwise procedure. The program also performs classification analysis.

SAS†

DISCRIM — classifies observations assuming a multivariate normal distribution within each class. It is not necessary to assume the classes have equal covariance matrices. The procedure computes linear or quadratic discriminant functions for classifying observations into two or more groups.

NEIGHBOR — is used for the same purpose as DISCRIM when the classes do not have multivariate normal distributions. A nonparametric nearest-neighbor method is used to classify observations.

CANDISC — finds linear combinations of the variables that best summarize the differences among the classes and computes scores for each observation on the linear combination. The technique performs canonical discriminant analysis and is related to both principal components and canonical correlation.

STEPDISC — performs a stepwise discriminant analysis to find a subset of variables that best reveals differences among the classes. Variables identified by this procedure can be used in any of the other procedures for more-detailed analyses.

BMDP‡

P7M — performs only stepwise discriminant analysis. A major emphasis is placed on developing classification functions. Also computed are coefficients for canonical variables (functions). Standardized coefficients are not computed.

*SPSS^x User's Guide 2nd ed. (New York: McGraw-Hill, 1986).
†SAS User's Guide: Statistics, Version 5 ed. (Cary, N.C.: SAS Institute, 1985).
‡W. J. Dixon and M. B. Brown, eds., BMDP-79: Biomedical Computer Programs P Series (Berkeley: University of California Press, 1979).

maximum number of discriminant functions that can be computed may also vary. However, these limits may exceed the size of problems facing marketing researchers in terms of what they can comprehend and interpret for users of the analysis.

It is beyond the scope of this book to illustrate each of the programs. We do, however, summarize some of the output of using the SPSS[x] program DISCRIMINANT (see Exhibit 13-1). Many of the measures computed are the same, or at least similar to, measures computed by other programs. The illustration involves use of the stepwise procedure, which can be summarized as follows:[24]

1. At stage 1 in the program separate F ratios are computed for each predictor. That is, a series of univariate analyses of variance across the groups are performed involving each predictor separately.

2. The predictor variable with the largest F ratio is entered first (assuming that it meets certain significance and tolerance levels for inclusion), and discrimination is effected with respect to this variable only.

3. A second predictor is then added on the basis of the largest adjusted (or "partial") F ratio, conditioned by the predictor variable already entered.

4. Each variable entered is then tested for retention on the basis of its association with other predictors in the equation.

5. The process continues until all variables that pass significance levels for inclusion and retention are entered.

6. At each stage in the stepwise procedure tests are made of intergroup separation (considered across all group centroids) and pairwise group separation for all distinct pairs.

7. At the conclusion of the stepwise procedure a summary of the predictors entered or removed, and associated Wilks' lambda (with its significance), are presented. Classification function coefficients, posterior probabilities of each case arising from each group, and classification results may also be shown.

8. For each canonical discriminant function computed the output shows its associated canonical correlation and Wilks' lambda, standardized coefficients, and, by option choice, the unstandardized coefficients.

AUTOMATIC INTERACTION DETECTION

One of the most interesting problems in associative analysis is the phenomenon of interaction in which the response to changes in the level of one predictor variable depends on the level of some other predictor (or predictors). When interaction effects exist, the simple additive property of individual predictor-variable contributions to changes in the criterion no longer holds.

The distinction between interaction effects and intercorrelated predictors is shown

---

[24]Features of stepwise procedures are discussed in Klecka, *Discriminant Analysis*, pp. 52–60.

Exhibit 13-1   Application of SPSS^x Discriminant Analysis

Management of a retail chain system was interested in consumers' attitudes toward the chain and other relevant aspects of the retailing environment. Data were collected from 175 consumers, 94 of whom could be categorized as frequent shoppers (VERS1) and 81 who were infrequent shoppers (VERS2). The consumers responded to a series of 12 Likert scales (LIKA to LIKL). The research question was concerned with whether these 12 attitude scales could discriminate between the shopper groups. The SPSS^x program DISCRIMINANT was applied to the data.

Although the analyst could have specified any prior probability the default option of 0.5 for each group was used. The analysis is conducted as a two-group discriminant analysis. Everything shown by the output represents what would be shown for n-groups, for each discriminant function computed.

All 12 scales were used for the analysis, but only 8 are shown in the illustration. Only four variables were included in the final analysis. The resulting discriminant function, although statistically significant, was only moderately significant on more pragmatic grounds. The canonical correlation was relatively small while Wilks' lambda tended to be relatively high. For classification purposes, the model was correct two-thirds of the time.

While this illustration may provide only modest results, it does illustrate most of the major dimensions of computerized discriminant analysis.

Wilks' Lambda (U-Statistic) and Univariate F-Ratio with 1 and 173 Degrees of Freedom

Variable	Wilks' Lambda	F	Significance
LIKB	0.97789	3.912	0.0495
LIKD	0.97814	3.866	0.0509
LIKE	0.99782	.3771	0.5399
LIKF	0.98323	2.951	0.0876
LIKG	0.95861	7.470	0.0069
LIKH	0.99504	.8628	0.3543
LIKI	0.99403	1.038	0.3096
LIKK	0.99968	.5590D-01	0.8134

First Step

At Step 1, LIKG was included in the analysis.

		Degrees of Freedom			Significance
Wilks' Lambda	0.9586074	1	1	173.0	
Equivalent F	7.470124		1	173.0	0.0069

Variables in the Analysis After Step 1

Variable	Tolerance	F to Remove	Wilks' Lambda
LIKG	1.0000000	7.4701	

Variables Not in the Analysis After Step 1

Variable	Tolerance	Minimum Tolerance	F to Enter	Wilks' Lambda
LIKB	0.9808719	0.9808719	2.4869	0.9449448
LIKD	0.9999750	0.9999750	3.6339	0.9387735
LIKE	0.9652846	0.9652846	1.2459	0.9517133
LIKF	0.9385830	0.9385830	1.0992	0.9525203
LIKH	0.8098111	0.8098111	.81453D-01	0.9581537
LIKI	0.9650519	0.9650519	.25495	0.9571886
LIKK	0.9813380	0.9813380	.18211D-01	0.9585059

F Statistics and Significances Between Pairs of Groups After Step
Each F Statistic Has 1 and 173.0 Degrees of Freedom.

	Group 1
Group	
2	7.4701
	0.0069

Last Step

At Step 4, LIKE was included in the analysis.

		Degrees of Freedom			Significance
Wilks' Lambda	0.9104462	4	1	173.0	
Equivalent F	4.180409		4	170.0	0.0030

Variables in the Analysis After Step 4

Variable	Tolerance	F to Remove	Wilks' Lambda
LIKB	0.8945690	4.58635	0.9350092
LIKD	0.9639610	3.8597	0.9311171
LIKE	0.8814719	1.7881	0.9200224
LIKG	0.9557594	6.3474	0.9444401

Variables not in the Analysis After Step 4

Variable	Tolerance	Minimum Tolerance	F to Enter	Wilks' Lambda
LIKF	0.9186928	0.8780329	.60240	0.9072124
LIKH	0.7740839	0.7740839	.19840	0.9093786
LIKI	0.9467602	0.8777749	.68906D-01	0.9100750
LIKK	0.9175810	0.8392064	.35425D-04	0.9104460

(*continued*)

Exhibit 13-1   Application of SPSS^x Discriminant Analysis (*Continued*)

F Statistics and Significances Between Pairs of Groups After
Step 4
Each F Statistic has 4 and 170.0 Degrees of Freedom.

	Group 1
Group 2	4.1804
	0.0030

Summary Table

Step	Action Entered	Removed	Vars in	Wilks' Lambda	Sig.
1	LIKG		1	0.958607	0.0069
2	LIKD		2	0.938773	0.0044
3	LIKB		3	0.920022	0.0025
4	LIKE		4	0.910446	0.0030

Classification Function Coefficients
(Fisher's Linear Discriminant Functions)

Vers =	1	2
LIKG	.4273735	.6062832
LIKD	1.103022	.8474887
LIKE	.2334551	.1095288
LIKG	1.158808	1.410825
(Constant)	−4.552408	05.329248

Canonical Discriminant Functions

Function	Canonical Correlation	After Function	Wilks' Lambda	Chi-squared	DF	Significance
		0	0.9104462	16.043	4	0.0030
1	0.2292					

Standardized Canonical Discriminant Function Coefficients

	Function 1
LIKB	0.57264
LIKD	−0.50711
LIKE	−0.36312
LIKG	0.64848

Unstandardized Canonical Discriminant Function Coefficients

	Function 1
LIKB	.2860773
LIKD	−.4085995
LIKE	−.1981587
LIKG	.4029761
(Constant)	−1.218941

Group Centroids

Group	Function 1
1	−0.28947
2	0.33592

Classification Results

Actual Group	No. of Cases	Predicted Group Membership 1	2
Group 1	95	68 71.6%	37 28.4%
Group 2	84	29 34.5%	55 65.5%

Percent of "Grouped" Cases Correctly Classified: 68.72%

Classification of Individual Cases

Case SEQNUM	MIS VAL	SEL	Actual Group	Highest Probability Group	P(D/G)	(G/D)	2nd Highest Group	P(G/D)	Discriminant Scores
1			1	1	0.9672	0.5424	2	0.4576	−0.2484
2			1***	2	0.9999	0.5488	1	0.4512	0.3360
3			1	1	0.9396	0.5604	2	0.4396	−0.3653
4			1***	2	0.7698	0.5031	1	0.4969	0.0433
5			1	1	0.4443	0.6624	2	0.3376	−1.0544

(continued)

Exhibit 13-1 Application of SPSS^x Discriminant Analysis *(Continued)*

Classification of Individual Cases

Case SEQNUM	MIS VAL	SEL	Actual Group	Highest Probability			2nd Highest		Discriminant
				Group	P(D/G)	(G/D)	Group	P(G/D)	Scores
6			1	1	0.7174	0.6039	2	0.3961	−0.6514
7			1	1	0.9671	0.5551	2	0.4449	−0.3307
.									
.									
.									
.									
.									
177			2	2	0.8892	0.5702	1	0.4298	0.4753
178			2	2	0.9247	0.5341	1	0.4659	0.2415
179			2***	1	0.6569	0.6162	2	0.3838	−0.7337
180			2***	1	0.0002	0.9254	2	0.0746	−4.0025
181			2	2	0.6705	0.6134	1	0.3866	0.7613
182			2***	1	0.2917	0.7016	2	0.2984	−1.3438
183			2	2	0.0336	0.8212	1	0.1788	2.4612

in Figure 13-4. Using an illustration drawn from public opinion research, assume that respondents are asked to rate the quality of some local municipality's bus service. Data are also collected on the respondent's extent of past usage of the service and whether he or she is working or not.

Suppose we wish to see if respondents' ratings of Y, the quality of the service (higher values indicating higher quality), are related to X_1, past usage of the service. However, we also suspect that the relationship between Y and X_1 might be dependent on whether the respondent is working or not (which can be denoted by a dummy variable X_2).

In Panel I we note the "classic" case of correlation between X_1 and X_2 but no interaction. We observe that Y is positively associated with changes in X_1 and that the slopes of the regression lines do not depend on the values of X_2 (working versus nonworking). Rather, it is the *intercept* that differs between the two cases, in the sense that respondents who are working report higher quality of service on the average than those who are not working. The correlation between X_1 and X_2 is indicated by the fact that average past usage by working respondents exceeds that of nonworking respondents.

Panel II shows the case of interaction without correlation between X_1 and X_2. Here we see that across the *total sample* of working and nonworking respondents, Y does not depend on X_1 (i.e., the total-sample slope is horizontal). However, *within* the separate levels of X_2, Y increases with increases in X_1, given that the respondent is not working, while it decreases with increases in X_1, given that the respondent is working. The average past usage is the same for both working and nonworking respondents, showing no correlation between X_1 and X_2.

Panel III shows the combined case of correlation and interaction. Across the total

Figure 13-4   Illustrations of Correlation and Interaction (Hypothetical Data)

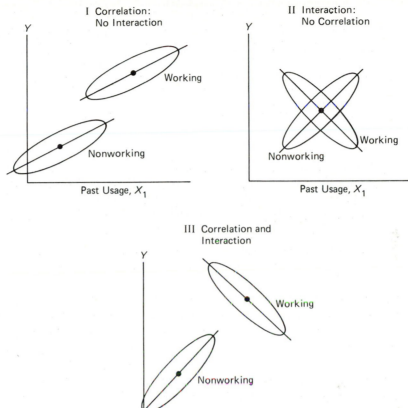

sample Y is positively associated with X_1. However, within the separate levels of X_2 we see that Y increases with increases in X_1, given that the respondent is not working, but decreases with X_1, given that the respondent is working. The positive association between Y and X_1, at the total-sample level, results primarily from the fact that *average* past usage is considerably higher for working respondents than it is for nonworking respondents.

In the analysis of observational and survey data one often finds cases in which the predictors are interactive as well as correlated. Survey data are the type of data in which the analyst would ordinarily use multiple regression, which, as we know, is a type of additive model. If the researcher suspects interaction-type effects, it is a common procedure to add cross-product terms (of the type X_1X_2 or $X_1X_2X_3$) to the regression model. Unfortunately, cross-product terms express only one form of interaction (a multiplicative one) and, furthermore, the cross products will generally be highly correlated with the original predictors.

If only a few (multiplicative-type) interactions are believed to exist, the researcher could introduce cross-product terms for only those predictors. A major problem, however, is that in exploratory analyses of observational and survey data one does not ordinarily know *which* predictors are interactive (and how they are interactive). *Automatic interaction detection* (abbreviated AID) is a sequential search routine, developed by Sonquist and Morgan, in which one starts out with a criterion variable that is either interval-scaled or dichotomous.[25] While the predictor variables might originally be (1) nominal-, (2) ordinal-, or (3) interval-scaled, these predictors are *all* recoded into *nominal* variables in which

1. Order across classes can be disregarded, or
2. Order across classes can be retained.

For example, if one of the original predictors is employment status (white-collar, blue-collar, unemployed) one may wish to treat this variable as an unordered polytomy. Some other variable such as age may be recoded into 18–20; 21–23; 24–26 years, etc. In this case one would probably wish to maintain order across classes. Each predictor variable can be designated by the researcher as unordered or ordered, independently of the rest.

It has been suggested that AID is often an appropriate technique to use when

- We do not want to make strong assumptions about relationships
- There are more than just a few potential explanatory variables
- There are a large number of observations

The first condition emphasizes the exploratory aspects of a study. The second condition recognizes that the use of cross tabulations would be cumbersome and overwhelming. The nature of AID is such that it has things in common with cross tabulations but is a technique that is at least more efficient than traditional cross tabulation analysis. For example, with 20 potential explanatory variables, in order to run all possible 3-way cross tabulations, more than 1,000 tables would be generated. The last condition emphasizes that a large number of observations are needed when there are many explanatory variables in order that there be sufficient cases to "fill" cells resulting from splits.

Basic Concepts of AID

Now, given a criterion, say, average weekly consumption of beer for sample individuals, the objective of AID is to perform a sequence of binary splits of the sample, choosing those splits (and predictor variables) that separate the sample into two subgroups that maximally account for criterion-variable variance at any given stage. For each candidate predictor variable, in turn, AID makes an exhaustive search of all allowable splits

[25]J. A. Sonquist, E. L. Baker, and J. N. Morgan, *Searching for Structure (Alias, AID-III)* (Ann Arbor: Survey Research Center, University of Michigan, 1971). A related procedure designed to handle a polytomous criterion variable is described in R. Messenger and L. Mandell, "A Model Search Technique for Predictive Nominal Scale Multivariate Analysis," *Journal of the American Statistical Association,* 67 (December 1972), 768–72. The original monograph on AID is J. A. Sonquist and J. N. Morgan, *The Detection of Interaction Effects,* Monograph No. 35 (Ann Arbor: Survey Research Center, University of Michigan, 1964).

on that variable and chooses the split that maximizes between-groups variation associated with the two groups so split. It then chooses from all of these "best splits" (conditioned by predictor) the *specific* predictor variable and, hence, the split that leads to the maximum of these separate maxima.

To see this algebraically, assume that Y denotes the criterion variable. With no information about the predictor variables we would fall back on the mean of Y, that is, $\bar{Y}$, to estimate individual response. The "error" sum of squares would then be

$$\sum(Y_i - \bar{Y})^2 = \sum Y_i^2 - \frac{(\sum Y_i)^2}{n} = \sum Y_i^2 - n\bar{Y}^2$$

Now, however, assume that the total sample has been split into two groups of n_1 and n_2 persons with respective means, $\bar{Y}_1$ and $\bar{Y}_2$. If so, the error sum of squares is

$$\left(\sum Y_{i1}^2 - n_1\bar{Y}_1^2\right) + \left(\sum Y_{i2}^2 - n_2\bar{Y}_2^2\right) = \sum Y_i^2 - \left(n_1\bar{Y}_1^2 + n_2\bar{Y}_2^2\right)$$

The *reduction* in variation by splitting into two groups is simply

$$n_1\bar{Y}_1^2 + n_2\bar{Y}_2^2 - n\bar{Y}^2$$

This gain in error reduction assumes, of course, that the subgroup means are indeed different.

Basically, then, AID performs a series of one-way analysis of variance-type computations (similar in spirit to our discussion in Chapter 12). After splitting the initial sample on the basis of the "best" predictor, the process is repeated on each of the two subsamples, and so on. At each step of the sequential splitting process AID looks for the best *available* split, not the best set of some number of final groups. The main result of this is a tree structure that shows, at each stage:

1. The predictor variable leading to the best binary split and how that predictor *is* split
2. The number of persons assigned to each of the two subgroups
3. The criterion-variable mean on each of the two subgroups

While other summary statistics (e.g., error sums of squares) can also be shown, the above outputs represent the principal ones. It should be emphasized that a basic assumption underlying the application of AID is that variables useful in explaining one part of the database are not necessarily those most effective for explaining another part.

A few other key considerations, in the nature of restrictions or criteria for the stopping of the splitting sequence, enter into the actual application of AID:

1. All partitionings of the sample may be subject to a requirement that the proportionate reduction in the criterion-variable sum of squares exceed some level (specified by the researcher). This is to guard against partitionings that do not appreciably reduce variation in the criterion variable.

2. To qualify for further splitting, a group must have a sum of squares greater than some level (specified by the researcher). This is to guard against splits that, pragmatically speaking, are not worth the effort, for example, where the group is already quite homogeneous.

3. In addition to the control parameters above, the researcher may place an upper limit on the total number of groups formed and/or the minimum number of persons (or objects) in each group.

A few caveats regarding the application of AID should be mentioned at this point.[26] First, AID is generally designed for really large samples, on the order of 1,000 or more. Since many versions of AID will take as many as 30 to 35 predictors, the program has ample opportunity to capitalize on chance variation in the data. Moreover, no statistial inferential apparatus is associated with the approach. This suggests the value of cross-validating results on new data or, possibly, double cross-validating by applying AID to separate halves of the sample.

Second, AID, being a sequential search procedure, does not specify an explicit model in the way, for example, that ANOVA does. In this regard it is often useful to use AID as an initial "screening" device to find those predictors that appear to be most prominent in accounting for criterion variation. This can then be followed by the formulation of an explicit dummy-variable regression model that includes main effect and interaction terms of specific interest to the researcher. Sonquist,[27] in particular, recommends the joint use of AID and multiple classification analysis, the latter being a type of dummy-variable regression model with some useful features for exploratory data analysis.[28]

Third, despite the explicit concern for interaction AID is found to be insensitive to various forms of interaction. Since AID only examines the immediate effect of a predictor on the between-group sum of squares and not future possible splits, any interactions that are not one-stage will not be identified. Later versions of the technique (AID-3) do have a look-ahead option to examine some of these interactions, but computation time is greatly increased.[29]

---

[26]An evaluation of the use of AID is presented in P. Doyle and I. Fenwick, "The Pitfalls of AID Analysis," *Journal of Marketing Research,* 12 (November 1975), 408–13.

[27]J. A. Sonquist, *Multivariate Model Building: The Validation of a Search Strategy* (Ann Arbor: Survey Research Center, University of Michigan, 1970).

[28]F. Andrews, J. N. Morgan, and J. A. Sonquist, *Multiple Classification Analysis* (Ann Arbor: Survey Research Center, University of Michigan, 1967). A strategy for the joint use of AID and MCA in a marketing context is discussed in L. T. Parsons and T. C. Ness, "Using AID and MCA to Analyze Marketing Data," Proceedings of the 1971 Educators' Conference, American Marketing Association, pp. 523–530.

[29]See B. B. Jackson, *Multivariate Data Analysis: An Introduction* (Homewood, Ill.: Richard D. Irwin, 1983), pp. 43–45.

An Industry Example of AID

One of the nice characteristics of AID is its simplicity of output, which facilitates ease of understanding on the part of researchers and managers alike. The output takes the form of a tree diagram, in which one can follow the result of each binary split as it takes place. This is illustrated in the brief case study that follows.

Rogers National Research is a Toledo-based consulting firm that specializes in marketing research for the automotive companies.[30] One of its annual studies involves a survey of various car troubles that new-car buyers have experienced over the six months preceding the survey. Among other things, the respondents are asked to rate their car's overall quality of workmanship, and list the number and type of defects experienced during the past six months of ownership.

Of particular interest to Rogers' clients is the extent to which a respondent is "make-loyal." That is, when asked to consider the next car purchase, does the respondent indicate plans to purchase another car of the current make (Chevrolet, Pontiac, Ford, Dodge, etc.) or some other make?

A large sample ($n = 4,364$) of respondents was available, involving their responses to 22 different questions regarding new-car workmanship, demographics, and so on. All respondents had recently purchased a compact car, either foreign or domestic. The criterion variable was whether the respondent indicated that he or she was make-loyal (coded 1) or not (coded 0) with respect to the next new car purchase.

AID was applied to this large data bank with the results shown in the tree diagram of Figure 13-5. At the top of the diagram we first note that the total-sample probability of being make-loyal is 0.27. That is, 1,178 out of the total of 4,364 respondents indicate that they are make-loyal. The first variable on which the total sample is split involves the respondent's rating of *overall quality* of workmanship of his or her present car. If rated good to excellent, the make-loyal probability in this subsample of 3,352 persons is 0.32; if rated fair to poor, the make-loyal probability for this subsample of 1,012 respondents is only 0.10. On the right-hand side of the tree, age is the next variable to enter, followed by number of defects, and then by a further split on quality of workmanship rating—this time between excellent versus good or very good. Finally, the name of the car manufacturer enters.

On the left-hand side of the tree diagram the only other predictor to enter involves the total number of reported defects. Notice, then, that this tree is *not* symmetrical and that different variables follow the initial split, based on quality of workmanship.

The upshot of all of this is that one can obtain a make-loyal probability as high as 0.68 if

- The owner's current compact car is made by either General Motors or Ford
- Overall quality of workmanship is rated excellent
- 0–3 defects are reported
- The respondent is 35 years of age or older

---

[30]The authors are indebted to Rogers National Research for permission to include this application of AID.

Figure 13-5   Automatic Interaction Detection—National Car Quality Survey

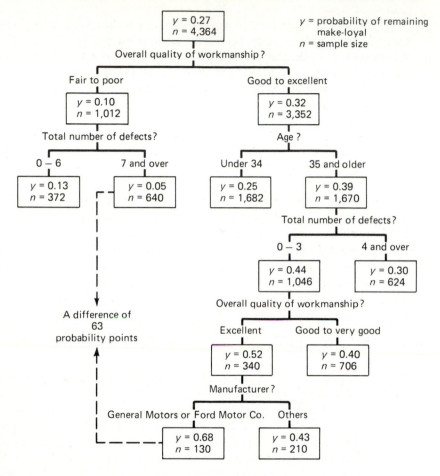

On the other hand, one can find a make-loyal probability as low as 0.05 if

- 7 or more defects are reported
- Overall quality of workmanship is rated fair to poor

In short, this type of information underscored the importance of certain types of quality control and led to a more detailed study of the kinds of defects that prompted the lowest incidence of make-loyal responses.

   Although not developed for such a purpose, a useful application of AID is *market segmentation analysis*.[31] This application provides the vehicle for discussing two addi-

[31]For example, see H. Assael and A. M. Roscoe, Jr., "Approaches to Market Segmentation Analysis," *Journal of Marketing*, 40 (October 1976), 67–76.

tional "limitations" of AID and how these can be overcome. First, a major feature of AID is that splits are limited to binary splits. The variables that represent bases for segmentation may need to be categorized in more than two classes in order to be meaningful. If this is the case and the researcher desires to use a procedure based on the logic of AID-type search, the method of *chi-square-based automatic interaction detection* (CHAID) can be used. Despite its not being limited to binary splits for the predictive variables and its advantages in computational aspects of the search heuristic, CHAID has had very limited use.[32]

A second consideration centers on using only one behavioral criterion variable, as AID uses. Pragmatically, it may be desirable to use multiple indicators. One alternative way of handling this for segmentation analysis has been *canonical* analysis. By doing this, however, the researcher moves from a technique giving results that are easy to understand, interpret, and communicate to others to a technique that is much more difficult to comprehend. To overcome this, MacLachlan and Johansson have proposed a multivariate extension of AID (MAID).[33] In large part, problems with MAID are the same as those associated with AID. This may very well be a major contributing factor to its low adoption of use. Much of the criticism that can be directed to MAID, and to AID as well, is less valid if both methods are viewed as an *exploratory* methodology, useful for *suggesting* groupings of customers to which marketing effort can be targeted profitably.

OTHER TECHNIQUES FOR CRITERION–PREDICTOR ASSOCIATION

Up to this point in the book, discussion of associative data analysis has emphasized the single criterion/multiple predictor techniques of

- Multiple regression
- Analysis of variance and covariance
- Two-group discriminant analysis
- Automatic interaction detection

Multivariate analysis of variance and covariance (discussed in Chapter 12) and multiple discriminant analysis (briefly described earlier in this chapter) are of the multiple criterion/multiple predictor variety. We say "multiple" criterion for the discriminant analysis because two dummy criterion variables were required to encode three groups and, in general, G-1 dummies are required to encode G criterion groups.

---

[32]See W. D. Perreault, Jr., and H. C. Barksdale, Jr., "A Model-Free Approach for Analysis of Complex Contingency Data in Survey Research," *Journal of Marketing Research,* 17 (November 1980), 503–15.

[33]D. L. MacLachlan and J. K. Johansson, "Market Segmentation with Multivariate AID," *Journal of Marketing,* 45 (Winter 1981), 74–84.

There are other techniques that deal with criterion–predictor association:

- Canonical correlation is a generalization of multiple correlation to two or more criterion variables.
- Probit and logit deal with predicting the level of a dependent variable that is nominaly- or ordinaly-scaled; the techniques differ only in the assumption made about the frequency distribution of the response.
- Path analysis/causal modeling involves techniques designed to identify causal relationships.

These techniques either are extensions or modifications of, or are considerably more complex than, ones we have already discussed in earlier chapters. Moreover, their application to marketing research has been much less than the methods already discussed. For these reasons descriptions of them are brief and nontechnical. More-detailed discussions will be found in the references cited.

Basic Concepts of Canonical Correlation

To illustrate the technique of *canonical correlation*, let us return to the radial tire study described in our discussion in Chapter 11 of stepwise multiple regression. As will be recalled, the criterion variable was the respondent's postexposure interest rating—after watching a set of TV commercials—of the firm's new brand of steel-belted radial tires. The main predictor variables were

X_1: general interest in the product class of steel-belted radials;

X_2: whether the firm's old brand was chosen as the respondent's last purchase of replacement tires; and

X_3: preexposure (before seeing the commercials) interest in the firm's new brand of steel-belted radials.

Now, however, let us assume that *two* criterion variables are involved·

Y_1: believability in the claims made in the firm's new TV commercial;

Y_2: postexposure interest in the firm's new brand (as before).

What we would like to find out is how highly correlated the *battery* of two criterion variables is with the *battery* of three predictors. Moreover, we would like to find a linear composite of the Y-variable set and a (different) linear composite of the X-variable set that will produce a maximal correlation.

This is what canonical correlation is all about. In terms of the classification in

Chapter 10, canonical correlation deals with (1) both description and statistical inference of (2) a data matrix partitioned into at least two criteria and at least two predictors where (3) all variables are interval-scaled and (4) the relationships are assumed to be linear. In more general terms, canonical correlation analysis can be used to investigate the following research questions:[34]

- To what extent can one set of two or more variables be predicted or "explained" by another set of two or more variables?
- What contribution does a single variable make to the explanatory power of the set of variables to which the variable belongs?
- To what extent does a single variable contribute to predicting or "explaining" the composite of the variables in the variable set to which the variable does *not* belong?
- What different dynamics are involved in the ability of one variable set to "explain" in different ways different portions of the other variable set?
- What relative power do different canonical functions have to predict or explain relationships?
- How stable are canonical results across samples or sample subgroups?
- How closely do obtained canonical results conform to expected canonical results?

The mathematics of canonical correlation are sufficiently complex that computer programs are a necessity. The major packages all have capabilities for performing the necessary calculations. Both BMD (P6M) and SAS (ANCORR) have specific canonical correlation programs, while in the SPSS^x package the multivariate analysis of variance program MANOVA does canonical correlation analysis.

We illustrate the use of this technique by applying BMD's P6M program and showing only highlights of the program. This program can handle a large number of variables and a virtually unlimited number of cases. In addition to finding the canonical correlations and linear composites, it provides

- Summary measures of means, standard deviations, etc.
- Input data correlations
- Tests of significance of the canonical correlations
- Canonical scores (analogous to discriminant function scores)
- Correlations of original variables with the linear composites (often called structure correlations)
- Bivariate plots for original variables versus their linear composites

[34]B. Thompson, *Canonical Correlation Analysis Uses and Interpretations* (Beverly Hills, Calif.: Sage, 1984), p. 10.

TABLE 13-10   Results of BMD–P6M Canonical Correlation

	Canonical Weights	Structure Correlations
Criterion set		
Y_1	−0.110	0.594
Y_2	1.069	0.997
Predictor set		
X_1	0.346	0.539
X_2	0.141	0.382
X_3	0.817	0.930
Canonical correlation	0.582	

INPUT CORRELATIONS FOR CANONICAL ANALYSIS

	Y_1	Y_2	X_1	X_2	X_3
Y_1	1.000				
Y_2	0.659	1.000			
X_1	0.202	0.315	1.000		
X_2	0.097	0.218	0.086	1.000	
X_3	0.321	0.539	0.226	0.258	1.000

Table 13-10 shows the results of applying P6M to the radial tire problem. In general with p criteria and q predictors, one can obtain more than a single pair of linear composites—up to a maximum of the smaller of p and q. Thus, in our case we would obtain two pairs of linear composites, uncorrelated across pairs, with the first pair exhibiting maximum correlation.[35] However, as it turned out, only the first pair of linear composites was statistically significant at the 0.05 alpha level; hence, only this pair of weights is shown.

Table 13-10 shows that the canonical correlation between the two batteries is 0.582. As is the case with multiple correlations, this measure varies between 0 (no correlation) and 1 (perfect correlation). Since *mutual* association between the pair of batteries is involved, we can say that the pair of linear composites account for $(0.582)^2$ or 34% of the shared variation between the two batteries.

The canonical weights for the criterion set show that Y_2 (postexposure interest) is the dominant variable in the criterion set; its canonical weight is 1.069. The dominant variable in the predictor set is X_3; its weight is 0.817. Since all variables are standardized to zero mean and unit standard deviation *before* the analysis, the weights are already in standardized form.

---

[35]In general, the canonical correlation of successive pairs decreases; that is, the first pair displays the highest correlation, the second pair the next highest, and so on. All composites are mutually uncorrelated *across* pairs.

What Table 13-10 really says is that if we formed a linear composite of the criterion variables using the canonical weights:

$$T_c = -0.110Y_{s1} + 1.069Y_{s2}$$

and another linear composite of the predictors, using the canonical weights:

$$T_p = 0.346X_{s1} + 0.141X_{s2} + 0.817X_{s3}$$

and took these two columns of numbers (the canonical scores) and correlated them, the result would be a *simple* correlation of 0.582 (the canonical correlation).

Also shown in Table 13-10 are the structure correlations—the simple correlations of each original variable with the canonical scores of its own battery's linear composite. Again we note that Y_2 is the most important variable (structure correlation of 0.997) in the criterion set and X_3 the most important variable (structure correlation of 0.930) in the predictor set. Indeed, as noted in the input correlation matrix, the *simple* correlation between Y_2 and X_3 is 0.539, almost as high as the correlation between the full batteries.

As indicated earlier, canonical correlation has not received the kind of attention that the techniques covered earlier have. Part of this lack of application is based on its difficulty of interpretation. Since it is a rather sophisticated technique, we refer the reader to other sources for further discussion of the procedure.[36]

Probit and Logit

In Chapter 11 we emphasized that multiple regression is a useful technique for estimating a dependent variable from a set of independent variables. A major assumption of standard regression analysis is that the dependent variable be continuous and at least interval-scaled. When the dependent variable is dichotomous, binary regression can be used.

What can the researcher do when the problem concerns estimating relationships involving dependent variables that are non-metric (i.e., nominal- or ordinal-scaled)? We often see regression used in this type of situation with the result of finding an unnecessarily high proportion of unexplained variance (i.e., a lower r^2), misleading estimates of the effects of the predictor variables, and inability to make statements about the probability

[36]For more-detailed discussion, see M. M. Tatsuoka, *Multivariate Analysis: Techniques for Educational and Psychological Research* (New York: John Wiley, 1971); M.S. Levine, *Canonical Analysis and Factorial Comparison* (Beverly Hills, Calif.: Sage, 1977); and B. Thompson, *Canonical Correlation Analysis: Uses and Interpretation* (Beverly Hills, Calif.: Sage, 1984).

of given responses. To overcome these problems, *probit* and *logit* have been developed. Although these techniques have been used extensively in several disciplines, they have not been as widely used in research on marketing-related problems.

Probit and logit deal with the same problem—predicting a dependent variable that is nominal- or ordinal-scaled. They differ solely in the assumption made about the frequency distribution of the response:

- In probit, the response is assumed to be normally distributed.
- In logit, a logistic distribution is assumed.

In addition to dealing with the same type of problem, the two techniques are related to each other in that mathematically each can be transformed to the other. Thus, it has been suggested that selection criteria might more realistically include personal preference, computational ease, and meaningfulness of interpretation.[37] Unfortunately, such criteria do not all lead to the same technique. When there is a single independent variable logit models are simpler to compute, but for multiple variables probit has an advantage that is derived from the properties of the multivariate normal distribution. Interpretability concerns seem to favor logit because the logistic can be directly interpreted.

Although direct application in marketing has not been widespread compared with other techniques, there have been applications and potential applications in areas such as consumer behavior (including new-product introductions). There have been at least three types of applications, which basically differ in degree of aggregation. Whether the analysis is at the *aggregate, segment* (e.g., benefits), or *individual* level, the process is the same. The analyst estimates a common set of parameter or attribute weights from scaled preference or choice data. A weighted combination of the parameters and the alternative's attribute values (objective or perceived) is used to estimate a choice probability for the alternative.

The research that has been reported about marketing applications seems to indicate that logit is the favored technique of the two.[38] In contrast, there have been few reported applications for probit. One recent application has been in forecasting for medical markets.[39] In this case conjoint analysis-derived utilities, patient/physician data, and market information were used to estimate market shares for existing products. The estimation model uses a variation of multinomial probit developed in a shares-of-choice model which forms the underlying mathematical structure of the forecasting model itself. Another application has been in examining the use of probit and logit in new-product introduction

---

[37]See P. Doyle, "The Application of Probit and Logit in Marketing: A Review," *Journal of Business Research,* 5 (September 1977), 235–48.

[38]See D. H. Gensch and W. W. Recker, "The Multinomial, Multiattribute Logic Choice Model," *Journal of Marketing Research,* 16 (February 1979), 124–32; S. J. Arnold, V. Roth, and D.J. Tigert, "Conditional Logit versus MDA in the Prediction of Store Choice," *Advances in Consumer Research,* Vol. VIII, 1980; N. K. Malhotra, "The Use of Linear Logit Models in Marketing Research," *Journal of Marketing Research,* 21 (February 1984), 20–31; and R. Schmalensee and J. F. Thisse, "Perceptual Maps and the Optimal Location of New Products," *Marketing Science Institute, Technical Working Paper No. 86–103,* 1986, pp. 12–14.

[39]C. Finkbeiner, "Tool Aids Forecasts for Medical Products," *Marketing News,* 20 (January 3, 1986), 40–41.

Figure 13-6 Hypothetical Causal Structure

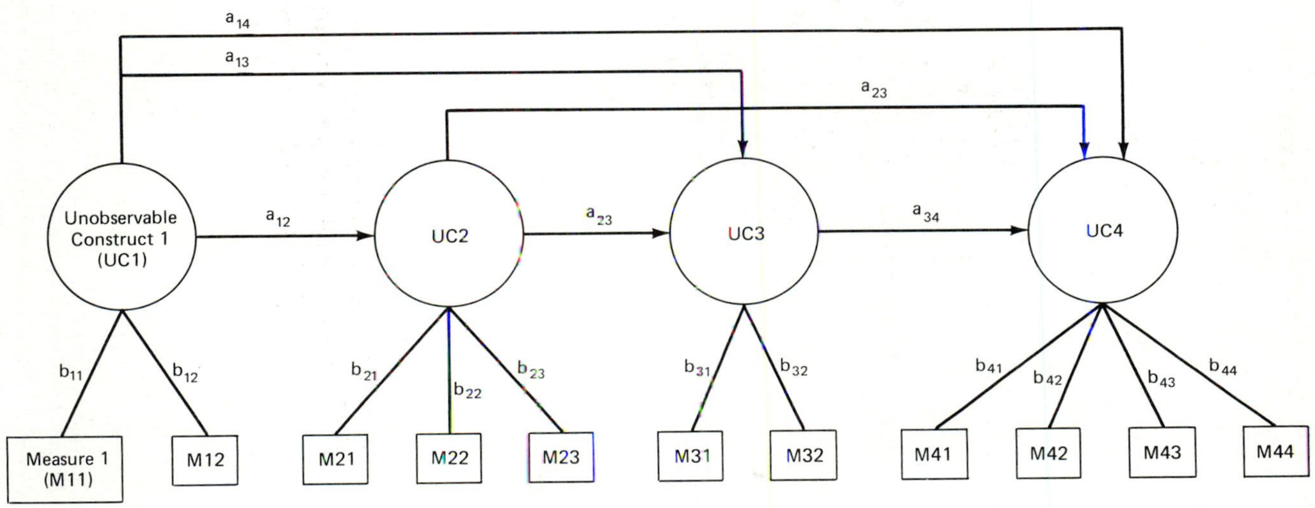

situations. Currim[40] compared *multivariate logit, independent probit,* and *generalized probit* models in the context of consumers' perceptions of transportation modes on several characteristics and their choices of modes. The first two models have a property known as the "independence of irrelevant alternatives" (IIA), since they lack consideration of product similarity and differences. That is, when a new product is introduced, it is assumed to obtain market share proportionately from all other brands, regardless of substitutability. The generalized probit model does not have this property. Using four criteria related to predictability of market share, the independent probit model out predicted logit and the generalized probit outpredicted independent probit.

How these techniques work and the underlying theories behind them tend to be technical. For a more detailed explanation we refer the reader to the references already cited and to the excellent introductory work of Aldrich and Nelson.[41]

Path Analysis/Causal Modeling

In recent years marketing researchers have become increasingly interested in the useful application of path analysis and structural equation modeling as an approach to *causal modeling.* Causal modeling provides the researcher with a systematic methodology for developing and testing theories in marketing.[42] From all this interest has emerged the development of *structural equation modeling* procedures.[43] These procedures blend two basic techniques:

- Factor analysis (to be discussed in Chapter 14)
- Simultaneous equation regression

Both of these techniques use multiple measures and simultaneous equation models to estimate the path of causation.

The essence of what happens with this type of analysis can be seen from a simple illustration. In Figure 13-6 we show a system with four unobservable constructs, each of which has more than one observable measure. In some situations the measures themselves may be correlated, which precludes finding a strong reliability from either simple indices or from regressions that relate the indices themselves as means of showing relations between the unobserved constructs.

---

[40]I. S. Currim, "Predictive Testing of Consumer Choice Models Not Subject to Independence of Irrelevant Alternatives," *Journal of Marketing Research,* 19 (May 1981), 208–22.

[41]J. H. Aldrich and F. D. Nelson, *Linear Probability, Logit, and Probit Models* (Beverly Hills, Calif.: Sage 1984).

[42]See R. P. Bagozzi, *Causal Models in Marketing* (New York: John Wiley, 1980).

[43]The November 1982 issue of the *Journal of Marketing Research* was a special issue on this topic.

To overcome this "problem" and to better estimate the relevant parameters, some rather complicated procedures have been developed which estimate both the links between the constructs(b_{ij}) and their measures and the links between the constructs themselves (a_{ij}) simultaneously. One widely used technique to estimate these parameters is LISREL. Another technique is PLS (partial least squares).[44] These techniques, and structural equation modeling in general, are highly technical methods of analyses and they are recommended only for experienced users. Since the number of such users is relatively small we do not discuss the techniques further.

SUMMARY

Chapters 11 and 12, as well as the current chapter, have all been concerned with various techniques for analyzing *between-set dependence:* regression, univariate analysis of variance and covariance, AID, two-group and multiple discriminant analysis, canonical analysis, probit and logit, and multivariate analysis of variance and covariance. At this point, it might appear that an almost bewildering array of techniques has been paraded before the reader.

Even at that, however, we have not discussed such extensions as canonical correlation of three or more sets of variables or tests for the equality of sums of squares and cross-products matrices. In addition, other related procedures, such as moderated regression, multiple-partial correlation, discriminant analysis with covariate adjustment, factorial discriminant analysis, to name a few, have been omitted from discussion.

What we have tried to do is to discuss the principal assumption structure of each technique, appropriate computer programs for applying it, and sufficient numerical applications to give the reader a feel for the kinds of output generated by each program.

Our coverage of so vast and complex a set of methods is limited in depth as well as breadth. The fact remains, however, that marketing researchers of the future will have to seek grounding in multivariate methodology, if current research trends are any indication. This grounding will probably embrace three facets: (1) theoretical understanding of the techniques; (2) knowledge of the details of appropriate computer algorithms for implementing the techniques; and (3) a grasp of the characteristics of substantive problems in marketing that are relevant for each of the methods.

Finally, we should reiterate the fact that all the preceding techniques display a penchant for capitalizing on chance variation in the data. One can hardly overemphasize the need to employ cross-validation procedures as well as the advisability of selecting criterion and predictor variables on the basis of conceptual relevance. Computer algorithms make it so easy to include as many variables as the researcher desires that one often develops a reluctance to think about *why* certain variables are included. Such temptations

[44]See K. G. Jöreskog and D. Sörbom, *LISREL VI Users' Guide,* 3rd ed. (Mooresville, Ind.: Scientific Software, 1984); K. G. Jöreskog and D. Sörbom, "Recent Developments in Structural Equation Modeling," *Journal of Marketing Research,* 19 (November 1982), 404–16; C. Fornell and F. L. Bookstein, "Two Structural Equation Models: LISREL and PLS applied to Consumer Exit-Voice Theory," *Journal of Marketing Research,* 19 (November 1982), 440–52; and J. S. Long, *Covariance Structure Models: An Introduction to LISREL* (Beverly Hills, Calif.: Sage 1983).

to "let the computer do the selection" are hard to resist but provide no substitute for hard thinking about the problem.

    Structural equation modeling and what this means to examining causation were briefly discussed at the end of this chapter. LISREL and PLS were identified as the two most widely used parameter estimation procedures.

ASSIGNMENT MATERIAL

1. Assume that the Jain Pool Co. has assembled income and lot-size data on a group of pool and nonpool owners living in southeastern Pennsylvania. In addition, data are available for each group on attitudes toward sun bathing, scaled from 0—"detest sun bathing," to 10—"extremely fond of sun bathing." the data are summarized below.

POOL OWNER	ANNUAL INCOME (THOUSANDS OF DOLLARS)	LOT SIZE (THOUSANDS OF SQUARE FEET)	ATTITUDINAL MEASURE
1	9.3	30.2	8
2	10.2	40.1	10
3	9.7	35.3	6
4	11.5	45.1	4
5	12.0	38.0	5
6	14.2	50.1	9
7	18.6	60.2	10
8	28.4	100.4	3
9	13.2	25.1	2
10	10.8	40.7	7
11	22.7	68.4	9
12	12.3	60.3	8

NONPOOL OWNER	ANNUAL INCOME (THOUSANDS OF DOLLARS)	LOT SIZE (THOUSANDS OF SQUARE FEET)	ATTITUDINAL MEASURE
1	8.2	30.2	2
2	7.8	40.2	0
3	11.4	44.8	1
4	16.3	50.6	4
5	12.4	42.5	8
6	11.5	60.3	0
7	6.8	39.7	6
8	10.4	35.4	4
9	14.2	42.6	3
10	11.6	38.4	2
11	8.4	30.2	4
12	9.1	25.7	5

Poor Risk	Annual Income (Thousands of Dollars)	Number of Credit Cards	Age	Number of Children
1	9.2	2	27	3
2	10.7	3	24	0
3	8.9	1	32	2
4	11.2	1	29	4
5	9.9	2	31	3
6	10.7	4	29	1
7	8.6	3	28	1
8	9.1	0	31	5
9	10.3	5	26	2
10	10.5	4	30	3

Equivocal Risk	Annual Income (Thousands of Dollars)	Number of Credit Cards	Age	Number of Children
1	14.4	4	34	4
2	14.7	7	33	2
3	13.6	3	41	1
4	10.3	1	37	1
5	14.9	6	39	0
6	15.8	5	37	3
7	16.0	4	36	5
8	11.2	2	35	3
9	12.6	8	36	2
10	14.7	3	29	4

Good Risk	Annual Income (Thousands of Dollars)	Number of Credit Cards	Age	Number of Children
1	18.6	7	42	3
2	17.4	6	47	5
3	22.6	4	41	1
4	24.3	5	39	0
5	19.4	1	43	2
6	14.2	12	46	3
7	12.7	8	42	4
8	21.6	7	48	2
9	26.4	5	37	3
10	19.4	9	51	1

a. Compute a two-group linear discriminant function using annual income, lot size, and attitude toward sun bathing as predictor variables.

b. How might the pool builder use the results of the function computed in part (a)?

c. Using the function computed in part (a), assign each of the 24 respondents to the class "pool owner" or "nonpool owner." Compare your answer with the known assignment. What is the percentage of correct classifications?

    d. The marketing researcher has received the following information about a new respondent not included in the original sample:
      (1) Annual income: $12,000
      (2) Lot size: 42,000 square feet
      (3) Attitude toward sun bathing: "8"
      Using the discriminant function, to which class would the respondent be assigned?

2. The credit firm of Maheshwari and Rao, Inc., has expressed interest in the possible use of discriminant analysis in the preliminary screening of credit applications. From past records the company has assembled information on three classes of married credit grantees: (a) poor risks, (b) equivocal risks, and (c) good risks. Additional information about a sample of credit grantees has also been obtained:

    a. Compute linear discriminant functions for a three-way analysis.
    b. Which variables appear to discriminate best among the three groups?
    c. Criticize the manner in which data were obtained for the three-way discriminant analysis.

3. Describe how a researcher might use automatic interaction detection to single out the best prospects for a firm specializing in selling classical records by mail.
    a. What criterion variable would you use?
    b. What predictor variables appear to be good candidates?
    c. How could the AID results be used as a preliminary approach to either multiple regression or two-group discriminant analysis?

4. Search the marketing research literature for individual applications of *canonical correlation, probit,* and *logit.*
    a. Why did each author use one of these techniques rather than multiple regression or analysis of variance and covariance?
    b. Describe other ways that the problem could have been handled.

5. How could canonical correlation be used to analyze the data that can be obtained from the questionnaires used by United Airlines (Case II-3)? What criterion and predictor variables would you select?

6. Using the variables to be examined by the United Airlines study (Case II-3), discuss how discriminant analysis might be used.

14

Factor Analysis and Clustering Methods

INTRODUCTION

In this chapter we focus on the case in which the data matrix has *not* been partitioned in advance into subsets of criterion and predictor variables. Rather, the analyst is interested in the whole set of interdependent relationships. Interest can center on the variables in the sense that the analyst may wish to summarize them (columns of the data matrix) in terms of a smaller set of linear composites that preserve most of the information in the original set. Factor analysis represents a class of techniques for achieving this objective.

On the other hand, the researcher may wish to focus his or her interest on the objects themselves. That is, the researcher may wish to partition the *rows* of the data matrix—where each row denotes an object—into homogeneous subsets of objects. In so doing the researcher is allowing the data themselves to suggest groups of objects. Cluster analysis is an appropriate set of techniques for this objective.

We first discuss factor analysis at an intuitive level using numerical examples. The discussion leads to the portrayal of points (objects or persons) in variables space and rotations of that space that satisfy certain criteria. This viewpoint underlies subsequent discussion of *principal components* as a major factor-analytic technique for summarizing multivariate data.

Attention then turns to a discussion of special topics and problems in factor analysis. We comment on such subjects as the rotation of principal components axes, other methods of factor analysis, the communality estimation problem, and statistical inference in factor analysis.

Clustering methods are introduced next. The fundamentals of cluster analysis are described in terms of questions concerning choice of proximity or similarity measure, clustering technique, and ways to define clusters.

Characteristics of various computer programs that have been proposed for grouping profiles are then described. This is followed by brief discussions of statistics for defining clusters and problems associated with statistical inference in this area. The chapter concludes with some empirical examples of cluster analysis.

BASIC CONCEPTS OF FACTOR ANALYSIS

Factor analysis is a generic name given to a class of techniques whose purpose often consists of data reduction and summarization. Used in this way, the objective is to represent a set of observed variables (or persons or occasions) in terms of a smaller number of hypothetical, underlying, and unknown dimensions which are called *factors*. This type of factor analysis is known as *exploratory factor analysis* and is the most common type used in marketing research applications. There are *common* factors that have effects shared in common with more than one of the observed variables and *unique* factors in which effects are shared with only one observed variable.

Factor analysis need not be confined to exploring the underlying dimensions of the data, however. It can be used to test specific hypotheses about the structure of a data set. When used for this purpose, it is referred to as *confirmatory factor analysis*.[1] Statistical tests can be used to determine if the data being analyzed are consistent with the imposed constraints reflected by the hypotheses or, in short, whether the data *confirm* the substantively generated model. There are times, however, when the confirmatory factor model can be used in an exploratory way.

The most widely used modes of exploratory factor analysis by marketing researchers are the *R* technique (relationships among items or variables are examined) and the *Q* technique (persons or observations are examined). Other modes of analysis are identified in Table 14-1, and these may be useful to the "creative" marketing researcher (also see Exhibit 14-1). For example, *S* and *T* techniques might be helpful in analyzing purchasing behavior or advertising recall data. The *P* and *O* techniques might be appropriate for looking at the life cycle of a product class, or perhaps even changes in demographic characteristics of identified market segments.

Factor analysis does *not* entail partitioning the data matrix into criterion and predictor subsets; rather, interest is centered on relationships involving the *whole* set of variables. In factor analysis:

1. The analyst is interested in examining the "strength" of the overall association among variables in the sense that he or she should like to account for this

---

[1]See J. Kim and C. W. Mueller, *Factor Analysis: Statistical Methods and Practical Issues* (Beverly Hills, Calif.: Sage, 1978), pp 46–60; and J. S. Long, *Confirmatory Factor Analysis* (Beverly Hills, Calif.: Sage, 1983).

association in terms of a smaller set of linear composites of the original variables that preserve most of the information in the full data set. Often one's interest will stress description of the data rather than statistical inference.

2. No attempt is made to divide the variables into criterion versus predictor sets.
3. The models are primarily based on linear relationships.
4. The models typically assume that the data are interval-scaled, although we shall briefly discuss the handling of nominal- and ordinal-scaled data as well.

The major *substantive* purpose of factor analysis is the search and (sometimes) test of constructs or "dimensions" assumed to underlie manifest variables. For example, a marketing researcher may collect a variety of consumer data on brand selection, store patronage, personality, and demographic variables. The main interest, however, might lie in the search for certain constructs, such as *private-brand proneness*. Proneness to purchase private brands may not represent an observable variable, but, rather, is to be *inferred* from (correlated) measures involving such observables as (1) the proportion of total purchases devoted to private-label brands, (2) attitude test scores on "thriftiness," (3) family size, (4) average amount of time per week devoted to shopping, and (5) store-switching behavior.

If studies should indicate that the observable variables are highly intercorrelated over repeated measurement occasions, we might attempt to develop a construct called private-brand proneness. This would entail the establishment of additional observable variables, subsequent testing, and so on. Much of the activity of the empirically oriented behavioral scientist is spent on just such pursuits in the domain of personality and cognitive theory. Factor analysis provides a means for the isolation of such constructs in addition to its "workhorse" role in data reduction.

TABLE 14-1   Modes of Factor Analysis

TECHNIQUE	FACTORS ARE LOADED BY	INDICES OF ASSOCIATION ARE COMPUTED ACROSS	DATA ARE COLLECTED ON
R	Variables	Persons	one occasion
Q	Persons	Variables	one occasion
S	Persons	Occasions	one variable
T	Occasions	Persons	one variable
P	Variables	Occasions	one person
O	Occasions	Variables	one person

Source: D. W. Stewart, "The Application and Misapplication of Factor Analysis in Marketing Research," *Journal of Marketing Research*, 18 (February 1981), 53.

Exhibit 14-1   Graphical Portrayal of Modes of Factor Analysis

The alternative modes of factor analysis can be portrayed graphically. The original data set is viewed as a *variables/persons/occasions* matrix (A). *R* -type and *Q*-type techniques deal with the variables/persons dichotomy (B). In contrast, *P*-type and *O*-type analyses are used for the occasions/variables situation and *S*-type and *T*-type are used when the occasions/persons relationship is of interest (C).

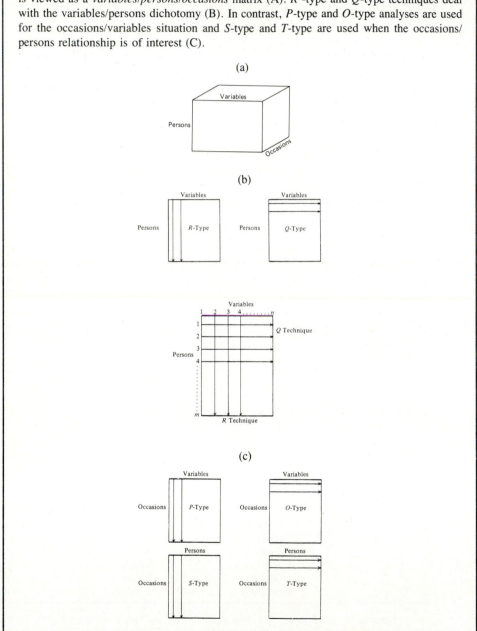

(a)

(b)

(c)

An Industry Application

To help motivate later discussion, let us consider an industry application in which factor analysis was used to help a firm's marketing researchers determine the basic dimensions of their company's image. While previous research had accumulated a lot of information on customers' perceptions of the firm, the researchers wished to learn if noncustomers employed similar frames of reference in evaluating the firm. That is, even though the firm might be rated below other firms along some of the image dimensions, were the dimensions themselves pretty much the same for the noncustomers?

The company in question is a large firm in the northeast that specializes in selling auto insurance policies by mail. Its growth had been rapid over the decade prior to the time the study was to be conducted. However, a tapering off of the rate of new-customer

TABLE 14-2 Statements Used in Image Study of Noncustomers

	DESCRIBES IT COMPLETELY					DOES NOT DESCRIBE IT AT ALL
	1	2	3	4	5	6
1. Will not cancel policy because of age or minor health problems.	1	2	3	4	5	6
2. Tries to handle claims equitably.	1	2	3	4	5	6
3. Difficult to do business with.	1	2	3	4	5	6
4. Provides excellent recommendations about what coverages should be purchased for individual needs.	1	2	3	4	5	6
5. Does not pay enough attention to its policyholders' problems.	1	2	3	4	5	6
6. Explains policies clearly and fully.	1	2	3	4	5	6
7. Tends to raise premiums without proper justification.	1	2	3	4	5	6
8. Its policies are better than others for older people.	1	2	3	4	5	6
9. Its coverage is generally renewable for life.	1	2	3	4	5	6
10. Takes a long time to settle claims.	1	2	3	4	5	6
11. Quick, reliable service—easily accessible.	1	2	3	4	5	6
12. A "good citizen" in the community.	1	2	3	4	5	6

acquisition served to renew interest in ways to attract additional policyholders. Accordingly, a survey was designed in which a sample of 380 noncustomers (who nonetheless claimed some familiarity with the firm) were interviewed. Among other things, each respondent was asked to evaluate the company on the 12 image-type statements appearing in Table 14-2. (These same statements had been employed in previous studies with the firm's customers.)

A glance at Table 14-2 suggests intuitively that some statements may be more or less tapping the same general constructs. For example, we would not be surprised if statements 1, 8, and 9 led to similar responses, since all three statements deal with whether older people are looked after in terms of their special needs. By the same token, statements 2, 4, 6, 11, and 12 all suggest quite positive things about a firm's general attitudes toward the public, particularly a firm's humanistic qualities. Conversely, statements 3, 5, 7, and 10 are rather pejorative about a firm's interaction with its public.

Therefore, it would not be unusual to find that respondent answers to statements 1, 8, and 9 were highly correlated; similarly, we might expect relatively high correlations of responses *within* each of the other two sets as well. However, would we also find that the *across-set* correlations are low? Are the conjectured image dimensions

- Relevance of policies for older people
- Humanistic and positive approach to its public
- Noncaring and negative approach to its public

more or less independent or are the second two "dimensions" really opposite ends of a single "desirable–undesirable" dimension?

Rather than trusting strictly to intuition, factor analysis systematically explores *which* variables exhibit high intraset correlations and low interset correlations, *how many* such sets there are (each set defining a dimension), and whether the dimensions can be considered as *uncorrelated* themselves.

Factor analysis has value only when correlations among subsets of the variables really exist. The higher these intraset correlations are, the better defined are the resulting factor dimensions.[2] Moreover, as we shall see, each original variable will receive a weight on each factor dimension that describes how much that variable contributes toward defining the dimension.

In the next section we show (for a much simpler data set) how one technique for doing factor analysis works. Insofar as the present example is concerned, it turned out that only three image dimensions were needed to account for over 80% of the variation in the original data.

As anticipated, statements 1, 8, and 9 defined the first dimension. However, only statements 10 and 11 defined (opposite ends of) the third dimension. The remaining statements 2, 4, 6, and 12 versus 3, 5, and 7 defined opposite ends of the second (good-

---

[2]It has been shown that factor analysis is responsive to the *relative* size of the observed correlations rather than to absolute size. This means that with data where the original variables are not very highly correlated, factor analysis will produce factors with high *loadings*. See A.S.C. Ehrenberg and G.J. Goodhardt, *Factor Analysis: Limitations and Alternatives* (Cambridge, Mass.: Marketing Science Institute, 1976), Report No. 76–116.

bad) dimension. Apparently, the speed with which the company handles its customer business is viewed differently from other evaluative aspects of its image.

The study also showed that the three image dimensions were common for customers *and* noncustomers, although the firm's *scores* on the variables defining the dimensions were generally better for customers. The most interesting result, however, was that the firm's scores on the first dimension (relevance of its policies for older people) were not appreciably different between customers and noncustomers; that is, the firm scored well with *both* groups.

This result prompted the company to design a special promotion to older insurance holders who were customers of *other* firms. The promotion outlined several new policies that were specially designed for senior citizens. The campaign was highly successful in attracting customers to the new policies and, in some cases, even switching policyholders completely away from their current companies.

Let us now turn to a simpler illustration that, nevertheless, covers the main concepts of factor analysis. This example deals with the performance characteristics of computer models. As such, all data are "hard," objective data on various aspects of computers' capabilities.

A Numerical Example

To illustrate the basic ideas of factor analysis it is much easier to work with a smaller data set. Table 14-3 shows a set of data involving only 15 rows and 6 columns (in contrast to the 380 rows and 12 columns that would be required to portray the image data based on Table 14-2).

TABLE 14-3 Standardized Data Matrix Used in Factor Analyses

COMPUTER NUMBER	DESCRIPTION	CHARACTERISTIC NUMBER					
		1	*2*	*3*	*4*	*5*	*6*
1	Philco 2000/210	−0.28	−0.36	−0.49	−0.52	−0.48	−0.27
2	Recomp II	3.51	3.61	−0.55	−0.60	−0.87	3.74
3	Honeywell 800	−0.39	−0.34	−0.55	−0.53	−0.59	−0.27
4	GE 225	−0.06	−0.28	−0.55	−0.57	−0.83	−0.26
5	RPC 301/354, 355	0.38	−0.27	−0.46	−0.50	−0.88	−0.27
6	Burroughs B5500	−0.43	−0.38	−0.55	−0.52	−0.48	−0.27
7	IBM 7040	−0.26	0.37	−0.55	−0.52	−0.59	−0.27
8	Univac 1004-1	0.70	0.68	−0.60	−0.61	−0.92	−0.27
9	CDC 3400	−0.47	−0.39	−0.37	−0.52	−0.48	−0.27
10	RCA 3301/3303	−0.28	−0.23	−0.02	−0.14	−0.77	−0.27
11	GE 635	−0.49	−0.39	−0.13	0.16	1.71	−0.27
12	IBM 360/65	−0.50	−0.39	1.32	2.47	1.08	−0.27
13	Univac 1108	−0.51	−0.39	0.36	0.16	1.70	−0.27
14	IBM 360/75	−0.51	−0.39	3.26	2.47	1.08	−0.27
15	CDC 6800	−0.52	−0.12	−0.13	−0.23	1.33	−0.27

In this case the units c⸱ association are all older digital computer models. Each model was originally measured oւ six different performance characteristics:

1. Execution time for addition, in microseconds;
2. Execution time for multiplication, in microseconds;
3. Minimum number of words that can be put in storage;
4. Maximum number of words that can be put in storage;
5. Maximum total storage; and
6. Cycle time in microseconds.

However, in Table 14-3 each of the six variables has been expressed as a *standardized* variate with zero mean and unit standard deviation. Intuitively, we would think that performance measures 1, 2, and 6 are indicants of *speed*. We would not be surprised if they exhibited high intercorrelation. Measures 3, 4, and 5 all seem to relate to computer *size or capacity* and may, in turn, be intercorrelated. However, this is all conjecture. Moreover, we do not know if speed and size can be considered as independent dimensions.

What *does* seem evident at the outset is the desirability of working with *standardized* data so that any differences in original measurement units—which are often arbitrarily chosen anyway—will not influence the analysis.

To simplify the problem even further, let us initially consider only the *first three columns* of the data matrix in Table 14-3. What we wish to do now is define some terms and then go on to factor-analyze the 15 × 3 data matrix obtained from the first three columns of the table.

Factor Scores

A *factor* of this 15 × 3 data matrix is simply a *liner combination* (or *linear composite*) *of the original scores*. For example, assume that we were to weight variable 1 by 0.5 and variables 2 and 3 by 0.1 each. Then a factor, F_1, could be written

$$F_1 = 0.5X_1 + 0.1X_2 + 0.1X_3$$

More generally, a factor can be shown as

$$F_i = a_1X_1 + a_2X_2 + \cdots + a_nX_n$$

where the a_i are the weights.

Each object has a *factor score*, where the weights are common for each object. For example, the factor score of the first computer is

$$F_{11} = 0.5(-0.28) + 0.1(-0.36) + 0.1(-0.49) = -0.225$$

In turn we could compute scores (using the same weights as above) for the other 14 computer models, giving us a new column of numbers, the factor scores. In general these factor scores will be different because the original scores are different across computer models.

But there is nothing magical about the particular weights chosen above. Any set of weights, the same or different over each column, plus or minus, might suffice. As a matter of fact, it is the purpose of various factor-analytic procedures to select these weights according to certain criteria. *The various methods of factor analysis are differentiated in terms of the bases upon which the weights are selected.*

How do we choose the weights for the first linear combination? As will soon be shown, we choose them so that the first column of factor scores has *maximum variance*. In the context of the total variance within the original data set, this means that this column of factor scores (i.e., the first factor) *explains* the largest portion of the total variance. Then, subject to the second set of factor scores being *uncorrelated* with the first, we choose a second set of weights so that the resulting second column of factor scores has maximum variance. This same principle will be invoked as we find additional linear combinations. In the present example, we shall be able to find three sets of factor scores; in general, with empirical data, we can find as many sets of (nonredundant) factor scores as there are columns to begin with (assuming that we have more objects than variables).

Factor Loadings

Suppose that we have gone ahead and found three factors (three sets of weights) and their associated factor scores. Assume that the linear combinations shown at the top of Table 14-4 were the ones actually used and that these, in turn, resulted in the three columns of (unstandardized) factor scores shown in the middle of the same table. We could then *correlate* each column of factor scores, in turn, with each of the three original variables in the data matrix, leading to the results shown in Table 14-5. A *factor loading* is defined simply as the correlation (across objects) of a set of factor scores with an original variable.

Let us examine this point more closely. The first set of weights in Table 14-4 are -0.68008, -0.67075, and 0.29596. (We discuss a bit later how these *particular* weights were obtained.) When these are applied to the three original variables, we obtain the first column of (unstandardized) factor scores shown in Table 14-4. For example, the first score of the first column is

$$0.28687 = -0.68008(-0.28) - 0.67075(-0.36) + 0.29596(-0.49)$$

Next, when we correlate this column, in turn, with each of the first three columns in Table 14-3, we obtain the first three rows of the first column shown in Table 14-5. We can then do the same thing with the other two sets of unstandardized factor scores shown in Table 14-4. Then we turn to Table 14-5 and note that performance variables 1 and 2

TABLE 14-4   Three Sets of Weights (Factors) and Resulting Factor Scores

Variable	Factor 1 Weights	Factor 2 Weights	Factor 3 Weights
1	−0.68008	0.17393	0.71223
2	−0.67075	0.24455	−0.70019
3	0.29596	0.95391	0.04966

UNSTANDARDIZED FACTOR SCORES

COMPUTER	Factor 1	Factor 2	Factor 3
1	0.28687	−0.60415	0.02831
2	−4.97125	0.96866	−0.05505
3	0.33051	−0.67563	−0.06702
4	−0.01577	−0.58269	0.21147
5	−0.21347	−0.43873	0.43685
6	0.38454	−0.69237	−0.06750
7	0.26222	−0.66036	0.04657
8	−1.10974	−0.28430	−0.00736
9	0.47172	−0.53007	−0.08005
10	0.33877	−0.12402	−0.03938
11	0.55636	−0.30461	−0.08238
12	0.99230	1.07682	−0.01749
13	0.71498	0.15933	−0.07229
14	1.57326	2.92567	0.07174
15	0.39565	−0.24380	−0.29279

COMPUTER	STANDARDIZED FACTOR SCORES		
1	0.19900	−0.63728	0.18226
2	−3.44843	1.02177	−0.35447
3	0.22926	−0.71267	−0.43154
4	−0.01094	−0.61464	1.36161
5	−0.14808	−0.46279	2.81279
6	0.26675	−0.73033	−0.43464
7	0.18190	−0.69656	0.29988
8	−0.76980	−0.29989	−0.04740
9	0.32722	−0.55913	−0.51544
10	0.23500	−0.13082	−0.25353
11	0.38593	−0.32131	−0.53041
12	0.68833	1.13586	−0.11260
13	0.49596	0.16807	−0.46544
14	1.09133	3.08609	0.46190
15	0.27446	−0.25716	−1.88523

TABLE 14-5   Correlations of Factor Scores (Table 14-4) with First Three Performance Variables of Table 14-3

Performance Variable	Factor 1	Factor 2	Factor 3	Sum of Squared Correlations
1	−0.98009	0.16491	0.11057	1.000
2	−0.96665	0.23187	−0.10870	1.000
3	0.42652	0.90445	0.00771	1.000
Sum of squared correlations*	2.07692	0.89898	0.02410	3.000
Cumulative proportion of total variation in performance variables	0.69230	0.99196	1.00000	

*This row also denotes the variance of the factor scores.

correlate highly (negatively) with factor 1, while variable 3 correlates highly with factor 2. None of the performance variables correlates very highly with factor 3.

These loadings (factor-variable correlations) in Table 14-5 are of interest in themselves. For example, variables 1 and 2 (execution time for addition and multiplication, respectively) are both indicants of "slowness." Since they both correlate highly (*negatively*) with the first factor, this suggests that the first factor is composed mainly of "speed." On the other hand, the fact that variable 3 (minimum number of words that can be put in storage) correlates highly with factor 2 suggests that the second factor is mostly a "capacity" dimension. Finally, the third factor appears to be mostly composed of error, since none of the original variables correlates highly with it.

However, things are not all this simple, particularly since variable 3 *is* correlated (0.296) with factor 1 and variables 1 and 2 *are* correlated (0.174 and 0.245) with factor 2. (We consider this point later in our discussion of rotating factor loadings to a "cleaner" structure.) Still, if we tried to account for the variance of the scores on factor 1 (scores appear in the first column in the middle portion of Table 14-4), which is 2.07692, we note from Table 14-5 that this also equals the sum of the squared correlations of each original variable, in turn, with factor 1. Thus, the contribution of each original variable to the variance of the scores on each factor is given by the *square of that variable's correlation (loading) with the factor*. In this way we can measure how important each variable is in defining each factor.

It is an interesting fact of the procedure that we can also turn the coin over and show how important each factor is in accounting for variance in each original variable. First, having found the three factors, can we use their scores to predict values on each of the original performance variables?

Recalling our discussion in Chapter 11 of beta weights in multiple regression, if *all* variables are in standardized form of zero mean and unit standard deviation *and* the predictor variables are uncorrelated, the least-squares estimate for, say, object i, on variable 1 would be

$$Z_{1i} = r_{1F_1}F_{1i} \; ; \; r_{1F_2}F_{2i} + r_{1F_3}F_{3i}$$

where r is a *simple correlation* between the variable and each factor in turn.

The first set of factor scores in Table 14-4 does *not* have unit standard deviation. The second set of scores *has* been standardized to unit standard deviation by dividing each of the entries of each column of the original set of factor scores by the square root of the column's variance (the mean of each column is already zero). The *variances,* incidentally, are 2.07692, 0.89898, and 0.02410, respectively, for factors 1, 2, and 3, as shown in Table 14-5. These are *also* the sum of the squared correlations between each factor and the performance variables.

Now, if we are interested in estimating the first computer model's original value (-0.28) on performance variable 1, our prediction formula is

$$Z_{11} = -0.98009(0.19900) + 0.16491(0.63728) + 0.11057(0.18226)$$

$$= -0.28$$

Moreover, if we examine Table 14-5 again, we can square each correlation of the first *row*:

$$(-0.98009)^2 = 0.96$$
$$(\;0.16491)^2 = 0.03$$
$$(\;0.11057)^2 = \underline{0.01}$$

$$1.00$$

and find the relative importance of each factor to the variation in each original variable. For example, in the case of variable 1 (execution time for addition) the first factor accounts for 96% of its variance.[3]

In effect, then, we can account for factors in terms of variables or variables in terms of factors. At this point it might seem strange to find the factors first and, having done so, to use the factors to estimate the performance variables that were employed to find the factors in the first place. As it turns out, however, two benefits are derived from such a representation:

1. The factors can be chosen so that their factor scores, unlike the original variables' scores, are *uncorrelated.*
2. The factors can be chosen sequentially, so that the first one accounts for most of the variability in the original data set, the second accounts for most of the residual variability, and so on.

---

[3]It is important to realize that in this example the three factors explain all the variance in the data set. In real-world applications, however, rarely will the factors explain all the variance.

Recapitulation

At this point we have gone through a whole series of computational steps and terminology that in their entirety may appear confusing. It would seem useful to recapitulate the procedure.

1. We first define a *factor* as a linear combination of the original variables. The weights used for the three factors "extracted" here are shown in the top portion of Table 14-4.

2. These weights are applied to the original data variables, yielding a set of three (unstandardized) factor scores for each object. These are shown in the middle portion of Table 14-4.

3. The factor scores are standardized to unit standard deviation by dividing each entry in each column by the square root of the column's variance. The variance of each column is shown in Table 14-5, while the standardized factor scores are shown in the bottom portion of Table 14-4.

4. Each column of factor scores (unstandardized or standardized—it makes no difference in this step) is then correlated with each of the columns of original variables, yielding the correlation matrix shown in Table 14-5.

5. When all scores are in standardized form and the factors have been chosen to be *mutually uncorrelated with each other,* the correlations of variables with factors—the factor loadings—can be viewed as regression coefficients to estimate the value of each computer model on each of the three performance characteristics. Generally speaking, the factors will diminish in importance in their estimating ability. That is, each set of factor scores accounts for a *diminishing proportion* of the variation in the original set of variables.

6. If we are willing to trade off some of the information in the original data matrix for a gain in data reduction, we would discard the last extracted factor first, the next-to-last second, and so on.

In the course of computing the various factor scores and factor loadings, we have been using a specific approach to factor analysis, called *principal components.* It is time to describe this procedure in more detail.

PRINCIPAL-COMPONENTS ANALYSIS

Principal-components analysis represents only one technique for extracting factors, or, in terms of this method, *components.*[4] This is the specific factoring technique that has been applied to the 15 × 3 matrix of Table 14-3 in order to find the factor scores of Table 14-4 and the factor loadings of Table 14-5.

---

[4]Some factor analysts discuss principal components as a model that is distinct from "factor" models. In practice, however, the more generic term of *factor analysis* is increasingly being applied to cover the principal-components procedure as well.

Exhibit 14-2   Some Concepts and Definitions of *R*-Type Factor Analysis

Factor Analysis:	A set of techniques for finding the number and characteristics of variables underlying a large number of measurements made on individuals or objects.
Factor:	A variable or construct that is not directly observable but is developed as a linear combination of observed variables.
Factor Loading:	The correlation between a variable and a factor. It is computed from correlating factor scores with observed manifest variable scores.
Factor Score:	A value for each factor that is assigned to each person. It is derived from a summation of the derived weights which are applied to the original data variables.
Communality (h^2):	The variance of each variable summarized by the factors, or the amount (percent) of each variable that is explained by the factors. The uniqueness component of a variable's variance is $1 - h^2$.
Eigenvalue:	The sum of squares of loadings of each factor. It is a measure of the variance of each factor, and if divided by the number of variables (i.e., the total variance), it is the amount of variance summarized by the factor.

Unlike some of the less structured factor-analytic procedures, principal-components analysis (in typical applications) leads to unique, reproducible results.[5] The objective is to portray a set of associated variables in terms of a set of orthogonal (mutually uncorrelated) linear combinations of those variables. The linear combinations are chosen so that each set of component scores accounts for a decreasing proportion of the total variance in the original variables, subject to being orthogonal with previously extracted components.

Let us consider the rationale underlying the method of principal components. Suppose that we return to the weights shown for each component at the top of Table 14-4. Of all the infinitude of weights that *could* be chosen to make up the factor scores (shown in the middle portion of Table 14-4), these are the *unique* weights that are found by application of the principal-components procedure. *These particular sets of weights yield unstandardized component* (i.e., factor) *scores whose variance is maximal, subject to each set of component scores being uncorrelated with previously obtained component scores.*

That is, no other set of weights could lead to a column of component scores with

---

[5]The method was first proposed by Karl Pearson in 1901. Its use in the analysis of associative data structures, however, is due to Harold Hotelling and is presented in the paper "Analysis of a Complex of Statistical Variables into Principal Components," *Journal of Educational Psychology*, 24(1933), 417–44, 498–520. Inasmuch as iterative methods are used in principal-components analysis, the term "unique" is used somewhat advisedly. Such procedures stop short of an exact solution and are subject to round-off error.

higher variance (in this problem) than the set -0.68008, -0.67075, and 0.29596. In our illustration, the total variance in the data (sum of the variances of the three standardized performance variables) is equal to 3; hence, each variable accounts for 33% of the total variance. The sum of the variances of the three components ($2.07692 + 0.89898 + 0.02410$) is also equal to 3. Note, however, that the proportion of total variation accounted for by the first component alone is 69%, and the first two components together account for almost all (99%) of the variance in the original set of data. Quite often, the analyst desiring parsimony would simply omit the last component, preferring to portray the data set in terms of only two components. In this case little information would be lost.

Geometric Aspects of Principal Components

Figure 14-1 shows, in general form, the geometric rationale of principal-components analysis. If the original variables are correlated, as they are in the illustrative problem of Table 14-3, then the points will not be uniformly scattered throughout the space. Rather, in three dimensions (for example), they will tend to follow an ellipsoidal pattern, as illustrated in Panel I of Figure 14-1. Notice that this figure looks like a flattened cigar.

If we put an axis P_1 through the longest direction of the ellipse, another axis P_2 through the second longest, and P_3 through the shortest, it turns out that those three axes *are* the principal-component axes of the data matrix. Note that they *are* at right angles (orthogonal) to each other, and furthermore, the variance (which is proportional to squared length) of P_1 exceeds that of P_2, which, in turn, exceeds that of P_3.

Of course, in limited samples of data, the flattened cigar shape is only approximated (if the variables are correlated). In two dimensions the pattern looks like an ellipse. In four and higher dimensions the pattern is hyperellipsoidal. While we cannot graph the latter case, the same idea holds mathematically: principal-components axes correspond to axes of the hyperellipse.

Figure 14-1   Geometrical Aspects of Principal-Components Factor Analysis

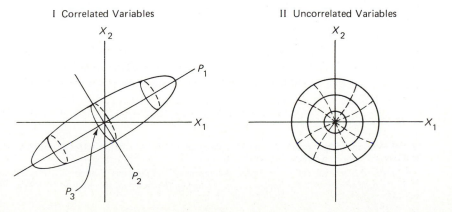

Panel II of Figure 14-1 illustrates why principal-components analysis is *not* applicable to data that are uncorrelated. In this case (assuming standardized variables), the points will trace out a spherelike figure. As we know, all directions through the center of a sphere lead to the same diameter and *no axis would display maximum variance*. Not surprisingly, no factoring method is relevant for this special case. However, this type of situation rarely arises insofar as empirical, nonexperimental data are concerned.

Geometrically speaking, it should be clear from Panel I that if we wish to discard any axis at all, the third axis P_3 is the best bet; little would be lost if the data were projected onto the plane formed by P_1 and P_2. Indeed, things could even by *improved* by projection if P_3 represented mostly an error dimension and the "intrinsic" dimensionality were only two dimensions.

We can now provide a geometric interpretation of the sets of weights that constitute the linear combinations of Table 14-4. For example, the first linear combination:

$$F_1 = -0.68008Z_1 - 0.67075Z_2 + 0.29596Z_3$$

constitutes a set of *direction cosines* that rotate the original three-dimensional space to the first principal-components axis; similarly, the second and third sets of weights are direction cosines for the second and third dimensions of the principal-components orientation.

Alternatives to Principal Components

Although principal components is widely used in marketing research study it is by no means the only technique used to extract the initial factors. Others include *principal factors, maximum likelihood, alpha factoring, image factoring,* and *least squares.*

An important difference among all these procedures, including principal components, is the nature of the value placed in the diagonal of the covariance or correlation matrix. This issue is, in reality, a problem of estimation of communality. For marketing researchers this appears to be of little practical concern, since there is strong evidence that most techniques lead to the same interpretations.[6] This is usually the case when there are a large number of variables and almost every one is expected to have a communality of least 0.4. Principal components uses 1.0 in the diagonals of the correlation matrix. Although this tends to produce higher loadings than alternative approaches, other results are similar. Thus when there are high communalities there are essentially no differences, and the choice of a procedure will not, by itself, affect results.[7]

---

[6]D. W. Stewart, "The Application and Misapplication of Factor Analysis in Marketing Research, *Journal of Marketing Research,* 18 (February 1981), 56.

[7]For more-detailed explanations of principal components and the other methods of factor extractions, see B. B. Jackson, *Multivariate Data Analysis: An Introduction* (Homewood, Ill.: Richard D. Irwin, 1983), Chap. 6; and Kim and Mueller, *Factor Analysis,* pp. 12–29.

COMPUTERIZED FACTOR ANALYSIS

In problems of realistic size the actual calculation of linear combinations, factor scores, and factor loadings is done by computer. One common strategy involves the following steps:

1. Compute the *full set* of principal components, including component loadings and scores.
2. Since the components will account for a decreasing proportion of the total variation in the data, keep only those component axes that cumulatively account for some appreciable percentage (e.g., 70% to 80%) of the total variability in the original data. Alternatively, a minimum absolute amount of variance that a factor should account for can be specified. The factoring process will stop when the next factor to be included has a variance less than this value. Computer programs typically set as a default value a variance of 1 for standardized data. However, this value can be varied.
3. Rotate the *retained* component solution to a more interpretable orientation. Recalculate factor loadings and scores in the rotated space.

As already shown, principal-components analysis orients the objects in variables space according to a definite set of criteria based on maximizing the variance of their projections on each axis, subject to maintaining orthogonality with previously "extracted" components. We now consider the possibility of rotating *this* orientation.

While principal-components analysis provides a useful tool from the standpoint of *data reduction,* it might *not* represent the best technique from an *interpretive* point of view. (Recall that one major purpose of factor analysis is the tentative identification of *constructs* underlying the manifest variables.) Interpretation is most often attempted at the *component-loading* level in which we are interested in the correlation of variables with components (see Table 14-5).

Easily interpreted component loadings are those in which each variable loads close to unity on one component and close to zero on all others. In this case the component whose variables show loadings close to unity can be interpreted in terms of whatever these particular variables appear to have in common.

Many criteria have been advocated for achieving interpretation of rotated components, and Thurstone[8] has been particularly active in this regard with his work on simple (or interpretable) structure. While the criteria of "interpretable" solutions differ among factor analysts, all seem to agree that it would be desirable to have *each variable load highly on one and only one factor.*

A variety of computer-based procedures have been advanced for rotating factor-loading matrices (as found initially by principal-components or some other factoring method). Generally these procedures can be divided into two groups—*orthogonal* versus *oblique* rotations. In orthogonal rotations the new axes must be mutually perpendicular

[8]L. L. Thurstone, *Multiple Factor Analysis* (Chicago: University of Chicago Press, 1947).

TABLE 14-6   Computer Programs for Factor Analysis

SPSS[x]

FACTOR   produces principal components analysis results and factor analysis results. There are six extraction techniques and several orthogonal and oblique rotation techniques. Factor scores can be calculated.

SAS

FACTOR   performs principal component and common factor analyses with orthogonal and oblique rotations. Factor scores are computed by a general SAS scoring program SCORE.

PRINCOMP   performs principal component analysis only and computes principal component scores.

BMDP

P4M   performs factor analysis of a correlation or covariance matrix. Is similar to SPSS[x] FACTOR procedure in having alternative extraction and rotation techniques.

and uncorrelated (just like the components were). Oblique rotations, as the name suggests, do not require the new axes to be uncorrelated; as such they are more precisely termed oblique "transformations" than "rotations."

As we showed for the criterion–perdictor association techniques in Chapters 11, 12, and 13, there are programs available from the major mainframe packages (see Table 14-6). The input data and output results are similar for all programs. These programs can handle large matrices of variables and cases.

Varimax Rotation

Varimax rotation of factor-loading matrices is an orthogonal procedure.[9] This procedure tends to produce some high loadings and some near-zero loadings on each factor. The Varimax technique leads to a new set of uncorrelated axes, keeping the *sum* of squared loadings for each row of the factor-loading matrix intact. Also the sum of cross products of loadings in any two rows of the rotated factor matrix equals the comparable quantity in the original factor-loading matrix. As such, the new axes account for (in total) just as much of the *common* variance as accounted for by the unrotated loading matrix. The Varimax rotation merely breaks up this variance in a different way.

When the original loading matrix has been obtained from a principal-components analysis, however, it is well to remember that successive "components" no longer account for maximum (residual) variance. That is, the variance-maximizing property of principal components, taken individually, is lost, although the retained components *as a group* account for the same proportion of total variance.

---

[9]H. F. Kaiser, "The Varimax Criterion for Analytic Rotation in Factor Analysis," *Psychometrika,* 23(1958), 187–200.

TABLE 14-7   Component-Loading Matrix—Six Performance Variables, Before Rotation of First Two Components*

	COMPONENT					
VARIABLE	*1*	*2*	*3*	*4*	*5*	*6*
	Before Rotation					
1	−0.914	−0.379	−0.039	0.014	−0.110	0.078
2	−0.873	−0.468	0.063	−0.006	−0.062	−0.093
3	0.604	−0.727	−0.268	−0.181	−0.006	0.003
4	0.625	−0.726	−0.211	0.190	0.003	−0.005
5	0.637	−0.464	0.614	−0.011	−0.027	0.011
6	−0.830	−0.522	0.093	−0.006	0.164	0.019
	Variance of Component Scores					
	3.453	1.908	0.508	0.069	0.044	0.015
	Cumulative Proportion of Total Variance					
	0.575	0.893	0.978	0.990	0.997	1.000

*Computed using an earlier version of BMD P4M.

Figure 14-2   Original and Varimax-Rotated Factor Loadings

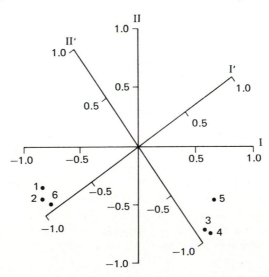

I, II — Original axes
I′, II′ — Rotated axes

A Numerical Illustration

As an illustration we apply one of the techniques to the *full* 15 × 6 matrix of Table 14-3. Since these programs provide a voluminous output, we restrict our attention to the component (factor)-loading matrix. This appears in Table 14-7.

We note from Table 14-7 that the first component accounts for almost 58% of the total variance, while the first two components together account for over 89% of the total variance. As we suggested earlier, factor analysts often retain all components whose component score variance exceeds unity. Indeed, the computer only provides output for those factors exceeding unity, or any variance value that was specified. In the case of Table 14-7 the first two components (with variances of 3.453 and 1.908, respectively) are the only ones that would be retained under this rule. The variables' loadings on the first two components of Table 14-7 are plotted in Figure 14-2. We see that the absolute value of all six loadings is rather high on component 1, and substantial loadings also appear on component 2. We wonder if a rotation of the two-space plot shown in Figure 14-2 can be found that will tend to yield, for each variable, *a high loading on one of the new axes and a low loading on the other*.

Varimax rotation of these components accomplished this objective rather well. The new axes are also shown in Figure 14-2, and the table of rotated loadings is shown in Table 14-8. We note that performance variables 1, 2, and 6 load heavily (negatively) on axis I', while variables 3, 4, and 5 load heavily (negatively) on axis II'. Moreover, we can interpret these axes quite easily as *speed* and *capacity* from our knowledge of the labels attached to the original variables.

Oblique transformations could also have been carried out on the loadings of Table 14-7.[10] However, in marketing research applications it is almost always the case that the procedure outlined above is followed: principal components and subsequent Varimax rotation of the loadings to improve interpretability. There is a good reason for this, since interpretation of the (rotated) factor-loading matrix is easier under this option than under any of the oblique options.

TABLE 14-8   Variables' Loadings on First Two
**   (Varimax-Rotated) Factors**

VARIABLE	COMPONENT 1	COMPONENT 2
1	−0.962	0.229
2	−0.982	0.133
3	0.062	−0.943
4	0.080	−0.955
5	0.243	−0.749
6	−0.979	0.064

[10]As a matter of fact, one of the oblique transformation options was applied for comparison purposes. Results were quite similar to those of Figure 14-2, although the resulting axes were slightly negatively correlated.

OTHER TOPICS IN FACTOR ANALYSIS

As stated earlier, many other procedures are available for factoring data.[11] In particular, the *common-factor model* is sometimes used in marketing. We comment briefly on this model and then turn to other topics in factor analysis.

Communalities and the Common-Factor Model

Our selection of principal-components analysis as *the* factor-analytic technique to consider for detailed exposition was based on its value as a *reproducible* procedure in accounting for common variance in a set of associated variables.

Other factoring methods, and, indeed, factoring theory, are often concerned *not* with accounting for common variance but with describing the *covariation* among the variables in terms of a small number of common factors *plus* a term representing a *unique factor* for each variable. As was shown, principal components represent linear combinations of *actual* variables; *in extracting components from the correlation matrix unities appear in the diagonal*.

In the common-factor model, numbers (i.e., the communalities) that are greater than zero but less than unity appear along the main diagonal of the correlation matrix to be factored. Each communality is initially estimated by the researcher and then the computer program adjusts these numbers so as to lead to the best fit of correlations estimated by the model to the actual (off-diagonal) correlations that one starts with.[12] The final communality estimates purport to be that part of the variance in each variable that is *held in common with the remaining variables*.

That is, the common factors account for only a portion of the variation in a single variable; the remainder of that variation is assumed to be ascribed to the variable *itself*.

Unlike the principal-components model the common-factor model does *not* produce exact factor scores. Rather, these factor scores also have to be estimated (usually by regression techniques), and there is no requirement that the estimated scores be uncorrelated across factors. In principal components, however, uncorrelated component scores are guaranteed by the model.

From a practical standpoint, the communality problem concerns *what values should be placed in the main diagonal of the original correlation matrix*, before factoring. Whether the common-factor model leads to a markedly different set of loadings than the principal-components model depends in large part of the *number* of variables. If the number exceeds 15 or so, both the components and common-factor models tend to produce similar results.

In marketing research applications it is not at all unusual to have at least 15 initial variables. Moreover, the components model is less susceptible to misinterpretation, since

---

[11]In addition to the references cited in a previous section of this chapter, a compendium of alternative methods can be found in H. Harmon, *Modern Factor Analysis*, 2nd ed. (Chicago: University of Chicago Press, 1960).

[12]The computer programs provide the capability for applying the common factor model (with communality estimates). Usually the starting value of the communality estimates is provided by each variable's R^2 with the remaining variables; this serves as a lower limit while unity represents the upper limit of the final communalities.

it entails linear combinations of *actual* variables. In the authors' view the components model has much to recommend it for the nonexpert in factor analysis.

Extensions of Basic Factor Models

A number of relatively new developments have taken place in factoring procedures. One particularly interesting methodology concerns what has become known as *confirmatory factor analysis*. In confirmatory factor analysis one can test hypotheses about how well the data fit certain specified patterns of factor loadings. In some instances the researcher may specify the full pattern of loadings, while in other cases he or she may fix only a portion of the pattern and allow the technique to solve for estimates of the unspecified factor-loading parameters. In the confirmatory factor model *all* common factors are assumed to be not correlated, some unique factors may be correlated, an observed variable may not have a unique factor associated with it, and the observed variables are affected by only *some* of the common factors.[13]

Congruence procedures are related techniques in which the researcher can match up two or more factor-loading solutions, either to a fixed-target pattern or to some compromise pattern formed from the original solutions themselves.[14] This approach can be useful in running double cross validations of factor solutions, in which the original sample size has been split into halves and separate analyses carried out.[15]

Factor Analysis in Prediction Studies

Factor analysis can sometimes be useful in multiple regression and other analyses of dependence structures, where the predictors are both numerous and highly correlated. If the predictors are first factor-analyzed and the criterion variable is regressed on the *full* set of factor scores, R^2 will be identical to that obtained from the usual multiple regression analysis.

However, the advantages of a preliminary principal-components analysis do *not* stem from extracting all components. Suppose that we wished to use only the higher-variance components as predictors on the assumption that these components represent the *stable* part of the common variance shared by the set of predictor variables. In this case we would be regressing the criterion variable on fewer predictor "variables," *with fewer degrees of freedom being lost* than in the regression case using all predictor variables.

Still, one could encounter difficulty in interpreting the regression coefficients, since the predictors would then represent linear combinations of the original set. In some cases

[13]For a good discussion of the differences between confirmatory and the usual (exploratory) factor analysis, see B. N. Mukherjee, "Analysis of Covariance Structures and Exploratory Factor Analysis," *British Journal of Mathematical and Statistical Psychology*, 26 (November 1973), 125–54.

[14]A somewhat detailed discussion of alternative factor comparison techniques is found in M. S. Levine, *Canonical Analysis and Factor Comparison* (Beverly Hills, Calif.: Sage, 1977).

[15]Still another variant of factor analysis involves so-called higher-order methods. For example, see Yoram Wind, P. E. Green, and A. K. Jain, "Higher Order Factor Analysis in the Classification of Psychographic Variables," *Journal of the Market Research Society*, 15 (1973), 224–32.

a more appropriate procedure would be to extract some relatively small set of components that account for most of the variance in the predictor set and then to select *actual* variables (with highest loadings on the components) as candidate predictors in the regression.

There is some danger associated with the above approach if one or more of the omitted variables just happens to be highly correlated with the criterion variable. The prudent analyst might do well to try out several regressions to see if R^2 changes very much as variables loading high on lesser components are dropped.

Empirically Derived Index Measures

A related use of principal-components analysis concerns the development of indexes for arraying various members of a data bank on some construct of interest. In a survey of shampoo purchase and use, for example, one might be interested in developing an index of "proneness" toward accepting a shampoo that promised "body" as a benefit, using such questionnaire items as (1) "body" appears in respondent's ideal set, (2) fineness of hair, and (3) hair thickness.

The first principal component of a data matrix has the property of maximally separating individuals along its dimension. As an *internal* criterion it could be used to order individuals as well as provide interval-scaled weights that indicate the importance of each of the contributory variables to the "proneness" measure. Many cases arise in marketing research where one needs a *single composite measure* of some construct but where no prior basis exists for weighting the variables making up the composite. If an empirically derived index is satisfactory, the first principal component can provide both the weights (e.g., -0.68008, -0.67075, and 0.29596, at the top of Table 14-4) and the index values (i.e., factor scores).

Other Types of Scales

Factor analysis is typically applied to interval-scaled data, although some analysts have employed dichotomous variables or mixtures of interval-scaled and dichotomous variables. If all data are nominal-scaled, the researcher could consider a set of techniques—latent-structure analysis—that are specifically designed for this type of situation.[16]

Researchers have also expanded the technique base to provide algorithms for factor-analyzing ordinal-scaled data.[17] However, many of these methods are subject to their own sets of problems (considered in Chapter 15). Moreover, there is reason to believe that simple integer-rank transformations (that are later treated as intervally scaled data) can provide useful and robust approximations.[18]

Finally, it should be mentioned that factor-analyzing *polytomous* variables that are coded into several dummy variables should generally be avoided (or at least used with

[16]P. F. Lazarsfeld and N. W. Henry, *Latent Structure Analysis* (Boston: Houghton Mifflin, 1968).

[17]J. C. Lingoes and Louis Guttman, "Nonmetric Factor Analysis: A Rank Reducing Alternative to Linear Analysis," *Multivariate Behavioral Research*, 2 (1967), 485–505.

[18]An investigation of this type of transformation in a related context is found in P. E. Green, "On the Robustness of Multidimensional Scaling Techniques," *Journal of Marketing Research*, 12 (February 1975), 73–81.

caution). This is because their intraset correlations are bound to be negative, strictly as a consequence of the category coding. In some instances this artifact can lead to difficulties in the interpretation of both factor loadings and factor scores.

Statistical Inference in Factor Analysis

Throughout this chapter we have had relatively little to say about the statistical significance of such entities as factor scores and factor loadings. For example, the analyst using principal-components analysis would like to know *how many* components to extract—that is, those that are statistically significant. Wilks[19] and Bartlett[20] have provided approximate large-sample tests for this problem. Other tests are also available.

Despite the effort expended by mathematical statisticians to develop statistical tests related to factor analysis, it is fair to say that relatively little application has been made of these tests by applied researchers. Rather, use of various rules of thumb (have ten times as many objects as variables, extract only those components whose variances exceed unity, rotate one-third as many components as there are variables, etc.) appears to be more prevalent. While the authors do not advocate the inviolate use of such ad hoc rules, the fact remains that (current) statistical significance tests do not appear to be extremely helpful either.

There are two reasons for this. First, distribution theory in factor analysis is quite complex, and few of the significance tests are available in easily applied form. Second, with a large number of objects relative to the number of variables, the number of *statistically* significant factors tends to equal the number of variables if one uses, say, principal-components analysis. In such cases components that account for a very small portion of total variability might still turn out to be statistically significant, even though their *practical* significance from an interpretive standpoint might be nil.

At the current state of the art—and factor analysis seems to display a certain "artistic" flavor—the authors are more inclined to view factor-analytic procedures as *descriptive* summaries of data matrices rather than inferential devices. While this objective may seem quite limited, it appears to be realistic, considering the stringency of assumptions underlying the currently available statistical tests and the complexity of their implementation.

Operational Issues

Three basic steps are implicitly involved in all factor analyses:

- Prepare the relevant covariance (or correlation) matrix
- Extract initial factors
- Rotate initial factors to a terminal solution

[19]S. S. Wilks, "The Large Sample Distribution of the Likelihood Ratio for Testing Composite Hypotheses," *Annals of Mathematical Statistics,* 9 (1938), 60–62.
[20]M. S. Bartlett, "Tests of Significance in Factor Analysis," *British Journal of Psychology,* 3 (1950), 77–85.

The first step is concerned with a broader question of whether a data set is appropriate for factor analysis even when the marketing researcher wants to identify dimensions within a set of data. The question of appropriateness is often overlooked because factors obtained from an analysis may seem to be readily interpretable and intuitively reasonable. Few computer programs provide any test for the appropriateness of a matrix for factoring. This issue of statistical significance was discussed in the previous section.[21]

The second step is more involved than choosing a method for extracting the factors. We have already discussed alternatives for doing this. Equally important is the decision of how many factors to extract. In the extreme case, there can be as many factors as there are variables (*R* - type analysis), as illustrated by Table 14-7. Depending on the method of initial extraction, different criteria may be used to answer this question:

- *Significance tests,* which focus on sampling variability.
- *Substantive significance,* which focuses on the minimum contribution a factor should make.
- *Interpretability and invariance,* which combines various rules and triangulates.
- *Eigenvalue specification,* which sets a minimum eigenvalue (usually 1 for a standardized data set) for a factor to be retained.
- *Scree test,* which is a graph of eigenvalues, and factoring is stopped where these begin to level off and form a straight, almost horizontal, line. This is illustrated in Figure 14-3.

The most widely used criterion in marketing research applications is eigenvalue specification. For further discussion of these criteria we refer the reader to the exposition by Kim and Mueller.[22]

The rotation question is concerned with a procedure for finding simpler and more easily interpretable factors. The most common orthogonal rotation procedure, Varimax, has already been discussed. One alternative is *Quartimax*. The Quartimax criterion may be most appropriate when a general factor is expected, as it tends to emphasize simplifying interpretation of variables. In contrast, Varimax simplifies factors.

BASIC CONCEPTS OF CLUSTER ANALYSIS

Like factor analysis, clustering methods are applied to intact matrices. The usual objective of *cluster analysis* is to separate objects into groups such that each object is more like other objects in its group than like objects outside the group. Cluster analysis is thus concerned ultimately with classification, and its techniques are part of the field of nu-

---

[21]Alternative tests of appropriateness are discussed briefly in Stewart, "Application and Misapplication of Factor Analysis in Marketing," pp. 56–58.

[22]Kim and Mueller, *Factor Analysis*, pp. 41–45.

Figure 14-3   Illustration of a Scree Test

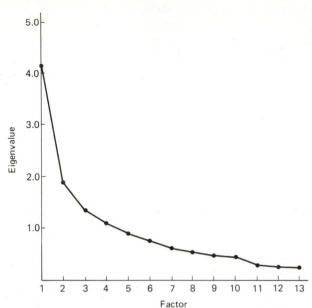

merical taxonomy.[23] In addition, cluster analysis can be used for (1) investigating useful conceptual schemes for grouping entities, (2) hypothesis generation through data exploration, and (3) hypothesis testing, or attempting to determine if types defined through other procedures are present in a data set.[24] Thus, cluster analysis can be viewed as a set of techniques designed to identify objects, people, or variables that are similar with respect to some criteria or characteristics. As such, it seeks to describe so-called natural groupings.

One of the major problems in marketing consists of the orderly classification of the myriad data that confront the researcher. The availability of household data from large consumer panels and the increasing detail with which corporate sales statistics are being recorded are illustrative of the growing need for a set of techniques that will automate, to some extent, the task of data reduction and classification.

The typical clustering procedure that we shall discuss assigns each object to one and only one class. Objects within a class are usually assumed to be indistinguishable from one another. Thus, we assume here that the underlying structure of the data involves

---

[23]For an elementary discussion of the field of numerical taxonomy, see R. R. Sokal and P. H. A. Sneath, *Principles of Numerical Taxonomy* (San Francisco: W. H. Freeman, 1963). More technical discussions may be found in Richard Stone, *Mathematics in the Social Sciences and Other Essays* (Cambridge, Mass.: MIT Press, 1966), Chap. 11; N. Jardine and R. Sibson, *Mathematical Taxonomy* (New York: John Wiley, 1971); and P. H. A. Sneath and R. R. Sokal, *Numerical Taxonomy* (San Francisco: W. H. Freeman, 1973).

[24]For a simplified discussion of the use of cluster analysis to achieve all these goals, see M. S. Aldenderfer and R. K. Blashfield, *Cluster Analysis* (Beverly Hills, Calif.: Sage, 1984).

an unordered set of discrete classes. In some cases we may also view these classes as hierarchical in nature, where some classes are divided into subclasses.

Primary Questions

Clustering procedures can be viewed as preclassificatory in the sense that the analyst has *not* used prior information to partition the objects (rows of the data matrix).[25] However, the analyst *is* assuming that the data are "partially" heterogeneous—that is, that "clusters" exist. This type of presupposition is different from the case in discriminant analysis where a priori groups of objects have been formed on the basis of criteria *not* based on profile resemblance in the data matrix itself. Given no information on group definition in advance, the major problems of cluster analysis can be stated as

1. What measure of interobject similarity is to be used, and how is each variable to be "weighted" in the construction of such a summary measure?
2. After interobject similarities are obtained, how are the classes of objects to be formed?
3. After the classes have been formed, what summary measures of each cluster are appropriate in a descriptive sense—that is, how are the clusters to be defined?
4. Assuming that adequate descriptions of the clusters can be obtained, what inferences can be drawn regarding their statistical reliability?

These questions constitute the main points of our discussion in this section of the chapter. Before proceeding, however, a few cautions should be raised:[26]

- Most cluster analysis methods are relatively simple procedures that are usually not supported by an extensive body of statistical reasoning.
- Cluster analysis methods have evolved from many disciplines, and the inbred biases of these disciplines can differ dramatically.
- Different clustering methods can and do generate different solutions to the same data set.
- The strategy of cluster analysis is structure-seeking, although its operation is structure-imposing.

Illustrative Profiles

Figure 14-4 portrays the performance profiles of three of the computers—models 1, 2, and 8 from the data of Table 14-3. If we were to try to cluster the models intuitively, we might say that models 1 and 8 exhibit fairly close profiles, while model 2 is quite

---

[25]We note that partitioning is performed in terms of the objects rather than the variables; thus, cluster analysis deals with intact data (in terms of the variables). Moreover, the partitioning is not performed a priori but is based on the object similarities themselves.

[26]See Aldenderfer and Blashfield, *Cluster Analysis*, pp. 14–16.

Figure 14-4   Performance Profiles of Computer Models 1, 2, and 8 (from Data of Table 14-3)

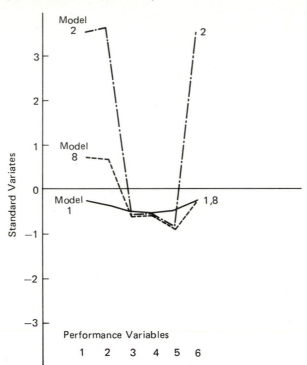

disparate. Still, we note that model 2 is quite close to model 8 on performance variables 3, 4, and 5; as a matter of fact, all three computers exhibit similar scores in these three variables.

While the profiles can be portrayed as shown in Figure 14-4, the reader can appreciate the problems encountered in plotting the profiles of all 15 computer models on the same grid. Imagine, then, the chaotic picture that would result if one wanted to cluster 100 computer models, each represented by 20 performance variables. The need for mechanistic clustering procedures becomes acute for problems of realistic size.

An alternative way to portray the data would be to consider the computer models as 15 points in six-dimensional space. While we cannot show this representation visually, we can still imagine each computer plotted in variables space. Natural measures of proximity, then, would be types of *distances* separating each pair of points. We discuss these various measures in a subsequent section of the chapter.

Choice of Proximity Measure

The choice of *proximity, similarity,* or *resemblance measure* (all three terms will be used synonymously here) is an interesting problem in cluster analysis. The concept of similarity always raises the question: Similarity with respect to what? Proximity measures are viewed in relative terms—two objects are similar, relative to the group, if their profiles across variables are "close" or they share "many" aspects in common, relative to those which other pairs share in common.

Most clustering procedures use pairwise measures of proximity. The choice of which objects and variables to use in the first place is largely a matter for the researcher's judgment. While these (prior) choices are important ones, they are beyond our scope here. Even assuming that such choices have been made, however, the possible measures of pairwise proximity are many. Generally speaking, these measures fall into two classes: (1) distance-type measures and (2) matching-type measures. We discuss the characteristics of each in turn.[27]

Distance Measures

A surprisingly large number of proximity measures can be viewed as distances in some type of metric space. We may recall from geometry the notion of Euclidean distance between two points in a space of r dimensions. The formula is

$$d_{ij} = \left[\sum_{k=1}^{r} (x_{ik} - x_{jk})^2 \right]^{1/2}$$

where x_{ik}, x_{jk} are the projections of points i and j on dimension k ($k = 1, 2, \ldots, r$).

Inasmuch as the variables in a data matrix are often measured in different units, the formula above is usually applied *after* each variable has been standardized to zero mean and unit standard deviation. Our subsequent discussion will assume that this preliminary step has been taken.

The Euclidean distance measure technically assumes that the space of (standardized) variables is orthogonal—that is, that the variables are uncorrelated. But in most data matrices the variables will be correlated. In cases where the original variables are highly correlated, some analysts follow a procedure of extracting the principal components of the matrix first and *then* finding the distance between pairs of points as referred to their scores on the (standardized) component axes:

$$d^*_{ij} = \left[\sum_{k=1}^{r} (y_{ik} - y_{jk})^2 \right]^{1/2}$$

---

[27]More generally, proximity measures have been categorized as *correlation coefficients, distance measures, association coefficients,* and *probabilistic similarity measures*. These are discussed in Aldenderfer and Blashfield, *Cluster Analysis,* pp. 16–33.

where y_{ik} and y_{jk} denote *unit variance* component scores of profiles i and j on component axis k ($k = 1, 2, \ldots, r$).

If we consider the square of each of these distance measures, the differences in the two approaches can be explained as follows:

1. Squared Euclidean distance in the original variables space has the effect of weighting each underlying principal component by that component's variance.

2. Squared Euclidean distance in the component space (where all components are first standardized to *unit* variance) has the effect of assigning *equal* weights to all components.

3. In terms of the geometry of the configuration, in the first case all points (computer models) are rotated to orthogonal axes with no change in their squared interpoint distance. The general effect is to portray the original configuration as a hyper-ellipsoid with principal-components axes serving as the axes of that figure. Equating all axes to equal length has the effect of transforming this hyperellipsoid into a hypersphere where all "axes" are of equal length.

However, if all the (standardized) variables are also uncorrelated, both d_{ij} and d^*_{ij} will be equivalent. An alternative procedure (in the case of the nonequivalence of d_{ij} and d^*_{ij}) is to perform a preliminary principal-components analysis and compute distances across the unit-variance dimensions involving only the larger-variance components. In this way the lesser components, which may be error variance, are *not* allowed to influence interpoint distance. This approach has much to recommend it.

Matching Measures

Quite often the analyst wishing to cluster profiles must contend with data that are only nominally scaled. The usual approach to this kind of situation employs attribute matching coefficients. Intuitively speaking, two profiles are viewed as similar *to the extent to which they share common attributes.*

As an illustration of this approach, consider the following two profiles:

	ATTRIBUTE					
OBJECT	*1*	*2*	*3*	*4*	*5*	*6*
1	1	0	0	1	1	0
2	0	1	0	1	0	1

Each of these objects is characterized by possession or nonpossession of each of six attributes, where a 1 denotes possession and a 0 nonpossession. Suppose we just count up the total number of matches—either 1, 1 or 0, 0—and divide by the total number of attributes. A simple matching measure can then be stated as

$$S_{12} = \frac{M}{N} = \frac{2}{6} = \frac{1}{3}$$

where M denotes the number of attributes held in common (matching 1's or 0's) and N denotes the total number of attributes. We notice that this measure varies between zero and one.

If weak matches (nonpossession of an attribute) are to be de-emphasized, the measure above can be modified to

$$S'_{ij} = \frac{\text{Number of attributes that are 1 for both object } i \text{ and } j}{\text{Number of attributes that are 1 for either } i \text{ or } j \text{ or both}}$$

In this case $S'_{12} = 1/5$. A variety of such matching-type coefficients are described by Sokal and Sneath.[28]

When similarity between cases described by dichotomies is being examined, the measures are known as *association coefficients*. Attributes need not be limited to dichotomies, however. In the case of polytomies, matching coefficients are often developed by means similar to the above by recoding the k-state variable into $k - 1$ dummy ($0 - 1$) variables. Naturally such coefficients will be sensitive to the variation in the number of states.

Finally, mention should be made of the case in which the variables consist of mixed scales—nominal, ordinal, and interval. Interval-scaled variables may be handled in terms of similarity coefficients by the simple device of computing the range of the variable R_k and finding

$$S^*_{ijk} = 1 - \frac{|x_{ik} - x_{jk}|}{R_k}$$

The measure S^*_{ijk} will then appropriately vary between 0 and 1, just like a similarity measure. This measure has been suggested by Gower[29] as a device to handle both nominal- and interval-scaled data in a single similarity coefficient.

Mixed scales that include ordinal-scaled variables present greater difficulties. If ordinal and interval scales occur, one can downgrade the interval data to ordinal scales and use a measure proposed by Kendall.[30] If all three scales—nominal, ordinal, and interval—appear, one is more or less forced to downgrade all data to nominal measures

---

[28]Sokal and Sneath, *Principles of Numerical Taxonomy*, pp. 128–41.

[29]J. C. Gower, "A General Coefficient of Similarity and Some of Its Properties," working paper, Rothamsted Experimental Station, England, 1968.

[30]See M. G. Kendall, "Discrimination and Classification," i *Multivariate Analysis*, ed. P. R. Krishnaiah (New York: Academic Press, 1966), pp. 165–85.

and use matching-type coefficients. An alternative approach would be to compute "distances" for each pair of objects according to each scale type separately, standardize the measures to zero mean and unit standard deviation, and then compute some type of weighted average. Such approaches are quite ad hoc, however.

Clustering Programs

Once the analyst has settled on some pairwise measure of profile similarity, he or she must still use some type of computational routine for clustering the profiles. A large variety of such computer programs already exists, and more are being developed as interest in this field increases. Each clustering program tends to maintain a certain individuality, although some common characteristics can be drawn out. Ball and Hall[31] have made a rather extensive survey of clustering methods. The following categories are based, in part, on their classification:

1. *Dimensionalizing the association matrix.* These approaches use principal-components or other factor-analytic methods to find a dimensional representation of points from *interobject* association measures. Clusters are then developed visually or on the basis of grouping objects according to their pattern of component scores.

2. *Nonhierarchical methods.* These methods start right from the proximity matrix and can be characterized as follows:
   a. *Sequential threshold.* In this case a cluster center is selected and all objects within a prespecified threshold value are grouped. Then a new cluster center is selected and the process is repeated for the unclustered points, and so on. (Once points enter a cluster, they are removed from further processing.)
   b. *Parallel threshold.* This method is similar to the preceding method except that several cluster centers are selected simultaneously and points within threshold level are assigned to the nearest center; threshold levels can then be adjusted to admit fewer or more points to clusters.
   c. *Optimizing partitioning.* This method modifies categories (a) or (b) in that points can later be reassigned to clusters on the basis of optimizing some overall criterion measure, such as average within-cluster distance for a given number of clusters.

3. *Hierarchical methods.* These procedures are characterized by the construction of a hierarchy or treelike structure. In some methods each point starts out as a unit (single-point) cluster. At the next level the two closest points are placed in a cluster. At the following level a third point joins the first two, or else a second two-point cluster is formed, based on various criterion functions for assignment. Eventually all points are grouped into one larger cluster. Variations on this procedure involve the development of a hierarchy from the top down. At the

---

[31]G. H. Ball and D. J. Hall, "Background Information on Clustering Techniques," working paper, Stanford Research Institute, Menlo Park, Calif., July 1968.

beginning the points are partitioned into two subsets based on some criterion measure related to average within-cluster distance. The subset with the highest average within-cluster distance is next partitioned into two subsets, and so on, until all points eventually become unit clusters.

While the above classes of programs are not exhaustive of the field, most of the more widely used clustering routines can be typed as falling into one (or a combination) of the above categories. Criteria for grouping include such measures as average within-cluster distance and threshold cutoff values. The fact remains, however, that even the "optimizing" approaches achieve only conditional optima, since an unsettled question in this field is *how many* clusters to form in the first place.

At this stage in the development of cluster analysis, the authors are of the opinion that clustering might best be approached in terms of a combination of dimensional representation of the points and techniques that group points in the reduced space (obtained from principal-components analysis or similar techniques). Alternatively, clusters based on the *original* distance measures may be embedded in the reduced space. This *dual* approach, if the dimensionality is small, enables the analyst to stay "close to the data" and possibly to augment the clustering results with visual inspection of the configuration.

Describing the Clusters

Once clusters are developed, the analyst still faces the task of describing them. One measure that is used frequently is the *centroid*—the average value of the objects contained in the cluster on each of the variables making up each object's profile. If the data are interval scaled and clustering is performed in original variables space, this measure appears quite natural as a summary description. If the space consists of principal-components dimensions, the axes cannot be described simply. Often in this case the analyst will want to go back to the original variables and compute average profile measures on these. The analyst can then construct average cluster profiles similar to the graphical portrayal in Figure 14-4.

If matching-type coefficients are used, the analyst may describe a cluster in terms of the group's modal profile on each of the attributes.

In addition to central tendency, the researcher may compute some measure of the cluster's variability, such as average interpoint distance of all members of the cluster from their centroid or average interpoint distance between all pairs of points within the cluster.

Statistical Inference

Despite attempts made to construct various tests of the statistical reliability of clusters, no fully defensible procedures are currently available. The lack of appropriate tests stems from the difficulty of specifying realistic null hypotheses.[32] First, it is not

[32]P. H. A. Sneath, "Some Statistical Problems in Numerical Taxonomy," *The Statistician,* 17 (1967), 1–8.

clear just what the universe of content is. Quite often the researcher arbitrarily selects objects and variables and is interested in concentrating on only that particular sample. Second, the analyst is usually assuming that "partial" heterogeneity exists in the first place; otherwise, why bother to cluster? Third, the clusters are formed *from the data* and not on the basis of outside criteria. Thus, one would be placed in the uncomfortable statistical position of "testing" the significance between groups formed on the basis of the data themselves. Finally, the distributions of objects and variables are largely unknown and it would be dangerous to assume that the variables conformed to some tractable model such as a set of multivariate normal distributions differing only in centroid locations.

Despite the formidable problems associated with statistical inference in cluster analysis, the analyst might try a few ad hoc procedures to provide rough checks on the clustering results. For example, the analyst might apply two or more different clustering routines to the same data and compare results across algorithms. Or, the analyst may wish to split the data randomly into halves, perform separate clusterings, and then examine the average profile values of each cluster across subsamples. Alternatively, the analyst may delete various columns (variables) in the original profile data, compute dissimilarity measures across the remaining columns, and compare these results with the clusters found from using the full set of columns (variables).

Still other procedures are possible. One could construct random profile data by sampling from some common multivariate distribution and comparing the partitioning found by this procedure with the original partitioning. A variation of the multivariate distribution sampling procedure in which a null hypothesis can be specified involves the use of contingency tables. Here, the null hypothesis is that there is no significant difference between the location of the data points and a distribution of points generated independently from the marginal distributions of each variable. The data are partitioned into cells (regions of the space) and counts made to obtain the observed frequency in each. The expected frequencies are calculated from the marginal distributions of each of the variables. A chi-square analysis is then performed to test for the significance of difference between observed and expected frequencies.

We continue to believe, at least in the present state of cluster analysis, that this class of techniques should be viewed as *preclassification,* where the object is to *formulate* rather than test categorizations of data. After a classification has been developed and supported by *theoretical research* and subsequent reformulation of classes, other techniques such as discriminant analysis might prove useful in the assignment of new members to groups identified on grounds that are *not* solely restricted to the original cluster analysis. Discriminant analysis, as an ad hoc device, may be used to find "optimal" weights for variables *after* performing the cluster analysis. In this case, however, its use would be *strictly* descriptive rather than inferential.

While the above caveats are not to be taken lightly, it seems to us that clustering techniques can still be useful—in ways comparable to the employment of factor analysis—as systematic procedures for the orderly preclassification of multivariate data. The results of using these approaches can be helpful and meaningful (after the fact), as will be illustrated in the next section.

APPLICATIONS OF CLUSTER ANALYSIS

So many different clustering programs are available that even a cursory description of them would easily exceed our scope. Let it suffice to say that BMD P Series includes four programs, SAS has seven programs, and SPSS[x] has one program. In addition, there are programs available for the PC such as the two clustering programs available in PC–MDS.[33] What we can describe are four applications of varying degrees of difficulty:

- A synthetic data problem, made up of only 12 points in two dimensions;
- A product-positioning study involving sports car brands;
- A performance-profile clustering of digital computers; and
- A foreign market analysis study of 71 countries.

A very simple application illustrating the nature of cluster analysis is shown in Exhibit 14-3.

Exhibit 14-3   A Simple Example of Cluster Analysis

We can illustrate cluster analysis by a simple example. The problem is to group a set of twelve branches of a bank into three clusters of four branches each according to the characteristics of the number of men who have borrowed money (X_1) and the number of women who have borrowed money (X_2). The branches are plotted in two dimensions in the figure. We use a distance measure of proximity, based on Euclidean distances in space.

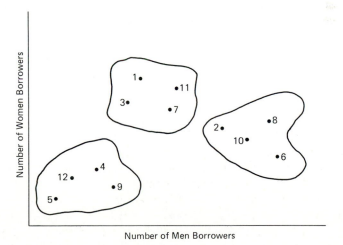

[33]See Scott M. Smith, *PC–MDS, Version 4.1*, 1987.

$$d_{jk} = \sqrt{(X_{1j} - X_{1k})^2 + (X_{2j} - X_{2k})^2}$$

where j and k are any two branches. Branches 2 and 10 appear to be the closest together. The first cluster is formed by finding the midpoint between branches 2 and 10 and computing the distance of each branch from this midpoint (this is known as applying the *nearest-neighbor algorithm*). The two closest branches (6 and 8) are then added to give the desired-size cluster. The other clusters are formed in a similar manner. When more than two dimensions (that is, characteristics) are involved, a computer program must be used for measuring distances and the clustering process.

Computerized Cluster Analysis

Let us start by illustrating one of the more popular clustering programs. Consider the standardized (artificial) data of Figure 14-5. In this case we have 12 points portrayed in two dimensions. Visually, it would seem that four clusters are present:

$$\{a, b\}$$
$$\{c, d, e, f, g\}$$
$$\{h, i, j, k\}$$
$$\{l\}$$

However, in most practical problems of interest, we cannot fall back on visual clustering. We could have hundreds of points in several dimensions (where each dimension is a

**Figure 14-5   Initial Configuration of Points for BMD—P1M
                        Cluster Analysis**

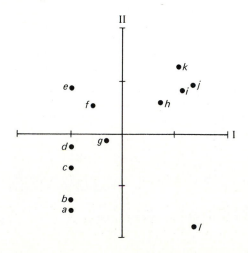

variable). Nonetheless, let us examine how various clustering rules would group the 12 objects represented as points in Figure 14-5.

BMD–P1M is one of the P series of biomedical programs.[34] Various measures of resemblance, including Euclidean distance, can be accommodated. The program is a hierarchical algorithm that starts out with each point as its own unit cluster and eventually ends up with all points in one undifferentiated cluster. Three amalgamation rules for building up the clusters are available.

Single Linkage

The *single-linkage,* or *minimum-distance, rule* starts out by finding the two points with the shortest Euclidean distance. These are placed in the first cluster. At the next stage a third point joins the already formed cluster of two if its shortest distance to the members of the cluster is smaller than the two closest unclustered points. Otherwise, the two closest unclustered points are placed in a cluster.

The process continues until all points end up in one cluster. The distance between two clusters is defined as the *shortest* distance from a point in the first cluster to a point in the second.

Complete Linkage

The *complete-linkage option* starts out in just the same way by clustering the two closest points. However, the criterion for joining points to clusters or clusters to clusters involves maximum (rather than minimum) distance. In other words, the distance between two clusters is the *longest* distance from a point in the first cluster to a point in the second cluster.

Average Linkage

The *average-linkage option* starts out in the same way as the other two. However, in this case the distance between two clusters is the *average* distance from points in the first cluster to points in the second cluster.

Results

The three amalgamation rules showed similar, but not identical, clusterings. For example, at the four-cluster level there was a difference in the placement of point *c* between the single- and average-linkage versus the complete-linkage rules:

SINGLE LINKAGE	COMPLETE LINKAGE	AVERAGE LINKAGE
{a, b, c}	{a, b}	{a, b, c}
{d, e, f, g}	{c, d, e, f, g}	{d, e, f, g}
{h, i, j, k}	{h, i, j, k}	{h, i, j, k}
{l}	{l}	{l}

[34]See W. J. Dixon and M. B. Brown eds., *BMDP: Biomedical Computer Programs* (Berkeley: University of California Press, 1979). While BMD–P1M is primarily designed to cluster variables, it is a simple procedure to reverse the role of variables and objects (as was done here).

Figure 14-6   Dendrogram From Complete-Linkage Clustering

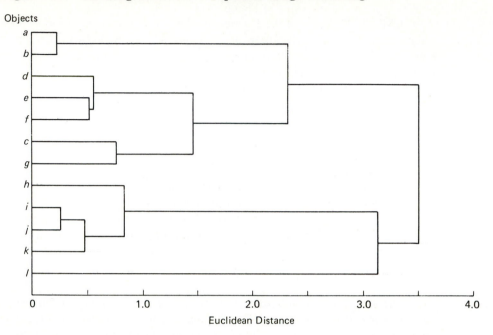

Since the program provides the full clustering sequence, it is easy to prepare a tree diagram (called a *dendrogram*). Illustratively, Figure 14-6 shows the dendrogram for the complete-linkage rule.

We note that points *a* and *b*, the closest pair, first join at a distance of 0.23. The next pair to join are points *i* and *j*, and so on. The last two clusters to merge are {*a, b, c, d, e, f, g*} and {*h, i, j, k, l*} at a distance value of 3.5. We note that the dendrogram provides a succinct and convenient way to summarize the clustering sequence.

Product-Positioning Application

Cluster analysis can be used in a variety of marketing research applications. For example, companies are often interested in determining how their products are positioned in terms of competitive offerings and consumers' views about the types of persons most likely to own the product.[35]

For illustrative purposes, Figure 14-7 shows the results of a pilot study in which interobject-distance data were developed for 7 sport cars, 6 types of stereotyped owners, and 13 attributes often used to describe cars. The distance data were based on respondents' degree-of-belief ratings about which attributes and owners "described" which cars. In this case a complete-linkage algorithm was also used to cluster the objects.[36]

[35]P.E. Green, "A Multidimensional Model of Product-Features Association," *Journal of Business Research,* 2 (April 1974), 107–18.

[36]S.C. Johnson, "Hierarchical Clustering Schemes, "*Psychometrika,* 32 (September 1967), 241–54.

Figure 14-7 Complete-Linkage Analysis of Product-Positioning Data

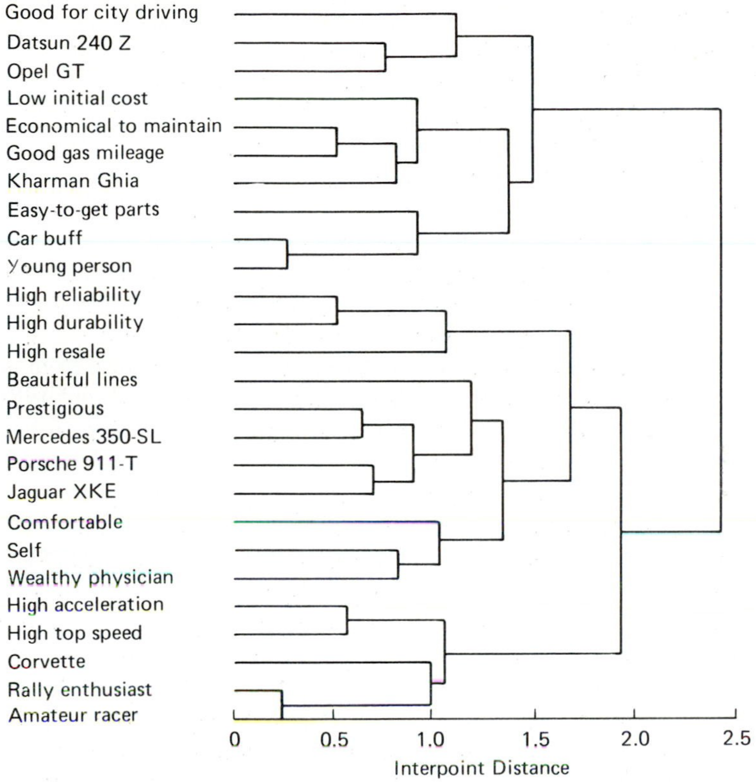

Looking first at the four large clusters, we note the *car* groupings:

- Datsun 240Z; Opel GT;
- Kharman Ghia;
- Mercedes 350-SL; Porsche 911-T; Jaguar XKE; and
- Corvette.

For example, the Corvette is seen as being in a class by itself with the attributes *high acceleration* and *high top speed*. Its perceived (stereotyped) owners are *rally enthusiast* and *amateur racer*.

Studies of this type can enable the marketing researcher to observe the interrelationships among several types of entities—cars, attributes, owners. The approach displays several advantages. For example, it can be applied to alternative advertisements, package designs, or other kinds of communications stimuli. That is, the respondent could be shown blocks of advertising copy (brand unidentified) and asked to provide degree-of-belief ratings that the brand described in the copy possesses each of the *n* features.

Similarly, in the case of consumer packaged goods, the respondent could be shown alternative package designs and asked for degree-of-belief ratings that the contents of the package possess various features. In either case one would be adding an additional set (or sets) of ratings to the response sets described earlier. Hence, four (or more) classes of items could be represented as points in the cluster analysis.

Performance Structure of the Computer Market

Computers, like many industrial products, such as electric motors, machine tools, and gas turbines, can be characterized by a set of performance characteristics. Assume that each computer model can be represented as a point in performance space. Some models will be "closer" to others in this performance space—that is, more competitive in terms of performance similarities.

Data for the cluster analysis reported here were obtained from published reports of first-time computer model installations made between 1964 and 1968. A sample of 47 models represented the objects for the grouping. Some 22 performance variables and features were used to develop the interobject similarity measures. These are shown in Table 14-9.

The actual analysis was rather complex and involved a combination of reduced-space analysis and hierarchical clustering. The former technique indicated that four basic dimensions appeared to underlie the data:

- Capacity
- Speed
- Orientation (scientific versus business)
- Elaborateness of features

TABLE 14-9   Performance Characteristics of 47 Computer Models

MEASURED VARIABLES	FEATURES DATA
1. Word length in binary bits	13. Floating-point representation
2. Likely fixed-point execution time: $a + b$ in microseconds	14. Binary arithmetic
3. Likely fixed-point execution time: ab in microseconds	15. Checking of data transfers
4. Likely fixed-point execution time: a/b in microseconds	16. Program-interrupt facility
5. Maximum number of index registers	17. Indirect addressing
6. Maximum number of input–output channels	18. Special editing capabilities
7. Minimum number of words in storage	19. Boolean operations
8. Maximum number of words in storage	20. Table lookup
9. Maximum total storage in digits	21. Storage checking
10. Maximum total storage in characters	22. Storage protect
11. Cycle time in microseconds	
12. Effective transfer rate in characters per second	

TABLE 14-10 Cluster Composition

CLUSTER 1	CLUSTER 5
Burroughs B2500	IBM 360/30
GE 415	IBM 360/40
GE 425	IBM 360/50
GE 435	IBM 360/65
Honeywell 1400	IBM 360/75
IBM 1130	IBM 360/44
	IBM 360/67
	RCA Spectra 70/35
	RCA Spectra 70/45
	RCA Spectra 70/55
	RCA 3301/3304

CLUSTER 2	CLUSTER 6
CDC 3100	GE 235
CDC 3200	Honeywell 200/120
CDC 3300	Honeywell 200/200
CDC 3400	IBM 360/20
Honeywell 1800	RCA Spectra 70/15
	RCA Spectra 70/25
	Univac 9200
	Univac 9300

CLUSTER 3	CLUSTER 7
CDC 6400	Honeywell 200/2200
CDC 6600	Honeywell 200/4200
CDC 6800	NCR 315 RMC
GE 625	
GE 635	
Honeywell 200/8200	
IBM 7092-II	
Univac 108	

CLUSTER 4	CLUSTER 8
Burroughs B300	Burroughs B3500
GE 115	Honeywell 200/1200
IBM 1401-G	RCA 3301/3303

Table 14-10 shows the eight-group clustering results from the hierarchical clustering. Various aspects of intermanufacturer competition are brought out. For example, cluster 5 shows rather clearly that segments of the IBM 360 computer series compete directly with segments of the RCA Spectra series (possibly a portent of RCA's eventual demise in the computer field). Cluster 3 brings out the competition among CDC, GE, Honeywell, IBM, and Univac. One notes, not surprisingly, that IBM has models in five out of the eight clusters. On the other hand, Honeywell has models in six of the eight clusters, an outcome that was not anticipated by the researchers.

The resulting clusters indicated which manufacturers competed with which other manufacturers in terms of similarity in the overall performance profiles of their machines. Moreover, the combination of reduced-space and cluster analysis provided a useful dual treatment of the data. The reduced-space phase provided help in summarizing the original variables in terms of a smaller number of dimensions, such as speed or capacity. The clustering phase permitted us to group machines according to their coordinates in the reduced, but still four-dimensional, space.

Foreign Market Analysis

Companies that are considering entering foreign markets for the first time as well as those considering expanding from existing to new foreign markets have to do formal market analysis. Often a useful starting point is to work from a categorization schema of potential foreign markets. Cluster analysis can be useful in this process.

To illustrate, we use the study by Green and Larsen.[37] In this study 71 nations were clustered on the basis of selected economic characteristics and economic change. The specific variables used were (1) growth in Gross Domestic Product, (2) literacy rate, (3) energy consumption per capita, (4) oil imports, and (5) international debt. Variables 1, 4, and 5 were operationalized as change during a specified time period.

Clustering was accomplished by use of BMDP's K-Means clustering routine. This routine is a nonhierarchical method that allocates countries to the group whose centroid is closest, using a Euclidean distance measure. A total of five clusters was derived based on the distance between countries and the centers of the clusters across the five predictor variables. The number of clusters selected was based on the criteria of total within-cluster distance and interpretability. A smaller number of clusters led to a substantial increase of within-cluster variability, while an increase in the number of clusters resulted in group splitting with a minimal reduction in distance. The composition of the clusters is shown in Table 14-11.

Validation Techniques

Once a solution has been obtained, the researcher may be interested in validating the results. Depending on the clustering method used, the analyst can select among five techniques: the *cophenetic correlation, significance tests on variables used to create clusters, replication, significance tests on independent variables,* and *Monte Carlo* procedures. Unfortunately, none of these has been widely used in marketing applications. Lack of use together with the technical nature of validation puts further explanation beyond the scope of this book.[38]

---

[37]R.T. Green and T.L. Larsen, "Export Markets and Economic Change," University of Texas at Austin, Department of Marketing Administration Working Paper 84/85-5-2, May 1985.

[38]See Aldenderfer and Blashfield, *Cluster Analysis,* pp. 62–74.

TABLE 14-11 Composition of Foreign Market Clusters

CLUSTER 1	CLUSTER 3	CLUSTER 5
Belgium	Ethiopia	Colombia
Canada	Ghana	Costa Rica
Denmark	India	Ecuador
Sweden	Liberia	Greece
USA	Libya	Hong Kong
Germany	Madagascar	Jordan
Netherlands	Mali	Mexico
UK	Senegal	Paraguay
Australia		Portugal
Finland		Venezuela
Norway		Yugoslavia
Switzerland		El Salvador
New Zealand		Iran
France		Tunisia
Ireland		Indonesia
Italy		Nigeria
Austria		Malawi

CLUSTER 2	CLUSTER 4
Cameroon	Brazil
Central African Republic	Chile
Egypt	Israel
Somalia	Japan
Togo	Korea
Zaire	Peru
Zambia	Philippines
Honduras	Singapore
Nicaragua	Spain
Morocco	Sri Lanka
Ivory Coast	Thailand
Tanzania	Turkey
Pakistan	Argentina
	Guatemala
	Kenya
	Uruguay

SUMMARY

This chapter has been concerned with two ways—factor analysis and clustering—to summarize associative information in interdependent data structures. Quite often reduced-space and cluster analysis can be usefully applied in tandem.

The factor-analytic method stressed here was principal-components analysis. This procedure has the property of selecting sets of weights for forming linear combinations of the original variables such that the variance of the obtained component scores is (sequentially) maximal, subject to each linear combination's being orthogonal to previously obtained ones. The principal-components model was illustrated on a small set of sample data. This was followed by a demonstration of Varimax rotation to improve interpretability of the component loadings. The concluding part of this section dealt with a miscellany of topics, such as communalities estimation, confirmatory factor analysis, factor analysis in prediction, index determination, statistical inference, and operational issues.

Cluster analysis was described in terms of four general questions: (1) selecting a proximity measure, (2) algorithms for grouping objects, (3) describing the clusters, and (4) statistical inference. In addition, three applications of clustering were briefly described.

ASSIGNMENT MATERIAL

1. The marketing research firm of Alpert and FitzRoy Ltd. is in the process of attempting to relate activity-interest test scores to "success" measures of applicants for retailing positions in a large Philadelphia department store. Activity-interest scores and success scores are available for a group of retailing personnel who have already been employed by the store. The activity-interest variables are: X_1—gregariousness, X_2—liking for outdoor sports, X_3—liking for music, and X_4—desire for travel. Higher values of the X_i or Y indicate higher interest or success, respectively.

   a. Conduct a principal-components analysis on the 14 × 4 matrix of activity-interest scores, utilizing the correlation matrix between variables as input.

   b. How would you interpret the first component?

   c. Rotate the component-loading matrix by means of the Varimax routine. How do you interpret the resulting loadings?

PERSON	X_1	X_2	X_3	X_4	Y^*
1	21	26	7	8	6.2
2	22	16	11	7	7.6
3	16	28	11	7	5.7
4	17	30	9	13	6.1
5	12	26	12	7	1.8
6	25	10	18	14	2.9
7	18	21	14	16	4.7
8	15	17	5	11	4.8
9	14	23	13	8	4.7
10	18	20	10	5	5.7
11	14	29	14	11	7.2
12	15	23	16	7	6.7
13	25	21	14	12	3.6
14	15	20	3	10	7.0

*Success measure.

2. Using the data of problem 1, compute component scores for each person on each of the (nonrotated) components.

    a. Assuming that you were required to arrive at a *single* index of activity-interest, how might you proceed? How would the 14 persons be arrayed in terms of this index?

    b. Conduct a multiple regression of the success measure Y versus the full set of component scores. Next, select the one variable that loads most highly on the first (unrotated) component and conduct a two-variable linear regression with Y as the criterion variable. Contrast the results of these findings in terms of accounted-for variance in Y.

    c. Conduct a multiple regression using scores on the first two (unrotated) components as predictors with Y as the criterion variable. Contrast the results of this step with those of the preceding analysis.

3. Discuss the similarities and differences among multiple regression, discriminant analysis, canonical correlation, and factor analysis in terms of (a) assumption structure and (b) objectives of the techniques.

4. The following data matrix was obtained from a study of potential benefits from using shampoo. The 19 benefits are portrayed in three dimensions and are derived from free-association techniques.

    a. Plot the coordinate values in three two-dimensional subspaces. What can be observed regarding benefit associations from these plots?

    b. Using a clustering program of your choice, cluster the 19 points. (Your routine may require preliminary computation of a distance measure between pairs of points.) How would you interpret the clusters?

Matrix of Reduced Space Coordinates

	COORDINATE		
BENEFIT	*I*	*II*	*III*
1. Body	−0.768	−0.274	−0.315
2. Fullness	−0.857	−0.240	−0.228
3. Holds Set	−0.116	−0.489	0.230
4. Bouncy	−0.113	−0.322	−0.769
5. Not Limp	−0.794	0.058	0.189
6. Manageable	−0.541	0.018	0.247
7. Zesty	0.651	−0.229	−0.425
8. Natural	0.088	0.782	−0.168
9. Clean	−0.006	0.381	0.045
10. Sheen	0.289	0.248	−0.312
11. Curly	0.257	−0.437	−0.178
12. Long	0.386	0.495	−0.433
13. Grooming Aid	0.480	−0.189	0.631
14. Soft	0.007	0.904	−0.216

Matrix of Reduced Space Coordinates (*Continued*)

	COORDINATE		
BENEFIT	*I*	*II*	*III*
15. Nice	0.317	−0.207	0.926
16. Combs Easily	−0.456	−0.229	0.504
17. Healthy	0.035	−0.344	0.349
18. Alive	0.707	−0.444	−0.129
19. Pretty	0.432	0.520	0.053

5. Examine the marketing literature for three applications of cluster analysis.
   a. What were the purposes of using cluster analysis by each of the authors?
   b. How would you critique the results of their analyses?
   c. What alternative multivariate methods can you propose for analyzing the data of these studies?

6. a. Use the data set given in problem 1 of the assignment material for Chapter 13 and conduct a cluster analysis of the people using the four variables shown. Pool ownership is to be a predictor variable and should be coded as follows: 1 = nonowner; 2 = owner. How would you interpret the resulting clusters?
   b. Do a factor analysis of these same data and interpret the results.

15

Multidimensional Scaling and Conjoint Analysis

INTRODUCTION

Up to this point our discussion of multivariate methods has not been tied in to any particular content area; rather, we have emphasized the *versatility* of the techniques across a wide spectrum of marketing problems. In the current chapter, however, we wish to describe two sets of multivariate techniques, *multidimensional scaling* and *conjoint analysis,* that are particularly well suited (and were originally developed) for measuring human perceptions and preferences.

As such, this chapter is something of a continuation of the psychological scaling material of Chapter 8. In the present case we shall be emphasizing *multidimensional* scales and *multiattribute* tradeoffs that often, but not necessarily, make use of ordinal data. The methodology considered here is of comparatively recent origin and the field is still undergoing development and trial application.

Multidimensional scaling (MDS) of perceptions and preferences is discussed first. An intuitive introduction to the topic is provided by using a geographical example involving a set of intercity distances. In particular, we show how MDS takes a set of distance data and tries to find a spatial configuration or pattern of points in some number of dimensions whose distances best match the input data. Attention then turns to the MDS of *subjective* data regarding persons' judged similarities and preferences of various stimuli. Various models for portraying these judgments are described and illustrated geometrically.

We next discuss ways in which MDS has been (and can be) applied to marketing problems. Comments are also made on the limitations of the methodology and the types of future research that may be anticipated in this field.

We then turn to a related methodology—conjoint analysis. In conjoint analysis we are concerned with the measurement of utilities—how people make tradeoffs in choosing among multiattribute alternatives. As with MDS, the fundamentals of the methodology are first described, including some empirical illustrations. This is followed by brief descriptions of applications and also a discussion of some current limitations and recent developments.

MDS FUNDAMENTALS

Let us start things off by taking a look at Panel I of Figure 15-1. Here we see a configuration of ten U.S. cities, whose locations have been taken from an airline map. By finding ruler distances between each city pair and converting these to miles, we could approximate the *numerical* interpoint distance entries of Panel II. (The distances were actually obtained from an airline atlas.) We recall from Chapter 14 that the Euclidean distance between a pair of points i and $j,$ in any number of r dimensions, is given by

$$d_{ij} = \left[\sum_{k=1}^{r} (x_{ik} - x_{jk})^2 \right]^{1/2}$$

In the present case, $r = 2$, since only two dimensions are involved. For example, we could find the distance between Atlanta and Chicago by (1) projecting their points on axis 1 (East–West), finding the difference, and squaring it; (2) projecting their points on axis 2 (North–South) and doing the same; and then (3) taking the square root of the sum of the two squared differences.

In short, it is a relatively simple matter to go from the map in Panel I to the set of numerical distances in Panel II. However, the converse is *not* so easy. And that is what MDS is all about.

Suppose that we are shown Panel II of Figure 15-1 without the labels so that we do not even know if the objects are cities. The task is to work backward. That is, we wish to find, simultaneously, the

- Number of dimensions and
- Configuration (or pattern) of points in that dimensionality

so that their computed interpoint distances most closely match the input data of Panel II. This is the problem of *metric* MDS.

Next, suppose that we were to take some order-preserving transformation of the 45 numbers in Panel II. For example, we could take the smallest distance (205 miles between New York and Washington) and call it 1. Then we could apply the same idea

Figure 15-1 Nonmetric MDS of Ten United States Cities

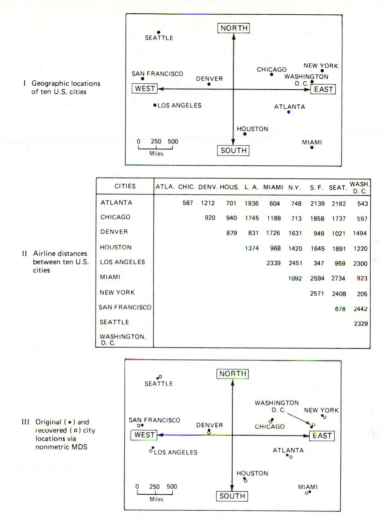

I Geographic locations of ten U.S. cities

II Airline distances between ten U.S. cities

CITIES	ATLA.	CHIC.	DENV.	HOUS.	L. A.	MIAMI	N.Y.	S. F.	SEAT.	WASH. D. C.
ATLANTA		587	1212	701	1936	604	748	2139	2182	543
CHICAGO			920	940	1745	1188	713	1858	1737	597
DENVER				879	831	1726	1631	949	1021	1494
HOUSTON					1374	968	1420	1645	1891	1220
LOS ANGELES						2339	2451	347	959	2300
MIAMI							1092	2594	2734	923
NEW YORK								2571	2408	205
SAN FRANCISCO									678	2442
SEATTLE										2329
WASHINGTON, D. C.										

III Original (•) and recovered (o) city locations via nonmetric MDS

and rank-order the remaining 44 distances up to rank 45 for the distance (2,734 miles) between Miami and Seattle. We could then find the

- Number of dimensions and
- Configuration of points in that dimensionality

so that the ranks of their computed interpoint distances most closely matched the ranks of the input data. This is the problem of *nonmetric* MDS.

In the error-free case (the situation considered here), it turns out that metric MDS methods can find, for all practical purposes, an exact solution. However, what is rather surprising is that, even after degrading the numerical data to ranks, nonmetric methods can achieve a virtually perfect recovery as well.

Panel III indicates that this is so by showing the results of applying a nonmetric algorithm to the ranks of the 45 numbers in Panel II.[1] As shown, even with only rank-order input information, the recovery of the original locations is almost perfect.

We should quickly add, however, that neither the metric nor nonmetric MDS procedures will necessarily line up the configuration of points in a North–South direction; all that the methods try to preserve are *relative* distances. The configuration can be arbitrarily rotated, translated, reflected, or uniformly stretched or shrunk so as to best match the target configuration of Panel I.[2] None of these operations will change the *relative* distances of the points.

Psychological Versus Physical Distance

The virtues of MDS methods are not in the scaling of physical distances but rather in their scaling of *psychological "distances,"* often called *dissimilarities*. In MDS we assume that individuals act as though they have a type of "mental map," not necessarily visualized or explicated, so that they view pairs of entities that are near each other as similar and pairs of entities far from each other as dissimilar. Depending on the relative distances among pairs of points, varying *degrees* of dissimilarity could be imagined.

We assume that the respondent is able to provide either numerical measures of his or her perceived degree of dissimilarity for all pairs of entities or, less stringently, ordinal measures of dissimilarity. If so, we can use the methodology of MDS to construct a *physical* map in one or more dimensions whose interpoint distances (or ranks of distances, as the case may be) are most consistent with the input data.

Not for a moment do we assume that this model *explains* perception. Quite the contrary: we only assume that it provides a useful *representation* of a set of subjective judgments about the extent to which a respondent views various pairs of entities as being dissimilar. Thus, MDS models are representations of data rather than theories of perceptual processes. That they can be interesting and useful is shown by the following example.

A Bostonian's View of the United States

A few years ago R. N. Shepard, one of the pioneers in the development of nonmetric scaling, was interested in persons' *subjective* judgments about the relative nearness of various U.S. states to each other. His experimental subjects were all long-term residents of Boston. Shepard obtained subjective data about how far each state was perceived for all distinct pairs of the 48 continental states and the data were scaled by nonmetric MDS.

Figure 15-2 shows a Bostonian's view of the United States as reflected in Shepard's

---

[1]See J. B. Kruskal and M. Wish, *Multidimensional Scaling* (Beverly Hills, Calif.: Sage, 1978).

[2]Techniques for doing this are called *configuration congruence* or *matching programs*. For example, see P. H. Schönemann and R. M. Carroll, "Fitting One Matrix to Another under Choice of a Central Dilation and a Rigid Motion," *Psychometrika*, 35 (June 1970), 245–57.

Figure 15-2 **"Map" of the United States Based on Subjective Judgments**

Source: Reproduced, with permission, from a research study of R. N. Shepard.

data. Notice that the eastern half of the United States is rather exaggerated compared with the western half. In particular, the northwestern portion looks rather pushed down. Still, it is remarkable that so much structure remains, considering the fact that the source of the input data was respondents' subjective judgments about relative distances. In short, perceptual *distortion,* while operative, was not severe enough to obliterate the general character of the geographic relationships among states. As noted, the respondents tended to exaggerate the size of areas nearer their homes and attenuate those farther away (and presumably of lesser importance).

CLASSIFYING MDS TECHNIQUES

As noted earlier, multidimensional scaling is concerned with portraying psychological relations among stimuli—either empirically obtained similarities or preferences (or other kinds of matchings or orderings)—as geometric relationships among points in a multidimensional space. In this approach one attempts to represent *psychological dissimilarity as geometric distance.* The axes of the geometric space are often (but not necessarily)

Exhibit 15-1   Selected MDS Programs

There are a number of computer programs available for conducting multidimensional scaling (MDS) analyses. These programs provide for a variety of types of input data. Versions of each are available for mainframe and microcomputers.* The following are the ones most widely used for marketing applications:

MDPREF is designed to do multidimensional scaling of preference or evaluation data. It is a metric model based on a principal-components analysis. Input data usually are stimuli evaluation data, although paired comparisons can be used in older versions of the model.

MDSCAL 5M constructs a configuration of points in space from information about the distances between points. Input data are proximities (similarities) of stimuli. Nonmetric and metric scaling can be performed, as can nonmetric and metric unfolding.

INDSCAL performs a canonical decomposition of N-way tables and analysis of individual differences in multidimensional scaling. Proximity data are input and the program produces up to a 7-way solution for 10 dimensions.

PREFMAP produces preference mapping analysis based on a generalization of the Coombsian unfolding model of preference. The program relates preference data to a multidimensional solution. Given a stimulus configuration and a set of preference scales, the procedure finds for each individual an ideal point in the given stimulus space.

PROFIT is a technique for fitting outside property vectors into stimulus spaces. Input data are the coordinates of stimulus points in k-dimensional space derived from an MDS procedure and sets of independently determined physical measures (properties).

KYST represents a blending of MDSCAL 5M and TORSCA 9. It includes the initial configuration procedure from TORSCA and has the capability of rotating solutions to principal components. The program handles metric and nonmetric scaling and unfolding and uses proximity input data.

*These programs for the microcomputer are found in S. Smith, *PC–MDS: Multidimensional Scaling and Conjoint Analysis,* Version 4.1, 1987.

assumed to represent the psychological bases or attributes along which the judge compares stimuli (represented as points or vectors in his or her psychological space).

Many different kinds of MDS procedures exist (Exhibit 15-1). Accordingly, it seems useful to describe a set of descriptors by which the methodology can be described.[3] These descriptors are

1. Mode—a mode is a class of entities, such as respondents, brands, use occasions, attributes of a multiattribute object.

[3]The descriptors are based on a subset of those listed by J. D. Carroll and P. Arabie, "Multidimensional Scaling," in *Annual Review of Psychology,* ed. M. R. Rosenzweig and L. W. Porter (Palo Alto, Calif.: Annual Reviews, 1980).

2. Data array—number of ways that modes are arranged. For example, in a two-way array of single mode dissimilarities, the entities could be brand-brand relationships, such as a respondent's rating of the *ij*th brand pair on a 1–9 point scale, ranging from 1 (very similar) to 9 (very different). Hence, in this case we have one mode, two-way data on judged dissimilarities of pairs of brands.

3. Type of geometric model—distance model versus a vector or projection model (the latter represented by a combination of points and vectors).

4. Number of different sets of plotted points (or vectors)—one, two, more than two.

5. Scale type—nominal, ordinal, interval, or ratio scaled input data.

Data Mode/Way

In marketing research most applications of MDS entail either single mode, two-way data or two-mode, two-way data. Single mode, two-way data are illustrated by input matrices that are square and symmetric, in which all distinct pairs of entities (e.g., brands) in an $I \times I$ matrix are judged in terms of their relative similarity/dissimilarity on some type of rating scale. The instructions can refer to pairwise similarity, association, substitutability, closeness to, affinity for, congruence with, co-occurrence with, and so on. Typically, only $I(I - 1)/2$ pairs are evaluated, since all self-similarities are assumed to be equal to each other and dissimilarity itself is assumed to be a symmetric relationship between members of a pair of entities.

MDS solutions based on single mode, two-way input data lead to what are often called "simple" spaces—that is, a configuration of only one set of I points. Pairs of points that are close together in this geometric space are presumed to exhibit high subjective similarity in the eyes of the respondent.

Another popular form of marketing research data entails input matrices that represent two-mode, two-way relationships. Examples include

1. I judges' preference ratings of J brands

2. Average scores (across respondents) of J brands rated on I attributes

3. The frequency (across respondents) with which J attributes are assumed to be associated with I brands

4. The frequency (across respondents) with which respondents in each of I brand-favorite groups pick each of J attributes as important to their brand choice

5. The frequency (across respondents) with which each of J use occasions is perceived to be appropriate for each of I brands

6. The frequency (across respondents) with which each of J problems is perceived to be associated with using each of I brands

These geometric spaces are often called "joint" spaces in which two different sets of points (e.g., brands and attributes) are represented. (In some cases three or more sets of entities may be scaled.)

Type of Geometric Model

In applications of single-mode, two-way data the entities being scaled are almost always represented as points (as opposed to vectors). However, in the case of two-mode, two-way data, the two sets of entities might each be represented as points or, alternatively, one set may be represented as points while the other set is represented as vector directions. In this latter case the termini of the vectors are often normalized to lie on a common circumference around the origin of the configuration.

The point-point type of two-mode, two-way data is often referred to as an *unfolding* model.[4] If the original matrix consists of *I* respondents' preference evaluation of *J* brands, then the resulting joint-space map has *I* respondents' ideal points and *J* brand points. Brand points that are near a respondent's ideal point are assumed to be *highly preferred* by that respondent. Although the original input data may be based on between-set relationships, if the simple unfolding model holds, one can also infer respondent-to-respondent similarities in terms of the closeness of their ideal points to each other. Brand-to-brand similarities may be analogously inferred, based on the relative closeness of pairs of brand points.

The point-vector model of two-mode, two-way data is a *projection* model in which one obtains respondent *i*'s preference scale by projecting the *J* brand points onto respondent *i*'s vector. The farther out (toward vector *i*'s terminus) the *projection* is, the more preferred that brand is for the respondent.

An Illustration of the Simple Model

We can illustrate the simple space model by means of Figure 15-3. This map is based on an MDS analysis of 42 respondents' averaged dissimilarity judgments regarding 15 bread/pastry items.[5] Each respondent was shown a list of 105 pairs of items—all distinct pairs of 15 breads/pastries, taken two at a time. For each pair, the respondent indicated his or her judgment of the items' similarity by rating the pair on an equal-interval scale ranging from 1 (very similar) to 9 (very different). Thus, the input data consisted of a single mode, two-way, half matrix of dissimilarity ratings on all distinct pairs, or 105 data values. The two-dimensional MDS configuration in Figure 15-3 represents the input data relationships as well. The first dimension separates sweet items (e.g., pastry, donut) from the less-sweet items (e.g., buttered toast). The second axis tends to separate plain-type items from toasted items.

An Illustration of the Unfolding-Type, Joint-Space Model

Figure 15-4 provides an illustration of two-mode, two-way scaling and involves an input matrix of 42 respondents' preferences for the same 15 food items. A simple unfolding

[4]C. H. Coombs, *A Theory of Data* (New York: John Wiley, 1964).

[5]Taken from P. E. Green and V. R. Rao, *Applied Multidimensional Scaling: A Comparison of Approaches and Algorithms* (New York: Holt, Rinehart & Winston, 1972).

Figure 15-3   Two-Space MDS Configuration Obtained from a Scaling of Judged Dissimilarities

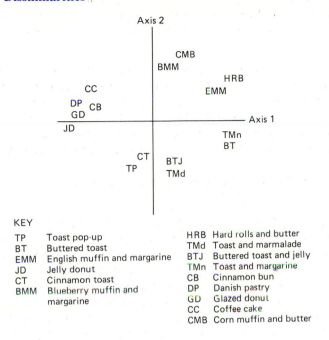

KEY

TP	Toast pop-up	HRB	Hard rolls and butter
BT	Buttered toast	TMd	Toast and marmalade
EMM	English muffin and margarine	BTJ	Buttered toast and jelly
JD	Jelly donut	TMn	Toast and margarine
CT	Cinnamon toast	CB	Cinnamon bun
BMM	Blueberry muffin and margarine	DP	Danish pastry
		GD	Glazed donut
		CC	Coffee cake
		CMB	Corn muffin and butter

model was applied to these data, leading to the joint space of ideal points and food items shown in the figure. Some indication of preference heterogeneity is noted by the fact that there are a large number of ideal points near the sweet items in quadrant 3 and also a concentration of ideal points is found around the nonsweet items in quadrants 1 and 4. It should be pointed out that the configuration of food items differs between Figures 15-4 and 15-3, reflecting the fact that different judgments are being sought (similarity versus preference). That is, in this case we do *not* apply a model in which the stimulus points (food items) assume fixed positions in the space, as obtained from some preceding analysis of judged similarities between food item pairs.

An Illustration of a Projection-Type, Joint-Space Model

Figure 15-5 illustrates a point-vector, joint-space model. In this case the food items are represented as points while various attributes (on which the food items were originally rated) are represented as vector directions. For example, if we were to project the food item points onto the vector "Inexpensive," we would find that buttered toast, toast and marmalade, toast and margarine, and buttered toast and jelly are all perceived to be inexpensive. On the other hand, glazed donut, danish pastry, cinnamon bun, and coffee cake are positioned at the other (expensive) end of the scale.

Figure 15-4   Two-Space MDS Configuration from Unfolding-Type, Joint-Space Analysis

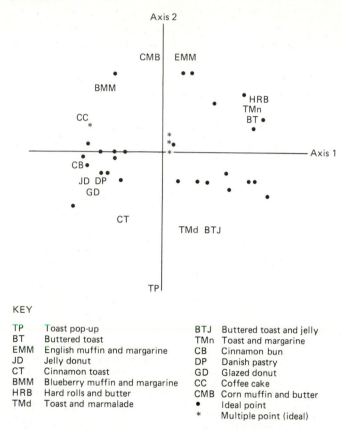

KEY

TP	Toast pop-up		BTJ	Buttered toast and jelly
BT	Buttered toast		TMn	Toast and margarine
EMM	English muffin and margarine		CB	Cinnamon bun
JD	Jelly donut		DP	Danish pastry
CT	Cinnamon toast		GD	Glazed donut
BMM	Blueberry muffin and margarine		CC	Coffee cake
HRB	Hard rolls and butter		CMB	Corn muffin and butter
TMd	Toast and marmalade		•	Ideal point
			*	Multiple point (ideal)

Type of Scaling Method

The scaling of the input data (namely, nominal, ordinal, interval, and ratio scale) also serves as a descriptor. As noted earlier, data that are interval-scaled or ratio-scaled are called *metric* and the corresponding scaling methods are called metric scaling. Data measured at the nominal or ordinal scale level, however, are called *nonmetric* and the corresponding scaling techniques are called nonmetric scaling.

Figure 15-3 (described earlier) is actually a metric MDS analysis of a set of dissimilarity data. By way of contrast, Figure 15-6 shows the results of scaling the *same* input data nonmetrically by working only with the ordinal properties of the input. As recalled, nonmetric MDS programs try to find a configuration whose *ranks* of derived interpoint distances most closely match the ranks of the original input data (in a space of reasonably low dimensionality).

An interesting byproduct of nonmetric MDS is a scatter plot of the original dissim-

Figure 15-5   Two-Space MDS Configuration from Projection-Type, Joint-Space Analysis

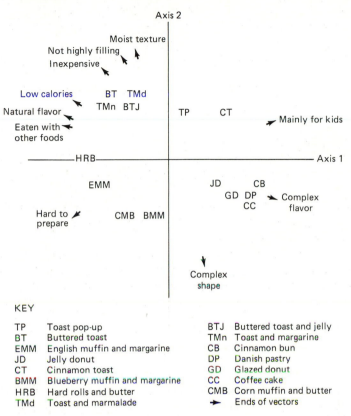

KEY

TP	Toast pop-up	BTJ	Buttered toast and jelly
BT	Buttered toast	TMn	Toast and margarine
EMM	English muffin and margarine	CB	Cinnamon bun
JD	Jelly donut	DP	Danish pastry
CT	Cinnamon toast	GD	Glazed donut
BMM	Blueberry muffin and margarine	CC	Coffee cake
HRB	Hard rolls and butter	CMB	Corn muffin and butter
TMd	Toast and marmalade	➤	Ends of vectors

ilarities on the derived distances, as shown in Figure 15-6. We note two things about Figure 15-6. First, the configuration does not differ all that much from the one in Figure 15-3, based on metric MDS. Second, the scatter plot in Figure 15-6 does not differ markedly from linearity, suggesting that metric methods can provide results that are close to nonmetric methods.

In the early days of MDS, a vast amount of attention was paid to the virtues of nonmetric versus metric scaling. From a conceptual viewpoint this distinction is very important and has spurred major advances in MDS over the past 20 years. However, from a practical, applied viewpoint, metric MDS methods usually produce results that are quite close to their nonmetric counterparts, particularly if integer-rank transformations are applied before the metric analysis is undertaken.[6]

Metric methods also offer the advantages of being less expensive in computer time

[6]See P. E. Green, "On the Robustness of Multidimensional Scaling Techniques," *Journal of Marketing Research*, 12 (1975), 73–81; and D. G. Weeks and P. M. Bentler, "A Comparison of Linear and Monotone Multidimensional Scaling Models," *Psychological Bulletin*, 86 (1979), 349–54.

Figure 15-6   Two-Space MDS Configuration from a (Nonmetric) Scaling of Judged Dissimilarities

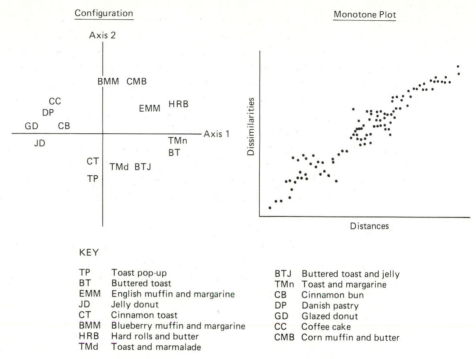

KEY

TP	Toast pop-up	BTJ	Buttered toast and jelly
BT	Buttered toast	TMn	Toast and margarine
EMM	English muffin and margarine	CB	Cinnamon bun
JD	Jelly donut	DP	Danish pastry
CT	Cinnamon toast	GD	Glazed donut
BMM	Blueberry muffin and margarine	CC	Coffee cake
HRB	Hard rolls and butter	CMB	Corn muffin and butter
TMd	Toast and marmalade		

and are robust over data sets that could lead to local optima or degeneracy under nonmetric analyses. Hence, it is somewhat ironic that the virtues of *metric* MDS have come to be appreciated in the aftermath of the significant theoretical strides that have accompanied the introduction of nonmetric MDS methods.

MARKETING APPLICATIONS OF MDS

To date, most MDS studies have been of a pilot-type or diagnostic nature, used to help marketing managers get some feel for how their brand is positioned in the minds of consumers, vis-à-vis competing brands. Some capsule illustrations follow.

Soft-Drink Slogans

A prominent producer of soft drinks wished to consider the adoption of a new slogan—one that would connote the distinct features of the brand. The firm's advertising department had prepared 15 candidate slogans and the problem was; Which one to choose?

A study of consumers' perceptions of these slogans and their association with various brands of soft drinks was undertaken. The study indicated that 11 of the 15 slogans were perceived as more closely associated with the images of one or more competitive brands than the firm's own brand. Had no comparison of brand-slogan congruence been attempted, it is conceivable that a slogan might have been chosen that would be more closely associated with a competitor's brand than with the company's own brand.

Computer-Firm Images

A large producer of electronic computers was concerned with the relationship between the physical characteristics of its hardware and data processors' perceptions. Computer models—the firm's and its competitors'—were first positioned geometrically in performance space (e.g., how long it would take the computer to perform a multiplication, size of core, etc.). Perceptual judgments of computer-model similarity were also obtained from the firm's sales personnel, its customers, and its noncustomers.

Of the three respondent groups, the sales personnel's perceptions agreed most closely with the objective (performance) positioning of the computer models. However, the firm's customers' perceptions of its computers disagreed with objective performance along a few of the key dimensions, suggesting that the salespeople were not emphasizing certain characteristics of the company's line that would enhance customer satisfaction. Perception of the firm's noncustomers had relatively little correspondence with the true performance characteristics of its computers. Quite the contrary: noncustomers perceived the firm's computer line as more or less undifferentiated from that of other firms.

The firm's noncustomers, to a large extent, evoked criteria other than physical performance in evaluating competitive models. Noncustomers were chiefly concerned with the prominence of the computer firm, the size of its technical support staff, and the various marketing services it could offer. Not surprisingly, the firm's noncustomers tended to be less technically sophisticated data processors—ones who would be attracted to a large, well-established (albeit higher-priced) computer supplier.

High-Nutrition Cereals

A marketer of a high-nutrition brand of cereal was becoming increasingly concerned over the relevance of his advertising toward promoting a cereal that both tasted good and had high nutritional value. Discussions with advertising agency personnel led to a new campaign that humorously stressed qualities of "good tasting" and high nutrition. The firm's marketing personnel wondered if this new message was getting across to the consumer.

A study of housewife perceptions of the firm's brand vis-à-vis other cereals was undertaken. The study indicated that the advertising goals *were* being achieved: while perceived as a high-nutrition cereal, the firm's brand plotted closer in "perceptual space" to good-tasting cereals than did any of the other high-nutrition brands. That is, consumers *were* perceiving the hybrid advertising appeal in ways desired by the company. In this case perceptions were measured for the purpose of *monitoring the results* of a basic change in advertising appeal.

Magazine Positioning

A large publisher of medical magazines was interested in the positioning of one of his journals.[7] A sample of physician readers of this and other medical magazines were asked to rank each of ten popular magazines on a series of criteria, such as

- Information useful for daily practice
- Best to read when in a hurry
- Greatest breadth of appeal

Figure 15-7 shows a joint-space map of the ten journals and the six vectors representing the criteria. As noted, the dimensions were labeled technical–nontechnical, and specialized–general. Contrary to expectations, the publisher found that his journal was evaluated as less technical and less general than originally believed. Along with corroborating information, this finding led to changes in editorial content and advertising solicitations.

Figure 15-7   Joint-Space Configuration of Medical Journals and Criterion Vectors

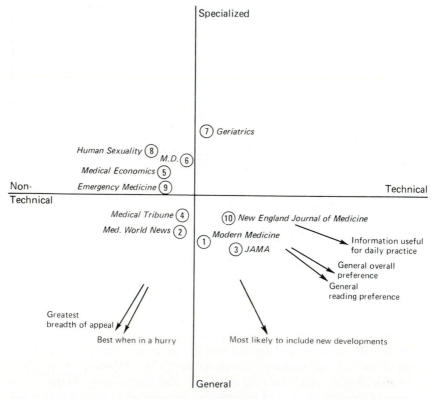

[7]This study (undertaken by P. E. Green) appears in Yoram Wind and P. J. Robinson, "Product Positioning: An Application of Multidimensional Scaling," in *Attitude Research in Transition*, ed. R. I. Haley (Chicago: American Marketing Association, 1972).

NEWER APPLICATIONS

While MDS methods are now being used as a data presentation tool in a variety of different businesses, much of their potential is yet to be realized. As illustrations of applications that offer substantial analytical promise, we can consider two areas: (1) market segmentation and (2) large-scale new-product development models.

Market Segmentation

One class of applications for MDS involves market segmentation. Suppose that one could characterize a product class and its buyers as points in a joint space whose dimensions are perceived product characteristics. Each brand could be represented as a stimulus point and each buyer as an ideal point in the same attribute space. Actually, however, this would be a "superspace" in the sense that different buyers could perceive the same stimuli differently as well as occupy different positions in the space that is perceived.

Conceptually, then, a market segment might be viewed as a subspace in which all members of the subspace perceive the stimuli similarly and occupy approximately the same ideal-point position. We could, logically, have the other three cases where (1) the stimuli are perceived differently but common ideal points exist,[8] (2) individuals exhibit similar perceptions but possess different ideal-point positions, and (3) neither stimulus perception nor ideal-point position is common over individuals. Further, we might be interested in the relationship of perception and/or ideal-point position to other characteristics of the buyer, such as the usual socioeconomic, personality, and demographic variables.

Partitioning the superspace of ideal points and stimuli into reasonably homogeneous subspaces—and identifying the characteristics of consumers who exhibit commonality of perception and preference—appear to be in the spirit of market-segmentation strategy. Perhaps such analysis would show "empty regions" where a high concentration of ideal points, but no "close" brands, are found. At the very least, the analysis should point out the competitive position of a firm's brand with other brands as viewed *perceptually* by different market segments, regardless of the brand's similarity with respect to physical and/or chemical characteristics.

From the manufacturer's point of view, the task is to modify its product, package, advertising, or whatever for the purposes of either (1) moving its brand toward some region in the space that has a high "concentration" of ideal points or (2) attempting to move the ideal points themselves toward its brand. We might also conceive of the possibility of changing the relative importance of the dimensions or even the number of dimensions, as might be the case in truly "innovative" brands. Or the manufacturer might try to move consumers (through "identification-with-reference-group" advertising) from an unfavorable market segment to a favorable one. Inasmuch as other brands also appear

---

[8]This case is "inadmissible," since we assume here that the arguments of the preference function are the perceived dimensions. For a general discussion of market segmentation issues, see Yoram Wind, "Issues and Advances in Segmentation Research," *Journal of Marketing Research*, 15 (1978), 317–37.

in the attribute space, the problem of estimating share of choices must be contended with as well.

While this approach is still speculative, a number of applications have already been carried out. Such spatial configurations have even been traced through time—a perceptual and preference characterization analogous to a Nielsen-type audit of goods movement.

Allied with this approach is the potential use of MDS in intracorporate research. Do the advertising department, field sales, product development staff, and firm's distributors have *congruent* images of the company's product or service? If so, do these perceptions agree with those of the ultimate buyers? If not, what are the implications of such inconsistency for the effectiveness of interrelated policy decisions regarding pricing, advertising theme, product design, and distribution practice?

Large-Scale New-Product Models

Some of the earliest applications of MDS have been in new-product development.[9] More recently, several researchers have proposed large-scale integrated procedures for new-product development and testing that are primarily based on MDS.[10] Although developed independently, the models are quite similar in several aspects:

1. Emphasis on developing perceptual maps by the use of consumer ratings on prespecified attribute scales
2. The general assumption of homogeneity of perceptions across consumers
3. Fitting of preference data into previously constructed perceptual maps via external (regression-type) methods involving ideal-point and/or vector representations of preferences
4. Incorporation of some function for relating probability of choice to distance from ideal point

In short, the models are designed to make *predictions* as to how new products positioned in the perceptual space will fare insofar as share of choices is concerned. It is not surprising that all the major textbooks on product policy discuss MDS methodology.[11]

With the development of more-sophisticated MDS models, such as three-way scaling (e.g., persons' preferences for brands across use occasions), product positioning models

---

[9]See V. J. Stefflre, "Market Structure Studies: New Products for Old Markets and New Markets (Foreign) for Old Products," in *Application of the Sciences in Marketing,* ed. F. M. Bass, C. W. King, and E. A. Pessemier (New York: John Wiley, 1969), pp. 251–68; and N. Morgan and J. M. Purnell, "Isolating Openings for New Products in a Multidimensional Space," *Journal of the Market Research Society,* 11 (July 1969), 245–66.

[10]E. A. Pessemier and H. P. Root, "The Dimensions of New Product Planning," *Journal of Marketing,* 37 (January 1973), 10–18; A. D. Shocker and V. Srinivasan, "A Consumer-Based Methodology for the Identification of New Product Ideas," *Management Science,* 20 (February 1974), 921–37; and G. L. Urban, "PERCEPTOR: A Model for Product Positioning," *Management Science,* 21 (April 1975), 858–71.

[11]E. A. Pessemier, *Product Management: Strategy and Organization* (New York: John Wiley, 1977); G. L. Urban and J. R. Hauser, *Design and Marketing of New Products* (Englewood Cliffs, N.J.: Prentice-Hall, 1980); and Yoram Wind, *Product Policy: Concepts, Methods, and Strategies* (Reading, Mass.: Addison-Wesley, 1982).

have taken on a strategic role that involves not only prediction of responses to new-brand introductions but (in some cases) optimizing the design of new products as well. Illustrations include models by Albers and Brockoff; DeSarbo and Rao; Gavish, Horsky, and Srikanth; Hauser and Shugan; Kamakura and Srivastava; and Zufryden.[12] Shocker and Srinivasan provide a useful review of these efforts.[13]

In sum, current research activity in MDS methods, including the increasing use of correspondence analyses for representing nominal data,[14] shows few signs of slowing down. In contrast, industry applications of the methods still seem to be emphasizing the graphical display and diagnostic roles that characterized the motivation for developing these techniques in the first place. The gap between theory and practice appears to be widening.

Limitations and Future Prospects

MDS methods still suffer from a number of limitations. For example, in the case of nonmetric methods all the methods are subject to the possibility of local optima and "degenerate" solutions where the answer is meaningless, even though the goodness-of-fit criterion has been satisfied. Fortunately, researchers are starting to learn that the older (metric) methods often provide good (and inexpensively run) approximations to the nonmetric versions. Simulation studies on the robustness of metric MDS methods have indicated that they generally produce good approximations in all but highly unusual circumstances.[15]

The content side of MDS—dimension interpretation, relating physical changes in products to psychological changes in perceptual maps—poses by far the most difficult problems for future research. However, two trends appear in the offing.

First, methodologists are developing MDS models that provide more flexibility than a straight dimensional interpretation. For example, recent models have coupled the ideas of cluster analysis and MDS into hybrid models of categorical-dimensional structure.

[12]S. Albers and K. Brockhoff, "Optimal Product Attributes in Single Choice Models," *Journal of the Operational Record Society*, 31, pp. 647–55; W. S. DeSarbo and V. R. Rao, "GENFOLD2: A Set of Models and Algorithms for the General Unfolding of Preference/Dominance Data," *Journal of Classification*, 2 (1984), 147–86; B. Gavish, D. Horsky, and K. Srikanth, "An Approach to the Optimal Positioning of a New Product," *Management Science*, 29 (November 1983), 1277–97; J. R. Hauser and S. M. Shugan, "Defensive Marketing Strategies," *Marketing Science*, 2 (Fall 1983), 319–60; W. A. Kamakura and R. K. Srivastava, "An Ideal-Point Probabilistic Choice Model for Heterogeneous Preferences," *Marketing Science*, 5 (Summer 1986), pp. 199–218; and F. S. Zufryden, "ZIPMAP: A Zero-One Integer Programming Model for Market Segmentation and Product Positioning," *Journal of the Operational Research Society*, 30 (1979), 63–70.

[13]A. D. Shocker and V. Srinivasan, "Multiattribute Approaches for Product Concept Evaluation and Generation: A Critical Review," *Journal of Marketing Research*, 16 (1979), 159–80.

[14]D. L. Hoffman and G. R. Franke, "Correspondence Analysis: Graphical Representation of Categorical Data in Marketing Research," *Journal of Marketing Research*, 23 (August 1986), 213–27; and J. D. Carroll, P. E. Green, and C. M. Schaffer, "Interpoint Distance Comparisons in Correspondence Analysis," *Journal of Marketing Research*, 23 (August 1986), 271–80.

[15]For a review of these developments, see P. E. Green, "Marketing Applications of MDS: Assessment and Outlook," *Journal of Marketing*, 39 (January 1975), 24–31. Also, for a more recent review, see L. G. Cooper, "A Review of Multidimensional Scaling in Marketing Research," *Applied Psychological Measurement*, 7, pp. 427–50.

Second, conjoint analysis, to be discussed next, offers high promise for relating changes in the physical (or otherwise controlled) aspects of products to changes in their psychological imagery and evaluation.[16]

FUNDAMENTALS OF CONJOINT ANALYSIS

Conjoint analysis, like MDS, is concerned with the measurement of psychological judgments, such as consumer preferences. However, one of the main distinctions between the two sets of methods is that in conjoint analysis the *stimuli are designed beforehand* according to some type of factorial structure.

In conjoint analysis the objective is to decompose a set of overall responses to factorially designed stimuli so that the utility of each stimulus attribute can be inferred from the respondent's *overall evaluations* of the stimuli.

In *metric* conjoint, the solution technique involves a type of analysis of variance in which the respondent's overall preferences serve as a criterion variable and the predictor variables are represented by the various factorial levels making up each stimulus. (Equivalently, design variables can be viewed as a set of dummy-valued predictors in the context of multiple regression.) In the *nonmetric* version of conjoint, the criterion variable is only *ordinal-scaled*.

Two principal methods for collecting conjoint-analysis data are in use. We illustrate each of these procedures first and then describe how conjoint data are analyzed.

Two-Factor Evaluations

Perhaps the simplest way to obtain tradeoff information for conjoint analysis involves a *two-at-a-time* procedure, as illustrated in Figure 15-8. This figure is drawn from an actual mail questionnaire, used in a survey that was undertaken in the early 1970s, right after the first wave of major gasoline price increases.[17] In particular, interest centered on the relative importance of miles per gallon in the respondents' purchase of their next new car.

Six factors, each described at three "levels," were under study:

- Miles per gallon
- Price
- Maximum speed
- Length
- Roominess
- Country of manufacture

[16]Typically, conjoint analysis deals with preference (and other dominance-type) judgments rather than similarities. However, more recent research has extended the methodology to similarities judgments.

[17]The study was conducted by Rogers National Research, Toledo, Ohio. The information in Figure 15-8 is reproduced with their permission.

Figure 15-8 Two-Factor-at-a-Time Evaluations

What is more important to you?

There are times when we have to give up one thing to get something else. And, since different people have different desires and priorities, the automotive industry wants to know what things are most important to you.

We have a scale that will make it possible for you to tell us your preference in certain circumstances — for example, gas mileage vs. speed. Please read the example below which explains how the scale works — and then

tell us the order of your preference by writing in the numbers from 1 to 9 for each of the six questions that follow the example.

Example:
Warranty vs. price of the car

Procedure:
Simply write the number 1 in the combination that represents your first choice. In one of the remaining blank squares, write

the number 2 for your second choice. Then write the number 3 for your third choice, and so on, from 1 to 9.

Price of Car	Years of warranty		
	3	2	1
$3,000	1		
$3,200			
$3,400			

Price of Car	Years of warranty		
	3	2	1
$3,000	1		
$3,200	2		
$3,400			

Price of Car	Years of warranty		
	3	2	1
$3,000	1	3	
$3,200	2		
$3,400			

Price of Car	Years of warranty		
	3	2	1
$3,000	1	3	6
$3,200	2	5	8
$3,400	4	7	9

Step 1 (Explanation)

You would rather pay the least ($3,000) and get the most (3 years). Your first choice (1) is in the box as shown.

Step 2

Your second choice is that you would rather pay $3,200 and have a 3-year warranty than pay $3,000 and get a 2-year warranty.

Step 3

Your third choice is that you would rather pay $3,000 and have a 2-year warranty than pay $3,400 and get a 3-year warranty.

Sample:

This shows a sample order of preference for all possible combinations. Of course, your preferences could be different.

For each of the following questions, please write in the numbers from 1 to 9 to show your order of preference for your next new car.

Price of Car	Miles per gallon		
	22	18	14
$3,000			
$3,200			
$3,400			

Maximum speed	Miles per gallon		
	22	18	14
80 mph			
70 mph			
60 mph			

Length	Miles per gallon		
	22	18	14
12 feet			
14 feet			
16 feet			

Roominess	Miles per gallon		
	22	18	14
6 passenger			
5 passenger			
4 passenger			

Made in	Miles per gallon		
	22	18	14
Germany			
U.S.			
Japan			

Made in	Price of car		
	$3,000	$3,200	$3,400
Germany			
U.S.			
Japan			

As can be observed from the sample instructions, the respondent is asked to rank the nine combinations of price and warranty (the latter being used only for illustrative purposes) from most to least preferred. We note the (hypothetical) respondent's decision to pay $3,200 for the car, rather than give up a year of warranty. This implies that, for the respondent, the utility decrease associated with a price change from $3,000 to $3,200 is less than the utility decrease associated with a change in warranty from three to two years.

If all pairs of tradeoffs are collected, the respondent must go through $6(5)/2 = 15$ such 3×3 tables. The problem, then, is to find a set of utility numbers—three numbers each for the six factors of Figure 15-8. These utility numbers are often called *part-worths*.

Having found the part-worths, we could then construct a *predicted* set of utilities for the 15 possible two-way tables, by adding the separate part-worths to find the total utility of any two-factor combination. The entries in each of the 15 prediction tables could then be ranked (1 to 9) so as to provide a counterpart set of tables. The objective is to find the separate utility numbers so that the correspondence between actual and predicted rankings is highest when considered across all 15 pairs (actual versus predicted) of tables.

Multiple-Factor Evaluations

While the two-factor-at-a-time approach makes few cognitive demands on the respondent and is simple to follow, it is both time-consuming and tedious. Moreover, it is conducive to respondents' losing their place in the table or developing some stylized pattern, just to get the job done. Most importantly, however, the task is unrealistic; real alternatives do not present themselves for evaluation on a two-factor-at-a-time basis.

The *multiple-factor approach* is illustrated by the two sample cards of Figure 15-9. Eighteen cards, in all, are made up according to a special type of factorial design (to be discussed later). The respondent is then asked to group the 18 cards into three piles (with no need to place an equal number in each pile) that are described as follows:

- Definitely like
- Neither definitely like nor dislike
- Definitely dislike

Following this, the respondent takes the first pile and ranks the cards in it from most to least liked, and similarly so for the second and third piles. By means of this two-step procedure, the full set of 18 cards is eventually ranked from most liked to least liked.

Figure 15-9   Multiple-factor Evaluations (Sample Profiles)

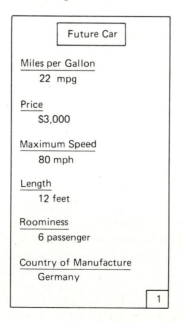
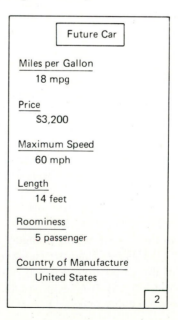

Again, the analytical objective is to find a set of part-worths for the separate factor levels so that, when these are appropriately added, one can find a total utility for each combination. The part-worths are chosen so as to produce the highest possible correspondence between the derived ranking and the original ranking of the 18 cards. While the two-factor-at-a-time and the multiple-factor approaches, as just described, assumed only ranking-type data, one could just as readily ask the respondent to state his or her preferences on (say) an 11-point, equal-interval ratings scale, ranging from like most to like least. Moreover, in the multiple-factor approach, a 0 to 100 rating scale, representing likelihood of purchase, could be used.

As may be surmised, the multiple-factor evaluative approach makes greater cognitive demands on the respondent, since the full set of factors appears each time. In practice, if more than six or seven factors are involved, this approach is modified to handle specific *subsets* of interlinked factors across two or more evaluation tasks.

Metric Versus Nonmetric Conjoint Analysis

Like MDS methods, conjoint analysis can be performed either metrically (via dummy-variable regression in which the criterion variable is assumed to be at least interval-scaled) or nonmetrically (by techniques, such as LINMAP or MONANOVA, where the criterion variable is assumed to be only ordinal-scaled).[18]

Moreover, like MDS, the initial impetus to conjoint analysis entailed the extensive use of nonmetric algorithms. Currently, however, ordinary dummy-variable regression is the most popular procedure, particularly in industry applications. The criterion variable is usually some type of preference or likelihood-of-purchase rating.

AN EXAMPLE OF METRIC CONJOINT ANALYSIS

The typical sequence that one goes through in implementing a conjoint study involves four steps:

1. Using one of a variety of data collection procedures sufficient data are obtained at the individual respondent level to estimate the part-worths of each person's utility function.
2. The matrix of respondent by attribute-level part-worths may then be related to other subject background data in an effort to identify possible market segments based on similarities in part-worth functions.
3. The researcher's client then proposes a set of product configurations that represent feasible competitive offerings. These products profiles are entered into a consumer choice simulator, along with the earlier computed individual utility functions.

---

[18]For a more extensive description of conjoint algorithms, see P. E. Green and V. Srinivasan's review paper, "Conjoint Analysis in Consumer Research: Issues and Outlook," *Journal of Consumer Research,* 5 (September 1978), 102–23.

4. While choice simulators differ, in the simplest case each respondent's individual part-worth function is used to compute the utility for each of the competing profiles. The respondent is then assumed to choose that profile with the highest utility (i.e., the choice process is deterministic).

Computation of the utilities is an important aspect of the whole procedure. We now turn to a simple example of how part-worths are computed.

A Numerical Example

Consider a situation in which a manufacturer of steel-belted replacement tires is interested in measuring consumers' tradeoffs among the following attributes:

- Brand
  - Sears
  - Goodyear
  - Goodrich
- Tread Life
  - 30,000 miles
  - 40,000 miles
  - 50,000 miles
- Price
  - $50/tire
  - $60/tire
  - $70/tire
- Sidewall
  - Black
  - White

Potential replacement tire purchasers are recruited and presented with the 18 alternatives shown in Figure 15-10. Each respondent is asked to rate each of the alternatives on a 0–10 scale, where 0 indicates absolutely no interest in purchasing and 10 indicates extremely high interest in purchasing.

Illustratively, Figure 15-10 shows the 18 evaluations made by one respondent. Although a total of $3 \times 3 \times 3 \times 2 = 54$ combinations of attribute levels could be made up, the respondent needs to evaluate only 18 of these. However, this specific set of 18 should be selected in a particular way, as will be noted later.

Figure 15-11 shows graphs of the implied values for each of the attribute levels; these can be obtained from an ordinary multiple regression program using dummy-variable coding. All one needs to do to estimate the respondent's original evaluations is to add each separate value (the regression coefficient) for each component of each described combination. (The regression's intercept term may be added in later if there is interest in estimating the absolute level of purchase interest.) For example, to obtain the respondent's estimated evaluation of card 1, one reads off the part-worths:

Value for Sears	= 2.4
Value for 30,000 miles	= 0
"Value" for $50 (i.e., a $20 cost saving)	= 1.7
Value for white sidewall	= 1.2
	5.3

In this instance we obtain an almost perfect prediction of the person's overall response to card 1. Similarly, we can find the estimated total evaluations for the other 17 options

Figure 15-10   Product Descriptions for Conjoint Analysis (Automotive Tires)

Card 1

<u>Brand</u>
    SEARS
<u>Tread Mileage</u>
    30,000 miles
<u>Price</u>
    $50
<u>Sidewall</u>
    White

Respondent's Rating . . . 5.2

Card 2

<u>Brand</u>
    SEARS
<u>Tread Mileage</u>
    40,000 miles
<u>Price</u>
    $60
<u>Sidewall</u>
    White

Respondent's Rating . . . 7.3

Card 3

<u>Brand</u>
    SEARS
<u>Tread Mileage</u>
    50,000 miles
<u>Price</u>
    $70
<u>Sidewall</u>
    Black

Respondent's Rating . . . 5.7

Card 4

<u>Brand</u>
    GOODYEAR
<u>Tread Mileage</u>
    30,000 miles
<u>Price</u>
    $60
<u>Sidewall</u>
    Black

Respondent's Rating . . . 4.8

Card 5

<u>Brand</u>
    GOODYEAR
<u>Tread Mileage</u>
    40,000 miles
<u>Price</u>
    $70
<u>Sidewall</u>
    White

Respondent's Rating . . . 7.2

Card 6

<u>Brand</u>
    GOODYEAR
<u>Tread Mileage</u>
    50,000 miles
<u>Price</u>
    $50
<u>Sidewall</u>
    White

Respondent's Rating . . . 9.3

Card 7

<u>Brand</u>
    GOODRICH
<u>Tread Mileage</u>
    30,000 miles
<u>Price</u>
    $70
<u>Sidewall</u>
    White

Respondent's Rating . . . 0.8

Card 8

<u>Brand</u>
    GOODRICH
<u>Tread Mileage</u>
    40,000 miles
<u>Price</u>
    $50
<u>Sidewall</u>
    Black

Respondent's Rating . . . 3.2

Card 9

<u>Brand</u>
    GOODRICH
<u>Tread Mileage</u>
    50,000 miles
<u>Price</u>
    $60
<u>Sidewall</u>
    White

Respondent's Rating . . . 6.4

Card 10

<u>Brand</u>
    SEARS
<u>Tread Mileage</u>
    30,000 miles
<u>Price</u>
    $70
<u>Sidewall</u>
    Black

Respondent's Rating . . . 2.2

Card 11

<u>Brand</u>
    SEARS
<u>Tread Mileage</u>
    40,000 miles
<u>Price</u>
    $50
<u>Sidewall</u>
    White

Respondent's Rating . . . 8.1

Card 12

<u>Brand</u>
    SEARS
<u>Tread Mileage</u>
    50,000 miles
<u>Price</u>
    $60
<u>Sidewall</u>
    White

Respondent's Rating . . . 8.3

Figure 15-10   Product Descriptions for Conjoint Analysis (Automotive Tires) (*Continued*)

Card 13	Card 14	Card 15
Brand	Brand	Brand
GOODYEAR	GOODYEAR	GOODYEAR
Tread Mileage	Tread Mileage	Tread Mileage
30,000 miles	40,000 miles	50,000 miles
Price	Price	Price
$50	$60	$70
Sidewall	Sidewall	Sidewall
White	Black	White

Respondent's Rating... 6.3   Respondent's Rating... 7.4   Respondent's Rating ... 7.3

Card 16	Card 17	Card 18
Brand	Brand	Brand
GOODRICH	GOODRICH	GOODRICH
Tread Mileage	Tread Mileage	Tread Mileage
30,000 miles	40,000 miles	50,000 miles
Price	Price	Price
$60	$70	$50
Sidewall	Sidewall	Sidewall
White	White	Black

Respondent's Rating... 2.2   Respondent's Rating... 4.3   Respondent's Rating... 5.7

and compare them with the respondent's original evaluations. The regression technique guarantees that the (squared) prediction error between estimated and actual response will be minimized.

The information in Figure 15-11 also permits the researcher to find estimated evaluations for *all* combinations, including the $54 - 18 = 36$ options never shown to the respondent. Moreover, all respondent's separate part-worth functions (as illustrated for one person in Figure 15-11) can be compared in order to see if various types of respondents (e.g., high-versus low-income respondents) differ in their separate attribute evaluations.

In short, while the respondent evaluates complete bundles of attributes the technique solves for a set of part-worths—one for each attribute level—that are imputed from the *overall* tradeoffs. These part-worths can then be combined in various ways to estimate the evaluation that a respondent would give to *any* combination of interest. It is this high leverage between the options that are actually evaluated and those that can be evaluated (after the analysis) that makes conjoint analysis a useful tool.

Reliability and Validity Checks

In carrying out a conjoint analysis it is useful to include the following ancillary analyses: (1) test–retest reliability, (2) a comparison of actual utilities with those of random respondents, and (3) an internal validity check on model-based utilities.

**Figure 15-11   Part-Worth Functions Obtained from Conjoint Analysis
(Hypothetical Data)**

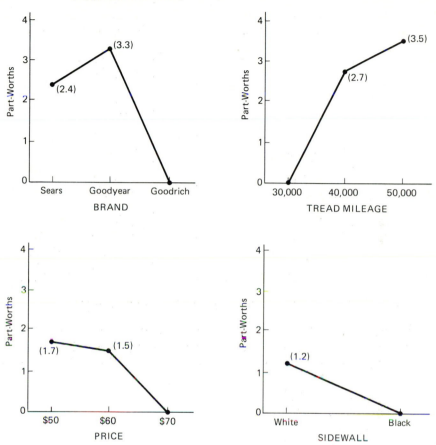

The test–retest reliability can be conducted by including a few replicate judgments (drawn from the original set of 18) at a later stage in the interview. The purpose here is to see if the judgments are highly enough correlated, on a test–retest basis, to justify the analysis of the respondent's data.

Random-respondent utilities are obtained by running a sample of pseudosubjects. The pseudosubjects' input data consist of random ratings or rankings, as the case may be. As the sample size increases we would expect, on average, *equal utilities* within each set of factor levels. However, any specific pseudosubject would depart from this expected value through sampling variability alone. By analyzing a sample of 100 or so pseudo-subjects, the researcher can develop a crude type of confidence interval around each set of averaged part-worths with which to compare real respondents' results.

The internal-validity check can be carried out by collecting a few new evaluations (drawn randomly from the 36 stimulus combinations not utilized in Figure 15-10). These constitute a hold-out sample. Their rank order is to be predicted by the part-worths developed from the calibration sample of 18 combinations.

OTHER ASPECTS OF CONJOINT ANALYSIS

The theoretical development of conjoint analysis in the behavioral sciences is of recent origin.[19] Its adaptation to marketing[20] is still going on. Even so, interest in the topic has grown rather dramatically. Some marketing consultants have developed considerable expertise and have made significant contributions to the field.[21] Commercial applications of conjoint analysis have entailed additional features of interest, some of which are briefly covered here.

Experimental Design

As mentioned earlier, if multiple-factor evaluations are used, highly fractionated factorial designs are pretty much a necessity if the researcher wishes to keep the stimulus set down to some reasonable number. *Orthogonal arrays* represent a special type of fractional factorial design that allows orthogonal estimation of all main effects (the type of model assumed in additive utility formulations) with the smallest possible number of combinations.

Orthogonal arrays are available for virtually any number of factors and levels within factor that the marketing researcher might need. As long as two-factor and higher-order interactions can be assumed to be negligible, orthogonal arrays represent the most efficient class of fractional factorial design that is available. Introduction to orthogonal arrays, and to other useful designs in the context of conjoint analysis, can be found elsewhere.[22]

Use of Visual Aids

Another problem in the application of conjoint measurement is the pragmatic one of getting across to the respondent what may be fairly complex concepts. Verbal descriptions of the type covered in Figure 15-8 are not only difficult for the respondent to assimilate but permit unwanted perceptual differences to intrude. For example, two respondents may have quite different perceptions of the car-length and car-roominess verbalizations.

Wherever possible, *visual props* can help in transmitting complex information more easily and uniformly than verbal description. As an illustration of the value of visual props, mention can be made of a study involving styling designs for future compact cars.

[19] R. D. Luce and J. W. Tukey, "Simultaneous Conjoint Measurement: A New Type of Fundamental Measurement," *Journal of Mathematical Psychology*, 1 (February 1964), 1–27.

[20] P. E. Green and V. R. Rao, "Conjoint Measurement for Quantifying Judgmental Data," *Journal of Marketing Research*, 8 (August 1971), 355–63.

[21] R. M. Johnson, "Tradeoff Analysis of Consumer Values," *Journal of Marketing Research*, 11 (May 1974), 121–27.

[22] P. E. Green, "On the Design of Choice Experiments Involving Multifactor Alternatives," *Journal of Consumer Research*, 1 (September 1974), 61–68.

In the course of preparing the questionnaire, rather complex experimental factors such as

- Overall size and interior layout
- Trunk size and fuel-tank capacity
- Exterior/interior width
- Interior spaciousness/visibility

had to be considered. To provide quick and uniform treatment of these style factors, visual props were prepared, as illustrated for two of the factors in Figure 15-12. (These can be projected on screens in full view of the respondents during the interview or made part of the questionnaire itself.)

Visual props work particularly well for the multiple-factor approach, since a relatively large amount of information can be communicated realistically and quickly by this means.

Other Models

So far our discussion has centered on the most widely applied conjoint model—a main-effects model using rankings or ratings. Other models, dealing with different types of data collection, criterion variables, or composition rules, are available.

For example, cases can arise in which the respondent is asked to compare each stimulus, in turn, with a standard one and indicate whether the test stimulus is liked better (or worse) than the standard. Following this, the respondent is asked to indicate his or her *intensity* of, say, liking, on a 4-point scale: like very much more, like much more, like somewhat more, like slightly more.

In other cases, the respondent may simply be asked to group the stimuli into a set of unordered classes: the product is appropriate for adult men, appropriate for adult women, appropriate for teenagers, and so on. In this case a special type of conjoint analysis, categorical conjoint measurement, can be called upon.[23]

Models that permit some or all two-factor interactions to be measured (as well as all main effects) have also been developed. These models again make use of various types of fractional factorial designs; specialized computer programs have been designed to implement them.[24] In short, the users of conjoint analysis currently have a highly flexible set of models and data collection procedures at their disposal.

Strategic Aspects

The output of conjoint analysis is frequently employed in additional analyses. Since most studies collect full sets of data at the individual respondent level, *individual utility*

---

[23]J. D. Carroll, "Categorical Conjoint Measurement," in *Multiattribute Decisions in Marketing,* ed. P. E. Green and Yoram Wind (Hinsdale, Ill.: Dryden Press, 1973), pp. 339–48.

[24]F. J. Carmone and P. E. Green, "Model Misspecification in Multiattribute Parameter Estimation," *Journal of Marketing Research,* 18 (February 1981), 87–93.

functions and importance weights can be computed. This fosters two additional types of analyses: (1) market segmentation and (2) strategic simulation of new factor-level combinations. Frequently, both kinds of analyses are carried out in the same study.

In segmentation studies, the respondents are usually clustered in terms of either their commonality of utility functions or their commonality of importance weights. Having formed the segments in one of these ways, the analyst can then determine how the segments

Figure 15–12   Illustrations of Visual Props Used in Conjoint Analysis

OVERALL SIZE/INTERIOR LAYOUT

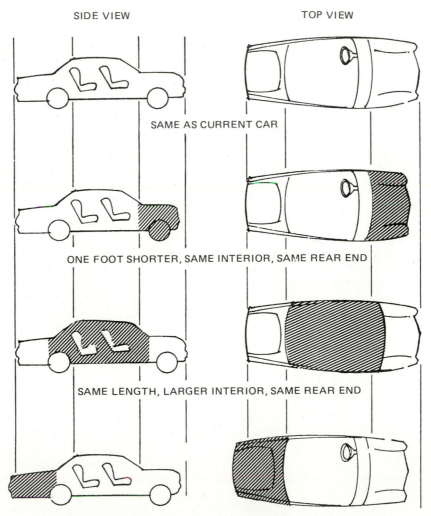

SIDE VIEW   TOP VIEW

SAME AS CURRENT CAR

ONE FOOT SHORTER, SAME INTERIOR, SAME REAR END

SAME LENGTH, LARGER INTERIOR, SAME REAR END

SAME LENGTH, SAME INTERIOR, LARGER TRUNK/FUEL TANK

Figure 15-12   (*Continued*)

EXTERIOR/INTERIOR WIDTH

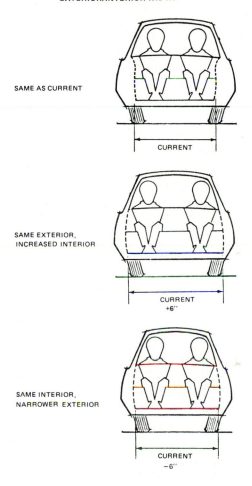

SAME AS CURRENT

CURRENT

SAME EXTERIOR,
INCREASED INTERIOR

CURRENT
+6''

SAME INTERIOR,
NARROWER EXTERIOR

CURRENT
−6''

differ with regard to other background data—product-class usage, brand-selection behavior, demographics, and so on.

Strategic simulations are also relatively easy to construct from conjoint-analysis
data by the simple device of including each individual respondent's utility function in a
computerized-choice model. Various combinations of factor levels can then be tried out
to see what their share of choices would be under different assumptions regarding competitive offerings and total-market demand.

The simulators can employ a variety of consumer-choice procedures, ranging from
having each consumer simply select the alternative with the highest utility to more
elaborate probability-of-choice rules where probability is related to utility differences in
the set of alternatives under evaluation.

APPLICATIONS OF CONJOINT ANALYSIS

Despite its recent development, conjoint analysis has already been applied to a wide variety of problems in product design, price elasticity of demand, transportation service design, and the like. Table 15-1 shows a representative list of applications. As can be noted, areas of application cover the gamut—products and services, as well as consumer, industrial, and institutional markets.

Perhaps the applications areas most conducive to conjoint analysis are those in which the product or service involves a relatively high resource commitment and tends to be "analyzable" by the purchaser (e.g., banking or insurance services, industrial products). Some idea of the range of possibilities may be gained from the capsule applications that follow.

TABLE 15-1   Sample List of Conjoint Applications

CONSUMER NONDURABLES

1. Bar soaps
2. Hair shampoos
3. Carpet cleaners
4. Synthetic-fiber garments
5. Gasoline pricing
6. Panty hose
7. Lawn chemicals

OTHER PRODUCTS

1. Automotive styling
2. Automobile and truck tires
3. Car batteries
4. Ethical drugs
5. Toaster/ovens
6. Cameras
7. Apartment design

FINANCIAL SERVICES

1. Branch bank services
2. Auto insurance policies
3. Health insurance policies
4. Credit card features
5. Consumer discount cards
6. Auto retailing facilities
7. High-tech maintenance service

OTHER SERVICES

1. Car rental agencies
2. Telephone services and pricing
3. Employment agencies
4. Information-retrieval services
5. Medical laboratories
6. Hotel design

INDUSTRIAL GOODS

1. Copying machines
2. Printing equipment
3. Facsimile transmission
4. Data transmission
5. Portable computer terminals
6. Personal computer design

TRANSPORTATION

1. Domestic airlines
2. Transcontinental airlines
3. Passenger train operations
4. Freight train operations
5. International Air Transportation Association
6. Electric car design

Designing Bar Soaps

In a consumer products study researchers related the psychological imagery of physical characteristics of actual bars of soap to end-use appropriateness; this study was conducted for the laboratory and marketing personnel of a diversified soap manufacturer.

Although the designing of a bar of soap—by varying weight, size, shape, color, fragrance type and intensity, surface feel, and so on—may seem like a mundane exercise, the fact remains that a cleverly positioned bar soap (for example, Irish Spring) can rapidly become a multimillion-dollar enterprise. Still, the extent of knowledge about the importance of such imagery is woefully meager.

The researchers formulated actual bars of soap in which color, type of fragrance, and intensity of fragrance were constructed according to a factorial design. All the other characteristics of the soap were held constant.

Respondents examined the soaps and assigned each bar to the end use that they felt best matched its characteristics: moisturing facial soap, deep-cleaning soap for oily skin, woman's deodorant soap, or man's deodorant soap. The data were then analyzed by conjoint analysis, leading to a set of psychophysical functions for each of the characteristics.

The study showed that type of fragrance was the most important physical variable contributing to end-use appropriateness. Rather surprisingly, the type of fragrance (medicinal) and color (blue) that appeared best suited for a man's deodorant soap were also found to be best for the deep-cleaning soap, even though deep-cleaning soap had previously been classed for marketing purposes as a facial soap in which floral fragrances predominated. On the other hand, fragrance intensity played a relatively minor role as a consumer cue for distinguishing among different end uses.

In brief, this study illustrated the feasibility of translating changes in various physical variables into changes in psychological variables. Eventually, more-detailed knowledge of these psychological transformations could enable a laboratory technician to *synthesize color, fragrance, shape, and so forth to obtain soaps that conjure up almost any desired imagery*. Moreover, in such other product classes as beers, coffees, and soft drinks it appears possible to develop a psychophysics of taste in which such elusive verbal descriptions as "full-bodied" and "robust" are given operational meaning in terms of variations in physical or chemical characteristics.

New Concept Descriptions

In many product classes, such as automobiles, houses, office machines, and computers, the possible design factors are myriad and expensive to vary physically for evaluation by the buying public. In cases such as these, the researcher usually resorts to verbalized descriptions of the principal factors of interest.

In the Rogers study (see Figure 15-8) it was found that consumer evaluations of attributes were highly associated with the type of car currently owned and the type of car desired in the future. Not surprisingly, gas mileage and country of manufacture were highly important factors in respondent evaluations of car profiles. Somewhat surprising, however, was the fact that even large-car owners (and those contemplating the purchase of a large car) were more concerned with gas economy than owners of that type of car had been historically. Thus, while they fully expected to get fewer miles per gallon than they could in compact cars, they felt quite strongly that the car should be economical compared with others in its size class.

Airline Services

One of the most interesting application areas for conjoint analysis is in the transportation industry, particularly airlines and other forms of passenger travel, where the service aspect is important to consumer choice.

As a case in point, a large-scale study of consumer evaluations of airline services was conducted in which consumer utilities were developed for some 25 different service factors such as on-ground services, in-flight services, decor of cabins and seats, scheduling, routing, and price. Moreover, each utility function was developed on a route (city-pair) and purpose-of-trip basis.

As might be expected, the utility function for each of the various types of airline service differed according to the length and purpose of the flight. However, in addition to obtaining consumers' evaluations of service profiles, the researchers also obtained information concerning their *perceptions* of each airline (that is, for the ones that they were familiar with) on each of the service factors for which the consumers were given a choice.

These two major pieces of information provided the principal basis for developing a simulation of airline services over all major traffic routes. The purposes of the simulation was to estimate the effect on share of choices that a change in the service configuration of the sponsor's services would have, route by route, if competitors did not follow suit. Later, the sponsor used the simulator to examine the effect of assumed retaliatory actions by its competitors. A procedure was also designed to update the model's parameters periodically by the collection of new field data.

Each new service configuration was evaluated against a base-period configuration. In addition, the simulator showed which competing airlines would lose business and which ones would gain business under various changes in perceived service levels. Thus, in addition to single, ad hoc studies, conjoint analysis can be used in the ongoing monitoring (via simulation) of consumer imagery and evaluations over time.

Recent Developments

Conjoint analysis has become a highly popular technique in a relatively short time. In 1982 a survey of business firms' use of conjoint analysis suggested that approximately 1,000 conjoint studies had been implemented subsequent to its introduction to marketing.[25] Since that time its popularity appears to have been sustained. With the recent introduction

---

[25]P. Cattin and D. R. Wittink, "Commercial Use of Conjoint Analysis: A Survey," *Journal of Marketing*, 46 (Summer 1982), 44–53.

of new software packages for the personal computer, conjoint methodology is now accessible to almost any interested user.[26]

New developments in data collection and analysis[27] and computer programs for easily finding orthogonal main effects plans[28] have been introduced. Conjoint methodology has also been extended to encompass use occasion and situation dependence in a series of dual conjoint designs, called componential segmentation.[29]

Perhaps the most interesting extension of the methodology, however, is the recent application of conjoint to the design of "optimal" products and product lines.[30] Thus, it now appears feasible to extend conjoint beyond the simulation stage (where one finds the "best" of a limited set of options) to encompass the identification of the best product (or line) over the full set of possibilities. These may number in the hundreds of thousands or even the millions. In sum, conjoint methodology, like MDS, appears to be moving into the product design optimization arena. Time will tell which technique receives the greater degree of industry application. Indeed, it may be that combining the analytics of conjoint with the display power of MDS offers the most useful approach from a pragmatic managerial viewpoint.

Still, conjoint analysis, like MDS, has a number of limitations. For example, the approach assumes that the important attributes of a product or service can all be identified and that consumers behave as though tradeoffs are being considered. In some products where imagery is quite important, consumers may not evaluate a product analytically, or, even if they do, the tradeoff model may be only a gross approximation to the actual decision rules that are employed.

Studies are needed on such questions as how many different factors can be allowed to vary in the multiple-factor data collection procedure and how this number depends on the way in which the information is communicated. Other studies are needed on the statistical robustness of the nonmetric models to errorful data as well as studies of how closely metric (ANOVA) models can approximate the more extensive nonmetric models.

In short, MDS and conjoint are still maturing—both as techniques that provide

---

[26]See "Adaptive Conjoint Analysis," Sawtooth Software, Ketchum, Idaho; and "Conjoint Analyzer," Bretton-Clark, 516 Fifth Avenue, New York, N.Y.

[27]P. E. Green, "Hybrid Models for Conjoint Analysis: An Expository Review," *Journal of Marketing Research,* 21 (May 1984), 155–59; P. Cattin, A. E. Gelfand, and J. Danes, "A Simple Bayesian Procedure for Estimation in a Conjoint Mode," *Journal of Marketing Research,* 20 (February 1983), 29–35; and N. K. Malhotra, "An Approach to the Measurement of Consumer Preferences Using Limited Information," *Journal of Marketing Research,* 23 (February 1986), 33–40.

[28]"Conjoint Designer," Bretton-Clark.

[29]See P. E. Green, J. D. Carroll, and F. J. Carmone, "Design Considerations in Attitude Measurement," in *Attitude Research Moves Ahead,* ed. Y. Wind and M. G. Greenberg (Chicago: American Marketing Association, 1977); and P. E. Green and W. S. DeSarbo, "Componential Segmentation in the Analysis of Consumer Trade-offs," *Journal of Marketing,* 43 (Fall 1979).

[30]F. S. Zufryden, "A Conjoint Measurement-Based Approach for Optimal New Product Design and Market Segmentation," in *Analytic Approaches to Product and Market Planning,* ed. A. D. Shocker (Cambridge, Mass.: Marketing Science Institute, 1977), pp. 100–14; P. E. Green, J. D. Carroll, and S. M. Goldberg, "A General Approach to Product Design Optimization via Conjoint Analysis," *Journal of Marketing,* 45 (Summer 1981), 17–37; P. E. Green and A. M. Krieger, "Models and Heuristics for Product Line Selection," *Marketing Science,* 4 (Winter 1985); and R. Kohli and R. Krishnamerti, "A Graph Theoretic Approach to Optimal Product Design," Graduate School of Business, University of Pittsburgh, 1986.

intellectual stimulation and as practical tools for product positioning, segmentation, and strategic planning.

SUMMARY

This chapter focused on two multivariate techniques that are special-purpose in nature: (1) MDS and (2) conjoint analysis. Both methods deal with the measurement of human judgments, and both are capable of handling data that are only of rank-order quality.

MDS methods are designed for portraying subjective similarities or preferences as points (or vectors) in some multidimensional space. Psychological distance is given a physical distance representation. In this part of the chapter we discussed metric and nonmetric MDS methods and ideal-point and vector preference models. A variety of applications were described to give the reader some idea of the scope of the methodology.

Conjoint analysis was described along similar lines. We first discussed the primary ways of collecting tradeoff data and then showed how such data are analyzed via a kind of monotonic analysis of variance. The importance of fractional factorial designs was discussed, as well as other practical problems in the implementation of conjoint analysis.

We next turned to some illustrative applications of conjoint analysis, including the design of new products and services. The chapter concluded with a brief description of future developments that could serve to increase the flexibility of the methodology.

ASSIGNMENT MATERIAL

1. Collect similarities data from people you know regarding a stimulus set of your choice—e.g., toothpaste brands, professors, automobiles, actors, vacation places, etc.
   a. Using an MDS program of your choice, scale the group data.
   b. Randomly divide your sample of respondents (make sure you have enough to do this) and scale the two subgroups' data separately. How do these subgroup scalings compare with the total group?
   c. Cluster-analyze the respondents by treating the similarities as profile data. Then separately scale the cluster averages. How do your configurations compare across clusters?

2. Describe three problems in marketing research (not mentioned in the chapter) that you feel might be amenable to MDS, and discuss how you would use MDS in each situation.

3. Describe three problems in marketing research (not mentioned in the chapter) that you feel might be amenable to conjoint analysis, and discuss how you would use conjoint analysis in each situation.

4. What types of consumer products do you think would *not* be amenable to conjoint analysis?

5. Suppose that you were asked to develop a set of factors for a prospective conjoint analysis of home mortgage types. What factors, and levels within each factor, can you suggest? Which approach—tradeoff or full profile—would you use? Defend your choice.

6. For the use of conjoint analysis, what conditions and situations dictate when tradeoff is the preferred approach and when full profile is preferred? Are there conditions in which only one approach can be used, since the other simply will not work?

CASES FOR PART IV

IV-1

ALVIN CONTROL SYSTEMS

Alvin Control Systems is a company that specializes in the production and sale of various types of control systems used by business firms and other organizations. The company has developed a new product which it expects to introduce on the market in about six months. The product is a type of fuel control system.

The fuel control system is a monitoring device that acts as a fuel-dispensing system for automotive vehicles. These systems accurately record the amount of fuel a vehicle consumes as well as other data necessary for operators of multiple vehicles (fleet managers). Such systems take into account such variables as engine tune, driver practices, and vehicle aerodynamic properties, that need to be controlled when comparing efficiencies of alternative vehicles.

The company is planning to market the monitoring device through a franchised distribution system. Prior to product introduction the company has decided that it needs some additional information on three major issues: (1) how to identify potential franchisees, (2) how to develop a training program for franchisees, and (3) how to develop a promotional campaign for the product. The first issue is being tackled by a consultant hired by the company for that purpose, and the third issue by the company's advertising agency.

Of concern now is developing a sales training program. The company realizes that it needs some relevant information about the potential market, including the characteristics of companies that have fleets of vehicles, the nature and characteristics of such fleets, and the characteristics of fleet managers. JB Associates, a full-service marketing research firm, has been hired to conduct a study having the following major objectives: (1) develop a profile of fleet control managers, (2) identify characteristics that determine the current "use status" of fuel-dispensing systems of fleets, and (3) identify the importance of various features in the purchase decision of fuel-dispensing systems.

The project director assigned by JB has decided that the best strategy to follow, given time and budget constraints, is to conduct a mail survey of fleet control managers in the western United States. The client itself is located in one of the states. The general approach to data collection will involve a four-contact system: preliminary notification, original mailing of questionnaire, a reminder post card sent one week after the first-wave mailing, and a follow-up second mailing of the questionnaire to those who had not responded sent one week after the reminder. All the usual mail survey techniques will be used, including cover letters, postage-paid return envelopes, monetary inducement, and so on. If the overall response rate is less than 55%, a telephone interview nonresponse validation will be done.

The sample used for the study will be a random sample of all registered motor vehicle fleets derived from lists available from the states' public utility (or similar type) agencies. The sample will be stratified on the basis of three size types, and sampling will be proportionate to the number of fleet within each size group. The total original sample size has been determined to be 849 fleets.

As shown in the following questionnaire, various question formats are to be used.

1. Develop a coding manual for the questionnaire that can be used for entering the data in a computer file.
2. Discuss alternatives for analyzing the data that will be obtained, given the objectives of the study and management intended use of the study results.

Questionnaire

This questionnaire is concerned with two areas:

1. COMPANY POLICY related to fuel consumption, and
2. Responsibilities of FLEET CONTROL MANAGERS.

Below are examples of questions concerning both areas. The time taken to respond to these and the remaining questions is greatly appreciated.

Q-1 In *your* opinion, which of the following statements most accurately reflects the impact that rising fuel costs have on your company's total operational costs? (Please circle number of your opinion.)

1 Increasing fuel costs have a greater impact on total operational costs than those related to other areas.

2 Increasing costs in all areas have the same impact on the total operational costs.

3 Increasing costs in other areas have a greater impact on total operational costs than increasing fuel costs.

Q-2 There are two ways of decreasing the costs your company has in the area of fuel: (1) REDUCING the number of vehicles in the fleet and the number of miles traveled per vehicle, or (2) INCREASING the EFFI-CIENCY of vehicles and controlling the amount of fuel consumed. Which option most accurately reflects your company's policy? (Please circle number of your opinion.)

1 Depend entirely on reduction

2 Depend mostly on reduction

3 Depend equally on reduction and increasing efficiency

4 Depend mostly on increasing efficiency

5 Depend entirely on reduction

Company Policy

The following statements pertain to areas such as fuel monitoring, staff responsibilities, and use of computerized systems. For each statement, CIRCLE the response that most accurately reflects the opinions of your company.

Q-3

A Current fuel-dispensing systems are not cost-effective.   AGREE DISAGREE

B Vehicle maintenance is the only way to conserve fuel.   AGREE DISAGREE

C Fleet control managers have the ultimate choice of the system by which fuel consumption is monitored and recorded.   AGREE DISAGREE

D To maintain accurate records, computerized systems must be developed in the areas of fuel consumption and vehicle maintenance.   AGREE DISAGREE

E In comparison, our fleet is more energy conscious than most fleets of comparable size.   AGREE DISAGREE

F The cost of fuel-dispensing systems is minimal compared with the amount saved in fuel consumption.   AGREE DISAGREE

Current Practices

Below is a list of ways in which fuel consumption can be reduced. For each item, please circle the response that most accurately reflects the practices of your company.

Q-4

	EXISTED/ PRACTICED PRIOR TO MY BECOMING FLEET CONTROL MANAGER	ADDED/ PRACTICED SINCE MY BECOMING FLEET CONTROL MANAGER	PLANNING TO ADD/ PRACTICE	DOESN'T EXIST AND NOT PLANNING TO ADD/ PRACTICE	DOESN'T APPLY TO COMPANY'S FLEET
A Devices to decrease aerodynamic drag	Existed	Added	Plan	No	NA
B Devices to control/ monitor vehicle speed	Existed	Added	Plan	No	NA

		Existed/ Practiced Prior to My Becoming Fleet Control Manager	Added/ Practiced Since My Becoming Fleet Control Manager	Planning to Add/ Practice	Doesn't Exist and Not Planning to add/ Practice	Doesn't Apply to Company's Fleet
C	Vehicle maintenance performed to increase efficiency	Existed	Added	Plan	No	NA
D	Conscious driving practices taught and/ or rewarded	Existed	Added	Plan	No	NA
E	Operational techniques undertaken to increase efficiency	Existed	Added	Plan	No	NA
F	Fuel-dispensing system	Existed	Added	Plan	No	NA

If you checked: EXISTED/PRACTICED PRIOR TO or ADDED/PRACTICED SINCE, please complete both sides of the YELLOW PAGE (Q7–10) and then the rest of the WHITE PAGES (Q18–28) in this questionnaire.

If you checked: PLANNING TO ADD/PRACTICE, please complete both sides of the BLUE PAGE (Q11–17) and then the rest of the WHITE PAGES in this questionnaire.

If you checked: NOT PLANNING TO ADD/PRACTICE, please complete the following question and then complete the rest of the questionnaire (WHITE PAGES).

Q-5   A fuel-dispensing system has not been installed, nor are plans being made to add a fuel-dispensing system. (Please circle number of your opinion.)

1 Our fleet is too small to realize the benefits provided by a fuel-dispensing system.

2 Existing systems cannot be easily tailored to meet our company's needs.

3 The cost of such systems outweighs the benefits.

4 There is no need for such systems; the current method of controlling fuel adequately meets our fleet's needs.

5 I have not heard of fuel-dispensing systems.

This section is to be completed *ONLY* if your fleet is CURRENTLY USING a fuel-dispensing system.

Q-6 For each of the features/attributes listed below, please circle your opinion for each item.

		EXTREMELY SATISFIED	SATISFIED	DISSATISFIED	EXTREMELY DISSATISFIED	DOESN'T APPLY TO FLEET
A	Overall accuracy of data	ES	S	D	ED	NA
B	Convenience of using system	ES	S	D	ED	NA
C	Records all data needed for fleet management	ES	S	D	ED	NA
D	Effectiveness of monitoring fuel consumed:					
	(a) By individual vehicle	ES	S	D	ED	NA
	(b) By individual driver	ES	S	D	ED	NA
E	Time saved in recording data as compared with previous method	ES	S	D	ED	NA
F	Cost efficiency	ES	S	D	ED	NA
G	System's capability of expanding	ES	S	D	ED	NA
H	Speed of data output	ES	S	D	ED	NA
I	Ease of entering data	ES	S	D	ED	NA

Q-7 System currently using (name) _____

Q-8 Year system was added _____

Q-9 How knowledgeable do you perceive *yourself* to be in the area of fuel-dispensing systems? (Please circle number of your opinion.)

1 Extremely knowledgeable

2 Somewhat knowledgeable

3 Slightly knowledgeable

4 Not at all knowledgeable

Q-10 If another fleet control manager were to ask your opinion of the system that you are currently using, what would you identify as

A The three most beneficial features/attributes (please list in order of importance, with 1 being the most important):

1 _____

2 _____

3 _____

B The two greatest limitations of the system:

1 _____

2 _____

This section is to be completed *only* if your company is CONTEMPLATING ADDING a Fuel-Dispensing System.

Q-11 Below is a list of features/attributes that a fuel-dispensing system may have. Please indicate how important each feature/attribute is in the final decision to purchase a fuel-dispensing system

		EXTREMELY IMPORTANT	IMPORTANT	SLIGHTLY IMPORTANT	NOT IMPORTANT	DOES NOT APPLY
A	Flexibility in programming	EI	I	SI	NI	NA
B	Ease of using system	EI	I	SI	NI	NA
C	Monitoring of amount of fuel:					
	(a) By driver	EI	I	SI	NI	NA
	(b) By vehicle	EI	I	SI	NI	NA
D	Decrease in time needed to record data	EI	I	SI	NI	NA
E	Cost-efficient	EI	I	SI	NI	NA
F	Speed of data output	EI	I	SI	NI	NA

Q-12 What systems have you evaluated or considered: _____

Q-13 Date you plan to purchase system: _____

Q-14 Price range considered for purchase of a fuel-dispensing system: ____
_____

Q-15 Please rank three features/attributes that have the greatest influence on your decision to purchase a fuel-dispensing system (with 1 being the most important):

1 _____

2 _____

3 _____

Q-16 Please list the two features/attributes that least influence your decision to purchase a fuel-dispensing system:

1 _____

2 _____

Q-17 What sources of information do you generally utilize in purchase decisions? (Please circle number of your opinion.)

1 Trade journals (specify): _____

2 Trade associations (specify): _____

3 Company reps

4 Other fleet control managers

5 Users of the system

6 Other (specify): _____

THE FLEET CONTROL MANAGER

The following set of questions refer to the fleet control manager's responsibilities in relation to maintaining the fleet.

Q-18 As a fleet control manager, what are *your* top two areas of concern in relation to the duties performed while at work:

1 _____

2 _____

Q-19 Below is a partial list of categories that contains duties normally performed by a fleet control manager. They may or may not reflect the responsibilities your company has assigned you as fleet control manager; therefore, please add or delete categories as they most accurately reflect your job duties.

	TASK CATEGORY	% OF DAY	EVALUATION				
A	Acquisition of vehicle	_____	A	B	C	D	E
B	Preventive maintenance of vehicles	_____	A	B	C	D	E
C	Demand maintenance of vehicles	_____	A	B	C	D	E
D	Monitoring fuel consumed	_____	A	B	C	D	E
E	Disposal of vehicles	_____	A	B	C	D	E
F	Labor negotiations	_____	A	B	C	D	E
G	_____	_____	A	B	C	D	E
		100%					

Next to the category title in the preceding table, please indicate:

1. The ESTIMATED TIME you would allot to each category if all tasks were performed on a DAILY BASIS. Assign percentage points that, when totaled, equal 100%.
2. Your EVALUATION OF EACH TASK according to the following letters. (Please circle *all* that apply to each task category)

A = tasks that *require the greatest accuracy*

B = tasks in which you would *prefer to change* the current method of completion and or recording

C = tasks over which you would *want to retain complete control*

D = tasks that are *currently using a computer*

E = tasks that *require the greatest amount of training/education*

Q-20 Below is a list of trade journals. For those to which you have access, please indicate whether the journal is a personal or a company subscription and the extent to which you normally read the journal. (Please circle the appropriate letter and number.)

		SUBSCRIPTION		AMOUNT OF JOURNAL READ			
		Company	*Personal*	<25% (1)	25–50% (2)	51–75% (3)	>75% (4)
A	California Trucker	C	P	1	2	3	4
B	California Fleet News	C	P	1	2	3	4
C	Commercial Car Journal	C	P	1	2	3	4
D	Fleet Owner (small-fleet edition)	C	P	1	2	3	4
E	Fleet Specialist	C	P	1	2	3	4
F	Owner Operator	C	P	1	2	3	4
G	Private Carrier	C	P	1	2	3	4
H	Others (specify):						
	_____	C	P	1	2	3	4

Q-21 What is your current job title? _____

Q-22 How many years have you been at this position? _____

Q-23 What type of company do you work for? _____

Q-24 How many years have you worked for this company? _____

Q-25 Total number of vehicles in fleet? _____

Q-26 Please identify the types of vehicles contained in your fleet (if more than one type, please indicate the precentage of each). Also identify the type of fuel consumed.

	TYPE	NUMBER	% OF FLEET	TYPE OF FUEL
A	_____	_____	_____	_____
B	_____	_____	_____	_____
C	_____	_____	_____	_____
			100%	

Q-27 What is the highest level of education that you have completed? (Please circle number of your opinion.)
1   High school
2   Technical school

3 College
   Degree earned: _____

Q-28 Please indicate: 1 Age _____
                       2 Sex _____

IV-2

MOUNT RUSHMORE INSURANCE COMPANY (B)

As discussed in Mount Rushmore Insurance Company (A), the company conducted a survey of customers and noncustomers to determine their reaction to a new concept of insurance. Data were obtained by telephone interviews. The marketing research manager has suggested that further insight into whether the new policy would be offered, its potential target market, and its marketing strategy could be obtained by multivariate analysis. The data set in Mount Rushmore Insurance Company (A) is to be used for such analysis.

1. Divide the sample into two groups: one group including respondents rating the concept "4" or "5" while the other group includes those rating it "1," "2," or "3."
   a. Run a two-group discriminant analysis with the predictor variables of respondent age, number of cars owned, and number of trips.
   b. Interpret the discriminant function.
   c. How well does the function classify the known membership of the sample?
   d. What changes, if any, occur when all six predictor variables are used for the discriminant analysis?

2. Factor-analyze the full 60×7 data matrix by principal components followed by Varimax rotation on those factors whose variance accounted-for values exceed unity.
   a. How would you interpret each set of rotated factor loadings?
   b. What other variables associated with that factor show high loadings for the concept-rating variable?
   c. Cluster-analyze the Varimax-rotated factor scores (after first finding interpoint distances in rotated factor space). Find three clusters of respondents.
   d. How would you interpret these clusters with regard to average concept ratings and Rushmore versus other company customers?

3. Having completed the various analyses, what should the marketing research manager recommend regarding (a) the wisdom of offering the policy, (b) its target market, and (c) future research needed before actual introduction of the policy?

IV-3

SYD COMPANY (D)

Some of the Syd Company's marketing managers were discussing the report presented by FC Associates covering the recent study that FC completed for Syd. It was noted that the level of analysis was not very sophisticated. Rather, most of the report dealt with findings based on cross tabulations and univariate/bivariate techniques.

After the discussion it was decided that perhaps there was value in having some "overall" analyses done using multivariate techniques. One manager had recently returned from a seminar given at a nationally recognized university in which it was continually emphasized that marketing problems are multivariable in nature.

The managers had decided to contact FC Associates and ask FC to conduct further analyses of the data they had collected in the shampoo study. Unfortunately, not one manager could definitively state which technique(s) ought to be used.

1. Referring to the A, B, and C cases as necessary, how can FC use factor analysis, discriminant analysis, multiple regression, and cluster analysis in analyzing the data set shown in Syd (B)?

2. For each of the techniques in question 1 that can be used, conduct the analysis and interpret the results.

16

Forecasting Procedures in Marketing Research

INTRODUCTION

As we have stressed throughout this book, the most pervasive characteristic of decision making is that it must take place under imperfect knowledge of the future; every decision is based on a forecast, whether or not formal techniques are used. The purpose of this chapter is to discuss the more formal nature of forecasting and its relationship to decision making under uncertainty. In doing so, we shall describe the classes of forecasting problems with which the market researcher must cope, the techniques that are available to assist him or her in this effort, and the evaluation of alternative forecasting techniques in terms of their values versus cost.

We first discuss the place of forecasting in decision making, what to forecast, and the role that marketing research plays in the gathering of information about the likelihood of alternative future events.

We then describe some of the more formal techniques of forecasting market potential, sales, and costs. The techniques discussed include persistence models, barometric forecasting, time-series decomposition, exponential smoothing, correlation models, econometric models, and polling. Although it is not our intent to provide a complete cataloging of available procedures, the reader should get from the discussion some flavor of the variety of techniques that are available for forecasting purposes.

We conclude the chapter with a discussion of the cost versus value of alternative forecasting procedures. We shall show that the solution to many business problems is not highly sensitive to forecast errors and, hence, that the value of the effort required to achieve greater forecast accuracy may not be justified by its cost.

THE NATURE OF FORECASTING

Why Forecasts Are Made

Any purposive activity in which there are uncertainties associated with future outcomes involves forecasting. The designation of one problem as being "more important" than another or the choice of one alternative as being "better" than another implies that forecasts have been made. The question is not *whether* we are to forecast but rather *what* we should forecast and *how* we are to do it. Forecasting can be viewed, therefore, as an *estimation or calculation of future events or developments, derived from a model, simple or complex, heuristic or analytic*. To put it another way, forecasting pertains to the formation of expectations about future states or processes of specific historical entities.[1]

There are two major reasons why forecasts are necessary:

1. Forecasts are made to help *identify* problems.
2. Forecasts are made to help *solve* problems.

The responsibility for forecasting sales for the firm typically rests with the marketing department. The purpose of the forecasts is often one of problem identification. Sales forecasts are usually made for each product and product line as well as for total company sales. They are frequently broken down by geographic area and type of customer as well. A sales forecast of this type is a form of *performance measurement*. It serves to identify products and/or sales areas that will not be performing at the level expected unless corrective steps are taken.

Sales forecasts are also used in setting *performance standards*. A forecast is implicit in any overall sales target or quota for a salesperson or a territory. Sales performance standards are usually established on the basis of a formal sales forecast. If later measurements indicate that the desired performance level has not been maintained, a problem is identified.

Forecasts are also made to help solve problems. The evaluation of alternative courses of action proposed as potential solutions to a problem always requires forecasts. Such evaluations usually involve forecasts of financial outlays as well as of sales. Should a new product be added to a product line that is not performing as well as it should? If it were added, what profit and discounted cash flow increments could be expected?

Considering both roles—problem identification and problem solving—a sales forecast is obviously a tool that is central to the marketing planning activity of a firm. Moreover, it must serve as the foundation of the marketing budget. In short, the sales forecast is critical for most activities of the firm: production activity, purchasing, personnel requirements, promotion, pricing strategy, managing the sales effort, and financial needs. As an illustration of forecasting for tactical planning, consider the forecasting technique developed by National Analysts, a major marketing research firm, for medical markets.[2]

---

[1]K. C. Land and S. H. Schneider, "Forecasting in the Social and Natural Sciences: An Overview and Analysis of Isomorphism," University of Texas at Austin, IC^2 Institute Working Paper 85-07-1, July 1985, p. 2.

[2]See C. Finkbeiner, "Tool Aids Forecasts for Medical Products," *Marketing News,* 20 (January 3, 1986), pp. 40–41.

The technique, called MEDICASTER, was developed primarily for non-durable medical products for which the doctor is the major decision maker. The market model represents existing product shares derived from the physician's decision processes, physician and patient characteristics, and market information. Using a market model for a product category, forecasts can be made in response to market changes such as new product introduction, competitor's response, and so on. The technique uses patients as the units of observation and relies on segmenting patients, patient-based conjoint analysis (discussed in the last chapter), market information about existing products, and a multinomial probit (discussed in Chapter 13) choice model to make its forecasts.

In addition to tactical and operational planning, the sales forecast is essential for sound strategic planning. However, in order to do this, forecasting effort needs to expand beyond predicting results of a set of predetermined strategic actions in an existing environmental structure. Strategic planning needs *strategic forecasting*, which is heavily concerned with predicting the structural environment within which the industry's business will be conducted.[3]

The Assumption of Stability

It is clear that any attempt to forecast the future assumes that past information is relevant and that the phenomenon under study possesses some regularity over space and time. By *stability*, however, is *not* meant that the phenomenon is necessarily constant through time or space, but only that the *rules* (or super-rules) for making the appropriate transformation are stable.

What to Forecast?

As was indicated earlier, one of the usual responsibilities of the marketing research department is to provide the factual data for the setting of marketing-related performance standards. Some of the more widely used standards in marketing include the following:

- *Profit* as a percentage of overall company sales, by product line, by product, by geographic area, by distribution channel, and by type of customer
- *Sales and/or market share targets* for the company as a whole, by product line, by product, by distribution channel, by type of customer, and by individual customer
- *Sales quotas* by geographic territory and by salesperson
- *Budgets* by type of marketing effort, by product line, and by geographic area

It is also the responsibility of the marketing research department to analyze and to make recommendations concerning prospective changes in the marketing-mix configuration, such as potential new products, changes in promotional budgets and/or media, increases or decreases in prices, and changes in the distribution system (Exhibit 16-1).

---

[3]See N. Capon and J. M. Hulbert, "Forecasting and Strategic Planning," Columbia University, Graduate School of Business, The Avis Rent a Car System, Inc., Working Paper Series in Marketing, No. 86-AV-1, January 1986.

Exhibit 16-1   Sales Forecasts Are Part of an Integrated Whole

Forecasts made by the marketing research department are part of an integrated whole of a firm's analytical forecasts. Below is a schematic of the flow of information and departmental responsibility for analytical forecasts that was once used by Eastern Airlines. Conditions in the industry and the firm during the past 10–20 years have undoubtedly led to changes in Eastern's forecasting structure. Even so, the system shown is a good illustration of the integrated nature of forecasting. Although the flow leads to financial analysis and forecasting total passenger revenue, the value of intermediate forecasts (passenger boardings, passenger forecasts by markets, special factors, etc.) for managerial questions seems clear.

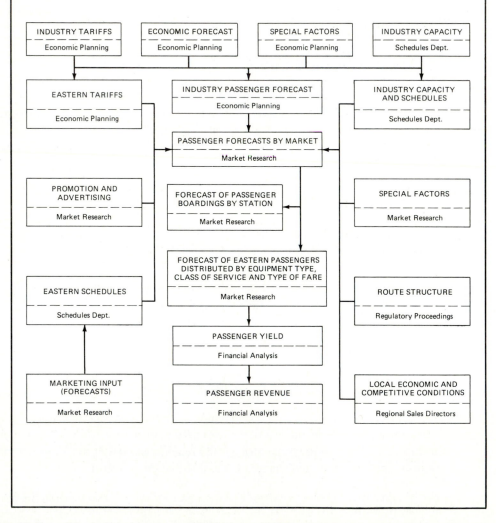

Source: W. Gross, "An Analytical Approach to Market Forecasting" *Georgia Business*, 30 (November 1970), 2.

A unifying concept by which the courses of actions of a profit-seeking firm can be evaluated is the cash-flow model (discussed in Chapter 3). This model requires that both revenues and financial outlays be forecasted over time. As such, consideration must be given to alternative uses of funds and the determinants of revenue and outlay flows.

Uncertainty in Forecasts

Decision makers may view the future in a variety of ways, depending on how sensitive the decision is to the unknown events of interest and how willing the manager is to "absorb uncertainty." For example, if a particular action is assumed to be superior to all other possible actions, irrespective of the course of future events, no forecast of these events is required. In other instances the consequences of a wrong decision may be quite sensitive to the unknown event(s) of interest and, hence, may justify the effort spent on reducing the manager's uncertainty. We can enumerate some of the major ways in which managers may treat uncertainty and their implications for marketing research activity.

At one extreme the manager may wish to view the future in *certainty-equivalent* terms. That is, he or she may be willing to assume only one possible outcome associated with a particular course of action, or in somewhat more subtle terms, the manager may be willing to replace an entire distribution of possible events by a single number (e.g., the mean of the distribution). If this is the desired act of behavior, only a single estimate might be requested from the marketing researcher. Probably all practicing marketing researchers have been exposed to the statement "Don't confuse me with ranges and probability numbers; all I want is your best single guess of what sales volume will be next year." This would be loosely akin to a "point" estimate.

In other cases the manager may wish to have the forecast expressed in terms of a *range of possibilities* with some statement about the likelihood that the "true" value will fall somewhere within the range. In still other cases the manager may only desire an expression of the chances that some outcome, say sales volume, will exceed a specified level.

In terms of the Bayesian approach outlined in earlier chapters, both of the above illustrations can be viewed as special cases of treating the class of unknown events in terms of a probability distribution. This distribution may be based on "relative frequency" notions or may reflect a more personalistic interpretation of the problem. The point to remember, however, is that *all* forecasts of future events are, in a sense, "acts of faith" that perceived past regularities will persist into the future. Creativity in model building is often displayed in the *level* of rules (or super-rules) at which stability is assumed. The comment "our business is changing too fast to model it" is rather naive. The challenge is to *upscale the level of abstraction* at which stability must necessarily be assumed.

Fortunately, many decisions do not require high accuracy in the prediction of future events or long time horizons over which events must be predicted. We have already seen in earlier chapters that the costs of wrong decisions may not be highly sensitive to changes in the unknown values of the parameters affecting the outcome. We have also seen that the process of sequential commitment frequently allows the decision maker more or less to "feel his way" by choosing courses of action that can be modified in the light of additional information. We shall amplify these remarks in later sections.

APPROACHES TO FORECASTING SALES

Two general approaches are available for forecasting sales of a firm. The first is a *derived forecast* that is made by first estimating market potential and then applying a forecasted market share for the firm. The result is a forecast of company sales for the period involved. The second approach is to forecast company sales directly without becoming involved in estimating market potential. This is known as a *direct forecast* of sales.

The term *market potential* has two different and commonly used meanings. It is sometimes understood to mean the amount of a product service that *could* be absorbed by the market during a specified period under *optimum* conditions of market development. It is also frequently used to mean the estimated amount of a product or service that *will* be absorbed by the market during a specified period.

The first of these definitions is the appropriate one to use in market planning. If a product is viewed as having considerably more potential than is currently being realized, an opportunity exists. With the proper changes in the marketing mix, sales may be increased.

The second usage of the term is synonymous with an industry sales forecast. That is, in forecasting the amount of a product or service that *will* be absorbed by the market in a specified period of time one is making a forecast of industry sales.

Our later discussion of sales forecasting techniques applies both to industry and to individual firm sales forecasts. It should be understood, therefore, that the terms "market potential" and "industry sales forecast" will have the same meaning unless otherwise specified. The term "sales forecast" will be understood to apply to the forecast for an individual firm.

Estimating Potentials

Before proceeding with our discussion of forecasting we make some further comment about market potentials. In addition to their use as the basis of derived forecasts, market and sales potentials are also useful for marketing planning and control. Uses of these estimates have been for such things as

- Setting sales quotas
- Buying advertising space and time
- Planning distribution
- Allocating advertising expenditures
- Structuring sales territories
- Finding "soft spots" (trouble areas) in a company's sales pattern

A number of techniques for estimating market potential are available to the analyst. These include the *chain-ratio method* (i.e., applying a series of ratios or usage rates to an aggregate measure of demand), *market survey, market test, corollary index* (single- or multiple-factor), and *market buildup*.[4]

---

[4]These are discussed in G. Churchill, N. Ford, and O. Walker, *Sales Force Management* (Homewood, Ill.: Richard D. Irwin, 1981), Chap. 5.

One of the primary tools used in market-potential estimation, and therefore commonly used in derived forecasting methods, is the *Standard Industrial Classification* (*SIC*) *system*.[5] The SIC system is particularly well suited to determining market potential for industrial products. It represents a uniform numerical coding procedure for classifying U.S. establishments by type of activity. For industrial marketers the system is highly useful for relating company activities to data produced by the federal and state governments, trade associations, publishing firms, and the like.

The SIC system divides U.S. firms into ten key divisions: (1) agriculture; (2) mining; (3) contract construction; (4) manufacturing; (5) transportation, communications, electric, gas, and sanitary services; (6) wholesale trade; (7) retail trade; (8) finance, insurance, and real estate; (9) services; and (10) public administration. These divisions, in turn, are divided into major groups (two-digit codes), groups (three-digit codes), industries (four-digit codes), and so on, in a hierarchical fashion, to seven-digit codes in some cases.

Figure 16-1 shows an illustration in the area of metalworking. As can be noted, the classification proceeds from major groups to groups to industries. The reporting of data by SIC code provides the industrial marketer with uniform statistics for estimating market potential and related tasks. Moreover, several business publications, such as *Iron Age*, regularly publish statistics utilizing the same codes. A number of market-survey firms, such as the Chilton Company, Philadelphia, and Dun and Bradstreet, New York, provide plant lists, coded by SIC, that can be used in preparing mail questionnaires. Moreover, *County Business Patterns*, published annually by the U.S. Department of Commerce, contains statistics at the county level for use in preparing market-potential figures by sales territory.

The SIC classification is also quite useful in conjunction with input–output tables, a topic discussed later in the chapter. In brief, the SIC codes (and accompanying statistics) are useful for a variety of market-potential estimation and forecasting tasks, including the measurement of market share, development of sales prospect lists, planning sales calls, and the like.

The SIC method is a major example of the buildup method. An example of a multiple-factor corollary index is the Index of Buying Power Method, which is useful for estimating potential demand for consumer goods. This method involves use of the Buying Power Index (BPI), which is published yearly by *Sales & Marketing Management* magazine. A geographic market's ability to buy is derived from a weighted average of population, income, and retail sales in that market. The BPI is a *general index* presented in the format as a geographic market's percentage of total U.S. retail sales potential.[6] Another approach based on demographics is presented in Exhibit 16-2.

FORECASTING TECHNIQUES

The marketing researcher is concerned with forecasts of both sales and costs. We will accordingly be concerned with the forecasting of both. The techniques used in forecasting market potential, sales, and costs share a common classification. The forecasting tech-

---

[5]Standard Industrial Classification Manual (Washington, D.C.: Government Printing Office, 1982).

[6]See R. P. Bagozzi, *Principles of Marketing Management* (Chicago: Science Research Associates, 1986), pp. 292–94.

Figure 16-1   How SIC Classifies Metalworking

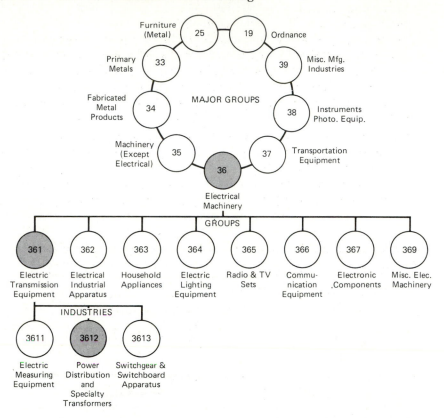

Source: From P. J. Robinson, C. L. Hinkle, and Edward Bloom, "Standard Industrial Classification for Effective Marketing Analysis," p. 21, Marketing Science Institute, November 1967, by permission.

niques used in forecasting these variables for existing products are those of *extrapolation, correlation, econometric models,* and *polling.*

1. *Extrapolation techniques.* These procedures utilize past changes in only the *variable of interest* as a basis for future projection of that variable; as such, the only "independent" variable is time. Illustrations of extrapolation techniques are various types of naive models, time-series decomposition, and exponential smoothing.

2. *Correlation techniques.* These procedures utilize past relationships between the variable to be forecasted and *other* variables (e.g., disposable income, customer inventory levels) that are thought to be related to the variable being forecasted. The forecast problem thus involves two major tasks: (a) quantifying the past relationship between the dependent variable and the predictor variables, and (b) forecasting values of the predictor variables as a necessary step before making a forecast of the dependent variable. In lead-lag models, the forecaster may be able to identify a fairly long and stable leading series early enough to forecast

Exhibit 16-2   Using Cluster Demographics for Potentials

Another approach to estimating potentials using a multiple factor index involves so-called demographic clustering techniques, such as ACORN by CACI, Inc. and ClusterPlus by Donnelley Information Services. These techniques provide total counts of households with similar rather than exact demographic profile matches. However, they give more depth than standard census reports which typically generate household counts (e.g., for the head of household) for only one or two characteristics at the same time.

One company, Continental Telecom of Atlanta, has extended demographic clustering to provide specific estimates.* For example, using the method it is relatively easy to estimate the potential number of households in a city (SMSA) where the head of household has a specific multiple-characteristic demographic profile. The method starts with demographic data obtained by using the ACORN system, which clusters consumers on the basis of the type of areas in which they live. Every U.S. census block/enumeration district (neighborhood) has been classified into one of 44 different types in accordance with the demographic, socioeconomic and lifestyle characteristics of the people living there. ACORN clusters are consistently defined throughout the country, so information obtained from one area can be applied to another.

A simple index score is developed for each neighborhood type based on matching the profile of that neighborhood against that of the target market, weighted by the relative importance to purchase intent of a profile characteristic. Earlier in the process a matrix of values is developed which relates each of the 44 neighborhood types to the national average for 48 demographic variables. Other SMSA relevant data also are used, e.g., total number of households and the percent of total households in each block group/enumeration district.

The resulting index values for each of the 44 area types represents the estimated number of households in each type that would actually be part of the target market. From this it is possible to develop estimates of a potential target market for any SMSA in the country.

---

*See R. F. Tomasino, "How to Use Cluster Demographics to Estimate Target-Market Potential," *Market News*, 18 (September 14, 1984), p. 42.

the lagged variable (without first forecasting the leading variable). If so, uncertainty still surrounds the stability of the functional relationship that links the two variables together.

3. *Econometric techniques.* These procedures are usually expressed as being "less empirical" than correlative models in the sense that they are based on some *underlying theory* about the relationships that exist among a set of economic variables. A set of equations may be stated that reflects how the phenomena should be interrelated (if the theory holds), and parameters of the models are estimated by statistical analysis of past data.

4. *Polling techniques.* Although all forecasting involves judgment, polling techniques are probably the least "formal" of the procedures enumerated above. As the name suggests, salespeople and executives may be polled with regard to the sales outlook and executives may be polled with respect to profit in the case of a new venture. These opinions may be "averaged" or combined in some manner as to reflect the opinions of company personnel closest to the market situation. Although this procedure is looked upon as less "scientific" than other techniques, it might more fairly be called *less explicit* in the sense that the process by which

Figure 16-2   Illustration of the Historical Analogy Technique

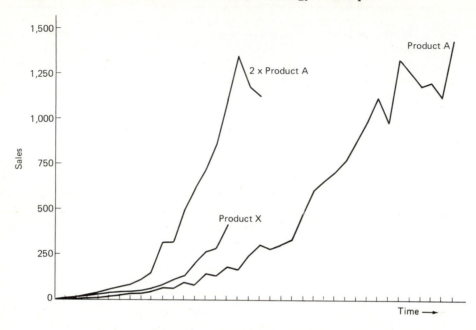

people make judgments from a variety of source data and experience is not understood. These procedures, however, may lead to fairly accurate forecasts and can serve as an independent check on the reasonableness of forecasts derived from more explicit models.

Since new products have no sales history, extrapolation as a method of sales forecasting is not possible. Correlation, econometric models, and polling techniques are applicable, however, as are *experimental techniques* and the use of *historical analogy*.

5. *Experimental techniques.* Test markets and controlled store tests (discussed in Chapters 6 and 18) are types of field experiments that are widely used to help forecast sales of new products. Laboratory experiments involving "purchasing" in a simulated-purchase situation have also been used for this purpose.

6. *Historical analogy.* The sales experience of an earlier, similar product is sometimes used as the basis for forecasting sales of a new product. A necessary assumption in using this approach is that the economic and market environment of the two products are either similar or that the effects of differences can be adequately reflected by adjustments to the sales data of the earlier product. An example of the application of historical analogy for forecasting the sales of a new product is the use of sales of black-and-white television sets for the first few years after their introduction to forecast sales of color television sets for a similar period. While this technique may appear to be most applicable to more aggregate measures (e.g., industry sales), it can be used for individual products that may be compared with industry-level data or with other products for which there are sufficient historical data. As shown in Figure 16-2, one approach is

to relate the product in question (X) to some other series (A), and comparisons can be made with the actual performance of A or to some multiple of A. In the example shown, X seems to be following a pattern similar to 1.5 times that of A.

Forecasting techniques, like any model, are difficult to test in the real world. Some analysts will attempt to test more formal models retrospectively. For example, they may divide the time series roughly into halves, calculate values for the parameters in the model by using the first half of the time series, and then use these values in forecasting the second half of the time series. Other researchers will employ two or more forecasting techniques and see if they arrive at forecasts that are more or less in agreement. The fact remains, however, that the observance of past regularities in the data provides no guarantee that these regularities will persist or that some other technique might not be more efficient in terms of lower total cost (forecast preparation cost plus the cost of forecast error).

Experimental techniques have been described elsewhere and historical analogy needs no further discussion. The first four of the techniques shown above do require additional discussion, however, and we now turn to that task.

Extrapolation Techniques

Market Potential/Sales Forecasting by Extrapolation

Extrapolation of past sales or market-share data can take a variety of forms. At one extreme are *persistence*, or *naive*, models, which merely use the value for the most recent period as a forecast for the next period. For short-range forecasts of sales data that are changing rather slowly over time, this simple and inexpensive procedure can provide reasonably accurate forecasts. Slight variations in the procedure involve extrapolating a trend for two or more periods. For example, if the most recent period's sales were 100 units and the next to the most recent period's sales were 80 units, sales forecasted for the next period would be $(100/80)(100) = 125$ units.

Persistence models are often used as a basis for evaluating other forecasting techniques. For example, Parker and Segura[7] used a five-year linear extrapolation to forecast sales for a home furnishings company and compared the results with those obtained from a regression model. For an 18-year forecasting period (1952–1970) the coefficient of determination for the extrapolation forecasts was 0.86, whereas that for the regression forecasts was 0.95.

Time-series decomposition techniques (trend and cyclical and seasonal analysis) and the fitting of various *growth curves* (logistic, Gompertz, modified exponential) are not far different in principle from the simple procedures enumerated above. The former set of procedures can be used for making short-range (less than one year) projections, intermediate-range (one- to five-year) projections, or longer-range (over five-year) projections. Growth curves are usually reserved for long-range projections where the trend of the series is deemed to be the sole component of interest for planning purposes.

The rationale underlying time-series decomposition is based on the assumption that the original data of a series are composed of a trend, cyclical component, seasonal

[7]G.G.C. Parker and E.L. Segura, "How to Get a Better Forecast," *Harvard Business Review*, 49 (March–April 1971), 99–109.

component, and an "irregular" component. A common functional form is to assume that these variables are multiplicative. Hence, the original data can be expressed as follows:

$$O = T \times C \times S \times I$$

where O = original data; T = trend component; C = cyclical component; S = seasonal component; and I = irregular component. Other functional forms (e.g., additive) can be used as well, and rather elaborate procedures (many of which are computerized) are available for isolating the assumed components. Of the available computer programs, one of the more comprehensive is the X-11 program developed by the Bureau of the Census.[8]

Growth curve forms of the traditional S-shaped variety are typically reserved for extrapolation of annual data for several years ahead on the assumption that these functional forms generally describe long-term behavior of many time series. Other variations of trend fitting use logarithms of the original data in a variety of functional forms: straight line, quadratic, and so on.

The mechanics underlying all the above procedures are reasonably simple, once a mathematical model to describe the past behavior of the series has been selected. The rub, or course, rests on *which* model (of a large variety of possible models) is to be selected. This choice must rest largely on empirical grounds and the use of limited retrospective tests of "goodness of fit."

For short-range forecasting, increasing attention has been given to an extrapolation technique known as *exponential smoothing*.[9] Exponential smoothing is an extrapolation technique that "smooths" the time series in a manner not unlike a moving average. Originally applied to inventory control problems, exponential-smoothing procedures combine the virtues of simplicity of computation and flexibility (associated with moving averages) with advantages that make their utilization particularly applicable to computer storage and computation. When hundreds of items have to be forecasted, as, for example, in inventory control systems, there are decided advantages in being able to update historical data rapidly.

Briefly stated, exponential smoothing is a type of moving average that represents a weighted sum of all past numbers in the time series with the heaviest weight placed on the most recent information. A fraction called a "smoothing constant" (and usually designated by the symbol α) is used to smooth the data. To see how this procedure is related to the conventional moving average (M_t), we first define this latter term as follows:

$$M_t = \frac{X_t + X_{t-1} + \cdots + X_{t-N+1}}{N}$$

[8]U.S. Department of Commerce, Bureau of the Census, "X-11 Information for the User," *Papers Prepared for the Seminar on Seasonal Adjustments of the National Association of Business Economists*, March 10, 1969.

[9]The primary references are R. G. Brown, *Statistical Forecasting for Inventory Control* (New York: McGraw-Hill, 1959); R. G. Brown, *Smoothing, Forecasting and Prediction* (Englewood Cliffs, N.J.: Prentice-Hall, 1963); and P. R. Winters, "Forecasting Sales by Exponentially Weighted Moving Averages," *Management Science*, 6 (April 1960), 324–42.

The moving average for the next period ($t + 1$) is found by adding X_{t+1} to the numerator series and dropping X_{t-N+1}. For example, assume that N, the number of periods in the average, is 7. The moving average for the tenth period is thus

$$M_{10} = \frac{X_{10} + X_9 + \cdots + X_4}{7}$$

The moving average for the next period (M_{11}) is then

$$M_{11} = \frac{X_{11} + X_{10} + \cdots + X_5}{7}$$

$$= M_{10} + \frac{X_{11} - X_4}{7}$$

If X_4 were not available for some reason, since we know that M_{10} was computed from a series of values containing X_4, we could substitute M_{10} for X_4 as a "best estimate" of this (now) missing value:

$$\overset{*}{M}_{11} = M_{10} + \frac{X_{11} - M_{10}}{7}$$

$$= \frac{X_{11}}{7} + \left(1 - \frac{1}{7}\right)M_{10}$$

where $\overset{*}{M}_{11}$ is used as an estimate of M_{11}. The simplest exponential model is merely a reflection of the above process and can be represented symbolically by

$$\overset{*}{S}_t = \alpha X_t + (1 - \alpha)\overset{*}{S}_{t-1}$$

where $\alpha(0 \leq \alpha \leq 1)$ takes the place of the ratio $1/7$ described above.

The determination of the correct numerical value to assign to α is, of course, the principal problem in using this technique. If the time series changes very slowly, we would like the value of α to be small so as to keep in the effect of earlier observations. If the series changes rapidly, we would like the value of α to be large so that the forecasts may be responsive to these changes. In practice, the value of α is often estimated by trying several values and making retrospective tests of the associated forecast error.[10] The value of α leading to the "smallest" forecast error is then chosen for future smoothing.

More elaborate formulations of the basic exponential-smoothing model enable the analyst to incorporate explicitly trends and seasonal elements of the time series. In special cases, the technique permits the use of statistical control procedures for signaling when the basic parameters of the model have changed.

---

[10]In special cases (stable autocorrelation functions), specific techniques are available for computing an "optimal" value of α (see Brown, *Smoothing, Forecasting and Prediction*, pp. 72–80). Of course, in economic series such stable autocorrelative functions are extremely rare.

The *Box–Jenkins model* is a computerized technique for trying various extrapolation models to see which one best fits the data.[11] If the process that generates the sales data is a reasonably stable one, the use of the Box–Jenkins program will indicate which extrapolative technique gives the best forecast. A general class of Box–Jenkins models for a stationary time series is the ARIMA, or autoregressive integrated moving-average models.[12] *Autoregressive* means a model in which a variable is a function of only its past values except for an error term disturbance. *Integrated* indicates that period-to-period changes in the level of the original variable are used rather than the absolute value of the variable itself. Finally, a *moving-average* procedure is used to eliminate any intercorrelations of the error term to its own past or future values.

Cost Forecasts by Extrapolation

Most manufactured products are produced by processes that have cost elements that are partially time-dependent. The price of materials, labor time per unit, labor rates, and overhead rates are examples. The same is true of salaries, travel, and media costs in marketing.

Extrapolations can be made of each of these cost elements using the same techniques as used for making extrapolations of sales data.[13] Such extrapolations are of use to the marketing researcher primarily in evaluating "no change" versus one or more "change" alternatives in a specific problem situation.

Correlation Techniques

Market Potential/Sales Forecasting by Correlation

The distinguishing feature of correlation techniques as applied to forecasting is that past changes in the variable to be predicted are related to other variables on the assumption that these historical associations will continue into the future. That is, the analyst is interested in examining *serial* correlation between the variable to be forecasted (say, company sales) and various "independent" variables (personal disposable income, distributor inventory levels, etc.) that might be expected to bear some plausible relationship to the variable to be forecasted. Illustrations are so-called lead-lag indicators and barometric indexes.

The essence of serial correlation techniques is that *if* a relationship is found to exist in the past and *if* this relationship can be expected to persist in the future, the series to be forecasted might be more accurately predicted by first predicting the levels of the predictor variables and then applying the historical functional relationship to predict the level of the dependent variable.

[11]G.E.P. Box and G.M. Jenkins, *Time Series Analysis, Forecasting and Control* (San Francisco: Holden-Day, 1970).

[12]A stationary time series is one whose average value does not change over time. See J. E Hanke and A. G. Reitsch, *Business Forecasting*, 2nd ed. (Boston: Allyn & Bacon, 1986), Chap. 10; and D. M. Bechter and J. L. Rutner, "Forecasting with Statistical Models and a Case Study of Retail Sales," *Economic Review of the Federal Reserve Bank of Kansas City*, March 1978, pp. 3–11.

[13]Cost extrapolation techniques are discussed in Nicholas Dopuch and J.G. Bunting, *Cost Accounting* (New York: Harcourt, Brace and World, 1969), Chap. 3.

As previously indicated, Parker and Segura[14] forecasted the sales of a home furnishings company using a regression model. Housing starts of the previous year (H_{t-1}), sales of the previous year (S_{t-1}), disposable income of the present year (I_t), and time (T) were used as predictor variables. The resulting equation was $S_t = 33.51 + 0.033H_{t-1} + 0.373S_{t-1} + 0.672I_t - 11.03T$; $R^2 = 0.95$ for a 22-year period.

The assumption behind this approach is that more accurate forecasts can be obtained by forecasting national income (and using the lagged values of the other predictor variables) than by forecasting the sales of the company directly. One of the dangers involved in using correlation techniques, however, is that the high autocorrelation in each series may give the appearance of high serial correlation (that is, one may be, in effect, correlating the trends of each series) when the other components of each series, say cyclical or seasonal, are not highly correlated. For long-range forecasting where emphasis *is* on the trend component, good results can sometimes be obtained by serial correlation procedures, but for shorter-range projections, reliance on high-correlation coefficients may be misleading because of the reason just mentioned. The central problem, of course, is to be able to forecast the predictor variables accurately.

The quest for "leading" series is one of the chief preoccupations of some professional forecasters. *Barometric,* or *indicator, forecasting* is the name applied to the use of such a series. If a "true" leading series can be found, for example, the analyst might be fortunate enough to have the actual (not forecasted) value of the predictor variable from which he or she could derive from a regression equation the predicted value of the criterion variable. Such occasions, where leading series consistently "lead," say, a firm's sales volume, by a sufficiently long period to be useful, are extremely rare.

Nevertheless, quite a bit of empirical work has been done on examining the relationships among various United States time series. The National Bureau of Economic Research has analyzed some 800 monthly and quarterly time series for consistent lead, coincidental, or lag relationships.[15]

On a more short-run basis, Albaum, Best, and Hawkins forecasted weekly sales of a bakery product (specifically hamburger buns) using a regression model.[16] Two predictor variables were used—average weekly high temperature (X_1) and a dummy variable to indicate whether the first of the month was on a Monday/Thursday/Friday or one of the other four days (X_2). The resulting equation was

$$\hat{Y} = 1028.6 + .0007X_1^3 + 172.4X_2$$

where $\hat{Y}$ was predicted weekly demand and X_1 and X_2 were as defined above. An observation set of 17 weeks was used to develop this *curvilinear model,* which had significant coefficients for the X_i and $R^2 = .79$. By using this forecasting model instead of the one that was used, the bakery would improve production and marketing efficiency by minimizing stockouts and returns.

[14]Parker and Segura, "How to Get a Better Forecast," p. 107.

[15]See G.H. Moore, *Statistical Indicators of Cyclical Revivals and Recessions,* National Bureau of Economic Research Occasional Paper 31 (New York).

[16]G. Albaum, R. Best, and D.I. Hawkins, "The Marketing of Hamburger Buns: An Improved Model for Prediction," *Journal of the Academy of Marketing Science,* 3 (Summer 1975), 223–31.

Finally, mention should be made of the use of various demographic series for long-range forecasting of total industry demand for such goods and services as geriatric care, baby food, new housing, and applicances. Despite some much-publicized errors, long-range forecasts of the total, sex, and age distribution of the population can provide interesting background material for long-range planning. That these time series could provide much help for forecasting *individual* company sales is obviously open to more question.

Cost Forecasting by Correlation

Forecasts of costs using correlation techniques are relatively common. The study cited earlier by Parker and Segura provides an example of regression analysis used for cost forecasting as well as for sales forecasting. They developed regression equations for "raw material costs," "wages and salaries," "other costs," "depreciation," "interest," "sales taxes," and "income taxes." Knowledge of such relationships is useful to the researcher when evaluating potential new products similar to the ones currently produced and marketed by the firm.

Econometric Techniques

Market Potential/Sales Forecasting by Econometric Models

Econometric techniques essentially entail explicit models about how the economy or a specific segment of the economy behaves. The usual econometric model involves a series of equations that have their origins in economic theory. Most of the models described in the literature deal with the macroeconomy and are used for forecasting GNP and its components.

The input–output model of the economy, alluded to earlier and developed by Leontieff,[17] is econometric in nature but assumes a somewhat different form. It is a way of organizing the national accounts in which the flow of goods and services between industries is shown. A matrix of industries as rows (87 industries in one version and 370 in another) and the same industries as columns has been prepared. Interindustry transactions have been determined empirically for each cell in the matrix. The value of the transaction shown in a single cell represents both an output of one industry—the industry of that row—and an input for an industry—the industry of that column. If one is interested in a particular industry, say Industry 43, Engines and Turbines (87 industry version), the distribution of outputs for that industry can be found by examining the row on which it is located and the distribution of inputs by examining the column.

The table is also provided in other forms to facilitate research use. A direct-requirements table has been prepared in which each cell entry is a coefficient obtained by dividing the dollar amount for that cell by the total of the column in which it is located.

---

[17]W.W. Leontieff, *Structure of the American Economy,* 1919–1929 (New York: Oxford University Press, 1951).

The result is an input coefficient. One can obtain the distribution of input coefficients for an industry by examining the column for that industry. A third form is a total-requirements table that shows the indirect as well as the direct requirements of each industry listed. The requirements are shown in coefficient form. This table permits the calculation of the total effect on all industries of a change in final demand on any one of them.

These forms of the input–output table permit forecasts of sales at the industry level to be made from GNP forecasts and forecasts of the effects of changes in final demand faced by a customer industry. An example of the forecasting of sales for an industrial product is given by Ranard.[18] For a GNP increase of 5% per year, sales for the motor vehicle industry were forecasted as increasing 3.9% per year. A 10% increase in demand for automobiles was estimated to require a 2.1% increase in steel output to meet direct and indirect requirements.

Given the reluctance of private firms to publicize the use of forecasting techniques that they find useful, it is difficult to estimate to what extent input–output and other econometric models have been used in practice. It is probably fair to say, however, that the individual firm's use of econometric models for forecasting sales is still somewhat limited. However, the available evidence on the accuracy of econometric model forecasts compared with that of forecasts by other methods indicates that the econometric forecasts are more accurate, particularly as the length of the forecast period increases.[19] So long as this conclusion continues to be supported by the experience of companies using econometric models, one can expect that their use in sales forecasting will experience substantial growth.

Cost Forecasting Using Econometric Models

Much empirical work has been done by econometricians to determine whether the relationships of costs to output postulated in theory exist in fact.[20] The methodology of statistical cost analysis has been developed to a considerable extent as a result and has carried over into practice.

A problem that always arises in evaluating new-product ventures is estimating production costs. Such estimates are usually required early in the evaluation in order to permit tentative prices to be set and conditional sales forecasts to be made.

A model that is widely used for this purpose in the electronic, appliance, aircraft, and shipbuilding industries is the *learning curve* model, sometimes called the *manufacturing progress function* and also known as the *experience curve*. Empirical investigations of the labor hours required to produce successive units of new products have indicated

---

[18]E.D. Ranard, "Use of Input/Output Concepts in Sales Forecasting," *Journal of Marketing Research,* 9 (February 1972), 53–58.

[19]See J. S. Armstrong and M. G. Groham, "A Comparative Study of Methods of Long-Range Market Forecasting," *Management Science,* 19 (October 1972), 211–21; R. F. Kosobud, "Forecasting Accuracy and Uses of an Econometric Model," *Applied Econometrics,* 2 (1970), 253–63; V. Zarnowitz, *An Appraisal of Short-Term Economic Forecasts,* National Bureau of Economic Research Occasional Paper 104 (New York, 1967); and D. M. Bechter and J. L. Rutner, *Economic Review of the Federal Reserve Bank of Kansas City,* March 1978.

[20]A definitive work in this area is J. Johnston, *Statistical Cost Analysis* (New York: McGraw-Hill, 1960).

that there is an exponential relationship between the hours required to produce the present unit, the hours required to produce the first unit, and the number of units that have already been produced. More specifically, the functional form of the relationship is

$$Y_i = Y_1 i^{-b}$$

where Y_i = labor hours required for the $i$the unit to be produced

Y_1 = labor hours required for the first unit

i = number of units produced thus far (including the ith unit); $i > 1$

$-b$ = rate at which the labor hours decline as the number of units produced increases

This equation may be expressed in logarithmic form as

$$\log Y_i = \log Y_1 - b \log i$$

In this form it is apparent that the function plots as a straight line.

The usual finding is that every time the number of units to be produced is doubled, the number of hours required to produce the last unit is reduced to a constant percentage of its former value. Thus, the term "80% curve" means that each time output is doubled, the number of hours required to produce the last unit is only 80% of the amount required before the doubling. If the amount required for unit 1 were 1 hour, for example, the amount required for unit 2 would be 0.80 hour, for unit 4, 0.64 hour, and so on.

The estimate of labor hours required to produce the ith unit therefore requires a determination of the slope of the curve and an estimate, or a measurement, of the time required to produce the first unit (or some unit before the ith one). Tables have been prepared of unit labor costs (and average cumulative total labor costs as well) for a wide range of learning curves.[21] If tables are not available, a graph of the curve at the learning rate desired can be prepared by making calculations for two values, plotting them on log-log paper, and drawing a straight line through them over the range of output of interest.

The values of the slope of the curves vary between industries and between companies within an industry. The Ford Motor Company experienced an 85% curve in producing the Model T from 1909 through 1923.[22] A study involving a number of industries reports values ranging from 67 to 86%.[23] This range of learning rates is wide enough to indicate that an investigation of rates in one's own company should be made before this cost forecasting model is used.

[21]See R.W. Conway and Andrew Schultz, Jr., "The Manufacturing Progress Function," *Journal of Industrial Engineering,* 10 (January–February 1959), 53, for an example of such a table.

[22]W.J. Abernathy and K. Wayne, "Limits of the Learning Curve," *Harvard Business Review,* 52 (September–October 1974), 111.

[23]R.W. Conway and Andrew Schultz, Jr., *Journal of Industrial Engineering,* 10, p. 54.

The labor hours per unit of product is, of course, only one element of the total product cost in a new-product venture. However, the other classes of production costs, material, and overhead are usually much easier to estimate. Material costs are relatively constant over wide ranges of output, and manufacturing overhead costs are typically allocated on a direct labor-hour base. The estimate of labor hours thus provides a basis for estimating overhead.

Polling Techniques

Market Potential/Sales Forecasting Using Polls

The job of forecasting individual company sales is fraught with so much uncertainty that it is not surprising that opinion polling is used by many firms, whether or not the procedure is formalized. In one sense, the personalistic forecasts obtained by polling can reflect any or all of the models discussed under the previous classifications. That is, it is possible that a business executive may be basing his or her opinion on some underlying model that involves extrapolation, correlation, or some type of personalistic econometric theory about how the firm's sales are affected by various economic variables. Although less *explicit,* it does not necessarily follow that forecasts obtained by polling techniques are less accurate than more formalistic techniques. As a matter of fact, serious study is being given to the so-called predictive expert in forecasting events for which no satisfactory alternative procedures are even available, let alone superior.

Some polling procedures are used to forecast *general* economic series, such as the McGraw-Hill survey of expenditures for plant and equipment and the Survey Research Center of the University of Michigan, which prepares surveys of consumer anticipations regarding the purchase of consumer durables. From the standpoint of individual firm planning, however, our concern is more with polling procedures of company executives, sales personnel, distributors, and the firm's consumers.

Executive polling procedures are used quite frequently in the development of long-range forecasts for the firm. Product managers and end-use experts may be asked to estimate sales levels for their particular product or market specialization, subject to a set of overall assumptions regarding various economic activities and competitors' behavior. One of the authors elicited sales executives' opinions regarding the implications of various pricing strategies on (1) competitors' retaliation, (2) market penetration, and (3) industry capacity changes. These opinions were expressed in terms of subjective probabilities. Although each group of executives was questioned independently, the agreement between groups was quite high. Although such consistency does not imply accuracy, it does suggest that personnel familiar with the marketing characteristics of a product do form similar judgments about the environments in which the firm operates. Furthermore, in this particular problem no alternative procedure existed for developing some of the inputs needed in the evaluation of pricing alternatives.

The polling of salespeople is a commonly used procedure to develop sales forecasts. Salespeople's estimates of sales for their particular districts may be next reviewed by the district manager, regional manager, and so on, and finally subjected to review by the firm's market analyst for consistency and correspondence with other sources of information.

Forecasts may also be developed by using "trade experts" drawn from the firm's distribution channels or directly from samples of customer groups. This procedure is used quite frequently in developing sales estimates for new products. In these cases no historical data are available for forecasting purposes, other than sales experience with broadly similar products or information about sales of the products with which the new-product candidate will compete.

One type of polling procedure, the Delphi method,[24] has achieved increasing application in recent years. The idea behind Delphi is simple: a group of experts are polled regarding their judgments about when each of some set of specified events falling within their area of expertise might happen. They may also be asked to state their degree of confidence in each judgment and the implications for present policies if the event were to occur. Typically, each participant "votes" in closed ballot and the results are tabulated and displayed in group form so that the participant can see what others (not identified) have forecasted. Successive rounds of voting, augmented by each participant's explication, in written but anonymous form, of assumptions underlying his or her judgments (for perusal by other participants) take place until results more or less stabilize in terms of a common understanding of the events being forecasted.

Cost Forecasting Using Polls

The use of polling in forecasting costs is less frequent than the other techniques that have been discussed. It is largely restricted to the polling of suppliers to obtain estimates of prices and of price changes for materials. By way of summary, polling procedures can be used effectively or can end up in a "pick a number" game, depending on the care with which opinions are assembled and the thoroughness with which checks for internal consistency and cross-checking with other information sources are carried out. Relying on the "objectivity" of more formal forecasting techniques can, however, result in as many pitfalls as naive treatment of more personalistic forecasts. The prudent marketing analyst may be well advised to consult several sources of information, whether or not some of this information may be based on intuition or hunch.

Recapitulation

In this section we have discussed various techniques for forecasting sales and costs. The emphasis has been on sales forecasting. Every sales forecaster should have in his or her "tool chest" each of the following:

- Facts, rumors, conjectures, and beliefs
- Statistical techniques
- Common sense and judgment

[24]See, for example, Olaf Helmer, *Social Technology* (New York: Basic books, 1966); and M. A. Jolson and G. L. Rossow, "The Delphi Process in Marketing Decision Making, *Journal of Marketing Research*, 8 (November 1971), 443–48.

Another way of viewing the alternative methods of forecasting demand is that they are based on *what people say* (e.g., polling), *what people do* (e.g., market test), and *what people have done*(e.g., time series, correlation, etc.). Which method is appropriate in any given application will depend on the availability of data, the extent of stability in demand (perhaps indicated by the product's life-cycle stage), the type of product, and the purpose of the forecast (i.e., how it is to be used).

We have not discussed any technique in great depth. To do so would expand the scope of this book beyond its intended audience. A good explanation of the time-series and correlation-based techniques will be found in the work by Hanke and Reitsch.[25] In contrast, polling techniques involve using methods discussed throughout this book.

FORECASTING MARKET SHARE

Market share is the percentage of industry sales made by the company over some stated time period. As described earlier, a derived forecast of company sales requires a forecast of industry sales and a market-share estimate.

Industry sales data are often, but not always, available on a historical basis from such sources as trade associations and government reports. When they are not available from these sources, they may be developed by the marketing research staff or, in some cases, purchased as part of the data supplied by a syndicated service (Neilsen, MRCA, and others).

In general, forecasts of market share may be made using the same techniques as described for market potential and sales forecasts. Data on market share over time comprise a time series that is susceptible, in principle, to the same kinds of treatment as a time series of sales. That is, one may extrapolate market-share data for forecasting purposes using the same persistence models (naive models, time-series decomposition, exponential smoothing, and others) as described for sales data. Correlation models appear to be at least as widely used for market-share forecasting as for sales forecasting. Econometric models and polling procedures can also be employed for this purpose.

PROBABILITY FORECASTING AND COST VERSUS VALUE OF INFORMATION

In this section we discuss two questions that can be classified under the general heading of "probability forecasting":

1. In "few action–few state" problems, how precise must be the probabilities associated with the occurrence of alternative states of nature?
2. In "many action–many state" problems, how is the best action chosen when the values assigned to alternative states of nature are subject to continuous variation?

---

[25]See Hanke and Reitsch, *Business Forecasting*.

We shall see that both questions are illustrative of "probability forecasting" in which the forecaster prepares not a single point estimate but a *probability* distribution (discrete or continuous) of possible values that the unknown parameter(s) of interest can assume.

Few Action–Few State Problems

As an example of the first class of problems, suppose that a new product planner is interested in marketing a food supplement, called Lottadyne, for baked goods. The product is made by a batch process that through equipment indivisibilities is restricted to the following annual capacities:

A_1: 1 million pounds

A_2: 2 million pounds

A_3: 5 million pounds

The conditional opportunity losses under S_1 ("high" sales) and S_2 ("low" sales) are shown in Table 16-1. As noted from the table, in this simplified example if S_1 obtains, act A_3 is the best course of action and is accordingly assigned a condition opportunity loss of zero. If S_2 obtains, however, act A_1 becomes the best course of action. Act A_2 is a kind of "hedging" act in the sense that the conditional opportunity losses associated with it are not extreme under either S_1 or S_2.

The problem facing the product planner is to estimate the probabilities of occurrence of S_1 and S_2, respectively. More appropriately, how precise must these estimates be? Suppose that $P(S_1)$ can vary over the interval 0 to 1. Then $P(S_2)$ is equal to $1 - P(S_1)$. If $P(S_1)$ were equal to 0.1, then the expected opportunity losses of the three acts would be:

$$EOL(A_1) = 0.1(6) + 0.9(0) = \$0.6 \text{ million}$$

$$EOL(A_2) = 0.1(3) + 0.9(3) = \$3.0 \text{ million}$$

$$EOL(A_3) = 0.1(0) + 0.9(8) = \$7.2 \text{ million}$$

TABLE 16-1 Conditional Opportunity Losses (Millions of Dollars)—Food-Supplement Problem

Act	State of Nature	
	S_1	S_2
A_1	6	0
A_2	3	3
A_3	0	8

**Figure 16-3 Expected Opportunity Losses (Millions of Dollars)—
Food-Supplement Problem**

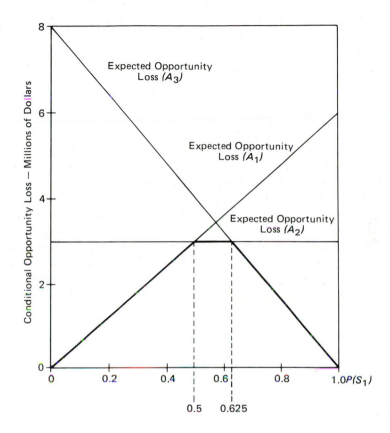

Clearly, under these conditions act A_1 (the low-capacity facility) would be preferable to the other courses of action. By assuming various values that $P(S_1)$ *could* have, we can construct the chart of expected opportunity losses shown in Figure 16-3.

We see from Figure 16-3 that if $P(S_1)$ is less than 0.5, then act A_1 is best, whereas if $P(S_1)$ is between 0.5 and 0.625, act A_2 is best. If $P(S_1)$ should exceed 0.625, then act A_3 is best. If $P(S_1)$ is exactly 0.625, either A_2 or A_3 could be chosen. These "indifference" points are determined by finding the points on the abscissa where the lines of expected opportunity loss intersect, that is, where

$$\text{EOL}(A_1) = \text{EOL}(A_2)$$

Letting $P(S_1) = P$, we have

$$6P + 0(1 - P) = 3$$

$$P = 0.5$$

Similarly, where E.O.L. (A_3) = E.O.L. A_2 then

$$OP + 8(1 - P) = 3$$

$$P = 0.625$$

The implication of these oversimplified calculations is that the product planner does *not* need to know the precise value of $P(S_1)$ but only that it falls in specific ranges. In terms of the assumptions of this problem, the same act (act A_1) would be chosen if $P(S_1)$ were, say 0.1, as would be chosen if $P(S_1)$ were, say 0.4. Although the illustration is simple, it does serve to demonstrate that in some marketing problems forecasts do *not* need to be made with high precision.

Many Action–Many State Problems

In more realistic cases, of course, a greater number of states of nature and courses of action are possible. For example, in inventory-control problems some "best" level of inventory may exist for each possible sales level. In production-planning problems the quantity of product produced may vary more or less continuously within a certain range.

To make the "many act–many state" case more specific, suppose that a promotion planner in the ethical drug field is interested in determining the "best" number of samples to produce for distribution to physicians by the firm's detailing salespeople. If physicians' requests for samples exceed the quantity produced, ill will incurred is assumed to be associated with unfilled requests as a function of the level of demand. If the number of samples produced exceeds the requests, there will be costs associated with excess production and inventory. For purposes of illustration, suppose that the imputed "cost" for each *unfilled* physician's request (for one sample) is $1.20 and suppose that the cost associated with each sample produced *in excess* of requests if $0.30. The promotion planner is interested in recommending some best level of sample production that minimizes expected cost under an uncertain demand for samples of the new product.

Assume that the upper panel of Figure 16-4 shows the promotion planner's probability distribution (expressed in histogram form) of the possible demand levels for samples of the new product. The planner is willing to believe that demand for the new drug samples will exceed 20,000 units and will be no higher than 80,000 units. The most "probable estimate" of demand (higher bar of the histogram) is that demand will be between 30,000 and 40,000 units.

The lower panel of Figure 16-4 shows the cumulative probability distribution derived from the histogram in the upper panel of the chart. The smooth curve in the lower panel of the chart is used to approximate cumulative probabilities *within* the histogram intervals. For example, the estimated probability of physician demand being less than 35,000 units is 0.45, as read from this curve.

To determine the best number of drug samples to produce, the promotion planner would like to find the appropriate balance point where the expected cost of underproducing just equals the expected cost of overproducing. We already know that both these costs are proportional to the difference between the amount produced and the amount requested.

Figure 16-4   Probability Distribution—Demand for Samples of New Drug Product (Thousands of Units)

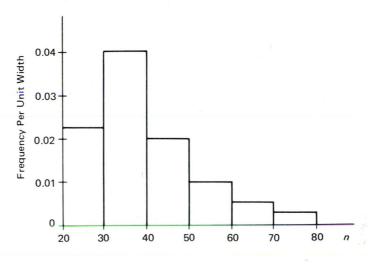

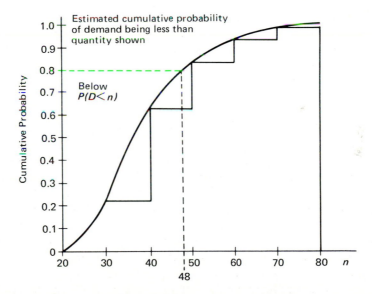

Fortunately, however, we do not have to construct a payoff table for *each* possible act and demand level. Instead, we may follow the principle "Keep increasing the production quantity until highest level n is reached for which the expected incremental cost of adding the nth unit is still less than the expected incremental cost of not adding the nth unit to the production level."

If we let D = demand level, C_o = \$0.30 = cost per unit of overproduction, and C_u = \$1.20 = cost per unit of underproduction relative to demand, we have, by application of the principle above,

$$C_0 P(D < n) < C_u[1 - P(D < n)]$$

$$[P(D < n)](C_o + C_u) < C_u$$

$$P(D < n) < \frac{C_u}{C_0 + C_u}$$

$$P(D < n) < \frac{\$1.20}{\$1.20 + \$0.30}$$

$$P(D < n) < 0.80$$

Returning to the lower panel of Figure 16-4, we note that the largest n for which $P(D < n) < 0.80$ is approximately 48,000 units. This represents the graphical solution to the problem. Had the promotion planner *not* considered the *asymmetry in the costs of over- versus underproduction,* he or she might have planned for either (1) a production level equal to the midpoint of the highest bar in the histogram (i.e., 35,000 units) or (2) a production level equal to the median or 0.5 cumulative probability level of the distribution (i.e., 36,000 units). In either case the promotion planner would have "underproduced" relative to the solution that takes into consideration the conditional costs of over- versus underproduction.

The essence of this problem is that forecasts should, in some cases, be *biased* to reflect the possible asymmetry of costs. In the present illustration we can see that *neither* the "most probable" (modal) forecast nor the median forecast necessarily represents the best level to plan for. As a matter of fact, in this illustration even the mean of the original probability distribution (39,300 units) would have provided too low a production level for minimizing expected total cost.

The preceding illustrations have demonstrated, first, that forecasts do not necessarily have to be precise to be useful and, second, that "best" single estimates of the unknown parameter do not necessarily lead to the best decision.

We can view the selection of forecasting procedures in the same general fashion as any other decision problem under uncertainty. Frequently, to achieve greater forecasting accuracy, the marketing researcher will have to employ more expensive forecasting procedures. The value of this increased accuracy for decision-making purposes should be balanced against the increased cost. The marketing researcher must continually ask, What would management do *differently* if a forecasting procedure yielding greater accuracy could be employed? Even if increased accuracy *can* be obtained, it is rarely obvious that the additional cost entailed is justified.

SUMMARY

The central theme of this chapter has been the treatment of forecasting activity within the framework of cost and value of information. We first discussed the general nature of forecasting and some of the problems associated with it.

Some of the major mechanistic techniques—exponential smoothing, correlation, trend analysis, and econometric models—were next briefly described. The role of less formal procedures—polling techniques—was also pointed out, and it was suggested that these techniques, though less formal, should not be summarily dismissed as being ineffective.

We concluded the chapter with a discussion of forecasting in the framework of decision theory. It was shown that (1) forecasts need not necessarily be highly accurate in order to support good decisions, and (2) depending on the nature of the forecast error, a "biased" estimate may lead to better results than "unbiased" estimating procedures.

ASSIGNMENT MATERIAL

1. The McKeon Company is a firm selling industrial supplies. Its marketing manager desires to find whether a useful forecasting formula can be developed by correlating its monthly sales with the ratio of unfilled orders to production for its major customers two months in advance. Data obtained for the preceding 12 months are as follows:

Month	Y, McKeon Sales in Time $t-2$	Month	X, Ratio of Unfilled Orders to Production in Time t
Jan.	$1.2 million	Mar.	1.15
Feb.	1.3	Apr.	1.20
Mar.	1.1	May	0.90
Apr.	1.0	June	0.80
May	0.8	July	0.75
June	1.2	Aug.	1.00
July	1.5	Sept.	1.35
Aug.	1.7	Oct.	1.40
Sept.	1.6	Nov.	1.65
Oct.	1.9	Dec.	1.80
Nov.	1.4	Jan.	1.45
Dec.	1.2	Feb.	1.20

  a. Prepare a scatter diagram for these data.
  b. Compute a linear regression equation.
  c. Assuming that the value of X in the next time period is 1.3, what is your estimate (using the regression equation) of McKeon's sales?
  d. What assumptions are you making in preparing the forecast in part (c)?

2. The Kerin Company is interested in using exponential smoothing for short-range forecasting purposes for inventory control. Monthly sales data (in millions of dollars) are shown below for a two-year historical period:

1985		1986	
Jan. 3.4	July 4.2	Jan. 4.4	July 5.8
Feb. 3.6	Aug. 3.9	Feb. 4.7	Aug. 6.0
Mar. 3.7	Sept. 3.8	Mar. 4.9	Sept. 5.7
Apr. 3.9	Oct. 4.1	Apr. 5.2	Oct. 6.2
May 4.2	Nov. 3.9	May 5.3	Nov. 6.4
June 4.7	Dec. 3.7	June 5.6	Dec. 6.7

a. Using smoothing constants of 0.1 and 0.2, respectively, prepare two exponential smoothings of these data. (Use the mean of the first three months, in each case, as a starting value for $\overset{*}{S}_{t-1}$. Then start the smoothing process in the fourth period.)

b. Compute the mean absolute deviation under each smoothing procedure for the period April 1985 through December 1986 according to the formula

$$\text{MAD} = \frac{1}{21} \sum_{t=4}^{24} |\overset{*}{S}_t - X_t|$$

where $\overset{*}{S}_t$ is the smoothed value and X_t the actual value for period t.

c. Compute the mean absolute deviation under each smoothing procedure for one-period-ahead forecasts according to the formula

$$\text{MAD} = \frac{1}{20} \sum_{t=4}^{23} |\overset{*}{S}_t - X_{t+1}|$$

Which value of the smoothing constant leads to the lower mean absolute deviation over the time series?

3. The marketing researcher for a breakfast food manufacturer is interested in determining the best number of premiums (a small toy) to order in conjunction with a forthcoming couponing campaign. If the number of requests for the premium should exceed its stock, the firm's policy is that the toy must be purchased on the open market to fill any demand excess. The opportunity cost per unit of demand unfilled by initial stock is $0.45. On the other hand, if too large a stock is ordered, the cost per unit of excess stock is $0.20. The marketing researcher's estimate of the demand distribution for the premium is as follows:

DEMAND LESS THAN OR EQUAL TO (UNITS)	CUMULATIVE PROBABILITY
50,000	0.00
60,000	0.10
70,000	0.35

(*continued*)

Demand Less Than or Equal to (Units)	Cumulative Probability
80,000	0.60
90,000	0.85
100,000	0.95
110,000	1.00

   a. Compute an estimated mean demand for the premium.
   b. Determine the best level of stock to order.
   c. In this problem, is the midpoint of the model demand interval a better or worse forecast than the estimated mean?

4. If it requires 75 minutes to assemble the first unit of a new appliance, what is the estimated time required for the 1,000th unit, given an 80% learning curve?

5. Given the following opportunity-loss table:

	State of Nature	
Act	S_1	S_2
A_1	9	0
A_2	4	5
A_3	0	7

   a. Construct a chart of expected opportunity losses as a function of the probability $P(S_1)$.
   b. If $P(S_1)$ is 0.6, which act leads to the lowest expected opportunity loss?
   c. Multiply all entries of the original table by 3. Does this change your answer to part (b)?

6. Which is the overall best approach to forecasting in marketing: "what people say," "what people do," or "what people have done"? Why?

17

Brand Positioning and Market Segmentation

INTRODUCTION

The basic question underlying many specialized procedures used in marketing research is simple; What makes people buy what brands or services? Depending on the resolution of this question are various decisions regarding changes in marketing mix variables—product, promotion, pricing, personal selling, packaging, distribution, after-the-sale service, and the like.

Over the years marketing researchers have developed a number of specialized procedures for dealing with such problems as advertising-copy testing, market segmentation, and new-product concept generation and testing, to name a few. These procedures have demonstrated their usefulness in helping marketers understand at least some of the reasons why people buy. This chapter (and Chapter 18 as well) is concerned with describing some of these methods in order to give the reader a flavor of the kinds of things that a marketing researcher may be called upon to do.

Both chapters offer more of a survey-type treatment than the material in Parts III and IV. For the most part, we do *not* delve deeply into the mechanics of the techniques but rather attempt to provide illustrations of their application and rationales for their development.

Brand positioning and market segmentation appear to be hallmarks of today's marketing research. From a marketing management viewpoint, market segmentation is the act of dividing a market into distinct groups of buyers who *might* require separate products and/or marketing programs directed to them. In contrast, brand (product) po-

672

sitioning is the act of developing a product and its associated marketing program to fit a place in the consumer's mind. The basis of product (or brand) positioning is segmentation "working" through market targeting which involves evaluating and selecting one or more of the market segments to serve:

| Market Segmentation | → | Market Targeting | → | Market Positioning |

From the perspective of research, *brand* (or *service*) *positioning* deals with measuring the perceptions that buyers hold about alternative marketplace offerings. *Market segmentation,* on the other hand, deals with determining which perceptions, preferences, characteristics, or other aspects of consumer choice might differ across buyer groups (see Exhibit 17-1). For example, a photofinisher did research to determine what consumers expect from film processing. Regarding one of its retail accounts, the photofinisher's

Exhibit 17-1   Using Research for Target Marketing

Marketers often face the problem of attracting new buyers to brands whose sales are declining. The first step, an obvious one, is to identify who these potential new buyers are. While it is very easy to simply say they are buyers of competitive brands, that is not sufficient to indicate what types of marketing activity would be most effective in attracting them.

What is necessary is an understanding of their purchasing behavior—for that will often provide "marketing handles" which one can utilize to reach these people. Learning how they shop, where they shop, what induces them to purchase, how loyal they are, how frequently they shop and how much they buy on each purchase occasion are all useful pieces of information for structuring market strategies.

As an illustration related to where people shop, Brand A was experiencing a decline in sales and there was a need to know which *target group(s)* presented the best *attraction* opportunity. By examining the purchase patterns of Brand A buyers compared to non-buyers of Brand A (target group) a substantial difference was discovered. Non-buyers of Brand A were making twice as many purchases in non-grocery outlets as were Brand A buyers, and about three times as many purchases in Discount Stores!

PERCENT OF CATEGORY SALES

TYPE OF STORE	BRAND A BUYERS	NON-BRAND A BUYERS	DIFFERENCE
Non-Grocery	21%	43%	105%
Grocery	79%	57%	
Discount Stores	12%	33%	175%

Furthermore, on a trend basis, non-grocery outlets were increasing their importance. Volume-wise they had a 26% increase in sales, accounting for 39% of total this year compared to 31% in the previous year. Even more significant was the increase in product category buyers who were not buying in non-grocery outlets (41% vs. 34%).

PERCENT OF CATEGORY VOLUME AND BUYERS ACCOUNTED FOR BY NON-GROCERY OUTLETS

QUARTER	VOLUME	BUYERS
1	31	34
2	32	35
3	32	36
4	35	38
5	39	41

This analysis indicated that by focusing its marketing efforts in grocery stores (the present targeting strategy), Brand A was essentially ignoring 40% of its potential buyers.

A regional analysis showed that market share in the South was weaker than in the rest of the country. Low sales in non-grocery outlets and the importance of such outlets in the South combined to depress sales in the region.

The message to marketing management was clear. There was a need to gain distribution in non-grocery outlets particularly in the South. A marketing program aimed at this would then be targeted to the areas of greatest need.

Source: Adapted from "The Importance of Target Marketing," *NPD Insights*, No. 10 (February 1982).

research showed that some of its customers wanted quick processing, others wanted photos for remembrance, and still others wanted high-quality prints. These three amateur photographer segments were to be satisfied by offering (1) one-day service for single standard-sized prints, (2) double prints of everything, and (3) oversized prints on glossy paper.

In either case we are interested in designing strategies that will enhance the company's offerings in terms of market share and earnings. Accordingly, the first part of the chapter describes a framework for examining prospective marketing strategies—market penetration, market development, product development, and diversification.

We then discuss a brand-positioning study that was undertaken by a large manufacturer of digital computers. We examine the congruence of the firm's product image across various groups—its salespeople, customers, and noncustomers.

Market segmentation is discussed next. We first describe the major methodological approaches to segmentation and then comment on the myriad bases or criteria that have been suggested for defining segments. Following this, two industry studies are discussed. The first study is a combined application of brand positioning and segmentation, undertaken for a Midwest brewery facing a severe loss in market share in one of its historically best trading areas. The second example is drawn from the auto insurance field and illustrates an application involving various consumer types that are identified in terms of perceptions, psychographics, and demographics.

In brief, the chapter tries to weave in some theoretical and methodological material with actual industrial examples that have been part of the authors' consulting experience.

MARKET STRATEGY FORMULATION

Brand positioning and market segmentation—indeed, any of the tools that are discussed in this and the succeeding chapter—ultimately are concerned with *strategy* formulation. *Marketing strategy* involves a simultaneous consideration of the firm's offerings and the market's wants and needs.

Ansoff's 2 × 2 Strategy Classification

More than 20 years ago Ansoff[1] developed a 2 × 2 table in which he considered four basic strategies in marketing:

- Market penetration
- Market development
- Product development
- Diversification

These four strategies were based on whether present or new products were made available to present or new markets.

Table 17-1 shows this schema. As noted, maintaining the same product line and the same markets (i.e., *market penetration*) suggests tactics that attempt to increase the intensity of usage among present customers by (1) promoting new end uses for the product, (2) increasing its disposability, (3) making it more price competitive with substitutes, and so on.

In *market development*, new classes of buyers (e.g., those from different geographic locations or different demographic backgrounds) are sought in an effort to broaden demand

TABLE 17-1 Ansoff's 2 × 2 Classification of Marketing Strategies

	PRESENT MARKETS	NEW MARKETS
Present products	Market penetration	Market development
New products	Product development	Diversification

[1] I. Ansoff, *Corporate Strategy* (New York: McGraw-Hill, 1965).

for the present product line. In *product development*, new items or modifications of the present ones are sought to increase the line's breadth of usage among present customers. Finally, in *diversification*, changes in products and markets are pursued simultaneously.

An Expanded Version

The 2×2 schema can easily be expanded by the simple idea of splitting products and markets into two subcategories: (1) *structural* and (2) *functional* characteristics. Table 17-2 shows the resulting 4×4 schema. (The term *offering* is used in Table 17-2 to cover both products and services.)

Structural characteristics of products include physical- and chemical-attribute levels, packaging, distribution, and price. "Structural" characteristics of persons refer to their demographic and socioeconomic characteristics. Although the latter characteristics are expected to change over time, they may be treated as fixed for relatively short time intervals. Moreover, it is reasonable to assume that demographic and socioeconomic variables moderate peoples' choices among offerings but, in turn, are pretty much independent of the firm's marketing strategies.

Functional characteristics of offerings pertain to the uses or purposes to which the products are to be put. (Included here are the symbolic values that offerings may display in a sociopsychological context.) Stretching the analogy a bit, functional characteristics of people pertain to one's style of living and one's perceptions and values in the marketplace.

Two different structural offerings (e.g., a mechanical pencil and a ballpoint pen) may serve the single function of facilitating written communication. Conversely, a single offering (e.g., a lemon-lime soft drink) may serve two or more functions, such as a midafternoon refreshment or a mixer with one's favorite bourbon at bedtime. The functions

TABLE 17-2   Expanded (4 × 4) Version of the Ansoff Schema

		PRESENT SEGMENTS		NEW SEGMENTS	
		Structural Characteristics	*Functional– Expressive Behavior*	*Structural Characteristics*	*Functional– Expressive Behavior*
Present offerings	Structural characteristics	MARKET PENETRATION		MARKET DEVELOPMENT	
	Functional– symbolic appeals				
New offerings	Structural characteristics	PRODUCT DEVELOPMENT		DIVERSIFICATION	
	Functional– symbolic appeals				

that an offering purports to fill are part of its array of promotional appeals, claims, and symbolic characteristics.

By the same token, two different demographic structures could display (within limits) a similar life-style, benefit-seeking pattern, or brand-preference profile. Conversely, a single type of demographic structure could manifest different goal-seeking and expressive behaviors.

The original Ansoff schema did not distinguish between structural and functional characteristics of offerings and markets. From the standpoint of strategy formulation, a more detailed classification might be preferred. For example, in the field of auto insurance one might want to distinguish between structural product development in which the actual policy's characteristics are altered (e.g., increased benefits, extended coverage, increased premium) and functional product development in which different appeals for selling the original policy are implemented. In turn, these appeals could be targeted to specific demographic groups, selected life-style segments, or different life-styles within a demographic group.

Depending on the empirical context, the interconnections between structure and function may be loosely or tightly coupled. For example, lowering an insurance policy's premium and offering the policy by mail may markedly change the offering's functional–symbolic character. Conversely, including a new restriction on claims (as part of the policy's fine print) may exert no effect whatsoever on the policy's image. Whatever may be the case, a general problem in strategy formulation is to achieve *congruence* between structure and functional–symbolic appeals. In particular, one may wish to find a specific structure that allows for a variety of believable functional–symbolic appeals, each one being attractive to a different market segment.

The value of the schema of Tables 17-1 and 17-2 is the guidance it provides for designing a brand-positioning or segmentation study in the first place. For example, consider the problem of a telephone company (e.g., Pacific Northwest Bell, a unit of U.S. West) wishing to increase revenues for long-distance usage within the area in which it offers long-distance service. Clearly, little can be gained by attempting to increase installed sets. For the most part, the market is pretty much saturated, although there always are possibilities of having people add additional telephone lines. What *can* be done (especially when considering competitive pressure from non-telephone-company long-distance services such as MCI and Sprint) involves such strategic aspects as

- Increasing the variety of appeals related to why people call long distance
- Changing the pricing or discount structure for further load leveling and increased overall demand
- Appealing to special demographic groups—senior citizens, college students, military service personnel—via special rates or gift certificates
- Appealing to special life-styles—the highly mobile, gregarious, and involved person—via special appeals or channels, such as direct mail

The reader can probably think of other illustrations where the permissible courses of action shape the kind of positioning or segmentation study that should be implemented. As basic as this point is, many research studies are launched and the data analyzed *before* the central ideal of formulating strategy alternatives even comes up. Accordingly, in each of the studies that follow we shall devote attention to the kinds of strategies that motivated the study design in the first place.

BRAND AND SERVICE POSITIONING

At any point in time the firm has some array of brands or services competing with other brands or service suppliers in the marketplace. A number of questions are associated with one's interest in the *status quo:*

1. How are our brands positioned in the minds of consumers and the trade vis-á-vis competing brands?
2. What kinds of people prefer our brands and how do these people compare with noncustomers in terms of brand perceptions and preferences, benefits sought, life-style, and demographics?
3. What appears to be happening to brand position from a more or less dynamic standpoint; that is, from what brands are we gaining customers and to what brands are we losing customers?

The three questions above are rather pervasive in any assay of the current (and short-range future) market position of the firm. Not surprisingly, a number of specialized procedures have been developed to help provide answers to these questions. We first take up the topic of brand and service positioning (Exhibit 17-2).

Exhibit 17-2   Repositioning an Automobile

One of the most successful foreign automobile manufacturers exporting to the U.S. market is Saab. In general, the U.S. importer, Saab–Scania of America, can sell every car it imports. The strategy followed by Saab is to produce a technologically superior product which is positioned in a small but growing and profitable market *niche.* Thus, Saab sells a relatively small number of cars, which are expensive and profitable.

During the 1950s and 1960s Saab's car market consisted of engineers, racing enthusiasts, and college professors. When the model 900 Turbo was introduced in 1979 the car was a big hit with "ski-resort owners and 'hippies' with golden retrievers." The company clearly needed new customers—e.g., those buying Volvos, BMWs and Audis. In order to expand the consumer market the following strategy was adopted:

- *Reposition* Saab as a luxurious, high-performance automobile
- Position it properly against its logical competition (BMW and Volvo)

Both advertising and marketing research were needed to achieve the repositioning. Moreover, research has confirmed the wisdom of the niche strategy and the specific repositioning. The luxury/sport segment and its corresponding consumer market is one of the fastest-growing in the auto industry.

Source: Adapted from B. Whalen, "'Tiny' Saab Drives Up Profits with Market-Niche Strategy Repositioning," *Marketing News,* 18 (March 16, 1984), Sec. 1., pp. 14–16.

One of the major activities pursued by contemporary marketing researchers is *brand* or *service positioning*. One approach to this problem is concerned with the development of perceptual and preference "maps" (as described in Chapter 15) of how consumers or industrial users "see" various brands as being similar or different and what combination of attribute levels they most prefer in their personal (or possibly household or organizational) choice of a product or service.

To illustrate the idea of brand/service positioning, we draw on a study undertaken for a large computer firm concerned with industrial users' evaluations of its offerings compared with other major competitors in the market.

A Computer Company Example

As is well known, the computer field is dominated by a few large-scale producers. International Business Machines, in particular, has enjoyed a commanding share of this market. Computers are highly complex from a technological point of view and their marketing requires sizable expenditures in providing the customer with technical backup, maintenance, and software capabilities. Computer users' views of alternative suppliers might be expected to include a variety of image characteristics that are not restricted to the performance features of competing computers.

One of the firms in this field was concerned with its positioning in the minds of computer users vis-á-vis competitive manufacturers.[2] In particular, the firm's management wished to know how its evaluation on a large number of attributes might compare with other firms in the field. In addition, the firm wished to learn how important each attribute might be in various users' (e.g., government, financial institutions, utilities) selection of computers and, in particular, whether these attribute "importances" might vary among present customers, noncustomers, and the company's own sales employees.

For purposes of these (and related) questions a sample of 310 computer users was drawn up in terms of

1. Current customers—130 respondents, half of whom held positions directly involved with data processing and half of whom were other customer-firm employees who played some role in equipment selection
2. Noncustomers (i.e., users of other firms' computers)—130 respondents, half data-processors, and half other employees with a stake in equipment selection
3. Sponsoring company's sales employees—50 respondents

In addition, the consumer group was stratified by end-use industry—fabrication, processing, utilities–communications, and so on.

A list of 15 attributes (including *overall* preference) was developed in cooperation with the sponsor's internal marketing research group. These appear in Table 17-3. Also shown in Table 17-3 are the eight firms that were to be evaluated with respect to each of the attributes.

[2]We are indebted to Robinson Associates, Inc., for permission to reproduce some of these materials.

TABLE 17-3   List of Attributes and Computer Firms Used in Supplier-Positioning Study

ATTRIBUTES

1. Favorableness of Performance/Cost Ratio
2. Provision for Utilizing a Large Number of Programming Languages
3. Reliability of Hardware
4. Extensiveness of Software Packages
5. Ease of Changeover from Other Systems
6. Quality of Education/Training
7. Quality of Technical Backup Services
8. Quality of Sales Presentations
9. Most Effective Use of Virtual Memory
10. High Acceptance by Systems Personnel
11. Innovativeness
12. Thoroughness and Speed of Service after the Sale
13. Flexibility regarding Price Negotiation
14. Suitability for Time Sharing
15. Your Overall Preference

COMPUTER FIRMS BEING RANKED

1. Burroughs
2. Control Data Corporation (CDC)
3. Honeywell
4. International Business Machines (IBM)
5. National Cash Register (NCR)
6. Radio Corporation of America (RCA)
7. Univac
8. Xerox (XDS)

Computer Manufacturer Evaluation

Each respondent, data processor, equipment specifier, or sponsoring firm employee was then asked to rank the eight computer firms with respect to each attribute, in turn, in accord with the following instructions (which were modified for the sponsoring firm's employees):

In this part of the questionnaire we are going to show you a set of cards—each card has the name of a computer firm. (HAND RESPONDENT THE SET OF 8 WHITE CARDS.)

Now we're going to mention various characteristics regarding computer manufacturers. For each such characteristic we'd like you to *rank* the various manufacturers in terms of how they stand relatively on each attribute, or characteristic.

For example, let's take the characteristic "performance/cost ratio." In your judgment, which of the computer manufacturers, in general, seems to offer the most favorable performance/cost ratio? Which next most? And so on. Don't be concerned if your knowledge of the various firms is limited. We're interested in your impressions, however vague they may seem to you. (HAVE RESPONDENT RANK THE 8 WHITE CARDS, IN TURN, FOR THE CHARACTERISTICS LISTED.)

In analyzing the rankings data obtained from this part of the questionnaire, we employed multidimensional scaling techniques of the type discussed in Chapter 15. For summary purposes, Figure 17-1 shows the total-sample results of respondent evaluations of the eight manufacturers in terms of a two-dimensional plot. The 15 attributes are represented by vectors in the same space. The scaling algorithm finds these point locations and the attributes' vector directions simultaneously so that the total-sample's rankings of the eight computer firms on each attribute can be estimated by merely dropping perpendiculars from each of the eight points onto each vector, in turn.

To illustrate, we consider the attribute "reliability of hardware," abbreviated as

Figure 17-1 Total-sample Perceptions of Computer Manufacturers and Attribute Directions

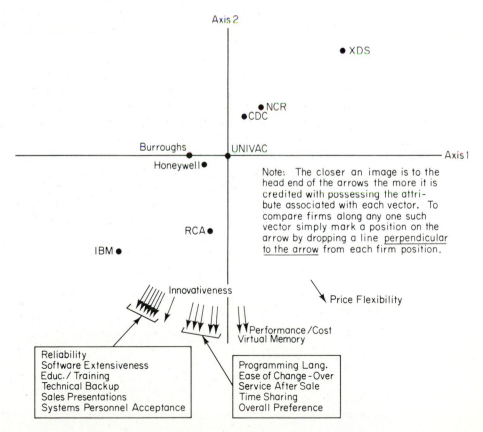

Note: The closer an image is to the head end of the arrows the more it is credited with possessing the attribute associated with each vector. To compare firms along any one such vector simply mark a position on the arrow by dropping a line perpendicular to the arrow from each firm position.

Reliability
Software Extensiveness
Educ./Training
Technical Backup
Sales Presentations
Systems Personnel Acceptance

Programming Lang.
Ease of Change-Over
Service After Sale
Time Sharing
Overall Preference

"reliability" in Figure 17-1. If we project each of the eight points onto this vector we obtain the scale-value ordering: IBM (first); RCA; Honeywell; Burroughs; Univac; CDC; NCR; and XDS (last). Although not described here, it turns out that each derived scale approaches interval-scale properties (where scale separations are meaningful) from input data that are only rank-ordered originally.

In terms of the problem at hand, the dominance of IBM is clearly indicated. On every attribute except "price flexibility," IBM ranks first insofar as the total sample is concerned. Interestingly enough, RCA ranks first on "price flexibility" and second on the remaining attributes.[3] Burroughs, Honeywell, and Univac are somewhat clustered, as are CDC and NCR. The Xerox Corporation's computers (XDS) represent a rather isolated point, quite possibly a result of their relative newness in the market and the resultant lack of respondent familiarity regarding their features.[4]

It is also of interest to point out that all 15 attributes are highly correlated, suggesting a type of "halo" effect. That is, if a respondent really has high regard for a firm he or she tends to rank the firm highly on *all* attributes. Only the attribute "price flexibility" appears to be highly distinguished from the others.

Attribute Importance

An additional question of interest to the firm concerned the relative importance that respondents would give to the attributes themselves in selecting a computer supplier. In particular, the sponsor wished to know if attribute importance varied by end-use industry— government, utilities–communications, educational–medical, financial, fabrication, process, transportation–retail—and by customer versus noncustomer, versus its own sales employees.

Accordingly, 14 of the 15 preceding attributes (excluding overall preference) were submitted for respondent evaluation in the following manner:

> Now we are going to show you 14 cards, each card bearing the name of a characteristic of computer manufacturers. (HAND RESPONDENT THE SET OF 14 GREEN CARDS SHOWING ATTRIBUTES.) What we would like you to do is group the cards into four piles, with approximately 3 cards per pile. The first pile should include those characteristics that you feel are *crucial* in your choice of a supplier.
>
> The second pile should contain those characteristics that are *highly important* to your choice of a supplier. The third pile should contain those characteristics that are *fairly important*. The fourth pile should contain those cards that are *not particularly important* to your evaluation of competing suppliers. (RE-CORD CARD NUMBERS OF SORTINGS IN RESPONSE FORM.)

---

[3]This study, which includes RCA, was undertaken *before* this company announced plans to discontinue its computer operations.

[4]Subsequent to this study, however, Xerox also dropped its XDS product line.

The ratings obtained by the above procedure, with the wording modified in the case of the sponsor's sales employees, were also analyzed via multidimensional scaling. In this case, however, the sample was partitioned twice, first by end-use industry (excluding the firm's employees' responses) and then on a customer versus noncustomer versus sales employee basis. In the latter case customer and noncustomer respondents were further subdivided into data processors (technically oriented, data-processing respondents, designated as the A group) and other equipment specifiers (e.g., controllers, engineers and other management personnel not directly involved in data processing, designated as the B group).

Figure 17-2 shows the results of this analysis, using the same type of analysis and diagram described earlier. In this case, however, attributes are represented as points (the things being rated) and respondent groups as vectors (the "things" performing the ratings).

As can be observed from Figure 17-2, the 14 attribute points reflect an underlying evaluative dimension that is almost unidimensional; that is, the attribute points lie very close to the horizontal axis of the figure.

The scale values of the 14 attribute points indicate that reliability of hardware is evaluated as the most important characteristic, followed by quality of technical backup services and extensiveness of software packages. Quality of sales presentations is viewed as least important. Note that the vector labeled "grand average" is almost coincident with the horizontal axis; this vector was developed from input data for the total sample.

Figure 17-2 Importance of Computer Manufacturer Attribute by Type of Respondent

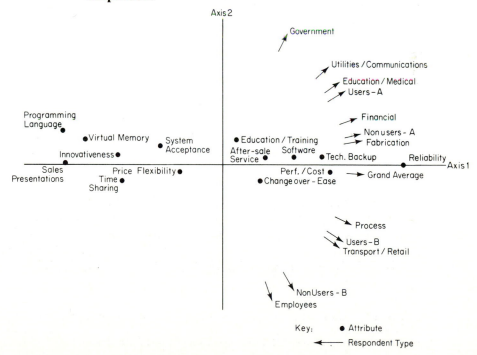

Insofar as end-user industry differences are concerned, we first examine the initial partitioning by industry class. Respondents in the government sector exhibit evaluations that are most highly separated from those in the transportation–retailing field. Even so, the rankings are virtually the same (e.g., for both groups reliability of hardware is viewed as most important), a reflection of the fact that little scatter of the points is found about the horizontal axis, although scale separations differ between the two groups.

When one examines the second basis for partitioning—users (groups A and B) versus nonusers (groups A and B), versus the sponsoring firm's sales employees—it seems that the main characteristic on which the groups' evaluations are separated is in terms of data-processing jobs versus other kinds of jobs. That is, both customers and noncustomers evaluate the attributes approximately the same, given the fact that they are respondents directly involved in data processing. However, their evaluations differ from those of respondents (group B) who are *not* directly involved in data processing. Interestingly enough, the sponsor's sales employees exhibit attribute evaluations that are close to those of the *non-data-processor respondents*.

In brief, the sponsor firm's customers evaluated the attributes about the same as noncustomers if one holds constant on type of job held by the respondent; attribute importance appears to be more a function of respondent job than it is of customer versus noncustomer status.[5]

Implications

The material abstracted here represented only a small part of the study. Based on other information collected in the study, the sponsoring firm's perceived position in the market was found to be considerably different from that based on the *objective* characteristics of its hardware vis-á-vis its competitors'. Moreover, from a total-sample standpoint, the sponsor firm tended to be rated highly on the *less important* attributes underlying supplier choice. And, those respondents who rated the firm most highly tended to be (1) highly technically trained data processors, (2) interested in performance/cost, (3) former IBM customers, and (4) data processors with high-level authority for choosing suppliers.

Unfortunately the sponsor's sales employees were (1) emphasizing the *less important* features of the product line; (2) failing to get across the story of the firm's superiority in specific aspects of performance/cost; and (3) catering more to the less sophisticated, nondata processor (group B respondents), who, in turn, were less likely to switch from the full-service features provided by IBM.

This example illustrates how market positioning can be used to examine the relationship between "objective" and "subjective" performance characteristics, on the one hand, and image contrasts among customers, noncustomers, and sales employees, on the other. In this case it appeared that the sponsor's salespeople were failing to capitalize on the firm's strengths with respect to the more sophisticated type of computer user. Instead,

---

[5]Although not discussed in detail here, the cosine of the angular separation between any pair of vectors represents a direct measure of the correlation between respondent group ratings. Thus, the vector denoting users-A is more highly correlated with the vector denoting nonusers-A than it is with users-B.

they were employing a sales strategy that was incompatible with the firm's image as a technical, performance/cost-oriented supplier that did *not* presume to provide the full service features of the industry giant IBM.

Other Applications

Although perceptual and preference mapping are powerful techniques for handling brand or service positioning, they are by no means the only useful techniques. Nor must

Figure 17-3   Comparative Profiles of Credit Union, PFF, and U.S. National Bank

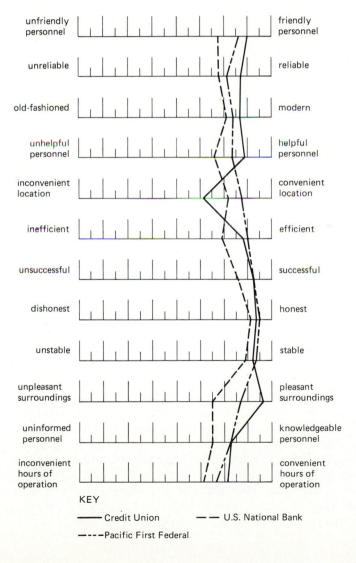

TABLE 17-4   Choice Criteria Average Scores for Comparative Motels*

MOTEL	AVERAGE SCORE FOR THE EIGHT "IMPORTANT" CHOICE CRITERIA	AVERAGE SCORE FOR THE FOUR "VERY IMPORTANT" CHOICE CRITERIA
Birger	3.88	4.00
Country Squire	3.69	3.63
Travelodge	2.88	3.38
Greentree	3.88	4.00
New Oregon	2.06	2.88
Ramada Inn	3.38	3.25

*Each criterion was scaled 1 to 5, with 1 representing *poor* and 5 representing *excellent*.

positioning techniques be as sophisticated or complex as those used to develop perceptual and preference maps. Sometimes a team can use simpler scaling techniques such as the semantic differential and numerical rating scales to provide data for assessing its present position.

As an illustration, a credit union was interested in determining how it had positioned itself in the minds of its members relative to other financial institutions in the county. A mail survey of 700 members of the credit union resulted in responses from 441 members. The members of the sample were asked to rate the credit union and one other financial institution (a commercial bank or savings and loan association) on 12 dimensions presented as a graphical positioning semantic differential. In addition to the credit union, sufficient responses were obtained for one savings and loan (the largest in the county) and three commercial banks. As the profiles show in Figure 17-3, the credit union was able to position itself in the minds of its members close to that of the largest commercial bank and the largest savings and loan in the county. Two apparently noticeable exceptions are the credit union's relatively inconvenient location and its relatively more pleasant surroundings.

Another illustration of a relatively simple approach that can be viewed as assessing positioning is provided by a study conducted for a motel (Birger). The motel's owner wanted to know how the motel was viewed compared with others that its customers perceived to be most similar to it. The sample for the mail survey that was used was drawn from the motel's records of customers who had stayed there during the two years prior to data collection. A total of 268 responses were received. Respondents were asked to evaluate 10 motels in the area on the basis of 12 criteria. In addition, survey members were asked to identify three motels most similar to the Birger. Five such motels were identified. The evaluation of the Birger and these motels is shown in Table 17-4. The Birger appears to be positioned closest to the Greentree and the Country Squire, regardless of the criteria used. Thus, although respondents identified five motels as being similar on an aggregate basis, when the individual criteria are used for evaluation the Birger appeared to be positioned close to only two other motels.

MARKET SEGMENTATION

To some extent the previous example of computer supplier positioning involved market segmentation in the sense that different types of respondents were found to view computer manufacturers differently. Product-service positioning and segmentation studies will often proceed hand in hand because we are usually interested in how products or services are perceived and evaluated by *different* groups of consumers.

The topic of market segmentation is a vast one and an interesting one for the marketing researcher. Market segmentation has been accepted as a strategic marketing tool for defining markets and thereby for allocating resources. No attempt will be made here to cover this field in depth, rather we shall discuss some basic concepts and then illustrate how one might go about doing a particular type of segmentation study.

Briefly stated, *market segmentation* is concerned with individual or intergroup differences in response to market-mix variables. The managerial presumption is that if these response differences exist, can be identified, and are reasonably stable over time, and if the segments can be efficiently reached, the firm may increase its sales and profits beyond those obtained by assuming market homogeneity. For example, DuPont's definition of a market segment is "a group of customers anywhere along the distribution chain who have common needs and values—who will respond similarly to the company's offerings and who are large enough to be strategically important to their business." At DuPont the segmentation process follows these steps:

- Group customers based on differences or similarities,
- Describe the groups or segments identified,
- Select target markets,
- Develop the competitive positioning of the offering to each segment, and
- Shape the total offering to achieve competitive advantage.[6]

Methods for Forming Segments

Two major problems arise in any market-segmentation study:

1. What method is to be used in carrying out the segmentation?
2. What base or criterion is to be used for defining the segments?

As it turns out, options for dealing with the first problem are quite limited; those for dealing with the second are quite varied.

Insofar as methods for forming segments are concerned, there are, basically, two:

1. *A priori segmentation,* in which the researcher chooses some cluster-defining descriptor in advance, such as respondent's favorite brand. Respondents are then

[6]See G. J. Coles and J. D. Culley, "Not All Prospects Are Created Equal," *Business Marketing,* May 1986, pp. 52–58.

classified into favorite-brand segments and further examined regarding their differences on other characteristics, such as demographics or product benefits being sought.

2. *Post hoc segmentation,* in which respondents are clustered according to the similarity of their multivariate profiles regarding such characteristics as purchasing behavior or attitudes. Following this, the segments may then be examined for differences in other characteristics, not used in the original profile definition. In post hoc segmentation one does not know the number of clusters or their relative size until the cluster analysis has been completed.

As an example of a priori segmentation, we might classify all respondents according to their stated favorite brand of beer or we might, if we were a financial institution, classify respondents on the basis of type of home mortgage. In either case, having done this, some technique such as multiple discriminant analysis might be used to determine if the groups differ in terms of average demographic profiles or life-style variables.

In post hoc segmentation, we prespecify only the set of variables on which consumers are to be clustered—benefits sought, problems encountered with the product, or whatever. We then take the consumers' response profiles on the whole *battery* of selected variables and clusters the respondents. Having done this, a technique such as multiple discriminant analysis (or simple cross classification, for that matter) can be employed to see if the various clusters differ with regard to demographics, product usage, and so on. In the preceding beer example, respondents could first be clustered on the basis of the commonality of their benefit-seeking profiles. We could then see if the various clusters differed significantly with regard to such things as weekly consumption of beer, favorite brand, and respondent age (see Exhibit 17-3).

In some studies a hybrid of the two approaches is used. For example, respondents could first be grouped according to favorite brand and then a clustering procedure employed to see if segments evincing common benefit-seeking profiles appear *within* each of the brand-favorite segments that were found via the a priori approach.

Figure 17-4 shows, in stylized form, hypothetical examples of each approach. To illustrate, assume that we have n consumers' consumption data (in cases, over some base period) of three brands of beer: A, B, and C. Under a priori segmentation we may elect to group people on the basis of the brand that enjoys the highest consumption rate. The second matrix is a simple transformation of the first in which an X appears under the brand for which consumption is highest for each respondent. (We note, for example, that the first two respondents are assigned to segment C.)

In post hoc segmentation, an extra step—computation of a matrix of interperson dissimilarity measures—is involved. Then, the actual grouping process is carried out by some type of clustering algorithm. To illustrate, assume that each of the n consumers responds to a set of needs-type attitude statements regarding beer consumption, on a 7-point agree–disagree scale. The first matrix shows the original response profiles. This matrix is transformed into an $n \times n$ symmetric matrix of dissimilarity measures in which each cell entry measures how dissimilar each pair of consumers is across the whole set of needs-type statements. This matrix is then submitted to a cluster analysis, yielding, in this illustrative case, four segments.

Figure 17-4   Alternative Ways to Form Segments

A Priori Segmentation

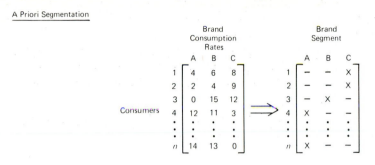

Post Hoc Segmentation

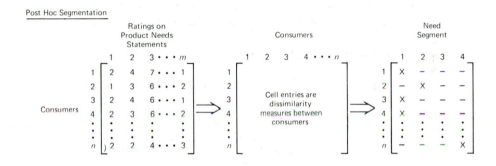

Hybrid Segmentation

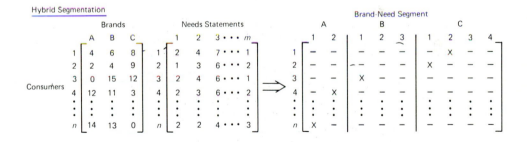

Hybrid segmentation starts out with both data sets. Respondents are first clustered by favorite brand. Following this, separate and independent dissimilarity-measure computations and cluster analyses are carried out *within* each favorite-brand segment. As seen in Figure 17-4, different numbers of clusters may emerge and, in general, the needs-type subgroups found by the hybrid approach differ from those found by the post hoc approach. (It should be mentioned that the order of this two-step process could be reversed.)

As can be noted from the preceding example, segmentation is an *aggregative* process insofar as matrices of individual data are concerned. Whether a single variable is selected for respondent assignment or whether a clustering is performed over a general measure of interperson dissimilarity, the net effect is to reduce the *n* original respondents to a

Exhibit 17-3   Nutritional Segmentation

NPD Research, Inc. has a service, National Eating Trends (NET), which monitors in-house food and beverage consumption among a nationally representative panel of households.* The NET service offers a nutritional segmentation based on *actual* food and beverage consumption behavior. NPD found that all households could be classified into one of five nutritional segments based on their in-home consumption patterns. These segments, and some of their food preferences, are

- *Kids Around:* hot dogs, presweetened cereal, soft drinks
- *Diet Conscious:* skim milk, sugar substitutes, diet magazine
- *Meat'n Potatoes:* whole milk, roast beef, boiled potatoes, gravy
- *Sophisticates:* alcoholic beverages, rye bread, swiss cheese
- *Naturalists:* fresh fruit, rice, natural RTE cereal, granola bars

In a study of snack foods it was desired to be able to segment on the basis of patterns of usage.† A convenience sample of 150 mothers were asked to rate each of 10 snack foods on 14 characteristics. They also indicated frequency of usage of the 10 foods. A cluster analysis of frequency of usage generated two major segments:

- *Healthies:* apples, oranges, raisins
- *Goodies:* potato chips, ice cream, candy, cookies

The other three foods—milk, snack crackers, and peanut butter sandwiches—did not relate, usagewise, to either segment.

A cluster analysis of the 14 characteristics illustrated segmenting on the basis of importance of features. Two major segments emerged:

- *Nutrition:* good for teeth/complexion, nourishing
- *Convenience:* easy to serve, eat out of hand, does not stain

*"Uncovering New Product Opportunities Related to Nutritional Segments," *NPD Insights,* 16 (May 1984).
†J. H. Myers and E. W. Forgy, "Getting More Information from Customer Surveys," *California Management Review,* 18 (Winter 1975), 66–72.

more manageable number of groups. In the process of doing this, information about detailed consumption of brands or detailed responses to needs-type statements is (willingly) discarded.

Two other points are worth making. First, in Figure 17-4, only persons were grouped into segments. While this is generally the way market segmentation proceeds, it is quite possible to take the obverse point of view and to cluster offerings. For example, in the case of a large number of brands, one could just as easily develop a dissimilarity measure for pairs of brands across persons' consumption profiles and cluster those brands that exhibit a relatively high commonality of usage. Just this kind of approach is frequently undertaken in the implementation of *positioning* studies. While this may not always be a useful thing to do, the point to be made is that one can cluster offerings just as readily as clustering people.

Second, the choice entities need not be products or services in the more narrow sense. They could be political candidates, legislative actions, charitable appeals, home site locations, or whatever.

Bases for Defining Segments

In contrast to the small number of segment-forming methods, the researcher has almost a surfeit of alternatives to serve as *bases for defining segments*. Some of the more popular bases are shown in Table 17-5. As can be observed, the bases run the gamut from highly brand-specific criteria to quite general and person-related criteria.

An illustration of a priori based segmentation would involve splitting the market for, say, toothpastes into favorite brands—Crest users, Colgate users, and the like. One could then see if the groups differed in terms of various background characteristics— sex, age, personality profile, and so on.

Alternatively, a post hoc segmentation could be carried out by clustering people on the basis of benefits sought and needs fulfilled. This would proceed by first preparing a large number (50 to 60) of statements, such as

- I'm more concerned than most of my friends about having an attractive smile.
- I often have problems of bad breath.

TABLE 17-5 Illustrative Bases for Defining Segments

Product-class behavior	*Brand-selection behavior*
Usage rate	Favorite brand
Number of different brands	Acceptable brand
used regularly	Disliked brand
Knowledge and experience	Store versus nationally
with product class	advertised brand
Brand-loyal versus brand switcher	
Product-class related attitudes	*Brand-related attitudes*
Benefits sought	Brand perceptions
Problems encountered in using	Brand preferences
product	
Attribute tradeoff functions	
Person-dominant attitudes	*Other bases*
Personality	Stage in life cycle
Psychographics	Social class
Life-style	Ethnic origin
Self-concept	Other demographics
Values	Region and city size
	Geographic mobility

- To me, the most important thing in toothpastes is their ability to prevent cavities.
- I have had a long history of problems with my teeth.
- I use a mouthwash almost every morning.

Respondents are asked to indicate their degree of agreement or disagreement with each statement on some, say, 7-point scale, ranging from *highly agree* to *highly disagree*.

The matrix of *n* persons' responses on the *m* statements is then transformed into an $n \times n$ dissimilarity matrix (see Figure 17-4 and Chapter 14), and respondent clusters are formed. The clusters are identified in terms of benefits sought and then cross-classified with other respondent background data. As R. I. Haley describes it, "the benefits which people are seeking in consuming a given product are the basic reasons for the existence of true market segments."[7] Haley provides an example of this viewpoint in the context of toothpaste brand choices; his classification is reproduced in Table 17-6.

As can be observed from the table, Haley describes four segments, denoted as The Sensory Segment, The Sociables, The Worriers, and The Independent Segment. The principal benefit sought is used to provide the *primary* basis for describing the market. Haley also looks at other characteristics of the resulting segments: demographics, special behavioral characteristics, brand favorites, personality characteristics, and life-style. From each composite description he then develops a shorthand label (e.g., "The Sensory Segment") for convenience of identification and discussion.

TABLE 17-6   Toothpaste Market Segment Description

SEGMENT NAME:	THE SENSORY SEGMENT	THE SOCIABLES	THE WORRIERS	THE INDEPENDENT SEGMENT
Principal benefit sought:	Flavor, product appearance	Brightness of teeth	Decay prevention	Price
Demographic strengths:	Children	Teens, young people	Large families	Men
Special behavioral characteristics:	Users of spearmint flavored toothpaste	Smokers	Heavy users	Heavy users
Brands disproportionately favored:	Colgate, Stripe	Macleans, Plus White, Ultra Brite	Crest	Brands on sale
Personality characteristics:	High self-involvement	High sociability	High hypochondriasis	High autonomy
Life-style characteristics:	Hedonistic	Active	Conservative	Value-oriented

Reproduced, with permission, from R. I. Haley, "Benefit Segmentation: A Decision-Oriented Research Tool," *Journal of Marketing,* 32 (July 1968), 30–35.

[7]R. I. Haley, "Benefit Segmentation: A Decision-Oriented Research Tool," *Journal of Marketing,* 32 (July 1968), 30–35.

An example of benefit segmentation for a service is provided by Moriarty and Venkatesan's study of potential financial-aid management information services for educational institutions.[8] As shown in Table 17-7A, four segments are described. In addition, to evaluate quantitatively the relative importance of the benefits to the segments, a Thurstone Case V scale analysis (discussed in Chapter 8) was performed for each segment. The results are reproduced in Table 17-7B.

These examples are good illustrations of how one primary basis, in this case the *principal benefit sought*, is used to define the market, and then other characteristics (e.g., brand preferences, life-style, etc.) are employed to describe the segments in ways that are potentially useful for copy design, media selection, package modification, and the like.[9]

In recent years there has been increasing interest in segmentation based on values and life-styles (i.e., on *psychographics*). In large part this has been due to the popularity of one syndicated scheme, Values and Lifestyles Segmentation (VALS), marketed by SRI International. VALS identifies four broad groups of consumers—need driven, outer directed, inner directed, and integrateds—which are then further divided into nine VALS types, with life-style data that distinguish among the types. Many marketers have found it beneficial to go beyond demographics in their segmentation. VALS combines demographics and attitudinal data, although it does have the same problems as any segmentation technique based on attitude discrimination. There have been many converts to VALS, and there are detractors. For instance, Sonia Yuspeh feels that syndicated segmentation schemes such as VALS are too simple, too remote, too rigid, and too unreliable; she favors using them as a descriptive tool rather than using them to select potential target segments.[10] Few people would argue against using psychographic data in conjunction with other data for purposes of segmentation. For example, Judith Langer has applied psychographic research to two demographic markets: the *affluent* and *young women*.[11] From this research have emerged six affluent segments and three young women segments.

POSITIONING AND SEGMENTATION COMBINATIONS—A BEER COMPANY EXAMPLE

Many marketing research studies (as illustrated by the previous computer image survey) are concerned with *both* product-service positioning and market segmentation. The first

---

[8]M. Moriarty and M. Venkatesan, "Concept Evaluation and Benefit Segmentation," *Journal of Marketing*, 42 (July 1978), 82–86.

[9]Another approach to the problem replaces the principal benefit sought with preferences for benefit bundles. See P. E. Green, Yoram Wind, and A. K. Jain, "Benefit Bundle Analysis," *Journal of Advertising Research*, 12 (April 1972), 31–36.

[10]See S. Yuspeh, "Syndicated Values/Lifestyles Segmentation Schemes: Use Them as Descriptive Tools, Not to Select Targets," *Marketing News*, 18 (May 25, 1984), Sec. 2, pp. 1ff; "SRI's Response to Yuspeh: Demographics Aren't Enough," *Marketing News*, 18 (May 25, 1984), Sec. 2, p. 1; and J. H. Mather, "No Reason to Fear 'Frightening' Reality of VALS," *Marketing News*, 19 (September 13, 1984), 15.

[11]See "Psychographic Research Segments Affluent, Young Women," *Marketing News*, 19 (January 4, 1985), 47–48.

TABLE 17-7 Financial-Aid Information Services Segment Description and Values of Benefits

(A) Description of Segments

Characteristics	Segment I	Segment II	Segment III	Segment IV
Principal benefits sought	Accuracy More time to counsel students Stored data Speed & time savings	Accuracy Consistency in award-making More time to counsel students Speed & time savings	Accuracy Consistency in award-making Better control of funds Cost savings	Accuracy Consistency in award-making More time to counsel students Better control of funds
Institution type (predominantly)	Public (54%) Private (46%) Four- and Two-year colleges	Public (64%) Private (36%) Four- and Two-year colleges	Public (56%) Private (44%) Vocational/Technical Schools	Public (68%) Private (32%) University Two-year colleges
Undergraduate enrollment	Under 1500	Under 1500	Under 1500	Over 1500
Number of financial aid applications processed/year	Under 500	Over 500	Under 500	Over 500

(B) Interval Scale Value of Service Benefits

	Segment I	Segment II	Segment III	Segment IV
6				
	5.80 -Accuracy	5.69 -Accuracy
	5.56 -Accuracy	
	5.39 -Consistency in award-making	
5.23 -Accuracy			
5				
4.13 -Consistency in award-making		
4				
		3.99 -Better control of funds	3.55 -Consistency in award-making
		3.93 -Cost savings	3.49 -Having more time to counsel with students
3.82 -Having more time to counsel with students			Better control of funds
			3.29 -Following guidelines for use of funds
3.58 -Stored data	3.44 -Following guidelines for use of funds	
3.29 -Speed & time savings	3.37 -Having more time to counsel with students	
3.20 -Better control of funds	3.27 -Speed & time savings	
3.07 -Following guidelines for use of funds	3.10 -Better control of funds	
	3.07 -Following guidelines for use of funds	3.00 -Speed & time savings	3.00 -Cost savings
3				
	2.77 -Cost savings	2.77 -Having more time to counsel with students	2.63 -Insures objectivity
2.84 -Consistency in award-making	2.70 -Stored data	

695

TABLE 17-7 Financial-Aid Information Services Segment Description and Values of Benefits

(B) Interval Scale Value of Service Benefits (*Continued*)

	SEGMENT I	SEGMENT II	SEGMENT III	SEGMENT IV
2	*2.50 -Better use of staff talent & consequently improved staff morale 2.25 -Allows waiting until last minute to process financial aid applications 2.04 -Cost savings	2.64 -Better use of staff talent & consequently improved staff morale 2.63 -Insures objectivity 2.12 -Simulation ability to assess potential policy changes	2.57 -Better use of staff talent & consequently improved staff morale 2.20 -Insures objectivity	*2.43 -Better use of staff talent & consequently improved staff morale Allows waiting until last minute to process financial aid applications 2.35 -Speed & time savings 2.13 -Stored data
	1.70 -Simulation ability to assess potential policy changes		1.61 -Simulation ability to assess potential policy changes 1.40 -Allows waiting until last minute to process financial aid applications	1.51 -Simulation ability to assess potential policy changes
1		.39 -Allows waiting until last minute to process financial aid applications	.14 -Stored data	
0				* These two service benefits have the same scale value.

*Reproduced, with permission, from M. Moriarty and M. Venkatesan, "Concept Evaluation and Benefit Segmentation," *Journal of Marketing*, 42 (July 1978), 82–86.

of these provides competitive information—which brands are seen as substitutible for which others—while the second emphasizes intergroup differences in perceptions or preferences. Accordingly, we now describe a second study in which both aspects were important to the firm's strategy.

A prominent midwestern beer producer was becoming increasingly concerned with the decline under way in share of market in one of its historically best sales areas. A new radio and spot television promotional campaign had recently been launched in an attempt to combat the situation, but, for unknown reasons, it was seemingly ineffective in stemming the decline.

The sponsor wished to know several things about the product, including its market position, the segments attracted toward the firm's beer, and the brand-switching tendencies of consumers in the market area that was declining in share. In particular, should the current promotional campaign be continued? Expanded in intensity? Changed in theme? Should the product formulation be changed? A new product developed?

A representative sample of male beer drinkers was drawn from the marketing area of interest and personal in-home interviews were conducted. Data were obtained on

1. Judged dissimilarities of 12 popular beers sold in the market area
2. Semantic differential ratings of the beers on a series of bipolar scales
3. Preference rankings of the 12 beers
4. Brand substitution, that is, other brands that the respondent would consider purchasing if the favorite were unavailable
5. Life-style and demographic data

The highlights of this study are illustrated next.

Brand Perceptions

For summary purposes, the data on judged brand dissimilarities for the total sample were scaled multidimensionally (see Chapter 15), resulting in the configuration shown in Figure 17-5. The 12 brands are represented by points and the various semantic differential (averaged) ratings are then fitted into the space via multiple regression, as an aid in interpreting the configuration. The horizontal axis of Figure 17-5 appears to be a type of premium-popular dimension with extremes represented, on the one hand, by Michelob, Budweiser, and Miller versus the sponsor's brand, Goebel, and Pfeiffer. The vertical axis appears to be a strength dimension. From the vector directions shown in the chart the sponsor's brand is perceived as strong and appealing to outdoor men. It is also perceived as the most filling of all the 12 brands.

Preference rankings of the 12 brands were transformed to paired comparisons and analyzed by Thurstonian Case V scaling. Prior to applying the scaling procedure, each respondent was classified, on the basis of length of time spent drinking the stated regular brand, as

1. Sponsor brand-loyal—had been drinking the sponsor's brand regularly for at least a year
2. Other brand-loyal—had been drinking a particular (competitive) brand regularly for at least one year
3. Switcher—others not meeting either of the above conditions

Thurstonian scales of preferences were then developed for each of the preceding segments and appear in Figure 17-6.

As can be noted from the figure, the sponsor's brand-loyal segment is *really* loyal in the sense that the second-place brand (Pabst) is positioned far below the favorite and, as a matter of fact, all 11 of the other brands are rather bunched at the low end of the scale.

Insofar as the remaining two segments are concerned, we note that Budweiser and Pabst appear as favorites in both cases. Moreover, the sponsor's brand fares rather poorly—third from last in the case of other brand-loyals and switchers. Hence, it became rather evident that the sponsor's brand exhibited little attraction potential from either other brand-loyals or switchers.

Figure 17-5   Perceptual-vector Spaces of Brand Positioning

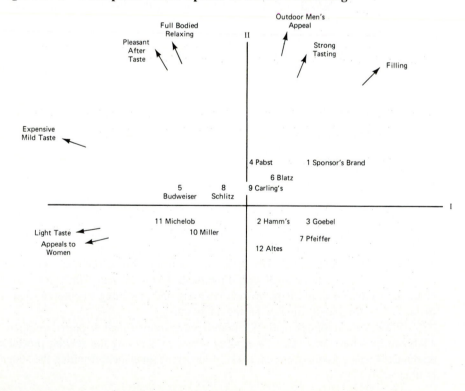

Figure 17-6   Thurstonian Scales by Beer-Drinker Class (Overall Preferences)

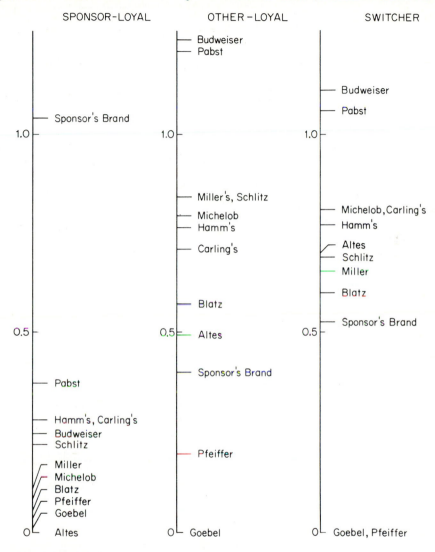

Segment Definition

The life-style and demographic information provided further background information for describing the three segments defined above. Multiple discriminant analysis (see Chapter 13) led to the following capsule descriptions of the segments:

Sponsor Brand-Loyal.   A heavier beer drinker than average; one who is fairly optimistic regarding future income increases; higher than average in self-confidence; generally perceives beer drinking as refreshing and rewarding rather than as escape or as a means of loosening up; moderate to conservative politically; higher proportion married and of foreign extraction; displays low interest in alcoholic beverages other than beer; working-class people, for the most part.

Other Brand-Loyal. Moderate beer drinker in terms of glasses consumed per week; feels somewhat rushed and in a hurry; somewhat opportunistic; enjoys beer most in a social setting; drinks other alcoholic beverages (rye and bourbon) as well as beer; drinks beer to enjoy parties more; higher-than-average income; likes to gamble; predominantly white-collar.

Switcher. Lower-than-average beer drinker in terms of glasses consumed per week; feels that life is too routine; does not enjoy planned activities; likes to try new things; enjoys beer drinking with others; most of this drinker's friends prefer liquor to beer; has not accomplished life's goals as yet; younger in age; below-average income; does not expect large income increases; fewer years in current job; tends to drink other alcoholic beverages (particularly vodka); both white-collar and blue-collar representation.

From the preceding capsule descriptions we get some idea of the sponsor brand-loyal type as steady, generally optimistic but settled individuals who view beer as a way of refreshing and rewarding themselves—individuals who are primarily beer drinkers and desire the stronger taste that the sponsor's beer exhibits.

Brand-Switching Tendencies

Data were also developed from the study on the question of what *other* brands the respondent would consider if, for some reason, the favorite brand were unavailable. The data represent the extent to which other brands are seen as *substitutes* if the respondent is unable to obtain the favorite. Analysis of this type of data can be useful from a diagnostic standpoint.

Table 17-8 shows the total-sample findings where row denotes current favorite brand and column denotes brands considered as substitutes if one's favorite brand cannot be obtained. For example, if the sponsor's brand is unavailable, respondents indicate that the major substitutes are Pabst, Hamm's, Carling's, and Budweiser (as might be inferred from Figure 17-5).

More important are the entries involving brands other than the sponsor's. In these cases the sponsor's brand receives highest frequency as an acceptable substitute only in the case of Budweiser drinkers (first column of Table 17-8). When one examines the *stability* of substitution—that is, the column frequency divided by the row frequency, shown only for the cases in which both frequencies are at least 15—the implications for the sponsor's brand are not favorable.

The sponsor's ratio of 0.3 (column total divided by row total) is the lowest of the group. The only other brand whose frequency of mentions as substitutes is less than the frequency of other acceptable brands is Schlitz (a ratio of 0.7). The other major brands, Hamm's, Pabst, Budweiser, and Carling's, all exhibit ratios of at least 1.0. Thus, drinkers of the sponsor's brand appear to exhibit a reasonably wide latitude regarding acceptable

TABLE 17-8   Brand-Substitution Frequencies—Conditioned Upon Favorite Brand

	BRANDS CONSIDERED AS SUBSTITUTES													
BRAND	*1*	*2*	*3*	*4*	*5*	*6*	*7*	*8*	*9*	*10*	*11*	*12*	*13*	*Total*
1. Sponsor's brand	—	20	5	22	15	1	4	7	20	3	—	—	—	97
2. Hamm's	1	—	—	9	1	1	—	—	—	5	1	—	—	18
3. Goebel	—	—	—	—	—	—	3	—	3	—	—	—	—	6
4. Pabst	6	3	—	—	15	6	—	1	4	3	1	1	1	41
5. Budweiser	8	5	—	5	—	1	—	2	2	4	4	3	—	34
6. Blatz	—	—	—	3	—	—	—	—	—	—	—	3	—	6
7. Pfeiffer	—	—	—	—	—	—	—	—	—	—	—	—	2	2
8. Schlitz	3	2	—	10	—	—	—	—	—	5	—	—	1	21
9. Carling's	3	1	—	15	5	2	1	1	—	2	—	3	4	37
10. Miller's	2	—	—	—	—	—	—	—	1	—	—	—	3	6
11. Michelob	—	3	—	—	3	—	—	—	—	—	—	—	—	6
12. Altes	2	3	—	6	7	—	—	1	3	—	1	—	—	23
13. Other	—	—	—	—	—	—	—	3	3	—	—	—	—	6
	25	37	5	70	46	11	8	15	36	22	7	10	11	303
Ratio*	0.3	2.1	—	1.7	1.4	—	—	0.7	1.0	—	—	—	—	

*Column frequency/row frequency.

substitute brands, but regular drinkers of competing brands do *not* generally consider the sponsor's brand as an acceptable substitute.

Note that this type of information can be supplementary to preference data in that one can highly prefer a brand yet *still consider a variety of other brands as acceptable* if for some reason one's favorite is unavailable. While the sample size underlying this particular table is small, the qualitative indication is that the sponsor's brand is *not* seen as an acceptable substitute by drinkers of many competitive brands.

Implications

Other findings of the study reinforced the observation already noted: the sponsor's brand attraction potential from other brands was not high. While a loyal segment existed— one composed of heavier, predominantly blue-collar drinkers—it was of interest to examine this profile against the type of promotional campaign recently introduced by the firm's advertising agency.

The promotional campaign, rather surprisingly, was addressed to the more affluent, sophisticated beer drinker and emphasized a folk-rock musical jingle with humorous, clever sales appeals. It did not seem to the research team that this type of advertising was at all congruent with either the beer's strong, masculine image or the life-style and demographic characteristics of its consumers. Moreover, although the campaign had been running for six months prior to the study, there was little indication that it was winning away customers of competitive brands. Thus, it seemed to be antithetical to current sponsor brand-loyals and ineffective in attracting new customers. Accordingly, the research team recommended that examination be made of alternative promotional campaigns that might have greater potential for the retention of sponsor brand-loyals. In addition, recommendations (based on evidence not reported here) were made for product development aimed at new brands that might be attractive to two new segments: (1) nonwhites and (2) younger beer drinkers.

However, insofar as the purpose of this chapter is concerned, the preceding study shows how the questions of product positioning, market segmentation, and consumer switching propensities can all be interrelated (and frequently are) in a single study.

SEGMENT-CONGRUENCE ANALYSIS

Our last topic for discussion in this chapter concerns an approach to market segmentation called *segment-congruence analysis*.[12] In carrying out segmentation studies it is not always clear what set of variables (e.g., brand favorite, benefits sought, psychographics, demographics) should constitute *the* base for defining segments, on either an a priori or post hoc basis. That is, one often finds an embarrassment of riches insofar as choice of a "distinguished" variable or set of (segment-defining) variables is concerned.

Segment-congruence analysis—which turns out to be simple in concept, if somewhat complex methodologically—is motivated by three principal problems:

1. In cases where it is not clear which variables should constitute the distinguished base, are the segments obtained from alternative bases mutually associated?
2. If so, which one of the bases makes the highest contribution to their mutual association?
3. In cases where one has preselected a distinguished base, how does the probability of a respondent's being a member of each of the segments formed from the distinguished base depend on membership in segments formed from the other bases?

We illustrate the approach with an example drawn from the auto insurance industry.

An Insurance Company Example

The sponsor of this study is a prominent northeastern insurance company, specializing in the selling of auto insurance by mail. The motivation for this study stemmed from the sponsor's interest in the types of people choosing its offerings versus those who did not. Various possible bases were proposed for defining the segments:

- Whether or not the respondent was a customer of the firm
- Commonality of respondents' images of their supplier

---

[12]P. E. Green and F. J. Carmone, "Segment Congruence Analysis: A Method for Analyzing Association among Alternative Bases for Market Segmentation," *Journal of Consumer Research,* 3 (March 1977), 217–22.

- Commonality of respondents' psychographic profiles
- Commonality of respondents' demographic profiles

In the first case, the segmentation could be based on a priori grounds, while in the latter three cases, post hoc methods would have to be used to develop the segments.

A survey was conducted among 534 respondents, each of whom had some type of auto insurance. Of the total sample, 155 were customers of the firm and 379 were noncustomers. The set of variables on which supplier-image segments were developed involved 13 attitude statements. Psychographic profiles were developed from 19 statements, while demographic profiles were based on 9 variables. Table 17-9 shows illustrations of the image and psychographic statements (as evaluated on a 6-point agree–disagree rating scale). Also shown are the 9 demographic variables.

Preliminary Data Processing

The first segmentation—the customer versus noncustomer grouping—required no additional processing, since information was already available on segment membership.

TABLE 17-9   Input Data for Alternative Segmentations

Illustrative image statements (13 in total)

1. Settles claims fairly.
2. Inefficient and hard to deal with.
3. Provides good advice about types and amount of coverage to buy.
4. Too big to care about individual policyholders.
5. Policies are especially good for retired persons.

Illustrative psychographic statements (19 in total)

1. For specific medical problems I usually go to a specialist rather than a general practitioner.
2. I usually look for the lowest possible prices when I shop.
3. I like to try new and different things.
4. My friends or neighbors often come to me for advice.
5. Most people don't realize the extent to which their lives are controlled by accidental happenings.

Demographics

1. Sex
2. Marital status
3. Education
4. Age
5. Employment status— retired versus working
6. Current (or previous) occupation—professional or management versus all other
7. Number of persons at current address
8. Number of years at current address
9. Family income

In the latter three cases, involving 13, 19, and 9 variables, respectively, a uniform segmentation procedure was followed:

- Each response battery of interest was factor-analyzed by principal components. Components whose variances exceeded unity were Varimax-rotated and unit-variance factor scores were obtained (see Chapter 14).
- The factor scores were than submitted to a hierarchical clustering program, and two-group through five-group clusterings were sought (see Chapter 14).

TABLE 17-10　Distribution of Frequencies Within the Multidimensional Contingency Table

INSURANCE-SUPPLIER SEGMENTS	IMAGE SEGMENTS	PSYCHO-GRAPHIC SEGMENTS	DEMOGRAPHIC SEGMENTS	FREQUENCY
1	1	1	1	5
2	1	1	1	52
1	2	1	1	12
2	2	1	1	22
1	1	2	1	11
2	1	2	1	46
1	2	2	1	9
2	2	2	1	16
1	1	1	2	18
2	1	1	2	59
1	2	1	2	29
2	2	1	2	42
1	1	2	2	34
2	1	2	2	111
1	2	2	2	37
2	2	2	2	31
				534

Insurance-supplier segments

1: Sponsor's customers

2: Other firms' customers

Psychographic segments

1: Controlled; conservative; old-fashioned
2: Risk taker; somewhat fatalistic; willing to try new things

Image segments

1: No specialization by age of insured
2: Caters especially to older people

Demographic segments

1: Primarily married couples; younger in age; larger number of household members
2: Greater incidence of widows and other single females; older in age; smaller number of household members

The analysis was carried out for the case in which all clusterings were maintained at the two-group level. This yielded a $2 \times 2 \times 2 \times 2$ contingency table of 16 cells. Table 17-10 (p. 713) shows the frequencies with which the 534 respondents were distributed across the 16 cells.

Table 17-10 also summarizes the principal differentiating characteristics of the separately obtained segmentations. In the case of insurance supplier, segment 1 members are customers of the sponsoring firm. The image segments consist of those who believe that their insurance supplier caters to older people (segment 2) versus those who do not make this distinction. The psychographic segments consist of those who are more or less risk takers and willing to try new things (segment 2) versus those who perceive themselves as more conservative and old-fashioned. The demographic segments are made up of those who are primarily older widows living alone (segment 2) versus those who are principally married couples, younger, and with larger household sizes.

Mutual Association across All Four Segmentations

Tests of mutual association across the four separate bases of segmentation were carried out by means of a generalized approach to chi-square analysis (see Chapter 10). The following hypotheses were tested by generalized chi square:

- All four clusterings are mutually independent.
- Insurance supplier is independent of the other three segmentations.
- Image is independent of the other three segmentations.
- Psychographics are independent of the other three segmentations.
- Demographics are independent of the other three segmentations.

As it turned out, all four segmentations exhibited *mutual* association. Moreover, if one had to select the most representative base of the four, it would be the one developed from the *supplier-image* data. At this point, then, it appeared that all four independently carried out segmentations exhibited association and, hence, could serve as useful predictor variables if the sponsor desired to select one of them as a distinguished base.

Analysis of the Distinguished Base

After reviewing the tests of mutual association the sponsor decided to choose the first base—sponsor's customers versus noncustomers—as the distinguished base. The problem then became one of developing a model for predicting the probability of membership in the segment representing the sponsoring firm's customers, given knowledge of the respondent's membership in the segments formed from the other three bases: image, psychographics, and demographics.

A relatively new approach, using what is known as a logit model, (see Chapter 13), was employed to find the necessary parameters. First, it turned out that image-segment membership was the primary variable for predicting whether the respondent was a customer or noncustomer of the sponsoring firm. Demographics were next in importance, followed by psychographics.

The results of the analysis can be interpreted by looking at the segments listed in Table 17-10. As recalled, two segments appear under each of the four bases of segmentation. As it turned out, the model's parameters indicated that *higher probabilities of being a sponsoring firm's customer* are associated with

- Being a member of image segment 2—caters especially to older people
- Being a member of psychographic segment 2—higher risk taker; somewhat fatalistic
- Being a member of demographic segment 2—female, widowed, older, small household size

In brief, a rather interesting profile emerges of the type of respondent most attracted to the sponsoring firm's auto insurance policies.

Table 17-11 shows the actual proportions that are customers of the firm versus those predicted by the model. Column (4) of Table 17-11 is derived from Table 17-10. For example, the first entry of column (4) is simply the ratio

$$\frac{5}{5 + 52} = 0.088$$

as obtained from the segment 1 of each of the predictor bases in Table 17-10. However, the model predicted a proportion of 0.125, leading to a residual of $0.088 - 0.125 = -0.037$.

TABLE 17-11   Results of Analysis in Which Sponsoring Firm's Customer is the Criterion Variable

(1)	(2)	(3)	(4)	(5)	(6)
OTHER SEGMENTATION BASES			SPONSOR'S	PROPORTION	
	Psycho-	*Demo-*	CUSTOMERS	PREDICTED	RESIDUALS
Image	*graphics*	*graphics*	(PROPORTION)	BY MODEL	[(4) - (5)]
1	1	1	0.088	0.125	−0.037
2	1	1	0.353	0.315	0.038
1	2	1	0.193	0.165	0.028
2	2	1	0.360	0.390	−0.030
1	1	2	0.234	0.195	0.039
2	1	2	0.408	0.439	−0.031
1	2	2	0.234	0.251	−0.017
2	2	2	0.544	0.520	0.024
			Mean absolute deviation		0.031

As noted from column (6), the model performs reasonably well; its mean absolute deviation is about 3 percentage points.

Implications

The implications of the study suggested that the type of customer drawn to the sponsor's offerings tended to be older than average, and in many cases widowed as well. Moreover, there was some tendency for customers to be greater risk takers, suggesting that they might be less concerned about the reliability and stability of firms that offer insurance by mail.

On the other hand, the results indicated that a way to attract *noncustomers* might be to emphasize the personalistic touch, perhaps by the availability of local personal contacts or company representatives that could be reached, on demand, by toll-free telephone numbers. In short, the company was provided with a useful target profile of *potential* customers that was described demographically and psychographically.

SUMMARY

This chapter emphasized two major types of marketing research studies: brand-service positioning and market segmentation. We started the chapter by describing various classes of marketing strategies: market penetration, market development, product development, and diversification. The detailed aspects of these strategies should influence the types of positioning studies undertaken by the firm.

Product positioning was illustrated by the digital computer study. In this case we were interested in how the sponsor's products were perceived vis-à-vis those of competitors. Moreover, we were also interested in the correspondence of these images across industry groups and across customers, noncustomers, and company sales personnel. The study showed that the company's salespeople were not emphasizing the firm's selective performance advantages and, moreover, were utilizing sales appeals that were attractive to those noncustomers who were *least* likely to switch computer suppliers.

The next section dealt with ways to form segments—the a priori, post hoc, and hybrid methods—and bases by which segments could be defined. A combination positioning–segmentation study, carried out for a midwestern brewery, was discussed as an example of how both approaches can be used to advantage. The study indicated that the firm's current promotional theme was out of step with the brand's loyal-customer base and also unattractive to new customers.

We concluded the chapter with a brief description of *segment-congruence analysis*. In this approach we examined the mutual association among alternative bases for defining segments and showed the results of a model for predicting the probability of membership in various classes of a specified segmentation base, given the respondent's membership in various background segments.

From our discussion it should be obvious that segmentation and positioning research may utilize any of the analysis techniques discussed in Parts III and IV of this book. In particular, discriminant, factor, and cluster analyses seem to be widely used. Less used are automatic interaction detection and logit. Finally, it has been suggested that there is great potential for using the probit model, its related methodology, and intention measurements for designing products for divergent segmentation preferences.[13]

ASSIGNMENT MATERIAL

1. Describe how you would go about developing a brand-positioning study for the toothpaste market.
   a. What are the major attributes by which toothpaste brands can be characterized?
   b. What procedures (see Chapter 15) might be used to develop brand-positioning maps?
   c. How might multiple discriminant analysis (see Chapter 13) be used to accomplish this purpose?
2. Make a search of the current journal literature and record the bases that researchers have used to segment markets.
   a. What are the respective advantages and disadvantages of these bases?
   b. How would you design a segmentation study for the marketing of bar soaps?
   c. How might respondents' reported brand substitutions (see Table 17-8 as an example) be utilized in this study?

3. Some researchers assert that benefits segmentation only plays back what advertisers have instilled in the respondents' minds. These critics believe that *problems-oriented* research, involving (1) problems experienced in using the products, (2) judged seriousness of each problem, and (3) the best brand for solving the problem, should be used instead of benefits-oriented research. Discuss the pros and cons of each method.
4. How would you describe the positioning that Mercedes Benz, BMW, Saab, Toyota, and Chrysler are attempting to achieve in the marketplace?
5. Does the credit union study provide data that would allow management to meaningfully segment its customers? Explain your answer.
6. For the motel study, show how management can segment its customers.

[13] See V. R. Rao and F. W. Winter, "An Application of the Multivariate Probit Model to Market Segmentation and Product Design," *Journal of Marketing Research,* 15 (August 1978), 361–68.

18

Evaluating New Marketing Strategies

INTRODUCTION

Brand positioning and market-segmentation activities, the main topics of the preceding chapter, are primarily concerned with measuring the firm's *current status*. A companion area of interest to the marketing researcher involves the evaluation of proposed *changes* to the present marketing program, such as new-product introductions, changes in promotion, pricing, packaging, or brand name. Within this class of activities are found procedures for new-concept generation and testing, advertising tests, package evaluations, price sensitivity, and so on. Emphasis is on changing the status quo, either the structural characteristics of the firm's offerings or their functional-symbolic characteristics. A number of tools have been developed to assist the researcher in the design and evaluation of new marketing strategies. We consider some of them here.

In addition to these specific tools, everything discussed in this book is applicable to the area of changing marketing strategies and the individual components of strategy. For instance, the research program used for the launch of the Mercedes-Benz 190 in the United States included focus groups, product clinics, measurements of consumer reaction after test drives, ad-impact and awareness studies, a survey of early buyers, and a follow-up survey. Continued research includes annual tracking studies to measure awareness and attitudes among owners and nonowners, car clinics to gather reaction to new models,

competitive analyses, copy testing, and geodemographic and life-style segmentation studies.[1]

Similarly, deregulation has increased the need for airlines to use research for information relevant to changing marketing strategy on such dimensions as price, promotion (including bonus programs), distribution (tickets can be sold by retailers and electronic systems), and the product itself (seat configuration, on board storage, etc.). These variables also interact with each other—e.g., the availability of a specified number of seats for full-fare and for discount-fare passengers. In addition, on-board storage may be increased to offset poor baggage service at certain airports. Illustrative of research done is that by United Airlines.[2] Conjoint analysis has been used to determine the relative importance of service attributes such as fare, scheduling, and on-board service. The company uses a syndicated service to track customer perceptions of competitive carriers. Such syndicated data are used to create performance ratings on key attributes and these ratings may provide management with "early-warning signals." Finally, United regularly uses studies to identify passenger demographics, preferences, demand for ground services, and so on.

The chapter starts with a discussion of new-product-planning evaluation. Such tools as the repertory and consumption grids are illustrated as devices for developing perceptual and use-occasion frameworks that consumers employ in dealing with various products or services. The frameworks, in turn, are useful in both new-product idea generation and promotional-theme planning.

Concept screening and testing are described next. By means of an industry example, we show how surveys can be set up for evaluating verbalized descriptions of new products rather quickly and economically. We conclude the section with a brief discussion of market testing, including test-market simulators.

The next principal topic includes procedures for testing various marketing-mix components—promotion, package, price, and so on. These research activities are also illustrated by industry examples.

The chapter concludes with a discussion of large-scale market planning models. An industry example of one such market simulator is presented, and we comment more briefly on other kinds of computer-based marketing models.

NEW-PRODUCT DEVELOPMENT AND TESTING

The procedures described in the preceding chapter—brand or supplier positioning and market segmentation—are primarily concerned with quantifying the *current* situation in the marketplace (i.e., what brands are competing with what others, what kinds of people

---

[1]Adapted from a talk by D. M. McCall at the 1984 American Marketing Association Marketing Research Conference and reported in "Research Played Role in Launch of 'Baby Benz,' " *Marketing News,* 19 (January 4, 1985), 20.

[2]Adapted from a talk by C. M. Lamar at the 1984 AMA Marketing Research Conference and reported in "Research Makes Skies Friendlier in Airline Business," *Marketing News,* 19 (January 4, 1985), 17–18.

favor what brands, and the patterns of brand substitution). Concomitant with the monitoring of current brand performance are various behind-the-scene activities aimed at changing the firm's status via new products, packages, promotional campaigns—in short, the generation and pretesting of *alternatives* to the present marketing mix.

New-product activities, including idea generation, concept testing, prototype testing, and test-market introductions, comprise a sizable undertaking on the part of many business firms. Not surprisingly, marketing research plays a key role in these product-centered activities.

New-product development (including modifications of existing products) is usually an expensive and time-consuming process. Billions of dollars (and other currencies as well) are spent annually for new-product research and development planning. While product-development procedures may vary greatly by company, many programs of this type involve formalized procedures for (1) idea generation, (2) concept screening and testing, (3) prototype construction and evaluation, (4) marketing-mix formulation (including packaging, promotion, and pricing), and (5) market testing.

In general, costs tend to increase as each succeeding stage in the product development process is implemented. It is not surprising, therefore, to find that the *timing* of market/marketing research is often such that the greatest effort is expended relatively early in the new-product project development. This type of timing pattern was supported by a study of 112 new industrial product situations.[3] In the aggregate, most companies in the situations studied utilized their market(ing) research sources relatively early in the development process, although there were significant differences in timing for the individual projects. Managers tended to do earlier research in situations involving

- Less situational similarity of the marketing tasks and decisions (in particular involving new customers,
- Greater uncertainty about the organizational buying and adoption process
- A resultant unfamiliar selling task
- Perceived less competitive advantage, less product uniqueness, more dominant competitors, and greater expected competitive response
- Higher risk to the adopting organization

In this section of the chapter we briefly describe four classes of procedures utilized in the idea-generation and concept-evaluation stages:

1. The repertory and consumption grids, as used in the development of constructs and use occasions by which consumers describe various products or services
2. Concept screening and testing procedures
3. Product idea screening by the firm
4. Test marketing

---

[3]R. A. More, "Timing of Market Research in New Industrial Product Situations," *Journal of Marketing,* 48 (Fall 1984), 84–94.

Repertory and Consumption Grids

Both the repertory and consumption grids are aimed at developing consumers' perceptual encoding schemes. In the former case we are interested in the verbal constructs that consumers use to describe similarities and differences among brands or schemes. In the latter case we are interested in (1) their perceived occasions of use, (2) their perceptions of interproduct substitution, and (3) their views about the types of users for whom the product may have particular appeal.

The *repertory grid* is based on Kelly's personal-construct theory in which individuals are assumed to develop over time a set of personalized constructs or "dimensions" with which they view entities or events.[4] From a marketing point of view, these constructs are typically product attributes. As a case in point, a major producer of frozen foods was recently interested in introducing a new type of toaster item that could be made up to taste like a variety of freshly baked products: blueberry muffins, Danish pastries, coffee cakes, and so on. The firm's marketing research director was particularly interested in the attributes of bakery items that consumers use to talk about and distinguish one product from another.

In this case, a series of focus-group interviews were set up and, in the course of these interviews, a repertory grid was developed. The typical procedure for developing a repertory grid of constructs is quite simple and involves the following steps:

1. The stimuli of interest—in this case the 20 bakery-type items shown in Table 18-1—are printed on a set of numbered cards.[5]

2. The respondent is asked to sort through the cards and remove any items with which he or she is completely unfamiliar.

TABLE 18-1   List of Food-Item Stimuli Used in Repertory-Grid Study

Stimulus	Stimulus
1. Toast pop-up	11. Cinnamon bun
2. Buttered toast (white)	12. Danish pastry
3. English muffin and margarine	13. Buttered toast (rye)
4. Jelly donut	14. Chocolate chip cookie
5. Cinnamon toast	15. Glazed donut
6. Blueberry muffin and margarine	16. Coffee cake
7. Hard rolls and butter	17. Apple strudel
8. Toast and marmalade	18. Toasted pound cake
9. Buttered toast and jelly	19. Corn muffin and butter
10. Toast and margarine (white)	20. Bagel and cream cheese

[4]See G. A. Kelly, *Psychology of Personal Constructs* (New York: W. W. Norton, 1955). Also see W.A.K. Frost and R. L. Braine, "The Application of the Repertory Grid Technique to Problems in Market Research," *Commentary*, 9 (July 1967), 161–75.

[5]The illustration is drawn from P. E. Green and F. J. Carmone, "The Effect of Task on Intra-Individual Differences in Similarities Judgments," *Multivariate Behavioral Research*, 6 (October 1971), 433–50.

3. Triples of cards are then selected (according to a prespecified sequence), and the respondent is asked to think of any way in which any two of the three items are similar to each other but different from the third.

4. The task is repeated for a new triple, and the respondent is asked for some new way in which any two of the stimuli are similar to each other and different from the third.

5. Constructs are recorded until the respondent fails to elicit any new ones as new triples are presented.

The construct sets of several individual respondents can be pooled (as was done in arriving at the 22 constructs shown as bipolar scales in Table 18-2) or maintained separately for each respondent. In either case the resulting stimuli and constructs can be set up in a grid or tabular fashion and respondents then asked to rate each stimulus (e.g., bakery item) on each construct.

The *consumption grid* also starts out with a set of stimuli, but in this case the respondent is presented with a *single stimulus* each time. For example, the respondent may be shown the first stimulus, "toast pop-up," and asked to *list all occasions in which*

TABLE 18-2   List of 22 Bipolar Scales Found From Repertory Grid

1.	Nonfruity flavor	1	2	3	4	5	6	7	Fruity flavor
2.	Easy to prepare	1	2	3	4	5	6	7	Hard to prepare
3.	Low crispness	1	2	3	4	5	6	7	High crispness
4.	Natural flavor	1	2	3	4	5	6	7	Artificial flavor
5.	Dry texture	1	2	3	4	5	6	7	Moist texture
6.	Complex flavor	1	2	3	4	5	6	7	Simple flavor
7.	Complex shape	1	2	3	4	5	6	7	Simple shape
8.	Not very filling	1	2	3	4	5	6	7	Highly filling
9.	Appeals mainly to kids	1	2	3	4	5	6	7	Appeals mainly to adults
10.	Served formally	1	2	3	4	5	6	7	Served informally
11.	Primarily breakfast item	1	2	3	4	5	6	7	Primarily non-breakfast item
12.	Soft texture	1	2	3	4	5	6	7	Hard texture
13.	High perishability	1	2	3	4	5	6	7	Low perishability
14.	Mostly eaten at home	1	2	3	4	5	6	7	Mostly eaten away from home
15.	High calories	1	2	3	4	5	6	7	Low calories
16.	Highly nutritious	1	2	3	4	5	6	7	Low in nutrition
17.	Drab appearance	1	2	3	4	5	6	7	Colorful appearance
18.	Usually eaten alone	1	2	3	4	5	6	7	Usually eaten with other foods
19.	Low general familiarity	1	2	3	4	5	6	7	High general familiarity
20.	Highly liked by men	1	2	3	4	5	6	7	Highly disliked by men
21.	Ordinary-occasion food	1	2	3	4	5	6	7	Special-occasion food
22.	Expensive	1	2	3	4	5	6	7	Inexpensive

this item would be appropriate for his or her consumption. For example, the respondent may say, "With coffee at breakfast." For each occasion elicited the respondent is then asked what *other products* might be appropriate for the same occasion, again elicited on a free-response basis. For the items thus elicited the respondent may be asked for new occasions, and so on.

The consumption grid thus involves free-response data for both use occasions and new items. One can start out with a small core set of items and expand both the item set and the occasion via sequentially obtained free responses. As a final step one can then present the *whole set of items and occasions* in grid fashion and have the respondent check off those occasions for which each item is appropriate. The net result of all of this is an items-by-occasions table in which each entry is coded 1 (denoting appropriateness) or 0 (denoting inappropriateness). Recent developments in scaling and clustering (see Chapter 15) permit this type of data to be portrayed as hierarchical clusters, at either the aggregate sample or subgroup levels.

Variations on the above procedure can be obtained via changes in instructions, for example: Who in the family would be most likely to consume this particular item? What other items would go well with this item? and so on.

The main purpose of the repertory and consumption grids is to find consumers' perceptual frameworks regarding brands or product substitutability or complementarity in terms of other facets (e.g., product attributes, use occasions, or user characteristics). The grids are often used in the generation of new-product concepts in the following manner:

1. Ideas for new products might be obtained by searching for new combinations of construct levels from the repertory-grid analysis (e.g., a blueberry-flavored bagel).

2. Ideas might be suggested by the substitution of existing attributes (e.g., a vanilla-chip cookie or a mocha- (nonfruit) flavored strudel).

3. The consumption grid may be used as a preliminary device to search for ways in which two nominally different products (e.g., chewing gum and soft drinks), used on similar occasions, might be made morphologically more similar—developing a chewing gum with a "carbonated" taste.

4. Ideas might be suggested by modifying products to encompass currently inappropriate use occasions—a cold-soup substitute for use occasions in which soft drinks are typically consumed.

5. Ideas might be suggested by complementarity motivations (e.g., a peanut-flavored pretzel as a cocktail party snack.)

The above procedures are hardly exhaustive of how repertory- and consumption-grid data can be used in idea generation. Possibilities for changing product form, mode of application, range of application, function, type of consumer to whom the product will appeal, and the like are illustrative of the uses of these procedures in concept generation.

Indeed, whole families of new concepts might be generated by a type of "cross-pollination" in which one imagines that foods can be (metaphorically) designed to serve the functions of music or visual art, that pet foods are designed like human foods, that clothing is designed to appeal to all five senses, and so on. While many of these metaphorical studies are carried out with executives (in "brain-storming" sessions) rather than with consumers, there is no compelling reason why consumers could not be used.

Concept Screening and Testing

New-product ideas (however obtained) are often subjected to consumer evaluation by means of procedures known as *concept screening* or *concept testing*.[6] The usual objective is to check for market acceptability of the ideas, usually expressed in verbal or pictorial form, *before* costly developments are undertaken to build actual prototypes. Concept testing is often undertaken in parallel with (or subsequent to) internal studies of technical feasibility.

Most concept-evaluation procedures exhibit the following characteristics:

1. A sample of potential buyers is presented with verbal or pictorial descriptions of the product—what its characteristics are, what functions it is designed to serve, its unique features compared with existing products. Control concepts (describing existing, but unidentified products) are often included as well.

2. Respondents are asked to rate each concept on various scales—degree of interest, intentions-to-buy, willingness to obtain the product versus an "equivalent" amount of cash.

3. Ratings may also be obtained on various prespecified attributes of the concept and respondents may be asked to list particular likes and dislikes about the concept, additional information that would be desirable to have about the concept, and so on.

From data obtained from tasks similar to the above, concepts are arrayed in terms of consumer interest. Often, normative data are also assembled over time on the relationship between various test scores from previous concept evaluations and the success rate of past product introductions (or between test and control concepts where market-share data are available for the latter).

Whatever the specific details of the procedure, the data are used as part of the basis on which the decision to undertake prototype development is made.

As with all research techniques, some potential problems may arise in concept research. At the analysis stage, a mistake that is often made is to concentrate on all respondents in the total target group. Yet, not every consumer can or will become a

---

[6]Concept screening usually entails a rather crude consumer evaluation of a relatively large number of ideas, while concept testing involves fewer concepts that are articulated in more detail; the latter procedure usually follows the preliminary application of concept screening. Illustrations of the use of multidimensional scaling, conjoint measurement, and related multivariate techniques are found in Y. Wind, "A New Procedure for Concept Evaluation," *Journal of Marketing,* 37 (October 1973), 2–11. A review of multiattribute research applied to new-product evaluation and concept evaluation is presented in A. D. Shocker and V. Srinivasan, "Multiattribute Approaches for Product Concept Evaluation and Generation: A Critical Review," *Journal of Marketing Research,* 16 (May 1979), 159–80.

brand user, regardless of how good the marketing program is. The prime target group consists of people who are likely to purchase the product (i.e., have a high interest in the concept) and are not being satisfied with existing alternatives.[7]

Another potential problem is related to respondent sampling and is one explanation why multiattribute techniques (and multidimensional scaling and related techniques) have limitations with respect to generating and evaluating "substantially new" product concepts. Very simply, the problem seems to be with using consumer evaluators who do not have real-world experience with the novel product concepts and attributes of potential interest. Rather, so-called lead users and high-benefit users have a greater ability to understand selected product attributes outside of the normally experienced range. *Lead users* are users whose present needs foreshadow the projectable future needs of the market being considered—i.e., individuals or firms who have needs that are not now prevalent among users of a given product but can be predicted to become general and to identify a commercially interesting market in the future. *High-benefit users* are users who have higher unmet needs for a given novel or familiar product attribute or concept than does the average user. Judgment and ingenuity are needed to find the needed lead users, and the process is essentially subjective in nature. That is, there is no precise formula for finding the group.[8]

An Illustration of Concept Evaluation

To illustrate the principles of concept evaluation, we describe a study conducted by a large producer of chemically based consumer items. The sponsor of this study had been engaged in a series of product-development and diversification efforts. The company's development department, assisted by outside sources, had come up with a set of 31 product concepts that were technically feasible to manufacture.

The problem at this point was to obtain rather gross consumer evaluations of the concepts—a type of concept screening—for later refinement and subsequent testing of the most attractive concepts from the consumer's point of view. A verbal description and artist sketch were prepared for each concept. Illustrations of four of these are shown in Figure 18-1.

A mail questionnaire was designed and sent to members of a national panel. The respondents consisted of men and women (one person per household) from demographically matched households. A total of 986 returns were received from women and 774 from men.

Each respondent was asked first to group the 31 concepts into those that were personally "interesting" versus those that were "not interesting." For each of the "interesting" ones the respondent was asked a series of questions, as shown in Figure 18-2.

---

[7]For further discussion of issues relating to analysis of concept testing data, see D. A. Schwartz, "Concept Testing *Can* Be Improved—and Here's How to Do It," *Marketing News*, 18 (January 6, 1984), Sec. 1, pp. 22ff.

[8]For a more-detailed discussion of lead users, see E. von Hippel, *Novel Product Concepts from Lead Users: Segmenting Users by Experience* (Cambridge, Mass.: Marketing Science Institute, December 1984), Report No. 84–109.

Figure 18-1 Illustrative Product–Concept Descriptions

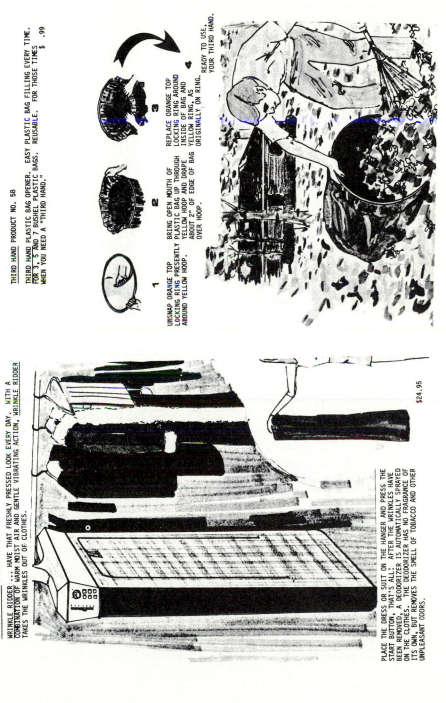

WRINKLE RIDDER PRODUCT NO. 64

WRINKLE RIDDER ... HAVE THAT FRESHLY PRESSED LOOK EVERY DAY. WITH A COMBINATION OF WARM MOIST AIR AND GENTLE VIBRATING ACTION, WRINKLE RIDDER TAKES THE WRINKLES OUT OF CLOTHES.

PLACE THE DRESS OR SUIT ON THE HANGER AND PRESS THE START BUTTON, THAT'S ALL! AFTER THE WRINKLES HAVE BEEN REMOVED, A DEODORIZER IS AUTOMATICALLY SPRAYED ON THE CLOTHES. THE DEODORIZER HAS NO FRAGRANCE OF ITS OWN, BUT REMOVES THE SMELL OF TOBACCO AND OTHER UNPLEASANT ODORS.

$24.95

THIRD HAND PRODUCT NO. 58

THIRD HAND PLASTIC BAG OPENER. EASY PLASTIC BAG FILLING EVERY TIME. FOR 3, 5 AND 7 BUSHEL PLASTIC BAGS. REUSABLE. FOR THOSE TIMES WHEN YOU NEED A "THIRD HAND." $ .99

1 UNSNAP ORANGE TOP LOCKING RING PRESENTLY AROUND YELLOW HOOP.

2 BRING OPEN MOUTH OF PLASTIC BAG UP THROUGH YELLOW HOOP AND DRAPE ABOUT 2" OF EDGE OF BAG OVER HOOP.

3 REPLACE ORANGE TOP LOCKING RING AROUND INSIDE OF BAG AND YELLOW RING, AS ORIGINALLY ON RING.

READY TO USE. YOUR THIRD HAND.

717

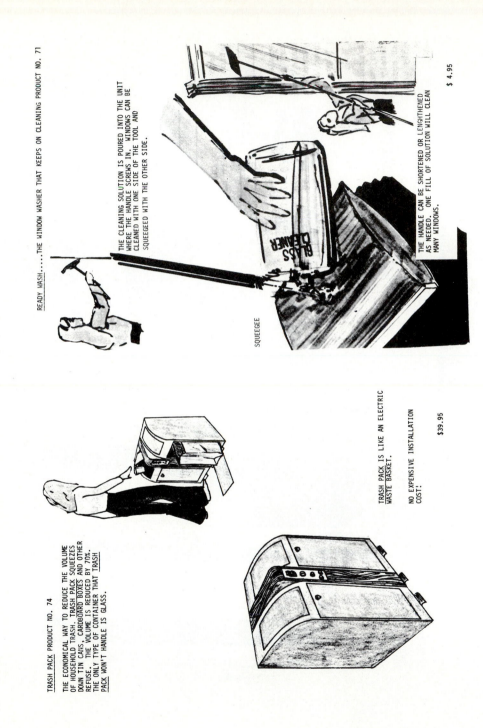

READY WASH.....THE WINDOW WASHER THAT KEEPS ON CLEANING PRODUCT NO. 71

THE CLEANING SOLUTION IS POURED INTO THE UNIT WHERE THE HANDLE SCREWS IN. WINDOWS CAN BE CLEANED WITH ONE SIDE OF THE TOOL AND SQUEEGEED WITH THE OTHER SIDE.

SQUEEGEE

GLASS CLEANER

THE HANDLE CAN BE SHORTENED OR LENGTHENED AS NEEDED. ONE FILL OF SOLUTION WILL CLEAN MANY WINDOWS.

$ 4.95

TRASH PACK PRODUCT NO. 74

THE ECONOMICAL WAY TO REDUCE THE VOLUME OF HOUSEHOLD TRASH. TRASH PACK SQUEEZES DOWN TIN CANS, CARDBOARD BOXES AND OTHER REFUSE. THE VOLUME IS REDUCED BY 70%. THE ONLY TYPE OF CONTAINER THAT TRASH PACK WON'T HANDLE IS GLASS.

TRASH PACK IS LIKE AN ELECTRIC WASTE BASKET.

NO EXPENSIVE INSTALLATION COST!

$39.95

Figure 18-2 Response Form Used for Each Product-Concept Description

1. From what you have seen and read, which word or phrase best describes your reaction to this product?

   Excellent ( )5   Good( )2
   Extremely good( )4   Fair( )1
   Very good ( )3   Poor( )0

2. What, if anything, do you think you might like about this product?

   _____

   _____

3. What, if anything, do you think you might dislike about this product?

   _____

   _____

4. If you were thinking of buying this product, what other information would you like to have about the product?

   _____

   _____

5. Where would you shop to buy this product?

   Grocery or   Variety store   ( )16
     supermarket   ( )11 Door-to-door, or
   Hardware store   ( )12 in-home sales person ( )17
   Department store ( )13 Mail-order
   Discount store   ( )14   catalog   ( )18
   Drugstore   ( )15 Trading
                               Stamp store   ( )19
                               Other   ( )20

6. If this product were available at a local store, how likely do you think you would be to buy it?

   Absolutely sure I would buy it   ( )6
   Almost sure I would buy it   ( )5
   Probably would buy it   ( )4
   Might or might not buy it   ( )3
   Probably would not buy it   ( )2
   Almost sure I would not buy it   ( )1
   Absolutely sure I would not buy it   ( )0

7. Would this product make a good gift?
                               YES( ) NO( )

Following this, the respondent was asked to imagine that he or she was given an extra $100 and had to select at least one of the items (but could select more than one) and keep the change. The respondent was then asked to select the item(s), he or she would choose.

Results of the study indicated that 5 of the 31 concepts received high evaluations from both men and women in terms of both single evaluation scores and inclusion in the set of products that the respondent would consider if $100 were available for spending.

Two of these five "winners" are shown in Figure 18-1, the "Wrinkle Ridder" and the "Third Hand." For purposes of contrast, the other two concepts—"Trash Pack" and "Ready Wash"—received scores (for both men and women) around the middle of the array of 31 items. These were not recommended for further testing.

The five "winners" and three (control) items were recommended for further testing, involving price experimentation and more articulated descriptions, as developed from an analysis of the open-ended responses (to questions shown in Figure 18-2 on likes, dislikes, and further information desired). Hence, concept evaluation can often involve a recycling of the research as the concepts undergo revision and further articulation, based on the results of earlier surveys.

Product Idea Screening by the Firm

As stated earlier, concept testing is often undertaken in parallel with or after internal studies. These internal studies include new-product screening evaluations. In addition to the widely used intuitive approach, there are four major formalized approaches:

- *Ranking* models that compare one product idea against others on some specified set of evaluation criteria—the highest-ranked product is selected.
- *Scoring* models that use criteria considered critical to a product's performance. Each idea is evaluated using these criteria, and those that exceed a minimum acceptable score (when summed across all evaluative criteria) are selected.
- *Economic* models that are based on deterministic or probabilistic payoffs, profits, R.O.I., etc.—the product meeting some desired level is selected.
- *Optimization* models that are based on selecting products that maximize some identified mathematical function—linear and dynamic programming are two approaches.

Of these approaches the ones most widely used by managers are scoring models. Such models are easy to use, easy to understand, and easy to communicate to others. To illustrate this approach a segment of a larger screening measurement instrument is shown in Figure 18-3. All an evaluator has to do is evaluate a product idea on each of 33 criteria which are categorized into the following major factors: *societal, business risk, demand analysis, market acceptance,* and *competitive.* In addition, an overall likelihood of success evaluation is made. Once data from such checklist approaches have been obtained from evaluators within the company, a type of summated score is obtained for each product idea. The criteria may or may not be differentially weighted.

Figure 18-3   New-product Screening Instrument

DIRECTIONS:

Check the response that best corresponds to your evaluation for each Criterion. Be sure you answer all questions. NOTE that "don't know" and "not applicable" responses are coded "DK" and "NA." Be SURE to use them when they are appropriate.

After each Factor group, a space is provided for your written comments relative to that section. If you have any specific information, or suggestions, use this space. These comments are highly useful in providing additional information and insights.

SOCIETAL FACTOR

1.   LEGALITY CRITERION: In terms of applicable laws (particularly product liability), regulations, product standards, this idea/invention/new product . . .

End Statements
{
_____ might not meet them, even if changed
_____ might require substantial revision to meet them   _____ DK
_____ might require modest revision
_____ might require minor changes   _____ NA
_____ will meet them without any changes
}

2.   SAFETY CRITERION: Considering potential hazards and side effects, the use might be . . .

End Statements
{
_____ very unsafe, even when used as intended
_____ unsafe under reasonably foreseeable circumstances   _____ DK
_____ relatively safe for careful, instructed users
_____ safe when used as intended, with no foreseeable hazards _____ NA
_____ very safe under all conditions, including misuse
}

3.   ENVIRONMENTAL IMPACT CRITERION: In terms of pollution, litter, misuse of natural resources, etc., use might . . .

End Statements
{
_____ violate environmental regulations and/or have dangerous environmental consequences   _____ DK
_____ have some negative effect on the environment
_____ have no effect on the environment if properly used   _____ NA
_____ have no effect on the environment
_____ have a positive impact on the environment
}

·
·

COMMENTS:

BUSINESS RISK FACTOR:

5.   FUNCTIONAL FEASIBILITY CRITERION: In terms of functions, will it actually do what it is intended to do?

{
_____ the concept is not sound; cannot be made to work
_____ it won't work now but might be modified   _____ DK
}

(continued)

Figure 18-3   New-product Screening Instrument (*Continued*)

End Statements {
_____ it will work but major changes might be needed
_____ it will work but minor changes might be needed   _____ NA
_____ it will work—no changes necessary
}

6.   PRODUCTION FEASIBILITY CRITERION: With regard to technical processes or equipment required for production, this invention might . . .

End Statements {
_____ be impossible to produce now or in the foreseeable future
_____ be very difficult to produce   _____ DK
_____ have some problems which can be overcome
_____ have only minor problems   _____ NA
_____ have no problems
}

•
•

COMMENTS:

DEMAND ANALYSIS FACTOR

13.   POTENTIAL MARKET CRITERION: The total market for products of this type might be . . .

End Statements {
_____ very small—very specialized or local in nature
_____ small—relatively specialized or regional in nature   _____ DK
_____ medium—limited national market
_____ large—broad national market   _____ NA
_____ very large—extensive national and possible international market
}

14.   POTENTIAL SALES CRITERION: Expected sales of this product might be . . .

End Statements {
_____ very small
_____ small   _____ DK
_____ medium
_____ large   _____ NA
_____ very large
}

15.   TREND OF DEMAND CRITERION: The market demand for products of this type appears to be . . .

End Statements {
_____ rapidly declining—product might soon become obsolete
_____ declining—potentially obsolete in near future   _____ DK
_____ steady—demand expected to remain constant
_____ growing slowly—modest growth opportunity   _____ NA
_____ rapidly expanding—significant growth opportunity
}

•
•

COMMENTS:

MARKET ACCEPTANCE FACTOR

19.   COMPATIBILITY CRITERION: Compatibility with existing attitudes and methods of use is . . .

{
_____ very low—will block market acceptance
_____ low—some conflict; will slow market acceptance   _____ DK
}

Figure 18-3   (*Continued*)

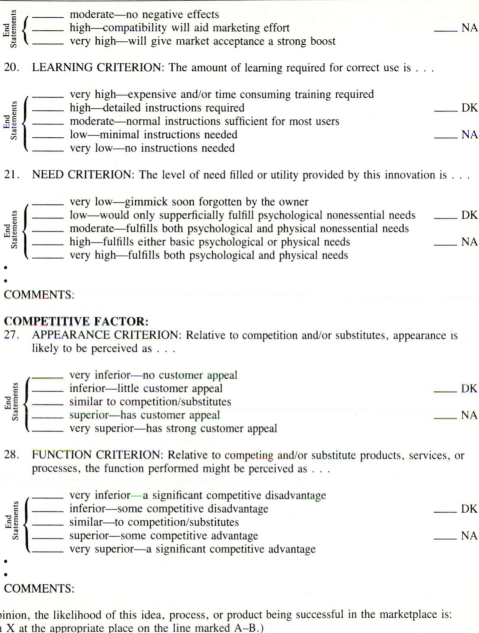

End Statements {
—— moderate—no negative effects
—— high—compatibility will aid marketing effort   —— NA
—— very high—will give market acceptance a strong boost
}

20.   LEARNING CRITERION: The amount of learning required for correct use is . . .

End Statements {
—— very high—expensive and/or time consuming training required
—— high—detailed instructions required   —— DK
—— moderate—normal instructions sufficient for most users
—— low—minimal instructions needed   —— NA
—— very low—no instructions needed
}

21.   NEED CRITERION: The level of need filled or utility provided by this innovation is . . .

End Statements {
—— very low—gimmick soon forgotten by the owner
—— low—would only supperficially fulfill psychological nonessential needs   —— DK
—— moderate—fulfills both psychological and physical nonessential needs
—— high—fulfills either basic psychological or physical needs   —— NA
—— very high—fulfills both psychological and physical needs
}

•
•

COMMENTS:

COMPETITIVE FACTOR:
27.   APPEARANCE CRITERION: Relative to competition and/or substitutes, appearance is likely to be perceived as . . .

End Statements {
—— very inferior—no customer appeal
—— inferior—little customer appeal   —— DK
—— similar to competition/substitutes
—— superior—has customer appeal   —— NA
—— very superior—has strong customer appeal
}

28.   FUNCTION CRITERION: Relative to competing and/or substitute products, services, or processes, the function performed might be perceived as . . .

End Statements {
—— very inferior—a significant competitive disadvantage
—— inferior—some competitive disadvantage   —— DK
—— similar—to competition/substitutes
—— superior—some competitive advantage   —— NA
—— very superior—a significant competitive advantage
}

•
•

COMMENTS:

In my opinion, the likelihood of this idea, process, or product being successful in the marketplace is:
(Place an X at the appropriate place on the line marked A–B.)

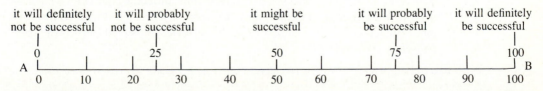

it will definitely not be successful	it will probably not be successful	it might be successful	it will probably be successful	it will definitely be successful
0	25	50	75	100

A └─┴─┴─┴─┴─┴─┴─┴─┴─┴─┘ B
0 10 20 30 40 50 60 70 80 90 100

Once a total score is obtained, there are basically four different ways in which to model the data:

- *Conjunctive Model,* which involves accepting or rejecting a product based on passing or not passing all the evaluative criteria. The product, in order to pass, would have to meet or exceed a specified minimum value for each of the criteria used.
- *Disjunctive Model,* which is based on accepting a product that exceeds specified levels on one or a few key criteria, regardless of its score on the others.
- *Lexicographic Model,* which is based on ranking the evaluation criteria in terms of their perceived importance. New-product ideas are compared criterion by criterion until there is an idea that is superior to the others on a criterion.
- *Linear Compensatory Model,* which is based on multiplying a product's score on a criterion and the importance weight for each criterion and then summing across all evaluative criteria. The product with the highest summated score is selected, or those products with scores above some cutoff value are selected, for further analysis.

Although the use of the linear compensatory approach seems to be most prevalent in practice, the other types of models should not be overlooked as viable alternatives. The ability to correctly screen out "unsuccessful products" may not be equal among the types of models, and each model's sensitivity to number of criteria, scaling values, and weighting schemes may also differ.

A study by Baker and Albaum illustrates these points.[9] A sample of 86 decision makers evaluated six product concepts representing consumer lighting products. All respondents were provided with graphic representations of the products and two pages of qualitative information pertinent to the subject areas covered by the checklist, which was the one illustrated in Figure 18-3. Respondents who recognized any product or who did not consider themselves technically competent or knowledgeable in the product category were omitted from the analysis. Two of the products were successful while four were unsuccessful; *success* was defined in terms of the lighting company's objectives for the product. Respondents also provided importance weights for each ctiterion.

The data for all criteria and the five most important criteria were modeled as conjunctive, disjunctive, lexicographic, and linear compensatory models. The following conclusions were reached:

1. The models demonstrated different degrees of accuracy. The most conservative model overall was the conjunctive model using the five critical criteria with a cutoff value of four.
2. The level of accuracy changes for models with different criteria or weighting scales values. Differences are rather dramatic, especially with the conjunctive and disjunctive models and less so with the lexicographic and the linear compensatory models.

[9]See K. Baker and G. Albaum, "Modeling New Product Screening Decisions," *Journal of Product Innovation Management,* 3 (March 1986), 32–39.

Based on this study it would appear that a fairly simple model, using a minimum number of evaluative criteria, might be useful for new-product idea screening. Which form the model might take could vary with the type of product and the nature of the company itself.

Prototype Evaluation and Market Testing

Concept screening, concept testing, prototype design, in-home use tests, and market tests can be viewed as a sequence of research steps in which the output of previous stages enters as input to subsequent ones. Of course, the possibility exists that a given stage may be recycled.

In concept screening and testing, one typically deals with verbalized or pictorial material only. In prototype and in-home test, one deals with the physical object, perhaps constructed in alternative forms, that can be tried out and compared with current products. A *prototype test* is any kind of evaluation that involves the physical product. *In-home tests* involve consumption of the prototype. In-home tests add a dimension to concept testing and often reveal situations not readily ascertainable from pure concept testing. For example, a food company was interested in examining alternative sales approaches for a new product. Concept testing of the approaches revealed that sales approach Y generated the most interest, although not significantly different from sales approach X. However, after trying the product in-home approach X was significantly the most acceptable. Another illustration of in-home testing is provided by a manufacturer of cleansers. Respondents were asked to use two new cleansers for two weeks; each was used for a different purpose for one week. Figure 18-4 shows the data collection form used in this in-home experiment.[10]

As one moves from concept screening to prototype tests, the "stimuli" become more realistic, but the research costs mount. The costs are particularly high in the *test-marketing* phase, where actual supplies of the product are placed on sale and alternative pricing, packaging, and promotional programs may be under test. (In general, the flexibility for program modification decreases as one moves through the sequence, although the similarity of the study to real marketing conditions increases.)

Another problem associated with full-scale market tests is the difficulty of controlling and monitoring the progress of the test. This problem is particularly acute in those cases in which marketing mixes are experimentally varied so that the researcher obtains information beyond that required for a "go, no go" decision.

A third problem concerns the fact that market tests can tip off one's competitors about the new-product candidate. Not only does this give them more lead time for developing strategies to combat the new entrant, but cases are known in which competitors have actually tried to thwart the market test itself by running special price promotions or other disruptive activities.

Finally, the amount of time required to assemble data on the results of the test

[10]This is a blind forced-choice test. For a discussion of this approach, see B. S. Buchanan and D. G. Morrison, *Measuring Simple Preferences: An Approach to Blind, Forced-Choice Product Testing* (Cambridge, Mass.: Marketing Science Institute, April 1985), Report No 85-33.

Figure 18-4   In-home Test of Two Cleansers

Use Product "M" First Then Use Product "G"
Test of Two New Scouring Cleansers

INSTRUCTIONS: You have been given two new cleansers. Be sure to open both cans at the same time. Do this right away and begin the test today using these products in place of your regular scouring cleanser. During the first seven days, use the product listed first at the top of your questionnaire for the work in your kitchen. Use this product every time you clean your sink, porcelain and tile, pots and pans, floor, etc.

During this first seven-day period, use the other product *in your bathroom*. Use it every time you clean your tub, sink, porcelain and tile, tile walls or floor, etc. At the end of this first seven days, switch the products, using the one you started with in the bathroom now in your kitchen and vice-versa. Make sure you use the products in the same manner and under similar circumstances. Please use the products for two weeks before you form a final opinion about them.

Vote your preference on each cleanser by placing a check mark (X) under "G" or "M." If you are unable to discern any difference whatsoever between the two products on any specific quality, place a check under "No Preference."

NOTE: Each of the first five questions under section 2 (Pots and Pans Test) refers to different types of pots and pans. Answer only those questions referring to the type of pots and pans you own. Do not check any answer for the types you do not own.

			PREFER		NO
			"G"	"M"	PREFERENCE
1.	*Porcelain and Tile Test*	Col.	(6)	(7)	(8)
	Which removed grease better from sink, etc.		( ) 1	( ) 1	( ) 1
	Which removed stains better from sink, etc.		( ) 2	( ) 2	( ) 2
	Which removed stains faster, more easily from sink, etc.		( ) 3	( ) 3	( ) 3
	Which made sinks, bathtubs and toilets cleaner & brighter		( ) 4	( ) 4	( ) 4
	Which made tile walls cleaner and brighter		( ) 5	( ) 5	( ) 5
	Which made tile floors cleaner and brighter		( ) 6	( ) 6	( ) 6
	Which did you prefer for amount of grittiness		( ) 7	( ) 7	( ) 7
	Which required less rinsing		( ) 8	( ) 8	( ) 8
	Which left less powder or dust on surface		( ) 9	( ) 9	( ) 9
	Which left surface freer from scratches		( ) 0	( ) 0	( ) 0
	All things considered which cleanser did you prefer for porcelain and tile		( ) X	( ) X	( ) X
2.	*Pots and Pans Test*				
	Which was better in removing scorched, burned or stained spots from:	Col.	(9)	(10)	(11)
	aluminum pots and pans		( ) 1	( ) 1	( ) 1
	stainless steel pots		( ) 2	( ) 2	( ) 2
	copper bottoms		( ) 3	( ) 3	( ) 3
	enamel pots and pans		( ) 4	( ) 4	( ) 4
	iron pots and pans		( ) 5	( ) 5	( ) 5

Which removed grease better from pots and pans	( ) 6	( ) 6	( ) 6
Which did you prefer for amount of grittiness	( ) 7	( ) 7	( ) 7
Which requires less rinsing	( ) 8	( ) 8	( ) 8
Which left surfaces freer from scratches	( ) 9	( ) 9	( ) 9
All things considered which cleanser did you prefer for pots and pans	( ) 0	( ) 0	( ) 0

3. *General*   Col.

	(12)	(13)	(14)
Which was easeir to shake from container	( ) 1	( ) 1	( ) 1
Which did you prefer for foaming	( ) 2	( ) 2	( ) 2
Which did you prefer for odor	( ) 3	( ) 3	( ) 3
Which did you prefer for color	( ) 4	( ) 4	( ) 4
Which appeared to be better for removing unpleasant odors from sinks, stoves, etc.	( ) 5	( ) 5	( ) 5
Which cleanser was more economical (went further)	( ) 6	( ) 6	( ) 6
Which cleanser was easier on your hands	( ) 7	( ) 7	( ) 7
Which was less irritating to nostrils	( ) 8	( ) 8	( ) 8
Which created less dustiness	( ) 9	( ) 9	( ) 9

(Col. 15)

4. Which cleanser did you prefer *over all* (Please check *one*)   ( ) 1   ( ) 2   ( ) 3

Col. (16) 1–10_ (17) 11–20_ (18) 21–30_ (19) 31–40_ (20) 41–50_ (21) 51–60_ (22) 61–70_

5. If you preferred one of the test products *over all* what are the principal reasons?

_____

_____

Col. (23)__ (24)__ (25)__ (26)__ (27)__ (28)__ (29)__

6. What if anything did you dislike about "G" _____

_____

Col. (30)__ (31)__ (32)__ (33)__ (34)__ (35)__ (36)__

7. What if anything did you dislike about "M" _____

_____

Col (37)

8. Have you used these products for cleaning woodwork or painted surfaces?

         Yes__ (1)   No__ (2)

If yes, please check preferred product:

	Col. (38–39)		
	Prefer		No
	"G"	"M"	Preference
Which did you prefer for cleaning woodwork	( ) 1	( ) 2	( ) 3
Which did you prefer for cleaning painted surfaces	( ) 4	( ) 5	( ) 6

9. What is your opinion of the strength of the odor in each cleanser? (Please check only *one* for *each* product.)

Figure 18-4   In-home Test of Two Cleansers (*Continued*)

Col. (40–41)

	ODOR MUCH TOO STRONG	ODOR SLIGHTLY STRONG	ABOUT RIGHT IN STRENGTH	ODOR SLIGHTLY WEAK	ODOR MUCH TOO WEAK
Test Cleanser "G"	( ) 1	( ) 2	( ) 3	( ) 4	( ) 5
Test Cleanser "M"	( ) 1	( ) 2	( ) 3	( ) 4	( ) 5

10. What is your opinion of the *quality* of the *odor* in each cleanser? (Please check only *one* for *each* product.)

Col. (42–43)

	VERY ACCEPTABLE	SLIGHTLY ACCEPTABLE	DON'T MIND IT (NEUTRAL)	OBJECT SLIGHTLY TO IT	OBJECT STRONGLY TO IT
Test Cleanser "G"	( ) 1	( ) 2	( ) 3	( ) 4	( ) 5
Test Cleanser "M"	( ) 1	( ) 2	( ) 3	( ) 4	( ) 5

11. What is your opinion of the grittiness of each product for *all purpose scouring cleansing*? (Please check *one* for *each* product.)

Col. (44–45)

	MUCH TOO GRITTY	SLIGHTLY GRITTY	GRITTINESS ABOUT RIGHT	NOT QUITE GRITTY ENOUGH	NOT NEARLY GRITTY ENOUGH
Test Cleanser "G"	( ) 1	( ) 2	( ) 3	( ) 4	( ) 5
Test Cleanser "M"	( ) 1	( ) 2	( ) 3	( ) 4	( ) 5

12. What is your opinion of the amount of foaming in each cleanser? (Please check only *one* for *each* product.)

Col. (46–47)

	MUCH TOO FOAMY	SLIGHTLY FOAMY	FOAMINESS ABOUT RIGHT	NOT QUITE FOAMY ENOUGH	NOT NEARLY FOAMY ENOUGH
Test Cleanser "G"	( ) 1	( ) 2	( ) 3	( ) 4	( ) 5
Test Cleanser "M"	( ) 1	( ) 2	( ) 3	( ) 4	( ) 5

13. Approximately how much of *each* test product was *left* in each container at the *end* of this two week test?

Col. (48–49)

	LESS THAN 1/4	1/4 TO 1/2	1/2 TO 3/4	MORE THAN 3/4
Test Cleanser "G"	( ) 1	( ) 2	( ) 3	( ) 4
Test Cleanser "M"	( ) 1	( ) 2	( ) 3	( ) 4

14. Please check below *each* cleanser that you have *tried* for Porcelain, Tile, Stainless Steel, Aluminum or Iron pots and pans or woodwork within the *past six months*.

Col. (50)

PLEASE CHECK EACH BRAND TRIED

Ajax	( ) 1	Bon-Ami	( ) 4
Bab-O	( ) 2	Comet	( ) 5
Old Dutch	( ) 3	Other	( ) 6 _____

(Please Specify)

Figure 18-4   (*Continued*)

Col. 51_____

15.   What is your FAVORITE BRAND of Cleanser?_____
(Brand Name)

Classification Data
(For Statistical Purposes Only)

16.   A. Please check your proper age group below:

Col. (52)

UNDER 25	25–34	35–44	45–54	OVER 54
( ) 1	( ) 2	( ) 3	( ) 4	( ) 5

B. How many adults *and* children are presently living in your household?

Col. (53)

One ( ) 1	Three ( ) 3	Five ( ) 5	Seven or more ( ) 7
Two ( ) 2	Four ( ) 4	Six ( ) 6	

NAME _____

STREET & NUMBER _____

CITY _____STATE_____

market is substantial—often 12 to 18 months or more before a go, no go decision is reached. Bearing in mind that additional lead time is then required for copy development and product placement, the total elapsed time can be significant. Recently, more efficient ways have been sought to (1) test marketing-mix alternatives at the same time that one is testing new-product acceptance and (2) reduce measurement cost, risks of competitive exposure, and the time lapse associated with test marketing.

Insofar as the first point is concerned, new services have been introduced to deal with comparative promotional mix evaluation. For example, Adtel, a Chicago research firm, offers a variety of test-market services, including dual-cable TV, where alternative copy experiments can be run at the time a new product is test-marketed. Other firms provide a series of in-home use tests where the respondent can "purchase" additional quantities of the product after their initial supply has been exhausted.

One of the latest trends in test marketing is to *simulate* the whole activity. A number of consulting firms are offering test-market simulators that attempt to predict the time path of market share and sales if the new product is introduced nationally under specified marketing-mix conditions. Typical inputs to these models include

- An estimate of initial trial probability;
- An estimate of first repeat-purchase probability;
- Empirical functions relating second and later repeat purchases to first repeat purchase; and

• Functions relating model parameters to the firm's advertising and promotion, price, and distribution coverage.

Initial trial probability is usually estimated from simulated market-choice tests, such as laboratory shopping experiments. Repeat purchasing is usually estimated from in-home use tests involving test and control products.

A test-market simulation costs but a fraction of the typical full-scale test-market study. Although there is not a great deal of information readily available about the simulators' accuracy in predicting market share and sales for new products and services that have been introduced by this means, there is evidence that an increasing number of companies are accepting the technique, although cautiously perhaps. As experience accumulates on their application, a more accurate evaluation of test-market simulators' benefits versus costs should be forthcoming.[11]

Another trend in test marketing is based on the use of *scanner-generated* data (discussed in Chapter 5 and 6). Research companies such as Information Resources, Inc., Burke, and A. C. Nielsen have available data from panels who purchase package goods in stores using scanners for checkout purposes. Although this technology requires capital, it still costs significantly less than conventional tests conducted in major markets. What does the future hold? Technologically, it has been suggested that people will gradually become accustomed to seeing and using such things as *in-home scanners, exposure meters* for commercial exposure data at both the household and individual viewer levels, and *electronic promotion services* operated from a kiosk and tied to scanners.[12] These techniques are still in the introductory stage, so it is too early to determine the extent to which they will have an impact on test-marketing practices.

TESTING COMPONENTS OF THE MARKETING MIX

Marketing researchers are frequently called upon to design and analyze tests of advertisements, package alternatives, and so on. These tests may be made in the context of either new products or existing products. The specialized procedures for carrying out this type of activity are myriad and no attempt will be made to catalog them. Rather, we provide a few illustrations of how such tests are designed and analyzed. The procedures described here are believed to be reasonably typical of the many kinds of techniques that are used in practice.

---

[11]For an evaluation of use of simulated test markets in pretest market models, see A. D. Shocker and W. G. Hall, "Pretest Market Models: A Critical Evaluation," *Journal of Product Innovation Management,* 3 (June 1986), 86–107.

[12]See J. R. Rhodes, "Technological Advances in Test Marketing: A Look to the Future," paper presented at the Sixth Annual Marketing Research Conference, American Marketing Association, October 1985.

Promotion Testing

Many firms, almost as a matter of routine, conduct tests of new TV commercials, radio spots, or print ads. These tests are often but not necessarily made in the context of new-product introductions. An illustration of the type of questionnaire used in these tests is shown in Figure 18-5. In this case the context involved changes in promotional theme for an existing product.

The purpose underlying this study was to examine consumer reaction to three new (test) commercials for auto batteries. A sample of 400 men—all between 18 and 65 years of age and all responsible for maintaining a car that was two years old or older—were selected and interviewed in central location facilities. Each respondent of the test group viewed one of the three test commercials (on a special type of color-sound projector) and three competitive commercials. A control group viewed a current commercial of the sponsor and the three competitive commercials. Hence, each set of test or control data was based on 100 respondents and all four were evaluated in the context of the same three competitive commercials.

Figure 18-5 shows portions of the questionnaire containing questions dealing with reactions to each commercial (order rotated across respondents). Also shown is the set of preliminary questions related to product-class familiarity, brand predispositions, product-attribute importance, and perceived-attribute uniqueness. (Not shown are the sections of the questionnaire dealing with life-style, previous auto battery purchases, demographics, etc.)

Part A is included to obtain information on brand awareness and interest, for comparison with test results. Part B is designed to record main idea playback, general impressions, believability, evaluation of product attributes, and buying interest for the brand advertised in each commercial, as reacted to separately. Part C is designed for direct comparison of all four commercials (each of which involved Part B-type responses). Here the respondent is placed in a position of having to compare the brands involved in all four commercials—one sponsor and three competitive—in terms of choosing among the four products being advertised. Hence, comparison data are available on a before-exposure basis (Part A), separate-exposure basis (Part B), and comparison basis after all four exposures (Part C). Responses include global-type, single-stimulus evaluations (e.g., degree of interest in the product), global-type comparison evaluations (e.g., which of the four batteries would you buy?), and attribute-type responses.

In this particular study only one of the three test commercials significantly outrated the sponsor's control commercial (as well as outrating the three competitive commercials). This particular test commercial scored well on recall of the main copy points, believability of claims, and product interest (Part B). Moreover, its share of choices in the comparison test of Part C was significantly higher than those of the other test commercials and control.

Interestingly enough, the winning test commercial emphasized reserve battery power and the ability to start the car under adverse weather conditions (in which other batteries might fail). Average price perceptions of the battery were also higher than those associated with commercials of competitive batteries, even though its average market price was about the same. Even allowing for the fact that the product had disproportionately high consumer awareness and interest (Part A responses), the winning test commercial displayed significantly higher brand scores. Finally, its comparative performance remained

Figure 18-5   Portions of Response Form Used in TV Commercial Testing: Part A—Awareness and Interest

1. You indicated that you had an automobile that was more than two years old. What is the exact make, model and year of this auto? (REPEAT FOR EACH AUTO OVER TWO YEARS OLD.) Did you buy this auto new or used?

Car	Make	Model	Year		New	Used
(a)	13-22	23-32	33-34	35		
(b)	36-45	46-55	56-57	58		
(c)	59-68	69-78	79-80	8		

Subj. No.   1-4
Card No. 2 5-6

2. Now I would like you to think about the different companies that make automobile batteries, or places where you can buy automobile batteries that you know of. Please tell me all the ones you know of. (PROBE WITH: What others?) (DO NOT READ LIST.)

A. Amoco _____ 9
B. Atlas _____ 10
C. Delco _____ 11
D. Exide _____ 12
E. Firestone Supreme _____ 13
F. Ford (not specified) _____ 14
    Motor Craft _____ 15
    Autolite _____ 16
G. Goodyear Power House _____ 17
H. Montgomery Ward's
    Riverside _____ 18

I. J.C. Penney's (not
          specified) _____ 19
    Survivor _____ 20
    Foremost _____ 21
J. Sears (not specified) _____ 22
    Die Hard _____ 23
    Allstate _____ 24
K. Shell Superlife _____ 25
L. Western Auto's Wizard _____ 26
M. Willard _____ 27
N. Willard-Exide _____ 28
    Other (SPECIFY)_____ 29

(HAND RESPONDENT CARD A.)

3. Imagine you were going to buy an automobile battery today. Please tell me which number on this card best describes how interested you think you would be in buying a _____(INSERT NAME) battery.

(REPEAT FOR EACH BRAND MENTIONED IN Q.2, AND FOR THE STARRED BRANDS, WHETHER OR NOT THEY WERE MENTIONED.)

	Not at all interested 0	10	20	30	40	50	60	70	80	90	Extremely Interested 100	
A. Amoco												30-32
B. Atlas												33-35
C. Delco												36-38
D. Exide												39-41
E. *Firestone Supreme												42-44
F. Ford (not specified)												45-47
*Ford-Motor Craft												48-50
Autolite												51-53
G. *Goodyear Power House												54-56
H. Montg. Ward's Riverside												57-59
I. J.C. Penney's (not spec.)												60-62
J.C. Penney's-Survivor												63-65
Foremost												66-68
J. Sears (not specified)												69-71
*Sears-Die Hard												72-74
Allstate												75-77
K. Shell Superlife												78-80
L. Western Auto's Wizard												8-10
M. Willard												11-13
N. Willard-Exide												14-16

Figure 18-5 *(Continued)*
Part B—Single Commercial Test

Commercial-- "Ford Motor Craft"

Show respondent Commercial--"Ford Motor Craft." When he finishes say...

1. What was the one main thing the advertiser was trying to tell you about this product? (PROBE WITH: What was the one main thing about this product they were trying
   to get across to you?) (PROBE FOR CLARIFICATION.)

   _____

   _____

   _____

2. What impressed you most about this product? (PROBE)

   _____

   _____

   _____

3. (HAND CARD B TO RESPONDENT.)
   Please look at this card and tell me which number on it best indicates how believable the things they say about this product are to you.

4. What are some of the things about this product you find hard to believe? (PROBE)

   _____

   _____

5. (HAND CARD C TO RESPONDENT.)
   I am going to read some statements that might be used to describe auto batteries.
   When I read each please look at this card and tell me to what extent you agree the
   statement describes the battery discussed in the commercial. Pick the big "yes"—
   if you agree completely. Pick the big "no" if you disagree completely. Or, you can
   pick any other size "yes" or "no" that best indicates how you feel.

   There are no right or wrong answers. We just want your opinions.

   Let's start. To what extent do you agree or disagree that the auto battery discussed in this commercial (READ FIRST STATEMENT)? Just read me the number corresponding to your opinion. (REPEAT FOR EACH STATEMENT.)

STATEMENTS	YES	YES	YES	NO	NO	NO	
A Starts car even in the coldest weather	6	5	4	3	2	1	11
B Won't wear down even when your engine is hard to start	6	5	4	3	2	1	12
C Has bigger plates and more acid	6	5	4	3	2	1	13
D Starts your car when other batteries won't	6	5	4	3	2	1	14
E Starts car even in the hottest weather	6	5	4	3	2	1	15
F Has a very strong battery case	6	5	4	3	2	1	16
G Guaranteed to be replaced free of cost	6	5	4	3	2	1	17
H Has twice as much power as new car batteries	6	5	4	3	2	1	18
I Has more power than you need until it's necessary	6	5	4	3	2	1	19
J Keeps your car away from the tow truck	6	5	4	3	2	1	20
K Has extra reserve power	6	5	4	3	2	1	21
L Is thoroughly tested to withstand punishment	6	5	4	3	2	1	22
M Has an easy-to-check water level	6	5	4	3	2	1	23
N Is guaranteed to hold a charge under normal use for as long as you own that car	6	5	4	3	2	1	24

6. (HAND CARD A TO RESPONDENT.)

Please look at this card and tell me which number on it best describes how interested you think you would be in buying the product described in the commercial.

Not at All   Extremely
Interested   Interested

0	10	20	30	40	50	60	70	80	90	100

25-27

7. Imagine you were going to buy the product exactly as it is described in the commercial. How much do you think it would cost? _____ 28-31

Part C—Comparison of Commercials

Subj. No.   1-4
Card No. 13 5-6

1. (a) If you were going to buy a car battery, which of the four auto batteries you
saw would you buy?

None	_____	8
Sears Die Hard	_____	9
Ford Motor Craft	_____	10
Goodyear Power House	_____	11
Firestone Supreme	_____	12

(b) Why would you select that one?

_____

_____

(c) Why wouldn't you select any one?

_____

_____

_____

2. (a) Which of the batteries you saw in the commercials has the best starting power?

Sears Die Hard	_____	13
Ford Motor Craft	_____	14
Goodyear Power House	_____	15
Firestone Supreme	_____	16

(b) Why do you think this battery has the best starting power?

_____

3. (a) Which of the batteries you saw in the commercials has the best reserve power?

Sears Die Hard	_____	17
Ford Motor Craft	_____	18
Goodyear Power House	_____	19
Firestone Supreme	_____	20

(b) Why do you think this battery has the best reserve power?

_____

_____

Figure 18-6   Ad-Tel Based Methodological Framework

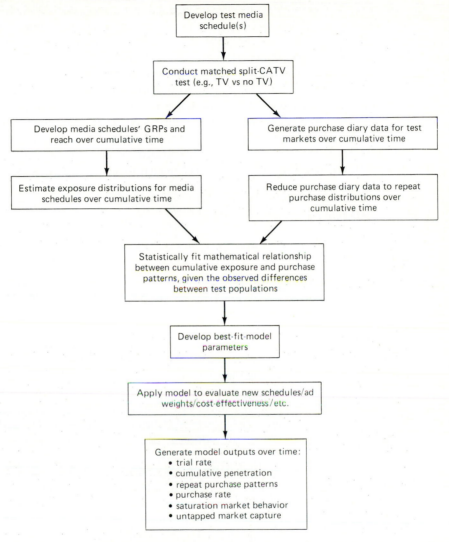

Source: F. S. Zufryden, "A Tested Model of Purchase Response to Advertising Exposure," *Journal of Advertising Research*, 21 (February 1981), 9.

high over various demographic subgroups, suggesting an appeal of general interest to virtually all classes of respondents.

It would take us too far afield to describe the techniques used in the analysis of the responses obtained in this study. Suffice it to say that testing procedures can be rather elaborate (as illustrated here), even for such a seemingly simple task as TV commercial evaluation.

In some testing situations the objective is to establish a mathematical relationship between advertising exposure, say from TV, and purchase behavior patterns. Although not limited to this, cable television provides a potential for testing under controlled conditions. For example, it has been suggested that a mathematical model can be used in conjunction with the AdTel split-cable TV experimental methodology, as illustrated in Figure 18-6.[13] AdTel uses an approach, based on a split-cable system, whereby matched (on demographics and psychographics) consumer populations within a single area, under normal conditions, receive alternative exposures of major media such as broadcast and print. In addition, there is matching of most marketing variables, including competitive marketing activities and store-shopping behavior. One advantage of using an AdTel-data-based model is that it controls for contaminants other than advertising effects. Among the potential industry applications are evaluating alternative media schedules and prediction of sales volume as a function of alternative media plans and resulting exposure patterns. Limited tests tend to support such models for enhancing a company's advertising decision-making process.

Packaging and Price Testing

The testing of alternative packages and prices often utilizes many of the same devices described earlier. To illustrate, a prominent manufacturer of carpet cleaning agents had developed a new type of foam cleaner, called *Lift Away,* made especially for spot cleaning. The cleaner was to be sprayed onto the carpet, worked in with an attached applicator, and left to dry. When dry, the same applicator would be used to brush away the dried foam (and the spot along with it).

The study summarized here was designed to test four alternative aerosol packages and two alternative prices for the new cleaner. A sample of 220 housewives (drawn from five cities) who had used a rug shampoo in the last 60 days was drawn. Color photographs of the four package designs were shown to the respondent (first with no accompanying price information), and the respondent was asked to rank the four packages in terms of personal preference. Figure 18-7 shows sketches of the four package designs and frequencies of choice.[14] As clearly indicated, the third alternative receives the highest frequency of first choices.

The sample was then split and each respondent was shown a set of 11 alternatives and her own brand—as determined from an earlier question—if not one of the stimulus brands. Group A received the lower-price information for the four test packages, whereas group B received the higher-price information.

In each group the respondent was asked to check

1. Those items she would consider purchasing on her next buying occasion (including her present brand, if desired)
2. Her most preferred item for future purchase
3. Her second most preferred item if she could not obtain her first choice

Prices of all existing brands were actual prices determined at the time of the study.

---

[13]See F. S. Zufryden, "A Tested Model of Purchase Response to Advertising Exposure," *Journal of Advertising Research,* 21 (February 1981), 7–16.

[14]Three of these packages (cans 2 through 4) were later used in a conjoint analysis, highlights of which are described in Chapter 15.

Figure 18-7   Frequencies of Preference for New Package Designs

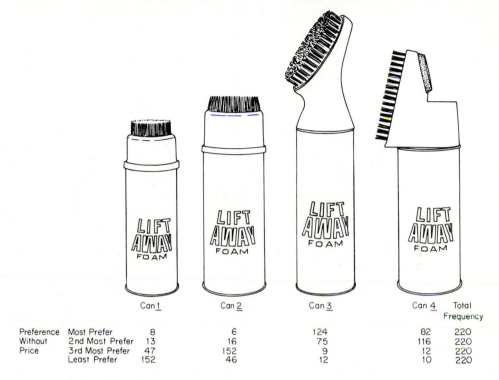

		Can 1	Can 2	Can 3	Can 4	Total Frequency
Preference	Most Prefer	8	6	124	82	220
Without	2nd Most Prefer	13	16	75	116	220
Price	3rd Most Prefer	47	152	9	12	220
	Least Prefer	152	46	12	10	220

Table 18-3 shows the results of this part of the study. Of the four test designs, the third alternative continues to receive the highest percentage of (1) considered purchases and (2) first-choice mentions, independent of price assignment. Not surprisingly, the percentage favoring alternative 3 declines from 25% (group A price conditions) to 14% (group B price conditions).

However, an examination of cost and volume considerations indicated that the higher price ($1.98) was justified, at least initially, from a profit standpoint. From other information obtained in the survey, an initial target group for promotion of the new product was found to involve

1. Relatively high social classes, living primarily in the Midwest and West
2. Higher-than-average education, socially oriented, and active in the acquisition of new products
3. Higher proportion owning pets

The packaging alternative and pricing strategy found from this study were used in the subsequent national introduction of the product that took place after market testing.

It is particularly applicable in package design research to use focus groups in which "quantitative" data can be incorporated. By including quantitative techniques it is possible

TABLE 18-3   Consumer Reactions to Various Lift Away Packages at Different Prices

GROUP A LOWER PRICES FOR LIFT AWAY	PRICE	PERCENTAGE OF RESPONDENTS WHO:		
		Would Consider	Chose as Most Preferred	Chose as Second Most Preferred
Lift Away 1	$ .88	65	2	6
Lift Away 2	$1.29	62	2	4
Lift Away 3	$1.41	83	25	17
Lift Away 4	$1.39	76	6	17
K2R	$1.59	72	17	21
Glory Spot	$ .77	68	9	13
Bissell Aerosol Rug Shampoo	$1.49	68	7	11
Dog Gone Carpet Kit	$3.98	7	1	2
Stain-Ex	$ .99	19	0	2
Out Carpet Spot Remover	$1.49	11	0	0
Abra-Cadabra	$0.79	10	0	0
Subject's brand		93	31	7
Total			100	100
GOUP B HIGHER PRICES FOR LIFT AWAY				
Lift Away 1	$1.19	61	2	8
Lift Away 2	$1.59	60	1	3
Lift Away 3	$1.98	79	14	18
Lift Away 4	$1.79	77	8	15
K2R	$1.59	69	14	14
Glory Spot	$ .77	70	13	19
Bissell Aerosol Rug Shampoo	$1.49	75	12	11
Dog Gone Carpet Kit	$3.98	13	1	3
Stain-Ex	$ .99	21	1	3
Out Carpet Spot Remover	$1.49	12	0	0
Abra-Cadabra	$0.79	12	1	0
Subject's brand		95	33	6
Total			100	100

to account for any effect of group dynamics, especially when there are more knowl-edgeable or more charismatic persons in the group. One useful approach is to have the focus group participants complete an evaluation form prior to the start of discussion.[15] Respondents are then shown each of the package designs under study and are asked to rate each on relevant attributes. After these evaluations are made, the focus group dis-cussion is started. Experience with this technique has shown that once people have stated

[15]K. Weiss, "Quantitative Results Possible From Focus Groups," *Marketing News,* 21 (January 2, 1987), p. 33.

their impressions in writing they tend to stay with them and explain their initial reactions. Since there will always be some people who change, the technique allows for determining whether the changes occurred between initial impressions and the later discussion. Also, tabulations of the ratings can be used to see if group dynamics have been operative. When multiple groups have been run, the sample becomes larger and more extensive analyses can be done with the ratings.

Of great concern to marketers has been testing for *price elasticity*. This often has a major influence on pricing strategy. Traditional approaches to answering questions about price elasticity are *econometric analysis, test marketing, direct questioning,* and *conjoint analysis.* One limitation that all these approaches share in common, although less so for conjoint analysis, is that they attempt to research a single variable when, in fact, sales (and profit) are affected by all aspects of the marketing program. Another approach is to use a *natural experiment* (discussed in Chapter 6). This approach, however, is restricted in that the conditions that create natural experiments do not commonly occur in all industries. Also, they do not necessarily occur *when* the price elasticity estimate may be needed.[16]

Until recently, conjoint measurement was considered the most accurate method of measuring price elasticity. New methodologies have been developed, based on behavioral models. These models can go beyond conjoint analysis to identify the price elasticities of each brand. Such behavioral models generally are proprietary, so few detailed results are reported. One such model is the Price Elasticity Measurement System (PEMS) developed by the Total Research Corporation. PEMS provides information on model validation, price elasticity variant pricing, product improvement effects, competitive price elasticities, and price simulation results.[17]

LARGE-SCALE MARKET SIMULATORS

Over the past few years, increasing attention has been given to the development of large-scale market simulators in which various strategies involving new or redesigned products or services are evaluated. One of the main applications of *conjoint analysis* (see Chapter 15) has been its use in developing input parameters to market simulators.[18] This type of application is illustrated in the context of a study involving airline services.

An Airline Company Example

The selection of an airline for domestic or transcontinental flights depends on a large number of service elements: departure time, number of stops en route, on-time

---

[16]See S.A. Neslin and R.W. Shoemaker, "Using a Natural Experiment to Estimate Price Elasticity: The 1974 Sugar Shortage and the Ready-to-Eat Cereal Market," *Journal of Marketing,* 47 (Winter 1983), 44–57.

[17]See J. Morton and M.E. Rys, "Price Elasticity Prediction: New Research Tool for the Competitive '80s," *Marketing News,* 21 (January 2, 1987), 18; and J. Morton and T.J. Dubanoski, "New Behavioral Model Measures Price Elasticity," *Marketing News,* 21 (February 27, 1987), 4.

[18]See, for example, L.D. Stranbe and B.J. Michaud, "Combine Microcompter Interviewing with Conjoint Analysis to Study Pricing Strategy," *Marketing News,* 17 (May 13, 1983), Sec. 2, pp. 10–11.

reliability, type of aircraft, on-board amenities, friendliness of the airline personnel, and so on. A few years ago, a prominent airline, specializing in domestic flights, was interested in finding out which of its services were most important to passenger choice and how it was perceived, vis-à-vis competing airlines, on each of several service dimensions.

Since evaluations of airline services (and perceptions of them as well) could be expected to vary by type of traveler, business versus nonbusiness, and by length of route, all data were collected according to a specific route–purpose combination, based on the trip last flown by the respondent.

Conjoint Analysis

Data were collected at central facility locations from respondents who had traveled by air during the past three months on one of the routes served by the study's sponsor. The total sample size was 680. The sponsor's identity was kept confidential during all interviews.

After collecting details of their last flight, the respondents were shown sets of pictures, each set describing one aspect of a hypothetical flight: ground services, in-flight services, physical decor of plane, and scheduling information. Wherever possible, visual props were used to illustrate the specific conditions. For example, Figure 18-8 shows two levels of one in-flight factor involving the placement and grooming of cabin attendants. Each set of sketches was prepared according to a fractional factorial design (see Chapter 15).[19]

Using the methodology of conjoint analysis, utility functions were prepared for each respondent. Some 15 different service factors were involved, as illustrated in Table 18-4. The "levels," or varieties, of each service factor ranged from two to five.

Illustratively, Figure 18-9 shows the utility functions obtained from business travelers on one of the longer hauls (two-hour flight time) for the four in-flight services listed in Table 18-4. As can be observed from the utility ranges, cabin attendants (placement and grooming) and type of food and beverages are the most important factors within this group of four.

Insofar as inputs to the market simulator are concerned, all utility functions were developed at the individual level, and each individual was classified by route and purpose of trip.

Airline Perception Data

Following the flight evaluation task all respondents were shown the names of airlines serving the particular route to which they had been assigned. They were then asked to check off all of those airlines with which they had travel experience over the route in question.

Following this they were shown, for each of the 15 factors, the set of levels appropriate for that factor. Then, for the airlines with which they had claimed familiarity

---

[19]Typically, in each scene there were four to six factors varying independently. Factors were interlinked over evaluations so that comparable utilities could be obtained for all components of the hypothetical flight.

Figure 18-8   Illustrative Levels for Factor Involving Cabin Attendants

I Two Attendants Up Front, Well-Groomed   II One Attendant Up Front, Well-Groomed
One Attendant in Galley, Badly Groomed

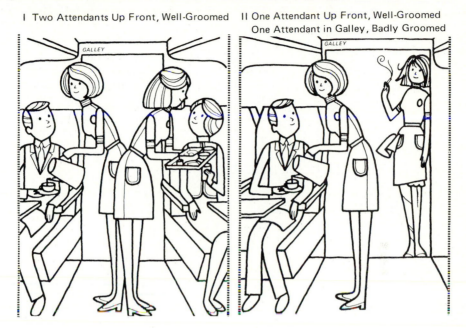

they were asked to select the factor level that most closely matched their perception of the airline's service level on that factor.

Since few respondents claimed familiarity with all airlines serving their route, the perception data were rather sparse (in addition to being crudely obtained). To increase the stability of the analysis these data were aggregated within route–purpose so that empirical probability functions were constructed across the levels of each factor. Each

TABLE 18-4   Airline Service Factors for which Utility Functions were Developed

Ground services

1. Quality of telephone service information
2. Courtesy and efficiency of check-in personnel
3. Length of waiting line for check-in

In-flight service

1. Cabin attendants (placement and grooming)
2. Type of reading material
3. Type of food and beverages
4. Type of entertainment

Physical decor

1. Amount of leg room
2. Seat width and comfort
3. Type of baggage racks
4. Type and number of lavatory facilities

Scheduling and other

1. On-time arrival reliability
2. Number of stops en route
3. Departure relative to ideal time
4. Type of aircraft: regular versus wide body

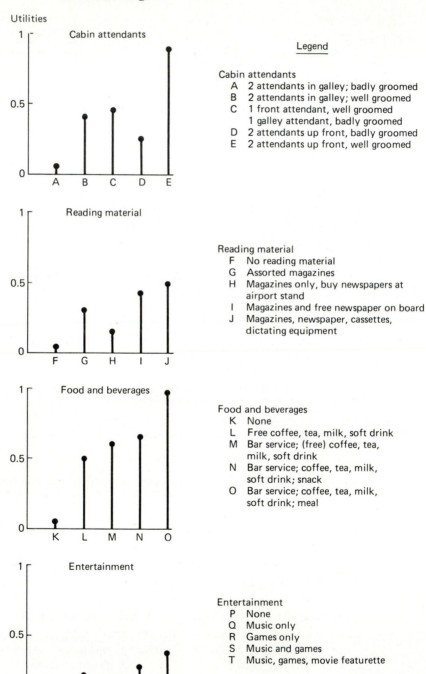

Utilities

Cabin attendants

Reading material

Food and beverages

Entertainment

Legend

Cabin attendants
A   2 attendants in galley; badly groomed
B   2 attendants in galley; well groomed
C   1 front attendant, well groomed
     1 galley attendant, badly groomed
D   2 attendants up front, badly groomed
E   2 attendants up front, well groomed

Reading material
F   No reading material
G   Assorted magazines
H   Magazines only, buy newspapers at airport stand
I   Magazines and free newspaper on board
J   Magazines, newspaper, cassettes, dictating equipment

Food and beverages
K   None
L   Free coffee, tea, milk, soft drink
M   Bar service; (free) coffee, tea, milk, soft drink
N   Bar service; coffee, tea, milk, soft drink; snack
O   Bar service; coffee, tea, milk, soft drink; meal

Entertainment
P   None
Q   Music only
R   Games only
S   Music and games
T   Music, games, movie featurette

function represented the empirically estimated probability that the factor would display each level of service, under each specific airline. In this way, a perceptual service-level profile—actually a probability distribution of such profiles—was developed for each airline–route combination.

Constructing the Simulator

The individual utility functions, classified by trip purpose and route, and the probability distribution of airline service profiles, classified by route, constituted the primary input data for the simulator. The simulator was constructed so that the following aspects of the problem could be examined:

- Effect on sponsor's share of airline choices (compared with the base case from survey) if various levels of its service are changed while all competitor's probability distributions remain the same
- Effect on sponsor's share (compared with base) if its service levels and selected competitors' levels are simultaneously changed
- Effect on sponsor's share (compared with base) if its service levels, competitors' service levels, and some of the utility functions themselves are simultaneously changed

While the simulator incorporated all three levels of capability, in practice most of the simulator's runs were carried out at the first level of analysis. The first-level simulation operated along the following lines:

- The user reads in the base-case service-level distributions.
- Random numbers are chosen and a particular service profile is selected for each airline's probability distribution by route.
- Each member of that route applies his or her specific utility function to all airlines on which familiarity had been claimed by that individual.
- The consumer chooses the airline with the highest utility (according to his or her specific utility function).
- The test case is next introduced (with its new probability distributions for the sponsor firm), while all competitive profiles remain as before.
- A choice is made under the test case, also on the basis of highest utility.
- Share of choices going to each airline are then compared, base versus test case, for each route—purpose and in-total.
- Tables and charts are provided by the simulator on the comparative performance of all test cases versus the base case (and versus each other, as well). It should be mentioned, however, that this simulator was quite crude by present standards.

Second-generation simulators of considerably greater sophistication have been proposed. For example, Frank J. Carmone, Drexel University, has developed a simulator call PRODSIM that has all the capabilities of the above and, in addition:

- Incorporates several different choice functions, including probability-of-choice mechanisms
- Allows the user complete freedom in specifying individual probability distributions over any service or product profile
- Provides brand-switching information regarding where new products or services will attract their business
- Can handle up to 30 different product or service factors with up to six levels per factor
- Provides interpolation possibilities for continuous factors
- Allows the user to systematically search for "optimal" service and product regions to aid in designing alternatives with high choice potential

In short, this program (and others like it) can be used on a more or less continuous market-planning basis. As new perceptual and utility data are collected, the simulator's parameters can be updated for future testing of competitive strategies. The analyst does not have to rely on access to a mainframe computer in order to run simulators. PRODSIM, for example, has been adapted to the microcomputer.

In the airline example the sponsor of the study tried out a wide variety of possible strategies and explored their implications on a cost–benefits basis. One decision involved the hiring of additional terminal check-in personnel to reduce customer waiting time. On the other hand, some (costly) services that had originally been planned for some routes were not implemented after the simulator indicated that their impact on increased demand would not justify their cost.

Other Computer-Based Models

A number of researchers have specialized in the construction of large-scale market-strategy models. Models now exist for advertising-budget determination, marketing-mix decisions, new-product forecasting and sales-call planning, to name a few.

These *second-generation* models are distinguished from earlier models by five important characteristics:

1. The models do not attempt to "optimize" in the traditional sense but rather try to search intelligently for good decisions, based on a realistic data-based, predictive model.
2. The models make liberal use of the manager's judgments in key areas when objective data are unavailable or too costly to obtain.
3. The models are user-oriented, allowing the manager to learn simplified versions of the model before complex ones—a type of evolutionary approach toward understanding the model.
4. The models are set up on time-share systems in which the manager has ready access to the algorithm via portable terminals and can communicate with the model by means of simple English commands.[20]

[20]L.M. Lodish, "Decision Models for Marketing Management,"*Wharton Quarterly,* 7 (Fall 1972), 53–56.

5. The models are easily adapted for changes in assumptions while providing rapid feedback on the consequences of changes in parameter values that the manager might wish to consider.

These modifications in the philosophy (as well as practice) of model building make a great deal of sense to the present authors and they augur well for continued progress in this area.

In addition to the above models, whose descriptions have been published, a number of other models have been developed on an intracompany or intraconsulting firm basis. In particular, a number of firms are currently experimenting with approaches to test market simulation, although details of these activities are not generally available.

Insofar as the motivation underlying this book is concerned, we note that the more recently developed models allow directly for the input of managerial judgments (frequently in the form of prior probabilities), a characteristic that is fully in accord with this book's presentation. Second, the models emphasize the need for data banks and systematic updating of parameter values. Clearly, the models are on the side of the marketing researcher, whose future role may well be even more important that his or her current contributions to marketing decision making.

SUMMARY

By dealing with specialized procedures for the design and evaluation of marketing strategies, we have tried to provide a broad sampling of the types of studies in which marketing researchers participate. While the examples are drawn mainly from the authors' own consulting experience, it is felt that they are representative of current efforts on the part of the more technically trained researcher. However, no attempt has been made to present all the implications of each study.

We discussed a variety of procedures, such as new-product generation, concept evaluation, product idea screening, ad testing, packaging, and pricing studies, aimed at examining proposed changes to the status quo. Capsule studies were used to illustrate the procedures in the form of actual marketing analyses. In cases where specialized techniques (multidimensional scaling, conjoint analysis, etc.) were used, the reader was referred to appropriate chapters for details.

We concluded the chapter with a discussion of large-scale marketing models, their characteristics, future potential, and relationship to the data input and analytical functions of the marketing researcher.

ASSIGNMENT MATERIAL

1. Design and carry out a small repertory-grid study in which the stimuli are brands of beer.

    a. What are some of the ways in which the resulting grid can be analyzed?

    b. How would you proceed to conduct a consumption-grid study using the same stimuli as used in the repertory grid?

2. Describe how you would set up a field experiment that considers simultaneously changes in brand name, packaging features, and pricing for a new cereal product (see Chapter 15).

    a. What factor levels would you use?

    b. How would you prepare the stimuli?

    c. What response measure would you select and what techniques for analysis seem appropriate?

3. Select from the literature some large-scale marketing model.

    a. Critique the model from the standpoint of managerial usefulness.

    b. How would you proceed to construct a model that simulated market testing in which you wish to obtain (1) first trial rate and (2) first repeat-purchase rate?

4. How would you go about trying to improve the (crude) simulator described in the airline study?

    a. How would you change the respondent-choice rule?

    b. How would you go about incorporating an explicit time path of share of choices?

    c. How would you plan to "test" the simulator's output?

5. Describe how you would go about using conjoint analysis to construct a simulator of network program selection in prime-time television viewing. What types of data would you collect? What are the control variables of interest?

6. Considering research and data collection needs as well as management decision making, which is the *best way* to model scoring data for product idea screening— conjunctive, disjunctive, lexicographic, or linear compensatory? Why? Would your choice change depending on the marketing variable of concern?

CASES FOR PART V

V-1

HANSON FOODS, INC.

Product H-2 is a variation of a common canned food item that is used regularly in over 80% of the households in the United States.* The product can be used as a cooking ingredient or eaten by itself. The normal retail price is between $0.70 and $0.75.

    The category of products into which product H-2 falls is dominated by three major brands. These three manufacturers share over 70% of the market with the remainder split

---

*Product H-2 is not identified in the case because to do so would have almost certainly identified the company that developed it. The company preferred to remain anonymous. A fictitious company name has also been used.

among many small canners and private-label brands. The total retail value of all brands sold in the product category is over $825 million per year. This is considerably greater than the retail value of such categories as peanut butter, jams and jellies, canned beans, canned peas, or packaged desserts.

Hanson Foods is one of the fastest growing, most aggressive companies in the industry. In the past year, sales of its regular item in this category (product H-1) had been growing at a rate three times faster than either of its competitors, but the brand was still third in market share. Brand K had been the historical market leader and was regarded by most consumers as the best-quality item in the product category. The retail price for brand K had been 0.75 per can for many years. This was normally 8 to 15 cents higher than either brand V or brand H-1. A large part of the total volume of brand H-1 was sold at specially reduced prices.

The popularity of brand K varied considerably in different regions of the country (Table 1). In many eastern areas, its market share was over 50%, while, in the West and South, the brand dropped to third position.

The development of product H-2 may be described as the result of an attempt to differentiate an existing product. Two years earlier, the management of Hanson and its advertising agency were faced with a problem common to many companies in the food industry. They were attempting to develop an advertising campaign that would differentiate brand H-1 from its competition, but the three major brands had essentially the same formulation. It was decided that product differentiation was needed, and, in order to accomplish this, the research and development people within the company were instructed to reformulate the product to incorporate some new and exotic spices. The copy strategy would emphasize the taste difference resulting from the new spices.

In the course of this development work, some interesting things began to happen. As various new spices were added to product H-1 and different flavor-intensity levels were evaluated by employee taste panels, it became apparent that some of these changes were perceived as completely new products.

It was quickly recognized that the introduction of a new product such as this

TABLE 1 Share of Market

	BRAND K (%)	BRAND V (%)	BRAND H-1 (%)	ALL OTHERS (%)
New England	37.0	10.1	12.5	40.4
New York	42.6	14.2	27.7	15.5
Middle Atlantic	37.6	11.7	13.6	37.1
East Central	27.2	17.4	17.3	38.1
West Central	25.6	24.7	14.6	35.1
Southeast	13.0	22.1	22.7	42.2
Southwest	11.6	35.4	25.6	27.4
Pacific	19.8	27.7	29.4	23.1
Total	25.3	21.4	20.1	33.2

could expand Hanson's shares of the market considerably and increase sales for the whole product category. The possibility of cannibalization existed because a new product might derive a major part of its sales from Hanson's current brand. But this strategy of fragmentation had been utilized in the soap industry with great success. New products were continually introduced for specialized uses, with resulting volume increases for the whole category. There was another danger that was not generally recognized by the company management. This new-product idea had originated in the research and development laboratories rather than having evolved from a discovered consumer need. This is a common cause of failure of many new consumer products by many manufacturers.

Further work by the research and development department resulted in three variations of product H-1, with distinctly different tastes resulting from different spices used. These products were retested by the employee taste panels, and the most popular formulation of the three was packed in limited quantities for consumer and market tests.

The next step was to find out if the idea made any sense to consumers. A small pilot study was conducted in which 24 respondents were asked for their reaction to the product idea. They were then given a sample can to use and the interviewer returned a week later to question them. The concept of product H-2 appeared to be well received by over three-fourths of the consumers contacted. The product seemed to live up to their prior expectations and there were no appreciable complaints about the flavor. The participants in the test were given a three-months' supply of the product and a further interview was conducted after eight weeks had elapsed. At this time, 64% of the respondents said, "If this were available, I would go out and buy some right away."

Further research was then conducted on a national basis to determine consumer acceptance of the concept and formulation. Depth interviews were used to probe top-of-mind meanings and associations generated by the concept. Then the respondent was given a can of the product and the interviewer returned a week later to measure the response to the product itself. Approximately 450 interviews were conducted in Los Angeles, Minneapolis, Atlanta, Philadelphia, Tacoma, Topeka, Columbus, and Bridgeport. The reaction to the product in this study is summarized in Table 2.

With this apparent consumer satisfaction with the product concept and formulation, the next step was to determine whether they would *purchase* the product with satisfactory regularity over a period of time. In order to measure this without going into an actual test market, an extended in-home usage test was conducted. Consumers in four cities,

TABLE 2 Respondent Study Results

	RESPONDENTS (%)
Would use	34
Probably would use	15
Might use	6
Probably would not use	15
Would not use	30

Sacramento, Baltimore, Milwaukee, and Jacksonville, were given the product to try for two weeks. If they had an interest in participating in the study, all competitive products were removed from their homes, and from then on they purchased their requirements from survey representatives. They were allowed to purchase product H-2 or any of the three major brands K, V, or H-1, as well as the strongest local brand in the area. Each family was contacted once a week for orders. The product was delivered to the participants' homes and a 10% discount on the normal retail price was given for all items purchased.

The response to product H-2 in this test was much better than had been anticipated, and the demand for it did not diminish appreciably in a 16-week test period. The management of Hanson had not previously been exposed to tests of this type, but representatives from the advertising agency who had observed the experience of other products in such tests were surprised to find a very high level of product usage and a negligible dropoff in demand.

On the basis of their previous experience with this type of extended use testing of new grocery products, the advertising agency projected first-year sales and market-share estimates for product H-2. The forecasts were based on different levels of distribution that might be achieved by the product in its first year:

- At 35% distribution, sales were estimated at 847,000 cases, or 8% of the market.
- At 45% distribution, sales were estimated at 1,220,000 cases, or 12% of the market.
- At 55% distribution, sales were estimated at 1,500,000 cases, or 15% of the market.

Distribution of 35% would mean that the product would be available for sale in stores doing 35% of the total grocery business in the United States. The agency believed that a distribution level of 45% was the most likely of the three if the product were introduced. Hanson management concurred in this judgment.

The Finance Department at Hanson was asked to make projections of profit (or loss) for the first three years after H-2's introduction, conditional on the distribution level achieved. Assuming that the distribution level achieved in the first year would be maintained over the full three-year period, their estimates were as follows:

	YEAR 1	YEAR 2	YEAR 3
35% distribution	($1,800,000)	($700,000)	($700,000)
45% distribution	($ 700,000)	$950,000	$1,200,000
55% distribution	($ 200,000)	$1,650,000	$2,000,000

These estimates were discussed by Hanson's management with the account executive from the agency. He recommended that they run a market test for H-2. He thought that the test should be conducted in four or five cities for a period long enough to determine trial and repeat-purchase rates. He estimated that such a test would cost $400,000 to $450,000.

1. Evaluate the concept and use tests conducted on the product.
2. What action should the Hanson management have taken?

V-2

*CURRENCY CONCEPTS INTERNATIONAL**

Dr. Karen Anderson, Manager of Planning for Century Bank of Los Angeles, settled down for an unexpected evening of work in her small beach apartment. It seemed that every research project Century had commissioned in the last year had been completed during her ten-day trip to Taiwan. She had brought three research reports home that evening to try to catch up before meeting with the bank's Executive Planning Committee the next day.

Possibly because the currency-exchange facilities had been closed at the Taiwan Airport when she first arrived, Dr. Anderson's attention turned first to a report on a project currently under consideration by one of Century Bank's wholly-owned subsidiaries, Currency Concepts International (CCI). The project concerned the manufacture and installation of currency-exchange automatic teller machines (ATMs) in major foreign airports.

CCI had been responsible for the development of Century Bank's very popular ATM ("money machine"), now installed in numerous branches of the bank as well as in its main location in downtown Los Angeles. The current project was a small part of CCI and Century Bank's plan to expand electronic banking services worldwide.

As she started to review the marketing research effort of Information Resources, Inc., she wondered what she would be able to recommend to the Executive Planning Committee the next day regarding the currency-exchange project. She liked her recommendations to be backed by solid evidence, and she looked forward to reviewing results of the research performed to date.

ACTIVITIES OF INFORMATION RESOURCES, INC.

Personnel of Information Resources, Inc., had decided to follow three different approaches in investigating the problem presented to them: (1) review secondary statistical data; (2) interview companies that currently engage in currency exchange; and (3) conduct an exploratory consumer survey of a convenience sample.

---

*This case was prepared by Grady D. Bruce, Professor of Marketing, California State University, Fullerton. Certain information in the case is disguised.
Copyright © by Grady D. Bruce

Secondary Data

The review of secondary data had three objectives:

1. To determine whether the number of persons flying abroad constitutes a market potentially large enough to merit automated currency exchange;
2. To isolate any trends in the numbers of people flying abroad;
3. To determine whether the amount of money that these travelers spend abroad is sizable enough to provide a potential market for automated currency exchange.

Using appropriate data published by the United States Departments of Transportation (*United States International Air Statistics*) and Commerce (*Survey of Current Business*), Information Resources concluded that Europe had the greatest market potential for introduction of the new system. As Dick Knowlton, coordinator of the research team, said, "Not only are all of the statistics high for Europe, but the short geographic distances between countries can be expected to provide a good deal of intra-area travel." This conclusion was reached by examining such data as (1) the number of people, particularly Americans, traveling from United States airports to foreign airports, (2) the number of Americans flying abroad to the top ten gateway cities during the past five years, (3) per capita spending by geographic area for the past five years and percentages of growth, and (4) the number of Americans, and growth rate, visiting geographic areas.

Company Interviews

In an attempt to better understand the current operations of currency exchange in airports, four major firms engaged in these activities were contacted. While some firms were naturally reluctant to provide information on some areas of their operations, several were quite cooperative. These firms, and a number of knowledgeable individuals whose names surfaced in initial interviews, provided the information that follows.

In both New York and Los Angeles, there is only one bank engaged in airport currency exchange: Deak-Perera. American Express, Bank of America, and Citibank, as well as Deak-Perera, are engaged in airport currency exchange in a variety of foreign locations. Approval of permits to engage in airport currency-exchange activity rests with the municipal body that governs the airport and is highly controlled. It appears that foreign currency exchange is a highly profitable venture. Banks make most of their profits on the spread in exchange rates, which are posted daily.

Both Citibank and Bank of America indicated that they attempt to ensure their facilities' availability to all flights. The more profitable flights were found to be those that were regularly scheduled, rather than chartered. The person more likely to use the facilities was the vacationer rather than the businessperson. Neither bank could give an exact figure for the average transaction size; estimates ranged from $85 to $100.

It was the opinion of bank/Deak employees, who dealt with travelers on a daily basis, that the average traveler was somewhat uncomfortable changing money in a foreign country. They also believed it to be particularly helpful if clerks at the exchange counter converse with travelers in their own language. A number of years ago Deak attempted to use a type of vending machine to dispense money at Kennedy Airport. This venture failed; industry observers felt that the absence of human conversation and assurance contributed to its lack of success.

Most of the exchanges perform the same types of services, including the sale of foreign currency and the sale of traveler's checks. The actual brand of traveler's checks sold varies with the vendors.

American Express has recently placed automated unmanned traveler's check dispensers in various American airports. This service is available to American Express card holders and the only charge is 1% of the face value of the purchased checks; the purchase is charged directly to the customer's checking account. As yet, the machines have not enjoyed a great deal of use, although American Express has been successful in enrolling its customers as potential users.

Methods of payment for currency purchases are similar at all exchanges. Accepted forms of payment include actual cash, traveler's checks, cashier checks drawn on local banks, Master Charge or Visa cards. When using a credit card to pay for currency purchase, there is a service charge added to the customer's bill, as with any cash advance.

Traveler Interviews

To supplement and complement the statistical foundation gained by reviewing secondary data sources, the consumer interview portion of the study was purposefully designed to elicit qualitative information about travelers' feelings toward current and future forms of exchanging currency. Approximately sixty American travelers were interviewed at both the San Francisco and Los Angeles International Airports, due to the accessibility of these locations to Information Resources' sole location. An unstructured, undisguised questionnaire was developed to assist in channeling the interview toward specific topics (see Appendix 1). Questions were not fixed and the question order was dependent on the respondent's answers. Basically, the guide served to force the interview conversation around the central foreign currency exchange theme. The interviews were conducted primarily in the arrival/departure lobbies of international carriers and spanned over four weeks, beginning in mid-December 1979. A deliberate attempt was made to include as many arriving as departing passengers to neutralize the effect of increasing holiday traffic. Additionally, to reduce interviewer bias, three different interviewers were used. Interviews were intentionally kept informal. And Dick Knowlton cautioned the interviewers to remain objective and "not let your excitement over the product concept spill over into the interview and bias the responses."

Results

The interviews were divided almost evenly between those who favored the concept and those who did not. Those who did perceive value in the concept tended also to support other innovations such as the automated teller machine and charging foreign currency on credit cards. Those who would not use the currency exchange terminals wanted more human interaction, generally did not favor automation in any form; and a fair proportion had had previous problems exchanging foreign currency. However, even those who did not favor the currency exchange idea did seem to prefer the system of having twenty-four-hour availability of the machines, and of using credit cards to get cash under emergency situations.

The respondents represented a diverse group of individuals ranging in age from eighteen to eighty years, holding such different positions as oil executive, photographer, housewife, and customs officer. Primarily bound for Europe, Canada, and Mexico, the interviewees were mainly split between pleasure-seekers and those on business. Only three individuals interviewed were part of tour groups, and of these three, only one had previously traveled abroad. The majority of the others had been out of the United States before and had exchanged currency in at least one other country. Many had exchanged currency in remote parts of the world, including Morocco, Brazil, Australia, Japan, Tanzania, and Russia. Only five individuals had not exchanged money in airports at one time or another. The majority had obtained foreign currency in airports and exchanged money in airports primarily in small denominations for use in taxicab fares, bus fares, phones, and airport gift shops, as well as for food, tips, and drinks. Most respondents agreed that a prime motive for exchanging money in airports was the security of having local currency.

Exchanging currency can become a trying ordeal for some individuals. They fear being cheated on the exchange rate; they cannot convert the foreign currency into tangible concepts (for example, "how many yen should a loaf of bread cost?"); they dislike lines and associated red tape; and many cannot understand the rates as posted in percentages. Most individuals exchange money in the airports, hotels, or banks, but sometimes there are no convenient facilities at all for exchanging currency.

People like to deal with well-known bank branches, especially in airports, because they feel more confident about the rate they are receiving. However, major fears of individuals are that the money exchange personnel will not understand English and that they will be cheated in the transaction. Furthermore, a few people mentioned poor documentation when they exchange currency in foreign airports.

The travelers were divided as to whether they exchange currency before or after they arrive in the foreign country, but a few said that the decision depended on what country they were entering. If a currency, such as English pounds, could easily be obtained from a local bank before leaving the United States, they were more likely to exchange before leaving. However, in no case would the traveler arrange for currency beyond a week in advance. Most preferred to obtain the foreign currency on relatively short notice—less than three days before the trip. Of the individuals on tours, none planned to obtain currency in the foreign airport. Apparently, the tour guide had previously arranged for the necessary transportation from the airport to the hotels, and there would only be enough time to gather one's luggage and find the bus before it departed, leaving no time to enjoy the facilities of the airport which required foreign currency. All three tour individuals did mention that they planned to obtain foreign currency once they arrived at the hotel. All individuals mentioned that they had secured their own foreign currency, but a few of the wives who were traveling with their husbands conceded that their spouses usually converted the currency in the foreign airport.

Very few of the interviewees had actually used an automated teller machine, but the majority had heard or seen the teller machines on television. Those who had used the automated machines preferred this convenience and were generally satisfied with the terminal's performance. Many of those who had not used the automated teller machines mistrusted the machine and possible loss of control over their finances. Concerns about security and problems with the machines breaking down were also expressed. One woman described the teller machines as being "convenient, but cold." Apparently, many people prefer having human interaction when their money is concerned.

As noted earlier, approximately thirty of the respondents would favor the exchange terminals over their normal airport currency exchange routine, while the same number would have nothing to do with the machines. However, the majority of potential users qualified their use by such features as competitive rates, knowing the precise charges, or knowing they could get help if something went wrong. Individuals who indicated no preference were included in the favorable category, simply because they would not refuse to try the machine. Most of the indifferent people seemed to indicate they would try such a machine if some type of introductory promotional offer was included, such as travel information, currency tips, or a better rate.

With virtual unanimity, the respondents felt that twenty-four-hour availability made the currency exchange machines more attractive, yet that alone would not persuade the dissenters to use the terminals. Some individuals felt that a machine simply could not give the travel advice that could be obtained at the currency-exchange booths.

The opportunity to charge foreign currency against a major credit card, such as Master Charge or Visa, was a definite plus in the minds of most respondents. One individual clearly resented the idea, however, feeling that he would "overspend" if given such a convenient way to obtain cash. Respondents offered a number of suggestions concerning implementations of the product concept and a number of specific product features:

1. Add information about the country.
2. Provide small denominations, and include coins.
3. Have it communicate in English.
4. Put in traveler's checks to get cash.
5. Put in cash to get foreign currency.
6. Post rates daily.
7. Keep rates competitive and post charges.
8. Have television screen with person to describe procedure.
9. Place the machines in hotels and banks.
10. Have a change machine nearby that can convert paper money.
11. Place machine near existing currency-exchange facilities for convenience when normal lines become long.
12. Demonstrate how to use the machine.
13. Use all bank credit cards.

1. *Should CCI and Century Bank have commissioned this research in light of the existing competitive situation?*

2. *Evaluate the approach taken by Information Resources, Inc. Was the research undertaken appropriate for the problem at hand? What else should have been done at this stage in the new-product decision process?*

3. *What additional research, if any, should be done?*

4. *Do the airport interviews of travelers give any clues as to how the market for automated currency exchange is segmented? How might these clues be investigated further?*

5. *State five hypotheses concerning consumer behavior that are suggested by the traveler interviews. Then explain how you would design research to investigate them (including, if appropriate, the wording of questions that would appear on a questionnaire).*

Appendix 1

INTERVIEW GUIDE FOR INTERNATIONAL TRAVELERS (U.S. CITIZENS)

These interviews should remain as informal as possible. The object is not to obtain statistically reliable results, but to get ideas that will help to stimulate research. These questions are not fixed; the order, however, is sometimes dependent on answers the respondents give.

(Introduce Yourself)

1. Are you going to be traveling to a foreign country? Arriving from a foreign country? A United States resident?

2. Where is/was your final destination?

3. Why are you traveling? (business, pleasure, a tour)

4. How often do you travel outside the United States?

5. Have you ever exchanged currency in a foreign country? (If no, go to #6.) Where? Does anything in particular stand out in your mind when you exchanged currency?

6. Have you ever changed money in an airport? (If no, go to #7.)

7. Where do you plan to exchange currency on this trip?

8. Where do you change money normally?

9. Have you ever had any problems exchanging currencies? Explain the circumstances.

10. Normally, would you change money before entering a country or after you arrive? If before, how long in advance? Where? (Probe.)

11. Are you familiar with Automated Teller Machines that banks are using? (If not, explain.) Have you used one of these machines?

12. What are you feelings toward these machines?

13. If a currency-exchange terminal, similar to an automated teller machine, were placed in your destination airport, would you use the machine or follow your normal routine?

14. Would 24-hour availability make the currency-exchange machines more attractive? Would you use the terminals at night?

15. None of the currency-exchange machines currently exists. What features or services could be provided so that you might choose to use a terminal rather than other currency-exchange facilities?

16. If you could charge the foreign currency received to a major credit card, such as Master Charge or Visa, would you be more likely to use the machine?

17. Demographics—Age range (visual) _____
    Occupation?
    Sex?
    Traveling alone?

Appendix A

Statistical Tables

TABLE A-1 Cumulative Normal Distribution—Values of Probability

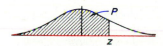

Values of P corresponding to Z for the normal curve. Z is the standard normal variable. The value of P for $-Z$ equals 1 minus the value of P for $+Z$, e.g., the P for -1.62 equals $1 - .9474 = .0526$.

Z	.00	.01	.02	.03	.04	.05	.06	.07	.08	.09
.0	.5000	.5040	.5080	.5120	.5160	.5199	.5239	.5279	.5319	.5359
.1	.5398	.5438	.5478	.5517	.5557	.5596	.5636	.5675	.5714	.5753
.2	.5793	.5832	.5871	.5910	.5948	.5987	.6026	.6064	.6103	.6141
.3	.6179	.6217	.6255	.6293	.6331	.6368	.6406	.6443	.6480	.6517
.4	.6554	.6591	.6628	.6664	.6700	.6736	.6772	.6808	.6844	.6879
.5	.6915	.6950	.6985	.7019	.7054	.7088	.7123	.7157	.7190	.7224
.6	.7257	.7291	.7324	.7357	.7389	.7422	.7454	.7486	.7517	.7549
.7	.7580	.7611	.7642	.7673	.7704	.7734	.7764	.7794	.7823	.7852
.8	.7881	.7910	.7939	.7967	.7995	.8023	.8051	.8078	.8106	.8133
.9	.8159	.8186	.8212	.8238	.8264	.8289	.8315	.8340	.8365	.8389

TABLE A-1   Cumulative Normal Distribution—Values of Probability (*Continued*)

Z	.00	.01	.02	.03	.04	.05	.06	.07	.08	.09
1.0	.8413	.8438	.8461	.8485	.8508	.8531	.8554	.8577	.8599	.8621
1.1	.8643	.8665	.8686	.8708	.8729	.8749	.8770	.8790	.8810	.8830
1.2	.8849	.8869	.8888	.8907	.8925	.8944	.8962	.8980	.8997	.9015
1.3	.9032	.9049	.9066	.9082	.9099	.9115	.9131	.9147	.9162	.9177
1.4	.9192	.9207	.9222	.9236	.9251	.9265	.9279	.9292	.9306	.9319
1.5	.9332	.9345	.9357	.9370	.9382	.9394	.9406	.9418	.9429	.9441
1.6	.9452	.9463	.9474	.9484	.9495	.9505	.9515	.9525	.9535	.9545
1.7	.9554	.9564	.9573	.9582	.9591	.9599	.9608	.9616	.9625	.9633
1.8	.9641	.9649	.9656	.9664	.9671	.9678	.9686	.9693	.9699	.9706
1.9	.9713	.9719	.9726	.9732	.9738	.9744	.9750	.9756	.9761	.9767
2.0	.9772	.9778	.9783	.9788	.9793	.9798	.9803	.9808	.9812	.9817
2.1	.9821	.9826	.9830	.9834	.9838	.9842	.9846	.9850	.9854	.9857
2.2	.9861	.9864	.9868	.9871	.9875	.9878	.9881	.9884	.9887	.9890
2.3	.9893	.9896	.9898	.9901	.9904	.9906	.9909	.9911	.9913	.9916
2.4	.9918	.9920	.9922	.9925	.9927	.9929	.9931	.9932	.9934	.9936
2.5	.9938	.9940	.9941	.9943	.9945	.9946	.9948	.9949	.9951	.9952
2.6	.9953	.9955	.9956	.9957	.9959	.9960	.9961	.9962	.9963	.9964
2.7	.9965	.9966	.9967	.9968	.9969	.9970	.9971	.9972	.9973	.9974
2.8	.9974	.9975	.9976	.9977	.9977	.9978	.9979	.9979	.9980	.9981
2.9	.9981	.9982	.9982	.9983	.9984	.9984	.9985	.9985	.9986	.9986
3.0	.9987	.9987	.9987	.9988	.9988	.9989	.9989	.9989	.9990	.9990
3.1	.9990	.9991	.9991	.9991	.9992	.9992	.9992	.9992	.9993	.9993
3.2	.9993	.9993	.9994	.9994	.9994	.9994	.9994	.9995	.9995	.9995
3.3	.9995	.9995	.9995	.9996	.9996	.9996	.9996	.9996	.9996	.9997
3.4	.9997	.9997	.9997	.9997	.9997	.9997	.9997	.9997	.9997	.9998

TABLE A-2   Upper Percentiles of the *t* Distribution

df \ $1 - \alpha$	.75	.90	.95	.975	.99	.995	.9995
1	1.000	3.078	6.314	12.706	31.821	63.657	636.619
2	.816	1.886	2.920	4.303	6.965	9.925	31.598
3	.765	1.638	2.353	3.182	4.541	5.841	12.941
4	.741	1.533	2.132	2.776	3.747	4.604	8.610
5	.727	1.476	2.015	2.571	3.365	4.032	6.859
6	.718	1.440	1.943	2.447	3.143	3.707	5.959
7	.711	1.415	1.895	2.365	2.998	3.499	5.405
8	.706	1.397	1.860	2.306	2.896	3.355	5.041
9	.703	1.383	1.833	2.262	2.821	3.250	4.781
10	.700	1.372	1.812	2.228	2.764	3.169	4.587
11	.697	1.363	1.796	2.201	2.718	3.106	4.437
12	.695	1.356	1.782	2.179	2.681	3.055	4.318
13	.694	1.350	1.771	2.160	2.650	3.012	4.221
14	.692	1.345	1.761	2.145	2.624	2.977	4.140
15	.691	1.341	1.753	2.131	2.602	2.947	4.073
16	.690	1.337	1.746	2.120	2.583	2.921	4.015
17	.689	1.333	1.740	2.110	2.567	2.898	3.965
18	.688	1.330	1.734	2.101	2.552	2.878	3.922
19	.688	1.328	1.729	2.093	2.339	2.861	3.883
20	.687	1.325	1.725	2.086	2.528	2.845	3.850
21	.686	1.323	1.721	2.080	2.518	2.831	3.819
22	.686	1.321	1.717	2.074	2.508	2.819	3.792
23	.685	1.319	1.714	2.069	2.500	2.807	3.767
24	.685	1.318	1.711	2.064	2.492	2.797	3.745
25	.684	1.316	1.708	2.060	2.485	2.787	3.725
26	.684	1.315	1.706	2.056	2.479	2.779	3.707
27	.684	1.314	1.703	2.052	2.473	2.771	3.690
28	.683	1.313	1.701	2.048	2.467	2.763	3.674
29	.683	1.311	1.699	2.045	2.462	2.756	3.659
30	.683	1.310	1.697	2.042	2.457	2.750	3.646
40	.681	1.303	1.684	2.021	2.423	2.704	3.551
60	.679	1.296	1.671	2.000	2.390	2.660	3.460
120	.677	1.289	1.658	1.980	2.358	2.617	3.373
∞	.674	1.282	1.645	1.960	2.326	2.576	3.291

df = degrees of freedom

Source: From Table III of R. A. Fisher and F. Yates, *Statistical Tables for Biological, Agricultural, and Medical Research,* published by Oliver & Boyd Ltd., Edinburgh, by permission of the authors and publishers.

TABLE A-3   Percentiles of the χ^2 Distribution

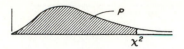

Values of χ^2 corresponding to P

df	$\chi^2_{.005}$	$\chi^2_{.01}$	$\chi^2_{.025}$	$\chi^2_{.05}$	$\chi^2_{.10}$	$\chi^2_{.90}$	$\chi^2_{.95}$	$\chi^2_{.975}$	$\chi^2_{.99}$	$\chi^2_{.995}$
1	.000039	.00016	.00098	.0039	.0158	2.71	3.84	5.02	6.63	7.88
2	.0100	.0201	.0506	.1026	.2107	4.61	5.99	7.38	9.21	10.60
3	.0717	.115	.216	.352	.584	6.25	7.81	9.35	11.34	12.84
4	.207	.297	.484	.711	1.064	7.78	9.49	11.14	13.28	14.86
5	.412	.554	.831	1.15	1.61	9.24	11.07	12.83	15.09	16.75
6	.676	.872	1.24	1.64	2.20	10.64	12.59	14.45	16.81	18.55
7	.989	1.24	1.69	2.17	2.83	12.02	14.07	16.01	18.48	20.28
8	1.34	1.65	2.18	2.73	3.49	13.36	15.51	17.53	20.09	21.96
9	1.73	2.09	2.70	3.33	4.17	14.68	16.92	19.02	21.67	23.59
10	2.16	2.56	3.25	3.94	4.87	15.99	18.31	20.48	23.21	25.19
11	2.60	3.05	3.82	4.57	5.58	17.28	19.68	21.92	24.73	26.76
12	3.07	3.57	4.40	5.23	6.30	18.55	21.03	23.34	26.22	28.30
13	3.57	4.11	5.01	5.89	7.04	19.81	22.36	24.74	27.69	29.82
14	4.07	4.66	5.63	6.57	7.79	21.06	23.68	26.12	29.14	31.32
15	4.60	5.23	6.26	7.26	8.55	22.31	25.00	27.49	30.58	32.80
16	5.14	5.81	6.91	7.96	9.31	23.54	26.30	28.85	32.00	34.27
18	6.26	7.01	8.23	9.39	10.86	25.99	28.87	31.53	34.81	37.16
20	7.43	8.26	9.59	10.85	12.44	28.41	31.41	34.17	37.57	40.00
24	9.89	10.86	12.40	13.85	15.66	33.20	36.42	39.36	42.98	45.56
30	13.79	14.95	16.79	18.49	20.60	40.26	43.77	46.98	50.89	53.67
40	20.71	22.16	24.43	26.51	29.05	51.81	55.76	59.34	63.69	66.77
60	35.53	37.48	40.48	43.19	46.46	74.40	79.08	83.30	88.38	91.95
120	83.85	86.92	91.58	95.70	100.62	140.23	146.57	152.21	158.95	163.64

For large degrees of freedom, $X^2 = \frac{1}{2}(Z + \sqrt{2v-1})^2$ (approximately) where v = degrees of freedom and Z is given in Table A-1.

Source: Adapted with permission from *Introduction to Statistical Analysis*, 2nd ed., by W. J. Dixon and F. J. Massey, Jr., Copyright 1957, McGraw-Hill Book Company.

TABLE A-4 Percentiles of the F Distribution

n_1 = degrees of freedom for numerator

$F_{0.90}(n_1, n_2)$ $\alpha = 0.1$

n_2 \ n_1	1	2	3	4	5	6	7	8	9	10	12	15	20	24	30	40	60	120	∞
1	39.86	49.50	53.59	55.83	57.24	58.20	58.91	59.44	59.86	60.19	60.71	61.22	61.74	62.00	62.26	62.53	62.79	63.06	63.33
2	8.53	9.00	9.16	9.24	9.29	9.33	9.35	9.37	9.38	9.39	9.41	9.42	9.44	9.45	9.46	9.47	9.47	9.48	9.49
3	5.54	5.46	5.39	5.34	5.31	5.28	5.27	5.25	5.24	5.23	5.22	5.20	5.18	5.18	5.17	5.16	5.15	5.14	5.13
4	4.54	4.32	4.19	4.11	4.05	4.01	3.98	3.95	3.94	3.92	3.90	3.87	3.84	3.83	3.82	3.80	3.79	3.78	3.76
5	4.06	3.78	3.62	3.52	3.45	3.40	3.37	3.34	3.32	3.30	3.27	3.24	3.21	3.19	3.17	3.16	3.14	3.12	3.10
6	3.78	3.46	3.29	3.18	3.11	3.05	3.01	2.98	2.96	2.94	2.90	2.87	2.84	2.82	2.80	2.78	2.76	2.74	2.72
7	3.59	3.26	3.07	2.96	2.88	2.83	2.78	2.75	2.72	2.70	2.67	2.63	2.59	2.58	2.56	2.54	2.51	2.49	2.47
8	3.46	3.11	2.92	2.81	2.73	2.67	2.62	2.59	2.56	2.50	2.50	2.46	2.42	2.40	2.38	2.36	2.34	2.32	2.29
9	3.36	3.01	2.81	2.69	2.61	2.55	2.51	2.47	2.44	2.42	2.38	2.34	2.30	2.28	2.25	2.23	2.21	2.18	2.16
10	3.29	2.92	2.73	2.61	2.52	2.46	2.41	2.38	2.35	2.32	2.28	2.24	2.20	2.18	2.16	2.13	2.11	2.08	2.06
11	3.23	2.86	2.66	2.54	2.45	2.39	2.34	2.30	2.27	2.25	2.21	2.17	2.12	2.10	2.08	2.05	2.03	2.00	1.97
12	3.18	2.81	2.61	2.48	2.39	2.33	2.28	2.24	2.21	2.19	2.15	2.10	2.06	2.04	2.01	1.99	1.96	1.93	1.90
13	3.14	2.76	2.56	2.43	2.35	2.28	2.23	2.20	2.16	2.14	2.10	2.05	2.01	1.98	1.96	1.93	1.90	1.88	1.85
14	3.10	2.73	2.52	2.39	2.31	2.24	2.19	2.15	2.12	2.10	2.05	2.01	1.96	1.94	1.91	1.89	1.86	1.83	1.80
15	3.07	2.70	2.49	2.36	2.27	2.21	2.16	2.12	2.09	2.06	2.02	1.97	1.92	1.90	1.87	1.85	1.82	1.79	1.76
16	3.05	2.67	2.46	2.33	2.24	2.18	2.13	2.09	2.06	2.03	1.99	1.94	1.89	1.87	1.84	1.81	1.78	1.75	1.72
17	3.03	2.64	2.44	2.31	2.22	2.15	2.10	2.06	2.03	2.00	1.96	1.91	1.86	1.84	1.81	1.78	1.75	1.72	1.69
18	3.01	2.62	2.42	2.29	2.20	2.13	2.08	2.04	2.00	1.98	1.93	1.89	1.84	1.81	1.78	1.75	1.72	1.69	1.66
19	2.99	2.61	2.40	2.27	2.18	2.11	2.06	2.02	1.98	1.96	1.91	1.86	1.81	1.79	1.76	1.73	1.70	1.67	1.63

n_2 = degrees of freedom for denominator

TABLE A-4 Percentiles of the F Distribution (Continued)

n_1 = degrees of freedom for numerator

n_2	1	2	3	4	5	6	7	8	9	10	12	15	20	24	30	40	60	120	∞
20	2.97	2.59	2.38	2.25	2.16	2.09	2.04	2.00	1.96	1.94	1.89	1.84	1.79	1.77	1.74	1.71	1.68	1.64	1.61
21	2.96	2.57	2.36	2.23	2.14	2.08	2.02	1.98	1.95	1.92	1.87	1.83	1.78	1.75	1.72	1.69	1.66	1.62	1.59
22	2.95	2.56	2.35	2.22	2.13	2.06	2.01	1.97	1.93	1.90	1.86	1.81	1.76	1.73	1.70	1.67	1.64	1.60	1.57
23	2.94	2.55	2.34	2.21	2.11	2.05	1.99	1.95	1.92	1.89	1.84	1.80	1.74	1.72	1.69	1.66	1.62	1.59	1.55
24	2.93	2.54	2.33	2.19	2.10	2.04	1.98	1.94	1.91	1.88	1.83	1.78	1.73	1.70	1.67	1.64	1.61	1.57	1.53
25	2.92	2.53	2.32	2.18	2.09	2.02	1.97	1.93	1.89	1.87	1.82	1.77	1.72	1.69	1.66	1.63	1.59	1.56	1.52
26	2.91	2.52	2.31	2.17	2.08	2.01	1.96	1.92	1.88	1.86	1.81	1.76	1.71	1.68	1.65	1.61	1.58	1.54	1.50
27	2.90	2.51	2.30	2.17	2.07	2.00	1.95	1.91	1.87	1.85	1.80	1.75	1.70	1.67	1.64	1.60	1.57	1.53	1.49
28	2.89	2.50	2.29	2.16	2.06	2.00	1.94	1.90	1.87	1.84	1.79	1.74	1.69	1.66	1.63	1.59	1.56	1.52	1.48
29	2.89	2.50	2.28	2.15	2.06	1.99	1.93	1.89	1.86	1.83	1.78	1.73	1.68	1.65	1.62	1.58	1.55	1.51	1.47
30	2.88	2.49	2.28	2.14	2.05	1.98	1.93	1.88	1.85	1.82	1.77	1.72	1.67	1.64	1.61	1.57	1.54	1.50	1.46
40	2.84	2.44	2.23	2.09	2.00	1.93	1.87	1.83	1.79	1.76	1.71	1.66	1.61	1.57	1.54	1.51	1.47	1.42	1.38
60	2.79	2.39	2.18	2.04	1.95	1.87	1.82	1.77	1.74	1.71	1.66	1.60	1.54	1.51	1.48	1.44	1.40	1.35	1.29
120	2.75	2.35	2.13	1.99	1.90	1.82	1.77	1.72	1.68	1.65	1.60	1.55	1.48	1.45	1.41	1.37	1.32	1.26	1.19
∞	2.71	2.30	2.08	1.94	1.85	1.77	1.72	1.67	1.63	1.60	1.55	1.49	1.42	1.38	1.34	1.30	1.24	1.17	1.00

TABLE A-4 *(Continued)*

$F_{0.95}(n_1, n_2)$ $\alpha = 0.05$

n_1 = degrees of freedom for numerator

n_2	1	2	3	4	5	6	7	8	9	10	12	15	20	24	30	40	60	120	∞
1	161.4	199.5	215.7	224.6	230.2	234.0	236.8	238.9	240.5	241.9	243.9	245.9	248.0	249.1	250.1	251.1	252.2	253.3	254.3
2	18.51	19.00	19.16	19.25	19.30	19.33	19.35	19.37	19.38	19.40	19.41	19.43	19.45	19.45	19.46	19.47	19.48	19.49	19.50
3	10.13	9.55	9.28	9.12	9.01	8.94	8.89	8.85	8.81	8.79	8.74	8.70	8.66	8.64	8.62	8.59	8.57	8.55	8.53
4	7.71	6.94	6.59	6.39	6.26	6.16	6.09	6.04	6.00	5.96	5.91	5.86	5.80	5.77	5.75	5.72	5.69	5.66	5.63
5	6.61	5.79	5.41	5.19	5.05	4.95	4.88	4.82	4.77	4.74	4.68	4.62	4.56	4.53	4.50	4.46	4.43	4.40	4.36
6	5.99	5.14	4.76	4.53	4.39	4.28	4.21	4.15	4.10	4.06	4.00	3.94	3.87	3.84	3.81	3.77	3.74	3.70	3.67
7	5.59	4.74	4.35	4.12	3.97	3.87	3.79	3.73	3.68	3.64	3.57	3.51	3.44	3.41	3.38	3.34	3.30	3.27	3.23
8	5.32	4.46	4.07	3.84	3.69	3.58	3.50	3.44	3.39	3.35	3.28	3.22	3.15	3.12	3.08	3.04	3.01	2.97	2.93
9	5.12	4.26	3.86	3.63	3.48	3.37	3.29	3.23	3.18	3.14	3.07	3.01	2.94	2.90	2.86	2.83	2.79	2.75	2.71
10	4.96	4.10	3.71	3.48	3.33	3.22	3.14	3.07	3.02	2.98	2.91	2.85	2.77	2.74	2.70	2.66	2.62	2.58	2.54
11	4.84	3.98	3.59	3.36	3.20	3.09	3.01	2.95	2.90	2.85	2.79	2.72	2.65	2.61	2.57	2.53	2.49	2.45	2.40
12	4.75	3.89	3.49	3.26	3.11	3.00	2.91	2.85	2.80	2.75	2.69	2.62	2.54	2.51	2.47	2.43	2.38	2.34	2.30
13	4.67	3.81	3.41	3.18	3.03	2.92	2.83	2.77	2.71	2.67	2.60	2.53	2.46	2.42	2.38	2.34	2.30	2.25	2.21
14	4.60	3.74	3.34	3.11	2.96	2.85	2.76	2.70	2.65	2.60	2.53	2.46	2.39	2.35	2.31	2.27	2.22	2.18	2.13
15	4.54	3.68	3.29	3.06	2.90	2.79	2.71	2.64	2.59	2.54	2.48	2.40	2.33	2.29	2.25	2.20	2.16	2.11	2.07
16	4.49	3.63	3.24	3.01	2.85	2.74	2.66	2.59	2.54	2.49	2.42	2.35	2.28	2.24	2.19	2.15	2.11	2.06	2.01
17	4.45	3.59	3.20	2.96	2.81	2.70	2.61	2.55	2.49	2.45	2.38	2.31	2.23	2.19	2.15	2.10	2.06	2.01	1.96
18	4.41	3.55	3.16	2.93	2.77	2.66	2.58	2.51	2.46	2.41	2.34	2.27	2.19	2.15	2.11	2.06	2.02	1.97	1.92
19	4.38	3.52	3.13	2.90	2.74	2.63	2.54	2.48	2.42	2.38	2.31	2.23	2.16	2.11	2.07	2.03	1.98	1.93	1.88
20	4.35	3.49	3.10	2.87	2.71	2.60	2.51	2.45	2.39	2.35	2.28	2.20	2.12	2.08	2.04	1.99	1.95	1.90	1.84
21	4.32	3.47	3.07	2.84	2.68	2.57	2.49	2.42	2.37	2.32	2.25	2.18	2.10	2.05	2.01	1.96	1.92	1.87	1.81
22	4.30	3.44	3.05	2.82	2.66	2.55	2.46	2.40	2.34	2.30	2.23	2.15	2.07	2.03	1.98	1.94	1.89	1.84	1.78
23	4.28	3.42	3.03	2.80	2.64	2.53	2.44	2.37	2.32	2.27	2.20	2.13	2.05	2.01	1.96	1.91	1.86	1.81	1.76
24	4.26	3.40	3.01	2.78	2.62	2.51	2.42	2.36	2.30	2.25	2.18	2.11	2.03	1.98	1.94	1.89	1.84	1.79	1.73

TABLE A-4 Percentiles of the _F_ Distribution (_Continued_)

n_1 = degrees of freedom for numerator

n_2 \ n_1	1	2	3	4	5	6	7	8	9	10	12	15	20	24	30	40	60	120	∞
25	4.24	3.39	2.99	2.76	2.60	2.49	2.40	2.34	2.28	2.24	2.16	2.09	2.01	1.96	1.92	1.87	1.82	1.77	1.71
26	4.23	3.37	2.98	2.74	2.59	2.47	2.39	2.32	2.27	2.22	2.15	2.07	1.99	1.95	1.90	1.85	1.80	1.75	1.69
27	4.21	3.35	2.96	2.73	2.57	2.46	2.37	2.31	2.25	2.20	2.13	2.06	1.97	1.93	1.88	1.84	1.79	1.73	1.67
28	4.20	3.34	2.95	2.71	2.56	2.45	2.36	2.29	2.24	2.19	2.12	2.04	1.96	1.91	1.87	1.82	1.77	1.71	1.65
29	4.18	3.33	2.93	2.70	2.55	2.43	2.35	2.28	2.22	2.18	2.10	2.03	1.94	1.90	1.85	1.81	1.75	1.70	1.64
30	4.17	3.32	2.92	2.69	2.53	2.42	2.33	2.27	2.21	2.16	2.09	2.01	1.93	1.89	1.84	1.79	1.74	1.68	1.62
40	4.08	3.23	2.84	2.61	2.45	2.34	2.25	2.18	2.12	2.08	2.00	1.92	1.84	1.79	1.74	1.69	1.64	1.58	1.51
60	4.00	3.15	2.76	2.53	2.37	2.25	2.17	2.10	2.04	1.99	1.92	1.84	1.75	1.70	1.65	1.59	1.53	1.47	1.39
120	3.92	3.07	2.68	2.45	2.29	2.17	2.09	2.02	1.96	1.91	1.83	1.75	1.66	1.61	1.55	1.50	1.43	1.35	1.25
∞	3.84	3.00	2.60	2.37	2.21	2.10	2.01	1.94	1.88	1.83	1.75	1.67	1.57	1.52	1.46	1.39	1.32	1.22	1.00

n_2 = degrees of freedom for denominator

TABLE A-4 (Continued)

n_1 = degrees of freedom for numerator

$F_{0.99}(n_1, n_2)$ $\alpha = 0.01$

n_2 \ n_1	1	2	3	4	5	6	7	8	9	10	12	15	20	24	30	40	60	120	∞
1	4052	4999.5	5403	5625	5764	5859	5928	5982	6022	6056	6106	6157	6209	6235	6261	6287	6313	6339	6366
2	98.50	99.00	99.17	99.25	99.30	99.33	99.36	99.37	99.39	99.40	99.42	99.43	99.45	99.46	99.47	99.47	99.48	99.49	99.50
3	34.12	30.82	29.46	28.71	28.24	27.91	27.67	27.49	27.35	27.23	27.05	26.87	26.69	26.60	26.50	26.41	26.32	26.22	26.13
4	21.20	18.00	16.69	15.98	15.52	15.21	14.98	14.80	14.66	14.55	14.37	14.20	14.02	13.93	13.84	13.75	13.65	13.56	13.46
5	16.26	13.27	12.06	11.39	10.97	10.67	10.46	10.29	10.16	10.05	9.89	9.72	9.55	9.47	9.38	9.29	9.20	9.11	9.02
6	13.75	10.92	9.78	9.15	8.75	8.47	8.26	8.10	7.98	7.87	7.72	7.56	7.40	7.31	7.23	7.14	7.06	6.97	6.88
7	12.25	9.55	8.45	7.85	7.46	7.19	6.99	6.84	6.72	6.62	6.47	6.31	6.16	6.07	5.99	5.91	5.82	5.74	5.65
8	11.26	8.65	7.59	7.01	6.63	6.37	6.18	6.03	5.91	5.81	5.67	5.52	5.36	5.28	5.20	5.12	5.03	4.95	4.86
9	10.56	8.02	6.99	6.42	6.06	5.80	5.61	5.47	5.35	5.26	5.11	4.96	4.81	4.73	4.65	4.57	4.48	4.40	4.31
10	10.04	7.56	6.55	5.99	5.64	5.39	5.20	5.06	4.94	4.85	4.71	4.56	4.41	4.33	4.25	4.17	4.08	4.00	3.91
11	9.65	7.21	6.22	5.67	5.32	5.07	4.89	4.74	4.63	4.54	4.40	4.25	4.10	4.02	3.94	3.86	3.78	3.69	3.60
12	9.33	6.93	5.95	5.41	5.06	4.82	4.64	4.50	4.39	4.30	4.16	4.01	3.86	3.78	3.70	3.62	3.54	3.45	3.36
13	9.07	6.70	5.74	5.21	4.86	4.62	4.44	4.30	4.19	4.10	3.96	3.82	3.66	3.59	3.51	3.43	3.34	3.25	3.17
14	8.86	6.51	5.56	5.04	4.69	4.46	4.28	4.14	4.03	3.94	3.80	3.66	3.51	3.43	3.35	3.27	3.18	3.09	3.00
15	8.68	6.36	5.42	4.89	4.56	4.32	4.14	4.00	3.89	3.80	3.67	3.52	3.37	3.29	3.21	3.13	3.05	2.96	2.87
16	8.53	6.23	5.29	4.77	4.44	4.20	4.03	3.89	3.78	3.69	3.55	3.41	3.26	3.18	3.10	3.02	2.93	2.84	2.75
17	8.40	6.11	5.18	4.67	4.34	4.10	3.93	3.79	3.68	3.59	3.46	3.31	3.16	3.08	3.00	2.92	2.83	2.75	2.65
18	8.29	6.01	5.09	4.58	4.25	4.01	3.84	3.71	3.60	3.51	3.37	3.23	3.08	3.00	2.92	2.84	2.75	2.66	2.57
19	8.18	5.93	5.01	4.50	4.17	3.94	3.77	3.63	3.52	3.43	3.30	3.15	3.00	2.92	2.84	2.76	2.67	2.58	2.49
20	8.10	5.85	4.94	4.43	4.10	3.87	3.70	3.56	3.46	3.37	3.23	3.09	2.94	2.86	2.78	2.69	2.61	2.52	2.42
21	8.02	5.78	4.87	4.37	4.04	3.81	3.64	3.51	3.40	3.31	3.17	3.03	2.88	2.80	2.72	2.64	2.55	2.46	2.36
22	7.95	5.72	4.82	4.31	3.99	3.76	3.59	3.45	3.35	3.26	3.12	2.98	2.83	2.75	2.67	2.58	2.50	2.40	2.31
23	7.88	5.66	4.76	4.26	3.94	3.71	3.54	3.41	3.30	3.21	3.07	2.93	2.78	2.70	2.62	2.54	2.45	2.35	2.26
24	7.82	5.61	4.72	4.22	3.90	3.67	3.50	3.36	3.26	3.17	3.03	2.89	2.74	2.66	2.58	2.49	2.40	2.31	2.21

n_2 = degrees of freedom for denominator

TABLE A-4 Percentiles of the F Distribution (Continued)

n_1 = degrees of freedom for numerator

n_2 \ n_1	1	2	3	4	5	6	7	8	9	10	12	15	20	24	30	40	60	120	∞
25	7.77	5.57	4.68	4.18	3.85	3.63	3.46	3.32	3.22	3.13	2.99	2.85	2.70	2.62	2.54	2.45	2.36	2.27	2.17
26	7.72	5.53	4.64	4.14	3.82	3.59	3.42	3.29	3.18	3.09	2.96	2.81	2.66	2.58	2.50	2.42	2.33	2.23	2.13
27	7.68	5.49	4.60	4.11	3.78	3.56	3.39	3.26	3.15	3.06	2.93	2.78	2.63	2.55	2.47	2.38	2.29	2.20	2.10
28	7.64	5.45	4.57	4.07	3.75	3.53	3.36	3.23	3.12	3.03	2.90	2.75	2.60	2.52	2.44	2.35	2.26	2.17	2.06
29	7.60	5.42	4.54	4.04	3.73	3.50	3.33	3.20	3.09	3.00	2.87	2.73	2.57	2.49	2.41	2.33	2.23	2.14	2.03
30	7.56	5.39	4.51	4.02	3.70	3.47	3.30	3.17	3.07	2.98	2.84	2.70	2.55	2.47	2.39	2.30	2.21	2.11	2.01
40	7.31	5.18	4.31	3.83	3.51	3.29	3.12	2.99	2.89	2.80	2.66	2.52	2.37	2.29	2.20	2.11	2.02	1.92	1.80
60	7.08	4.89	4.13	3.65	3.34	3.12	2.95	2.82	2.72	2.63	2.50	2.35	2.20	2.12	2.03	1.94	1.84	1.73	1.60
120	6.85	4.79	3.95	3.48	3.17	2.96	2.79	2.66	2.56	2.47	2.34	2.19	2.03	1.95	1.86	1.76	1.66	1.53	1.38
∞	6.63	4.61	3.78	3.32	3.02	2.80	2.64	2.51	2.41	2.32	2.18	2.04	1.88	1.79	1.70	1.59	1.47	1.32	1.00

n_2 = degrees of freedom for denominator

Source: Adapted with permission from *Biometrika Tables for Statisticians*, Vol. I, 2nd ed., edited by E. S. Pearson and H. O. Hartley, Copyright 1958, Cambridge University Press.

TABLE A-5 Short Table of Random Numbers

```
46  96  85  77  27  92  86  26  45  21  89  91  71  42  64  64  58  22  75  81  74  91  48  46  18
44  19  15  32  63  55  87  77  33  29  45  00  31  34  84  05  72  90  44  27  78  22  07  62  17
34  39  80  62  24  33  81  67  28  11  34  79  26  35  34  23  09  94  00  80  55  31  63  27  91
74  97  80  30  65  07  71  30  01  84  47  45  89  70  74  13  04  90  51  27  61  34  63  87  44
22  14  61  60  86  38  33  71  13  33  72  08  16  13  50  56  48  51  29  48  30  93  45  66  29

40  03  96  40  03  47  24  60  09  21  21  18  00  05  86  52  85  40  73  73  57  68  36  33  91
52  33  76  44  56  15  47  75  78  73  78  19  87  06  98  47  48  02  62  03  42  05  32  55  02
37  59  20  40  93  17  82  24  19  90  80  87  32  74  59  84  24  49  79  17  23  75  83  42  00
11  02  55  57  48  84  74  36  22  67  19  20  15  92  53  37  13  75  54  89  56  73  23  39  07
10  33  79  26  34  54  71  33  89  74  68  48  23  17  49  18  81  05  52  85  70  05  73  11  17

67  59  28  25  47  89  11  65  65  20  42  23  96  41  64  20  30  89  87  64  37  93  36  96  35
93  50  75  20  09  18  54  34  68  02  54  87  23  05  43  36  98  29  97  93  87  08  30  92  98
24  43  23  72  80  64  34  27  23  46  15  36  10  63  21  59  69  76  02  62  31  62  47  60  34
39  91  63  18  38  27  10  78  88  84  42  32  00  97  92  00  04  94  50  05  75  82  70  80  35
74  62  19  67  54  18  28  92  33  69  98  96  74  35  72  11  68  25  08  95  31  79  11  79  54

91  03  35  60  81  16  61  97  25  14  78  21  22  05  25  47  26  37  80  39  19  06  41  02  00
42  57  66  76  72  91  03  63  48  46  44  01  33  53  62  28  80  59  55  05  02  16  13  17  54
06  36  63  06  15  03  72  38  01  58  25  37  66  48  56  19  56  41  29  28  76  49  74  39  50
92  70  96  70  89  80  87  14  25  49  25  94  62  78  26  15  41  39  48  75  64  69  61  06  38
91  08  88  53  52  13  04  82  23  00  26  36  47  44  04  08  84  80  07  44  76  51  52  41  59

68  85  97  74  47  53  90  05  90  84  87  48  25  01  11  05  45  11  43  15  60  40  31  84  59
59  54  13  09  13  80  42  29  63  03  24  64  12  43  28  10  01  65  62  07  79  83  05  59  61
39  18  32  69  33  46  58  19  34  03  59  28  97  31  02  65  47  47  70  39  74  17  30  22  65
67  43  31  09  12  60  19  57  63  78  11  80  10  97  15  70  04  89  81  78  54  84  87  83  42
61  75  37  19  56  90  75  39  03  56  49  92  72  95  27  52  87  47  12  52  54  62  43  23  13

78  10  91  11  00  63  19  63  74  58  69  03  51  38  60  36  53  56  77  06  69  03  89  91  24
93  23  71  58  09  78  08  03  07  71  79  32  25  19  61  04  40  33  12  06  78  91  97  88  95
37  55  48  82  63  89  92  59  14  72  19  17  22  51  90  20  03  64  96  60  48  01  95  44  84
62  13  11  71  17  23  29  25  13  85  33  35  07  69  25  68  57  92  57  11  84  44  01  33  66
29  89  97  47  03  13  20  86  22  45  59  98  64  53  89  64  94  81  55  87  73  81  58  46  42

16  94  85  82  89  07  17  30  29  89  89  80  98  36  25  36  53  02  49  14  34  03  52  09  20
04  93  10  59  75  12  98  84  60  93  68  16  87  60  11  50  46  56  58  45  88  72  50  46  11
95  71  43  68  97  18  85  17  13  08  00  50  77  50  46  92  45  26  97  21  48  22  23  08  32
86  05  39  14  35  48  68  18  36  57  09  62  40  28  87  08  74  79  91  08  27  12  43  32  03
59  30  60  10  41  31  00  69  63  77  01  89  94  60  19  02  70  88  72  33  38  88  20  60  86

05  45  35  40  54  03  98  96  76  27  77  84  80  08  64  60  44  34  54  24  85  20  85  77  32
71  85  17  74  66  27  85  19  55  56  51  36  48  92  32  44  40  47  10  38  22  52  42  29  96
80  20  32  80  98  00  40  92  57  51  52  83  14  55  31  99  73  23  40  07  64  54  44  99  21
13  50  78  02  73  39  66  82  01  28  67  51  75  66  33  97  47  58  42  44  88  09  28  58  06
67  92  65  41  45  36  77  96  46  21  14  39  56  36  70  15  74  43  62  69  82  30  77  28  77

72  56  73  44  26  04  62  81  15  35  79  26  99  57  28  22  25  94  80  62  95  48  98  23  86
28  86  85  64  94  11  58  78  45  36  34  45  91  38  51  10  68  36  87  81  16  77  30  19  36
```

TABLE A-5 Short Table of Random Numbers (*Continued*)

69	57	40	80	44	94	60	82	94	93	98	01	48	50	57	69	60	77	69	60	74	22	05	77	17
71	20	03	30	79	25	74	17	78	34	54	45	04	77	42	59	75	78	64	99	37	03	18	03	36
89	98	55	98	22	45	12	49	82	71	57	33	28	69	50	59	15	09	25	79	39	42	84	18	70
58	74	82	81	14	02	01	05	77	94	65	57	70	39	42	48	56	84	31	59	18	70	41	74	60
50	54	73	81	91	07	81	26	25	45	49	61	22	88	41	20	00	15	59	93	51	60	65	65	63
49	33	72	90	10	20	65	28	44	63	95	86	75	78	69	24	41	65	86	10	34	10	32	00	93
11	85	01	43	65	02	85	69	56	88	34	29	64	35	48	15	70	11	77	83	01	34	82	91	04
34	22	46	41	84	74	27	02	57	77	47	93	72	02	95	63	75	74	69	69	61	34	31	92	13

Source: Adapted with permission from *A Million Random Digits* by The Rand Corporation, Copyright 1955, The Free Press.

TABLE A-6 Short Table of Random Normal Deviates

$\mu = 0, \sigma = 1$

−0.670	0.518	0.387	0.523	0.641	1.243	0.322	−2.607	−1.097	−0.012
−2.912	1.448	1.343	−0.122	0.726	−0.617	0.609	2.319	−0.450	−1.197
−0.028	−0.790	0.057	1.425	1.940	1.161	−0.878	−0.716	−0.244	−1.151
−1.257	0.774	0.003	0.388	1.060	1.028	−0.236	1.172	0.442	−0.157
2.372	−1.376	−1.318	1.236	0.738	0.337	−0.534	0.090	0.886	0.676
−0.970	0.438	−0.672	−0.180	0.667	1.370	−0.481	0.329	0.842	0.449
−1.228	0.129	−0.426	−0.165	0.028	2.696	1.201	−1.351	0.724	−1.017
−0.369	0.310	0.432	0.237	0.884	−1.224	0.539	0.852	0.497	−0.283
1.161	1.219	1.615	0.336	1.100	−0.528	0.161	0.278	0.675	−1.143
−0.284	2.609	0.792	1.825	−0.249	1.654	0.621	0.979	−1.472	−1.173
−0.578	−0.789	0.106	0.832	−0.597	0.496	−0.561	−1.033	−0.578	−0.378
0.074	0.261	−0.766	−1.046	0.361	−0.043	−1.927	1.527	0.605	1.475
0.230	0.046	0.978	−1.901	1.162	−0.545	0.697	1.151	2.033	0.080
2.162	−0.562	1.190	0.925	−1.057	0.015	−1.371	1.067	−1.080	−1.129
−1.020	−1.130	−0.315	0.628	−0.140	2.050	−0.030	−0.629	0.128	−1.221
1.323	−0.836	−0.284	−0.249	−0.768	1.242	−1.879	−0.417	0.013	−0.502
2.329	1.884	0.033	0.598	−0.217	0.260	0.431	−1.914	0.205	1.155
2.761	1.800	−0.562	0.714	−0.407	0.009	−0.724	−1.168	0.247	1.166
−0.232	0.605	−0.023	−0.531	0.542	−0.155	0.697	1.037	−0.316	−0.003
−0.742	0.210	−0.741	−1.099	0.158	2.112	−0.765	−0.319	−0.247	0.345
−1.410	0.413	0.705	1.444	1.057	−0.843	0.043	−0.571	−0.001	0.203
2.272	−0.719	0.679	2.007	−0.180	0.698	−1.137	0.688	−0.571	−0.100
2.832	0.925	−1.350	1.529	−0.260	−1.007	−2.350	−1.501	0.289	1.522
−1.086	−0.558	−0.973	−1.285	−0.021	0.077	0.915	−0.241	−0.249	−0.529
0.134	1.815	0.313	1.571	−0.216	2.261	0.696	−0.130	0.393	0.017
0.783	0.600	−0.745	1.127	−0.684	−0.519	0.125	−0.499	1.543	−0.082
0.174	−0.897	0.575	−0.751	0.694	−2.959	0.529	1.587	0.339	−0.813

TABLE A-6 (*Continued*)

			$\mu = 0, \sigma = 1$						
−1.319	0.556	2.963	1.218	1.199	−1.746	1.611	0.467	−0.490	0.202
1.298	−0.940	−1.143	−1.136	−1.516	0.548	0.629	0.250	−1.087	0.322
−0.676	−1.107	−1.483	0.278	0.493	−0.442	1.078	−0.336	−0.177	−0.057
−1.287	0.775	−1.095	1.161	−1.877	1.874	1.703	−1.619	−0.725	−1.407
0.260	−0.028	−1.982	0.811	0.999	1.662	0.908	1.476	−1.137	−0.945
0.481	1.060	1.441	0.163	0.720	1.490	−0.026	−0.502	0.427	−0.351
0.794	0.725	1.971	0.384	−0.579	−1.079	−1.440	−0.859	−0.346	0.007
0.584	−0.554	1.460	0.791	−0.426	−0.682	0.430	1.922	−2.099	0.221
−0.114	0.379	−0.698	1.570	−0.511	−0.725	0.680	−0.591	−1.091	0.357
−1.128	−1.707	0.921	−0.859	−1.566	1.523	−0.900	−0.988	0.264	0.282
0.691	0.153	0.076	1.691	0.553	0.457	−1.107	0.322	0.633	0.007
1.115	0.777	−0.738	0.868	1.484	−0.792	0.950	−0.842	−0.192	0.620
−0.389	0.559	0.670	−0.315	1.234	0.475	1.117	1.286	−0.649	−1.880
0.330	0.750	−0.642	0.148	−0.608	0.866	−1.720	0.653	−0.210	−0.959
−0.333	−0.084	1.239	−0.049	−0.095	−0.197	−0.213	−1.420	−0.491	0.102
1.718	1.111	−0.548	−0.653	1.534	−0.456	−0.395	1.614	−0.531	−0.785
−0.182	0.620	1.178	−1.071	0.444	−0.072	−1.001	1.325	−0.302	−1.119
1.260	−1.192	0.182	−0.397	−0.705	−1.085	−1.492	1.642	0.673	−0.707
−1.204	−1.725	1.695	1.473	0.665	−0.489	0.020	0.267	1.230	0.865
−0.619	0.307	−0.226	−0.096	0.987	−1.195	−1.412	0.433	2.052	0.022
−0.272	−0.096	0.137	−0.361	0.653	−0.156	1.309	−0.480	−0.397	1.302
0.245	−0.690	0.493	−1.123	1.465	0.132	0.582	−0.429	0.225	0.125
0.101	−0.855	0.782	−1.040	2.113	−1.423	−1.010	0.158	0.106	−1.232

Index